Contemporary Issues in SPORT MANAGEMENT

SAGE was founded in 1965 by Sara Miller McCune to support the dissemination of usable knowledge by publishing innovative and high-quality research and teaching content. Today, we publish over 900 journals, including those of more than 400 learned societies, more than 800 new books per year, and a growing range of library products including archives, data, case studies, reports, and video. SAGE remains majority-owned by our founder, and after Sara's lifetime will become owned by a charitable trust that secures our continued independence.

Los Angeles | London | New Delhi | Singapore | Washington DC

Edited by
TERRI BYERS

Contemporary Issues in SPORT MANAGEMENT

A Critical Introduction

Los Angeles | London | New Delhi
Singapore | Washington DC

Los Angeles | London | New Delhi
Singapore | Washington DC

SAGE Publications Ltd
1 Oliver's Yard
55 City Road
London EC1Y 1SP

SAGE Publications Inc.
2455 Teller Road
Thousand Oaks, California 91320

SAGE Publications India Pvt Ltd
B 1/I 1 Mohan Cooperative Industrial Area
Mathura Road
New Delhi 110 044

SAGE Publications Asia-Pacific Pte Ltd
3 Church Street
#10-04 Samsung Hub
Singapore 049483

Editor: Chris Rojek
Editorial assistant: Delayna Spencer
Production editor: Tom Bedford
Copyeditor: Audrey Scriven
Proofreader: Camille Bramall
Indexer: Silvia Benvenuto
Marketing manager: Michael Ainsley
Cover design: Shaun Mercier
Typeset by: C&M Digitals (P) Ltd, Chennai, India
Printed and bound by CPI Group (UK) Ltd,
Croydon, CR0 4YY

Introduction © Terri Byers 2016
Foreword © Earle F. Zeigler 2016
Chapter 1 © Oliver Rick, Callie Batts-Maddox and David L. Andrews 2016
Chapter 2 © Patrick A. Reid and Daniel S. Mason 2016
Chapter 3 © Antonio Davila and George Foster 2016
Chapter 4 © Wladimir Andreff 2016
Chapter 5 © Chris Gratton, Donfeng Liu, Girish Ramchandani and Darryl Wilson 2016
Chapter 6 © Gabriela Tymowski, Terri Byers and Fred Mason 2016
Chapter 7 © Russell Holden 2016
Chapter 8 © Kevin Carpenter 2016
Chapter 9 © Andrea Geurin-Eagleman 2016
Chapter 10 © Shannon Kerwin 2016
Chapter 11 © Danny O'Brien and Ben Corbett 2016
Chapter 12 © Andrew Byers and Dene Stansall 2016
Chapter 13 © Jiandong Yi 2016
Chapter 14 © Kamilla Swart 2016
Chapter 15 © Jason Bocarro and Michael Edwards 2016
Chapter 16 © Mark McDonald and Kirsty Spence 2016
Chapter 17 © Annelies Knoppers and Agnes Elling-Machartzi 2016

Chapter 18 © Leigh Robinson and Mathieu Winand 2016
Chapter 19 © Aaron Smith and Bob Stewart 2016
Chapter 20 © David Forrest 2016
Chapter 21 © Elwyn Cox 2016
Chapter 22 © Andrew Harvey and Haim Levi 2016
Chapter 23 © Ian Brittain 2016
Chapter 24 © John Beech 2016
Chapter 25 © Sebastian Kopera 2016
Chapter 26 © Olan Scott, Katherine Bruffy and Michael Naylor 2016
Chapter 27 © Jonathon Edwards 2016
Chapter 28 © Stacey Hall 2016
Chapter 29 © Ryan Scoats and Eric Anderson 2016
Chapter 30 © Joerg Koenigstorfer 2016
Chapter 31 © Terri Byers and Alex Thurston 2016
Chapter 32 © Nicolas Chanavat and Guillaume Bodet 2016
Chapter 33 © Kate Westberg, Constantino Stavros, Bradley Wilson and Aaron Smith 2016
Chapter 34 © Christos Anagnostopoulos and Dimitrios Kolyperas 2016
Chapter 35 © Terri Byers 2016

First published 2016

Library of Congress Control Number: 2015941454

British Library Cataloguing in Publication data

A catalogue record for this book is available from the British Library

ISBN 978-1-4462-8218-2
ISBN 978-1-4462-8219-9 (pbk)

MIX
Paper from responsible sources
FSC® C013604

At SAGE we take sustainability seriously. Most of our products are printed in the UK using FSC papers and boards. When we print overseas we ensure sustainable papers are used as measured by the PREPS grading system. We undertake an annual audit to monitor our sustainability.

CONTENTS

ABOUT THE EDITOR AND CONTRIBUTORS

EDITOR

Terri Byers joined the University of New Brunswick in July 2014, after 19 years of teaching and researching in the United Kingdom. She has authored/co-authored a variety of publications, including books such as *Key Concepts in Sport Management* (Sage), as well as journal articles in *European Sport Management Quarterly*, *International Sport Management and Marketing*, *Corporate Governance* and the *Journal of Leisure Research*. She has won over $1m CAD in funding for her research and worked on projects totalling more than $2m CAD. Current research interests are devoted to non-participation in sport and how sport organizations innovate to increase participation.

CONTRIBUTORS

Christos Anagnostopoulos is an Associate Professor in Sport Management at Molde University College (Norway) and an Associate Lecturer in Management at the University of Central Lancashire (Cyprus). He holds a PhD from Coventry University and a Master's from his research into sport management and the business of football from Birkbeck, University of London. He is an Early Researcher Awardholder of the European Association for Sport Management, and head of the sports unit at the Athens Institute for Education and Research. His research falls within the fields of organizational behaviour and strategic management. He is notably interested in corporate social responsibility in and through sport, as well as in the management of team sport organizations.

Eric Anderson is an American sociologist known for his research on sport, masculinities, sexualities and homophobia. He shows an increasingly positive relationship between gay male athletes and sport, as well as a growing movement of young heterosexual men's masculinity becoming softer and more inclusive.

Wladimir Andreff is Professor Emeritus at the University Paris 1 Panthéon Sorbonne, Honorary President of the International Association of Sports Economists and the European Sports Economics Association, and incumbent

President of the Scientific Council at the Observatory of the Sports Economy (French Ministry for Sports). He has published over 130 scientific articles, edited four volumes (including *Contemporary Issues in Sports Economics: Participation and Professional Team Sports*, Edward Elgar, 2011) and authored five books on sports economics (most recently, *Mondialisation économique du sport*, De Boeck, 2012).

David Andrews is Professor of Physical Cultural Studies in the Department of Kinesiology at the University of Maryland. Utilizing a form of radical contextualism derived from cultural studies' conjoined intellectual and political sensibilities, his work looks to illuminate and complicate the role of physical culture in the (re)production of the late capitalist formation. His publications include *The Blackwell Companion to Sport* (edited with Ben Carrington, 2013, Blackwell), and *Sport and Neoliberalism: Politics, Consumption, and Culture* (edited with Michael Silk, 2012, Temple University Press).

Callie Batts-Maddox received her PhD in Physical Cultural Studies from the University of Maryland. She lived in north India for two years while conducting research for her doctoral dissertation, and also spent time working as a youth baseball coach and yoga instructor in Delhi. Her previous work has appeared in *Sport in Society*, the *International Journal of Cultural Studies*, the *Review of Education, Pedagogy and Cultural Studies* and the *Journal of Tourism and Cultural Change*.

John Beech is an Honorary Research Fellow at Coventry University in the United Kingdom, where he was previously Head of Leisure, Sport and Tourism Management. He regularly lectures in Austria, Croatia, Germany and Finland, and is an International Professor at the Russian International Olympic University in Sochi, Russia. He received the Football Supporters' Federation Writer of the Year Award for the season 2009/10, and his research has been reported in the *Financial Times*, the *Times*, the *Independent*, the *Observer*, the *Glasgow Herald*, the *Daily Express*, France's *Le Parisien*, Germany's *Frankfurter Algemeine Zeitung* and *Handelsblatt*, Austria's *Die Presse*, and Spain's *Expansión*.

Jason Bocarro is an Associate Professor in the Department of Parks, Recreation and Tourism Management at North Carolina State University. He has published over 40 peer-reviewed research journal publications spanning a number of disciplines, including medicine, sociology, public health, psychology, parks and recreation, exercise science and education, as well as book chapters and practitioner-based publications. His research has been featured in *Time Magazine*, the *Guardian*, national public radio and *USA Today*.

Guillaume Bodet is Professor of Sport Marketing and Management within the School of Sport Sciences at Université Claude Bernard Lyon-1 (Université de Lyon). He is a member of the Centre for Research on Innovation in Sport

(CRIS EA 647) and the Laboratory of Vulnerability and Innovation in Sport (L-Vis) as well as a Visiting Fellow at Loughborough University, UK. His research primarily deals with consumer behaviour regarding sport organizations, sporting events and sport brands. He has published many articles in peer-reviewed journals such as *European Sport Management Quarterly*, the *International Journal of Sports Marketing and Sponsorship*, *Journal of Retailing and Consumer Services* and *Psychology and Marketing*.

Ian Brittain is a research fellow in the Centre for Business in Society at Coventry Business School. He is an internationally recognized expert in the study of disability and paralympic sport and has attended the last four summer Paralympic Games in Sydney, Athens, Beijing and London. He is an experienced researcher and has published widely in a variety of books/book chapters and journals. He has also presented at a variety of national and international conferences, and has been successful in a number of large grant applications, including two Marie Curie International Incoming Fellowships for Dr Leonardo Mataruna from Brazil and Professor Jill Le Clair from Canada, for which he acts as Scientist in Charge.

Katherine Bruffy is a Lecturer on Sport Management and Programme Leader in the Department of Sport at the Unitec Institute of Technology, Auckland, New Zealand. Katie's passion for sport began as a youth swimmer and continued through her time as a collegiate synchronized swimmer. She began teaching in higher education in 2006 at the Ohio State University, where she also earned her PhD researching sport nostalgia. Particular research areas of interest include sport marketing, consumer behaviour, governance and sport development. Katie has worked within these research areas as a consultant for the Skycity Breakers Basketball Team, Auckland Mystics Netball Team and Auckland Cricket.

Andrew Byers, as a specialist in reproductive biology, has an interest in all aspects of animal breeding. His current research focus is on the effect of environmental pollutants which impact on reproductive health, but more broadly he has an interest in issues around animal health, welfare and ethical breeding practices. He has worked as an academic at a number of UK universities and is currently affiliated with the University of Nottingham School of Veterinary Medicine and Science.

Kevin Carpenter is an independent legal and sports consultant with experience across a broad range of disciplines, including regulatory, commercial, dispute resolution, competition and intellectual property. He advises individuals, sports governing bodies and public organizations on all aspects of sports law, business and policy. He has a focus on integrity, governance, regulatory and disciplinary matters, and makes regular public appearances internationally delivering presentations and commenting in the media on topical sports issues. He has published across a range of journals and produces a regular blog that is published by the international sports law resource LawInSport.

Ben Corbett spent 15 years in the sports industry before completing his PhD in Strategic Sport Management at Griffith University. He is currently a Lecturer at the Institute for Sports Business at Loughborough University in London. Ben's research interests include strategy, governance and high performance management.

Elwyn Cox is an experienced business consultant, project manager, curriculum advisor and lecturer. He has lectured at the University of Winchester for over 10 years, moving from the Business School to develop a Sport Management programme. Providing high-quality learning experiences for students has been his passion and his research has centred on practical pedagogic issues. He has also presented internationally on his views and research. Current projects include establishing a specialist sport sponsorship research centre focusing on the hybrid sport sponsor, and local sponsors in financing UK sport.

Antonio Davila has a dual appointment as Professor of Entrepreneurship and Professor of Accounting and Control at IESE Business School. He is the Alcatel Lucent Chair of Technology Management and has also been a professor at the Harvard Business School during 2013 and 2014, teaching in the MBA core curriculum. Before coming to IESE, he was a faculty member at the Graduate School of Business, Stanford University, after receiving his doctorate from the Harvard Business School. He teaches courses in innovation management, entrepreneurship, management accounting and control, and sports management at the Master's, doctoral and executive education level.

Jonathon Edwards is an Assistant Professor in the Faculty of Kinesiology at the University of New Brunswick (UNB), Canada. He teaches courses in sport marketing and sponsorship that include branding and brand management for the MBA in the Sport and Recreation Management programme at UNB. Jonathon uses applied qualitative research to explore sport delivery systems through institutional theory, and has published in a variety of sport management journals, spoken at a number of academic and practitioner's conferences, and conducted research on behalf of national sport organizations.

Michael Edwards is an Associate Professor in the Department of Parks, Recreation and Tourism Management at North Carolina State University. His research interests centre on social inequality in access to physical activity and sport environments, and sport's impact on community health and development. In 2011, he received the Oak Ridge Association Ralph E. Powe Junior Faculty Achievement Award, being recognized as one of the top 30 junior researchers in the USA. He has also spent over a decade managing professional baseball organizations in the United States and has received national recognition as Minor League Baseball *Executive of the Year* on two occasions.

Agnes Elling-Machartzi, PhD, has 25 years' experience in sport and academia, and is currently at the Mulier Institute's Centre for Research on Sports in Society in the Netherlands. Her research interests include sports and social inclusion/exclusion (gender, sexuality, ethnicity) and changing socio-psychological meanings in grassroots and elite sports biographies. Widely published in Dutch and English, Agnes is currently involved in a three-year research project on the development of women's football and (new) media, funded by the Netherlands Organization for Scientific Research (NWO).

David Forrest is a Professor of Economics at the University of Liverpool Management School. He has contributed extensively to the academic literature on both sports economics and the economics of gambling, and is a board member at both the *Journal of Sports Economics* and *International Gambling Studies*. He advises international agencies and sports federations on match-fixing issues. As a member of Britain's Responsible Gambling Strategy Board, he is also active in evaluating policies towards issues related to problem gambling.

George Foster is the Konosuke Matsushita Professor of Management at the Graduate School of Business, Stanford University. His areas of research, teaching and advising include entrepreneurship, sports management and globalization. He is the author or co-author of seven books or major reports and over 50 articles. He was a two-term member of the Global Agenda Council on Sports and Society for the World Economic Forum and has led or co-led two major World Economic Reports ('Global Entrepreneurship and the Successful Growth Strategies of Early-Stage Companies' and 'Entrepreneurial Ecosystems Around the Globe and Company Growth Dynamics'). One hallmark of his teaching at Stanford is the multiple senior executives from entrepreneurial ventures and the sports landscape that co-teach individual sessions. Over 60 executives regularly join his MBA classes each year for individual sessions. He has directed multiple executive programmes for the NFL and the NBPA, and is a co-author with Bill Walsh (the three-time Super Bowl winning coach) of *The Business of Sports*.

Andrea Geurin-Eagleman is a Senior Lecturer in Sport Management at Griffith University in Brisbane, Australia. She has published extensively on the topics of sport communication and marketing, specifically focusing on media portrayals of athletes of differing race, gender and nationality, as well as athletes' and sport organisations' use of social media. Her work has appeared in over 30 peer-reviewed academic journal articles and she has presented her research at numerous conferences around the world. She currently serves on the editorial boards of seven academic journals, and in 2015 was named a North American Society for Sport Management (NASSM) Research Fellow, recognizing her outstanding research contributions in the field of sport management.

Chris Gratton is Emeritus Professor of Sport Economics and Director of the Sport Industry Research Centre at Sheffield Hallam University. He currently has six academic books in print, the latest of which is *The Global*

Economics of Sport, which was published in 2012. His main research interests are: the estimation of the economic benefits of hosting major sports events; the estimation of the economic importance of sport including the construction of sport satellite accounts; and the analysis and modelling of large sport participation surveys.

Stacey Hall is an Associate Professor of Sport Management at the University of Southern Mississippi (USM). She has been published in international sport management, homeland security and emergency management journals, and has co-authored two textbooks—*Global Sport Facility Operations Management* and *Security Management for Sports and Special Events*. Stacey has also been referred to as one of the leading experts in sport security, with interviews in *USA Today, ESPN the Magazine, CBS New York* and *ESPN Outside the Lines*.

Andrew Harvey is a Researcher and Programme Manager at Birkbeck Sports Business Centre, University of London. In 2013 he won research funds from the European Commission to conduct an original empirical study of 1,500 professional football players across Europe as part of a project led by FIFPro, the world professional footballers' union. The results of the project informed a Good Practice Guide, entitled "Protect our Game." Andy has appeared regularly on television and radio to discuss his research findings. He is currently Programme Manager for the FIFPro Executive Education programme, and in addition to researching match-fixing, has published widely on sport, gender and sexuality.

Russell Holden runs In the Zone Sport and Politics Consultancy, providing insight into the interplay between sport and politics both in the UK and overseas, and offering teaching, research, consultancy and broadcasting expertise. He previously taught at Cardiff Metropolitan University and regularly lectures at the University of Worcester and Southampton Solent University. He has written widely on the politics of sport, more especially on the political economy of cricket, and has co-edited a special edition of *Sport and Society* ("Sport, Community and Citizenship" (Routledge)). He is also the co-founder of the United Kingdom Political Studies Association Sport and Politics Research Group.

Shannon Kerwin is an assistant professor in the Department of Sport Management at Brock University who teaches and conducts research in the area of management and leadership in sport, specifically looking at how personal and organizational values align in order to enhance important organizational outcomes, the role of conflict in the effectiveness of volunteer boards of directors, and how leadership is developed and fostered within the context of team/organizational culture.

Annelies Knoppers is a Professor in the Department of Governance and Organization Studies at the University of Utrecht in the Netherlands. Her research focus is on diversity and gender in sport organizations with the use of critical theory. Her emphasis is specifically on the gendering of positions of leadership. She has conducted this research in the USA and the Netherlands and has looked at coaches and sport managers in both paid and voluntary positions. After conducting more than 25 years of research on this topic, she has concluded that very little has changed in that time because the same issues keep reappearing. Possibly the users of this text can make a significant difference on this issue!

Joerg Koenigstorfer is a full Professor and holds the Chair of Sport and Health Management at Technische Universität München (Germany). In his research, Joerg investigates the managerial decisions of sport and health companies, and their impact on consumers and welfare. The results of these studies have been published in scientific journals (such as the *Journal of Marketing Research*, *Journal of Public Policy and Marketing*, *Appetite*, *British Journal of Nutrition*, *Physiology and Behavior*, *Journal of Sport Management*) and cited by various mass media outlets.

Dimitrios Kolyperas is a Lecturer in the Marketing and Retail division of Stirling Management School, Stirling University. His PhD focused on corporate social responsibility in football clubs as well as sports marketing. Dimitrios also holds an MBA from Cardiff University. His current research interests concentrate on sport management and marketing, corporate governance, as well as corporate social responsibility. He is currently the Programme Director of the BA in Marketing at Stirling University while remaining a fan of sport, in particular basketball.

Sebastian Kopera is an Assistant Professor at the Jagiellonian University in Kracow, where he researches and teaches e-business and e-commerce issues in sport and tourism industries. His current interests focus on the application of social media as a tool supporting innovation-oriented knowledge transfer and acquisition.

Haim Levi is a Research Associate at the Birkbeck Sport Business Centre, University of London, specialising on issues relating to sporting integrity. He has worked on several anti-match-fixing related projects, among them the Transparency International initiative 'Staying on Side' which was funded by the European Commission, as well as the international football players' union FIFPro's initiative (Protect Our Game Good Practice Guide for Professional Football Players' Associations) to tackle match-fixing in football. Haim had written business school case studies on a variety of sport governance and regulatory issues for classrooms in different academic and executive education programmes. He is currently part of the Financial Crime team at Deloitte UK.

Dongfeng Liu is Professor and Associate Dean at the School of Economics and Management at Shanghai University of Sport in China. His main research interests include sport events management, sports events evaluation, sport and urban development, and sport policy studies. He has over 30 publications to his name including books, refereed journal articles, refereed conference articles, and industry reports.

Daniel S. Mason is a Professor of Physical Education and Recreation and adjunct with the School of Business at the University of Alberta. His research focuses on sports leagues and franchises, cities, events and infrastructure development. His work has been published in the *Journal of Sport Management*, *Journal of Urban Affairs*, *Economic Development Quarterly*, *Managing Leisure*, *Economic Inquiry*, *Contemporary Economic Policy*, *Tourism Management* and *Urban Studies*. He was named a North American Society for Sport Management Research Fellow in 2004.

Fred Mason is an Associate Professor in Kinesiology at the University of New Brunswick, and teaches sport history, sport sociology and media studies related to sport. He has longstanding interests in the history of para sports, and in how sports media coverage connects to gender, disability and multi-cultural discourses. His work has been published in a variety of journals including the *International Review for the Sociology of Sport*, *Sport in Society*, *Sport History Review*, the *Canadian Bulletin of Medical History* and the *Electronic Green Journal*. He is currently engaged in a multi-year ethnographic project on ultrarunning in Canada.

Mark McDonald is an Associate Professor in the Mark H. McCormack Department of Sport Management at the University of Massachusetts Amherst, where he received a PhD in 1996. He has given more than 45 academic presentations and published 28 journal articles in such respected journals as the *Journal of Sport Management*, *Sport Marketing Quarterly*, *International Journal of Sports Marketing and Sponsorship* and *European Sport Management Quarterly*. He also received the NASSM Distinguished Sport Management Educator award in 2009. His research interests include experiential learning pedagogy, leadership, and leadership development.

Michael Naylor is currently a sport management Lecturer at Auckland University of Technology in New Zealand. Previously, he spent time in the United States and Canada as both a practitioner and scholar in the sport industry. His research interests include sport marketing, consumer psychology and social media. The projects he undertakes are based in a variety of participant and supporter contexts around the world.

Danny O'Brien is an Associate Professor and Head of Programme, Sport Management, in the School of Health Sciences at Bond University, Gold Coast, Australia. Danny has presented his work at over 30 international conferences and published many book chapters and articles in journals such as the *Journal of Sport Management*, *Sport Management Review*, *European Sport Management Quarterly*, *Annals of Tourism Research*, *Journal of Sustainable Tourism* and *European Journal of Marketing*. He is also an active reviewer for several sport management journals and is the Associate Editor for *Sport Management Review*.

Girish Ramchandani is a Reader at Sheffield Hallam University's Sport Industry Research Centre. His principal area of research is the evaluation of major sports events, and he has published widely on their economic, sport development, and elite performance outcomes. He is currently engaged by UK Sport to evaluate around 40 international sporting events until 2019.

Patrick A. Reid is a doctoral student in the Faculty of Physical Education and Recreation at the University of Alberta. He has been involved in sport management for more than 40 years. As a former Vice President of the Canadian Amateur Hockey Association and former Director General of the Sport Medicine and Science Council of Canada, Pat is currently assisting the City of Edmonton as the Executive Director of the Edmonton Combative Sports Commission, which governs professional mixed martial arts, boxing and wrestling events in the city.

Oliver Rick is currently on the faculty of the University of Massachusetts, Boston. He is a graduate of the Physical Cultural Studies programme, and has published on a broad number of topics in sports management. In particular his research interests have focused on global sport media and policy. In addition, during his time at the University of Maryland, Rick has crafted a second research focus, studying urban physical activity practices, cultures and policies. Building on this research he has several forthcoming publications that critically analyze the development of bicycling within urban settings, as well as the impacts of active transportation and recreation policies.

Leigh Robinson is Head of Sport at the University of Stirling. She works extensively with Olympic sport organizations and has a specialist research profile in the area of the effectiveness of National Federations and National Olympic Committees in developing sport systems. Leigh is editor (along with others) of *The Routledge Handbook of Sport Management*, *Managing Olympic Sport Organisations* and *Managing Voluntary Sport Organisations*. She is also a member of the board for sportscotland and the Director for Governance and Compliance for Commonwealth Games Scotland.

Ryan Scoats is a PhD candidate at the University of Winchester, where he also lectures part-time. His work focuses on the meanings people attach to threesomes and their interpretations of their experiences. Other research interests include masculinities, sport, sexualities, identity and consensual non-monogamy.

Olan Scott is an Assistant Professor in Sport Management at University of Canberra. He gained his PhD from Griffith University, Australia, where he explored the framing of sport broadcasts through the analysis of commentator narrative. Olan is heavily involved in industry-focused research including social media marketing, fan engagement and other media-related projects with organizations in Australia, Canada and New Zealand. Olan has attracted funding from industry partners and competitive grants (both internal and external). He is also a board member of the Canberra Cavalry Australian Baseball League team since 2015. He has been a lecturer in a variety of sport management courses, including sports marketing, sport management and development, and social media.

Aaron Smith is Professor and Deputy Pro-Vice Chancellor, Industry Engagement, at RMIT University in Melbourne, Australia. He has research interests in the management of psychological, organizational and policy change in business and sport. Aaron holds doctorates in both organizational change and cognitive science, and has written on cognitive and popular science as well as philosophy of science. He has also consulted in policy, governance, marketing, leadership, change management, human resource and performance management for a diverse range of organizations.

Kirsty Spence, Associate Professor, has worked in the Department of Sport Management at Brock University, in St Catharine's, Ontario, Canada, since 2004. Kirsty has accrued experience developing leaders within a university setting through developing and teaching curricula using experiential learning pedagogy as well as through research publications. Her teaching and research work has been specifically guided by use of Ken Wilber's All Quadrant, All Level (Integral) Model and the Leadership Development Framework (LDF) for over a decade. Kirsty was also certified as Master Integral Coach™ through Integral Coaching Canada® in 2011, which has also served as an excellent complement to inform her teaching and research practices.

Dene Stansall is horse racing consultant for the campaign group Animal Aid. He has written and lectured extensively on issues relating to the use of horses in sport, and counselled the Royal Society for the Prevention of Cruelty to Animals' (RSPCA) Scientific, Academic and Technical Committee. He has also addressed the Associate Parliamentary Group on Animal Welfare in the UK Parliament. He is frequently requested to comment in the mainstream media.

Constantino Stavros is an Associate Professor in Marketing, at the School of Economics, Finance and Marketing at RMIT University, located in Melbourne, Australia. He possesses a global understanding of marketing, particularly in the application of strategic concepts in communication, and the development and function of marketing both through and of sport.

Bob Stewart is Professor of Sport Policy in the College of Sport and Exercise Science at Victoria University, Melbourne Australia. Bob has a special interest in player regulation in professional team sports, and the ways in which the forces of neoliberalism and hyper-commercialism shape the structure and conduct of contemporary sport. Bob is the sole author of *Sport Funding and Finance* (Routledge, 2015); co-author – with Aaron C.T. Smith – of *Rethinking Drug Use in Sport: Why the War Will Never be Won* (Routledge, 2014); editor of *The Games are Not the Same: The Political Economy of Football in Australia* (Melbourne University Press, 2007); and lead author of *Australian Sport: Better by Design? The Evolution of Sport Policy in Australia* (Routledge, 2004).

Kamilla Swart is an Associate Professor in the Tourism and Event Management Department, Faculty of Business and Management Sciences, Cape Peninsula University of Technology. Her research interests include sport and event tourism, with a specific focus on mega-events and event policies, strategies and evaluations. She was instrumental in driving the 2010 Fédération Internationale de Football Association (FIFA) World Cup Research Agenda and served as the City of Cape Town's Research Coordinator for 2010.

Alex Thurston is a final year PhD candidate at Loughborough University, studying sport policy and small voluntary sport clubs. He completed a Master's at Coventry Business School examining control in swimming clubs using qualitative methods.

Gabriela Tymowski is an Associate Professor in the Faculty of Kinesiology at the University of New Brunswick, Fredericton, Canada. Her teaching and research expertise lies in the field of applied ethics with a focus on vulnerable populations, primarily children and animals, in sport. She has studied and/or lectured in Australia, England, the USA, South Korea, Barbados and Greece with the International Olympic Academy. Her most recent publication is 'The virtue of compassion: Animals in sport, hunting as sport, and entertainment' (edited by J. Gillett and M. Gilbert, *Sport, Animals and Society*, Routledge, 2014).

Kate Westberg is an Associate Professor in Marketing at RMIT University in Melbourne, Australia. Kate's research focuses on the controversial issues that can arise in professional sport and the resulting implications for managing the sport brand and key stakeholders. In addition to athlete transgressions, she is also interested in exploring the implications resulting from the association of sport with 'risky consumption' products such as gambling, alcohol and unhealthy food.

Bradley Wilson has a keen interest in sponsorship, branding, understanding image transfer and methods advancements research. He has multiple affiliations (as Associate Professor of Communication, Branding and Urban Creative Cultures, Facultad de Administración, Universidad de los Andes, Colombia; Senior Lecturer in Advertising. School of Media and Communication, RMIT University, Australia; and Visiting Professor of Department of Services Management, Universität Bayreuth, Germany) and also serves on four editorial advisory boards.

Darryl Wilson is a Principal Lecturer at Sheffield Hallam University. He teaches economics and research on the Sport Business Management-related degrees. His current research interests include measuring success at major sporting events, with a particular focus on the Commonwealth Games, and he has published several journal articles in this area.

Mathieu Winand is a Lecturer in Sport Management in the School of Sport at the University of Stirling and Programme Director of the MSc in Sport Management. He is also an Associate Researcher at the Belgian Olympic Chair, Université Catholique de Louvain. His expertise is in the area of sport governance, performance management, innovation in sport and sport policy.

Jiandong Yi is Deputy Director of the general planning and legal affairs department of the Beijing 2022 Olympic Winter Games Bid Committee and Director of the Research Centre of Sport Governance and Sport Development in Wuhan Sport University. In 2012–2013 he was a Visiting Scholar at the Weatherhead East Asian Institute of Columbia University and focused on the area of sports economics and management. Previously he gained his doctoral degree in Humane and Sociological Science of Sports at Beijing Sport University (1999–2002). His research interests include sports system reform, sporting culture and sport governance. He is currently hosting a major national research project on the reform of western sport governance and modernization of China's sport governance.

FOREWORD

There has never been a more appropriate time to have a book like *Contemporary Issues in Sport Management* appear. Hence I congratulate the editor Terri Byers for her enterprise and zeal. The use of a "three-layer approach," to identify the current issues facing sport management and those who manage it, is both important and timely.

As we can appreciate, sport as a phase of human physical activity has assumed greater or lesser importance, starting with primitive societies and continuing in later societies up to the present day. Sport of varying types has been used by people of all ages in a variety of ways as the human species has evolved and these creatures lived out their lives. Sport has literally become a social force, impacting on society both generally and as a vital concern, for those desiring to employ it professionally in a variety of ways.

However, as is the case with so many facets of life on Earth, such involvement can be used beneficially or misused to the subsequent improvement or detriment of humankind. It is my belief that we are using it well in some ways, *but that we are also abusing it badly in others!* In the case of competitive sport, I believe we have gradually and increasingly done the latter (i.e. perhaps approaching a stage where we could overall be doing more harm than good with it). Conversely, in the case of related physical activity (i.e. regular exercise or "physical activity education") in the developed world, I believe humans are too often *"abusing it by first not understanding it and then by not using it more intelligently"*! (Ironically, in the "undeveloped world," people often get *too much* "exercise" just to stay alive!)

As I see it, we are often abusing sport, or certain people are "using us," but not to the world's best advantage. People are not getting the most value from it. Indeed they may often even be experiencing negative effects or disvalue from it. In the case of exercise, in the so-called advanced societies, we are using it insufficiently and therefore not to its best advantage either. How this has happened since earliest times is difficult to understand.

Please understand this: I don't for a moment argue here that the proper use of sport and related activity throughout the planet's affairs could be a panacea for all of the world's ills, the elixir that would create a heretofore unknown era of good will and peace worldwide. I do believe, however, that wisely employed it could enrich lives "healthwise" and "recreationally" for many more millions than it is doing so presently. In addition, I would also assert that *the wise use of exercise, sport and sound health practices throughout people's entire lives would indubitably go a long way toward keeping them happier and healthier in lives that become extended by years because of this type of life practice.*

What I am arguing is that, employed properly and correctly, sport and physical activity—as one of a number of vital social forces (e.g. nationalism, ecology)—could contribute to the improvement of the current situation enormously. Moreover, I believe that the active use of competitive sport worldwide to promote what have been called *moral* values, traits or attributes, as opposed to so-called *socio-instrumental* values, would create a social force of such strength and power that humankind might be helped as it confronts the social and physical devastation looming ahead. At the very least, I believe such active promotion would delay to a considerable degree the onset of what promises to become an increasingly destructive societal situation.

Such an "untenable societal scenario" has been described vividly by Walter Truett Anderson in the essay "Futures of the Self," taken from *The Future of the Self: Inventing the Postmodern Person* (1997). He sketched four different scenarios as postulations for the future of earthlings in this ongoing adventure of civilization. Anderson's "One World, Many Universes" version is the most likely to occur. This is a scenario characterized by high economic growth, steadily increasing technological progress and globalization combined with high psychological development. Such psychological maturity, he predicts, will be possible for a certain segment of the world's population because "active life spans will be gradually lengthened through various advances in health maintenance and medicine" (Anderson, 1997: 251–3).

The systemic-change force mentioned above that is shaping the future, this all-powerful force, may well exceed Earth's ability to cope. As gratifying as such factors as "globalization along with economic growth" and "psychological development" may seem to the folks in a coming "One-World, Many Universes" scenario, there is a flip side to this prognosis. Anderson identifies this image as "The Dysfunctional Family" scenario. All of these benefits of so-called progress are highly expensive and available now only to relatively few of the seven billion plus people on Earth. Anderson foresees this as "a world of modern people happily doing their thing; of modern people still obsessed with progress, economic gain, and organizational bigness; and of postmodern people being trampled and getting angry" (ibid.: 51). As people get angrier, present-day terrorism in North America could seem like child's play.

Hence, the charge I have given myself is to make the case that the social phenomenon known as competitive sport is largely being used incorrectly, and the social phenomenon known as developmental physical activity (and related health education) is being employed insufficiently and inadequately. Both of these activities promoted one way or another through physical activity education and related health instruction could combine to provide much greater value to humankind. They could be a social force that used properly could go a long way to the creation of a better, more peaceful world. *Presently I believe that the relationship between these two aspects (i.e. sport and exercise) of a potentially most powerful social force is "out of joint" in the developed world. It must be rectified for the ultimate good of humankind!*

So far so good, you may say. But just how does this situation that I describe have a relationship to this new introductory text edited by Terri Byers? It does in this way. Those experienced management scholars, who have been invited to contribute to this text, have provided a wide variety of contexts and settings that individually and totally identify the necessary theory and practice that professional students must understand if they hope to obtain employment and subsequent success in the field of sport and physical activity management.

As I said at the outset, sport and related physical activity have become a vital force, a *sine qua non* if I may, as the world moves ahead in this twenty-first century. Everything considered, I feel that I must conclude by saying that we can use it very well, well, fairly well or not well at all. The many chapters and cases in this book can provide you with a solid and complete underpinning as you enter a lifelong career as a young professional. The editor has constructed a text that enables us as readers to understand a wide variety of issues that are important to the business and management of sport, but without neglecting the implications of our actions as managers within our field (sport), society and different groups. The book also encourages sound business skills with responsible decision-making practices to encourage you not only to "make an impact" but to also think critically about what impact you are making!

The editor Terri Byers gets you off to a "rousing start"! Whatever happens thereafter is up to you.

Earle F. Zeigler, PhD, LLD, DSc

Hon. Past President, North American Society for
Sport Management (1986)

ACKNOWLEDGEMENTS

Firstly, my biggest thank you goes to all the chapter authors who have provided their expertise and enthusiasm to this edited text. There are over 50 authors who have contributed to this text and I am indebted to them for their insightful contributions. Those who read this book should appreciate the international scope of expertise these academics and industry professionals have brought to an increasingly complex subject—the management of sport. Included in that are my sincere thanks to Earle F. Zeigler for his thoughtful foreword: his experience of our sport management community is legendary! Many thanks also to Sage, especially Chris Rojek, Gemma Shields, Delayna Spencer and Tom Bedford, for the opportunity to produce something 'a little bit different', and for all the support provided throughout the writing and production of this text.

In addition I would like to thank colleagues and friends for supporting me, whether they realized it or not! My gratitude goes to Trevor Slack, who has always encouraged and inspired me to write and work hard—it was over 20 years ago that the Slack family took me under their wing as a graduate student in England and I have always been grateful for their continued support. Special thanks go to CARNiVAL (EU-funded project) partners Jöerg Koenigstorfer, Kamilla Swart and Jason Bocarro for their input into this book and their collegiality over the past years, which has made international collaborations like this possible and enjoyable. Thanks also to the reviewers who provided encouraging feedback on the chapter drafts.

Finally and most importantly, thank you to Andrew and Lochlan—family make everything worthwhile.

Terri Byers

INTRODUCTION

Welcome to the first book specifically devoted to discussing and analyzing 'contemporary issues' in sport management. This text is an innovative approach to introducing the subject of sport management and offers readers an engaging, informative but challenging introduction to some of the most pressing contemporary issues in our industry. Chapters written by over 50 academic experts and emerging leaders in sport management research as well as some industry professionals provide students new to sport management education with a unique insight into a wide variety of issues and some management tools to contribute to our industry in an effective and responsible, sustainable manner. A careful read through this book will show you WHAT many of the pressing issues in the field of sport management are, how these many issues are *interrelated*, and how you can analyze and assess problems using a wide variety of academic research and theories to develop effective solutions to these challenges. This book encourages you to THINK about issues, problems and situations, and consider the implications (short, medium and long term) of your choices and decisions.

As an introduction this text does not cover advanced theories of management or extensively use comparative perspectives to analyze issues. We do have cases and "thinking points," and consider different contexts, from around the globe, from China, Australia, Norway and the Middle East to the UK, Germany, the USA and Canada. What is important to recognize is that this book shows you how theories that have been developed outside of sport and inside the sporting context can help managers make better decisions, develop a deeper understanding, create more sustainable business and avoid making costly mistakes. It also encourages developing sport managers to think critically, seek evidence and access information to inform their decisions and question current practices in order to improve the leadership and management of sport in today's society. By introducing sport management through the contemporary issues in the field, readers will firstly gain an appreciation of the challenges they may face in managing sport. The chapter authors have included cases from around the globe so readers will get a feel for the sizable global nature of the industry. Various disciplines such as sociology, economics, management and psychology are used to analyze cases and illustrate how being a sport manager is a multi-disciplinary task. Accessing theory from various knowledge disciplines can help us be more effective, critical managers. We will also become aware of how "interconnected" the issues in this book are and their importance to the effective management of sport. How issues are connected is explained in the next section describing the structure of the book. Enjoy reading and good luck with your future endeavours in sport management.

STRUCTURE OF THE BOOK

The book's structure rests on three levels of analysis: global, national and organizational. These are then interconnected to help demonstrate the complexity of management in a sporting context. A final fourth part draws together the different levels of analysis in a chapter entitled "Employability in Sport Management" to reiterate the essential linkages between all the chapters presented in the book. The text is structured this way to allow us to communicate the forces which influence the management and practice of sport. These global, national and organizational forces do not operate independently, and so within each chapter we show the interrelationship between the global, national and organizational, or the interrelationship between chapters within a part, through highlighting in bold those concepts which overlap with other chapters in the book. For instance, if you read the chapter on globalization, you will notice words such as **technology**, **political** and **economic** in heavier type because these concepts are integral to understanding globalization, and you should read the other chapters on these topics with this in mind. For example, the chapter on mega sport events is related to chapters on globalization, politics, sponsorship and economy, and so you will understand how the management of these sport events is complex but integrated.

Part One: Globalization

The first part of this book begins with the "big picture": global issues. The issues covered in this section affect virtually *all* sport organizations, sports and nations. You may not deal with these issues on a daily basis, but they are a crucial part of the external environment of all sport organizations, and so understanding this environment allows you as a sport manager to monitor trends in technology, corruption, politics, economics and ethical practices. This part begins by examining the concept of globalization itself. In the first chapter, the authors present the term "glocalization" to demonstrate the complex nature of understanding the globalization of sport and its significant impact on managers of sport. Chapter 2 takes a look at one of the most prevalent and fundamental concepts in sport management, commercialization. It explores the relatively quick emergence and commercialization of mixed martial arts and the Ultimate Fighting Championship. An essential chapter that illustrates the links between commercialization, globalization, branding, governance and the media—you will immediately begin to see how interesting yet complex the management of sport can be. Chapter 3 introduces you to the impact of technology and innovation in sport , focusing on the world of professional sport where innovation can be a key strategic advantage to business survival and success. A fascinating chapter linked to gambling/betting, doping in sport, stadium management and much more, as it illustrates the pervasive use of technology and importance of the proactive drive to innovate in the sport industry. Chapter 4 focuses on a truly global (but unfortunate) issue for sport managers: corruption. This chapter provides an introduction and some of the research on corruption in sport, but concentrates on demonstrating an economic perspective and encourages you to think about how this information can be used to combat corrupt practices of match fixing in modern sport. With links to chapters on trust and control in sport, gambling and betting and doping, this chapter sets the scene for new sport managers' need to develop a critical view of the industry. Chapter 5 complements the preceding chapters on globalization and commercialization by illustrating how a basic economic understanding of the sport industry is essential to managers of sport. The focus here is on the sponsorship and broadcasting of major events and the changing economic business environment in which global sport operates. Chapter 6 represents an introduction to ethics in sport and the many ethical issues which arise for sport managers as a result of the increasing commercialization and globalization of sport. It introduces you to a framework for making ethical decisions in sport management in the context of commercialization pressures, and raises awareness of the broad scope of ethical issues in sport, including managing the development of a sport, the impacts and moral issues of 'sport' hunting, and ethical issues in sport innovation and entrepreneurship. Chapter 7 is concerned with the politics and governance of sport, which introduces you to the "realities" of sport governance and politics. Chapter 8 focuses on international sport law and the issues in a North American and European context. Chapter 9, on media and communications, introduces you to the importance of media training for athletes, coaches and sport managers. Chapter 10, on Human Resource Management (HRM) in sport, focuses on the key skills and tasks for an HR manager, while also encouraging you to appreciate a strategic approach to managing human resources in order to maintain or improve the management of sport organizations. Chapter 11, on strategic management, gives a concise overview of its key principles and applies these to the analysis of creating and managing a sport organization's strategy.

Part 1 ends with a controversial and little talked about subject, the use of animals in sport. Chapter 12 highlights the delicate nature of the use of animals in sport. Animals do not volunteer to be involved in sport and we have a responsibility to ensure their welfare. Do we even have the right to involve them? While many students may not directly go into sport management involving animals, grasping the issues presented in this chapter is crucial for a comprehensive and thorough understanding of sport management contexts. This chapter also illustrates nicely the link to understanding ethics in sport and sport management, i.e. the prevalence of corruption including doping across different sport sectors. Many people are indirectly involved in sport using animals, such as corporate days or sponsorship relations at the races, and so a knowledge of the issues in this regard is relevant for responsible management development.

Part Two: National Issues

The second part of the book introduces a variety of issues that may manifest differently in different countries, that are influenced by global issues, and that therefore provide a cultural context to working in the industry. Each chapter does not have the scope to cover the many various international contexts so often a limited number of countries will be used to illustrate the importance of the topic. You may want to consider how, for example, match fixing, policy or participation take place in different countries compared to those mentioned in the chapter. There is even an argument for some of these chapters being seen as "global" issues—match fixing for example is a problem globally and could be explained in this way. However, for the purpose of this introductory book it is presented with examples primarily from the UK. Chapter 13 is on sport policy and focuses primarily on sport policy development in China, where this is relatively new and concentrates on achieving the goals of the Chinese government. While the use of sport to achieve government objectives is not new or unique, it is new to the Chinese government, and so we can analyze their attempts to learn about the management of sport in this context and compare these to other countries' success in using sport in this way. Chapter 14 on mega sporting events introduces the complexity of organizing and the politics of securing the rights to host events such as the Olympics and World Cups. Very topically, the chapter begins to assess the challenges that arise with measuring and ensuring positive legacies from these events. Chapter 15 focuses on participation in sport, the historical development of increased interest in sport participation, trends in participation and the implications for managers of these trends. With key relevance to sport funding, policy, globalization and control chapters, this chapter illustrates a number of contemporary issues within such aspects as sustained participation, relations to elite sport, access / equity and accountability with regard to the benefits of participation.

Chapter 16, on leadership, provides a comprehensive introduction to a concept which scholars have struggled for decades to define and theorize about. The authors focus on transformational leadership and provide guidance on how to meet the challenges of providing effective leadership in sport management. Chapter 17, on gender, discusses several current debates in the gender and sport domain. You will recognize here the implications of commercialization and professionalization on women's football. Gender is an important nuance of sporting life and managers must increasingly be sensitive to how this is influenced by and influences sport experiences as well as its role in shaping those experiences. Chapter 18 on performance management is a no-nonsense introduction to a vital task for sport managers—the evaluation and management of an organization's performance. A practical chapter linked to chapters on control and strategy, you will enjoy this insight into how and how not to manage performance.

Chapter 19, on doping, points to an unfortunate reality in sport and provides the tools and knowledge for you to think about the implications of doping in sport: it also confirms the seriousness of the problem. The challenge for future managers is to be critical of existing systems and values that may not be effective in eradicating doping and to provide innovative solutions to a long-standing problem which threatens the future of all sport. Chapter 20 on gambling and sports betting gives an international flavour to the introduction of this topic: the legal status of betting in several countries is explained and the implications for sport managers are discussed.

As the chapter illustrates the interconnectiveness of managing sport, you will notice that reading the chapters on law, technology, economy, match fixing and funding will further enhance your understanding of the issues around gambling and betting in sport.

Chapter 21 looks at funding for sport and, while it focuses on the context of sport in the UK, it also makes some comparisons with other countries, which can help you appreciate there are different funding models/options, each of which comes with advantages and disadvantages. This chapter highlights a fundamental problem with all funding for sport that comes via government—the transient and short-term nature which makes planning and sustainable performance a significant challenge for managers. Chapter 22 on match fixing takes an in-depth look at various cases from England, Finland and Turkey, which hint at the global scale of the match fixing problem but also show how this manifests at a national level. Chapter 23 on disability sport introduces you to some of the problems faced by disabled athletes and the challenges they face in participating in sport. The chapter encourages you to think about what sport managers can do to provide greater inclusivity within the sport system for these athletes.

Part Three: Organizational Issues

Part 3 takes a closer look at management in sport and what happens inside various types of organizations and sports. These contemporary issues are multi-disciplinary, covering sociological issues and organizational/management structure issues as well as marketing and ethics, with clear links to previous chapters indicated by bold text as was discussed earlier. These issues are of more immediate concern to sport managers and so you will begin to get a feel for tasks and knowledge relevant to managing a successful sport organization. Chapter 24 is concerned with ownership and has clear links to the financing/funding of sport. It covers different types of ownership in sport organizations and their inherent strengths and weaknesses, as well as how the external environment may serve to regulate ownership and the implications this has for sport managers.

The two chapters that follow are concerned with social media. We have provided two chapters on this contemporary issue as it is one of the most prevalent, rapidly expanding and misunderstood tools in sport management—until now. While social media are often adopted as a fast, free and presumably more effective than traditional marketing method of reaching consumers and members, there are challenges and implications to using this technology which sport managers need to be aware of in order to manage their impacts successfully. Chapter 25 is concerned with the role of social media in sport and outlines some of these challenges, but also provides insight into the opportunities presented by this form of marketing. The chapter highlights the complexity of the social media concept from a sport management research perspective, and particularly discusses the challenges and risks associated with managing social media. To provide a balance, the authors also acknowledge and discuss that there are still many opportunities for research in social media and that this is much needed to inform sport management practice. Chapter 26, on the importance and application of social media, provides a more hands-on instructional analysis of this tool. This chapter takes you through the various approaches for developing and implementing social media marketing strategies, and encourages an appreciation of the importance of a strategic approach to building relationships through social media, brands and marketing practices.

Chapter 27, on brand management, adopts a step-by-step approach to how to build a brand, recognize successful brands and how a sport manager can establish brand loyalty. With clear links to chapters on trust, sponsorship and loyalty in particular, the author, through cases studies on rebranding Reebok and the challenges of building a brand, provides an excellent introduction to the concept of brand management in sport. Chapter 28, on crisis management, is an interesting revelation on the current reality of managing sport events and provides you with key tools to supply safe and effective sport event products. The importance of understanding chapters on media and communication, sport law and control becomes apparent when reading this chapter. Chapter 29 on sexuality and homohysteria is another fascinating yet little talked about subject in the sport management world. The authors reveal some crucial links to chapters on gender, media and governance, and encourage sport managers to consider their role in proactively engaging with this subject. Chapter 30 on loyalty focuses on defining fan loyalty and relates this to the concept of customer lifetime value from the perspective of different stakeholders. The authors demonstrate the importance of loyalty in the management and marketing of sport. Chapter 31, on trust and control, in sport introduces two very complex, yet rarely mentioned concepts relevant to sport managers. Control is paradoxically necessary for sport managers yet misunderstood, and trust is integral but easily damaged, so not easily repaired. Via links to chapters on corruption, player transgression, ethics, doping, animals, match fixing and governance in particular, this chapter illustrates nicely the complexity and challenges of being a manager in different sport contexts. Chapter 32 introduces the importance of sponsorship to sport and begins to discuss the role of sponsorship in corporate social responsibility (CSR). Chapter 33 on athlete transgression illustrates the fragile nature of brands, sponsorship relations and the role sport managers have in managing the actions of their athletes. The implications of transgressions are also discussed as well as tools/strategies for managing such occurrences. With important relevance to other chapters on crisis management, media and communication as well as commercialization and trust, this chapter is essential if you wish to work in high profile, elite/professional sport. Chapter 34 on CSR, the final chapter in this section, provides a comprehensive introduction to this rapidly evolving issue in sport. It makes a particular distinction between the CSR *of* sport and *through* sport, and discusses key managerial issues in the implementation of CSR. Essential, practical, but grounded in theory and evidence, this chapter is a fitting end to the book as it relates to globalization and media, participation, mega sporting events, economy, ownership, ethics—in short, almost every preceding chapter!

These chapters represent contemporary issues as found in the media, in practice and in the academic realm, and have been selected because they are prominent and, in some cases, because they are not prominent enough and require your attention! We now turn to the final part, which draws on all the material presented thus far. The section on employability challenges you to consider and reconsider what you do and do not know, and encourages you to make a difference in the sport industry.

Part Four: Employability

This final part focuses on employability in sport and draws on all chapters in this book. If you are seeking employment in the sport industry, or wish to manage a sport club, a stadium or a National Governing Body, or perhaps are a sport entrepreneur who sees an opportunity in this growing industry, it is vital you recognize that the labour market is global and also understand how globalization affects us as employers and employees.

This part consists of a single concluding chapter that examines contemporary issues and the employability "race" in sport management. It outlines the nature of the industry and the essential skills and knowledge you will need to be successful, as well as offering a reminder that innovation, ethical decision making and social responsibility do not always have to be at odds with economic gain, long-term growth and financial stability. Think for yourself, think outside the box, and be critical in and of your decisions as a manager of sport!

CHAPTER STRUCTURE

The contemporary issues introduced at each of these levels are firstly illustrated through evidence from the media. To do this, each chapter provides three quotes which demonstrate the significance of their topic in the news and help you the reader begin to understand why the concept/issue has been selected for the book and why the concept is important to sport managers. Specific Learning Outcomes, which indicate what knowledge you should gain from the chapter, are followed by an introduction to each chapter. The authors for each chapter have constructed a number of case studies and/or "thinking points" to contextualize the contemporary issues, and they also supply some relevant theory / discussion (Tools for Analysis) to help "analyze" the issue and develop a deeper understanding of it and how sport managers may think about dealing with problems and developments in their field. This leads on to an "Action Learning" section, which encourages you to consider the case studies/thinking points and the "Tools for Analysis" together and answer some challenging questions which you may face as the manager of a sport, programme or event. Some chapters focus on a particular sport and others will illustrate a contemporary issue as it applies to different sports or different countries.

Chapter authors have also been afforded some flexibility in some cases in order to present the subject in the manner in which they felt most appropriate.

Therefore, all chapters are not rigidly structured identically. Some cases are long and others quite short, some chapters have two cases while others have four or five, depending on the need. In some cases you will find "thinking points," which are shorter cases for consideration.

Some chapters are longer than others as we did not want to stifle an author's interpretation and presentation of their material and nor did we want to force authors to cover aspects of their subject that were not integral to their chosen focus. This variability provides for interesting reading and encourages you to pay attention to the content of each chapter rather than provide the "cookie cutter" style that is common amongst introductory texts. This also helps develop your ability to embrace diversity—a skill you will very much need as a sport manager in these contemporary times as illustrated by our final chapter on employability!

Overall, this book exposes you to a wide variety of issues and the opinions, perspectives and views of over 50 academics/practitioners: it is our pleasure to write on these subjects and we would encourage you to continue to read beyond the theory and ideas presented here. This is an "introduction" to the management of sport and so with your critical thinking skills you should be able to search and find other authors who also focus on these issues, and in time, begin to construct your own informed opinions and innovative practices to make a meaningful contribution to sport.

PART ONE
GLOBAL ISSUES

PART MAP

1

GLOCAL SPORT: IMPACT ON CORPORATIONS AND INSTITUTIONS

OLIVER RICK, CALLIE BATTS-MADDOX AND DAVID L. ANDREWS

> Perhaps the reason that it [the IPL] continues to capture the global cricketing imagination despite all the caveats is that, unlike so many other sporting competitions around the world, it could genuinely be won by any of the teams taking part.
>
> (*The Wall Street Journal*, 7 April 2015)

> As popular and annoying as Justin Bieber, the Indian Premier League makes its presence felt once more.
>
> (*The Hindu*, 8 April 2015)

> Only the IPL has the ability to entice, draw in, make you jump around like a "Belieber" and yet make you feel like you have just wasted three hours of your life all in one single match.
>
> (*International Business Times*, 7 April 2015)

LEARNING OUTCOMES

Upon completion of this chapter, students will be able to:

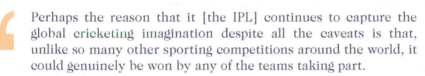

- Understand a comprehensive definition of glocalization.

- Conceptualize the complexity of global interconnectivity.

- Understand the interaction of the local and global as playing a role in sport management at many levels, as being fundamental to the formation of institutions, events and labor flows.

- Discuss ways in which the concept of local "authenticity" and untethered global identities are used to structure and market sports globally.

INTRODUCTION

Globalization is a complex and diverse process, and one which—whether we realize it or not—impacts on virtually all aspects of our lives, including sport. However, sport is not simply a passive receptor molded by the forces of globalization. The cultural, political and economic significance of sport render it a contributory element to the very nature of contemporary globalization. As a result, within this chapter, our aim is to examine the specificities of globalization, as they are manifest within, and through, the practices and institutions underpinning contemporary sport culture. In more specific terms, our aim is to outline the relationship between sport and globalization.

Globalization has been characterized as the condition of increasingly complex interconnectivity between peoples and places around the globe (Tomlinson, 1999). Although this complex global interconnectivity has long historical antecedents, recent developments in communications and logistic technology have increased the speed at which these forms of globalization are advancing. Today life is defined by its globally interconnected nature, where we routinely interact with goods, people and media from around the world in our day-to-day lives. Whereas in earlier phases within communications technology, social and cultural life was centered almost exclusively on the local, today, while we may be emplaced within the local, we are, almost unavoidably, simultaneously implicated in social and cultural networks and relations that are truly global in scale. Hence, to be an effective manager of sporting events, teams and institutions, one is compelled to be attentive to how sport is impacted by, and impacts upon, the global.

Within this overarching process of increasing global interconnectivity, sport has played a role in facilitating the globalizing process, whilst also being wholly shaped by it. Sport was once defined by its local specificities, where there existed a multitude of relatively parochial sport forms that were associated with particular nations, regions or even municipalities. Facilitated by a period of sporting standardization, or sportization (Maguire, 1999), centered in Britain during the late nineteenth century, the sporting system became increasingly rationalized and uniform both within, and between, nations. This sporting standardization allowed for the possibility of national and international sporting competition, since it transformed sport from being an incoherent patchwork of locally expressed activities, into becoming a highly bureaucratic and rationalized global system. Having evolved for more than a century, the global sport order now constitutes a comprehensive network of events and competitions stretching around the world. As such in this chapter we discuss the specificities of this sporting globalization, and examine how international sport forms have developed out of what were once predominantly local expressions of competitive physical activity.

As previously noted, globalization is a complex process, and sport as a global entity is intricately intertwined with the global flows and interconnections constitutive of the global condition. Numerous scholars have discussed sport's position as both producer and product of the global (e.g. Andrews and Grainger, 2007; Andrews and Ritzer, 2007; Bairner, 2001; Campbell, 2011; Harvey et al., 1996). However, what is also clear is that, whilst sport plays an important role in the formation of global interconnections, it still maintains its rootedness in the local. Indeed the global flows and relations that define our times are underpinned by local contexts. In other words, whilst there is increasing global interconnectivity, the local continues to matter. The process of becoming global has not resulted in an homogenization of sporting forms, leading to exact replication of sporting practices and institutions around the world. Instead, and as in other aspects of contemporary culture, we suggest sport is currently informed by a complicated interaction between the local and the global, leading to what has been widely referred to as a sporting glocalization (Cho, 2009; Giulianotti and Robertson, 2004; Kobayashi, 2012). Certainly some dimensions to sporting business, governance and practice exhibit commonalities wherever they are enacted, yet the peculiarities of specific regional and national cultures mean that sport is not uniformly represented, manifest or experienced in the same way everywhere. We therefore want to resist any approaches to global sport that conceptualize it only as resultant of "the compression of the world and the intensification of consciousness of the world as a whole" (Robertson, 1992: 8). Instead this chapter explains and demonstrates throughout our case studies, that "the globalization that we are now faced with is far from simplistic and one-sided" (Silk and Falcous, 2005: 450). Instead we agree with Silk and Falcous when they go on to state that "globalization is disordered, full of paradox and the unexpected, and of irreversible and juxtaposed complexity" (2005: 450). Sport at times combines local dimensions with global processes and flows, so that "In spite of globalization, sports remain inherently connected to national and local roots" (Cho, 2009: 321). Sport not only maintains local roots, but also in many senses the global nature of sport relies upon the continuing presence of the local.

Sport managers should be aware that sport can no longer be defined by a simple uni-directional process of global homogenization, but instead should be attentive to the mutual interpenetration of the local and the global as the glocal. It is important to understand that "the corporate strategy of glocalization manifests and articulates the complexities of the global cultural economy at large," of which sport is an important part (Kobayashi, 2012: 45). In other words the running of sporting entities of any size and scale will be most effective when those involved recognize that any sporting corporation, institution or practice exists at the nexus of global forces and processes, and local experiences and expectations.

Exploring the international expansion of road cycling, and its local histories

Professional road cycling events have a long history, one that is understood to have burgeoned primarily from a traditional Western European center that includes France, Belgium, the Netherlands, Spain and Italy in particular (Witherell, 2010). The top tier of road cycling has always been commercialized; teams have always been identified by their major sponsors, and events often started as corporate marketing exercises (Sarrantonio, 2005). Indeed the Giro D'Italia's iconic pink leader's jersey was meant to represent the pink *La Gazzetta dello Sport* newspaper, its primary sponsor (Fotheringham, 2013). Yet, despite this historical center, cycling has at various points in the twentieth and twenty-first centuries also spread to be included in events around the world. Indeed Australia and the USA held international cycling events as early as the first half of the twentieth century. However, within the modern cycling era, under the comprehensive governance of the Union Cycliste Internationale (UCI), cycling has gradually experienced a more extensive global diffusion. A greater variety of countries have come to host teams and events at various levels of cycling in its many disciplines. Clearly developments in communications technologies have come to underpin the capability of sports media, logistics and marketing to incorporate and take advantage of more national markets. From track cycling world cup events in Columbia, to road cycling World Tour events in China, mountain bike world cup events in South Africa, and cyclocross world cup events in the Czech Republic, cycling as a professional sport, especially road cycling, has clearly come to have a truly global reach. However, whilst there have been identifiable shifts towards a global structure to the sport, from its governing body down, that have surpassed the global nature of cycling as a sport previously, cycling still maintains its local meaningfulness. As an example, races such as Liege-Bastogne-Liege are still a major part of the cycling calendar, a race that started well over 100 years ago in the Wallonian region of Belgium. Additionally this desire to maintain these locally meaningful dimensions to events has meant even the slightest changes to long-standing race routes can invoke resistance and consternation from fans (Rogers, 2012).

The locally resonant and historical dimensions to many of cycling's events, teams and institutions continue to exist alongside the increasingly global presence of professional cycling. However, this is not merely a co-presence of the global and local, but global networks around cycling that have drawn on these local elements. Companies leverage names such as "Roubaix," the name of the finishing town in the famous "monument of cycling" Paris-Roubaix, in selling products around the world. Recently Specialized (a US bicycle and cycling goods manufacturer), Café Roubaix Bicycle Studio (a bike shop in Alberta Canada) and Advanced Sports International (a US based multinational that owns multiple production groups around the world) have been involved in an extended legal battle over the rights to the valuable name (MacMichael, 2013). The local resonance of the town "Roubaix" as an integral part of the symbolism of the race, "Paris-Roubaix" has been utilized to build global branding and underpin cultural and economic flows around the world. Indeed the value of the local in growing cycling globally, for sports goods companies, or for the building of sport media spectacles, has even led to attempts to create new local meaningfulness by which to continue this global growth. In other words, the celebration and therefore the importance of the local significance of cycling for the success of the sport as a corporate entity globally have also meant that there have been various attempts to create new "classics" in cycling's traditional centers and beyond. The "Strade Bianche" race is only a few years old, but with its course through the compacted chalk roads of Tuscany in Italy it has drawn on romanticized images of cycling's history to build its reputation. Utilizing many of the same roads as the L'Eroica event (one in which cyclists tour the region on classic bicycles and are often adorned in classic cycling clothing) it ties into the nostalgia of this event to frame its appeal to a particular cycling history (Inring.com, 2012). The Strade Bianche race and the L'Eroica event attract global audiences, and attendance, through their ability to expound upon a romantic imaginary of cycling that is based on the particularities of cycling in its traditional locals, i.e. those of Western Europe.

Clearly cycling is a sport that has seen a new found global reach, in events, teams, production and marketing. Yet, whilst the sport has become global, it also draws upon and resonates with local cultures and histories. This is specifically the case with many European races, whose histories and symbolic value have been used in building events and branding products worldwide. In this sense cycling, and particularly road cycling, is a truly glocal sporting practice and institution. It is not only the continued presence of the local alongside an increasingly global nature of the sport, but also the continued reliance of the global on the local and an ability to create new global locals that make cycling glocal. Cycling as a global entity both draws on local histories (such as specialized bicycles' use of Roubaix for branding products) and forms new local specificities through races like the Strade Bianche or North America's "one-day classic" the tour of Battenkill (Clapp, 2012). Professional road cycling's local elements have underpinned and become highly influenced by the increasingly global diffusion of the sport.

TOOLS FOR ANALYSIS

Utilizing glocalization as the analytical framework, the development of professional cycling competition can be seen to be reflective of both globalizing tendencies and the continuation of local particularities. For road cycling specifically, standardization of the format, the creation of an international governing body and the aggregation of races into a World Tour have resulted in a truly global sporting competition. However, at the same time races of particular local significance remain as celebrated events within the World Tour calendar, and the cultures of cycling's historic centers are still very much celebrated and used to extend and promote the sport globally. Cycling has relied particularly on developments in communications technology (Thibault, 2009) to facilitate its global growth and its connection to the local. Notably road cycling competitions, often started as corporate events as well as utilizing an almost exclusively trade team format, have drawn on these technologies to advertise products and companies locally, nationally and now globally. With no stadia to charge admissions, and very little revenue sharing for television rights, cycling's ability to be a setting for marketing is its main economic interest for investors. As Thibault reiterates, the "progress in communication technologies has enhanced the ability of exchange among individuals, organizations, and governments" (2009: 2), and it is that exchange that cycling has enhanced and relied upon to initiate and maintain its role as a corporate sport. Certainly for other sports, advertising and their mediation are important, but for very few other sports are these so central. Cycling's glocal nature is facilitated by a multitude of media and transportation technologies, and it is this technological advancement that has meant contemporary road cycling is at the center of a "reflexive and mutually reinforcing relationship between the global and the local" (Kobayashi, 2012: 45).

Local cultures and histories become folded into the production and practice of sport globally. Sporting events may be global, but each is produced in a manner designed to resonate with the popular sensibilities of the host city, region or nation. Whilst the governing body of cycling looks to expand into new media markets, it also continues to rely on a sense of history, nostalgia and authenticity that is produced through cycling events founded over 100 years ago in Western Europe. Indeed as discussed in the case study above, races like the "Strade Bianche" have gained rapid popularity by their ability to mimic the celebrated historical races that accompany it in the World Tour calendar.

In being able to effectively analyze cycling as a global corporate sporting entity, sport managers and marketers need to understand and accentuate cycling as a globally localized property. This involves more than the coincidental interplay of local events with the establishment of global tours that extend to new national settings, but also necessitates understanding how the elaboration and/or imitation of cycling's local resonances are used to promote the sport. Cycling relies heavily on its media presence for revenue, and as such the ability of cycling teams and event managers to increase the global visibility of the sport, whilst maintaining its mediated richness through the local, is fundamental to its success. For road cycling "branding is subject to substantial glocalization," the complex interplay of universalizing and localizing forces (Giulianotti and Robertson, 2004: 555). Ultimately the global growth of professional road cycling, as well as its many attendant profit-making entities and cultural expressions that exist across the world, rely upon an extended celebration of its historical locals and the production of new global locals. In this sense road cycling is an expression of glocal sport, wholly the product and producer of an intertwined local and global sporting expression.

- In what ways are sporting leagues and events increasingly being more considerate of their local histories as they become more global?
- In what ways can sport managers balance the inclusion of elements that reflect the local alongside the interests in accessing global markets?
- As new events are added to a sporting series; for instance, new races as part of the UCI cycling calendar, how can these include the local elements of these new events within the identity of the sport?
- Should protectionist policies be used to protect local investments in global sports? Should teams be allowed to heavily protect their cultural presence in the sport through policies that might ultimately inhibit the global development of that sport?

CASE STUDY 1.2

The IPL

Inaugurated in 2008, the Indian Premier League (IPL) has quickly become one of the world's most successful and spectacularized sporting leagues, and a robust example of the complexities of globalization. In 2010 it was valued at $4.13 billion and was the second highest paying league in the world, topped only by the National Basketball Association in the United States (Mitra, 2010). Its growth as an indigenous Indian creation with an undeniable global presence has catapulted India into the global sporting economy and has also signaled the shift of cricket control and power away from the West to the East (Gupta, 2009).

The IPL is arguably the most visible and marketable iteration of Twenty20 cricket, a shortened form of the sport created in 2003 by the England and Wales Cricket Board to revive interest in the game, increase attendance and appeal to television audiences (Jackson, 2007). Instead of lasting for five days like a traditional Test match or an entire day like the 50 overs per side format, a Twenty20 match takes approximately three hours to complete, with each team limited to a single innings with a maximum of 20 overs. Buoyed by the new form's popularity in England, other countries soon adopted the format and established domestic professional leagues, including South Africa, Australia, New Zealand and the West Indies. In 2007, the International Cricket Council (ICC) launched the first Twenty20 World Cup held in South Africa and broadcast live to a worldwide television audience of nearly 400 million people (Hopps, 2007). In the World Cup final, India defeated Pakistan in an exciting and politically charged match that cemented Twenty20's place as a legitimate and popular sport form with global potential.

Energized by India's World Cup victory and drawn by the financial promise of the

Twenty20 format, the Board of Control for Cricket in India (BCCI) created the IPL as a six-week domestic league, initially composed of eight city-based teams privately owned through a franchise system. This private ownership structure is complemented by an annual player auction, in which local and international cricket stars are literally put up for sale, like "cattle in a meat market" (Vasu, 2011: 46). In 2013, Australian cricketer Glenn Maxwell drew the highest paycheck when the Mumbai Indians paid $1 million to retain his services for the six weeks of the season (www.iplt20.com). Cricketers from various nations play in the IPL, making the league an international product operating in a global marketplace.

IPL matches are elaborate entertainment spectacles that incorporate elements of corporatized global sport such as live music performances, celebrity appearances, fireworks and cheerleaders, all of which contribute to the "razzmatazz and glitz of a cricketing revolution" (Starick, 2008: 58). The unrelenting "sportainment" of the IPL certainly captivates the Indian public, but the league also taps into a sense of the changing Indian condition and functions as a glocalizing force in which the global and local intermingle. Much of contemporary Indian culture, including film, television, literature, food, leisure and sport, has been glocalized. So much so that a growing middle class have been characterized by their "glocal competence" (Brosius, 2010: 13) in blending global and local influences in their everyday lives. The IPL constitutes a form of sporting glocalization because the league is global in much of its organizational, structural and production elements, while being simultaneously local in terms of its packaging and presentation for an Indian audience. It is a space where "globalized Indianness" (Brosius, 2010: 329), a sense of transnational cosmopolitanism, can be realized and displayed. Cricket in India, and particularly the IPL, are a metaphor for the processes and products of globalization while also operating as an important site for the instantiation of the postcolonial nation (Mehta et al., 2009; Wagg and Ugra, 2009).

While the IPL certainly benefits from globalization in terms of wider exposure, the participation of international cricketing stars and financial gain, it is an event that does not necessarily depend on globalization for success. It is important to note here that the IPL is an outstanding example of an "Indian product acquiring international brand recognition" (Gupta, 2009: 204), and this sense of Indianness serves as a vehicle for the expression of nationalism in and through the IPL. Displays of nationalism function as a response against the IPL's intense engagement with globalization, corporatization and elements of Westernization deemed threatening to traditional Indian culture. Cultural spaces in India, including sport, are increasingly being framed by competing "discourses of Indianness and globalization" (McDonald, 2003: 1563), and the IPL has become a site for the expression of tension between the two, even as it continues to exist as a "strange hybrid of the English village green, Bollywood, and the Super Bowl" (Rowe and Gilmour, 2009: 172).

TOOLS FOR ANALYSIS

Cricket certainly displays some similar processes of corporate glocalization to those that were discussed with cycling. Of course, the diffusion and distribution of cricket around the world have variously been attributable to the spread of sport-focused corporate and commercial interests. However, we now look to also discuss this corporate present in relation to cricket's important and distinct colonial histories. The prominence of cricket as a sport in India, as well as in Pakistan, Bangladesh, Sri Lanka and the West Indies, is intimately tied in with the historical former presence of imperialist powers. The spread of cricket is intimately bound up with the rampant colonialism of the nineteenth and early twentieth centuries. Differently put, the histories of colonization experienced by many nations have impacted on their post-colonial sporting pastimes and passions. Although often imposed upon colonized populations, many times sporting practices have become incorporated into the cultures and sensibilities of the local.

Cricket in India has played many roles in relation to the nation's colonial past. Being at different times a symbol of British rule, as well as the increasing integration of Indian and British cultures, today cricket sits at the center of an Indian national culture, and a key expression of what it means to be Indian. Cricket in India has become a focal point for national identity, a means by which India can express its cultural, political and economic status both inwardly and outwardly, and present itself as a vibrant nation that is no longer defined by its colonial past. As such, sports managers who are aware of the glocal nature of sport can understand the complex post-colonial relations of sport for nations such as India. Cricket has become global through various processes, not only by the continued impact of a colonial past, but also more recently through a corporatization of the sport. It has grown from an amateur pastime of gentleman, into a multi-million dollar corporate sport entity played at the top level by highly salaried professionals. This shift to a corporate sporting entity has extended from cricket's histories, leading to the present-day shift in cricket's core nations to some of its historical peripheries. India in particular has become an economic and cultural center for cricket, which in turn has not only re-oriented cricket's global networks, but also reflected and impacted on its various local expressions. The sport is no longer an extension of Britishness throughout the commonwealth, but is practiced in specifically Indian ways. The formation of the IPL has created the foremost professional cricket league in the world. The IPL in itself is an expression of local Indianness, drawing on local celebrities and media culture, whilst blending this with Americanized league structures and forms of spectacularization. Cricket in India has been resultant of the overlap of British colonial histories and Americanized corporate sport structures, as well as the specificities of Indian politics, culture and economics.

There is the possibility that local sporting cultures can be exploited for corporate and commercial gain, but we must not deny the agency of local communities to adapt, propagate and protect their own sporting forms and practices in the face of globalization. As Giulianotti and Robertson (2007: 134) discuss within this glocal conception, there is a "challenge [to] the assumption that globalization processes always endanger the local", so that instead this approach "both highlights how local cultures may critically adapt or resist 'global' phenomena, and reveals the way in which the very creation of localities is a standard component of globalization." Certainly the ability of nations like India to build strong communities around cricket, a communal identity that is cognizant of indigenous histories and culture, shows how this results in sometimes positive and conversely negative outcomes. Cricket as a local expression of a global sport in India continues to relate to its colonial past, whilst also expressing the global significance of an independent contemporary India. Indeed through the IPL the country has been able to impact upon the formation of local cricketing expressions in the sport's new frontiers, as well as its historical centers. Without analysis that utilizes this glocal conception as a central theoretical tool, the complex power relations of sport in post-colonial nations may be misunderstood as merely the remnants of imperial pasts, rather than expressions of the complex interplay between imposed colonial sporting formats and expressions of new found nationalisms.

ACTION LEARNING

- How would you look to preserve valued elements of local culture within corporate sporting practices, without perpetuating insularity in the sport?
- With recognition of the problematic colonial histories of sport in many developing and post-colonial nations, what are some of the ways in which you can develop new forms of global interconnectivity that will support instead of marginalize these nations?
- Sport may be purported to have enduring local dimensions that have historic attachments, but what work is done to maintain a local nature in sport in the face of increasing globalizing processes?
- Many international governing bodies for sport implement policies that serve to protect what are seen as the traditional homes of various sports. As these tend to be predominantly Western nations, discuss the need to think critically if tradition is worth preserving over the more equal opportunities for all nations in sport.

CONCLUSION

It is important to recognize the effects upon sport that derive from globalizing processes, and the role sport has played in furthering global interconnectivity and flows. However, as has become clear throughout the case studies and analyses, any approach to considering sport within a global framework must always also recognize the enduring presence of the local. As Giulianotti and Robertson (2007: 134) state, this glocal approach encourages conceptualizing a "simultaneity or co-presence of both universalizing and particularizing tendencies in globalization." Not only may local identities, institutions, communities and cultures continue to be present within the global, but they may also come to play a role in how the global develops. Indeed the use of local languages and images by a global sporting corporation like Adidas, Nike or Puma is an example not only of how the local is maintained within the global, but also of how the local impacts upon or is utilized by these globalizing forces. To not pay sufficient attention to the ways in which the local interpenetrates these globalizing forces is to fail to consider the likely role of local cultures. As sports managers start to develop a complex understanding of the glocalization process they will be able to approach the structures of contemporary sport in a more nuanced way. Put differently, by attempting to consider how sport is the outcome of the interaction of global and local forces, sports managers can better conceptualize how sport is structured across, within and between nations in a complex manner. This in turn should underpin better-informed modes of managing events, teams and leagues that are more responsive to the glocal, instead of being ignorant of the continuation of the local within global processes and flows. Adopting glocalization as the central analytical framework nurtures a more nuanced understanding of the role that is played by global networks of interconnections in shaping the societies in which we live.

REFERENCES

Andrews, D.L. & Grainger, A.D. (2007) Sport and globalization. In G. Ritzer (ed.), *The Blackwell Companion to Globalization*. Malden, MA: Blackwell. pp. 478–97.

Andrews, D.L. & Ritzer, G. (2007) The global in the sporting glocal, *Global Networks*, 7(2): 135–53.

Bairner, A. (2001) *Sport, Nationalism, and Globalization: European and North American Perspectives*. Albany, NY: State University of New York Press.

Brosius, C. (2010) *India's Middle Class: New Forms of Urban Leisure, Consumption and Prosperity*. New Delhi: Routledge.

Campbell, R. (2011) Staging globalization for national projects: global sport markets and elite athletic transnational labor in Qatar, *International Review for the Sociology of Sport*, 46(1): 45–60.

Cho, Y. (2009) The glocalization of U.S. sports in South Korea, *Sociology of Sport Journal*, 26: 320–34.

Clapp, D. (2012) ROAD magazine—July 2012 : Tour of the Battenkill. Available at: www.bluetoad.com/display_article.php?id=1088366 (last accessed 25 December 2013).

Fotheringham, W. (2013) What's facing Sir Bradley Wiggins at the Giro d'Italia—our race guide. Available at: www.theguardian.com/sport/2013/apr/27/bradley-wiggins-giro-d-italia-guide (last accessed 18 November 2013).

Giulianotti, R. & Robertson, R. (2004) The globalization of football: a study in the glocalization of the "serious life", *British Journal of Sociology*, 55(4): 545–68.

Giulianotti, R. & Robertson, R. (2007) Forms of glocalization: globalization and the migration strategies of Scottish football fans in North America, *Sociology*, 41(1): 133–52.

Gupta, A. (2009) India and the IPL: cricket's globalized empire, *The Round Table*, 98(401): 201–11.

Harvey, J., Rail, G. & Thibault, L. (1996) Globalization and sport: sketching a theoretical model for empirical analysis, *Journal of Sport and Social Issues*, 20(3): 258–77.

Hopps, D. (2007) Cricket: India on top of the world after Gambhir snuffs out Pakistan attack, *The Guardian*, 25 September, p. 8.

Inring.com (2012) Strade Bianche, the modern race that's a classic. Available at: http://inrng.com/2012/03/strade-bianche-classic-italy/ (last accessed 18 November 2013).

Jackson, J. (2007) How Bill Midgeley changed the world, *The Observer*, 23 September, p. 14.

Kobayashi, K. (2012) Corporate nationalism and glocalization of Nike advertising in "Asia": production and representation practices of cultural intermediaries, *Sociology of Sport Journal*, 29(1): 42–61.

MacMichael, S. (2013) Café Roubaix could keep name after Fuji owner wades into Specialized row | road.cc. Available at: http://road.cc/content/news/100452–caf%C3%A9–roubaix-could-keep-name-after-fuji-owner-wades-specialized-row (last accessed 25 December 2013).

Maguire, J.A. (1999) *Global Sport: Identities, Societies, Civilization*. Cambridge: Polity.

McDonald, I. (2003) Hindu nationalism, cultural spaces, and bodily practices in India, *American Behavioral Scientist*, 46(11): 1563–76.

Mehta, N., Gemmell, J. & Malcolm, D. (2009) "Bombay sport exchange": cricket, globalization and the future, *Sport in Society*, 12: 694–707.

Mitra, S. (2010) The IPL: India's foray into world sports business, *Sport in Society*, 13(9): 1314–33.

Robertson, R. (1992) *Globalization: Social Theory and Global Culture*. London: Sage.

Rogers, N. (2012) Opinion: New Flanders route is blasphemous. Available at: http://velonews.competitor.com/2012/03/news/opinion-new-flanders-route-is-blasphemous_211331 (last accessed 18 November 2013).

Rowe, D. & Gilmour, C. (2009) Global sport: where Wembley Way meets Bollywood Boulevard, *Continuum*, 23(2): 171–82.

Sarrantonio, A. (2005) The Florentine-article » The Giro d'Italia … not just another cycling race. Available at: www.theflorentine.net/articles/article-view.asp?issuetocId=1347 (last accessed 27 December 2013).

Silk, M.L. & Falcous, M. (2005) One day in September/a week in February: mobilizing American (sporting) nationalisms, *Sociology of Sport Journal*, 22: 447–71.

Starick, P. (2008) Cheerleaders, movie stars, rock 'n roll, fireworks: welcome to the Indian Premier League revolution, *Sunday Mail*, 20 April, p. 58.

Thibault, L. (2009) Globalization of sport: an inconvenient truth, *Journal of Sport Management*, 23: 1–20.

Tomlinson, J. (1999) *Globalization and Culture*. Chicago, IL: University of Chicago Press.

Vasu, A. (2011) Going once … going twice … sold!, *Sports Illustrated India*, 2(4): 40–7.

Wagg, S. & Ugra, S. (2009) Different hats, different thinking? Technocracy, globalization and the Indian cricket team, *Sport in Society*, 12(4/5): 600–12.

Witherell, J.L. (2010) *Bicycle History: A Chronological Cycling History of People, Races, and Technology.* Cherokee Village, AR: McGann.

USEFUL WEBSITES

http://global-sport.eu
http://inrng.com

2

THE COMMERCIALIZATION OF SPORT

PATRICK A. REID AND DANIEL S. MASON

> Promoters circling one another as M.M.A. takes root in Asia.
> (*New York Times*, 18 May 2013)
>
> UFC buys out rival Strikeforce.
> (*Toronto Globe and Mail*, 12 March 2011)
>
> Garry Cook: UFC has scratched surface in Europe – desire is to reach 1 million fan base.
> (*London Telegraph*, 24 October 2013)

LEARNING OUTCOMES

Upon completion of this chapter, students will be able to:

- Understand the process of commercialization and how it applies to sport, as well as discuss the benefits, challenges, and positive and negative impacts.

- Identify a top sports brand worldwide and discuss how **branding** has a significant role in the commercialization of sport.

- Trace the global expansion of a sport and discuss how that sport develops a global presence.

- Discuss how a sport achieves legitimacy with the public and why this is a key aspect for sport managers.

INTRODUCTION

Increasingly, sport is known as much for its value as an entertainment product to be consumed as for any intrinsic value it might have. As a result it has become a multi-billion dollar industry worldwide, where savvy marketers attempt to promote their respective sports properties to a mass market. This process is known as commercialization. *Commercialization of sport is the process of exploiting a sports property for an* economic *return, usually through print and electronic* media*, advertising and marketing and promotion, within a mass market.*

A very successful example of commercialization in the sport industry today is the growth of the professional sport of Mixed Martial Arts (MMA). This chapter will review the development of MMA more generally, and the Ultimate Fighting Championship (UFC) company more specifically, into a commercialized entertainment product.

What is interesting in studying this particular sport is that in a very short time, in sport development years, MMA has gained a level of legitimacy with a significant global sport audience, mainly driven by the UFC. On 16 November 2013, the company's 20th anniversary, the UFC held their event 167. It featured Canadian Georges St. Pierre versus American Johnny Hendricks. The estimated pay-per-view audience was 625,000 buys, a number significantly higher than that which Manny Pacquaio versus Brandon Rios drew in their WBC boxing event a week earlier (see MMAfighting.com).

The commercial development of the sport has been so rapid that the combative sports commissions charged with responsibility for the governance of the sport at the state, provincial and national level now lag behind in standardizing its rules, regulations and operating procedures. The purpose of this chapter is to discuss the process of commercialization of a sport and the positive and negative consequences of this phenomenon in the sport industry.

CASE STUDY 2.1

Mixed Martial Arts

MMA is considered one of the fastest growing sports in the twenty-first century. (Downey, 2007; Snowden and Shields, 2010; McCarthy, 2011). A combination of striking (with the fists, feet, elbows, shins and knees) and grappling ('wrestling' in either a vertical or horizontal position), the combative sport of MMA has captured the attention of competitors and fans worldwide (Snowden and Shields, 2010). In its initial stages, MMA was created to answer fight fans' question of who would win in a fight between a boxer and a wrestler. An initial pay-per-view show developed by Sport Entertainment Group (SEG) turned one show, *'The Superfight'*, into a series as fighters from other combat sports entered the competition for what SEG was calling 'the ultimate fighter' (McCarthy, 2011).

Viewers responded to the event with a great deal of curiosity. Many were fans of the individual fighting disciplines whose fighters were entering the contest, and were keen to see how their respective styles would hold up against those of others. However, without weight classes and advertised as a hand-to-hand combat sport without rules MMA was an interesting spectacle, but not considered a sport (McCarthy, 2011). Due to the contrast in fighting styles, many fighters were grossly overmatched and some fights saw brutal, one-sided outcomes. These events were considered so barbaric that a US senator (John McCain of Arizona) initiated a nationwide campaign to ban those activities that he labelled 'human cockfighting' (Cava, 2006). Cain managed to convince his fellow senators in 47 out of 50 states to ban MMA (Watanabe, 2012). As a result the events moved 'underground' in the USA and unsanctioned fights continued to be staged that attracted a cult-like following among fans. In other words, even though the events were not being acknowledged as legitimate sporting contests in many jurisdictions, they remained very popular amongst a small but dedicated group of fans. Without changes, MMA would be a niche entity at best as a form of sporting entertainment.

As a result of the restrictions in the USA, the UFC staged its events overseas, attracting an increasing number of spectators and consumers as it began to build its global **brand**. However the promotion showed that the major financial markets for the combative sport of professional boxing were in major cities in the USA, like Las Vegas and Atlantic City, so the UFC capitulated to public and legislative demands and decided that new rules and an event structure were required if MMA was to gain recognition as a legitimate sport. In doing so, the UFC sought to make the sport more respectable and draw in new viewers who would have otherwise been turned off by the violence of the sport. To do so, they copied rules, in some respects, from the sport of professional boxing (McCarthy, 2011), and the UFC was able to gain a toe-hold in the world of major commercial professional sport.

However, the lengthy legal battle to secure sanctioning with athletic commissions took a financial toll on SEG, leaving it on the verge of bankruptcy. In 2001 two brothers, Frank and Lorenzo Fertitta, who were executives of Station Casinos, together with their business partner Dana White, purchased the UFC from SEG for US$2 million and created the company Zuffa LLC as the parent entity controlling the UFC (Santos et al., 2013). It was at this point that the UFC seemed poised to become a more mainstream sport.

TOOLS FOR ANALYSIS

Suchman (1995) stated that 'legitimacy is a generalized perception or assumption that the actions of an entity are desirable, proper, or appropriate within some socially constructed system of norms, values, beliefs and definitions'. He argued that achieving legitimacy would enhance the commercial viability of organizations, as their actions would be more widely accepted and condoned.

ACTION LEARNING

- Discuss why achieving legitimacy is important to the viability of sport organizations.
- Discuss why rules and regulations in a sport are important in the pursuit of legitimacy.

- Discuss legitimacy in terms of concepts like power and leadership and how this might apply to other sport organizations you are familiar with.

CASE STUDY 2.2

Zuffa LLC

Having discussed the emergence of MMA more generally, we now focus more specifically on the UFC and its parent organization Zuffa. Lorenzo Fertitta had been a former member of the Nevada State Athletic Commission (NSAC). The UFC made a strategic alliance with the NSAC and together they created the current rules for MMA. This initiative was led by well-known MMA referee John McCarthy, and former Olympic wrestler and UFC commissioner Jeff Blatnick. The NSAC then adopted the agreed-upon rules for MMA, giving the sport some initial legitimacy, illustrated by the fact that many athletic commissions in both the USA and Canada then adopted the same rules governing this new sport and many changed their names to 'combative sport commissions' in step with acceptance of the sport of MMA (McCarthy, 2011).

As MMA gained in popularity, other promoters were attracted to the commercial opportunity they imagined existed with MMA. Organizations that had previously staged boxing events traded in their boxing rings and purchased MMA cages (MMA used to be called 'cage fighting'). The attraction was so popular that smaller promotions developed and became a feeder-system of talented competitors interested in competing for the lucrative contracts being offered by the UFC. Community-based fitness and training centres that had previously attracted young athletes interested in amateur combative sports, or young adults who took combative sport classes for general fitness or self-defence purposes, were joined by a growing number of athletes interested in training for competitive MMA.

With the popularity of competitors from around the world competing in UFC televised events, local MMA events continued to grow in popularity. Promoters used the economic model of the UFC where fighters were paid a small appearance fee with larger bonuses for winning. Initial cost investments to the promoter were relatively small. To ensure audiences were entertained and would want to return for subsequent events, financial bonuses were offered by the promoters to the fighters for 'best fight of the night', 'best knock-out of the night' and 'best submission win of the night'. Such bonuses ensured a high entertainment value for paying spectators (Snowden and Shields, 2010).

For example, in Canada in 2013 the City of Edmonton municipal commission governed more professional combative sports shows (professional MMA, boxing and wrestling) than any other Canadian commission and has done so for the past number of years. With four promoters staging professional MMA events, another half-dozen promoters staging professional wrestling events and one promoter staging professional boxing events, more than 70 combative sports events are held annually within the City of Edmonton jurisdiction (Reid, 2013).

Although these smaller events may be held independent of the UFC, the organization maintains a strong influence and presence throughout the sport. MMA events are usually held in an actual cage structure that is a unique commercial component to the sport. A small number of promoters stage MMA events in a modified boxing ring, which has better sight lines for spectators, but entanglement of fighters with the ropes changes the dynamics of the event, so few such rings exist. The UFC uses an eight-sided cage they call (and have patented) 'the Octagon'. Because of the patent, they collect royalties from any promoter who uses an eight-sided cage for their local events (because of this cost, some promoters have developed and use six-sided and ten-sided cages). The cage is made of metal chain link fencing coated with black vinyl. It has two doorways on opposite sides where the fighters enter and exit. The top edge of the cage, the corners and doorways are heavily padded for fighters' protection. The cage sits on a metal frame that is approximately 1.2 m above floor level. The cost of a cage can typically range from US$20,000 to US$40,000 and is a commercial property created specifically for MMA (Gentry, 2005; Snowden and Shields, 2010.)

The vinyl floor covering the mat inside the cage provides a commercial opportunity for the event promoter. Sponsors' names and logos are usually either printed within the vinyl floor covering or applied as giant stickers. The UFC has been able to create its own unique image by virtue of its use of the distinctive Octagon design. This allows the UFC not only to differentiate itself from other MMA promotions, but also to benefit financially from royalties paid for other promoters using the Octagon for their own promotions.

The UFC has also built other elements into the fan experience surrounding a fight. While smaller promoters will regularly host events in one locale, the UFC takes its events to various cities throughout the world. The length of time the fighters are in any one city for an event is quite short. To assist promotion of an event, the UFC has expanded the scope of the fighters' official weigh-in, held a day prior to the competition, making this a spectacle all of its own. Fighters compete in ten different weight classes. Each must attend an official commission regulated weigh-in, where he/she must weigh in at (or under) the fight weight category they wish to compete in the following night. The UFC uses this opportunity to introduce the fighters to the public, so the weigh-in is advertised as an open forum where spectators can attend for a nominal fee and watch their favourite fighters weigh in and stage a fighter-to-fighter 'face-off' photo opportunity. The idea of the open forum weigh-in has grown in popularity, with thousands of spectators now attending the weigh-in at UFC events. At this the promoter will usually have UFC merchandise for sale (Gentry, 2005; McCarthy, 2010).

To further stretch the presence of an event in a city, a press conference is usually held on the Wednesday, the day before the weigh-in. In major cities, and for special events, the UFC also stages a 'Fan Expo'. This consists of 2 days when fighters can be seen in training sessions, perhaps take part in autograph signing sessions, and where other industry icons are present, discussing the combative sport industry and selling the latest merchandise. Introduced in 2009, the UFC Fan Expo is operated by Reed Exhibitions, one of the world's largest event organizers. Running from 10 a.m. through to 6 p.m. each day, individual day tickets are sold for approximately US$50, with a two-day ticket selling for closer to US$75 (Gentry, 2005). Thus the weigh-in and Fan Expo provide two additional opportunities for the UFC to generate revenues and expand its fan base.

Selling tickets for events is another area where promoters have been commercially creative. This also provides an opportunity for the UFC to create a different experience for certain spectators, and charge them accordingly. For example, the cage or Octagon is centrally located in the arena. The first 10 feet around the cage make up the 'technical zone' and are controlled by the local athletic commission. Within this 10-foot section are the working officials (judges), the ringside physicians, the timekeeper, scorekeeper, executive director, the working print and electronic media, the television production team and the announcers' table. On occasion there are also a few chairs for presidents of corporations sponsoring the event (McCarthy, 2011).

Just outside of the technical zone is floor-level seating that extends in all directions away from the cage. These seats command the highest price and that price will fluctuate depending on the calibre of fighters on the evening fight card, whether there is a title fight being contested, or whether there is a grudge match that is usually hyped through social media by the fighters (McCarthy, 2011).

The UFC realized that the demand for tickets was always high as events continued to be sold out in advance. Taking commercial advantage of this situation, the UFC created a UFC Fight Club Ultimate membership ($75) and Elite membership ($150), which allowed a subscriber priority access to the pre-sale of tickets (a maximum limit of six). Membership also includes a magazine subscription, a discount on select merchandise and a few other items, but the main benefit remains first access to the pre-sale of tickets. This creative commercial arrangement attracted spectators in general and also spectators living in close proximity to where UFC events were being scheduled. Even though UFC events usually sold out, and ticket revenue was always known in advance of the show, the addition of this 'club' arrangement generated considerable additional revenues on top of the price for tickets (Gentry, 2005).

The discussion above has shown how the UFC has been able to position itself and its parent promotion company, Zuffa LLC, as the largest and most commercially successful mixed martial arts organization globally. Based in Las Vegas, Nevada, Zuffa LLC owns, operates and controls the internationally recognized sport of MMA as it is known today through its UFC entity. In addition, Zuffa LLC pursued the purchase of longstanding MMA rival promotions PRIDE, World Extreme Cagefighting and StrikeForce, and their respective stable of fighters, and succeeded in purchasing these by early 2011 (Tainsky et al., 2012).

With a commercial strategy that capitalized on digital television, satellite broadcasting and the explosion in social media via the internet (to be discussed in Case Study 2.3), Zuffa LLC and their trademark event UFC copied the commercial success of professional boxing and only broadcast their most significant events on pay-per-view (PPV) television. The UFC ventured to other continents staging events, building their international brand and consumer following, and generating millions of dollars. In 2008, *Forbes Magazine* reported the estimated value of the UFC brand name had reached the $1 billion (US) mark (Miller, 2008) with more recent estimates closer to $2 billion (US) (Tainsky et al., 2012).

Dana White, the president and a shareholder of Zuffa LLC, is the most successful MMA sport promoter ever. With the financial backing of the Fertitta brothers, in less than 4 years he took a fledgling MMA company that was financially in the red and turned it into a billion dollar institution. He continues to be the face of the organization as he strives to create ultimate fighter events on five continents (Snowden and Shields, 2010).

TOOLS FOR ANALYSIS

The American Marketing Association defines a **brand** as 'a name, term, sign, symbol or design or a combination of them intended to identify the goods and services of one seller or one group of sellers and to differentiate them from those of other sellers'.

ACTION LEARNING

- Discuss how the UFC has been able to differentiate its brand from other MMA and boxing promotions.
- Describe the brand created by Zuffa LLC and compare it to the brand of (1) a team sport; (2) a winter sport; (3) an amateur Olympic sport.

- Discuss the similarities and the differences between a sport brand and an individual athlete brand and the specific complications that might arise for each.

CASE STUDY 2.3

Reaching New Audiences in the UFC

As the operators of the UFC were developing MMA, they were aware they needed to cultivate a new viewing audience interested in this edgy, combative sport which featured, and promoted, consensual violence. A key characteristic of the product remains '*competition*' (Coakley, 2009). MMA developed into a gladiator-style competition. Two fighters were locked in a fenced-in cage, fighting with basically their bare fists

(4-ounce gloves), and able to kick or knee their standing opponent in the face or head. Yet the unique competition attracted fans. Borrowing from the sport of professional boxing, the UFC created championship belts that in turn identified champions with whom the public could identify (Shilbury, 2012).

The model for UFC events was to host an event with a series of scheduled fights (the 'fight card'), sell tickets to spectators then televise the event on PPV television, where viewers paid specifically to watch the event at home. As discussed above, tickets to attend live events are expensive, and unless one was friends with an existing MMA fan who bought a PPV event to watch, it would be difficult to bring in new fans to the sport. The major commercial breakthrough for Zuffa LLC/UFC was their investment in creating their own reality television programme called 'The Ultimate Fighter' (TUF), which aired in the US on Spike TV and became the network's first major success. This programme was available to cable TV subscribers who had Spike as part of their existing programming. Each episode showed the contestants (fighters) living together and engaging in a series of elimination fights that culminated in a series finale (also shown on Spike's regular channel). The programme allowed viewers a chance to get to know fighters' personalities as well as see them in action. Much of the show focused on their training experience, which allowed viewers to gain more respect for fighters' athleticism and the commitment they had to their profession. It also gave prospective fans a chance to see what the UFC was all about without having to commit to attending an event or paying to watch an event on PPV.

With the success of TUF, Zuffa began rebranding and repositioning MMA as a mainstream sport that included its own regularly recurring reality television programme. The popularity of MMA and the UFC soared: UFC 52, held in 2005, set the record for an MMA event at the time with a gate attendance of 14,274 and an estimated 300,000 PPV purchases of the event (Watanabe, 2012).

UFC 75 was held on the same night at one of the leading division one college football games in the USA (Oregon vs. Michigan) and a NASCAR race. UFC 75 drew the most viewers (2.5 million) compared to the college football game (2.3 million) and NASCAR (2.1 million). The finale of 'The Ultimate Fighter' Season 3 gained a higher viewership than the Major League Baseball playoffs (Oakland Athletics and the Detroit Tigers), with 1.6 million viewers compared to 1.1 million viewers (Watanabe, 2012). In terms of spectator appeal, the UFC version of MMA was now a mainstream sport.

According to independent research, the UFC generates far greater revenue through PPV than by the sale of tickets to events. Tainsky et al. (2012) reported that UFC 83 in Montreal, QC, generated US$5.1 million in gate revenue and US$23.8 million in PPV revenues (530,000 PPV purchases at US$44.95 each). A Standard and Poor's report stated that PPV revenues accounted for nearly 75% of total UFC revenues (Ashville, 2008).

Seven of the ten most popular PPV events in 2010 were UFC telecasts, with the other three being boxing events (Tainsky et al., 2012). A recent report suggested the UFC collected 50% of PPV revenue, with the remaining portion shared by cable and satellite PPV providers (Ashville, 2008).

Meanwhile, the UFC continues to offer some events on network television. On 12 November 2011 the UFC broadcast the first live MMA fight ever shown on the FOX television network. The show attracted the largest audience to ever watch an MMA event in the USA, drawing a rating of 5.7 million viewers and peaking at 8.8 million (Mendoza, 2011). Not only did it illustrate that the UFC had achieved some level of legitimacy with a sports viewing audience, as the viewership surpassed that of every US college football game except one in 2011, the viewing demographic achieved also showed a 4.3 rating for 18–34 year olds (which surpassed 65% of the playoff and World Series baseball games shown on FOX) and surprisingly achieved a number one ranking among women in its time slot (Mendoza, 2011).

Although PPV was the main source of revenue for the UFC, followers of UFC through PPV in the USA were less inclined to purchase events covered outside of the country. In response the UFC has provided free television coverage of a number of their off-shore events, exposing the sport to new consumers at no cost (Watanabe, 2012).

The strategies described above have all contributed to the rapid increase in popularity in MMA generally, and the UFC specifically. This has been achieved by carefully cultivating new audiences and providing additional opportunities for fans to follow the sport through free televised events and other programming.

TOOLS FOR ANALYSIS

Previous research examining major professional sports leagues suggests that successful sports leagues sell their product to four distinct groups. First are the fans who support the UFC by attending events, following events on social media and purchasing UFC merchandise. The second group is composed of television and other media companies that purchase the rights to show events as a programming option. Third are communities that create combative sports commissions, develop local combative sports clubs and vie to host the UFC events. The final group is made up of the corporations that provide revenues through sponsorship of the UFC and associating with MMA as a sport (Mason, 1999).

What is it that attracts fans to a new sport, particularly a combative sport? Park et al. (2011) have suggested it is *sport fan exploratory curiosity*, a process of 'seeking sensational and novel stimulation from sports, players, teams, or any sport-derived produces by engaging in exploratory behavior'. Applying the curiosity and arousal research of Berlyne (1960, 1966, 1971) and Zuckerman (1994) to a sport context, they surmised that curiosity is evoked by (sport) boredom that motivates an individual to seek an increased level of (sport) arousal, to the point of motivating that individual to seek the source of such stimuli. MMA is clearly a sport that stimulates arousal!

- Based on the information provided in this chapter, assess the degree to which the UFC has successfully marketed its product to each of these groups to achieve commercial success.
- Identify one or more groups that you feel have been underserved and develop a new strategy for the UFC to pursue in order to reach them.

- Global media companies are increasingly involved in the promotion of key sports. Discuss the advantages and disadvantages of a reliance on the media and how this might impact on the relationship the UFC has with fans, corporations and the cities that host events.

CONCLUSION

The corporation Zuffa LLC has developed the sport of MMA and more specifically Zuffa LLC's own signature event, the UFC, into a highly successful commercial product. The commercial value of Zuffa LLC is reported to be $2.2 billion, which rivals such well-known sport organizations/brands as the New York Yankees baseball organization (2.3 billion) and Barcelona Football Inc. (2.6 billion) (Forbes, 2014). Zuffa LLC and the UFC are an excellent success story in the commercialization of sport in the twenty-first century. It remains to be seen how Zuffa will be able to maintain its popularity and build on its existing fan base and revenue streams.

REFERENCES

Ashville, R. (2008) UFC pay-per-view revenue up, buys flat; UK expansion turns profitable. MMApayout.com. Available at: http://mmapayout.com/2008/07/s-p-rating-a-closer-look/ (last accessed 13 January 2011).

Berlyne, D. E. (1960) *Conflict, Arousal, and Curiosity*. New York: McGraw-Hill.

Berlyne, D. E. (1966) Curiosity and exploration, *Science*, 153: 25–33.

Berlyne, D. E. (1971) *Aesthetics and Psychobiology*. New York: Appleton-Century-Crofts.

Cava, M. R. D. (2006) Ultimate fighting wins loyalty, *USA To-Day*, 5 December.

Coakley, J.J. (2009) *Sports in Society: Issues and Controversies* (10th edn). New York: McGraw-Hill.

Downey, G. (2007) Producing pain: techniques and technologies in no-holds-barred fighting, *Social Studies in Science*, 37: 201–26.

Forbes (2014) Top 10 Lists 2014. Available at: www.forbes.com/lists (last accessed 18 September 2015).

Gentry, C. (2005) *No Holds Barred: Ultimate Fighting and the Martial Arts Revolution*. Preston: Milo Books.

Mason, D. S. (1999) What is the sports product and who buys it? The marketing of professional sports leagues, *European Journal of Marketing*, 33(3,4): 402–18.

McCarthy, J. (2011) *Let's Get It On! The Making of MMA and its Ultimate Referee*. Aurora, IL: Medallion.

Mendoza, J. (2011) UFC on FOX scores big, most-watched UFC event ever. MMA Payout.com: the Business of MMA. Available at: http://mmapayout.com/2011/11/ufc-on-fox-scores-big-most-watched-ufc-event-ever (last accessed 18 september 2015).

Miller, M. (2008) Ultimate cash machine, *Forbes Magazine*, 10 April.

Park, S.-H., Mahony, D. & Kim, Y. K. (2011) The role of sport fan curiosity: a new conceptual approach to the understanding of sport fan behaviour, *Journal of Sport Management*, 25: 45–56.

Reid, P. A. (2013) Personal communication, 10 December.

Santos, C. A., Tainsky, S., Schmidt, K. A. & Shim, C. (2013) Framing the octagon: an analysis of news-media coverage of mixed martial arts, *International Journal of Sport Communication,* 6: 66–86.

Shilbury, D. (2012) Competition: the heart and soul of sport management, *Journal of Sport Management*, 26: 1–10.

Snowden, J. & Shields, K. (2010) *The MMA Encyclopedia*. Toronto: ECW Press.

Suchman, M. C. (1995) Managing legitimacy: strategic and institutional approaches, *Academy of Management Review,* 20 (3): 571–610.

Tainsky, S., Salaga, S. & Santos, C. A. (2012) Determinants of pay-per-view broadcast viewership in sports: the case of the Ultimate Fighting Championship, *Journal of Sport Management*, 27: 43–58.

Watanabe, N. M. (2012) Demand for pay-per-view consumption of Ultimate Fighting Championship events, *International Journal of Sports Management and Marketing*, 11 (3–4): 225–38.

Zuckerman, M. (1994) *Behavioral Expressions and Biosocial Bases of Sensation Seeking*. New York: Erlbaum.

USEFUL WEBSITES

http://bjmuta.com (Big John McCarthy Ultimate Training Academy)
http://mmafighting.com (statistics on MMA, social media site)
http://UFC.com (Ultimate Fighting Championship)

3

TECHNOLOGY AND INNOVATION
ANTONIO DAVILA AND GEORGE FOSTER

> Pietersen's dismissal in the third Test was another controversial one this series. The Hot Spot technology did not record an edge, although sound detectors picked up a clear noise as the ball passed the bat.
>
> (*Sydney Morning Herald*, 8 August 2013)
>
> At a cost of £250,000 per ground, 14 cameras have been installed at Wembley and all 20 Premier League stadiums for the new season.
>
> (*The Telegraph*, 8 August 2013)
>
> Super Bowl XLVII will include cameras in the media box devoted to helping team trainers and physicians spot unusual behavior in players that suggests they may have suffered a head injury …
>
> (*National Geographic*, 2013)

LEARNING OUTCOMES

Upon completion of this chapter, students will be able to:

- Understand the impact that technology is having on the practice and the business model of professional sports.

- Discuss how technology affects how sports organizations relate to fans and sponsors, how on-field decisions are made and how athletes prepare for a top performance.

- Consider how a framework for thinking about technology in sports is useful and how technology is shaping this amazing industry.

INTRODUCTION

Technology and business innovation are transforming professional sports. Football is considering for the first time whether to use goal-line technology (Hawk Eye and Goalref) to determine whether a goal has been scored. Broadcasting of National Football League (NFL) and National Hockey league (NHL) games on North American television is constantly introducing new technology support to improve fans' experience, such as first and ten line or the puck tracking system. New stadiums such as San Francisco's 49ers Santa Clara Stadium are being equipped with the latest wireless technology to give fans at the stadium an even better experience. Big data are helping teams optimize their revenues. Advancements in health are helping players personalize their training, avoid injuries and speed up the recovery process.

This chapter provides a framework for you to think about the impact of technology and innovation in sports (see Table 3.1). Technologies encompass almost every aspect of science including not only biology and related fields such as medicine, but also nutrition and training, information technology ranging from communications to statistics, and material technology. However, innovations in social sciences and the business aspects of sports are also important: new ways to set prices, bundle sporting products, design stadium experience or manage sports.

TABLE 3.1 *Innovations in sport*

Aspects of the sports world that innovations shape	Main actors in the sports world that benefit from the innovation	Activities that the innovation influences
On-field—pre-game	Players, coaches, teams, agents and sports agencies	Player selection
	Coaches	Analyze and define game plans
	Trainers	Peak performance, injury recovery
On-field—within game	Referees	Referee support technology
	Players and trainers	Health monitoring
	Coaches	Game decisions

Aspects of the sports world that innovations shape	Main actors in the sports world that benefit from the innovation	Activities that the innovation influences
Broadcasting	Fans	Better at-home experience: better images, more information, simultaneous viewing
	Broadcasting companies— television, internet, mobile	Deliver new products and improved existing ones
Stadium and off-field management	Fans	Better at stadium experience: unique content, access to broadcasts, data and analysis
	Teams	Better revenue and cost management
	Sponsors	Better information and marketing to fans

ON-FIELD INNOVATIONS

Pre-game technologies encompass a broad set of fields. Player selection (human resource management) has evolved with the adoption of statistical tools to analyze players and predict their performance within a given team. This approach became popular with the book (and then the movie) *Moneyball,* which described how the Oakland As used this to deliver beyond expectations given their budget. Data analysis is also having a profound impact on how plays are selected in sports such as American football. Software is now widely used in football to analyze game plans and opponents. Coaches, managers and sports managers are the people adopting these technologies.

Another aspect of pre-game technologies is related to players' health, i.e. maximizing their physical strength and minimizing the time to recovery in case of injury. Nutrition, personalized training sessions, and data gathering and analysis of players' vital signs are all fields that are contributing to better and safer sports' practice. Smart jerseys (jerseys that record and analyze a player's health during training) are combined with data management software to prevent injuries and optimize training.

Injury recovery technologies involve both sports medicine and intelligent systems to minimize a player's time off the field given their health and injury history. Investing in injury recovery technologies has a player's health aspect to it, but also an economic aspect. The size of the contracts in the most important professional sports means that the costs accrued by losing a player for a few games are very significant.

Both injury recovery and peak performance also involve the use of performance enhancing drugs (doping). A race between advances in drug development and drug detection has marked the history of sport for decades. Often, performance enhancing drugs are beneficial for short-term sporting performance but dangerous as regards a player's long-term health. The World Anti-Doping Agency (WADA) and the work of **law** enforcement agencies represent constant efforts to **control** and eradicate inappropriate use of these technologies.

Within the game, technologies are used to improve the decision making of officials, teams, coaches and players. Some pre-game technologies are also being used during the game. Data analysis for decision making is utilizing real time for play selection. Health information recorded through GPS, video or smart clothes technology is used to make decisions on whether to substitute players. Miles run during the game are used to detect players getting tired.

Referees are also benefiting from technology. Video replays have been used for quite a long time in American football or in track and field, and Hawk Eye is now fully accepted in tennis. The objective of technology is to increase the number of right calls. Games such as cricket or football can be strongly influenced by a bad call from the referee. The adoption of technology aid systems (or the decision on which technology to adopt) depends not only on the values and culture of individual sports, but also on the trade-off between the cost of the technology and the delay in the game vis-à-vis the benefits that come from increased accuracy. For instance, Major League Soccer (MLS) has ruled out cross-the-line cameras as too costly, while the English Premier league (EPL) has introduced them. Over time as the cost of technology lowers, this argument will shift towards more technology in sports. Sports such as football have more conservative cultures that are reluctant to adopt technology and do so only to react to large mistakes such as England's crucial goal that was disallowed against Germany in the South Africa World Cup. Other sports such as cricket, in its adoption of sound meters and heat meters, are much more proactive.

BROADCASTING INNOVATIONS

Technologies to enhance home experience have improved very significantly over the past few years (**the role of the media**). High definition TV, integration of the internet and television, the increase in the number of cameras to capture more angles of the action and virtual reality are some of the technologies that are making watching sports a better experience. The future holds technologies such as augmented reality or 3D that will make watching sports an even more engaging entertainment experience.

Sports such as Formula One and MotoGP have built-in cameras in their cars and motorcycles to introduce new perspectives for the producer and viewers alike. Formula One have also experimented with the option of having the viewer become the producer and thus select the piece of the action to watch: a fan could choose to watch the head of the race, the battle for fifth place, or the action in boxes.

Broadcasting technology also allows an audience to simultaneously follow several games. The NFL's Red Zone gives fans watching a particular game the option to switch to another game where an important play has happened. Technology also offers the alternative of split screens or picture-in-picture to follow several games at the same time.

Technology advances are opening new alternatives for advertising (**brand management**). The perimeter advertising boards around football stadiums or basketball courts are now used to display various advertisements sequentially. The teams and leagues are selling time for displaying adverts on these boards. New technology can process the images from a game and change the content of the boards for different markets. So, even if people at the stadium are seeing a beer advertisement on the boards, people at home in a particular market may see a car advert, while people in another market may see a bank advert. The technology replaces actual content with virtual content.

STADIUM AND MANAGEMENT INNOVATIONS

While there is nothing comparable to live sports in a stadium, the advances in broadcasting technology are catching up. As watching sports at home becomes ever more engaging, the experience in the stadium must also improve if sports events are to continue attracting people. Technology in stadiums is an important aspect of this effort to make the in-stadium experience more attractive.

The San Francisco 49ers finished construction of their new Levi's stadium in Santa Clara, California, which opened in the summer of 2014. The stadium sits in the middle of Silicon Valley and, as you would expect, it has the latest information technology for fans to enjoy the game. The 49ers hired a former Facebook Chief Financial Officer (CFO) to lead the efforts in having a state-of-the-art stadium in terms of technology.

Wi-Fi technology allows fans in the stadium to enjoy most of the advances in broadcasting technology. Large broadband will give them access to the same broadcasting alternatives as people at home who enjoy the most expensive subscription. Teams and leagues can even create content that is exclusive to people at the stadium and make their experience even more unique. However, the cost of embedding Wi-Fi technology in a stadium can range from US$10 to $20 million and this can be an expensive proposition for a lot of teams.

Another key aspect of stadium technology is selling and pricing tickets. Advances in **communication** and information technology are giving teams new ways to keep the value they generate. Revenue management includes a set of tools such as dynamic pricing, adaptive pricing or product bundling that will take advantage of demand information to increase the attendance and revenue per available seat. Teams are also using technology to operate in secondary markets. Season ticket holders who are not going to a specific game and want to sell their tickets can do so through the team's website or an affiliated website. The margin on these tickets was previously going to some market maker, but now the team will keep this. Managing the secondary market also gives the team control over pricing to avoid these tickets being sold below their face value and thus hurting regular ticket sales. A further improvement to ticketing is the possibility of buying better tickets when a game has already started. Fans can purchase better tickets during the game if these are available. The prices for these tickets decrease as the game progresses. An additional innovation in ticketing is options, i.e. fans pay for the option to buy a ticket if the team makes it to a certain game in a knockout competition.

Teams are also using technology to gather more information about who is at the stadium and then utilizing this information to provide a better service for sponsors and fans. The ideal situation would be one where paper tickets have been replaced by electronic tickets. This ticketing policy would have an email or Facebook link for every fan entering the stadium. Moreover, it would allow keeping track of each fan's interaction with the team to better target offers not only from the team itself but also from sponsors.

Sponsors such as mobile phone companies can also track phone use at an event to compare their market share at that event to their market share in the region. This information can then be used to undertake focused marketing campaigns at the event and measure their impact.

Another innovation in **sponsorship** is micro-sponsorship. A company buys a block of sponsorship space that it then resells in smaller pieces to smaller companies that cannot afford (or are not interested in) a full sponsorship package.

Magazines are also innovating to better target sports fans. For instance, a magazine now offers the issue linked to the opening of the season with a corresponding cover for each one of the teams. Each fan buys the cover for their team and collectors buy all of the different covers! Teams are also leveraging new technologies with new business models. Teams now sell apps and ring tones for fans to customize their mobile devices. The information of fans using mobile devices has become a hot commodity. Fans have very special relationship with sports and the information from this is valuable to many parties: teams and leagues want to know more about their fans to engage more deeply with them, sponsors want this information to better target their messages and device manufacturers also want this as well as the websites that fans visit or could visit.

Fantasy sports and betting are also building on new technologies. Internet betting and **gambling** companies now collect a lot of information on people's betting. The internet has created more liquid markets that have opened up multiple possibilities for people to bet. Legal and more expanded betting options can also become a source of additional revenue for sports. But, more importantly, statistical analysis of betting patterns can identify potential **match fixing** and help maintain the integrity of the game as well as help people with gaming addictions, reduce crime and increase tax collection.

THINKING POINT 3.1

Marketing Innovations

A European football team is considering various options for increasing revenues. The team has learned that some teams in the top American sports leagues are using innovative ways to price their tickets. The techniques are new to sports but they are adapted from industries such as those for hotels and airlines. They are identified under the concept of revenue management. Thus far the team has been using variable pricing. The team decides on ticket prices for the coming season (starting in September) the previous May. The marketing manager then sets the prices so that the sum of all games is higher than the price of a season ticket. She has also taken into account seat locations at in the stadium and the quality of opponents to set these prices.

The additional options she is contemplating are as follows:

- *Dynamic pricing* where prices evolve over time as the kickoff time approaches according to a preset formula that contemplates the following variables: standing of opponent, day of the week, time of day, standing of the team, time to kickoff and the weather forecast.
- *Adaptive pricing* where prices evolve over time depending on the demand for tickets at a particular point in time.
- *Bundling different products on the ticket* such as merchandising or food and beverages to offer a wider range of alternatives to fans.
- *Offering the possibility of blocking seats next to the one purchased for a fee, so friends can subsequently buy these.*
- *Offering the possibility of buying the option of having a ticket for the Champions League final if the team happens to reach it.*

TOOLS FOR ANALYSIS

Revenue management, dynamic pricing and adaptive pricing are some of the most recent innovations in stadium management. Revenue management refers to different tools such as the alternatives presented to the marketing manager in the case study above that improve teams' ability to capture more of the value that they create. These are intended to sell the right product to the right person, at the right price, at the right time. Dynamic pricing is a particular tool where prices move in a predetermined way as other variables change. For instance, prices change as weather predictions change, or as the quality of the rival changes. Adaptive pricing is a tool that adapts prices to demand. As websites become a more important distribution channel for tickets, the number of visitors and their conversion into customers is a very good estimate of demand. When demand goes up, ticket prices will follow suit. As demand weakens, prices will move down.

While these tools can be helpful to improve revenues and separate various market segments, they work best when people have good information about customers. This idea leads quickly to the importance of customer relationship management systems (CRMs). These are databases that record any interactions a team has with customers, from their visiting the website, buying one or multiple tickets, the frequency with which they come to the stadium, to which games, at what time, against which teams, the other things they buy at the stadium, etc. The more information there is about a customer and the customers who are similar to that individual, the easier it becomes to predict behavior and personalize offerings. The various tools for revenue management discussed in the case study, i.e. dynamic pricing, adaptive pricing, product bundling, seat selection and options, can be analyzed from the cost benefit perspective. The benefits of such tools mean teams keep more of the value they create and this value now stays on the table (i.e. revenue from people who would have come to the game if the price had been right or that goes to scalpers who take advantage of the high demand for certain games).

The cost side of these tools has more dimensions that need to be considered. There are costs associated with putting together the technology: the software necessary to collect information, to analyze the information and to communicate with fans. But implementing technology often has costs associated with fans and society accepting the technology. For instance, fans can feel uncomfortable with prices changing every day. They have experienced this happening in hotels, but they haven't done so in sports. Season ticket holders may also notice that some games are cheaper than what they paid for them. Again, communication is important here to have them understand that game prices are not equal across rivals.

ACTION LEARNING

- How would you evaluate the quality of information in a sports organization that is considering adopting revenue management tools?
- How would you implement revenue management in a sports organization? Where would you start?
- Research question: Identify on the web teams that are implementing different revenue management tools. What are the fans' comments? How are the teams communicating their new pricing policies?
- Thinking point question: Analyze the type of information that the marketing manager in Thinking Point 3.1 above needs to set up the pricing alternatives, as well as the pros and cons of each of these options.

THINKING POINT 3.2

FIFA

Football governing bodies have traditionally been conservative in terms of adopting new technologies. The latest issue has been the adoption of goal-line technology to help referees 'see' goals. Similar technologies are present in other sports such as ice hockey or tennis. But the debate in football has been going on for many years now and it is only now that some of these governing bodies are starting to implement this technology. The EPL is the first league to do so.

Discussions at FIFA—the international football federation—are still going on about adopting this technology as well as other technologies. Off-side is the other rule that has raised more controversy. Linesmen are supposed to know the position of the forward when the ball leaves the foot of the midfielder, i.e. they have to see two different parts of the field at the same time and make a judgment on the spot that will often involve less than a few inches—a feat that is challenging if not impossible. Technology to ease the work of linesmen and diminish the number of mistakes (sometimes critical for the game) has been proposed.

TOOLS FOR ANALYSIS

The role of technology in sports is a controversial topic and goal-line technology is just one example. This specific case has given rise to a significant debate within the football family after the referee of the England versus Germany 2010 World Cup missed a ball that had gone several feet into the German goal. Making the right call would have tied the game.

The benefits of technology such as the one discussed in this section are aligned around the idea of the integrity of the game. An accurate technology will help referees who have to make decisions in tenths of a second and who might not have seen the action as clearly as they would have liked. Referee decisions are very visible today with broadcasting technologies that allow analysts and fans to review a certain play several times and see if the referee made a bad call. Because of the nature of certain sports such as football, these mistakes can dramatically influence the outcome of a game. The integrity of the game is threatened because the win does not go to the best team but to the team that happen to benefit from the referee's mistake.

Confronting these benefits are the costs of adopting technology. One argument against adopting technology is that the accuracy that it offers is not good enough. The technology would not solve the problem, merely shift it from a person to a machine. Most of the technologies that are considered for supporting referees are accurate enough to improve decision making. Another argument is that the technology is too costly. The goal-line technology solution that the EPL has adopted requires a £250,000 investment per stadium. Considering that unclear goals are rare, this is a very large amount of money. FIFA has extended this argument by saying that football should be the same whether it is the World Cup or an amateur league game. Playing the same game is agreed to be more engaging for the grass roots. Technology creates two footballs: elite football and the rest. Another argument that has been sometimes proposed is that referees' mistakes are part of the game and removing them would also remove an integral part of what the game is about. Finally, using technology to review plays requires the game to stop. Certain sports such as American football, tennis, cricket or even basketball have stopping periods built in. But for football this would mean introducing a break for reviewing a play that currently does not exist.

ACTION LEARNING

- What arguments would you use to support the adoption of off-side technology in football?
- How would you evaluate the adoption of a new technology in your favorite sport? What tests would you perform? To whom would you talk? What criteria would you use for selecting the technology?

- Research question: Identify technologies in your favorite sports that are being used to improve refereeing. How was the process of adopting the technology? How did fans react to the adoption of the technology?
- Thinking point question: In Thinking Point 3.2 what arguments support the adoption of technology and which ones go against it?

CONCLUSION

The relationship between sports and technology goes back to the early years of competition. The transformation of professional sports into a business benefited from the introduction of radio and then television. This intimate relationship has continued to grow and the internet, Big Data, high-resolution TV and mobile devices are expanding the way fans watch sports and giving smaller sports the opportunity to reach audiences all over the world. Sports and technology conferences such as Massachusetts Institute of Technology (MIT) Sports Analytics are now widely attended. Sports and medical technology have also evolved together. Sports medicine is now an established field that includes issues ranging from nutrition to optimizing training and drug detection. Finally, innovations in business models are also shaping the way sports capture more of the value they generate. New sponsorship models, revenue management or the creation of new sports that emphasize the entertainment aspect to attract fans, are innovations that do not necessarily have technology at their center but create significant value.

This chapter has provided a way to think about innovation, technology and sports. Innovations impact on the game directly. Pre-game activities such as player selection and game plans as well as players' health are quickly evolving because of technology. Game activities such as referee support, game tactics and players' performance are the second area of influence. Broadcasting and the at-home fan experience is another aspect of sports that is quickly evolving through a combination of technology and business innovation. Finally, stadium innovations include technologies that enhance the in-stadium fan experience as well as having an impact on the business side including ticketing, and marketing and sponsorship. These latter innovations go beyond the stadium and also include tech-nologies and ideas that affect third parties, such as websites, betting or sports agencies.

BIBLIOGRAPHY

Can, H., Lu, M. & Gan, L. (2011) The research on application of information technology in sports stadiums, *Physics Procedia*, 22: 604–9.

Davila, A. and Kaminsky, G. (2013) Revenue management and dynamic pricing, Sports Management Notes, IESE Business School.

Kolt, G.S. (2011) Innovation and translation in sports medicine and sports science research, *Journal of Science and Medicine in Sport*, 14(2): 93–4.

National Geographic (2013) NFL looks to helmet technology to combat concussions. Available at: http://news.nationalgeographic.com/news/2013/13/130202-football-concussions-nfl-super-bowl-safety-head-injuries-health (accessed 22 October 2015).

Trabal, P. (2008) Resistance to technological innovation in elite sport, *International Review for the Sociology of Sport*, 43(3): 313–30.

Turner, P. (2012) Regulation of professional sport in a changing broadcasting environment: Australian club and sport broadcaster perspectives, *Sport Management Review*, 15(1): 43–59.

Yoshida, M., James, J. D. & Cronin, J. J. Jr (2013) Sport event innovativeness: conceptualization, measurement, and its impact on consumer behaviour, *Sport Management Review*, 16 (1): 68–84.

USEFUL WEBSITES

www.udobu.com
www.pogoseat.com
www.netsuite.com
www.stubhub.com

CORRUPTION IN SPORT

WLADIMIR ANDREFF

> Is the Olympic games safe from Asian match fixing gangs?
> (Inside the Games, 3 December 2013)
>
> Tracking corruption in the Sochi Olympics.
> (ABC News, 29 January 2014)
>
> Major Games: Let sport triumph, not corruption.
> (Transparency International, 5 February 2014)

LEARNING OUTCOMES

Upon completing this chapter, students will be able to:

- Understand how an economic analysis of sport corruption can inform sport managers about the multifaceted nature of the concept of corruption in sport.

- Understand how corruption distorts sporting outcomes, infringes the rules of the game, destroys outcome uncertainty, dampens sport credibility and undermines sport integrity.

- Discuss how corruption may be combatted in sport through prohibition, sanctions, regulation, taxation and coordination between these policy tools.

INTRODUCTION

Corruption in sport is understood as any illegal, immoral or unethical activity that attempts to deliberately distort the outcome of a sporting contest for the personal material gain of one or more parties involved in that activity (Gorse and Chadwick, 2013). From an economic standpoint, corruption in sport was initially meant to refer to any action that aims at and succeeds in earning money by distorting the outcome of sport contests by means of bribery/throwing a game for money or non-monetary compensation. Nowadays, corruption in sport has extended to other unethical behaviors such as distorting the allocation of mega-sporting events, biasing decisions made by sport governing bodies and fixing bet-related matches. Corrupt sport dates back to the earliest centuries when sporting events emerged. Maennig (2006) reports documented cases of bribing competitors at the Olympic Games in 388, 332 and 12 BC. Corruption scandals have increased in modern sports, namely in boxing, US college basketball, South Korean, Swedish and Turkish basketball, English, Indian, Kenyan and South African cricket, French handball, Australian and English rugby, African, Asian, European and Latin American football, Japanese sumo wrestling, Austrian, Russian and Serbian tennis, South Korean volleyball, and Chinese and English snooker. With growing money inflows attracted into sport and the globalisation of the sports economy (Andreff, 2008; 2012a), nowadays corruption can plague, to some extent, any and all facets of sport business. Corrupt sport has become such a significant criminal economic activity that it deserves a deeper focus on the most global opportunity for corruption – sport betting scandals related to match fixing. With the emergence of online betting, the latter is the spearhead of borderline economic behaviour and, in many occurrences, of naked criminality, which is out of reach of both national governmental regulation and sanctions designed by national and international sport governing bodies.

A TYPOLOGY OF SPORT CORRUPTION

A typology of corrupt sport is featured below that may be useful for understanding and preventing corruption. It starts with cases currently considered as *petty corruption* between sport insiders. In some cases, corruption operates without significant amounts of money, which is known as *barter corruption*. Corruption may also affect the highest *sport governing bodies*, with some well known cases illustrated. With increased inflows of money into sport, new forms of corruption emerged through first sport *betting scandals*. With economic and sport globalisation, global criminal networks entered the sport gambling business; now they organise match fixing on a wide scale related to *global online fraudulent sport bets*. In the face of huge international betting scandals related to match fixing, the enforcement of a *global taxation* levied on sport bets is recommended.

PETTY CORRUPTION: ON-THE-SPOT CORRUPTION BETWEEN SPORT INSIDERS

The most ancient type of corrupt sport is the one spontaneously emerging during the course of a sporting contest between two competitors or two teams. Competitor A bribes competitor B to let him/her win. Or perhaps competitor A would bribe opponent B to accept helping him/her to win in the face of a third opponent. Such on-the-spot corruption is not planned in advance and occurs when an opportunity of securing a win randomly appears in the progress of a sport contest. It is a sort of petty (as distinct from heavily criminal) corruption that distorts a sporting outcome without endangering anyone's life or creating a huge societal issue. For instance, in long-distance cycling races like the Tour de France, in some circumstances winning a stage happens to be bargained between two riders who finish ahead of the peloton, eventually with one rider bribing the other (Andreff, 2014). Caruso (2008) evidenced spontaneous cooperation between rivals in sport contests. In a football match, players from the two teams speak to each other – just like two cycling riders at the end of a stage – or simply signal to the opponents, by kicking the ball aimlessly and lazily, their willingness to exert less effort and fix the result. Such corruption usually involves monetary payments. Winning a Tour de France stage is bargained in the range of €100,000 with a variance depending on race circumstances and the type of (mountain or not) stage. This kind of corruption emerges between sport insiders (athletes/players, coaches, referees, umpires and sport managers from the club level up to international sport governing bodies), and not one of the corrupt or the corruptors will operate from outside the sports industry.

BARTER CORRUPTION: BUYING A SPORT WIN WITHOUT CASH

Another type of petty corruption between sport insiders works without money. In such barter corruption, an athlete or team A on the brink of being relegated downward in the sporting hierarchy, and thus in absolute need of a win, offers an athlete or team B a bribe to win; this bribe is not paid in cash but later on with some planned losses accepted by A in further matches against B. Barter corruption is difficult to detect since there is no money flow or material indices. A fascinating methodology consists of the creative use of existing data sources (Duggan and Levitt, 2002) to detect corruption in Japanese professional sumo wrestling. The incentive structure of promotion in sumo wrestling leads to gains from trading between wrestlers on the margins for achieving a winning record against their opponents. The authors show that wrestlers win a disproportionate share of the matches when they are on the margins. Increased effort cannot explain the findings. Match rigging disappears in times of increased media scrutiny. Wrestlers who are victorious when on the bubble lose more frequently than would be expected the next time they meet that opponent, suggesting that part of the payment for throwing a match is a future payment-in-kind. Reciprocity agreements between stables of wrestlers appear to exist, suggesting that collusive behaviour is not carried out solely by individual actors.

Corruption in Japanese Sumo Wrestling with Payment-in-kind

A sumo tournament involves 66 wrestlers participating in 15 bouts each. A wrestler who achieves a winning record (eight wins or more) is guaranteed to rise up the official ranking; a wrestler with a losing record will fall in the ranking. The critical eighth win results in a promotion rather than relegation. A dataset of over 64,000 wrestler matches (32,000 bouts) between January 1989 and January 2000 shows that 26% of all wrestlers finished with exactly eight wins compared to only 12% with seven wins. Distinguishing between match rigging and wrestler effort, a statistical analysis has shown an excess win likelihood of between 12–16% for wrestlers on the bubble. There is thus a significant probability that in a match involving a wrestler on the bubble, the two wrestlers will collude in favour of the former's win – this represents match rigging and corruption though without any immediate money at stake. If this assumption were to be correct, one must find some sort of compensation provided to the wrestler who colluded to lose the match.

The likelihood that the two wrestlers will meet again soon is high: in the dataset, 74% of the wrestlers who meet when one is on the margin for eight wins will face one another again within a year. From this comes a second statistical test that confirms collusion-corruption. The wrestler who was on the margins in the last meeting is statistically less likely to win than would otherwise be predicted. This statistical finding is consistent with the fact that part of the compensation for throwing a match is non-monetary and consists of the opponent promising to return the favour in the next meeting. Corruption here occurs with a payment-in-kind. The statistical evidence is that wrestlers who were on the bubble do much worse in the next meeting with the same opponent, losing 10% more frequently than would be expected, which is consistent with the match rigging hypothesis. In 2000, the Japanese press published articles where two former sumo wrestlers made public the names of 29 wrestlers they alleged to be corrupt and 14 wrestlers who they claimed refused to rig matches. The conclusion? A creative use of data can reveal the evidence of corruption (see more details in Duggan and Levitt, 2002).

TOOLS FOR ANALYSIS

The Japanese Sumo Association attempted to eliminate the economic basis of match rigging in 2000 by changing the incentive structure for wrestlers on the margins; moreover the level of public scrutiny increased. Both changes led to a significantly lower number of rigged matches until 2003 (Dietl et al., 2010). However, from 2003 to 2006, the abnormally high winning probabilities of wrestlers on the margin in bubble matches reappeared, as well as their loss in the next match with the same opponent, with an abnormally high probability. This confirmed Duggan and Levitt's findings that the structure of promotion-relegation provides sumo wrestlers with incentives to rig matches. Comparable corrupt behaviour is *tanking* in US college basketball (Balsdon et al., 2007) or in closed leagues with a rookie draft system based on reverse-order-of-finish picks for new players entering the league. At a certain moment in the sporting season, some teams are no longer in contention for the play-offs; they then choose to deliberately underperform and unexpectedly lose games to go down the ranking and therefore improve their pick position on the reverse-order-of-finish draft. This sort of match rigging is called 'tanking', i.e. obtaining quality players at higher draft picks. As long as players are pressurised to throw games without monetary bribes, this is still barter corruption. All the types of corrupt sports that follow below to some extent involve sport outsiders, often termed 'corruptors' or 'criminals'.

The statistical detection of sport corruption is fascinating but it requires a detailed dataset that is not available across all sports. Moreover, the same creative use of data would not work with team sports since it is much more difficult or impossible to detect in statistics from a match between two teams where one of the players has thrown the match. However, once detected in this way, is corruption more credible than if detected through the emergence of a match-fixing scandal in the media? And even if it were to be convincing enough, the next question is: could a wrestler or a player be sued in a court for corruption only on the basis of such statistical evidence? These questions open new avenues for reflection and debate about sport corruption.

ACTION LEARNING

- Could you imagine sport contests in which the competitors were not able to talk together and communicate in order to avoid petty corruption? Which ones? Are new communication technologies a hindrance or a facilitator to petty corruption?

- In which sports (beyond sumo wrestling) do you think that a creative use of databases could be replicated in view of detecting barter corruption?

CORRUPTION AT THE LEVEL OF SPORT GOVERNING BODIES

Corrupt sport insiders may belong to governing bodies. A major case in point happens to emerge when allocating mega-sporting events such as the Olympics and FIFA World Cup, or appointing someone to an honorary VIP position in a sport governing body (Maennig, 2005). Widespread rumours about such corruption are numerous but difficult to verify empirically. Sticking to evidence unearthed after a report written by a FIFA general secretary, a complaint introduced to the court in 2002 accused the FIFA president of corruption and embezzlement as regards diverting funds toward some FIFA members, namely the incumbent presidents of CONMEBOL (the Latin American football confederation) and CAF (African football).[1] In the same vein, bribery was well-documented when allocating the 2000 Olympic Games to Sydney. A peak of corruption was reached in the allocation of the 2002 Winter Games to Salt Lake City, to such an extent that it triggered a widespread reform of the International Olympic Committee (IOC) and the exclusion of IOC executive committee members in 1999. In 2010, FIFA suspended two executive members suspected to have sold their votes for allocating the 2022 World Cup to Qatar, and the Qatari president of Asia's football confederation (AFC) under the presumption of fraud. Executive members of sport governing bodies and government' ministers were also revealed to have participated in betting scandals in Taiwanese baseball (Lee, 2008).

CASE STUDY 4.1

Candidate Cities Bribing IOC Members for Votes

Following huge growth in the number of candidatures for hosting the Olympics during the mid-1980s, candidate cities attempted to influence IOC members in ways that were ethically questionable. A fairly significant number of IOC members accepted favours from candidate cities or even demanded for themselves or their entourage valuable gifts of all kinds, study grants, free vacations and flight tickets, paid internships and jobs, or even cash. These practices were made public in the media as of 1986 when electing the 1992 Olympic cities, although they probably existed before that date (notably regarding the election of Seoul over Nagoya for the 1988 Games) but in a more undetectable way. Illicit embezzlements and bribes had already occurred in 1991 when Nagano won the bid over Salt Lake City for the 1998 Winter Olympics. Around the same time, suspicion fell on Robert Helmick, a former president of the International Swimming Federation and the architect of the Atlanta victory for 1996. The head of the 2000 Sydney candidature committee openly admitted various questionable aspects of lobbying, including the use of 'agents' in charge of obtaining votes or grants to African national Olympic committees awarded on the eve of the vote. The Sheridan Report published in 1999 also established that Sydney 2000 bribed VIPs to become the Olympic host city. In September 1993, just before the IOC cast its votes, the Australian Olympic Committee had offered AUS$65,000 to two IOC members, the representatives for Kenya and Uganda.

▶

---

[1]More about this case can be found in the book by Jennings (2006).

Four enquiry commissions were created in 1999 regarding the attribution of the 2002 Winter Games, which came out with around 30 IOC members in office (out of 104) who were implicated to varying degrees in vote rigging. Four of them resigned of their own accord, 10 were officially reprimanded with varying degrees of severity and around 10 were called into question by the media but escaped any form of action by the IOC. The six excluded IOC members were Augustin Arroyo (Ecuador), Zein el-Abdin Gadir (Sudan), Sergio Santander Fantini (Chile), Jean-Claude Ganga (Congo), Lamine Keita (Mali) and Paul Wallwork (Samoa). The infamous Mr Kim Un-yong (South Korea), a former President of the International Taekwondo and Judo Federations, and a former IOC Deputy President, was censured in 1999 and eventually resigned in 2005, under strong pressure. Unveiling naked corruption has triggered a reform of the IOC attribution rules (for more details, see Chappelet and Kübler-Mabbott, 2008, and Andreff, 2012b).

TOOLS FOR ANALYSIS

The question here is whether the reform of IOC attribution rules was enough to put a brake on corruption. According to Chappelet and Kübler-Mabbott the changes were going in the direction of improving IOC governance. Nevertheless, rumours were still circulating about corruption in the course of the attribution process of the 2014 Winter Games to Sochi and 2016 Summer Games to Rio de Janeiro. What would happen if Doha were to be a candidate to host the Games in the near future? Is there any way out from this third type of corruption? As suggested in Andreff (2012b), the first step would be to change the allocation mode for global mega-sporting events. One option could be to design a rotation rule across continents and countries to host a given mega-sporting event – FIFA has taken a step forward on this path since the attribution of the 2002 World Cup to two Asian countries, then to South Africa in 2010. However this may not be enough as a corruption-hedging recipe. Another more radical option would be to uproot corruption in the allocation of mega-sporting events with a new regulation that weeds out city candidatures. This would consist of fixing once and for all a single site for each such event (as Greece unsuccessfully suggested with Olympia for the 1996 Summer Games). However, one would suspect that such an option would be resisted by the IOC as well as multinational companies for the sake of their own private financial interests and revenues.

ACTION LEARNING

- How do you understand the relationship between corruption and the quality of governance in sport governing bodies?

- Should the latter be submitted to a regular or permanent auditing of their decisions and expenditures?

BETTING SCANDALS AND POINT-SHAVING: THE ADVENT OF MAJOR FRAUDS

Before sport economic globalization and online betting, a major opportunity for corrupt sport to emerge was already present in sport gambling, which provided an opportunity for fraud since it created an incentive to lose a sport contest through match fixing in the hope of making money against the likelihood of a sport performance. The 1964 betting scandal in British football is a case in point. The Italian black market for football bets – *Totonero* – developed alongside the official and controlled *Totocalcio*; some matches were usually rigged in relation to *Totonero* betting. More recently, AS Roma was found to corrupt referees in 1999. The *Calciopoli* case in the 2000s revealed significant referee corruption. In 2006 some of Juventus Turin's managers were convinced of rigging 18 matches by corrupting referees, and the club was then relegated for this (see Case Study 4.3 below). In 2011, the justice system revealed that 47 individuals in the *Calcioscomesse* case, including some criminals from outside football, had developed an entire system of illicit bets related to match fixing in the *Serie B* (second division) and *Lega Pro* (third division). In Spanish and Portuguese football in 2004, and in Brazilian football in 2005, several club managers and referees were arrested and sued for organising fix-related bets. The Japanese *yakuzas*, which control the baseball betting system, are also known to fix matches. Even in the German *Bundesliga*, a referee, Robert Hoyzer, received a jail sentence for having rigged matches in 2004 whereby he himself was betting on the results along with Croatian punters and criminals. All of this created a base for global betting networks connected to match fixing that then emerged subsequently.

In North America, point-shaving is a specific kind of corrupt sport in which an athlete is promised money in exchange for an assurance that the team will not cover the point spread. The corruptor then bets on that team's opponent and pays the corrupt player with proceeds from a winning wager. Few cases of point-shaving have been documented. However, the practice has been found to be widespread in National Collegiate Athletic Association basketball by comparing bet and game outcomes with those in professional sports (Wolfers, 2006). In examining 44,120 men's college basketball games played between 1989 and 2005, Wolfers offers evidence that point-shaving occurs far more frequently than previously believed and estimates that at least 1% of games involve gambling corruption. Borghesi's (2008) results suggest that unusual patterns previously suspected to be indicators of point-shaving are ubiquitous throughout sports and unlikely to be caused only by corruption. Line shading by sports bookmakers may explain the anomalies in game and bet outcome distribution as well. Legal and illegal gambling markets are thus intertwined because illicit bookmakers often balance their positions by placing bets at legitimate sports bookmakers.

Referee Match Rigging in Italian Football *Serie A*

Rigging a match plays a crucial role in its outcome. For example, in the 1994–1995 championship, one minute before the end of a Juventus–Brescia match, the referee offered a non-existing penalty to Juventus. In Italian *Serie A*, the assignment of referees was extremely complex and highly discretionary. Matches were classified on different levels (the so-called *griglie*) depending on their importance for the championship final outcome. Many referees in each *griglia* were selected on the basis of (non-publicly) evaluating their past performance. In May 2006, a major scandal was uncovered by Italian prosecutors after tapping phone conversations as part of an investigation at Juventus with regard to the 2004–2005 football season. They found that the general manager of this football club, Luciano Moggi, had had a great deal of contact with referees, football federation officials and journalists during the 2004–2005

TABLE 4.1 *Matches likely to have been rigged by Juventus managers before the 2004–2005 season*

Season	Match day	Match	Result	Rigged episode
1994–1995	18	Juventus–Brescia	2–1	Last minute irregular penalty
1996–1997	20	Juventus–Perugia	2–1	Perugia was denied penalty
1997–1998	3	Juventus–Brescia	4–0	Brescia was denied penalty
1997–1998	11	Juventus–Lazio	2–1	Penalty for Juventus
1997–1998	19	Juventus–Roma	3–1	Referee favours to Juventus
1997–1998	21	Juventus–Sampdoria	3–0	Inexistent goal for Juventus
1997–1998	25	Juventus–Napoli	2–2	Referee favours to Juventus
1997–1998	30	Empoli–Juventus	0–1	Empoli was denied a goal
1997–1998	31	Juventus–Inter	1–0	Inter was denied penalty
1999–2000	33	Juventus–Parma	1–0	Parma was denied goal
2001–2002	3	Juventus–Chievo	3–2	Penalty for Juventus
2001-2002	14	A.C. Milan–Juventus	1–1	Penalty for Juventus
2001–2002	15	Inter–Chievo	1–2	Inter was denied penalty
2002–2003	17	Chievo–Juventus	1–4	Two penalties for Juventus
2002–2003	20	Juventus–Empoli	1–0	Penalty for Juventus
2002–2003	29	Juventus–Roma	2–1	Penalty for Juventus
2003–2004	10	Modena–Juventus	0–2	Referee favours to Juventus
2003–2004	16	Sampdoria–Juventus	1–2	Referee favours to Juventus
2003–2004	24	Brescia–Juventus	2–3	Referee favours to Juventus

championship, won by Juventus. These contacts were finalised to rig matches by choosing referees favourable to Juventus. Referees were then selected by a team of former referees with whom Moggi had extensive phone conversations.

The tricky strategy used by Moggi was to ask referees to give a red card to the most important players on a rival team during the match directly before the rigged match in order to minimise the risk of a loss or a draw in the latter. For instance, Jankulowski was given a red card for futile reasons in the Udinese–Brescia match, and consequently missed the following match he should have played against Juventus. Thus the rigged match resulted in a seemingly 'fair' outcome despite the fact that one or two key players were out of the game and this could have significantly affected the result. In other cases, the referee in matches under investigation offered a penalty kick or neglected an offside presumably in favour of one team. In all of these occurrences, tapped phone conversations certified direct contacts between the managers of the corrupting team, the official selecting referees and sometimes the referees themselves. Corrupting managers were threatening to destroy referees' reputations if they had not complied with their requests.

A total of 78 matches (i.e. about two fixtures per week) were likely to have been rigged. These did not only involve Juventus, but were also mostly in favour of Juventus since they were favourably conditioning the outcomes of other Juventus matches. Other teams involved in the scandal were A.C. Milan, Fiorentina, Lazio and Reggina. A.C. Milan was accused of having influenced the assignment of linesmen for its match against Chievo Verona in April 2005, while Fiorentina's owner and Lazio's chairman were accused of having used a match rigging method similar to Moggi's for referee designation. The Italian Football Federation decided that Juventus should be relegated to *Serie B* (second division) with a nine-point deduction for the 2006–2007 championship; the sanctions were eight points for A.C. Milan; 15 points and exclusion from the Champions League for Fiorentina; three points and exclusion from the UEFA Cup for Lazio; and 15 points for Reggina. Very low pecuniary sanctions were sentenced to those managers presumably involved in match rigging. Moggi was fined €30,000, while his annual wage with Juventus at that time was in the range of €2.7 million. Most of these sanctions had small effects on the involved teams' budgets. Effectively it was the fans of those teams caught for corruption who were *de facto* the major losers since their favourite team was relegated (for more details see Boeri and Severgnini, 2008).

TOOLS FOR ANALYSIS

The aforementioned telephone calls were tapped as part of an investigation into the use of doping by the Juventus team. Sport corruption is often unveiled only by chance. Referee assignment is the weakest link in the sport chain which is targeted by corruptors. Sport insiders must always be involved for sport corruption to operate smoothly. Thus the cure, if any, must be applied first within the sport movement itself. A question then arises: are the above-mentioned sanctions harsh enough to prevent sport corruption from being a revolving process? Juventus's relegation was a rather significant sanction but its effect was not long-lasting as the team was promoted the next year in *Serie A*. And what of the fine of 0.01% of the corrupting manager's annual revenue? Why not envisage a life-ban for the corruptors and corrupt from the football world to uproot corruption? Short of lifelong sanctions, match rigging had been virulent in (Italian) football even before 2004–2005 (see Table 4.1).

ACTION LEARNING

- Is it conceivable to prohibit sport betting for the sake of sport integrity? Would not such a prohibition be frustrating to consumers – those who were keen on or attracted to betting? And would not such prohibition fuel even more illegal activity in the sport gambling market?

MATCH FIXING-RELATED BETS AND GLOBAL ONLINE FRAUDULENT SPORT BETTING NETWORKS

Globalisation has brought about increased **economic competition** in the sport gambling market due to both the internet and market deregulation. Punters now have direct access to foreign bookmakers, while the gambling business must be liberalised under pressure applied by international organisations such as the World Trade Organization (WTO) or European Union (EU). The volume of sporting bets has skyrocketed, along with the opportunities for fraud (Forrest et al., 2008). With globalisation came product differentiation in the bets offered, such as live **betting** (currently 60% of all placed bets), in-play betting, handicap betting, spread betting, proposition betting and betting exchanges, all of which encompass new risks. As a result, frauds often materialise in spot fixing instead of match-outcome fixes.

Match and spot fixing has become the most widespread form of corrupt sport in recent years. Fraudulent networks of punters and criminals rig matches by bribing players or referees or place bets on the fix via the internet. Despite the surveillance of 30,000 games per season in 43 European football leagues, such corrupt business is skyrocketing: in 2011 about 10% of matches were felt to be suspicious, while in 2012 about 700 games were found to be rigged, primarily in lower professional divisions. Many of these fraudulent networks are based in Asia, namely China, Malaysia, Singapore and the Philippines, where betting outlays are not limited, and in some central Eastern European countries. Interpol dismantled 272 of such irregular bookmakers in 2007, arrested 1,300 people suspected of organising bets on fixed matches in Asia and seized US$16 million in cash in 2008. Before cracking down on these networks, Interpol assessed the volume of irregular bets at $1.5 billion. Talk of corrupt sport in 2013 cannot avoid focusing on **match fixing** connected to irregular betting.

By the 1960s, with a growing interest in football and an increased demand for bets, a second form of betting was introduced with football pools or Toto-betting: all bets placed were pooled and the winners shared the money between them less charges. Thus the fixtures and results were utilised by a growing number of independent betting providers and the football property rights were moderately attenuated. In the twenty-first century, with football globalisation and the invention of the internet, a third type of betting emerged with betting platforms: anyone can offer a bet on any game in the world and punters can take up the bet and bet against it by choosing from the various products mentioned above in the sport betting market. National betting regulation can be easily circumvented through global online betting possibilities. Today the fixtures and results are used by so many providers that football property rights are completely attenuated (Dietl and Weingärtner, 2012).

Then there is the over-use of those public goods which consist of football fixtures and results, and as for any public good the variable cost of offering a single new bet is negligible, i.e. close to nil. Coupled with new sport-betting products, this has resulted in explosive market growth, with the situation becoming uncontrollable for football. This extensive usage of a public good by the gambling industry, and the possibility of betting high sums, increase the likelihood of match fixing. The direct cost of prevention and investigation against match fixing grows and by the same token the indirect cost of more frequent betting scandals rises. This new analysis ends with examining various solutions for football getting rid of these external costs for fix-related betting.

CASE STUDY 4.3

The Match Fixing Technology of Gambling Corruptors

The journalist and academic Declan Hill has spent over 10 years getting close to and observing from within some of the match fixing networks operating in soccer; the outcome has been his famous book *The Fix* (Hill, 2008). He inferred from this long-lasting experience a sort of check list of all that a gambling network has to do to successfully fix a match and pocket a huge amount of money from betting on the fix.

Let us call it the five-stage technology of successful bet-related match fixing.

Stage 1: Access. The first problem that confronts a gambling corruptor is how to gain access to the players or the referee. The easiest access is to be a soccer insider working with a league, a club or some governing body. Otherwise a second method of ensuring access to players relies on 'runner-arranged contacts'. Corruptors have to employ 'agents', known as 'runners', to access players or referees.

Stage 2: The set up. There are two options here. In some highly corrupt Asian leagues, corruptors will use a fast and direct approach (for instance, a telephone call) to the targeted player or referee. In leagues with low corruption, corruptors face a more difficult job. A counterfeit intimacy method must often be implemented. The idea is to find a player/referee weakness (he likes drugs or expensive watches or blonde prostitutes, etc.) and then exploit it to compromise the targeted match fixer. Once the latter has accepted gifts or money, he is ripe for corruption.

Stage 3: Calling the fix. Since the ultimate goal of fixing is profit maximisation two fixes must go together: fixing the game and fixing the gambling market. To fix the latter corruptors have to find out the spread of the betting market and place the bet that will ensure the greatest profit. They must also make completely sure that players will deliver that result by following their instructions. In the gambling market, corruptors will usually not place a bet in their own names, and will preferably use third parties known as 'beards', 'mules' or 'runners'. Technically there are many ways of legally rigging the betting market, while some other possible methods are dishonest and fraudulent; corruptors must choose the most appropriate method each time. Finally, it is crucial that corruptors signal to the corrupt players or referees what is to be done on the pitch without attracting any attention, and then give a signal that they have understood (for instance, shooting the ball offside or into the corner, etc., with live betting).

Stage 4: Performance. For the most part, players do not perform fixes by deliberately losing matches. They simply underperform at the appropriate time in the game to achieve the desired result, or referees take a wrong decision as if it were a slight mistake in judgement.

Stage 5: Payment. Over 70% of the payments to corrupt players in gambling fixes are in cash, often in stepped amounts. An initial symbolic payment settles the deal that a player will take part in fixing a match. The main payment is reserved for after the match once the fix has been achieved (for more details see Hill, 2009).

TOOLS FOR ANALYSIS

The **technology** of match fixing related to betting is rather sophisticated. In practice, a corruptor cannot operate alone through the five aforementioned stages. Thus corruptors act within hidden networks that are not easy to detect. Nowadays, sport corruption is far removed from initial petty corruption and has reached a high degree of networking and organisation. Since it is not possible to put a policeman on the tail of any potential match fixer, and even less so for potential fraudulent gamblers, combatting this last type of sport corruption therefore requires sophisticated technology (i.e. electronic surveillance to instantly check unbelievable odds) and coordination between a network of various international organisations. In recent years increasing cooperation has been apparent in the fight against betting-related match fixing, namely between the United Nations (UN), the Council of Europe, the EU, Interpol and Sport Accord. Would this be enough to detect such sophisticated match fixing? Alas not, because as you will have noticed a sport insider (player, referee) must always be involved as a match fixer: in practical terms a fix cannot materialise without some active participation from inside the sport. Thus combatting match fixing must come first and foremost from within the sport movement's governing bodies as they have obviously not done enough so far.

CASE STUDY 4.4

Some Football Leagues are More Affected by Match Fixing than Others

Following on from Declan Hill's works, a Fixed-Match Database (FMD) has gathered evidence about 301 fixed matches in 60 different countries and 55 different soccer leagues and cup games; data are structured along with 39 quantitative and qualitative variables. A second database (FMD2) only selects 137 games with the highest degree of certainty that a fix actually occurred. Next, these games were matched with a randomly selected control group of 130 honestly played games. From this comparison, the aspects that point up wide-scale match corruption are: leagues marked by high relative exploitation of players (low wages, non-payment of wages); an expectation of official corruption; and the presence of large illegal gambling networks. Country ranking on the World Bank's Corruption Perception Index (CPI) does not affect the presence of high levels of match fixing in the country. Singapore, ranked fifth in the CPI index, has a soccer league that suffers from high levels of corruption, as do countries like Vietnam, which is ranked 106 places below it on the CPI listings. Some leagues defend their product quality by actively sanctioning players or coaches who suggest that any match corruption may be going on. On the other hand, some football associations themselves may be corrupt organisations (e.g. those in Colombia or Brazil).

From the database, it is also possible to pinpoint who has detected match corruption. The largest number of fixes (42%) was revealed by police investigations. Confession by a participant in the media and independent media investigations represent about 18% each in total detection. Outside confessions make up slightly over 10% of detection occurrences. One finds betting patterns, and spectators below 5%, and the football association administration at only 2%. This confirms that most football associations do not publicise corruption cases, and on the contrary attempt to blur or hide them. If transparency is not present this always facilitates and triggers extensive corruption (for more details see Hill, 2010).

TOOLS FOR ANALYSIS

One variable of course does not appear on the database, i.e. the overall inflow of money at stake in each federation-fixed match. The richer a federation is the higher the probability of attracting corruptors and criminals drawn by the apparently unlimited amount of money on tap. The greatest numbers of detected corruption cases have been in football, cricket, tennis and snooker (i.e. wealthy sports). Therefore an economist would infer that a radical option to eradicate sport corruption seems to be to draw a final halt to the inflow of money in sports. The question here is whether this is feasible or even realistic when rich sports are so much more financially awash and economically globalised. That is the reason why less comprehensive solutions are looked for, such as prohibitions, sanctions, regulations and taxation (see the conclusion below).

ACTION LEARNING

- Could sport hedge against economic market globalisation, in particular sport betting and gambling? (See also below.) Are the various sports evenly threatened by betting-related match fixing? Which ones seem safer to you? Which ones seem most exposed to the above-described match fixing technology?

COMBATTING MATCH FIXING: WHAT IS TO BE DONE?

All economic analyses conclude that the more money there is flowing in to sport, the greater the sport corruption. Since a drastic money withdrawal from sport, however appealing, is an unrealistic solution with current sport economic globalisation, other options must be looked at. One of these is the *prohibition* of those activities that most likely channel corruption, for instance sport betting. Some countries have opted for prohibiting sporting bets: for example, the USA, Brazil, Cuba, Indonesia, India, Malaysia and several Commonwealth of Independent States (CIS) countries. Another group still maintains a state monopoly over sport betting, made up of countries such as Canada, Chile, China, Colombia, Japan, South Korea, Singapore and a few European countries (Finland, Greece, Hungary, the Netherlands, Norway and Portugal). The bulk of irregular fix-connected sport bets emanate from China, Malaysia and Colombia. National prohibition or a state-owned betting system generates, in a global sport betting market, a worldwide black market that is primarily based in those countries where punters have to circumvent a legal impossibility to bet or a legal possibility to bet under state control only. A safety valve was created in countries like the USA with a local exemption to overall betting prohibition in Delaware and Nevada: the outcome has been that illegal bets overall – and not only sporting bets – are 99 times bigger than legal ones (AGA, 2012).

Standard counteracting policies against corruption are sanctions that raise the cost of corruption, and regulation that increases corruption prevention, surveillance and detection. In terms of *sanctions*, criminalisation of corruptors and corrupt activities is seen as the major tool by which to combat match fixing and illegal or irregular betting (UNODC and IOC, 2013). Maennig (2008) advocates sanctions that would maximally worsen the bad reputation of corrupt sport insiders, and by the same token would increase the ex-post non-monetary costs of corruption: corruptors and corrupt insiders would have to be more cautious to avoid detection and sanction so the expected value of the direct monetary costs of corruption would increase. When it comes to *regulation*, the target may be either the price to pay or the volume of sport corruption. Regulation maintains some ex-ante control over potential corrupt activities, for example, as regards sport betting delivering licences to gambling operators (in Panama, the UK and most European countries). For Maennig, controls over sport bets must be strengthened in order to make punters more aware of their responsibilities. In some countries, gambling operators are imposed with the payment of a property right to offer sport bets (1% to 2.5% of bets), or certain kinds of bets are forbidden such as spread betting, which favours match fixing.

Another option for public regulation would be to fix a very high minimum price for sport bets that would put a ceiling on and reduce the rate of return to punters: at the end of the day this would deflate the volume of bets and thus the likelihood of match fixing. Fine-tuning a regulation can diminish the number of betting scandals though not definitely phase them out. Moreover, domestic regulation against sport corruption and match fixing enforced on a national basis would crowd out corruptors and match fixers to those countries without regulation or where regulation is usually circumvented. Illegal bets would then migrate to China, Colombia or Malaysia: in fact, this has already happened. Last and not least, the more significant the regulation, the more crucial the issues in enforcing it and avoiding the regulators themselves becoming interested in corrupt business.

Dietl and Weingärtner (2012) follow up on work by Coase (1960) in assuming that transaction costs are nil or negligible, and thus the identity of whoever holds the property rights on an asset does not matter. They suggest an original solution to resolve the issue of external costs borne by football due to completely attenuated property rights on public goods (i.e. fixtures, results). This is to find a reallocation of property rights over sport betting that would nullify the external costs for football, once it has been recognised that the objective is a 'social optimum, but also with regard to the optimum outcome for the game of football and its institutions' (1960: 10). And since 'the government will always aim for the social optimum rather than the football optimum' (ibid.: 12), they do not view regulation or taxation as the best solution. Therefore they would advocate allocating the property rights over sport bets to productive football institutions rather than the exploitative betting providers. A complete elimination of betting scandals simply requires that football institutions stop selling any property rights to the gambling industry.

Is such a radical solution realistic? For example, would football's (sport) institutions decide to deprive themselves from attracting money into their industry through sport betting? Would they cut themselves free from the godsend of betting simply to clean up betting scandals? Here the issue of good or bad governance of sport clubs and governing bodies arises, in particular with regard to football (Andreff, 2007). If the transaction costs are not nil, the allocation of property rights over public goods (fixtures, results) to football's (sport) private institutions – a solution that must be called 'privatisation' – often leads, in different contexts, to embezzlement, cheating, asset grabbing … and corruption (Andreff, 2005). Combatting corruption by creating new opportunities for corruption is paradoxical to say the least. Eventually, such a privatisation drive would not phase out the illegal sport betting market, since those bookmakers or operators who had not paid for the rights to use sport results for offering bets would now become 'unofficial betting providers' (2005: 15). Betting scandals will continue. Finally, if we actually consider betting scandals as a social issue, it is debatable whether to look for a football (sport) social optimum instead of an overall social optimum (for all industries and the whole of society). The latter has no chance of coinciding with the specific aspirations of football's (sport) institutions and industry.

Dietl and Weingärtner (2012) contend that taxation of bookmakers and betting operators whose receipts would compensate football for the burden of its external costs is likely to significantly reduce the quantity of betting scandals, but they point out that the tax must be extremely high and perhaps so high that it would dissuade all football betting. Such taxation would not necessarily affect bookmakers' behaviour in such a way that they would avoid those types of bets that facilitate match fixing. At a more basic level also, domestic taxation in a national betting market would not be efficient in the face of global fix-related sport-betting markets. Thus we would suggest a new tool to combat fix-connected sporting bets, a so-called *global 'Sportbettobin' tax* with a variable tax rate (see Appendix 1). This is inspired by the famous Tobin (1978) tax, and closer to the sports industry, the so-called 'Coubertobin' tax (Andreff, 2001, 2004, 2010). The former targeted a slowdown in global financial transactions and international capital flows, while the latter was actively proposed with the aim of hindering and scaling down the flourishing international trade (transfers) in athletes below the age of 18 from developing to developed countries. One interesting aspect of the latter is its variable rate, which increases when the age of a transferred athlete goes down, whereas the Tobin tax was designed with a 1% fix rate and its first ongoing implementations retain an even lower rate.

In order to adapt the concept to sport betting, one must first sketch the threshold over which the 'Sportbettobin' tax should be levied, i.e. the amount of bet winnings that triggers taxation, say at the lowest 1% rate. A low tax rate may have a sort of moralising impact on punters as well as a low threshold for winnings above which the tax is levied. But we cannot expect to actually slow down sport betting on fixes only with such a moralising effect. The debate remains open as to how high this threshold should be: €50,000, 100,000, 500,000 or 1 million? It would be more efficient to put a brake on fix-connected sport betting with a variable tax rate rising above the moralising 1% level. A tax rate growing with the amount of winnings above the threshold is likely to dissuade the number of bets placed by match fixers or crowd out criminals using those bets to enrich themselves; they would move away from sport corruption and focus on some other criminal activity. If the highest rate of taxation is fixed high enough, the worst of fix-connected sport betting would vanish since the tax would confiscate the bulk of winnings and lower match fixing profitability enough to cause it to dry it up. With such a tax, the hyper-gains on rigged bets would shrink due to the hyper-taxation of winnings.

What would the revenues from the 'Sportbettobin' tax be used for? Overall the fiscal receipts would first finance more efficient and widespread surveillance systems of online sport betting and match fixing. It might also help some countries, and especially the Asian and less developed ones where betting on fixes is the most concentrated, to implement rigorous surveillance systems. Which body would be accountable for levying the 'Sportbettobin' tax? Various options may be envisaged such as a specific worldwide organisation (like a World Fund for the Tax on Sport Betting) or a branch of an existing intergovernmental body under the aegis of the UN (as with the United Nations Development Programme or the World Bank). In any case, it should not be an international sport governing body (an international sport federation or the IOC), firstly because it would consist of plenty of sport insiders, who as the most greedy may also be corrupt, and secondly because the accountability of public taxation must never fall into a private body's hands. Levying a global tax must remain the responsibility of a public governing body.

CONCLUSION

Beyond the aforementioned steps to cleanse sports of match fixing corruption, a more general worldwide anti-corruption programme should be further elaborated on. Obviously athletes, sportsmen and women, coaches, sport managers and governing bodies must be involved in and receive good incentives for such involvement. However these are probably not enough. As recently stated on the 'Play the Game' network, corrupt sports organisations cannot be trustworthy partners in the fight against match fixing and corruption. On the whole, sport needs better governance to deal effectively with global challenges, such as creating more transparent and sustainable mega-events, recruiting more people for physical activity, protecting children against abuse and providing equal rights for women. And even sport organisations and governing bodies must admit that, to some extent, government interference may help in combatting sport corruption, for example the international taxation on sport betting mentioned above.

REFERENCES

AGA (2012) Sport wagering fact sheet, American Gaming Association, retrieved from www.americangaming.org/industry-resources/research/fact-sheets/sports-wagering.

Andreff, W. (2000) Financing modern sport in the face of a sporting ethic, *European Journal for Sport Management*, 7(1): 5–30.

Andreff, W. (2001) The correlation between economic underdevelopment and sport, *European Sport Management Quarterly*, 1(4): 251–79.

Andreff, W. (2004) The taxation of player moves from developing countries. In R. Fort & J. Fizel (eds), *International Sports Economics Comparisons*. Westport, CT: Praeger. pp. 87–103.

Andreff, W. (2005) Post-Soviet privatisation in the light of the Coase Theorem: transaction costs and governance costs. In A. Oleynik (ed.), *The Institutional Economics of Russia's Transformation.* Aldershot: Ashgate. pp. 191–212.

Andreff, W. (2007) French football: a financial crisis rooted in weak governance, *Journal of Sports Economics*, 8 (6): 652–61.

Andreff, W. (2008) Globalization of the sports economy, *Rivista di diritto ed Economia dello Sport*, 4 (3): 13–32.

Andreff, W. (2010) Why tax international athlete migration? The 'Coubertobin' Tax in a context of financial crisis. In J. Maguire & M. Falcous (eds), *Handbook on Sport and Migration.* Abingdon, Routledge. pp. 31–45.

Andreff, W. (2012a) *Mondialisation économique du sport. Manuel de référence en Economie du sport.* Brussels: De Boeck.

Andreff, W. (2012b) The winner's curse: why is the cost of mega sporting events so often underestimated?. In W. Maennig & A. Zimbalist (eds), *International Handbook on the Economics of Mega Sporting Events.* Cheltenham: Elgar. pp. 37–69.

Andreff, W. (2014) Economie du cyclisme: succès commercial et équilibre compétitif du Tour de France. In J. Guillaumé & J.-M. Jude (eds), *Le vélo et le droit: transport et sport*, «Colloques et essais». Paris: Fondation Varenne, LGDJ.

Balsdon, E., Fong, L. & Thayer, M. A. (2007) Corruption in college basketball? Evidence of tanking in post-season conference tournaments, *Journal of Sports Economics*, 8 (1): 19–38.

Boeri, T. & Severgnini, B. (2008) The Italian Job: match rigging, career concerns and media concentration in Serie A, IZA Discussion Paper, Bonn.

Borghesi, R. (2008) Widespread corruption in sports gambling: fact or fiction?, *Southern Economic Journal*, 74 (4): 1063–9.

Caruso, R. (2008) Spontaneous Match-Fixing in Sport: Cooperation in Contests. In P. Rodriguez, S. Késenne & J. Garcia (eds), *Threats to Sports and Sports Participation*, Ediciones de la Universidad de Oviedo. pp. 63–82.

Chappelet, J.-L. & Kübler-Mabbott, B. (2008) *The International Olympic Committee and the Olympic System: The Governance of World Sport.* Abingdon: Routledge.

Coase, R. H. (1960) The problem of social cost, *Journal of Law and Economics*, 3(1): 1–44.

Council of Europe (2008) Why sport is not immune to corruption, Enlarged Partial Agreement on Sport, December.

Dietl, H. M. & Weingärtner C. (2012) Betting scandals and attenuated property rights – How betting related match fixing can be prevented in future, Working Paper no. 154, Institute for Strategy and Business Economics, University of Zurich.

Dietl, H. M., Lang, M. & Werner, S. (2010) Corruption in professional sumo: an update on the study of Duggan and Levitt, *Journal of Sports Economics*, 11(4): 383–96.

Duggan M. & Levitt S.D. (2002) Winning isn't everything: corruption in sumo wrestling, *American Economic Review,* 92(5): 1594–605.

Forrest, D. (2012) The threat to football from betting-related corruption, *International Journal of Sport Finance*, 7 (2): 99–116.

Forrest, D., McHale, I. & McAuley, K. (2008) 'Say it ain't so': betting-related malpractice in sport, *International Journal of Sport Finance*, 3(3): 156–66.

Gorse, S. & Chadwick, S. (2013) The prevalence of corruption in international sport: a statistical analysis, report prepared for the Remote Gambling Association, Centre for the International Business of Sport, Coventry University Business School.

Hill, D. (2008) *The Fix: Soccer and Organized Crime.* Toronto: McClelland & Stewart.

Hill, D. (2009) How gambling corruptors fix football matches, *European Sport Management Quarterly*, 9(4): 411–32.

Hill, D. (2010) A critical mass of corruption: why some football leagues have more match fixing than others, *International Journal of Sports Marketing and Sponsorship*, 11(3): 221–35.

Jennings, A. (2006) *Foul! The Secret World of FIFA: Bribes, Vote Rigging and Ticket Scandals.* London: Harpersport.

Lee, P.-C. (2008) Managing a corrupted sporting system: the governance of professional baseball in Taiwan and the gambling scandal of 1997, *European Sport Management Quarterly*, 8(1): 45–66.

Maennig, W. (2005) Corruption in international sports and sport management: forms, tendencies, extent and countermeasures, *European Sport Management Quarterly*, 5 (2): 187–225.

Maennig, W. (2006) Corruption. In W. Andreff & S. Szymanski (eds), *Handbook on the Economics of Sport.* Cheltenham: Elgar. pp. 784–94.

Maennig, W. (2008) Corruption in international sports and how it may be combated. In P. Rodriguez, S. Késenne & J. Garcia (eds), *Threats to Sports and Sports Participation*. Ediciones de la Universidad de Oviedo. pp. 83–111.

Paul, R. & Weinbach, A. P. (2011) Investigating allegations of point shaving in NCAA basketball using actual sportsbook betting percentages, *Journal of Sports Economics*, 12(4): 432–47.

Preston, I. & Szymanski, S. (2003) Cheating in contests, *Oxford Review of Economic Policy*, 19(4): 612–24.

Reiche, D. (2013) The prohibition of online sports betting: a comparative analysis of Germany and the United States, *European Sport Management Quarterly*, 13(3): 293–314.

Tobin, J. (1978) A proposal for international monetary reform, *Eastern Economic Journal*, 4(3–4): 153–9.

UN Global Compact (2013) Fighting corruption in sport sponsorship and sport-related hospitality: a practical guide for companies, draft for consultation, July.

UNODC & IOC (2013) *Criminalization Approaches to Combat Match-Fixing and Illegal/Irregular Betting: A Global Perspective*, United Nations Office and Drugs and Crime and International Olympic Committee, Vienna/Lausanne, July.

Wolfers, J. (2006) Point shaving: corruption in NCAA Basketball, *American Economic Review*, 96(1): 279–83.

USEFUL WEBSITES

American Gaming Association: www.americangaming.org/industry-resources/research/fact-sheets/sports-wagering

Council of Europe, Enlarged Partial Agreement on Sport: www.coe.int/t/dg4/epas

www.economist.com/blogs/gametheory/2011/11/corruption-sport

European Lotteries: www.el-sport.org

Financial Action Task Force on Money Laundering: www.fatf-gafi.org/fr

Interpol, Integrity in Sport – http://www.interpol.int/Crime-areas/Integrity-in-Sport/Integrity-in-sport

Money laundering through the football sector, FATF report: www.fatf-gafi.org/NCCT_fr.htm

Play the Game: www.playthegame.org/news/news-articles/2014/eu-ministers-will-
discuss-sports-governance-before-signing-match-fixing-convention
Transparency International: www.transparency.org/topic/detail/sport
United Nations Office on Drugs and Crime: www.unodc.org

APPENDIX 1: A 'SPORTBETTOBIN' TAX

A simple model of a Tobin tax adapted to sport betting that should be dissuasive and likely to de-link bets from match fixing is:

$$T_b = G \cdot [t + s_x \cdot G_x]$$

with

T_b: overall fiscal receipts derived from levying the 'Sportbettobin' tax;

G: gains drawn from sport betting;

t: the first tax rate over the lowest threshold that triggers tax enforcement, say 1%;

$s_x > 1$ (x being variable): a super-tax at a variable rate which depends on different higher thresholds from the first one, i.e. a super-tax varying with the taxation tranche;

G_x: different thresholds of betting gains that delineate upper taxation tranches (and thus rates).

For example, assume that the first threshold for levying the tax is $G_x = G_a = €50,000$: with a 1% tax rate someone having bet and gained €60,000 would pay $T_b = 0.01 \times (60,000 - 50,000) = €100$.

If the gain jumps over a second threshold $G_b = €100,000$, the winner also has to pay the super-tax s_x, say at a 5% rate. A winner who had gained €200,000 would pay an overall tax $T_b = 0.01 \times (100,000 - 50,000) + 0.05 \times 150,000 = €8,000$.

If the gain passes over a third threshold $G_c = €1$ million, the tax reaches a 30% rate. A winner of €2 million would pay $T_b = 500 + 0.05 \times 950,000 + 0.30 \times 1,000,000 = €348,000$.

Assuming that the tax must be nearly prohibitive over some very high threshold, say $G_d = €10$ million, then the rate is as high as 90%. A bet winner gaining €20 million would pay an overall tax $T_b = 500 + 0.05 \times 950,000 + 0.30 \times 9,000,000 + 0.90 \times 10,000,000 = €11,748,000$ (over 55% of its gains). Winning €100million a match fixer would be levied as a punter €82.748.000; at this level, the tax is confiscatory. A match fixer (and of course any punter) would quit the match-fixing business ahead of reaching such heavy taxation.

5

THE GLOBAL ECONOMICS OF SPORT

CHRIS GRATTON, DONGFENG LIU, GIRISH RAMCHANDANI AND DARRYL WILSON

Sky and BT Sport have paid a record £5.136bn for live Premier League TV rights for three seasons from 2016–17. The figure represents a 70% increase on Sky and BT's current £3bn deal.

(BBC, 10 February 2015)

Broadcast rights are becoming more expensive as television providers and advertisers chase after the big audiences that live events such as American football games and awards shows attract.

(*Financial Times*, 6 October 2014)

That the 2012 Olympics were a success is not in doubt. But will the £8.7bn that was spent on them deliver the legacy that was promised – and in particular, are we any fitter or healthier?

(*Guardian*, 26 July 2013)

Upon completion of this chapter, students will be able to:

- Understand how globalization has affected the sports market.

- Understand the key economic theories that affect sponsorship and the broadcasting of major sports events.

- Recognize the changing economic business environment in which global sport industries operate.

INTRODUCTION

Today we have a globalized commercial market for sport. Fifty years ago this was not the case. In this chapter we attempt to analyse the forces that gave rise to the globalized sport market situation that we now have.

It is the development of television technology and its spread across the globe that changed the nature of sport production and consumption and hence the economics of sport. The FIFA World Cup was televized for the first time in 1954, and the Rome Olympics in 1960 were the first Games to take advantage of the 'Eurovision link' to broadcast live around Europe (Whannel, 2005). Television broadcasting has significantly increased the global popularity of both events, and contributed significantly to the globalization of sport in general.

Whannel (2005) argued that within a television landscape where much is recorded, safe and predictable, only news and sport offer uncertainty, risk and 'liveness', as well as a powerful sense of being there as these happen, and it is this feature which has driven exponential growth in the demand for televized sport.

The television industry has to rely on high viewing rates to obtain advertising revenue, or, in the case of pay television, subscription revenue. The potential for huge audiences, even during the day and late at night, and usually during the slack summer season in the case of the summer Olympic Games, has led to growing competition between television networks for exclusive broadcasting rights for major sport events.

The explosive growth of television sport and the huge sums of money generated by broadcasting rights fees have changed the economics of sport, turning it into a highly commercialized commodity. Sponsorship has also had a similar effect.

Popular sporting events that can attract a global audience via broadcasting become ideal vehicles for corporate sponsors seeking to raise the global profile of their brands. Smart (2007) argues that such events transcend cultural differences, and being universal in appeal, open up access to consumer markets around the world in a way that few other social and cultural practices can equal. As such, they offer multinational corporations a unique platform for brand building and global marketing.

From the late 1970s and early 1980s, corporate sponsorship of global sport events began to grow dramatically. FIFA was the first global sports organization for which corporate sponsorship became a major source of revenue generation, with the World Cup becoming the main tournament for securing lucrative global commercial sponsorship agreements and for auctioning the sale of global television broadcasting rights (Smart, 2007). They began with the 1978 World Cup in Argentina, for which contracts were negotiated with six major corporate sponsors, including Coca-Cola and Gillette, which established a template that would be followed in subsequent tournaments.

It is generally recognized that the 1984 Los Angeles Olympics were a watershed in the commercialization of the Olympic Games and provided a model in financing major events in general. Until then global sporting events such as the Games were increasingly considered to be a financial burden for organizers. It was Peter Ueberroth, head of the Los Angeles Olympic Organizing Committee, who made history. Unlike the organizers at Montreal's 1976 Olympics, who had sold sponsorship rights to 628 'official' partners, Ueberroth drastically reduced the number of sponsors to 34 but managed to hike the price to an unprecedented US$4 million minimum per corporation. The total sponsorship and licensing revenue reached a record high of US$126.7 million, compared to US$7 million at the 1976 Games. Ueberroth showed how establishing a limited number of product categories and guaranteeing exclusive sponsorships in each category could trigger bidding wars between rival companies and thus maximize sponsorship revenue. The 1984 Games have been described as inaugurating the most successful era of corporate sponsorship in Olympic history.

Commercialization and globalization, prompted by global television media and multinational corporations (MNCs), have radically transformed the nature of modern sport, turning it from an amateur-based playful activity into a serious multi-billion dollar global business and established industry. The major globalizing forces are: the increasing globalization of media coverage of major sports events (e.g. the Olympics, World Cup); the creation of new global sports events (e.g. the Cricket World Cup, Rugby World Cup) driven by the eagerness of global sports organizations to promote their sport; global television coverage of what were formally domestic events (e.g. the English Premier League); global recognition of the top athletes competing in these events; and the association of these athletes with global sports brands (e.g. Nike, Adidas). The characteristics of the global sports market that emerged were: an escalation in the price of broadcasting rights to the top sports events; global marketing of major sports products by using images (not words) that were recognizable worldwide; sports celebrities becoming the most important part of these images; an escalation in the price of sponsorship deals for events and athletes by both sport (e.g. Nike, Adidas) and non-sport (e.g. Coca-Cola, McDonalds) sponsors. Gratton et al. (2012) have analysed how this global market for sport has emerged and this chapter condenses the contents of that book.

MEDIA

Over the past two decades, perhaps the most striking development in the sport industry has been the rapid evolution of the broadcast demand for sport. This can be best illustrated by what has happened to the broadcasting rights for the English Premier League from its inception in 1992. Even though this is part of the market-driven sector, this example is important for stressing just how significant the economic relationship between sport and the media has become, and this is covered in Case Study 5.1.

The escalation in the price of broadcasting rights for sport has not only been happening in football. The sale of broadcast rights to the Olympics has seen a similar spectacular rise over the past two decades. Olympic broadcast partnerships have provided the Olympic Movement with an unprecedented financial base and helped to ensure the future viability of the Olympic Games. The global broadcast revenue figure for the 2008 Olympic Games in Beijing represents a threefold increase from the 1992 Barcelona broadcast revenue less than two decades earlier. Similarly, the global broadcast revenue figure for the 2006 Olympic Winter Games in Turin also represents a threefold increase from the 1992 Albertville broadcast revenue less than two decades earlier.

The collective global value of the latest 2010 Vancouver Winter Games and 2012 London Summer Games' broadcast rights fee is estimated to be around US$3.83 billion. This figure is $1,258 million (or almost 1.5 times) greater than the cumulative broadcast revenue earned from the 2006 and 2008 Olympics.

The broadcasting rights fees for the Olympics have been growing at a phenomenal rate but the income for the IOC from broadcasting has been growing even faster since it has taken a bigger percentage for itself over recent decades. In the 1972–1980 period the IOC took 10% of the broadcasting rights income, whereas the local organizing committee for the games received the other 90%. In the 2006–2010 period the IOC took 51% leaving the local organizing committee with 49%. The 90% going to the host city in 1972 would be 90% of $17.8 million, which was the rights fee for the Munich summer Olympics or $16 million. In 2008, the broadcasting rights fee income was $1.74 billion. The 49% of this received by Beijing would be $853 million, or over 53 times the amount received by Munich in 1972. Although the absolute amount of income received by the host city from broadcasting rights has continued to rise, it is clearly the case that the IOC has benefited most from the exponential growth in broadcasting income over the past 20–30 years. If we take the example above, in 1972 the IOC's share of the broadcasting rights fee was $1.78 million. In 2008 it was $0.89 billion or 500 times the amount they received in 1972.

Since 2010 there has been no percentage distribution and the local organizing committee receives a guaranteed amount from the IOC, which effectively means the latter receives more than 51% of the broadcasting income. The Summer Olympics have become the largest televized event on the planet and they continue to grow. The Beijing Olympics, in total, attracted about 4.7 billion TV viewers worldwide, which equates to over two thirds of the world's population, surpassing the 3.9 billion who watched the 2004 Athens Games and the 3.7 billion who watched the 2000 Sydney Games. London expanded the global market further to 4.8 billion, but also showed that the audience was now reaching a natural plateau at just below 5 billion (although 88% of the UK's population watched some of the Games).

Olympic broadcasters not only offer programmes on traditional television but have also taken up opportunities created by new media technology, such as offering live programmes through the internet, mobile phones and multiple television channels. This process began during the first decade of the twenty-first century and developed rapidly. The IOC launched its own internet channel in 2008, which was available on the YouTube platform for 77 countries in Asia, Africa and the Middle East, where the Olympic Games internet rights had not been sold.

During the 2008 Beijing Games, the IOC's official website and other related websites drew 105 million unique viewers, while there were more than 21 million views on the IOC digital channel. Globally, the Beijing Games attracted more than 265 million video views and in excess of 1.2 billion page views on official rights-holding internet and mobile phone platforms. During the 2010 Vancouver Winter Games, total global output across traditional media, free-to-air and pay television, reached 24,000 hours. Internet and mobile communications reached 26,000 hours, which was at least a hundred-fold increase from the 2006 Turin Games, when new media rights were exploited in only 23 countries. Mobile video downloads at Vancouver reached two million, more than six times the 301,000 for the 2008 Beijing Games. This underscores the global growth of new media and social media, and successful utilization of these platforms by the IOC and Olympic Games organizers.

The website of the American broadcaster NBC attracted 46 million unique users during the 2010 Winter Games, an increase of 33 million compared with the 2006 Turin Games. The NBC's mobile platform attracted 87.1 million page views, 52 million more than during the Beijing 2008 Games, and provided 2 million mobile video streams, which was a six-fold increase on the Beijing Games. In the UK, the BBC delivered 50 million video streams from the 2008 Games, compared to just 2.4 million during Athens 2004. Forty-five per cent of the BBC's online audience engaged with video from its Olympic site. Around 13% of the UK adult population watched video content from the Beijing Games on the internet, while around 1–2% did so during the 2004 Games.

Over recent years the IOC has become much more professional in maximizing the income it earns from the sale of Games broadcasting rights and as a result that income has grown dramatically. Because of the size of the global television audience, sponsors are keen to be associated with events with such global reach. Hence sponsorship income has grown alongside growth in broadcasting rights fees.

CASE STUDY 5.1

Broadcasting Rights Fees in the English Premier League

The first televized live Football League matches were shown in 1983. The annual rights fee for the 10 matches shown live in that season was £2.6 million. Deals for 1983–85 and 1986–88 were joint deals with the BBC and ITV, with the annual rights fee rising slightly to £3.1 million in the 1986–88 period. A major escalation came when ITV pushed up the annual fee to £11 million in 1988–92 for its exclusive coverage, with a large increase in the number of live televized matches to 18 per year. However, this was nothing compared to what happened when the Premier League was formed in 1992 and the rights were sold to pay-per-view satellite television.

The first Premiership deal with BSkyB covering the period 1992 to 1997 was for £304 million and the number of live televized matches increased more than threefold to 60 per season. The 1997 to 2001 deal was for £670 million, giving the Premier League nearly three times the annual income of the previous deal. The 2001–04 deal of £1.1 billion was again with BSkyB, as was the 2004–07 deal. Both these deals involved more live matches per season. The fact that there was no increase in the price BSkyB paid for the 2004–07 rights was seen by many as an indicator that the boom time for broadcasting rights was over. By 2004, for many English Premier League clubs, broadcasting income was already the single most important source of income.

During the life of the 2004–07 contract the European Commission intervened on the grounds that BSkyB was in a monopoly position in relation to the control of broadcasting rights for live Premier League games. It insisted that when the rights for the 2007–10 period were auctioned that at least one of the packages offered went to a different broadcaster. As a consequence, of the six packages offered by the Premier League for the 2007–10 period BSkyB secured only four of them, consisting of a total of 92 live matches. BSkyB paid £1.3 billion for these games at a cost of £4.76 million per game compared with an average cost per game over the 2004–07 period of £2.47 million per game, a 93% increase in the cost to BSkyB. The other two packages went to an Irish television station, Setanta. Their packages consisted of 46 live games per year at a total cost of £392 million, or £2.8 million per game – considerably less than the cost to BSkyB but more than BSkyB paid for each game over the 2004–07 period. The total income to the Premier League from the new deal was £1.7 billion over three years, a massive 67% increase compared to 2004–07.

This was not the end of the increase in revenue from broadcasting rights for the 2007–10 period. The Premier League sells the international rights separately, territory by territory. These were sold for the 2004–07 period for a total of £320 million, which was more than the Premier League was paid for its domestic rights for the first five years of its life. The international rights for 2007–10 sold for £625 million, a 95% increase on the previous deal. In mid-2009 Setanta ceased trading in Britain after it was unable to meet a payment deadline to the Premier League amongst a number of sporting organizations and its allocation of matches for the 2009–10 season was subsequently sold to the Disney-owned ESPN. The domestic television rights deal covering the period 2010–13 increased in value to £1.8 billion – a relatively modest increase, but overall the intervention by the European Commission resulted in a considerable escalation in the price of domestic broadcasting rights by increasing the competition in the auction for rights.

The rights to the Premier League for 2013–16 were sold for a total (domestic and international) price of £5.5 billion compared to the £3.2 billion for the 2010–13 period, a 72% increase. This suggests that it is the level of competition for the rights rather than the state of globalization that determines their price.

Competition for the domestic broadcasting rights increased greatly in the latest bidding when British Telecom (BT) entered the fray. The result was a vast increase to £3.0 billion for the domestic rights for the 2013 to 2016 period. BT's entry into the sports rights market also signals a new commercial strategy in the use of the rights. Whereas Setanta and ESPN were using the broadcasting rights to sell subscriptions to their channels in the same way as Sky does, BT will provide free Premier League football to its broadband customers. It is using the rights to sell subscriptions not to its TV channels but to its broadband service where it competes with Sky head-on.

Meanwhile the income for the international rights continued to increase as, by 2013, 212 countries across the world were receiving live Premier League broadcasts. The international rights fees more than doubled to £1.4 billion for 2010–13, and increased a further 80% to £2.5 billion for the 2013–16 period. These staggering rates of increase in income to top class sport occurred as the British economy was experiencing its worst economic crisis of the post-war period.

TOOLS FOR ANALYSIS

Why has sport seen such an escalation in the price of broadcasting rights? Todreas (1999) provides a possible explanation that relates more to the development of the television industry than that of the sports industry. His explanation is mainly in the context of the US market. Todreas points to the supply chain of television programmes which consists of 'conduit' and 'content'. 'Conduit' refers to the distribution of programmes to consumers by the television companies. He refers to this as the downstream end of the supply chain. 'Content' consists of the upstream suppliers, in our case the teams and leagues that produce sports contests. As television markets have developed, he argues that value 'migrates upstream', i.e. profitability switches from the owners of the conduit to the owners of the content.

To explain this, he identifies three eras in the history of television: the broadcast era (for the USA, late 1940s to early 1970s); the cable era (early 1970s to early 1990s); and the digital era (early 1990s to the present). He also points out that in the broadcast era it was the television stations that owned the conduit that were highly profitable because of their monopoly power. There were few suppliers and these tended not to compete directly with each other but instead operated more as a cartel. The cable era saw some expansion of operators at the conduit end of the supply chain, but cable licences were restricted with often only one granted for each municipality.

The digital era, however, brought in new competitors in the distribution of programmes and new ways (e.g. telephone, internet) of distributing content. This new competition reduced margins and profits, and destroyed value in the conduit and increased value in the content. The new technology changed the methods of distribution but it did not change the process of content creation. Sports teams and leagues supplying content were in a strong bargaining position. There was increased competition for the limited supply of sport content.

If this was the situation in the USA, the situation was even more favourable for sports content owners in new markets targeted by the new generation of broadcasters. Sports programmes almost uniquely had this ability to attract the size and characteristics of audiences most attractive to distributors, sponsors and advertisers. These audiences were also willing to pay a premium price to broadcasters to receive more of the sports content than had been previously supplied by the old free-to-air networks. As these developments were taking place, in Europe in particular, governments were stepping back from the old regulatory distribution systems and liberalizing television in order to encourage the development of the new digital technology. However, it was not long before these same governments stepped in to regulate what they perceived to be the adverse effects on sports broadcasting from the new television landscape.

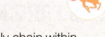

LEARNING ACTIVITIES

- How has broadcasting within the EPL evolved over the past two decades?
- What does economic theory tell us about the type of market that major events operate in?

- How does the supply chain within broadcasting operate?

SPONSORSHIP

The Olympic Partners (TOP) programme is the worldwide sponsorship programme managed by the IOC. The IOC created the TOP programme in 1985 in order to develop a diversified revenue base for the Olympic Games and establish long-term corporate partnerships that would benefit the Olympic Movement as a whole. The TOP programme operates on a four-year term in line with the Olympic quadrennium. The TOP programme generates support for the Organizing Committees of the Olympic Games and Winter Olympic Games, the National Olympic Committees (NOCs) and the IOC. The TOP programme provides each Worldwide Olympic Partner with exclusive global marketing rights and opportunities within a designated product or service category. The global marketing rights include partnerships with the IOC, all active NOCs and their Olympic teams, and the two Organizing Committees of the Olympic Games and the Games of each quadrennium. The TOP Partners may exercise these rights worldwide and may activate marketing initiatives with all the members of the Olympic movement that participate in the TOP programme.

The revenue from the TOP programme in 1985–1988 covering the Calgary Winter Olympics and the Seoul Summer Olympics was US$96 million. This had risen to $663 million by the 2001–04 period covering Salt Lake City and Athens. For the 2005–08 period (Turin/Beijing) it increased further to $866 million.

Though less in total than the amount raised through the sale of broadcasting rights, the rate of growth in sponsorship income has mirrored that from broadcasting. This is no coincidence. Sponsors are attracted to events that draw large television audiences. The Summer Olympic Games and the Football World Cup attract the largest cumulative television audiences on the planet, with both events gaining the attention of over two thirds of the world's population. As a result these events are sponsored by global corporations aiming to enhance their global market position. The majority of these sponsors are non-sport corporations simply because most major global corporations are in the non-sport sector. These sponsors are not promoting sport. They are promoting their products that are marketed on a global basis with the events that have the largest global reach.

It is not only events that attract sponsorship. Teams, kit, stadia and the athletes themselves are all targets for sponsors, although the sponsors' motivation is that all of these aspects will be showcased through broadcasting at major events.

Total sponsorship has continued to grow throughout the 2002–14 period with no sign of a reduction due to the global economic crisis. However, the number of sponsors withdrawing from sponsorship deals has increased from 2008 onwards although up to now other sponsors have been found to replace them, with the result that total sponsorship income has continued to increase.

GLOBAL SPORTS ORGANIZATIONS

As we have seen with the example of the Olympics, the global sports organizations (GSOs) that own the rights to a major sports event have benefited enormously from the rise in broadcasting and sponsorship income.

With the enormous sums obtained through broadcasting rights, corporate sponsorship and other commercial activities, many GSOs have become exceedingly rich. Even the IOC, arguably the most powerful GSO in the world, had little income until broadcasting revenue started in the 1960s. Before that rich men ran the IOC and paid their own expenses. The IOC earned US$3.5 billion overall from broadcasting, sponsorships, licensing and other commercial income between 1997 and 2000. FIFA's revenues have grown to over US$4 billion in the four-year cycle between World Cups. As *The Economist* (2011) pointed out (under a photograph of a line of pigs each with its snout in a trough), in the four years up to 2010, after its contribution to the costs of the World Cup in South Africa, FIFA made a profit of $631m and kept a handsome $707m for its own operating expenses, while dispensing $794m to its 208 grateful member football associations, many of them poor and dependent on FIFA's largesse. For the International Rugby Board (IRB), its revenue from broadcasting the World Cup increased from a mere £1 million in 1987 to £45 million in 1999, and over the same period sponsorship income rose from £2 million to £17 million.

The commercial income of the IOC and FIFA has expanded massively over the past 30 years but these GSOs are still mainly in the role of supplying the Olympics and the World Cup just as they were three decades ago. The difference now is that the demand for these events from host cities, broadcasters and sponsors has increased, and since there is only one monopoly supplier and supply is fixed, this increase in demand has led to the huge rise in commercial income.

GSOs' growing economic power and their new role of revenue generation and distribution have given rise to the argument that the ends and means of the GSOs have become inverted: sport is 'no longer their objective but a means to other more economically oriented organizational ends' (Forster and Pope, 2004). As a result, their status of being not-profit-making has increasingly been called into question. Questions have been raised over their capacity 'to act simultaneously as regulatory institutions and as commercial entities in the negotiation of sponsorship and broadcasting rights' (Lee, 2005). This is particularly controversial when there is a lack of transparency and accountability in the global governance of sports and sporting events and when 'representatives of governing hierarchies have frequently been accused of bribery and corruption' (Lee, 2005). The Salt Lake City Olympics scandal involving bribery in the bidding process eventually led to the resignation of four IOC members and expulsion of another six. In late 2010, FIFA awarded Qatar the 2022 World Cup amid allegations that the decision was influenced by bribes. In 2011, Sepp Blatter was re-elected president of FIFA unopposed after his only rival, Qatar's Mohamed Bin Hammam, withdrew after allegations of bribery. How to compromise the responsibility of non-profit governance as sport governing bodies with their newly assumed commercial role is going to be one of the most salient challenges that GSOs will continue to face in the future.

MAJOR EVENTS

What has given the major GSOs their economic power has been their exclusive ownership of major sports events. As some of these have become global sports events over recent decades so the monopoly power of the GSOs has increased, in particular in the global broadcasting market and in the global sponsorship market for the rights to broadcast and sponsor these events. The two most powerful GSOs, the IOC and FIFA, own the two most popular sports events on the planet, the Olympics and the Football World Cup. Not only do the majority of the world's population watch these events live on television, but also major cities and countries all over the world compete intensely to host these events.

A broad range of benefits has been suggested for both the country and the host city from staging major sports events, including urban regeneration legacy benefits, sporting legacy benefits, tourism and image benefits, and social and cultural benefits. The direct economic impact benefit, however, is the reason most cities have put forward as the reason for their wanting to host events. It is well known that cities and countries compete fiercely to host the Olympic Games or the Football World Cup. However, over recent years there has been increasing competition to host less globally recognized sports events in a wide range of other sports where spectator interest is less assured and where the economic benefits are not so clear cut.

Cities staging major sports events have a unique opportunity to market themselves to the world. The massive escalation in fees for broadcasting rights means broadcasters give blanket coverage at peak times for such events, enhancing the marketing benefits to the cities that stage them.

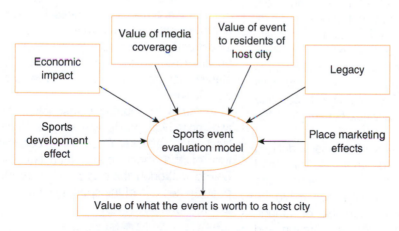

FIGURE 5.1   *Towards an event evaluation model*

Such benefits might include a notional value of exposure achieved from media coverage and the associated place marketing effects related to hosting and broadcasting an event. Figure 5.1 outlines the broad range of benefits that hosting an event may generate. As indicated earlier economic impact has been the main focus of impact over the recent past but this is now changing to a focus on legacy. Because of the importance now given to legacy benefits from hosting major sports events these are the subject of Case Study 5.2.

The Legacy of Beijing 2008

In the existing literature on the social and long-term impact of sport events, the concept of legacy has been used with increasing frequency. The popularity of the word 'legacy' is largely due to its association with the Olympic discourse, referring to the long-lasting impacts of the Olympic Movement and Olympic Games. In 2000, the Olympic Games Global Impact (OGGI) project was launched by the IOC to improve the evaluation of the overall impacts of the Olympic Games on the host city, its environment and its citizens, as well as to propose a consistent methodology to capture the overall effects of hosting the games (Gratton and Preuss, 2008). The concept of 'legacy', together with the concept of 'sustainable sports development', has become an essential part of the IOC's and the Organizing Committee of the Olympic Games' (OCOG) vocabulary.

Despite the lack of a clearly defined concept, more and more authors tend to agree that legacies from major sports events such as the Olympics could be positive or negative, tangible or intangible, intended or untended (Gratton and Preuss, 2008; Mangan, 2008; Masterman, 2009), and authors have proposed different perspectives on possible event legacies. Gratton and Preuss (2008) proposed the following definition of legacy: 'Legacy is planned and unplanned, positive and negative, intangible and tangible, structures created through a sport event that remain after the event'.

Infrastructure

Infrastructure obviously means not only the sport infrastructure for competition and training, but also the general infrastructure of a city such as airports, roads, telecommunication, hotels, housing (for athletes, media and officials), entertainment facilities, parks, etc.

Beijing 2008 is often referred to as the most expensive Olympics ever staged, with the oft-cited figure of $40 billion for infrastructure investment. For the Beijing Olympics there was substantial upgrading of the infrastructure in general, and of transportation in particular. The newly built airport terminal increased capacity by 24 million. Three new underground lines and one new express link from the airport to the city were also built. These transport improvements were the main cost for the infrastructure investment for the Games, but they remain today and provide substantial benefits for those who live in or visit Beijing.

In terms of sporting infrastructure the two most high profile venues, the Bird's Nest and the Water Cube, have become two of the main tourist attractions in Beijing, although there is criticism of the post-Games use of the sporting infrastructure for sport.

Knowledge, skill development and education

The host population gains knowledge and skills from staging a mega sport event. Employees and volunteers develop skills and knowledge in event organization, human resource management, security, hospitality, service, etc.

What is noteworthy is the unprecedented scale of volunteers involved in the Beijing Games , as 1.7 million people served as volunteers in Beijing and the co-host cities, which was the highest number in Olympic history, as well as in China's history for a single event, involving 100,000 people (including 30,000 Paralympics volunteers), games volunteers providing direct services in the official venues, 400,000 city volunteers providing visitor information, translation assistance, etc., through designated volunteer posts, and 1 million 'society volunteers' engaging in routine services, plus 200,000 cheerleading volunteers.

Image

Mega sport events have tremendous symbolic significance and form, and contribute to repositioning or solidifying the image of a city, region and country. There is little doubt that the Beijing Olympics had a huge beneficial effect on China's image in the rest of the world. The opening ceremony amazed the world in its ambition and spectacle. Nothing like it had ever been seen before. The Bird's Nest stadium and the Water Cube also set new standards for international sporting venues and provided wonderful images that that were seen worldwide. Despite China's opening up in recent decades it was still a country that many people were not familiar with. The Olympics managed to change that since two thirds of the world's population saw Beijing and China every day for the best part of three weeks in August 2008.

Networks

Major sports events require close cooperation between the international sport federation, the national sport federation, the local organizing committee, politicians, the media and a multitude of other organizations. The networks created through these interactions can provide a lasting legacy from the event.

Due to the massive scale and multi-year preparation and organization needed, the Beijing Olympics greatly promoted the international exchange in politics, culture, economics and sport, and helped to build networks and links between China and the world.

Culture

Gratton and Preuss (2008) indicated how major events can leave a cultural legacy:

> Mega sport events produce cultural ideas, cultural identity and cultural products. Opening ceremonies especially include a cultural-artistic aspect which is a condensed display of the host country's culture. A positive cultural image, increased awareness, new infrastructure and additional tourist products, combined with the soft factor of better service quality have a great potential to increase tourism in the long-term.

The Beijing Games were a celebration of both Olympic culture and Chinese traditional culture. The Olympic education project alone involved 400 million students from 400,000 schools across the country. From 2003 to 2008, the Ministry of Culture, the State Administration of Radio Film and Television, the State Physical Culture Administration, the Beijing government and the Beijing Organizing Committee jointly held the 2008 Olympic Cultural Festival on an annual basis. The final year Festival lasted nearly three months throughout the

Olympic and Paralympic Games of 2008, featuring a series of important cultural activities including both China's national and world-class artistic performances.

Emotion

Mega events generate pride for the population of the host city and country. In China, the Olympics were deliberately used to increase the confidence and self-esteem of the Chinese people. Part of this was related to the staging of the games: the pride that comes from the association of this global event with your own country. This was reinforced by the demonstration of Chinese culture at the opening ceremony. The euphoria generated in China by their topping the medal table added further to the country's sense of national pride, self-esteem and confidence.

TOOLS FOR ANALYSIS

The argument on why cities bid to host major events has over recent years been based on the economic development paradigm set out in Figure 5.2. That is, events will influence people living outside the host city and country to visit or invest in the city or country either during the event itself or in subsequent years because the place marketing effects of seeing the event on television will generate more tourism in the longer term.

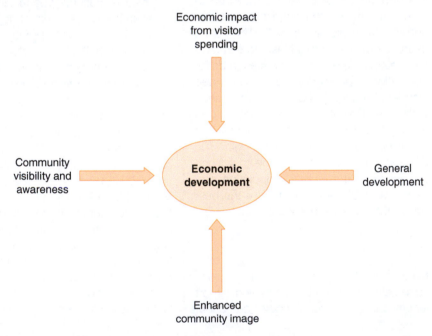

FIGURE 5.2   *Economic development paradigm*
Source: Crompton (2004)

CONTEMPORARY ISSUES IN SPORT MANAGEMENT

The American sport economics literature, however, has argued consistently that no evidence exists to suggest such economic benefits from hosting events ever actually materialize. As Crompton (2004) states:

> The prevailing evidence is that substantial measurable economic impact has rarely been demonstrated. This is causing the focus of the argument for public subsidy to be redefined, away from economic impacts and economic development towards the psychic income benefits. This is the new frontier.

This literature is mainly concerned with the economic impact of teams in the major four American team sports, American football, ice hockey, baseball and basketball. Other economists have shown that major events do generate a substantial economic impact. The Football World Cup in Germany in 2006 generated an economic impact of €2.56 billion, an average of €40 million from each match (Preuss et al., 2009).

There is little evidence to suggest that the Olympics, summer or winter, generate a significant economic impact. During the period July to September 2012 there were 4% less visits to the UK by overseas residents than in the same period in 2011. A similar pattern was observed in Beijing in 2008, Athens in 2004 and Sydney in 2000.

In contrast to the economic argument which focuses on audiences external to the host city or country, psychic income focuses internally on the host

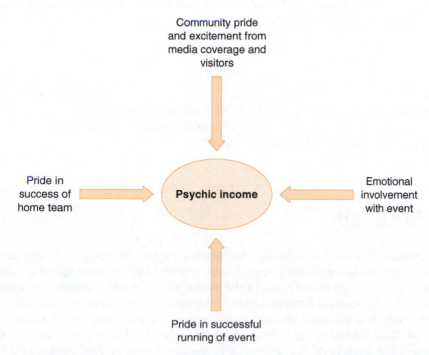

FIGURE 5.3 *Psychic income paradigm*
Source: Crompton (2004)

city or host country residents, and refers to the emotional and psychological benefit residents receive from hosting as indicated in Figure 5.3.

Such emotional benefits have also been identified by Gratton and Preuss (2008) as a key part of the legacy of major events. In addition in the last few years sport economists have adopted the methodology developed in the economics of happiness literature to analyse the effect of hosting major events on national pride and social wellbeing. Some studies have examined the willingness to pay (WTP) for both hosting sports events and success at sporting events and found that both may be substantial. Atkinson et al. (2008) explored the willingness of citizens in London, Manchester and Glasgow to host the 2012 London Olympic Games. They found the average WTP was highest among Londoners (£22), about twice as much as in Glasgow and Manchester, and was £2 billion for the UK population as a whole. Sussmuth et al. (2010) found similar levels of WTP for German citizens for the 2006 World Cup. Wicker et al. (2012a,b) found significant levels of willingness to pay for both Olympic success and World Cup success amongst German citizens.

Kavetsos and Szymanski (2010), using Eurobarometer data for 12 European countries, showed that hosting major events had a significant impact on national pride. Kavetsos (2012), using Eurobarometer data for 16 countries, also found significant effects on national pride from hosting major events. De Nooij et al. (2013), using a social cost–benefit analysis of the recent Netherlands World Cup bid, found that a greater sense of happiness, national pride, harmony and national identity was the main economic benefit to the hosts from staging a World Cup rather than economic impact.

The evidence cited above suggests that the 'old' economic paradigm is no longer the main benefit of hosting major events. The 'new' psychic income paradigm is increasingly becoming more important.

LEARNING ACTIVITIES

- Describe legacy/sustainable sports development.
- Is hosting a major sports event detrimental or beneficial to a host city/nation?

- How will legacy/sustainable sports development evolve in the future?

CONCLUSION

Globalization of the sport market has given us some very positive outcomes. Sports consumers worldwide can access unprecedented coverage of all the major sports events taking place in the world. The sports fan, whether living in Australia, China, North America or just about anywhere else with access to digital technology, can follow all the matches of top world teams such as Manchester United, Real Madrid or Barcelona. He or she can also follow every major golf tournament from both the American Professional Golfers' Association (PGA) Tour and the European Tour. Similarly, in other major sports events, wherever they take place, these can be watched live by most of the world. Fans worldwide now have much greater knowledge of the top players in a wide range of sports and what is going on at the very top level in those sports. There are no national barriers to discussions about sport when fans from different countries meet. This broadening of knowledge may also have led to less security issues around major football events such as the World Cup and the European Championships, with those staged so far in the twenty-first century being characterized by a carnival atmosphere, with fans from different countries celebrating together at 'fanfest' sites set up in the host cities for those of them without tickets.

Sport has also benefitted from the globalization of sport. Thirty years ago most of the football clubs in the top division in England were virtually bankrupt and the majority of their income that came from gate receipts and gates had fallen consistently from reaching their peak in 1948. Football was a declining industry. Today, broadcasting revenue is the main source of income to the English Premier League closely followed by sponsorship and commercial income. The very fact that 212 countries take live coverage of the English Premier League automatically increases their attractiveness to sponsors who seek such worldwide coverage. The same applies to the other major global sports events. During the post-2008 world recession sport was one of the few industries not to suffer a major cutback in revenue. Not only has sport received massive increases in income over recent years, but this income has also proved remarkably stable in challenging world economic conditions.

Sport has also massively increased its profile as an area of economic, social and cultural activity. It has to be taken seriously even by those who do not like sport. It is now a major global industry. In most developed economies it accounts for around 2% of GDP, in some a lot more. Much of the rise in the economic importance of sport in recent years is due to the developments we have discussed in this chapter.

Whatever the arguments relating to the costs and benefits of the globalization of sport there is no possibility of going back to the sort of national sports markets we had 30 years ago. It is unlikely that the pace of globalization in the sport market will continue in the next 20 years at the rate it has over the past two decades due to the simple fact that it has already touched most of the world. It is certainly the case that new developments in technology and in sport will provide greater opportunities for further globalization.

REFERENCES

Atkinson, G., Mourato, S., Symanski, S. & Oxdemiroglu, E. (2008) Are we willing to 'Back the Bid'? Valuing the intangible impacts of London's bid to host the 2012 summer Olympic Games, *Urban Studies*, 45(2): 419–44.

BBC (2015) Premier League TV rights: Sky and BT pay £5.1 bn for live games. Available at: www.bbc.co.uk/sport/0/football/31357409 (accessed 18 September 2015).

Crompton, J. (2004) Beyond economic impact: an alternative rationale for the public subsidy of major league sports facilities, *Journal of Sport Management*, 18: 40–58.

de Nooij, M., van den Berg, M. & Koopmans, C. (2013) Bread or games?: A social cost–benefit analysis of the world cup bid of the Netherlands and the winning Russian bid, *Journal of Sports Economics*, 14(5): 521–45.

Economist, The (2011) The awfulness of FIFA: an embarrassment to the beautiful game. Available at: www.economist.com/node/18774796 (accessed 18 September 2015).

Financial Times (2014) Value of US sports broadcast rights up 18.7%. Available at: www.ft.com/cms/s/0/57def478-4b1c-11e4-8a0e-00144feab7de.html#axzz3Y2Wh3pNb (accessed 6 October).

Forster, J. & Pope, N.K.L. (2004) *The Political Economy of Global Sporting Organisations.* London: Routledge.

Gratton, C. & Preuss, H. (2008) Maximising Olympic impacts by building up legacies, *International Journal of the History of Sport*, 25(14): 1922–38.

Gratton, C., Liu, D., Ramchandani, G. & Wilson, D. (2012) *The Global Economics of Sport*. London: Routledge.

Kavetsos, G. (2012) National pride: war minus the shooting, *Social Indicators Research*, 106: 173–85.

Kavetsos, G. & Szymanski, S. (2010) National well-being and international sports events, *Journal of Economic Psychology*, 31: 158–71.

Lee, J. (2005) Marketing and promotion at the Olympics, *The Sport Journal*. Available at: www.thesportjournal.org/article/marketing-and-promotion-olympic-games (accessed 6 October).

Mangan, J. (2008) Prologue: guarantees of global goodwill: post-Olympic legacies – too many limping white elephants? *The International Journal of the History of Sport*, 25(14): 1869–83.

Masterman, G. (2009) *Strategic Sports Event Management: An Olympic Edition.* Oxford: Butterworth-Heinemann.

Preuss, H., Kurscheidt, M. & Schütte, N. (2009) *Ökonomie des Tourismus durch Sportgroßveranstaltungen: Eine empirische Analyse zur Fußball-Weltmeisterschaft 2006.* Wiesbaden: Gabler Verlag.

Smart, B. (2007) Not playing around: global capitalism, modern sport and consumer culture, *Global Networks*, 7(92): 113–34.

Sussmuth, B., Heyne, M. & Maennig, W. (2010) Induced civic pride and integration, *Oxford Bulletin of Economics and Statistics*, 72(2): 202–20.

Todreas, T.M. (1999) *Value Creation and Branding in Television's Digital Age.* Westport, CT: Quorum.

Whannel, G. (2005) The five rings and the small screen: television, sponsorship, and new media in the Olympic Movement. In K. Young and K.B. Wamsley (eds), *Global Olympics: Historical and Sociological Studies of the Modern Games.* London: Elsevier.

Wicker, P., Hallman, K., Breuer, C. & Feiler, S. (2012a) The value of Olympic success and the intangible effects of sports events: a contingent valuation approach in Germany, *European Sport Management Quarterly*, 12(4): 337–55.

Wicker, P., Prinz, J. & von Hanau, T. (2012b) Estimating the value of national sporting success, *Sport Management Review*, 15(2): 200–10.

6

ETHICAL BEHAVIOR AND VALUES IN SPORT

GABRIELA TYMOWSKI, TERRI BYERS AND FRED MASON

England's 2018 World Cup bid slammed in ethics report.

(*The Melbourne Age*, 2014)

NFL chief asked to resign over handling of violence against women.

(*The Melbourne Age*, 2014)

Sport fandom is an ethical minefield—one we must each navigate alone.

(*The Guardian*, 2014)

LEARNING OUTCOMES

Upon completion of this chapter, students will be able to:

- Define ethics and sport ethics.

- Identify ethical issues which may be faced by sport managers.

- Understand five considerations for ethical decision making.

- Follow an ethical decision-making framework to guide decision making in the sport management environment.

INTRODUCTION

Increasing pressures of commercialization, professionalization, **globalization** and commodification of sport have seen calls to action from academics, practitioners and others who are concerned about sport at all levels. From children's sport through the ranks of amateur sport to elite sport, unethical practices including exploitation, **corruption**, cheating, **doping**, discrimination and a lack of fairness, appear to be on the rise (Morgan, 2006). This perception is certainly supported by mass media coverage, as rarely do stories of the aforementioned **transgressions**—in addition to others such as **gambling** and human trafficking—escape the headlines. Furthermore, other contemporary concerns in society generally such as those about the environment and social justice permeate sport as well (McNamee, 2010). As one of humankind's most fundamental institutions, sport, and those who lead and manage it, are increasingly confronted with the pressures to demonstrate that they are indeed worthwhile and responsible (Zeigler, 2007). While increasing commercialization and professionalization of sport have brought forth great opportunities for development through a global sport economy, with benefits also come some disadvantages and new challenges, particularly in the ethical realm.

The purpose of this chapter is to introduce readers to the theme of ethics in the management of sport. Future sport managers will need the skills and knowledge to guide their decisions on a wide range of ethical issues in sport environments, decisions which have the potential to affect athletes, coaches, parents, spectators, sponsors, managers and others involved directly and indirectly in sport. Sport managers need to be equipped to make the best decisions when faced with difficult situations, and also need to be prepared to make proactive decisions where possible to prevent problems from occurring at all. They also need to perform their duties honestly, professionally and ethically. The goal of sport ethics is to improve the lives of those involved in and affected by sport.

Ethical issues in sport may be understood as conflicts of values, conflicts of interest, or conflicts of rights and obligations. These conflicts may arise when institutional needs and organizational and personal values are not in alignment. Ethical challenges may be related to persons, policies and places. Sport ethics falls within the category of applied ethics, a sub-category of ethics encompassed by the discipline of philosophy.

Ethics is the branch of philosophy that deals broadly with what is morally right and wrong. It may also be called moral philosophy. Both ethics and morality may refer to embedded social regulations and cultural and historical traditions which manage behavior, and to some degree, a person's character. Simply put, ethics refers to standards of behavior that guide us towards right action in the many situations and relationships in which we find ourselves—as friends, partners, parents, coaches, community members, professionals or sport managers. The ultimate goal of ethics is to help improve the lives of people and others affected by our actions, such as **animals** and the environment. The challenges of ethics lie primarily in the gray area of behavior between what may be considered acceptable or right action and what may be held to be unacceptable action. Theories developed throughout our history have aimed to guide how we ought to act.

Theories of ethics are concerned with standards for right conduct and moral evaluation, and try both to give an account of right action and explain what makes that action right. Ethics tries to answer questions such as "how should one live?" and "how ought one to act?" In contrast to theories of action we have virtue theory, which focuses on character evaluation and establishing the criteria for evaluating an individual's character. Virtue ethics asks "what is involved in being a good or virtuous person?" One's character may be revealed through motives, intentions and actions, each of which may be influenced by moral values such as honesty, respect, fairness, justice, humility and compassion. Whether these are theories of right action or of character evaluation, moral theories provide moral guidance and the evaluation of human conduct.

Ethical issues in sport are as diverse as the millions of people of all ages who **participate** actively in sport as well as those who are coaches, parents, spectators, fans, critics and managers of sport. The sport industry ranges widely from recreational and grassroots levels to health and fitness, intercollegiate athletics, professional sport and facility management. The nature and challenges of sport may vary dramatically between each segment. For example, the purposes of sport at the professional level focus on sport as entertainment and money-making, quite different from sport at the amateur levels. Ethical issues facing managers include those related to the commercialization, professionalization, **globalization** and commodification of sport. Managers of sport are faced with ethical questions on a daily basis within each of those realms, about equity, access, professionalism, the treatment of athletes, exploitation, **media** access and coverage and conflicts of interest, as well as competing demands from the public, athletes, parents, sponsors and their own staff, including supervisors and owners. Given the myriad ethical questions and circumstances in which sport managers may find themselves, what is the best course of action for ethical decision making?

CASE STUDY 6.1

Ultrarunning

Ultrarunning, also known as ultramarathoning, is by definition running in events longer than the marathon distance of 42 kilometers (26.2 miles). While the length of races varies depending on the venue and terrain, standard distances include 50 kilometers, 50 miles, 100 kilometers and 100 miles. There are also 6-, 12- and 24-hour events where competitors run loops over a set course, covering as much distance as possible in the set time limit, and stage races where participants cover longer distances over several days. The distance is not the only challenge, as races typically occur on trails, and often involve rugged terrain and significant elevation gains and drops.

Ultrarunning has been around in its current form since the 1970s. One of the earliest continuing races is the Western States Endurance Run, originating in 1974 and formalizing as an event in 1978 (Hoffmann and Wegelin, 2009). Ultrarunning has traditionally been a small subculture, with small fields of locally based runners, an ethos of community support and little fanfare other than in specialized magazines. David and Lehecka (2014) describe the culture of ultrarunning as "the spirit of the trail," where completion of the race is stressed over competition, and personal transformation and a sense of community are highly valued. Speed has never been a real goal, as times are essentially meaningless when comparing one course to others.

However, ultrarunning has experienced exponential growth in recent years (Hoffman et al., 2010). *Ultrarunning Magazine* (2014) reports that the number of ultra-distance races in the USA increased from 293 races in 2004 to 1,296 in 2014. Part of the popularity of ultrarunning has resulted from, and continues to reinforce, trends towards commercialization of the sport. There are now ultrarunning-oriented product lines from sports companies, increasing attention from mainstream media companies and a recent rash of ultrarunner autobiographies and non-fiction books, some of which have sat on bestseller lists for extended periods of time (Jurek, 2012; Karnazes, 2006; McDougall, 2009). Traditionally, ultrarunning races have not offered prize money, and many of the older races still do not do so. However, there are now highly commercialized race series with major sponsorship deals that offer prize money and appearance fees (David and Lehecka, 2013).

Some elite ultrarunners are sponsored by shoe and gear companies, manufacturers of specialized nutrition and even beer companies, making a career as a professional trail and ultrarunner increasingly possible.

One of ultrarunning's first breakout stars, Catalan-born runner Killian Jornet, has a long-standing relationship with Salomon. Jornet had great racing success at a young age (27 years old at the time of writing, unusual for a sport where most runners peak in their late 30s and early 40s), winning both Western States and the major European mountain race Ultra Trail de Mont Blanc (UTMB) in 2011. In his own writing (Jornet, 2013) and Salomon's advertisements related to him (e.g. Salomon, 2012), Jornet is constructed as a force of nature, a highly competitive individual, and someone on a spiritual quest.

Jornet and Salomon partnered to produce the YouTube series "Killian's Quest" (later given out on DVD at Salomon-sponsored trail races), a series of short videos of Jornet running up and down mountains or training with other recognizable people in the sport. This culminated in an advertising campaign centering on his 2011 season and his assistance in helping Salomon design shoes. He has since gone on to tackle his own projects, for example one called "Summits of My Life," where he is attempting to complete "fastest known times" (FKTs) for ascending and descending major mountain peaks of the world, all filmed by GoPro camera and released on the web. At the same time, he remains a highly visible Salomon-sponsored athlete. Salomon has gone on to produce other trail and ultrarunning videos on their YouTube channel Salomon TV, and now sponsors numerous trail runners, including a group of young athletes from around the globe known as the Salomon Running Academy.

All of this sponsorship means more attention and prize money and a greater focus on elite athletes. This offers the possibility of better organized races, bigger fields, and professional careers in the sport. But ultrarunning has never been particularly about elite athletes or mass fields. Longstanding ultrarunners are worried that it is going to change the core values of the community. Recent media articles quote race directors complaining about a large number of runners who not understand the subcultural norms, which include easygoing attitudes and approaches to race organization (Uhan, 2015).

Much of this change appears to stem from the commercialization of ultrarunning, such as Salomon's involvement; Salomon used to be a skiing-focused company, but has become heavily involved in ultrarunning because it offers a marketing niche. Many within the sport worry that ultrarunning will become like triathlon, which started as small fields of athletes interested in extreme endurance challenges. It is now a highly elite, competitive and expensive sport in which to participate, and has such a commercialized third-party presence that the governing bodies are effectively no longer in control (Phillips and Newland, 2014). Furthermore, there are environmental limits in ultrarunning, where many wilderness areas in which races occur may support only a limited number of runners. This had led to the need for qualifying races and large entry lotteries for many of the most popular races, often limiting the opportunities for longstanding participants.

TOOLS FOR ANALYSIS

Ethical decision making

Identifying moral standards on which everyone would agree is difficult. Theories of right action are not universal, and no one theory has yet been found to be absolute. Thus, rational inquiry into ethical issues is put forth as an approach to making ethical decision, using a framework for thinking ethically. The following framework, adapted from the Markkula Centre for Applied Ethics (2009b), serves as a guide for ethical decision making for sport managers. It is not a template: ethical decision making is a process based on reason and logic in the identification of an ethical issue, careful compilation and consideration of the circumstances, an evaluation of alternatives, making a decision and testing it, and then circumspect reflection on the process. Following these steps will guide one towards ethical decision making.

Identification of an ethical situation

1 Might this decision or situation be harmful to an other (person, animal, the environment), individually or collectively? Does this decision involve a choice between a good and bad alternative, or perhaps even between two "good" options or between two "bad" options?

Gather the facts

2 What are the relevant circumstances of the situation? What do you know, and what do you not know? Do you know enough about the situation to make a decision?

3 Who are the stakeholders in this situation? Who has an important stake in the outcome?

4 What are the options for action? Have all the relevant persons and groups been consulted?

5 Who will be, and who might be, affected by the outcomes of decisions? How might they be affected?

Evaluate the alternatives

6 Evaluate the alternatives by considering the following approaches to ethical decision making:

- Which option will produce the most good and do the least harm? (The Utilitarian Approach)

Utilitarian theory holds that the ultimate standard of what is morally correct depends on the greatest amount of good for the greatest number. Those who use the utilitarian approach make ethical decisions based on what they anticipate to be the short- and long-term consequences for the majority. Utilitarians try to maximize the utility, satisfaction, benefit or happiness for the greatest number.

- Which option best respects the rights of all who have a stake? (The Rights Approach)

The rights approach aims to protect and respect the moral rights of those affected, based on the view that humans have a dignity based on their human nature, and on their ability to choose freely their life choices. This dignity includes the right to be treated as an end and not merely as the means to others' ends.

- Which option treats people equally or proportionately? (The Justice Approach)

Justice as fairness supports equal rights and equality of opportunity while providing the greatest good to those least advantaged. Right action treats all equals equally, and unequals unequally but is fairly based. Not everything has to be equal, so long as each person has an equal opportunity to achieve a desired outcome.

- Which option best serves the community as a whole, not just some members? (The Common Good Approach)

The Common Good approach posits the view that life in a community is a good in itself, and that our actions ought to contribute to that life. This view considers the overlapping relationships of a community or society as being the basis of ethical reasoning, and therefore respect and compassion for all others—particularly the most vulnerable—are requirements for this reasoning. Some of the common conditions which are important for this approach would be having effective health care, legal systems, police and fire departments, and public recreation facilities.

- Which option leads me to act as the sort of person I want to be? (The Virtue Approach)

Virtue ethics focuses on the character of an individual, and asks "what would a virtuous person do in this situation?" and "would this action be that of a morally excellent person?" Virtues are dispositions that guide us to act in accordance with the behavior of a morally virtuous character. Examples of virtues include honesty, compassion, fairness, integrity, self-control, prudence and courage.

Make a decision and test it

7 Considering all these approaches, which option best addresses the situation?

8 If I told someone I respect which option I have chosen, what do I think they might say? Would they support my decision?

Act, and then reflect on the outcome

9 How can my decision be implemented with the greatest care and attention to the interests of all stakeholders?

10 How did my decision turn out and what have I learned from this specific situation?

ACTION LEARNING

- How has the commercialization of ultrarunning impacted on the participants of this sport?
- Should sport managers be concerned with the changes seen in ultrarunning as the sport has become increasingly commodified?

- How best should sport managers promote the sport of ultrarunning while maintaining its traditional roots, and ethos of community and humility?

Hunting as Sport

For thousands, even millions, of years, the vast majority of humans have hunted animals for subsistence in order to survive. Subsistence hunting is not feasible anymore for the vast majority of the general human population today as a means of survival, and for those who do eat the animals they kill, this is usually a supplement to their diets rather than an exclusive means of feeding themselves. Nowadays, as people in much of the western world have achieved stable enough lives that they have leisure time available for recreation, some people pursue and kill animals purely for their own pleasure, as entertainment (Tymowski, 2014). "Sport" hunting is rather a misnomer for this activity, since definitions of sport typically require that the participants engage in these activities voluntarily (Boxill, 2003; Suits, 1988). Animals are not free to choose whether or not they participate, and thus are not acting autonomously (Singer, 1990). As such, given that participation in sport must be free and voluntary, "sport" hunting cannot be classified as a sport when not all those involved have consented, and cannot consent to such an activity. Only the humans are participating voluntarily and enjoying the process of stalking and killing: the animals are pursued, terrified and usually killed. However, given the prominence that "sport" hunting has on television sports channels, in magazines and in commerce, this activity appears to fall within conventional notions of sport.

The commercialization of hunting wildlife has led to it being a hugely profitable industry (Sorenson, 2010). A wide variety of products and services are available to hunters in stores and through online shopping. Governments of countries around the world permit the killing of animals for sport. Canada is the only country that allows the killing of polar bears, and it has become a popular "sport" for elite (and wealthy) hunters. While hunting is restricted to Aboriginal communities via a system of licenses, communities may choose to sell their licenses to others wishing to kill animals for sport. That opportunities to hunt animals are available on eBay, an online site selling everything from clothing to jewelry to even a human kidney at one time, has commodified the killing of animals, for the pleasure and entertainment of humans.

The commercial hunting of wild animals has had a profound global impact on the environment (Richards, 2014). Wildlife have been commercially exploited, some to the point of extinction, if not endangerment. Animals have been exploited as human resources, typically in a manner which presupposes there to be an endless supply. Even when researchers have implored governments to stop, or at least limit, the killing of animals for sport, governments have argued from economic development perspectives that hunting is an important economic driver. That hunting for sport is highly controversial is without argument, and governments have repeatedly put forth the paradoxical justification that killing animals for pleasure and entertainment both promotes conservation efforts by managing animal populations, and also by promoting economic development, always a political tool (Sorenson, 2010; Van de Pitte, 2003). Sport managers may find themselves in the midst of an ethical quagmire when it comes to sport hunting, and need to be prepared to make strong ethical decisions regarding this issue.

TOOLS FOR ANALYSIS

Sport entrepreneurship, innovation and social responsibility

Sport has changed dramatically over the past few years. **Innovations** in technology, entrepreneurship, commercialization and increasing awareness of social responsibility have significantly impacted on the ways in which sport is managed, consumed, marketed, and in many ways have transformed it into the "business" of sport. Entrepreneurs have brought innovation to sport in interesting and transformative ways. For example, consider how, over the past several decades, traditional outdoor sports such as surfing, skating, alpine skiing and rock climbing have been "indoorized" where they are now available in safe, predictable and controlled indoor settings (van Bottenburg and Salome, 2010). Other sports such as white water kayaking and canoeing now take place in artificial settings, with concrete "rivers," recycling water pumps, and enormous demands for both energy and water (Salome et al., 2013). It does seem ironic that in an age when social and environmental responsibility is seen as increasingly important in sport and in society, entrepreneurship has commodified a nature sport into one that defies its origins. Salome et al. (2013) point out that entrepreneurs have created entirely artificial environments where the activities are controlled, predictable, efficient and calculable, and are marketed as sensational and adventurous outdoor lifestyle sports, despite being artificial and distant from the original "natural" version of the sport. An example here is Ski Dubai, a ski and snowboard resort built within an enormous climate-controlled shopping mall in the United Arab Emirates. The UK also offers a number of indoor "dry" snow centres. Despite the artifice of these now-indoor versions of outdoor adventure sports, corporate environmental responsibility (CER) overlays these kinds of commodified nature sports via the entrepreneurs who have developed them. Innovation and entrepreneurship must embrace these areas of concern—corporate environmental and social responsibility—and must do so within a framework of sustainability as well.

CER has come about as a response to concerns about environmental impacts, and the responses from organizations to "green" their facilities and practices (Salome et al., 2013). Pressure from public and environmental organizations has led to increased environmental legislation and regulation, and attention from organizations at many levels. Environmentally oriented business management and awareness of the environmental impact of organizations have resulted in increased CER, as part of a greater concern with social responsibility. There are clearly conflicts between **economic** values and environmental concerns, where the latter may be more costly than maintaining the status quo, and thus there is often tension between the two values. It is possible for socially responsible organizational activities to benefit both the organization and society (Babiak and Wolfe, 2009). Babiak and Wolfe (2009) have concluded that social responsibility has been emphasized to such a degree in other industries, and more recently in sport, that it will remain an important issue for sport organizations and managers well into the future. As Ratten (2011: 57) noted, "sport is an entrepreneurial process as innovation and change are key elements of sport": sport will change as entrepreneurs effect change in sport, and those involved in sport management must be prepared to face rapid change.

Sport-based entrepreneurship is a useful theoretical framework for understanding sport management, and the marketing of sport in particular (Ratten, 2011). Ratten argues that it is useful for sport managers to have an entrepreneurial orientation towards their profession, in order to understand proactive, innovative and risk-taking behavior by those involved in sport, and most particularly to understand the "different perspectives from athletes, coaches, community, corporation, country and region" (2011: 66). There are a variety of types of sport-based entrepreneurship including community-based, social, ethnic and international. Each of these areas contributes to sport and its development in different ways, some areas of which are yet to be explored, and given the dynamism of sport, sport managers must be prepared to react to these areas and perspectives as they develop and change. Their roles will change also as entrepreneurship is multi-faceted, and must be inclusive within their communities, whose roles too must be flexible. Community-based entrepreneurship entails a community behaving corporately in the roles of both entrepreneur and an enterprise focused on a common goal (Ratten, 2011). There will be ethical challenges to change, and sometimes the rapid pace will make decision making difficult, but proactive planning will help sport managers prepare for the future.

ACTION LEARNING

- In what ways as a sports manager can you help foster an environment that promotes kindness and compassion?
- In the role of sport manager, identify and evaluate the ethical dimensions of "sport" hunting.
- Using the virtue ethics approach, how might a person of virtuous character approach "sport" hunting?
- Should sport be used to pursue economic value at the expense of all else?

- When sport prioritizes profit-making over other values, how might that influence the way sport is managed? Consider the impact of that approach on athletes, coaches, spectators and others.
- How might sport managers promote ethical behavior in sport?
- How might environmental responsibility compete with other sport values?
- What kinds of ethical challenges might a community-based sports entrepreneurship pose?

CONCLUSION

Sport is enjoyed by millions of people around the world, and will continue to be enjoyed, despite the many ethical challenges facing those who participate, manage and consume it. Sport adds joy and meaning to the lives of those involved at every level, and perhaps the best way to ensure that joy continues is to identify ethical issues that may endanger the benefits conferred by and through sport for individuals at every age, at every level of sport from amateur levels to the ranks of professional sport, and to manage those issues. Problems are best prevented, and when these occur, they need to be managed well. Using an ethical framework to promote the interests of those involved and affected by sport's challenges is a valuable approach to that end. Decisions need to be ethically defensible, and thus sport managers need to learn about the ethical dimensions of sport and how to make ethical decisions, as well as provide leadership in this realm. This chapter has provided an introduction to ethics in sport management, a framework for ethical decision making, and further reading and resources for additional education on the subject.

Sport managers may wish to begin their deliberations of the next steps for sport by considering Earl Zeigler's question that he posed for those in the profession of sport management: "What kind of sport should the profession promote in order to help shape the world in the 21st century?"(2007: 316). Consideration of ethical decision making is relevant for many areas of sport management that are beyond the scope of this chapter, and we would encourage students to consider the ethics of sport management in the context of sport governance, mega sporting events, the impacts of sport on society, innovation, technology and sport entrepreneurship, to name but a few.

REFERENCES

Babiak, K. & Wolfe, R. (2009) Determinants of corporate social responsibility in professional sport: internal and external factors, *Journal of Sport Management*, 23: 717–42.

Boxill, J. (2003) The moral significance of sport. In J. Boxill (ed.), *Sport Ethics: An Anthology.* Hoboken, NJ: Wiley-Blackwell. pp. 1–14.

David, G.C. & Lehecka, N. (2013) The spirit of the trail: culture, popularity and prize money in ultramarathoning, *Fast Capitalism,* 10(1). Available at: www.fastcapitalism.com.

DeSensi, J.T. & Rosenberg, D. (2011) *Ethics and Morality in Sport Management,* 3rd edn. Morgantown, WV: Sport Management Library, Fitness Information Technology, Inc.

Hoffman, M.D., Ong, J.C. & Wang, G. (2010) Historical analysis of participation in 161 km ultramarathons in North America, *International Journal of the History of Sport*, 27(11): 1877–91.

Hoffman, M.D. & Wegelin, J.A. (2009) The Western States 100–Mile Endurance Run: participation and performance trends, *Medicine and Science in Sports and Exercise*, 41(12): 2191–8.

Hums, M.A., Barr, C.A. & Gullion, L. (1999) The ethical issues confronting managers in the sport industry, *Journal of Business Ethics,* 20(1): 51–66.

Jornet, K. (2013) *Run or Die.* Boulder, CO: Velo.

Jurek, S. (2012) *Eat and Run: My Unlikely Journey to Ultramarathon Greatness.* Boston, MA: Mariner.

Karnazes, D. (2006) *Ultramarathon Man: Confessions of an All-night Runner.* New York: Tarcher.

LaFollette, H. (2007) *The Practice of Ethics.* Malden, MA: Blackwell.

Markkula Centre for Applied Ethics (2009a) Making an ethical decision. Available at: www.scu.edu/ethics/practicing/decision/making.pdf.

Markkula Centre for Applied Ethics (2009b) Framework for ethical decision making. Available at: www.scu.edu/ethics/practicing/decision/framework.html.

McDougall, C. (2009) *Born to Run: A Hidden Tribe, Superathletes, and the Greatest Race the World has Never Seen.* New York: Knopf.

McNamee, M. (2010) *The Ethics of Sports.* London: Routledge.

Morgan, W.J. (2006) *Why Sports Morally Matter.* New York: Routledge.

Phillips, P. & Newland, B. (2014) Emergent models of sport development and delivery: the case of triathlon in Australia and the US, *Sport Management Review,* 17: 107–20.

Ratten, V. (2011) Sport-based entrepreneurship: towards a new theory of entrepreneurship and sport management, *International Entrepreneurship Management Journal,* 7: 57–69.

Richards, J.F. (2014) *The World Hunt: An Environmental History of the Commodification of Animals.* Berkeley, CA: University of California Press.

Salome, L.R., van Bottenburg, M. & van den Heuvel, M. (2013) 'We are as green as possible': environmental responsibility in commercial artificial settings for lifestyle sports, *Leisure Studies,* 32(2): 173–90.

Salomon (2012) Trail running, for me, is not about running (32pp. brochure), Kalistene Printing.

Seth, H. & Babiak, K.M. (2010) Beyond the game: perceptions and practices of corporate social responsibility in the professional sport industry, *Journal of Business Ethics,* 91(3): 433–50.

Singer, P. (1990) *Animal Liberation,* 2nd edn. London: Thorsons.

Sorenson, J. (2010) *About Canada—Animal Rights.* Halifax: Fernwood.

Suits, B. (1988) Tricky triad: games, play, and sport, *Journal of the Philosophy of Sport,* 15: 1–9.

Thornton, P.K., Champion, W.T. & Ruddell, L. (2012) *21.* Sudbury, MA: Jones & Bartlett.

Tymowski, G. (2014) The virtue of compassion: animals in sport, hunting as sport, and entertainment. In J. Gillett & M. Gilbert (eds), *Sport, Animals and Society.* New York: Routledge. pp. 140–54.

Uhan, J. (3 March 2015) Modeling values in the ultrarunning community, *Ultrarunning Magazine.* Available at: www.ultrarunning.com/featured/modeling-values-in-the-ultrarunning-community.

Ultrarunning Magazine (2014) 10 year growth of ultrarunning events and races. Available at www.ultrarunning.com/data/10-year-growth-of-ultrarunning-events-and-races.

Van Bottenburg, M. & Salome, L. (2010) The indoorisation of outdoor sports: an exploration of the rise of lifestyle sports in artificial settings, *Leisure Studies,* 29(2): 143–60.

Van de Pitte, M. (2003) The moral basis for public policy encouraging sport hunting, *Journal of Social Philosophy,* 34(2): 256–66.

Zeigler, E. (2007) Sport management must show social concern as it develops tenable theory, *Journal of Sport Management,* 21: 297–318.

USEFUL WEBSITES

http://cces.ca
www.nassm.com/InfoAbout/NASSM/Creed
www.olympic.org/ethics-commission
http://sportsethicist.com/
www.tidesport.org
http://portal.unesco.org/education/en/ev.php-URL_ID=2223&URL_DO=DO_
    TOPIC&URL_SECTION=201.html
www.wada-ama.org

7

POLITICS AND SPORT GOVERNANCE

RUSSELL HOLDEN

> It is our belief that concentrating power in the hands of the few can lead to greater corruption risks. The ICC should operate in a manner that reflects integrity and fair-play as well as the true spirit of the game.
>
> (Deryck Murray Trinidad and Tobago Transparency Institute, April 2012)

> Whereas cricket used to be a symbol and example in the West Indies of anti-colonial struggle and hence attracted a real following, today it is nothing more than expression of gold-digging individuals.
>
> (John Passant, 1 December 2009)

> The Union [Samoan] is functioning properly despite its faults, but we are still running and the teams are competing at international level – all the teams – so we need to sit down with them and discuss what the real issues are. Their responsibilities are to play when we ask them and leave the administration to the Union.
>
> (Paimang Jensen, quoted in V. Wylie, 27 November 2014)

Upon completion of this chapter, students will be able to:

- Comprehend the concept of sport governance (extending beyond the promotion of equal opportunity, widening participation and fair play), and how governance is driven by political issues and why sport has to be regulated.

- Understand the changing nature of sport governance with particular reference to the growing impact of globalisation that is inextricably linked to national and international sport.

- Begin to conceptualise how rugby union and cricket provide an interesting comparison of governance, as they possess very different histories of professionalism.

- Gain a thorough insight into the consequences of weak and ineffectual governance.

INTRODUCTION

Whilst clubs and athletes compete for victory in sporting competition, sport requires organisation and systems of governance to ensure the viability and fairness of such competition for its credibility. In addition, this guarantees the continued interest of the fans and the on-going commitment of sponsors. At the international and global level, governance is essential for decisions regarding the continued existence and functioning of **sporting mega-events**. As sport involves and revolves around contested power struggles between and amongst nations (Marjoribanks and Farquharson, 2013) as well as powerful individuals (manifest through political parties or sporting bodies), it is imperative that the issue of governance is viewed within the prism of politics. This is a reality that has to be appreciated by all those involved in the management and provision of sport at a local, national and, most critically of all, an elite international level.

Sport is rule-governed and regulated (Giulianotti, 2005; Guttmann, 2005) and the making and breaking of governance rules is central to the operations and dynamics of sport governance. Although this chapter is not concerned with the realities of poor governance, it is critical to how governance relates to the politics of international sport that we understand the consequences which problems such as inadequate monitoring, the lack of transparency and succession planning can have on the decision-making process and its consequent implications.

WHY DOES SPORT HAVE TO BE REGULATED?

As Woodward (2012: 43) comments:

> It is hardly surprising that sport speaks so volubly of equity and justice framed by impartiality; each game even has its own arbiter in the form of at least one referee or umpire.

Governance, as Horne et al. (2013) suggest, involves the making, breaking and changing of rules of engagement, and provides the mechanism through which power operates. Thus, in tackling issues of governance, questions arise concerning where the power or the capacity to act to enable change occurs. Sport is ruled and governed by a range of national and international bodies, yet these rules are often broken and the governance of sport is concerned with measures to reduce these transgressions (Horne et al., 2013).

To fully appreciate the political realities of sport governance within an international setting, the enormous differences in opportunity, wealth, democracy and models of professional sport need to be acknowledged (Jarvie and Thornton, 2012). The agenda for regulation and governance is essentially driven by the transformation of global sport by finance capital and the erosion of democratic power by unaccountable market power impelled by the forces of neo-liberalism.

Horne et al. (2013) rightly suggest the realities and structures of governance in sport, be these at a local, national, international or global level, display increased control and the dominance of economic power, as evidenced through the rise of global capital and international media conglomerates. Yet this begs the question of the degree to which governments can, and indeed prove able to, **control** this manifestation of increasing power.

In seeking to explain the realities of governance, a theoretical context is essential. The realist or neo-realist perspective is the one most suited to the on-going analysis as the governance of international sporting bodies will always reflect the needs of the dominant governing bodies of sport. Therefore, cooperation and institutional decisions are heavily constrained by issues of power and the needs of vested interests. Although this approach sometimes lacks the nuance needed to fully appreciate the fluidity of identities and challenges to the existing order, dominant interests constantly prevail. An interesting case in point is the emergence of India as the key power-broker in international cricket. The establishment of the Indian Premier League (IPL) provides a notable example of this, with its complex interlocking with the Board of Cricket and Control India (BCCI), which administers cricket throughout India (Asthill, 2013).

However, the accepted framework for regulation and governance is framed by a 'Northern' agenda, despite the huge differences in opportunity, wealth, democracy, sporting taste and models of professional sport that prevail beyond the confines of the G8 countries. [1] As international sport becomes increasingly **commercialised**, its freedom is evermore restricted with the need for **law** and forms of regulation intensifying. Sporting autonomy becomes more of a myth as its separation from a range of political and societal issues becomes less possible. In the cases of Pakistan, Sri Lanka and Zimbabwe, the political authorities, and in some cases the heads of state, have overtly interfered with the administration of the game and the selection of the team captain. [2]

It appears that **ethical** concerns over honesty, fairness, justice and responsibility often take a back seat to the demands of vested interests. The difficulties that the World Anti-Doping Agency (WADA) is currently facing in exploring controversies regarding **doping** of athletes and the unfair advantage that they, in the cases of Jamaica and Kenya, can accrue, give credence to this reality. The International Amateur Athletics Federation (IAAF) has spoken out strongly against what it deems to be a heavy-handed approach by WADA, particularly in the case of Jamaica.

GOVERNANCE AND THE SPORT – POLITICS OVERLAP

Governments are increasingly aware of the power of sport as a policy and catalyst for transformation, integration and even inspiration, with many utilising it as a vehicle for promoting and selling complex and potentially unpopular policy. Sport has a long political history, and sport and politics have long been enmeshed at different times in different places across the globe (Woodward, 2009). In both historical and contemporary terms, it needs to be viewed in the context of colonialism and neo-colonial history. It has played its part in nation-building and the forging of identity, with cricket and rugby union both having enjoyed pivotal roles.

Governance of sport is embedded in the politics of sport, as power operates at different levels. At a minimum, sport is not divorced from the social forces that influence it. It is a strong focus for political interventions, whilst parties and leaders strive to identify with these interventions, as exemplified by Prime Minister Blair's use of the 2012 Olympics as a political tool. [3]

 Of course, £9bn is in one sense a lot of money but, in another sense, you're regenerating an entire part of the country, creating thousands of jobs and there's massive amounts of investment coming in. (Gibson, 2012)

In contrast, the Russian President Vladimir Putin viewed the 2014 Sochi Winter Olympics as a tool for both domestic and foreign policy, recognising the value of a two-pronged strategy to showcase the Russian state, culminating with the 2018 FIFA World Cup. The case of China, too, is relevant in this context, with the authorities carefully using the Beijing Olympics as a device for projecting national interest, which influenced the governments of most Olympic participants to substantially tone down their concerns over the suppression of human rights both internally and in Tibet.

Consequently, sport can be utilised as a transmission mechanism for ideological values (Hoolihan, 2008; Coakley & Pike, 2009). As Hoolihan and White (2002) distinguish, politics in sport can direct our attention to the use made by government of sport as well as the process by which public policy is made, and it can also lead to the way in which sport organisations promote their own sectional interests in working with financial backers and vested interests. The Bahrain Formula 1 (F1) race is an interesting case in point. Now in its 10th year, the race continues, with F1 maintaining its links with its key business allies despite the ever-growing concerns regarding human rights abuses perpetrated by the powerful governing royal family:

> Politics is none of our business, is the incessant refrain. This is about sport, they cry, as the often violent efforts by the ruling Sunni monarchy to snuff out demonstrations by the Shia minority are conveniently swept aside. (Brown, 2014)

The argument by pro-government groups is that the Bahrain Grand Prix generates more than £300 million for the Bahrain economy, yet the race itself, attended by a modest 28,000 in 2013, remains the province of an elite.

CASE STUDY 7.1

International Cricket

Any examination of the realities of international cricket, whether in terms of issues of principle or *realpolitik*, must acknowledge a distinctiveness about the game in comparison to other sports, where, in many instances, the role of the US has been and continues to remain significant.

The first major challenge to the governance of cricket in the twenty-first century came with the 2003 Cricket World Cup. In this instance cricket's governing body, the International Cricket Council (ICC), decided to schedule some of the tournament matches in Zimbabwe, despite the regime's patent disregard for fundamental human rights and possible threats to the security of the players.

To explore the complexity of the Zimbabwe question, the role and actions of the governing body of international cricket and its response to this issue need consideration. However, this only becomes meaningful when viewed in the context of the impact of the ICC's behaviour on a national cricket authority, which, in this instance, was the England and Wales Cricket Board (EWCB) and its response to the crisis with regard to the guidance offered to the team management about whether to play in Zimbabwe.

The ICC is the governing body for international cricket. Full Members are drawn from current and former Commonwealth nations. Having been renamed the International Cricket Conference in 1965, it adopted its current name of the International Cricket Council in 1989. At that point, it took over the role of the MCC by administering aspects of the game on behalf of the Test-playing nations. However, the MCC retained responsibility for the laws of the game. Currently, the ICC has 105 Members (10 Full, 36 Associate and 59 Affiliate). The 10 Full Members are the governing bodies for cricket of a country recognised by the ICC from which representative teams are qualified to play official Test cricket.

Over the past decade, the financial balance of the world game has changed with the commercial success of the ICC's Cricket World Cup, the World Twenty20, and the Champions Trophy, as well as the IPL, the Champions League and other Twenty20 tournaments (Gupta, 2004). The base of its financial success has been in the Indian subcontinent where cricket is the dominant sport. It is there that the devotion to cricket generates the financial success, which gives the sport the funding it needs to develop new opportunities. This success is to be welcomed, as cricket (along with other international sports) cannot afford to ignore the potential to increase its revenues.

However, cricket's new-found affluence must be tempered with maintaining and enhancing the integrity of the game, both on and off the field. Cricket's values need to keep pace with the changing financial landscape. Whereas recent publicity has focused largely on on-field issues, there is a need to be just as vigilant concerning off-field behaviours. In effect, protecting and maintaining the reputation of cricket is fundamental to the long-term sustainability and effective governance of the game. It may be everyone's responsibility, but the ICC has, and should have, a lead role to play. Repositioning the ICC to proactively shape the overall governance of the game rather than its current reactive role on behalf of the Full Members is critical. The global function of the ICC is to undertake the administration, development, coordination, regulation and promotion of the game of cricket worldwide in cooperation with its members.

The Strategic Plan for 2011–2015 also implies a broad role for the ICC. However, many of its existing governance arrangements reflect the membership structure that has long been in place. The ICC has no substantive control over the Future Tours Programme (FTP), as Full Members determine their own bi-lateral arrangements, and hence the ICC is in no position to ensure its fairness. They are, however, expected to support the FTP through provision of umpires and officials on behalf of the Full Members, as well as to try and embed common playing conditions across all international matches. The latter has proved to be extremely difficult with the BCCI unwilling to agree to the use of the 'Decision Review System'.

Critically, the Strategic Plan for 2011–2015 also initiated a governance review. As Lord Woolf notes in his review, those interviewed have repeatedly come back to the question of whether the role of the ICC is to act in the best interests either of its Full Member boards or the international game. There is a significant, although not unanimous, body of opinion that believes it is essential the ICC is positioned and empowered to promote, develop and act in the best interests of the international game. This view was echoed by respondents to the consultation, who, irrespective of their country of origin, advocated a global parent body role for the ICC. To date, no conclusive discussion has been led by the ICC to confirm and clarify that this is the role it should play.

The review was delivered in 2012. It suggested a series of reforms to make cricket's governance more transparent and better equipped to oversee a global sport. Since then, there has been no formal response from the ICC to the Woolf recommendations. However, in early 2014 the ICC proposed a new structure that is now being accepted. The current proposals bear little or no relation to the principles outlined in the Woolf report, which, in itself, only represented standard corporate governance practice. The proposals are notable for ignoring other wider indicators of good governance such as accountability, transparency, participation, consensus, equity and inclusiveness. It is difficult to see how the proposed changes are in the interests of the game as a whole. They create a concentration of power in the 'Big Three' (India, Australia and England), with no oversight or effective avenue for the other Full, Affiliate and Associate members to hold them to account, reinforcing concerns that the creation of reserved places in the top tier is open to abuse, rather than serving the best interests of the game. As Berry suggests:

> The Big Three would henceforth concentrate all decision-making in their own hands on the grounds of providing strong leadership and stability. (Berry, 2014)

The entrenching of a privileged position for the 'Big Three' appears to be an abuse of entrusted power for private gain, giving them disproportionate, unaccountable and unchallengeable authority on a wide variety of constitutional, personnel, integrity, ethical and developmental matters. This is clearly contrary to the needs of good governance and totally removed from the sentiments conveyed by Lord Woolf and his team.

TOOLS FOR ANALYSIS

Any examination of the ICC has to be conducted in the context of the changing nature of international sport, where the new commercial realities of a game (cricket) that is ever more global are reflected in the power centre having relocated to South Asia from its longstanding base in England. This has presented an additional challenge to those who formerly controlled the game, as it overturns the orthodox model of globalisation and economic development which maintains that the dynamics of the process are spurred on by the forces of wealth from traditional geographical locations, i.e. the developed economies. With the power base of cricket now firmly entrenched in South Asia, the old order has been overthrown in both sporting and commercial terms.

International cricket presents an interesting case study of the politicisation of international sports governance in the running of the ever-expanding game (unusually, one with three distinct formats), as its administration for many years was underpinned by colonial influences which have been shaken to the core, not only by the growing status of South Asian cricket, but also by the role of India through its governing body, the BCCI. However, critical to the development of the game has been the rise of a transnational community able to support its favoured team across national boundaries. The spread of **technology** enables the provision of real-time coverage of the sport, be it via satellite, cable, web or podcast, and this helps to satisfy the increasing demands of the Indian diaspora and their continued passion to devour cricket coverage.

HEGEMONY OF COMMERCE

Having noted how the administrators of international cricket have struggled to keep pace in responding to the commercial imperative, it is necessary to view sport in terms of the globalisation thesis (Berry, 2006: 6). This will help to determine an understanding of how globalisation has impacted on the game and its governance, even if it is only viewed as a continuation or extension of the modernisation processes. As Beckles (1998) suggests, this process in terms of cricket has passed through three stages, with the globalised period having followed those of colonialism and nationalism.

A substantial literature exists on **globalisation**, and, more specifically, its impact on sport (Allison, 2005), and this material can be distilled into two distinct perspectives. The first concentrates on the imperialist rationale, stressing the unequal relationship between the culturally dominant, primarily western capitalist economies and the developing countries. The emergence of this relationship is spurred on by western economies wishing to extend the markets for capitalist products, which include sports such as cricket and rugby union, as exemplified within their recent strategic reviews. [4] Consequently, an alternative theoretical perspective on globalisation has evolved, which places an increased emphasis on the interconnection and interdependency of all global areas and the weakening of cultural coherence in individual states. Bairner (2005) takes this further by suggesting that sport is now bound up with a network of interdependent chains marked by uneven power relations. As a result, sport is best perceived as a set of global power networks in which the practice and consumption of elite modern sport can best be understood. Cricket, and to a lesser extent rugby union, are locked into a set of global networks largely driven by commercial interests, thus intensifying the commodification of the respective games. Rugby union is especially concerned to spread the game as geographically wide as possible, most notably beyond the confines of former British and French colonial interests. This will assist in capturing a wider television audience beyond the four-yearly World Cup that will generate more capital for the expansion of coaching and the process of talent identification. With the growth of rugby union in the US, as a consequence of investment and good fortune, the sport may take a new turn.

> There are thousands of American footballers and basketball players who are not going to gain a professional NFL or NBA contract, but who are increasingly realising that there is a global sport that potentially suits their skills perfectly. (*Guardian*, 25 March 2014)

For cricket, the apex of this development is the 50-over World Cup competition held every four years, with the new Twenty/20 format generating rapidly growing interest. Cricket features amongst a list of sports, including baseball, basketball, ice hockey and rugby union, which may appear to be globalised in terms of intensity and impact, but in reality only have a grip on certain geographical areas. Thus, the globalisation of sport is an uneven process, within which the place of cricket is distinctive. Yet sport's constant use of the nation as a rallying point and focus creates an uneasy tension when advocating the globalisation argument. The globalisation of sporting practices in terms of the spread of certain games around the world has, paradoxically, fuelled nationalism, which has manifest itself within cricket's governing body, the ICC, and, to a less potent extent, within the International Rugby Board, as witnessed in the negotiations to reform the existing annual European knock-out tournament. [5]

A key element of globalisation has been the flow of wealth, technology and ideas from the core to the periphery. Yet cricket disproves this model with the non-western nations now in a position to determine the format of the game, its content (international touring schedules) and venues, whilst conceivably moving to reshape the rules of the international game through its voting power within the ICC. This new reality was evident in the glorification of the heroes of Australia's cricketing dominance over the period 1995–2005 on the Asian sub-continent (notably Steve Waugh, Shane Warne and Brett Lee). [6]

Even though sport is less sympathetic to globalisation than other cultural forms such as music and film because of its dependence on passionate national differentiation (Rowe, 2003), the commodification of cricket has led to a geographical, if not an ideological, relocation of power, with the driving mechanism for this being the activities of operatives like the Murdoch Global Cricket Corporation (MGCC). The MGCC has capitalised on the migration of labour, with the spread of technology helping to extend the notion of global entertainment. Indeed, it was the actions of the Indian media mogul Mark Mascarenhas, who was able to secure the true market value for international cricket when he was successful in his bid of $8.5m by his company World Tel for the 1996 World Cup, that took cricket to a new level of commercial activity. His efforts were undoubtedly boosted by the rapid growth of technology , the interest of transnational TV networks, the commercial possibilities of the one-day game and the opportunity to have an advertisement screened at the end of each over. In paying $22.5m to secure the television rights for India for the 2003 and 2007 World Cups, and three ICC Champions Trophies in 2002, 2004 and 2006, this was seven times more than the amount paid by Murdoch's STAR Sports network.

- How can the ICC best reconcile its desire to extend cricket without further empowering the strong cricketing nations?
- How can the governance of cricket be structured in such a way as to ensure

comprehensive governance, as opposed to a concentration of power in limited hands?
- Does the existing governance structure of the ICC actively promote transparency and democratic decision making?

CASE STUDY 7.2

The International Rugby Board and the Rugby World Cup

The IRB has overseen the development of rugby union since 1886. Despite being in its infancy, professional rugby union is a sport that its governing body estimates has 3.5 million playing the game at some level. Although it still needs to be vigilant about the draw of its rival, rugby league, and the possibility of code-switching by players, the game is prospering. However, as recently as 2011, it was financially hamstrung by a trio of its most powerful constituent members, who threatened to pull out of the 2015 World Cup due to a dispute concerning a serious projected loss of income.

As with cricket, rugby union at elite level is played by a limited number of nations, yet it has a better (though far from ideal) distribution of revenue, a greater appetite for growth and a more systematic method for allocating fixtures among its members – a reflection of a more effective form of governance than operates within cricket. The comparatively recent advent of professionalism in the game has brought with it a set of administrators who

are more adept, yet far from revolutionary, in responding to the contemporary pressures central to effective sport governance.

The IRB, which is based in Dublin, has 205 members. While the ICC currently has a board of 16 (a President, Vice-president, CEO, the Presidents of each of the 10 Full Members and of three Associate Members), the IRB's council comprises 27 (a Chairman, two seats for each of the eight founding countries – England, Scotland, Ireland, Wales, Australia, New Zealand, South Africa and France – and a seat each for Argentina, Canada, Italy and Japan). The remaining six members come from rugby's six world regions, which are roughly in line with the six continents. This regional representation is lacking within the ICC.

The council meets twice a year and formulates the IRB's overall strategy, admits or expels members and selects the hosts for the World Cups. To pass a decision usually requires a simple majority of the council, but changes to the IRB bye-laws or the laws of the game need the votes of two-thirds of the council. A 10-person Executive Committee is derived from the IRB's council and the Executive Committee is responsible for the management and operation of the IRB. The ICC's new

Executive Committee, as a consequence of the proposed new structure will comprise just five members.

Outside the boardroom, the IRB also now appears more willing than cricket to spread its resources. Members are divided into three tiers, according to whom they compete against. There are 10 tier-one countries, eight in tier two and the remainder are in tier three. The IRB's tier-one members are divided into six northern hemisphere countries and four southern. The former compete in the Six Nations tournament, and the latter in the Rugby Championship, both annual competitions. Three southern-hemisphere countries, New Zealand, Australia and South Africa, are also involved in a separate company called SANZAR, which oversees the Super Rugby competition, played between franchises in the three countries. These 10 tier-one countries also play each other during the year, during two defined calendar periods. Tours in the southern hemisphere take place around June, while visits to the northern hemisphere happen in November and December. Not all countries play each other every year but generally a tour consists of three matches against three countries, thus demonstrating a fairer system than the one on offer in cricket, though the schedule could be further reformed. In September 2012 the IRB announced a series of matches in the November block, which increased the participation of tier-two and -three sides.

The IRB illustrates its commitment to growing the game in different countries through its World Cup formula. The World Cup is a 20-team event in which countries are divided into four pools of five teams each. The quarter-finalists all automatically qualify for the next World Cup, but there are incentives for the other teams in each group too, because the ones that finish third also go through to the next tournament. An additional step has been taken to ensure the smaller teams have better chances against the big boys. At the 2015 World Cup, the IRB will make a scheduling change so as to give the minnows a week's break between matches, rather than just the three days most of them have had at previous World Cups. This should improve the performance levels of the lower ranked nations.

TOOLS FOR ANALYSIS

While rugby union has shown more willingness to expand than cricket, particularly through the vehicle of the seven-a-side format which will enter the Olympics in 2016, its leadership is keen to ensure that the sport is sustained through the promotion of wider competition, seeking to make certain that the sport's competitiveness is retained, as this will guarantee a spectacle that broadcasters and fans are keen to devour, at the same time as generating much-needed cash for future investment. Entrance to the Olympic family will intensify the exposure of the sport, and the existing leadership within the sport both at IRB and national levels is showing itself capable of capitalising on its new status, as laid out in the IRB's current Strategic Plan, which runs until 2019, though the emphasis on the Olympics displeases the rugby purists.

However, this apparent modernity within the game's administrators is recent, as eight nations have long held a hegemonic role in the game's governance

(Harris, 2010). This powerful core group of nations share a common colonial heritage (aside from France), i.e. the English language. The inherent conservatism of this group resulted in the sport waiting until 1987 for its first world cup, close to 60 years after football first initiated the idea. The failure to develop as a truly global game despite the intensifying forces of globalisation is evidenced by the venues selected for host nation status and the limited numbers of nation-states taking part. Those that governed the sport lacked the desire to export it as in some cases they feared being beaten at their own game. This reality persisted amongst some governing unions even in the professional era, although New Zealand's unwillingness to schedule a test match in Samoa until 2015 smacks more of arrogance and a desire to control a domestic game and its development structure which it has exploited for its own purpose in talent identification and personnel recruitment for the All Black national side.

Also as Woodward (2012) suggests the animosity evident between the southern nations (colonial upstarts) and the home nations, let alone amongst the latter and France, did not help progress the sport or its organisational and management ethos. The cost was the strangulation of the sport, as the power-brokers feared democratisation and the opening up of the game's administration could lead to the ultimate loss of power and control over the destiny of the sport they had created. As the southern nations hold on international rugby tightens, the demand for governance reform grows. Although the English Rugby Football Union have shown willing to change, if only to maximise the opportunities of being tournament hosts in 2015, other governing bodies remain reticent to confront complex and game-changing issues. Instead, they prefer to view the seven-a-side model as the solution to an ageing audience and the need to secure television funding as a lever for deferring some critical decisions concerning the future structure and organisation of the game's traditional format.

ACTION LEARNING

- Does the effective governance of rugby hinge on more open public scrutiny?
- Is effective governance easily achievable within the context of the rivalry and different perceptions of the game that persist in the northern and southern hemispheres?
- At what point, and in what ways, will the resistance to a dramatic overhaul be overtaken by the commercial interests that increasingly underwrite the sport?

CONCLUSION

With sport increasingly susceptible to **corruption**, the extent to which international sporting governance is committed to fairness, international justice and social reform is open to question. **Globalisation** and the increasing tendency to **brand** sport as entertainment present new challenges for governance. Unless those involved in the process of sport regulation (which, at different times, may involve sports fans, sports stars and government) appreciate the complexity of *realpolitik* and the need to engage with the political process locally, nationally and internationally, the essence of good governance will be lost.

The pressure to veer from the prime responsibilities of effective governance is great in an era when it is increasingly tough to address match fixing, the notion of fair play and transparency, as the desire to generate multi million dollar revenues to secure the future of sports can create the conditions in which corruption can thrive. For those involved with the UK launch of the 2014 Tour De France, a golden opportunity presented itself to reclaim a sport that has paid an enormously high price for its inept governance, whilst 2015 offers major opportunities for both cricket and rugby union. Disputes concerning the composition of the World Cup continue, and the IRB will be sorely tested by the all-Ireland bid to host the 2022 tournament, yet as an effective governing body they should be constantly vigilant concerning issues of monitoring, transparency and succession planning.

NOTES

[1] The term 'northern' is used in this context to cover what are termed the 'developed economies', which paradoxically include some other economies from the southern hemisphere.

[2] Details of the complicated internal operations of the cricketing authorities of the countries identified are chronicled in the annual *Wisden Cricketer's Almanack*.

[3] The most detailed and contemporary source is Jefferys (2012).

[4] Full details are available in the two recent reviews undertaken by Lord Woolf for cricket, and the IRB for Rugby Union.

[5] Within the protracted discussions regarding the new version of the Heineken European Cup glimmers of nationalist sentiment were evident in the utterances of the key negotiators.

[6] Waugh, Warne and Lee have been, and in the case of the last two remain, heroic figures within India. The IPL has helped to prolong the high profile of Warne and Lee.

REFERENCES

Allison, L. (2005) *The Global Politics of Sport: The Role of Global Institutions in Sport.* London: Routledge.

Asthill, J. (2013) *The Great Tamasha: Cricket, Corruption and the Turbulent Rise of Modern India.* London: Wisden Sports Writing.

Bairner, A. (2005) Sport and the nation in the global era. In L. Allison (ed.), *The Global Politics of Sport: The Role of Global Institutions in Sport.* London: Routledge.

Beckles, H. (1998) *The Development of West Indies Cricket: Volume 2, The Age of Globalization.* Kingston: The University of West Indies Press.

Berry, S. (2006) Organising chaos: what is the point of the ICC?, *Wisden Cricketer,* 3(6).

Berry, S. (2014) Big Three's ICC coup is all about money. *The Daily Telegraph,* 7 February.

Brown, O. (2014) F1 Steers clear of uglier realities in Bahrain where the nightmare of the forgotten ones goes on and on, *The Daily Telegraph*, 2 April.

Coakley, J. & Pike, E. (2009) *Sports in Society: Issues and Controversies.* Boston, MA: McGraw Hill

Giulianotti, R. (2005) *Sport: A Critical Sociology.* Cambridge: Polity.

Gibson, O. (2012) Blair tells 2012 critics to show 'a bit of pride', *Guardian,* 25 July.

Gupta, A. (2004) The globalization of cricket: the rise of the Non-West, *International Journal of the History of Sport,* 21(2): 257–76.

Guttmann, A. (2005) *Sport: The First Five Millennia.* Boston, MA: University of Massachusetts.

Harris, J. (2010) *Rugby Union and Globalization: An Odd-Shaped World.* Basingstoke: Palgrave.

Hoolihan, B. (2008) *Sport and Society: A Student Introduction.* London: Sage.

Hoolihan, B. & White, A. (2002) *The Politics of Sport Development: Development of Sport or Development Through Sport.* London: Routledge.

Horne, J., Tomlinson, A., Whannel, G. & Woodward, K. (2013) *Understanding Sport, A Socio-Cultural Analysis.* Abingdon: Routledge.

Jarvie, G. & Thornton, J. (2012) *Sport, Culture and Society.* Abingdon: Routledge

Jefferys, K. (2012) *Sport and Politics in Modern Britain: The Road to 2012.* Basingstoke: Palgrave.

Majoribanks, T. & Farquharson, K. (2012) *Sport and Society in the Global Age.* Basingstoke: Palgrave.

Rowe, D. (2003) Sport and the repudiation of the global, *International Review for the Sociology of Sport,* 38(3): 281–94.

Woodward, K. (2009) *Embodied Sporting Practices: Regulating and Regulatory Bodies.* Basingstoke: Palgrave Macmillan.

Woodward, K. (2012) *Planet Sport.* Abingdon: Routledge.

Woolf, Lord & Price Waterhouse (2012) *An Independent Governance Review of the ICC.* London: HMSO.

USEFUL WEBSITES

www.espncricinfo.com/magazine/content/story/717833 www.irb.com/aboutirb/organization/index.html
www.transparency.org.uk

8

INTERNATIONAL SPORT LAW
KEVIN CARPENTER

ASADA doping decision makes a mockery of doping scandal investigation.

(*Guardian Online*, 21 April 2015)

Perth Glory call of court action against Football Federation Australia's salary cap breach sanctions.

(*Guardian Online*, 14 April 2015)

Amateur snooker player found guilty of match-fixing.

(BBC Sport online, 2 April 2015)

LEARNING OUTCOMES

- Appreciate why laws and regulations matter in the world of sport.

- Identify whether sporting regulations and/or the law apply to a situation and how the two sit together.

- Understand the use of Alternative Dispute Resolution (ADR) in sport and the role of the Court of Arbitration for Sport (CAS).

- Learn what sport managers have done well (or otherwise) when the law becomes involved in sport and apply good practice.

INTRODUCTION

Sport does not operate in a vacuum. It is subject to the same laws as other sectors of society. Yet each sport in each country has its own unique, and often complex, set of rules and regulations that govern the sport and all those involved in it. This multi-layered legal and regulatory framework can provide sport managers with challenges outside of their comfort zone. The term 'sport law' covers a multitude of legal disciplines. It is often the case that practising 'sport law' in reality means applying expertise in a particular legal area to a sporting context. For example, advising a football club on a contractual agreement with a local, national or international business to sponsor the team's shirt is simply applying contract law to sport **sponsorship**.

Certain aspects within 'sport law' do however require specialist knowledge such as doping, **match fixing** and financial fair play. When it comes to disputes in sport, be they as a result of on-the-field or off-the-field activities, not only can issues be decided by the court system of the country in question but they may also be heard by specialist sport tribunals. These tribunals can be within the sport themselves (i.e. a disciplinary hearing) or external to the sport, the principal of which being the Court of Arbitration for Sport (the CAS). This was originally established under the auspices of the International Olympic Committee (IOC) back in 1984, but later became a completely independent body in 1994, with its seat (its base for legal purposes) being in Lausanne, Switzerland. The CAS is therefore subject to Swiss laws, particularly those regarding arbitration proceedings and public policy (i.e. important legal principles including fundamental rights, good faith and proportionality). In addition to its permanent seat in Switzerland, it also operates an ad hoc division at major sporting events when asked to do so, principally at the Olympic Games. The CAS will hear any dispute which is either directly or indirectly linked to sport, however the majority of cases that come before it concern disputes in relation to eligibility, integrity and governance. It has both an ordinary and appeals arbitration division. The ordinary division hears cases where both parties have agreed to submit to a private dispute resolution procedure. The latter hears appeals to the decisions of sport governing bodies (SGBs) where the CAS will examine whether the rules of an SGB are reasonable and being applied and interpreted lawfully and whether any penalties imposed are necessary, reasonable and proportionate. What the CAS will not rule upon are in-game or on-field decisions of match officials unless bad faith or illegality can be proven.

Sport as a sector is becoming increasingly commercial and as that trend continues then so will sport laws be needed and called upon to regulate that growth and keep order.

THINKING POINT 8.1

The New Orleans Saints and 'Bountygate'

On 7 February 2010 the New Orleans Saints beat the Indianapolis Colts 31–17 to win Super Bowl XLIV, the first National Football League (NFL) Championship in their franchise history.

Soon after their victory the NFL began investigations into the Saints following allegations from an anonymous tip-off that the team had deliberately attempted to injure opposing players in their play-off run to Super Bowl XLIV in return for direct financial reward. These allegations amounted to what was in essence a bounty programme, funded by the players themselves, that became known as the 'bountygate' scandal.

Following extensive investigations and the collection of hard irrefutable evidence the NFL issued heavy sanctions in the spring of 2012 to a number of key Saints staff, both playing and non-playing, including Head Coach Sean Payton (one year suspension), then Defensive Coordinator Gregg Williams (indefinite suspension) and 3× Pro Bowl Linebacker Jonathan Vilma (one year suspension).

After many legal cases, including both sporting tribunals and the civil courts, the players' suspensions were finally overturned on 11 December 2012 as the appeals officer laid the blame squarely at the feet of the Saints' coaches and management.

TOOLS FOR ANALYSIS

Leaving aside the disciplinary action taken against the management and coaches, professional sports in the USA are operationally and legally unique in world sport as each one is governed by a Collective Bargaining Agreement (CBA). CBAs in US professional sport can be described as the labour blueprint between the players and the owners, and are a mechanism which attempts to ensure harmony between labour (employment) law and antitrust (competition) law. In European sport perhaps the most famous sports law case, the Bosman case, was all about the relationship between employment and competition law (HRM, a human resource management issue) at the supra-European level. The CBA covers the complete range of relationships and issues between the management of the league and their athlete employees, including the team discipline which was at the heart of 'bountygate'.

Professional sports in the USA also have very powerful players' unions and commissioners. In the NFL ('the League') the union is made up of the National Football League Players' Association (NFLPA) and the Commissioner Roger Goodell. The latter acts as the chief executive officer of the sport, appointed by the teams/franchise owners, and holds broad powers to manage and govern the sport. This includes disciplinary matters, with a wide discretion as to both guilt and sanctions, and there are very limited situations in which he can be challenged. The NFLPA discovered this first-hand once the suspensions were handed down to the Saints players by Commissioner Goodell.

It is important to remember that the processes in place in the CBA allow Commissioner Goodell to act as prosecutor and judge and the NFLPA agreed to this when signing the CBA into force at the time. Nevertheless, the claims brought by the NFLPA, on behalf of or by the players themselves, attempted in a variety of ways to show that Goodell had acted outside his authority as commissioner. Firstly under the League rules, with the allegations of intent to injure opponents, and secondly under the CBA as the additional monies paid through the bounty programme breached the salary cap rules.

These claims included filing a formal challenge with the League, suing the League in the federal court and a further three rounds of appeals. The federal judge was sceptical about the exercise of power by the commissioner but declined to give a ruling. Ironically Commissioner Goodell had the power to hear the first appeal under the CBA, which unsurprisingly he dismissed. The second was heard by two retired federal judges and a law professor who ordered the commissioner to adjust the punishments because his disciplinary role was limited to the allegations to injure opponents, not the salary cap, which under the CBA had to be left to the 'special master' as judge. However, Commissioner Goodell did not climb down far and therefore the third and final appeal, to an appeal officer appointed by Commissioner Goodell who was a former NFL Commissioner himself, led to the suspensions being vacated in their entirety.

With safety being paramount in the inherently violent sport of American football, especially in light of the serious concussion litigation lawsuits that have recently been settled by the League, Commissioner Goodell, as the supreme voice about the best interests of the sport, continues to make safety his principal policy to ensure the long-term viability of the NFL.

ACTION LEARNING

- What are the advantages and disadvantages to having the head of an SGB acting as an administrator and judge?

- Research similar cases and how they have been dealt with in a European football league (i.e. the Premier League) where there is no concept of CBAs.

Sanctions for First Time Doping Offences

Since 2010 the sanctions meted out to athletes found guilty of a doping offence for the first time have been at the top of the sporting regulatory political agenda and under the sporting legal spotlight.

As the World Anti-Doping Agency's Anti-Doping Code (WADC) currently stands, athletes are subject to a mandatory minimum period of ineligibility (ban) of two years upon having been found guilty of a first-time offence. Therefore, depending on when they get banned, the athlete in question may not miss an Olympic Games as these occur every four years. Despite this, it was felt by many stakeholders in sport that those found guilty should miss at least one Olympic Games as part of their punishment. To counter the restrictions on this under the WADC, the International Olympic Committee (IOC) introduced the so-called 'Osaka Rule' into the Olympic Charter, the effect of which was that any athlete who had a doping suspension from 1 July 2008 of more than six months was automatically barred from participating in the next Olympic Games regardless of when the ban expired.

However, in a case in October 2011, notionally between the US Olympic Committee and the IOC concerning the banned former Olympic champion LeShawn Merritt, the CAS determined that the 'Osaka Rule' was invalid and unenforceable. The CAS's reasoning was that the 'rule' was not an eligibility criteria for competing in the Games, rather it was an additional sanction and therefore not compliant with the WADC to which both the USOC and IOC are signatories.

This issue was then further clarified when the British Olympic Association (BOA) lost a similar case on appeal to CAS against WADA regarding the BOA's bye-law which operated to impose a lifetime ban for a British athlete having been found guilty of any doping offences. Once again CAS found this to be an additional sanction rather than eligibility criteria.

TOOLS FOR ANALYSIS

Doping is one of the most contentious topics in global sport and is a significant challenge for sport managers. This case shows that SGBs do not have complete autonomy over how they run and govern their sport. Once SGBs voluntarily (in name but not always in reality due to external factors such as political pressures) sign up to regulations like the WADC then all signatories have to abide by the sport law in place, even if an individual SGB signatory does not agree with certain aspects of the regulatory regime. Not only have the IOC and BOA fallen foul of this in recent years, but so has the world governing body of football, FIFA. This is particularly important with a global threat to sport such as doping, as the WADC's goal is to ensure 'that all athletes and members of the "athlete entourage" benefit from the same anti-doping procedures and protections, no matter the sport, the nationality, or the country where tested, so that athletes may participate in competition that is safe and fair'. With each new version of the WADC, each signatory, and any other stakeholders or interested parties, have the opportunity to take their place in the consultative process. The Code Review Process extends over two years and is designed to update and amend the WADC according to the wishes of its signatories and stakeholders. As a sport manager this is a real and serious way in which your voice representing your sport can participate and be heard in the sporting legislative process.

The multi-layered sporting legal systems that sport managers have to understand and be prepared for were evident in relation to the bye-law as it was first challenged by the disgraced sprinter Dwain Chambers in the civil courts of England and Wales in 2008. This case was brought prior to the CAS's ruling on the IOC's Osaka Rule in USOC v IOC. The English High Court was of the opinion that although the bye-law did appear to be in contravention of the WADC, it was nevertheless justified by the Osaka Rule. The court also rejected Chambers' challenge that the bye-law and ban were an unlawful restraint of trade, ruling that the denial of participation in the Olympics was only a speculative loss to his livelihood. Before commencing expensive legal proceedings, whether within the realms of sporting justice or civil/criminal justice, sport managers need to consider carefully the risks and whether alternative ways to achieve their goals would be better, for example lobbying other sporting bodies to support a change in the regulations. The decision of the BOA to go to the CAS to defend its bye-law in light of the USOC v IOC decision is a salutary warning in this regard. There was never any real prospect that their case was likely to succeed and it was not at all a surprising outcome.

Following the two rulings at the heart of this case study the Code Review Process has resulted in the latest draft of the new 2015 WADC setting the period of ineligibility for a first offence at four years, which will cover an Olympic cycle.

ACTION LEARNING

- Research the evolution of the relationship between FIFA and WADA.
- Find the redline of the 2015 WADC against the 2009 WADC and consider whether you think each amendment is a positive step or not?

How the Mighty have Fallen: Lance Armstrong Finally Comes Clean (Ironically)

Having overcome his battle with cancer and returning to win an unprecedented seven consecutive Tour de France cycling titles, despite many suspicions and rumours about doping, Lance Armstrong became revered around the world not only for his cycling achievements but also the work he did through his Livestrong charity.

However his world came crashing down when on 24 August 2012 the United States Anti-Doping Agency (USADA), led by its courageous and tenacious Chief Executive Officer Travis Tygart, imposed a sanction of lifetime ineligibility and disqualification of all the competitive results Armstrong had achieved since 1 August 1998. This was followed by a devastating 200-page Reasoned Decision published by USADA on 22 October 2012, setting out in meticulous detail the doping programme operated by Armstrong and the teams he had cycled for.

Up until this point Armstrong had aggressively defended and pursued anyone who sought to insinuate that he had doped, but the evidence set out by USADA was undeniable and he went on to admit to systematic doping throughout his career, not to the authorities, but to Oprah Winfrey on worldwide television.

TOOLS FOR ANALYSIS

The demise of Lance Armstrong has made the sport of cycling front, back and middle page news across the world for all the wrong reasons. However, he has not been the only actor in this dark sporting macabre that has drawn fire from many quarters. The International Cycling Union (UCI), the world **governing** body for cycling, has been widely criticised on a number of fronts for allowing him, and other dopers in the sport, to prosper for many years. It has become evident, both as a result of what was written in the Reasoned Decision and in the media, that there were serious failings by the UCI and its executives, which were at least a result of wilful blindness if not deliberate ignorance, to the doping culture that purveyed cycling during Armstrong's period of dominance.

Legally the Armstrong affair throws up a number of interesting issues for the managers involved, whether at the governing body (UCI), regulator (WADA and USADA) or team level. One legal issue for sport managers to consider when dealing with a number of different bodies within a sport is who has jurisdiction over a particular matter that arises. There is some doubt in the Armstrong case whether it was the UCI rather than USADA who were the proper body to investigate and charge him, as the majority of the charges arose prior to the WADC coming into force in 2004 (to which USADA is a signatory). This was raised by Armstrong in a civil case that he brought to restrain USADA's arbitration proceedings back in 2012, but as he lost overall he did not pursue some of the unresolved jurisdictional issues. Unfortunately for sport managers this means there is a still a significant amount of uncertainty as to which authority has jurisdiction in a major international doping scandal.

It is also important for sport managers to be aware of any limitation periods that may apply which restrict the period of time for which a claim may be brought. In Armstrong's case the limitation period under the WADC was eight years, but USADA disapplied this on the basis of a deliberate concealment by Armstrong of his cheating using a CAS decision and a US arbitral decision. However it is not clear why US law applied given that prior to 2004 the applicable anti-doping rules were those of the UCI, who are governed by Swiss law. An additional limitation period issue that arose is that back in 2005 Armstrong gave evidence under oath whereby he said categorically he was not a drugs cheat. Under US criminal law this would normally lead to a perjury charge. However, Armstrong has been smart in that the limitation period for such a charge is also eight years and therefore he falls just outside that, although he could still face civil perjury charges but this will not lead to imprisonment.

Often the most contentious aspects of a disciplinary finding are the sanctions handed down. The lifetime ban from all sports that USADA placed upon Armstrong is problematic principally due to the fact that the majority of the findings relate to pre-2004 when the first WADC was introduced, and such a broad sanction was not available under the UCI's anti-doping rules in force at the time. As with most sporting superstars Armstrong made the majority of his personal wealth, thought to be around $125 million, through sponsorship deals rather than his prize money. But given his admission to Oprah there is a substantial risk that the money paid under these deals will be recovered by using either so-called express morality clauses in the contracts, namely statements (called warranties) by Armstrong that he was not a drug cheat, or this could be impliedly included depending on the governing law of each contract.

A far bigger potential exposure for Armstrong is under the US False Claims Act. The principal sponsor of his cycling team during his seven victories was the United States Postal Service, which is a government entity, and under this act claims can be made against not only Armstrong, but also against managers and executives within the team, to recover monies paid to the team. On top of that any damages awarded can also be trebled. This would not be possible in many countries outside the USA, including the UK. The legal fallout from the Armstrong scandal, and his subsequent television admission, will rumble on for many years to come, and will clarify some of the issues mentioned above that sport managers of the future will do well to be aware of.

ACTION LEARNING

- Investigate how many other sports people have received lifetime bans for doping since the introduction of the WADC in 2004.

- Research what happened when Armstrong attempted to compete in a triathlon soon after his ban from USADA.

For the First Time the CAS Finds Itself Not Top of the Sporting Justice System

In 2007 professional footballer Francelino Matuzalem da Silva took the decision to unilaterally terminate his contract with Shakhtar Donetsk of the Ukraine and join Real Zaragoza of Spain. However he did this without just cause and with two years remaining on his contract. Unsurprisingly Shakhtar were not too happy about this and wanted some financial recompense. FIFA agreed with them, as did the CAS and the Swiss Federal Supreme Court (FSC) upon appeal, eventually awarding Shakhtar nearly €12 million in compensation for breach of contract, which Matuzalem and Zaragoza together were then liable for.

This was not the end of the matter, however. When Matuzalem and Zaragoza were unable to pay, and therefore Shakhtar could not enforce the financial award made in their favour, FIFA's Disciplinary Commission slapped a ban on Matuzalem in relation to any football-related activity until he paid the award in full. The CAS supported FIFA upon appeal. What Zaragoza, FIFA and CAS did not bank on was that being based in Switzerland CAS were subject to Swiss law as interpreted and administered by the FSC.

The FSC held that Matuzalem's interest not to face an indeterminate ban from football, and therefore his livelihood, clearly outweighed FIFA's interest in becoming the private enforcer of a monetary claim. Therefore the FSC quashed a decision of the CAS for the first time as the CAS's decision violated Swiss public policy.

TOOLS FOR ANALYSIS

The Matuzalem series of cases pulls together a number of sport law strands that we have discussed already: the role of the CAS and how it fits with the 'normal' courts of the land, the relationship between players and clubs, and the legality of sanctions. For sport mangers, the Matuzalem series introduced yet another avenue of legal recourse for parties to turn to. This introduces even greater risk when disputes arise by showing how Swiss law can influence the legal relationship between sporting parties who have no direct connection to Switzerland, with the player being from Brazil and the two clubs based in the Ukraine and Italy. However being indirect members of FIFA through their national associations, with FIFA's rules and regulations providing the opportunity to appeal to the CAS, then CAS football awards remain reserved for the FSC.

Cases such as Matuzalem's involving breach of contract and/or compensation have often arisen in football over the years and ended up before the CAS. However, given decisions of the CAS do not create binding precedents for subsequent CAS cases and panels (the doctrine of precedent being the policy of courts to abide by or adhere to principles established by decisions in earlier cases) there is an additional layer of uncertainty in this area. Given the player was entirely at fault for having left his original club, Shakhtar, one may view FIFA's ban as proportionate, and now that the FSC have overturned that decision Shakhtar are being unfairly prejudiced. The FSC addressed this issue in a number of related ways. Swiss law provides that an arbitral award can be set aside if incompatible with public policy, public policy having both a substantive and procedural element. To fail on substantive grounds the decision has to be rendered in disregard of a fundamental principle of law, with this case centring on the rights of Matuzalem to enter into a contract with Zaragoza against the restriction placed upon him by FIFA via the ban. The FSC decided that FIFA's ban was so excessive that it cancelled out Matuzalem's economic freedom and therefore the CAS's upholding of it could legitimately be set aside. Essentially the FSC said the wide-ranging ban prevented Matuzalem from earning an income which would allow him to pay back the liability to Shakhtar.

It is surely right that sport, having such a crucial role to play in society, should be subject to scrutiny on the grounds of public policy. However this does not sit easily with the notion that a footballer can walk out on a club without proper notice and without just cause. These are the sort of complex legal, commercial and ethical challenges sport managers have to face on a regular basis. The FSC also pointed out to the parties that yet another set of legal principles had to be considered. The New York Convention is an international legal instrument which provides a regime for the enforcement and recognition of arbitral awards between contracting states. Crucially there are far more contracting states to the convention than countries who are likely to enforce a private court action from a foreign country. Therefore the CAS said Shakhtar should have gone down this route, using the CAS award it already had for the clear breach of contract as the basis, rather than going back to FIFA and the CAS undertaking a private enforcement action. Sport managers should take note as arbitration (not just at the CAS) is increasingly the preferred way to settle sporting disputes across the world.

ACTION LEARNING

- Consider why the CAS, and other sporting bodies such as the IOC and FIFA, are based in Switzerland.

- Research what is meant by *lex sportive*.

CONCLUSION

The cases we have looked at are a drop in the ocean when considering the multitude of legal issues facing modern-day sport worldwide. This can be seen in the acknowledgement of a separate discipline of sport law, and a sporting court, the CAS, given the unique nature of the sector. It is distinctive in that any legal dispute in sport, be it internal to the sport or involving the normal courts of the land, rarely involves a single set of sport 'laws' or principles. These can be national, regional or international. It is also an area of the law where alternative dispute resolution using specialist 'judges' is becoming increasingly popular. A further unique element to sport is the role it plays in wider society and therefore the media attention it receives. Legal and disciplinary disputes in sport are played out in the glare of the media and public eye more than in any other sector.

Sport has always been left to govern itself and thus to its own devices, meaning there are often amateur attitudes and management to the legal challenges associated with an ever-more professional and commercial industry. Therefore sport managers have to make increasing provision in their plans and budgets for legal advice in a number of areas, be it employment, commercial, IP, discipline or regulatory ... the list goes on.

Wherever there is money there are legal disputes, so as more money floods into sport, sport law will become a vital part of the sporting fabric and sport lawyers invaluable to all stakeholders in the industry.

BIBLIOGRAPHY

Bandini, P. (2012) Tagliabue's verdict on NFL bounties leaves Commissioner Goodell the Loser. Available at: www.theguardian.com/sport/2012/dec/11/paul-tagliabue-nfl-bounties-roger-goodell (last accessed 2 July 2013).

Beloff, M., Kerr, T., Demetriou, M. and Beloff, R. (2012) *Sports Law*. Oxford: Hart.

CAS 2011/A/2658 British Olympic Association (BOA) v. World Anti-Doping Agency (WADA).

CAS 2011/O/2422 United States Olympic Committee (USOC) v. International Olympic Committee (IOC).

Gandert, D. (2012) The battle before the Games: the British Olympic Association attempts to keep lifetime ban for athletes with doping offences, *Northwestern Journal of International Law and Business,* 32(4): 53–80.

Griffan, F. (2013) Bountygate and the NFL Commissioner: a legal analysis, *LawInSport.com*, 29 January.

Gut-Schweizer, E. and Gasser, C. (2013) Switzerland: Ordre Public/Personal Freedom-Discussion of Decision 4A_558/2011 (= 138 III 322). Dated 27 March 2012 by the Swiss Federal Supreme Court, *International Sports Law Review*, 1: 31–3.

Hunter, A. and Segan, J. (2013) Lessons from Lance. Sports Law Conference presented by Blackstone Chambers, London, May.

Holder, L. (2013) Judge dismisses Jonathan Vilma's defamation lawsuit against Roger Goodell. Available at: www.nola.com/saints/index.ssf/2013/01/judge_helen_berrigan_dismisses.html (last accessed 2 July 2013).

James, M. (2013) *Sports Law*. Basingstoke: Palgrave Macmillan

Levy, R. (2012) Swiss Federal Tribunal overrules CAS Award in a landmark decision, *LawInSport.com*, 11 October.

Lines, K. (2012) From a small cede a mighty code may grow: an analysis of CAS 2011/A/2658 BOA v. WADA. Available at: http://sportslawnews.wordpress.com/2012/09/01/from-a-small-cede-a-mighty-code-may-grow-an-analysis-of-cas-2011a2658-boa-v-wada/ (last accessed 10 December 2013).

Nixon, A. (2012) BOA lose bye-law appeal, *LawInSport.com,* 4 May.

Singh, S. (2013) British Olympic Association v World Anti-Doping Agency: an examination of the ethical issues governing anti-doping initiatives, *The Columbia Journal of European Law Online,* 19.

Voser, N. and George, A. (2012) Landmark ruling of Swiss Supreme Court setting aside CAS award for violation of substantive public policy. Practical Law Company. Available at: http://uk.practicallaw.com/1-519-2649?service=arbitration (last accessed 11 July 2013).

WADA (2012) Questions and answers on the Code Review Process. Available at: www.wada-ama.org/En/Ressources/Questions-reponses/Processus-de-revision-du-Code (last accessed 5 July 2013).

USEFUL WEBSITES

http://link.springer.com/journal/40318
www.lawinsport.com

9

MEDIA AND COMMUNICATIONS

ANDREA GEURIN-EAGLEMAN

> The athletes have realised that they're a **brand** and that they're going to lose a lot of money if they're not acting appropriately on social media.
>
> (Mark Cuban, Owner of the Dallas Mavericks NBA team, 19 March 2014 at SXSW event)
>
> In today's media-saturated society, athletes' words carry less weight... Virtually anyone can have a Twitter account, where offensive or controversial tweets generally enjoy 15 seconds of fame before being shoved out of the public's increasingly short attention span by another 'shocking' comment.
>
> (Journalist Rob Vogt in *The Global Times*, 25 March 2015)
>
> We love television but the future is not just about television. It's about television complemented with all of the other platforms that we have.
>
> (Alan Wurtzel, President of Research and Media Development for NBC Universal, 12 February 2014)

Upon completion of this chapter, students will be able to:

- Define and explain the term 'sport communication' and identify the various sport communicators and communication methods they utilise.

- Understand the differences between traditional media and new media when communicating sport-related news.

- Provide examples of the ways in which communication campaigns can impact on sport entities.

- Demonstrate how policies and **laws** impact on athletes' and sport organisations' communication.

- Explain the concept of media training for athletes and employees of sport organisations.

INTRODUCTION

Sport communication is a broad topic that involves several different communicators and forms of communication. The term 'sport communication' is defined by Pedersen et al. as 'a process by which people in sport, in a sport setting, or through a sport endeavour, share symbols as they create meaning through interaction' (2009: 430). Additionally, Pedersen et al. (2007) developed the Strategic Sport Communication Model (SSCM), which outlines three components involved in the sport communication process. These include personal and organisational communication in sport (e.g. intrapersonal, interpersonal, small group, intraorganisational and interorganisational communication), sport mass media (e.g. publishing and print communication, electronic and visual communication, and new media), and sport communication services and support (e.g. advertising, public relations, crisis communication and research).

It should be noted that, although the **media** play a large role in the concept of sport communication, members of the media are not the only people involved in the sport communication process. This process involves senders (sport communicators) who communicate messages and recipients (audience members) who receive such messages (Pedersen et al., 2007). Any person who communicates with or in a sport entity qualifies as a sport communicator. Therefore, sport stakeholders such as coaches, athletes, fans and sport organisation employees can be sport communicators along with the media.

This chapter discusses sport communication from a global perspective, as both cases within the chapter focus on international sport organisations. The first case highlights the communication methods employed by the

International Federation of Associated Wrestling Styles (FILA) in its attempt to reinstate the sport of wrestling in the Olympic Games. This case focuses on the power of not just sport organisations, but also sport fans and stakeholders, to create change via sport communication. The second case discusses a Russian law and its potential impact on the 2014 Winter Olympics in Sochi, Russia. It raises issues relating to athletes' communication rights and sport organisations' responsibilities to educate their athletes about the laws of other nations in order to protect such athletes from harmful consequences.

CASE STUDY 9.1

Olympic Wrestling's Social Media Campaign

Wrestling has a rich history with the Olympic Games, as it was one of the sports contested at the first modern Games in 1896 (*Athens 1896*, n.d.) and also existed at the ancient Olympic Games as early as 708 BC (Irving, 2013). These facts made it all the more shocking when the International Olympic Committee (IOC) voted in February 2013 to eliminate the sport of wrestling from the Olympics, beginning in 2020 (Hendricks, 2013). According to an IOC official, the decision was made not because of anything wrong with wrestling, but rather due to positive aspects offered by other sports (Irving, 2013). The IOC limits the number of sports contested at the Olympics to 28 (Grohmann, 2013).

The international wrestling community swiftly responded to the news with a social media campaign led by wrestling's international governing body, the International Federation of Associated Wrestling Styles (FILA). Primarily utilising Facebook and Twitter, FILA encouraged wrestlers, fans and supporters to submit photos of themselves in a wrestling stance so that FILA could upload them onto their Facebook page.

A total of 371 photos were posted to two albums on the organisation's page. Participants in the photo promotion were quite varied, and included children, wrestling club members, national team members from various countries, a bride and groom on their wedding day, a young boy and his dog, characters from Disney World and former Olympic wrestlers. Additionally, FILA called on wrestling stakeholders to post photos on their own social media accounts and to use the hashtag #TakeAStance in wrestling-related social media posts (FILA, 2013). FILA also released a special edition brochure to help plead its case for keeping wrestling as an Olympic sport. Every member of the IOC received a printed copy of the brochure and it was also available in digital form on the FILA website (Condron, 2013).

Along with its social media campaign involving fans and international wrestling stakeholders, FILA quickly made several organisational changes, including the resignation of then-president Raphael Martinetti of Switzerland and the appointment of Serbia's Nenad Lalovic as his replacement (Wilson, 2013). Additionally, women and athletes were given a greater role in decision making within the organisation and two weight classes were added for women. Rule changes were also adopted which made the sport easier to understand from a spectator's perspective (Longman, 2013; Wilson, 2013).

FILA's social media campaign and swift organisational changes resulted in a positive result for the organisation and wrestling stakeholders worldwide: just six months after it was announced that wrestling would be excluded from the 2020 Olympics, the IOC executive board held a secret ballot vote and wrestling was reinstated (Wilson, 2013). With 49 votes, wrestling received overwhelming support for reinstatement over its competitors, as baseball-softball received 24 votes and squash received 22 (Wilson, 2013). IOC President Jacques Rogge was quoted as saying, 'Wrestling has shown great passion and resilience in the last few months. They have taken a number of steps to modernize and improve their sport' (Wilson, 2013: para. 7).

TOOLS FOR ANALYSIS

Since the advent and subsequent popularity of the internet, media channels tend to fall into one of two categories: traditional and new media. Although many sport organisations increasingly utilise new media as a communication tool, traditional media still offer strengths as well. It is important for sport communicators to understand the differences between the two forms, as well as the potential benefits and risks that each pose. Traditional media typically refers to media channels that are not on the internet such as print and electronic media (Stoldt et al., 2012). The term 'print media' refers to news sources such as newspapers, magazines, and books. 'Electronic media' refers to sources such as television and radio. 'New media' are defined as online or internet outlets such as organisational websites, news websites, blogs and social media sites like Facebook and Twitter. This term can also refer to new technologies such as smartphones and tablets. Sport organisations and athletes can communicate their messages via traditional and new media channels using methods such as publicity, in which journalists report on the organisation/athlete in a news-related form; advertising, which is a form of communication in which the organisation pays to have its message published; or organisation-created communication pieces such as brochures, newsletters, magazines, videos or web content that the organisation creates and publishes itself.

According to Zimmerman et al. (2013: 108), in recent years traditional print media have experienced a declining consumer base and an 'ongoing demise'. This is due to many factors, such as the economic crisis globally, the increase in media consolidation, and possibly also to the popularity of new media. Zimmerman et al. illustrated the rise of new media and decline in the consumption of traditional print media in not just one global region, but in four different countries, i.e. the USA, China, Germany and Israel. Still, Kiousis (2001) found that media consumers rated newspapers as having the most credibility when compared to websites or television news, so this seems to be at least one advantage that traditional print media have over other communication forms.

Regarding electronic media, Irwin et al. (2008) discussed the merits of using television and radio as advertising outlets for sport organisations. One benefit of electronic media is television's power to create effective images in the minds of consumers due to its visual and audio features. Although radio only has the capability to deliver audio, it can be useful for targeting specific audiences and is more cost effective than television.

In contrast to traditional media, the popularity of new media for sport communication purposes is continually increasing. One of the greatest differences between utilising traditional and new media as sport communication outlets is the interactive nature of new media, allowing for much more two-way communication between senders and receivers. For example, when an article appears in the newspaper about a local rugby team, readers cannot easily respond to the article or ask the rugby team or journalist questions about it. When the same story is posted on a news website, however, the reader will likely have the option to post a comment or question at the end of the article, to which the journalist, team or other readers can respond. Additionally, new media are often viewed by sport organisations as a more affordable means of communication than traditional media, and organisations can control their message better when they produce this and then post it on their website or social media outlets like Facebook or Twitter (Eagleman, 2013).

The FILA case study above and the information about traditional and new media in sport communication should assist students in completing the following action learning exercises.

ACTION LEARNING

- FILA used new media and social media to help the sport of wrestling win its reinstatement in the Olympic Games. Along with new media, what traditional communication methods could an organisation use to achieve the desired result? What are the strengths and weaknesses of each type of communication (traditional vs. new)?
- This case explained how an international sport federation used social media to communicate its case to the IOC. Assume that you work in the communications department of your national sport organisation for the sport of wrestling (e.g. USA Wrestling if you live in the USA). Develop a communications plan that you could implement from a national perspective to help save the sport of Olympic wrestling. What similarities and differences would exist between your plan and the one implemented by FILA?
- FILA is the international governing body for the sport of wrestling, but several other wrestling governing bodies and organisations exist at national and regional levels. Using the internet, conduct research on these organisations and their communication efforts to reinstate wrestling in the Olympic Games. What methods did other organisations utilise? How did these efforts differ from FILA's campaign?

Russia's Anti-Gay Law and the 2014 Winter Olympics

The 2014 Winter Olympics took place in Sochi, Russia, in February 2014. This marked the first time Russia had hosted the Games since Moscow served as the host city for the 1980 Summer Games (*Sochi, 2014*, n.d.). Athletes from 85 countries competed for a total of 98 medals in Sochi and an estimated 3 billion television viewers were expected to watch the Games (*Official Spectator Guide*, 2013).

In June of 2013, just eight months before the Sochi Games, Russia's government passed a bill banning 'propaganda of non-traditional **sexual** relations' (Mills, 2013: para. 3). According to a report by the Associated Press (2013), the law was passed in an attempt to 'promote traditional Russian values as opposed to Western liberalism' (para. 4) and under the law, fines would be issued to anyone who provided information to minors about the lesbian, gay, bisexual, and transgender (LGBT) community or to any person or organisation that held a gay pride rally.

The bill made news headlines worldwide, as media and sport officials immediately wondered what impact it would have on the 2014 Olympic Games. Many public figures called for the IOC to change the location of the 2014 Olympics or for countries to boycott the Games. For example, British broadcaster Stephen Fry compared Vladimir Putin's treatment of gay people to Adolph Hitler's treatment of Jewish people. He stated, 'An absolute ban on the Russian Winter Olympics of 2014 in Sochi is simply essential' (Stallard, 2013: para. 4). Fry went on to suggest that the Olympics should be held in a previous Winter Olympics host city, such as Salt Lake City in the USA or Lillehammer in Norway. While US President Barack Obama said he would not pursue a boycott of the Games, his name was noticeably absent from the US Olympic delegates list for Sochi. Instead, the list included two openly gay athletes: Caitlin Cahow, a former hockey player, and Billie Jean King, a legendary tennis player. The delegation included no current senior US political figures and Koring (2013: para. 2) called it, 'the most serious slap to Russian Olympic sensibilities since President Jimmy Carter ordered a boycott of Moscow's 1980 Summer Games over the Soviet invasion of Afghanistan', demonstrating that the **politics of sport** when concerned with **mega-events** such as the Olympics have a long and **global** history.

The IOC's response to the controversy was that it did not have the authority to discuss Russia's laws and that the law did not violate the IOC's Olympic Charter, which states that 'all segregation is completely prohibited, whether it be on the grounds of race, religion, colour, or other, on the Olympic territory' (BBC News 2013: para. 7). The Olympic Charter also bans political demonstrations in Olympic venues and sites (Sneed, 2013). IOC spokespeople said that they were convinced there would be no discrimination against athletes or spectators in Sochi (Mills, 2013).

In November 2013 New Zealand speed skater Blake Skjellerup, the only openly gay athlete set to compete in Sochi, said that he would not shy away from the issue and planned to wear a rainbow badge with an image of a speed skater and the words 'Blake Skjellerup – Proud 2014' (CNN, 2013: para. 6). He was selling the badge to raise funds for his Olympic trip to Russia and said that he would openly express his feelings and emotions while in the country (CNN, 2013). Athletes such as Skjellerup raise many questions for national Olympic sport organisations. Many questioned to what extent athletes would be able to speak about the law without facing punishment by the Russian government, as a Russian official in charge of preparations for the Olympics, Dmitry Kozak, stated, 'If people of traditional sexual orientation spread propaganda of non-traditional sex to children, then they will also be held accountable' (Sneed, 2013: para. 13). Some believed this statement meant athletes could be fined, arrested or deported if they were found to have violated the law regardless of their own personal sexual orientation (Sneed, 2013).

TOOLS FOR ANALYSIS

High-profile athletes such as Olympians or members of professional teams often communicate regularly with several sport stakeholders, such as the media, sponsors, sport governing bodies, fans and community members. In the past, athletes' primary mechanism for communicating their opinions on topics relating to their career or their sport was via interviews with traditional news media outlets. With the relatively recent popularity of new media, however, athletes now regularly take to their own websites, Facebook pages, Twitter accounts and other online social media outlets to post their thoughts before ever speaking to traditional journalists. With new media, opinions and pictures can be disseminated to millions of people within seconds at the click of a button. Everything that members of an organisation post online, be it athletes, coaches or other employees, has the potential to impact on the reputation of not just the individual athlete or employee, but the organisation as a whole. In the case of Sochi 2014, it seems that sport organisations and athletes may face consequences more serious than a damaged reputation if they speak out against Russia's anti-gay law during the Olympic Games.

It is common for sport organisations, including those responsible for sport governance, to hold media training sessions with athletes in order to prepare them for what to expect in interviews and to provide guidance or tips on how to respond to questions. Kelly (2012) advises that for organisations to truly have successful media training sessions, coaches must be included.

Additionally, both coaches and athletes must understand the importance of interacting with the media and how they can potentially help the entire sport organisation.

The increasing use of new media by athletes, coaches and sport organisation employees means that such media training is now more important than ever, and sport organisations must train their members not only in how to communicate with the media, but also in how to effectively and responsibly use new media and social media. Some organisations have created **social media** guidelines for athletes and employees to follow. For example, the IOC has its own guidelines for athletes and those holding Olympic credentials at the 2014 Sochi Games. The policy encourages athletes and credentialed personnel to post to new media and social media sites, but asks that they do so in a first-person diary format instead of assuming the role of journalist. The policy also states, 'Postings, blogs and tweets should at all times conform to the Olympic spirit and fundamental principles of Olympism as contained in the Olympic Charter, be dignified and in good taste, and should not be discriminatory, offensive, hateful, defamatory or otherwise illegal and shall not contain vulgar or obscene words or images' (International Olympic Committee, 2013: 1).

The information presented in the case above, along with the information on sport organisation media training, will help you complete the following action learning activities.

ACTION LEARNING

- Conduct an internet search to find at least two sport organisations that have social media or new media guidelines for their athletes, coaches and/or employees. Next, visit the IOC's website to download a copy of their guidelines for the 2014 Sochi Olympics. Compare the three guideline documents. What are their similarities and differences? What changes, if any, do you believe the three organisations should make to their policies and why?

- Imagine that you are a communications manager for a sport national governing body whose athletes would have competed in the 2014 Sochi Olympics (e.g. Ice Speed Skating New Zealand). What additional information do you feel that you would have needed to know about Russia's new law in order to have held a media training session with your athletes prior to the Games?

- Based on your answer to the previous question, conduct internet searches to seek the answers to your questions about Russia's law. Based on your findings, what information and advice would you have provided to your athletes in their media training session?

CONCLUSION

This chapter highlighted two cases involving international sport organisations and the utilisation of communication methods to deal with the issues presented in the cases. Additionally, this chapter helped readers develop an understanding of the differences between traditional and new media and the importance of media training for sport organisation employees in the age of new/social media. It is evident that new media are rapidly changing the sport communication landscape, and sport organisations and constituents must quickly adapt to these changes in order to remain effective in their communication efforts. Still, sport communication reaches far beyond the concept of new media, as we must remember that it also includes intrapersonal, interpersonal, small group, intraorganisational and interorganisational communication, publishing and print communication, electronic and visual communication, advertising, public relations, crisis communication and research (Pedersen et al., 2007). Additionally, anyone who communicates with or in a sport entity is a sport communicator.

REFERENCES

Associated Press (2013) Russian anti-gay bill passes, protesters detained. Available at: www.cbsnews.com/news/russian-anti-gay-bill-passes-protesters-detained (last accessed 20 December 2013).

Athens 1896 (n.d.) Athens 1896. Available at: www.olympic.org/athens-1896-summer-olympics (last accessed 16 December 2013).

BBC News (2013) IOC dismisses Sochi Games gay law concerns. Available at: www.bbc.co.uk/news/world-europe-24288074 (last accessed 20 December 2013).

CNN (2013) Sochi 2014: Gay athlete promises defiant stance at Games. Available at: http://edition.cnn.com/2013/11/20/sport/sochi-2014-skjellerup/ (last accessed 20 December 2013).

Condron, B. (2013) FILA releases brochure as part of campaign to save Olympic wrestling. Available at: www.fila-official.com/index.php?option=com_content&view=article&id=1032:fila-releases-brochure-as-part-of-campaign-to-save-olympic-wrestling&catid=60:actualite&Itemid=100235&lang=en (last accessed 16 December 2013).

Eagleman, A.N. (2013) Acceptance, motivations, and usage of social media as a marketing communications tool amongst employees of sport national governing bodies, *Sport Management Review*, 16(4): 488–97.

FILA (2013) FILA encourages all Olympic wrestling fans to #TakeAStance to save Olympic wrestling. Available at: www.prnewswire.com/news-releases/fila-encourages-all-olympic-wrestling-fans-to-takeastance-to-save-olympic-wrestling-218691241.html (last accessed 16 December 2013).

Grohmann, K. (2013) Wrestling's shortlist return was no error – IOC.
Available at: http://uk.reuters.com/article/2013/05/31/uk-olympics-rogge-idUKBRE94U0HC20130531 (last accessed 16 December 2013).

Hendricks, M. (2013) IOC cuts wrestling from 2020 Olympics. Available at:
http://sports.yahoo.com/blogs/olympics-fourth-place-medal/ioc-cuts-wrestling-2020-olympics-125709336-oly.html (last accessed 16 December 2013).

International Olympic Committee (2013) IOC social media, blogging, and internet guidelines for participants and other accredited persons at the Sochi 2014 Olympic Winter Games. Available at: www.olympic.org/Documents/social_media/IOC_Social_Media_Blogging_and_Internet_Guidelines-English.pdf (last accessed 2 January 2014).

Irving, J. (2013) How wrestling lost the Olympics. Available at: www.nytimes.com/2013/02/16/opinion/how-wrestling-lost-the-olympics.html (last accessed 16 December 2013).

Irwin, R.L., Sutton, W.A. & McCarthy, L.M. (2008) *Sport Promotion and Sales Management* (2nd edn). Champaign, IL: Human Kinetics.

Kelly, T. (2012) Being prepared to take advantage of athletic success. In G.C. Stoldt, S.W. Dittmore & S.E. Branvold (eds), *Sport Public Relations* (2nd edn). Champaign, IL: Human Kinetics. pp. 146–8.

Kiousis, S. (2001) Public trust or mistrust? Perceptions of media credibility in the information age, *Mass Communication and Society,* 4(4): 381–403.

Koring, P. (2013) Obama sending gay athletes to Sochi as Harper says he'll skip Olympics. Available at: www.theglobeandmail.com/news/politics/harper-and-obama-to-skip-sochi-winter-olympics/article16045167/ (last accessed 20 December 2013).

Longman, J. (2013) Wrestling, with revamped rules, returns to Summer Games. Available at: www.nytimes.com/2013/09/09/sports/olympics/wrestling-is-restored-to-the-olympics.html (last accessed 18 December 2013).

Mills, L. (2013) IOC satisfied Olympic charter respected for Sochi. Available at: http://bigstory.ap.org/article/ioc-fully-satisfied-over-russias-anti-gay-law (last accessed 20 December 2013).

Official Spectator Guide (2013) Available at: www.sochi2014.com/en/games/spectator/guide (last accessed 20 December 2013).

Pedersen, P.M., Laucella, P., Miloch, K. & Fielding, L. (2009) The juxtaposition of sport and communication: defining the field of sport communication. In J. Nauright & S. Pope (eds), *The New Sport Management Reader.* Morgantown, WV: Fitness Information Technology. pp. 429–44.

Pedersen, P.M., Miloch, K.S. and Laucella, P.C. (2007) *Strategic Sport Communication.* Champaign, IL: Human Kinetics.

Sneed, T. (2013) Athletes face challenges in speaking out against Russia's anti-gay laws. Available at: www.usnews.com/news/articles/2013/10/04/athletes-face-challenges-in-speaking-out-against-russias-anti-gay-laws (last accessed 20 December 2013).

Sochi 2014 (n.d.) Sochi 2014. Available at: www.olympic.org/sochi-2014-winter-olympics (last accessed 20 December 2013).

Stallard, K. (2013) Stephen Fry: Ban Russia Olympics over gay laws. Available at: http://news.sky.com/story/1125815/stephen-fry-ban-russia-olympics-over-gay-laws (last accessed 20 December 2013).

Stoldt, G.C., Dittmore, S.W. & Branvold, S.E. (2012) *Sport Public Relations* (2nd edn). Champaign, IL: Human Kinetics.

Wilson, S. (2013) Wrestling wins IOC vote for place in 2020 Olympics. Available at: http://news.yahoo.com/wrestling-wins-ioc-vote-place-2020-olympics-155605812-spt.html (last accessed 18 December 2013).

Zimmerman, M.H., Tamir, I., Ihle, H., Nieland, J.U. & Tang, J. (2013) A global crisis? International perspectives on the state of print sport media. In P.M Pedersen (ed.), *Routledge Handbook of Sport Communication*. New York: Routledge. pp. 108–17.

10

HUMAN RESOURCE MANAGEMENT IN SPORT

SHANNON KERWIN

Former Pan Am Games CEO Ian Troop, who was fired last month, will receive $534,800 in severance. The package was agreed upon Friday by the TO2015 board of directors and Troop.

Troop, who was paid $390,000 a year to helm the 2015 sports extravaganza, was unexpectedly sacked Dec. 13 over what sources told the Star were "leadership issues." His severance package is a far cry from some estimates of up to $1 million.

(*The Toronto Star*, 31 January 2014)

Those involved in hirings and firings [within NCAA basketball]—from coaching and athletic director standpoints—have seen the etiquette involved in these processes change drastically in the past 15 years or so, and they can list many of the reasons why...

(*USA Today SPORTS*, 4 November 2014)

Sarah Thomas, a native of Mississippi who began her officiating career in high school, worked [American football] games before leaving to continue her career in pharmaceutical sales. She was then contacted by Conference USA, and began working for the conference in 2007. She became the first woman to officiate a [college American football] bowl game in 2009. Thomas then joined the NFL's Officiating Development Program, worked some New Orleans Saints' training camps, and also officiated a NFL preseason game last August.

(*Sports Illustrated*, 5 April 2015)

LEARNING OUTCOMES

Upon completion of this chapter, students will be able to:

- Develop their ability to define and discuss the importance of recruiting, managing and developing personnel in the sport industry.

- Develop their ability to discuss appropriate skill-enhancing, motivation-enhancing and opportunity-enhancing Human Resource Management (HRM) strategies within a given sport context.

- Develop their ability to critically review HRM strategies to determine best practices and areas for improvement.

INTRODUCTION

A sport manager is charged with managing paid staff, volunteers and paid (or non-paid) interns during the course of his/her sport management career. In sport meccas, such as the USA, intercollegiate athletics and professional sport are the main employment sectors where paid staff and interns make up a large portion of human resources (see Chelladurai, 2006). However, in countries such as Canada, the UK and Australia, sport sectors include thousands of non-profit, voluntary-based sport clubs that operate through volunteer boards of directors and (oftentimes) minimal numbers of paid staff (see Hoye and Cuskelly, 2007). As such, the strategies for recruiting, managing and developing personnel in these contexts may be quite different from their American counterparts.

Within the **global** sport industry, it is becoming increasingly difficult to attract and retain employees and volunteers, as competing opportunities may deter personnel from committing to one sport organization for a given length of time. Thus, competing opportunities may increase personnel mobility, which makes it important to understand the factors that impact the motivation and commitment of paid staff, volunteers and interns and will in turn influence operational (customer service, productivity, **innovation**) and financial outcomes (Jiang et al., 2012).

Drawing from the behavioral perspective of HRM, human capital theory and the resource-based view of the firm (Barney, 1991; Becker, 1964; Becker and Huselid, 1998; Jackson et al., 1989; Mahoney and Pandian, 1992), the focus of this chapter is on how sport managers can (1) use HRM practices to influence paid staff, volunteer and intern (i.e. personnel) behaviors, (2) manage their personnel to strengthen skills, knowledge and ability associated with human resources and (3) create a competitive advantage through optimizing human resources. Skill-enhancing, motivation-enhancing and opportunity-enhancing HRM strategies that have been adopted and validated in previous management literature will be discussed (Bailey et al., 2001; Batt, 2002; Gardner et al., 2011; Huselid, 1995; Liao et al., 2009; MacDuffie, 1995; Subramony, 2009), while recruiting, managing and developing sport personnel will be addressed as the main functions of a human resource manager in sport.

Skill-enhancing HRM strategies are designed by human resource managers to ensure appropriately skilled personnel are recruited and selected within sport organizations. Comprehensive recruitment, rigorous selection and extensive training are all key components of how sport managers can enhance the skills among their human resources. For example, the sport manager should directly link the training and orientation process to job descriptions (postings) as well as the interview and selection procedures. To ensure there is synergy in communication and that all personnel are equipped with the proper tools and knowledge associated with their role, skill-enhancing HRM strategies are essential practices of any sport manager.

Motivation-enhancing HRM strategies are adopted to strengthen personnel's ability to achieve personal goals. Competitive compensation, incentives and rewards, access to benefit plans, opportunities for promotion and job security are factors that may increase motivation in sport employees. For example, sport marketing employees within an athletic department may be more motivated to achieve their goals if their HR manager communicates the promotional opportunities available within the athletic director's office. Further, the motivation of a membership coordinator within a local field hockey club may be enhanced if there are rewards attached to attracting and retaining new members.

Within sport organizations, as managers often operate with reduced budgets and limited resources, volunteers and unpaid interns comprise a large majority of sport personnel. As such, motivation-enhancing strategies (primarily associated with monetary benefits) may not be easily altered by a sport manager given the tight budgets and strict policies associated with financial resources. In cases where budgets are a primary concern, sport managers may turn *to opportunity-enhancing HRM strategies* that are designed to empower personnel to use their skills and provide motivation to achieve organizational objectives. For example, flexible job design, the creation of work teams, employee involvement, information sharing and performance appraisals are essential practices that can be adopted by a human resource manager when attempting to develop paid staff, volunteers and interns. Specifically, a demotivated sport information director within a national sport organization may be inspired to work harder if his/her manager uses job design to enrich (i.e. provide more meaning and importance to) his/her tasks. In this case, the manager gives the sport information director more responsibility in terms of the magnitude of the tasks he/she is given, thus supplying a greater sense of utility and accomplishment within his/her role.

Thinking Point 10.1 and Case Study 10.1 illustrate examples of where sport managers must enhance their human resources by recruiting, managing, and developing their employees, volunteers and interns. For sport managers, it is important to critically review which skill-enhancing, motivation-enhancing and opportunity-enhancing HRM strategies may be the most appropriate in any given context. It is possible to use more than one strategy, and so the personnel a sport manager is managing, as well as the sport setting for which a sport manager is operating within, will be determining factors regarding which strategies are ultimately chosen. Because of this, sport managers must constantly communicate with their personnel to determine (1) what is needed by the organization, (2) what is expected by personnel and (3) what is missing to achieve optimal levels of motivation, satisfaction, commitment and individual performance.

THINKING POINT 10.1

Recruiting and Managing Sport Event Volunteers

The International Canoe Federation's Junior and Under 23 Canoe Sprint World Championship is an annual sport event held at various locations across the globe. The event is host to 63 countries, includes more than 1,600 athletes, officials, coaches and team staff, and occurs over a four-day period. In order to operate such an event, the steering (planning) committee (consisting of volunteers, paid staff and interns) must recruit, manage and develop over 250 event volunteers. The steering committee meets approximately once a month for the year and a half prior to the games.

In the summer of 2013, the international competition was held in Canada for the first time. As such, the steering committee was charged with recruiting volunteers in a region that (1) had not hosted a canoe/kayak event of this magnitude, (2) had a fragmented interest in the sport of canoe/kayak, (3) had hosted other national non-sport events in the past and (4) is geographically proximate to a large metropolitan city. Further, given that a sport event of this magnitude had not

been previously held in the region, training and managing of the volunteers became a "learn-as-you-go" process for many of the paid staff and volunteers on the steering committee.

As the recruiting and managing process began, the steering committee received the following information:

- Volunteers were to be recruited in the following positions: Accreditation, Anti-Doping, Athlete Services/Security, Boat Control, Catering, Ceremonies, Festivals and Merchandise, International Federation Services, Logistics, Medical, Operations and Volunteer Services, Printing, Social Functions, Sport Information, Transportation/Airport Shuttle and Water Safety.
- Individuals interested in roles within Anti-Doping, Boat Control, Medical, Transportation and Water Safety MUST possess specific certification and training protocol to serve in these capacities.
- The budget for the event allowed for volunteers to receive a volunteer package that included a mini-backpack, volunteer t-shirt and jacket. The more shifts for which a volunteer worked, the more t-shirts he/she received in his/her volunteer package.

ACTION LEARNING

- As a steering committee member, what skill-enhancing HRM strategies could be used to help recruit volunteers in this case? Please consider ALL the information you have been given above when responding.

- As a steering committee member, what motivation-enhancing HRM strategies could be used to manage the volunteers once they are onsite at your event to ensure they are motivated and committed to their role and the success of the event?

TOOLS FOR ANALYSIS

A sport manager who adopts *skill-enhancing HRM strategies* will begin by critically reviewing the processes and procedures around recruitment. Recruitment of volunteers in particular has become an issue worldwide as the increasing number of sport events (both large and small) that require a substantial body of volunteer personnel is being met with decreasing numbers of individuals willing to serve (Berkeley, 2013; NSW, 2008; Special Olympics Ontario, 2013). For a sport manager, recruiting can be quite difficult for small and large sport events. Specifically, sport managers need to recruit sport event volunteers for (1) small, local events where he/she is drawing from the local community, as well as (2) large international mega sporting events where sport managers recruit volunteers from across the globe.

Recent research suggests that individuals may be drawn to sport by the sense of community that is felt within the sport community (see Warner et al., 2013). As such, when recruiting volunteers it may be useful for sport managers to assess the common interest that brings individuals together to give their time to an event. However the challenge is for sport managers to determine the common interest of the population that he/she is targeting for recruitment. For example, a sport manager may find that this common interest is tied to the act of volunteering and giving back to the community (rather than a specific connection to sport). For larger, international events, the common interest may lie within the sport itself and a desire to contribute to the development of a sport and its athletes.

No matter the context, a sport manager's role is to determine who he/she is attempting to recruit and what the common interest may be of paid staff, volunteers and/or interns in order to leverage that common interest through advertising and communication (e.g. recruitment advertisements, web-blasts, word-of-mouth). For example, if a steering committee has identified that individuals in the community hosting their event typically volunteer in cases where these are benefiting the community as a whole, it would be important to (1) contact other community organizations who use volunteers in an attempt to access their volunteer database, and (2) create an electronic poster with details about the event, specifically focusing on how it will contribute to the community. In this case, the message sent out should be strategically aligned with the common interest identified in the community.

Further, *motivation-enhancing HRM strategies* are adopted by a sport manager once personnel enter a sport organization's workforce to strengthen personnel's efforts toward achieving individual goals. It is necessary to recognize that competitive compensation, access to benefit plans, opportunities for promotion and job security are factors that may increase motivation in sport employees; however, the same effect may not occur for sport volunteers. In relation to sport volunteers specifically, it is imperative that sport managers ensure constant communication with volunteers during their volunteer tenure, as poor scheduling, feelings of being useless in the process (or skills going unused) and perceptions of a lack of care from administration can cause volunteers to drop out, reduce their efforts and perform at less than optimal levels. Within motivation-enhancing strategies, **communication** regarding reward structures (formal **control** mechanisms) and incentives is often essential for maintaining satisfied sport volunteers. For example, most sport volunteers receive a volunteer package that includes volunteer information regarding the event and each volunteer's role, and oftentimes includes merchandise or giveaways associated with the event. This is typically a well-received incentive/reward if the packages are given in a fair and equitable manner. In the case of volunteers and interns, it is not the size or monetary value of the incentive/reward that matters, but rather the process by which it is received. For example, if sport managers are clear in communicating what is included in the package and how the quality and quantity of contents were decided upon by sport managers, sport volunteers will typically view these "perks" as fairly distributed. As such, if communication is high between volunteers and sport managers regarding the decision processes associated with these "perks," increased motivation and effort may result.

ACTION LEARNING

- You are struggling to recruit volunteers from the local canoe/kayak community specifically for your transportation committee. You have done some research and determined that the common interest among your potential pool of volunteers is to enhance the image of the local community that is hosting the event. What potential "extra" recruitment strategies could you as a sport manager use to recruit enough volunteers specifically for the transportation committee during the four days of the event?

- The 2018 FIFA World Cup is to be held in Russia for the first time. Complete an online search to determine: (1) the total number of volunteers needed to host the World Cup of Football; (2) the number and title of committees that require volunteers for the event; and (3) a volunteer recruitment strategy for the 2018 FIFA World Cup in Russia.

Training and Performance Appraisals among Sport Interns

In exit interviews with over 150 unpaid sport interns, approximately 65% indicate they are at least satisfied with the training and feedback received from their manager or HR manager within their sport industry placement. As such, the growing concern for proper communication between paid staff and interns during their entry into a position and continuation through to performance is one that must not go unnoticed by human resource management personnel. The following information is given to you regarding a particular placement within a national governing body in Canada (Golf Canada, 2011):

Job posting

Golf Canada is looking for qualified applicants to serve as event operations interns within our Championships Division. The four (4) interns will travel as two teams extensively throughout Canada during the internship and will help conduct Junior Championships, Golf Canada's National Men's and Women's Amateur Championships and the National Women's Tour. Other exciting opportunities may include assisting the Championships Division with such events as the Professional Men's and Women's Open Championships. The internship will be for a total of four months. Most days will begin between 5:00–6:00 a.m. and end between 8:00–10:00 p.m. every day of the week, including weekends and holidays.

If you are not a morning person, require eight hours of sleep nightly, or have difficulty being away from your family or friends for extended periods of time, this internship is not for you. Interns will learn everything that is involved with running a successful golf event.

Some of the duties and responsibilities include:

- *General tournament and golf course setup and preparation*
- *Administrative tasks*
- *Starting and scoring of players*
- *Media and public relations*
- *Moderating equipment inventory, maintenance and replenishment*
- *Delivering high quality customer service to all partners, participating facilities, volunteers and players*
- *Public speaking*
- *Driving the equipment truck and trailer to various events sites across Canada*

Scenario

The board of directors for Golf Canada has recognized that it is imperative that their operations interns are adequately trained so that they (1) can harness the skills needed to complete their duties, and (2) understand their role and what is required of them to ensure world class golf events take place across the country. Further, the board has acknowledged a performance gap in the previous season's group of interns. Thus, the board is proposing the performance appraisal process be reviewed with a specific recommendation for appraisals to occur following each event. The purpose of multiple appraisals would be to facilitate interns' development during the internship and enhance effectiveness. Currently, one performance appraisal takes place at the end of an intern's tenure, where each of the eight duties and responsibilities listed above are rated on a scale from 1 (unsatisfactory) to 7 (satisfactory).

ACTION LEARNING

- What is involved in accomplishing each of the duties and responsibilities listed above? Would the performance appraisal look the same at each time point?
- How would each of the duties and responsibilities listed in the job description be addressed through a training schedule for the interns?
- How would each of the duties and responsibilities be assessed during a performance appraisal of the interns?

TOOLS FOR ANALYSIS

Given the fast-paced, ever-shifting world of sport management, it is very easy to forget the basic functions of communication that are so vitally important to the role of managing human resources. In particular, what is communicated to employees, interns and volunteers during training and performance appraisal, and how this communication is received, will have a significant impact on an individual's ability to do his/her job, and on his/her motivation to do a job well and perform at a high level of competency. As such, the basic tenets of training and delivering performance appraisals to sport personnel are provided below.

TRAINING PERSONNEL

Training of paid staff, volunteers and interns may be particularly relevant in the sport industry. Specifically, in an Australian study of community sport volunteers, it was uncovered that retention of sport committee and board members was directly associated with training and support (Cuskelly et al., 2006). Given the importance of training in the sport sector and the statistics associated with (extreme) variability in the training actually provided to sport personnel, it is important to utilize this vital HRM practice to reduce turnover, increase personnel's motivation and enhance human resources within the sport workplace (Taylor et al., 2008).

Within any sport industry position, a sport manager should provide some form of training and orientation outline that consists of a number of key steps (Smith and Mazin, 2004):

1 *Review human resource forms and policies* (e.g. the payroll forms and pay periods for paid staff, the volunteer policies and procedures, volunteer contracts where appropriate, internship waiver forms, the organizational mission and values).

2 *Introduce the workspace* (e.g. information about computers, email systems, phones, office space/keys, passcodes, entrances/exits, the lunchroom) *and co-workers* (e.g. who does the individual report to, and who reports to the individual, if appropriate?).

3 *Review and discuss the job description, expectations* (for both personnel and employer) *and short-term goals.*

4 *Explain any specific organizational or industry jargon.*

If adopted, sport managers must ensure these steps are taken for each new personnel member (e.g. employee, volunteer and intern). In larger organizations or in contexts where large numbers of volunteers are entering the organization for a given period of time, these steps can be reviewed in groups, rather than individually, to ensure maximum use of time and resources.

Within training it is also important to acknowledge that you will be developing both hard and soft skills within your personnel. *Hard skills* are measureable and often encompass the technical skills required to complete a job. For example, the Director of Finance for the United States Olympic Committee (USOC) would need to be trained on the specific software required to run the accounting system for the USOC. *Soft skills* are associated with personal development and are much harder to measure or quantify, however these are just as important as hard skills when assessing how personnel are trained. For our Director of Finance example, this individual may be trained in both hard and soft skills. For instance, he/she would be trained on the computer software required for accounting procedures (hard skill) and also trained in the process of critical thinking and communication (soft skill), as this individual will have to both critically assess budgets and effectively communicate relatively large dollar amounts to a number of paid staff and interns.

The initial phase of providing a training program for new personnel includes identifying the training needs of the particular role(s). Here, sport managers should return to the job description/posting and review the required skills, duties and responsibilities that have been outlined for a given position. These factors will be broken down into hard and soft skill requirements and then included in the training program outline (see above). Following the identification of skills to be included in training, it is time to decide on the process for delivering the training material. The following are provided as a list of potential delivery tactics (Berman et al., 2001; Smith and Mazin, 2004):

On-the-Job Training—an individual is given hands-on experience with a skill related to their job description and provided with feedback and evaluation as they complete the task associated with a given skill (this can be intermittent or continuous).This tactic can be useful for employees, volunteers and interns.

Mentoring—new or novice personnel are "matched" with an experienced employee or manager in their unit/department to develop the new personnel through on-going, periodic conversations and discussions regarding the nature of the job and development opportunities. This tactic is most useful for employees or interns.

Demonstration of skills through video or role play—a facilitator shows the new personnel how to accomplish a skill or task themselves, either in person or via video. This tactic can be useful for employees, volunteers and interns.

Lectures—the sport manager explains facts, policies, procedures and organizational values. This tactic is useful for employees, volunteers and interns, however it should be used in conjunction with other tactics to facilitate learning.

Group discussion—in a group setting led by a sport manager, which allows employees (new and old) to share ideas, expectations, concerns and experiences. This tactic can be useful for employees, volunteers and interns, however it is not typically seen with large groups of volunteers due to time constraints.

Self-assessment—new personnel are given the opportunity to complete a task/skill and rate themselves on an established scale or measure. This tactic can be useful for employees, volunteers and interns, however it is not typically seen with large groups of volunteers due to time constraints.

Online resources—internal or external manuals or guides may be used by sport managers to supplement (or be used commensurately alongside) training materials. This tactic can be useful for employees, volunteers and interns. Due to time and budget constraints, this may be the optimal training tactic for large groups of volunteers or employees. In this case, designing contingencies (e.g. tests associated with an online resource) to ensure individuals are reading the training material is essential.

When selecting a specific delivery tactic, it is important to assess your sport context to determine which of these may be most suitable. For example, if you have a position that requires the soft skill of critical thinking (e.g. a sport market analyst) it would be appropriate to complete on the job training or mentoring as a portion of the training to ensure that individuals are able to work through problems and receive feedback where required.

Upon conducting an effective training program, the communication given by a sport manager MUST be consistent with what was communicated in terms of required skills and responsibilities in the job description (e.g. a sport marketer requiring strong communication and human relation skills), which then MUST be consistent with what will be evaluated in the performance appraisal.

PERFORMANCE APPRAISAL

Major criticisms of formal appraisals (Smith and Mazon, 2004) are that there is a lack of communication, a lack of training and discomfort with negative conversations. However, by creating a system where communication is connected during recruitment (job description), training (managing) and appraisal (developing), personnel will receive valuable feedback that may enhance motivation and individual development. For example, an intern who receives a properly communicated appraisal from his/her direct manager that details his/her strengths, provides an outline of weaknesses, and also provides steps and suggestions for improvement, should be met with positive outcomes (e.g. acceptance of the appraisal content). Further, an operations manager who is given regular feedback regarding his/her role after each event in a given sport season will have the opportunity to improve upon his/her weaknesses and build on successes. With a performance appraisal, sport managers will (Smith and Mazon, 2004):

- Identify key skills, duties and responsibilities related to the individual's role.
- Identify organizational and personal goals.
- Discuss previous positive and negative appraisals.
- Discuss gaps in performance and recommend strategies for closing such gaps.
- Capitalize on strengths.
- Set up a communication process and training needs.
- Set the objectives for the next appraisal.

Due to the short tenure of event volunteers within a sport organization, the above steps are often limited to employees, long-term volunteer board members and interns. Despite the time and budgetary constraints associated with performance appraisal among sport event volunteers, it is vital that sport managers continuously communicate with event volunteers. Discussions regarding strengths and weaknesses between sport managers and volunteers are relevant to a volunteer's satisfaction with his/her volunteer experience, where guidance from sport managers regarding strategies to improve on weaknesses is always appropriate.

Furthermore, for all sport personnel, it is crucial to address who will conduct the appraisal and how this will be done. Firstly, the person doing the appraisal will often determine whether or not the personnel receiving the appraisal will deem the process fair and equitable. For example, if due to scheduling conflicts a sales intern is given a performance appraisal by the manager of the operations department, the intern may (1) not take the appraisal seriously as the manager of operations would not be viewed as an expert on a sales intern's performance, and (2) begin to question the nature of his/her relationship with the direct supervisor whom he/she believes should be the one delivering the appraisal. Wherever possible, sport personnel should receive their appraisal from their direct supervisor/manager or someone they work with on a regular basis who is above them in the organizational hierarchical structure.

Secondly, concerns around fairness and justice processes may be linked to how the performance appraisal is conducted. Particularly in situations where a performance appraisal is given regarding poor performance, it is imperative to ensure the process of delivering that appraisal is perceived as fair to reduce any potential negative feelings with the appraisal. For example, wherever possible, appraisals should be delivered in person. If an appraisal is given over the phone or via email, the reasons for this particular style of delivery should be carefully thought out by the manager giving the appraisal and these reasons should then be clearly articulated to the individual receiving the appraisal. For instance, a sales representative for the Toronto Marlies minor league ice hockey team (a semi-professional league in Canada) who receives his/her performance appraisal via email (without any explanation for this mode of communication) may perceive the process of appraisal to be less valid, ignore the areas for suggested improvement and thus continue to record a poor sales performance for the Marlies. More specifically, Brown et al. (2010) found employees who had negative experiences with the process of their performance appraisal were more likely to be dissatisfied with their job, less committed to the organization and be more likely to contemplate leaving the organization.

To conclude, when delivering a performance appraisal in person or over the phone, two-way communication is enhanced that allows for a proper dialogue regarding gaps in performance, recommended strategies for closing these gaps and tips for how an individual can capitalize on their strengths.

ACTION LEARNING

- Conduct a literature review on issues associated with interns as human resources in the sport industry. Provide a brief summary of how these issues may impact on our recruiting, managing and developing human resources in the sport industry.
- Prepare a performance appraisal for the job duties and responsibilities listed in Case Study 10.1. Firstly, pair up in groups of two and have one student be the manager and the other be the intern. As the sport manager, you are required to provide the intern with a performance appraisal that indicates poor performance regarding customer service and administrative tasks. Secondly, write a report regarding the difficulties associated with giving a performance review that highlights a poor performance and some strategies that may be used to ensure your intern continues developing from the appraisal, rather than becoming demotivated.

CONCLUSION

Sport managers are facing increasing pressures to maximize the potential of their human resources (employees, volunteers and interns) in an industry that is rife with budget cuts, time constraints and increased pressure to perform at an optimum level with limited resources. Whether this is the for-profit, non-profit or public sector of sport in Canada, the USA, Australia or China, it is imperative that sport managers understand the basic functions of recruiting, managing and developing personnel to ensure human resources are leveraged to achieve a **strategic** competitive advantage. Without a clear human resource management system, it is difficult for sport organizations to fulfill their organization's corporate or business level strategies.

This chapter highlighted the importance of understanding skill-enhancing, motivation-enhancing and opportunity-enhancing HRM practices that are particularly relevant to today's contemporary global sport context. Specifically, recruiting, training, delivering performance appraisals and providing reward/incentive systems were topics discussed and related to issues facing contemporary sport managers. It is vital that any aspiring sport manager critically review the strategies that are most relevant to their personnel, organization and industry sector, and continuously communicate with personnel to ensure that HRM strategies are (1) known, (2) understood and (3) perceived as fair within the sport management workplace.

REFERENCES

Bailey, T., Berg, P. & Sandy, C. 2001. The effect of high performance work practices on employee earnings in the steel, apparel, and medical electronics and imaging industries. *Industrial and Labor Relations Review, 54*: 525–543.

Barney, J. 1991. Firm resources and sustained competitive advantage. *Journal of Management, 17*: 99–120.

Batt, R. 2002. Managing customer services: human resource practices, quit rates, and sales growth. *Academy of Management Journal, 45*: 587–597.

Becker, G.S. 1964. *Human Capital: A Theoretical and Empirical Analysis.* Chicago, IL: University of Chicago Press.

Becker, B.E. & Huselid, M.A. 1998. High performance work systems and firm performance: A synthesis of research and managerial implications. In G.R. Ferris (ed.), *Research in Personnel and Human Resources Management*: 53–101. Greenwich, CT: JAI Press.

Berkeley, G. 2013. Popular sport club makes volunteer plea. Retrieved from www.worcesterstandard.co.uk/2013/08/05/news-Popular-sports-club-makes-volunteer-plea-79878.html on October 18, 2013.

Berman, E.V., Bowman, J.S., West, J.P. & Van Wart, M. 2001. *Human Resource Management in the Public Sector: Paradoxes, Process, and Problems.* Thousand Oaks, CA: Sage.

Brown, M., Hyatt, D. & Benson, J. 2010. Consequences of the performance appraisal experience. *Personnel Review*, *39*(3): 375–396.

Chelladurai, P. 2006. *Human Resource Management in Sport and Recreation,* 2nd edn. Champaine, IL: Human Kinetics.

Cuskelly, G., Taylor, T., Hoye, R. & Darcy, S. 2006. Volunteer management practices and volunteer retention: a human resource management approach. *Sport Management Review, 9*: 141–163.

Gardner, T.M., Wright, P.M. & Moynihan, L.M. 2011. The impact of motivation, empowerment, and skill-enhancing practices on aggregate voluntary turn-over: the mediating effect of collective affective commitment. *Personal Psychology, 64*: 315–350.

Golf Canada, 2011. Tournament Operations Internship. Retrieved from www.golfcanada.ca on October 18, 2013.

Hoye, R. & Cuskelly, G. 2007. *Sport Governance.* Oxford: Elsevier.

Huselid, M.A. 1995. The impact of human resource management practices on turnover, productivity, and corporate financial performance. *Academy of Management Journal, 38*: 635–672.

Jackson, S.E., Schuler, R.S. & Rivero, J. 1989. Organizational characteristics as predictors of personnel practices. *Personnel Psychology, 42*: 727–786.

Jiang, K., Lepak, D., Hu, J. & Baer, J. 2012. How does human resource management influence organizational outcome? A meta-analytic investigation of mediating mechanisms. *Academy of Management Journal, 55*(6): 1264–1294.

Liao, H., Toya, K., Lepak, D.P. & Hong, Y. 2009. Do they see eye to eye? Management and employee perspectives of high-performance work systems and influence processes on service quality. *Journal of Applied Psychology, 94*: 371–391.

MacDuffie, J.P. 1995. Human resource bundles and manufacturing performance: organizational logic and flexible production systems in the world auto industry. *Industrial and Labor Relations Review, 48*: 197–221.

Mahoney, J.T. & Pandian, J.R. 1992. The resource-based view within the conversation of strategic management. *Strategic Management Journal, 13*: 363–380.

NSW, 2008. Help! We need more volunteers. Retrieved from www.dsr.nsw.gov.au/sportsclubs/news_article.asp?id=20 on October 18, 2013.

Smith, S. & Mazon, R. 2004. *The HR Answer Book: An Indispensable Guide for Manager and Human Resources Professionals*. New York: American Management Association.

Special Olympics Ontario, 2013. Volunteers. Retrieved from http://ottawa.specialolympicsontario.ca/volunteers on October 18, 2013.

Subramony, M. 2009. A meta-analytic investigation of the relationship between HRM bundles and firm performance. *Human Resource Management, 48*: 745–768.

Taylor, T., Doherty, A. & McGraw, P. 2008. *Managing People in Sport Organizations: A Strategic Human Resource Management Perspective.* Oxford: Elsevier.

Warner, S., Kerwin, S. & Walker, M. 2013. Examining sense of community in sport: developing the multidimensional "SCS" scale. *Journal of Sport Management, 27*(5): 349–362.

USEFUL WEBSITES

Sport England, Human Resources http://archive.sportengland.org/support__advice/governance_framework_tool/4_human_resources.aspx

British Columbia, Canada, Human Resource Guide for Community Sport: Managing Employees
www.bcsummerswimming.com/docs/ReferenceGuides-HumanResourcesGuideCommunitySport.pdf

How to make a human resource policy guidebook
http://smallbusiness.chron.com/make-human-resource-policy-guidebook-11183.html

HR best practices
www.eco.ca/pdf/ECO_HR_BestPractices_Report.pdf

11

STRATEGIC MANAGEMENT

DANNY O'BRIEN AND BEN CORBETT

There is no doubt that Olympic qualification has added another dimension to the [Sevens Rugby] Series and enabled us to reach out, engage and inspire new audiences in new markets around the world.

(Brett Gosper, World Rugby CEO – WorldRugby.org, 2015)

What we've been able to do is take advantage of some of that [market] fragmentation but also really develop a brand.

(Scott Dickey, President and CEO, Competitor Group – USNews.com, 2013)

I know that as much growth as we've seen, we have a long way to go before we can sustain four franchises in Europe. On the other hand, I believe it's our manifest destiny to expand.

(Adam Silver, NBA CEO – Sports.Yahoo.com, 2015)

LEARNING OUTCOMES

Upon completion of this chapter, students will be able to:

- Demonstrate a broad understanding of strategic management principles.
- Understand the importance of analysing organizational opportunities and threats in the context of the sport organization's strengths and weaknesses.

- Discuss issues in implementing sport organizational strategy.

- Demonstrate their knowledge of contemporary issues within strategic sport management.

INTRODUCTION

Strategy is about decision making, long-term impacts, integration and focus, the implementation of decisions, creating value for customers and key stakeholders, and outperforming competitors. The objective of strategic management is to develop a competitive advantage over rivals. Ideally, over an extended period of time, a sport organization can create sustainable competitive advantage. Competitive advantage comes from an organization's ability to perform activities more effectively than rivals can.

The strategic process may begin with an external and internal environmental analysis, from which an identification of strengths, weaknesses, opportunities and threats (SWOT) can be made. A visual representation of this process is referred to as a SWOT analysis. From this, decisions regarding strategic method and direction can be made. In some, but not all, sport organizations, a formalized strategic plan is produced. In implementing this strategic plan, on-going environmental analysis assists in making decisions regarding resource allocations and appropriate organizational structures. Once strategies are implemented, mechanisms of strategic **control** are required to ensure goals and objectives are being met. These control mechanisms provide for strategic evaluation throughout each step in the process, and adjustments can be implemented as and when required. In this chapter, rather than the complete strategic management process, our focus is on the sub-components involved in environmental analysis, and strategy evaluation and selection.

CASE STUDY 11.1

Rugby Sevens Olympic Inclusion and the Australian Rugby Union

Rugby 'Sevens' has been in existence since 1883. Until recently, it had been widely viewed as less serious and more social than the traditional 15-a-side version of the game. The International Rugby Board (IRB) initially campaigned for Sevens' Olympic

inclusion in 2005, but this effort failed due to the lack of a women's game, and, to a lesser extent, the argument that only a handful of countries were genuinely competitive.

In 2009, the IRB finally won its bid for 2016 Olympic inclusion. The emergence and competitiveness of women's Sevens was a requirement from the IOC for Olympic inclusion, so the IRB introduced the women's Rugby World Cup Sevens in 2009. Eighty nations competed to earn one of the 16 spots. The IOC was present in Dubai for the

2009 RWC Sevens not only to witness the highly competitive women's competition, but also to see that the men's competitive gap was closing. Kenya, Wales, Argentina and Samoa were the men's semi-finalists, proving the game had opened itself up to a wider global population. Olympic inclusion has many implications for national governing bodies, including financial support from national Olympic committees, media and sponsors; changes to regulatory and development structures; and the potential for the pride and notoriety of an Olympic medal. Traditionally successful Olympic nations, but non-traditional rugby nations, such as China, Russia, Canada and the USA, have significantly increased their investment in rugby as a direct result of Olympic inclusion.

With the 2016 Olympic Games funding cycle beginning in 2013, the Australian Rugby Union (ARU) faced a strategic dilemma. Firstly, Australia places a high priority on Olympic success, and routinely has the best medal count per capita of any nation. Secondly, Australia is traditionally one of the most successful rugby nations, continually placing in the top five of IRB world rankings, and winning two Rugby World Cups in 1991 and 1999. In addition, Australia has five teams in the Super Rugby competition, the premiere professional rugby competition in the southern hemisphere.

However, the ARU has never matched its 15-a-side success in men's Sevens. The ARU's past Sevens strategy has been to use the IRB Sevens World Series as a development tool for aspiring 15-a-side players. Consequently, the ARU has invested little in Sevens' development. Meanwhile, the growing economic significance of Sevens is evident at the international level, with 18% of the IRB's 2012 revenue attributed to Sevens. However, in Australia, Sevens represents only 2% of revenues, and that includes funding from the Australian Sports Commission and the Australian Olympic Committee. The ARU was seemingly at the forefront of women's Sevens development when it won the 2009 Women's Sevens Rugby World Cup and instituted a National Women's Sevens Championship in 2012; however, in 2013 the Australian women's team was lagging behind New Zealand, the USA and Canada.

As of 2013, Australia has lacked a true domestic Sevens competition structure to help identify and develop new Sevens athletes. While there are several Sevens carnivals run by independent operators and state governing bodies, there is nothing like the structures seen in competing nations such as the UK, the USA, New Zealand and even Kenya. Australia is also unique with four codes of professional football competing for the same athletes and fans, with rugby union the third most watched code behind Australia Rules Football and rugby league and just ahead of soccer. There is some evidence that the Olympic inclusion of Sevens is attracting more youth participation and 'code-hoppers' in many countries, including some rugby league and netball converts.

TOOLS FOR ANALYSIS

This chapter provides tools for identifying the strategic issues in this case, and indeed, in most sport organizations. Strategic issues may be problems or opportunities that could materially impact on the competitive position of the sport organization. Competitive positioning can be determined after internal and external environmental analyses.

External environments

Organizations do not exist within a vacuum, rather they impact on and are impacted on by other constituents in their environment. An organization's environment can be broken down into the general and task environments. The general environment includes areas that may not have an immediate impact on the organization, but instead have a more indirect influence. These broader influences include economic, political, sociocultural, legal, demographic, ecological, and **technological** trends and forces.

The task environment includes aspects of the environment that directly impact on an organization's decision making and performance on a more intimate basis. The task environment may include competitors, suppliers, athletes' groups, customers or fans, and legislative agencies. Figure 11.1 demonstrates that the sport organization is encompassed and directly influenced by the task environment, which is itself enveloped by the general environment.

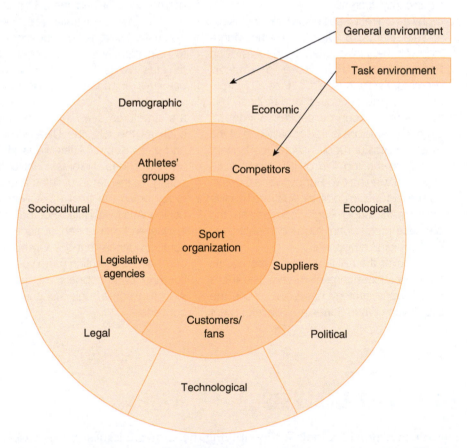

FIGURE 11.1 *The general and task environments of a sport organization (adapted from Slack, 1997, p. 134)*

Sport organization environments are very complex and always evolving, with instability in both general and task elements. This instability was originally described by Emery and Trist (1965) as environmental turbulence, which encompasses the level, nature and speed of change. One constant about an organizational environment is that it is always changing.

The notion of a turbulent environment is not, on its own, necessarily worrisome for management; it is the environment's level of predictability that can stress managers. Turbulence that is cyclical or linear is predictable, and can often be managed without changes to the organizational structure. However, unpredictable environmental turbulence can 'jolt' an organization into change (Laughlin, 1991). For example, the Olympic inclusion of Rugby Sevens is a major environmental jolt that has demanded a response from rugby governing bodies around the world.

Internal environment

The internal factors that can influence how well a sport organization navigates its strategic path through times of environmental change include its resources and capabilities, core competencies and the extent of structural inertia.

Resources and capabilities

A sport organization's resources refer to its tangible and intangible assets. Tangible resources can include stadia, equipment, office buildings, land and cash. Intangible resources may include **brand**, image, reputation, coaching and athletic know-how, and culture. These intangible resources typically take a great deal of time to develop, and may be extremely difficult for competitors to imitate. For these reasons, intangible resources are often considered to be more valuable as they can form the basis for core competencies and sustainable competitive advantage.

A sport organization's capabilities are the processes, systems or procedures used to manage its resources for industrious use. In the preceding case study, the key resources available to the ARU could be described as mostly intangible, including a long history of winning international tests, a strong brand, coaching expertise and robust ties to private high schools for youth development. However, some would agree that the ARU has been resting on these resources for too long, while competitors, with comparable resources, have been more innovative in developing competencies like attracting and developing talent, expanding brand reach, engaging with fans and media, and leveraging the Olympic status of Sevens rugby in ways the ARU has yet to exploit.

Core competencies

Stemming from an organization's resources and capabilities are its core competencies. A competence is a characteristic or collection of characteristics possessed by all or most organizations in a specific industry sector. A core competence is a unique asset that allows an organization to achieve greater value and therefore reach a competitive advantage. Competencies become core when they become the source of the sport organization's competitive advantage, as illustrated in Figure 11.2.

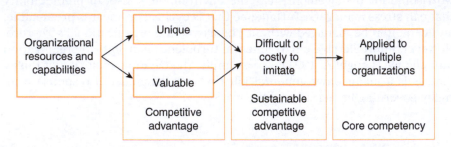

FIGURE 11.2 *Organizational resources and capabilities leading to competitive advantage (adapted from Harrison and St. John, 2014, p. 49)*

Inertia

Not all organizations that have identified a strategic option in line with core competencies can actually enact the strategy. This is due to the concept of inertia. Inertia stems from an organization's momentum and manifests as resistance to a change in strategy. There are some external variables that contribute to organizational inertia, which include **legal** and fiscal barriers to entry and exit, the cost of acquiring new information about the environment and legitimacy constraints. Alternatively, some theorists conclude that organizations will continue on an inertial path until environmental turbulence forces a strategic change. Huff et al. (1992) define inertia as management's level of commitment to the current strategy, and further discuss that an environmental shock is the primary antecedent for organizational change.

To use the case study example, Olympic inclusion has pressured rugby union's governing bodies to develop, and in some cases create, Sevens rugby programmes in order to remain competitive internationally. Change can be seen in both traditional and non-traditional rugby governing bodies. For example, non-traditional rugby nations like the USA, Russia and China have changed from amateur, participation-based models to investment in high performance. Meanwhile, traditional rugby nations, like England, South Africa and France, have been nimble in diverting resources from the 15-a-side game into Rugby Sevens. However, Australia's inertial response to the Sevens challenge has delayed significant strategic action, and left it lagging behind its key competitors. This demonstrates the constant need to survey the environment. A common tool for environmental surveillance is SWOT Analysis.

SWOT Analysis

The acronym, SWOT, stands for Strengths, Weaknesses, Opportunities and Threats, and is depicted in Figure 11.3.

FIGURE 11.3   *SWOT Matrix*

Strengths are internal factors that include the resources, capabilities and core competencies that provide the basis to achieve organizational strategies and derive an advantage over rivals. Examples include financial resources such as Olympic funding, human capital such as elite technical staff, and facilities such as state-of-the-art weight rooms and recovery labs. Weaknesses limit a sport organization's abilities to properly enact strategy or pursue new strategies. Just as financial resources, human capital and facilities can be the strengths of one sport organization, they may be a source of weakness in another if it lacks, for example, key stakeholder support, experienced athletes or state-of-the-art facilities.

Opportunities are environmental conditions that present an organization with a means to develop new products and/or services, and a platform for competitive success. For example, Olympic inclusion has led to public schools accepting rugby as part of the curriculum in many countries, providing new opportunities to introduce children to the sport at a critical developmental age. How a focal sport organization reacts to opportunities depends on its internal strengths and weaknesses. Finally, threats are environmental conditions that have the potential to undermine an organization's ability to achieve its strategic objectives. For example, while Olympic inclusion presents many opportunities, for foundation unions such as Australia, it also presents a significant threat. For example, pressure from its own Australian Olympic Committee has forced the ARU to divert resources away from its core competency of men's 15-a-side into women's rugby and Sevens.

- What are the key opportunities that Olympic status brings to the ARU?
- How can the ARU leverage its strengths to take advantage of these opportunities?
- How might Olympic status be viewed as a threat by the ARU?

- What weaknesses does the ARU have that might exacerbate any threats posed by Olympic inclusion?
- Diagrammatically present your answers to the above questions as a SWOT Analysis.

CASE STUDY 11.2

Competitor Group, Inc.

Competitor Group, Inc. (CGI) is an endurance sport media and events company, specializing in running, triathlon and cycling. CGI manages over 80 events in North America and Europe, and the Rock 'n' Roll Marathon Series is its flagship property. Additional events include the National Football League Run Series, Muddy Buddy, TriRock Series and others. Over 680,000 people participate in CGI events each year.

CGI's media platform includes five publications (*Competitor*; *Triathlete*; *Inside Triathlon*; *Women's Running*; and *Velonews*) with a combined monthly circulation of 800,000. Competitor.com was launched in 2009 as the main web portal for the events and print media, merging 18 different websites. Competitor.com has 2.5 million unique visitors per month and CGI's properties have over 900,000 social media followers.

CGI's competitive advantage lies in its core competencies of: (1) brand equity with endurance enthusiasts; (2) only national year-round marketer in combined running, cycling and triathlon space; and (3) economies of scale with digital, print and event assets allowing for operational savings, 'cost-free' marketing, and leverage with non-endemic sponsors and advertisers.

A growth investment firm, Falconhead Capital, owns CGI. Falconhead's mission is to build CGI through acquisition and organic growth, with an end-goal of selling the company at a high multiple. The initial purchases of Elite Racing (Rock 'n' Roll Marathon Series) and the magazines have been followed by purchases of one-off events (e.g. the Las Vegas Marathon), additional media (e.g. Windy City Publications), and most recently, the Triathlete.com URL. CGI also grows organically via green fielding events (i.e. TriRock), building online content and increasing distribution.

With rapid growth (five events in 2008 to over 80 in 2013), CGI faces the possibility of diminishing returns, i.e. a point where events begin to cannibalize each other and exclusive series sponsors cannot extend their fee or afford activation for additional events in the same geographic area. Looking at this situation through an investor's eyes, the dilemma thickens.

The optimal time to sell a company is not when it has reached its growth capacity, but rather, when it is on an upward curve. Falconhead needs to show success in both past and current growth, as well as potential for future growth.

CGI has proven its capability for growth through the endurance industry in North America and Europe. To continue growth, CGI is contemplating two options: (1) CGI can use the same industry defragmentation model it used with endurance sport and expand into buying other individual 'competitor' sport products (e.g. kayak, rock climbing, etc.); or (2) CGI can stick to the product it knows, but expand by purchasing endurance sport products in the Asia-Pacific region.

TOOLS FOR ANALYSIS

Strategy evaluation and selection

STRATEGIC DIRECTION Influences on strategic direction include internal and external stakeholders, the broad and task environments, and organizational history and inertia. The organization's mission, vision and business definition encapsulate its strategic direction. *Mission* defines the organization's purpose, what it does and why it exists. *Vision* is what the organization desires to be in the future. *Business definition* outlines the sport organization's products, markets, functions served and resource transformation processes.

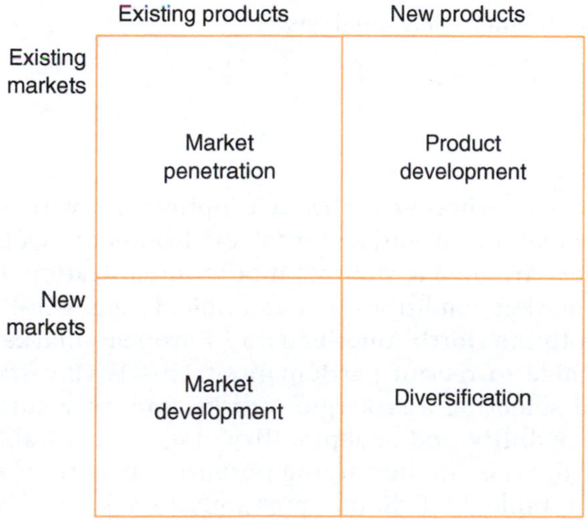

	Existing products	New products
Existing markets	Market penetration	Product development
New markets	Market development	Diversification

FIGURE 11.4 *Ansoff (1957) matrix of strategic directions*

The four primary strategic directions are illustrated in Figure 11.4. *Market development* entails bringing an existing product to a new geographic, demographic or psychographic market, as exemplified by expanding the Rock 'n' Roll Marathon to the Asia-Pacific. *Product development* entails introducing a new product in the current market, exemplified by CGI placing a TriRock triathlon event in a current Rock 'n' Roll Marathon city or region. *Diversification* involves a sport organization spreading its risk by investing in a new business area or product line to reach a larger market, exemplified by CGI's creation of the online media portal, competitor.com. In that example, CGI's diversification was 'related' (lower risk), as the target consumer was the same (runners). An unrelated (higher risk) diversification may be to include rugby tournaments in CGI's event profile. Finally, *market penetration* is increasing market share in the current market with existing products.

Strategic method

Strategic method refers to the way organizations approach the strategic direction. If the strategic direction is the route an organization takes towards competitive advantage and profitability, then the strategic method is the vehicle by which the organization travels (see Table 11.1).

Suitability-Feasibility-Acceptability

Once the strategic direction and methods have been identified, the sport organization must then evaluate each possibility before selecting the strategic option or options. One popular technique is the Suitability-Feasibility-Acceptability (SFA) analysis.

Suitability

Suitability refers to whether a strategic option fits with the organization's core competencies and external environment. Options may be unsuitable if they are inconsistent with other organizational strategies or unpredictable market conditions. For example, is the Asia-Pacific market similar enough to the North American and European markets in the way CGI has been able to recruit participants? This is the first step when evaluating and selecting a strategic option, and only suitable options move to the feasibility and acceptability stages. A suitability analysis utilizes SWOT to assist in identifying potential directions and methods as described in Table 11.1. Some questions to ask while performing a suitability analysis include:

- Will this option exploit opportunities and minimize threats?
- Will this option utilize the organization's strengths and/or reduce its weaknesses?
- Will this option achieve the organization's objectives?
- Will this option enhance competitive advantage?

Describe some external and internal conditions where certain strategic directions and methods are more appropriate.

TABLE 11.1 *Strategic directions and methods (adapted from Evans et al., 2003 p. 272)*

Strategic option	External environment	Internal resources/ competencies
Directions		
Market penetration	Gain market share for advantage	Exploit superior resources and competencies
Product development	Exploit knowledge of customer needs	Exploit research and development
Market development	Current markets saturated	Exploit current products
	New opportunities for geographic spread, entering new segments, or new uses	
Diversification	Current markets saturated or declining	Exploit core competencies in new arenas
Methods		
Internal development	First in field	Learning and competence development
	Partners or acquisitions not available	Sole financial responsibility
Merger/acquisition	Speed	Acquire competencies
	Supply–demand	Scale economies
	Price to earnings ratios	
Joint venture development	Speed	Complementary competences
	Industry norm	Learning from partners

Feasibility

Feasibility refers to whether a strategic option is achievable. The option may be suitable, but the organization may be lacking the resources or capabilities to actually follow through on it. In addition, external factors such as government regulations and negative customer reactions may prevent the strategic option from moving forward. Some questions to ask while performing a feasibility analysis include:

- What is the likelihood of implementing this option?
- Does the organization have the tangible and intangible resources necessary to pursue this option?
- Does the organization have the competencies necessary to pursue this option?
- What environmental factors may prevent this option from being successful?

Acceptability

Acceptability refers to whether a strategic option will attract support from key internal and external stakeholders. Internal stakeholders may include employees and the board. Employees must enact the strategy. For example, CGI employees may not fully buy in to the new strategic option if it negatively affects their daily duties. Organizational inertia often precludes a shift in strategic direction because employees do not accept the change. The board and CEO must decide which option will have a superior return on investment to the organization, and whether the level of risk is within the organization's security level. External stakeholders that need to accept the strategy include customers and suppliers, as each may choose to conduct business with other organizations. For example, if a sports team decides to cut its overall salary by developing players instead of signing expensive free agents, then some sponsors may not see as much value in the franchise. Some questions to ask while performing an acceptability analysis include:

- Will the employees willingly enact this option?
- What is the likely return on investment of this option?
- What is the likelihood and impact of the risks associated with this option?
- Will this option cause the organization's current customers and/or suppliers to reduce transactions?

A tool to assist with the analysis of different strategic options is the SFA Ranking Matrix depicted in Table 11.2. After identifying at least two strategic options, systematically score each criterion on a scale of 1–5 (1 = low, 5 = high) on the option's ability to achieve each goal. Provide a brief rationale for each score because several managers may repeat this process with different perspectives before coming together to make a decision. Ultimately, after such a methodical evaluation, one option will emerge with a superior total score to the alternative/s.

TABLE 11.2 *SFA Ranking Matrix*

	Option 1 Method: Direction:		Option 2 Method: Direction:	
	Score	Rationale	Score	Rationale
Suitability				
Achieves objectives				
Enhances competitive advantage				
Uses strengths				
Hides weaknesses				
Exploits opportunities				
Averts threats				
Sub-total				
Feasibility				
Likelihood of implementation				
Have the capabilities and resources				
Environment allows it				
Sub-total				
Acceptability				
Risk level				
Return on investment				
Stakeholders				
Sub-total				
TOTAL				

ACTION LEARNING

- Perform a SWOT analysis on CGI.
- Should CGI expand the 'competitor' umbrella to include other individual lifestyle sports? If so, what other sports would be a good fit? Why?
- Should CGI expand into the Asia-Pacific region? If so, which cities should they target? Why?

- Name and explain the strategic direction and method for each option depicted in Questions 2 and 3.
- Using an extended version of the SFA Matrix (Table 11.2), perform an SFA analysis and determine which option CGI should pursue.

CONCLUSION

The strategic process should be perpetual. Internal and external environmental scanning through the tools discussed in this chapter, such as SWOT and SFA Analysis, assist in identifying, evaluating and selecting strategic methods and directions with the intent of developing competitive advantage. Organizations must continually adapt to market conditions through the strategic process or risk competitive obsolescence.

REFERENCES

Ansoff, H.I. (1957) Strategies for diversification. *Harvard Business Review,* 35: 113–124.

Emery, F.E. & Trist, E. (1965) The causal texture of organizational environments. *Human Relations,* 18: 21–32.

Evans, N., Campbell, D. & Stonehouse, G. (2003) *Strategic Management for Travel and Tourism.* Oxford: Butterworth-Heinemann.

Harrison, J.S. & St. John, C.H. (2014) *Foundations in Strategic Management* (6th edn). Mason, OH: Thomson South-Western.

Huff, J.O., Huff, A.S. & Thomas, H. (1992) Strategic renewal and the interaction of cumulative stress and inertia, *Strategic Management Journal,* 13: 55–75.

Laughlin, R.C. (1991) Environmental disturbances and organizational transitions and transformations: some alternative models. *Organization Studies,* 12: 209–232.

Slack, T. (1997) *Understanding Sport Organizations: The Application of Organization Theory.* Champaign, IL: Human Kinetics.

USEFUL WEBSITES

Competitor Group, Inc. case websites
http://competitor.com

Media kit
http://cgimediakit.com

Australian Rugby Union case websites
http://rugby.com.au
http://irb.com

12

ANIMALS IN SPORT

ANDREW BYERS AND DENE STANSALL

> Her Majesty's horse may have failed a drugs test but this is no Tour de France Moment.
>
> (*The Telegraph*, 2014)
>
> 1,000 racehorses a year in UK abattoirs. Shocking failures in checks. How do we know thoroughbreds aren't in our food?
>
> (*The Independent*, 18 February 2013)
>
> Dope-testing of horses to be doubled at stables during 2014.
>
> (*Guardian*, 22 December 2013)

LEARNING OUTCOMES

Upon completion of this chapter, students will be able to:

- Gain a broad understanding of the current use of animals in sport and the many issues that arise for sport managers.

- Draw parallels to human sport from examples of contemporary issues in equestrian sport.

- Critically examine the practices related to the supply of animals for sport.

- Critically discuss the **governance** of animals in sport.

INTRODUCTION

The use of animals in sport has a historical foundation dating back millennia. The list of animals currently and previously used in sport is long, with horses and dogs most notable. The *Circus Maximus* was infamous for the horrific injuries caused to horses and chariot riders. The racing, supported by a boisterous and baying crowd, created a scene that would not be far removed from today's Aintree Grand National in England where contemporary equine athletes fall and die. The notable difference is that now the race organizers are placed under pressure from stakeholders (**sponsors**, public, animal rights groups) to take steps to evaluate and manage the **risks** for horses (and riders). Our changing culture removes French Bulldogs, the most popular modern breed, far from the brutal sports of the baiting ring for which it was originally bred. This horrific form of entertainment provided 'sport' for the masses and aristocrats alike in the not so distant past, but the taint of the past can be found in the present with the re-emergence of some of these blood sports. Michael Vick, a professional athlete himself, provides a high profile example with his convictions related to dog fighting and **gambling**. In comparison to their human counterparts, animals in sport have a more brutal past but hopefully a more humane future. The welfare of animals in sport can be compromised as they play a utilitarian role within a human cultural system. The animals' natural instincts, attributes and behaviour are disregarded. Exploitation can be legal or illegal under **law** or through regulation and **governance** of the sport. The distinction between the two is often a thin line governed by a subjective set of rules that are most often **controlled** and determined by the sport itself.

A further burden on animals is the use of drugs to optimize performance or, on the contrary, to hinder performance for corrupt gambling, or to mask injuries and thereby potentially exacerbate them. Campaigning has increased public awareness and given rise to scrutiny and pressure, thus demanding greater transparency from the sport's regulator. The willingness to response to criticism of those in a position to **control** any change has been varied.

In democratic countries, governments hopefully act to appease the sensibilities of the majority. In western countries, dog fighting, bear baiting and hare coursing, for example, were once legal (or were not illegal) but became illegal as the tide of public opinion turned against them. Animals such as horses and dogs are used in sport globally, with other animals such as camels (racing in the Middle East), ostriches (racing in Australia) and bulls (fighting in Spain) still being exploited for entertainment. These practices are 'largely' self-regulating and considered part of a nation's culture, providing **economic** benefits as well as an opportunity for public entertainment.

Use of the term 'sport' should be questioned when referring to blood sports and utilising animals as prey for the pursuit and pleasure of humans. But for the context of the discussion a broader definition can be accepted, and a number of parallels and differences between human and animal participation in sport discussed. Animals in sport present unique **ethical** issues but it is also surprising how many issues are common across species. While these issues are vast, this chapter focuses on horse racing. This industry provides ample examples of important issues for sport managers and an opportunity for the critical thinker to consider this sector directly or as a novel case study to better understand broader issues. Whether one is working directly in the racing industry, or perhaps involved peripherally through corporate **sponsorship**, partnership or **ownership**, there are many interesting and challenging aspects to the use of animals in sport.

CASE STUDY 12.1

Government Policy, Economic Gains and Animal Welfare Consequences

In 1969 the Irish Finance Minister, Charles Haughey, introduced tax exemptions for the Irish horse-breeding industry. He was, in addition to being a politician, a thoroughbred horse breeder and stud owner. The financial benefits of the legislation placed Irish breeders in a favourable position over their competitors in Britain. Not only providing a marked business advantage, it also put a focus on Ireland as the place to invest in horses and racing. It did, however, open the floodgates to a racehorse breeding industry that would see unregulated expansion and over-production in the following decades.

The welfare consequences for the horses of over 40 years of intensive Irish breeding became immediately present and persistent. None more extreme, than those seen during the global economic recession at the end of the first and start of the second decade of the twenty-first century. In 1969 Ireland and Britain together registered some 6,227 (Popham, 2002) thoroughbred foals from a combined mare population of 12,226 (Morris, 1990). The 2007 registered foal returns from Ireland alone reached a peak of 12,961 from an active broodmare population of some 20,700 (Bull and Griffin, 1985). As dramatic as its rise, so was its decline. A decrease in the demand for mares and foals was to follow, resulting in dire consequences for thousands of horses. The term the industry uses for unwanted surplus animals is 'wastage' and the high breeding levels contributed to this 'wastage'.

Ireland's ascent to become the leading thoroughbred breeding nation in Europe was spurred on by direct internal government support through tax expenditure and deregulation, and indirectly by European Union financial assistance. It allowed entrepreneurs to establish vast breeding empires and cottage industry breeders not only to survive but to thrive – for a time! Traditionally horses were bred to race in a sporting environment. But opportunists saw a further reason for breeding, which was the bloodstock sales market. This lucrative parallel industry, fundamentally driven by monetary gain, saw horses traded like commodities in a practice called pin-hooking (i.e. buying young horses and selling them at a profit before they race).

Most notably, in 2006 a young colt called The Green Monkey (Racing Post, 2014) was purchased for $425,000 and subsequently sold for $16 million to the Irish-based racing and stallion barons Coolmore. He never won a race and was retired after three disappointing runs. Foal production created buoyancy in the bloodstock markets and parallel growth. Under the hammer went unraced foals, weanlings and yearlings to global buyers who looked to speculate. Not only did Irish bloodstock markets see a boom, so also did those in England. Annually thousands of young horses born in Ireland were transported to English bloodstock sales. The average priced yearling in England in 1976 was under 10,000 guineas, and this rose to more than 42,000 guineas in just five years (Lowther, 2014) (£1.05 = a guinea).

As Ireland's mare population grew, so did its impressive stallion roster. This not only attracted Emerald Isle mares but also mares from across Europe as the 'go to' place. It eventually ignited breeders from North America and Australasia who initiated a programme for shuttling top stallions to mares on those continents. The horse market was further buoyed up by improvements in the Irish economy during the 'Celtic Tiger' (Berry, 2003) years from 1995 to 2000. This was due to historical and continuous financing from the European Union and US corporate investment in the Republic. It made for a wealthier population and, for many, the opportunity to speculate in racehorse ownership. The economic boom however proved a house of cards and the inevitable collapse had profound implications for those equine athletes that had been created for sport and speculative profit.

TOOLS FOR ANALYSIS

Government policy aimed at economic gains was successful (see Case Study 12.1) but the downside to this was increasingly evident – animal welfare declined. The vast majority of owners, then as now, would never recover their horse's keep and training costs. Thousands of mediocre racehorses had flooded onto the market and into the limited racing calendars in Britain and Ireland. 'Banded' races were the epitome of this, i.e. large fields of horses raced for meagre prize-money returns – a direct consequence of over-production. Failed racehorses, which are the majority, were easily replaced, leading to a huge surplus in horses.

Ireland by 2007 had the highest equine-to-human density of any European population, with an average of 27.5 sport and leisure horses per 1,000 people (Leadon et al., 2012). Breeding horses had been seen as an investment and borrowed money had financed and underpinned many ventures, but these were now looking naïve in the extreme when Ireland hit a dramatic economic downturn in 2008 (Whelan, 2013). The market for horses was about to reach rock bottom with devastating effects. At this juncture a financial and welfare crisis was emerging: breeders were now left with thousands of pregnant mares, newly born foals, yearlings waiting to go to the sales and young two-year-old horses looking to enter training, as well as a population of store horses (older unraced animals who would usually go for jump racing). Alarmingly, and despite this, thoroughbred horse breeders continued to produce foals for racing in their thousands for which there was, literally, a dying market.

Ireland's solitary horse abattoir was soon unable to 'process' the huge number of racing industry horses, Irish sport horses and other leisure and mixed breed horses that came through its gates. Slaughter figures (Driver, 2013) rose exponentially from just over 2,000 in 2008 to over 24,000 in 2012. Abattoirs sprung up almost overnight to cater for the demand for the disposal of unwanted horses (Griffiths, 2011). In the crudest terms, Irish and British horseracing had gone from a sport to a food producer. Young foals to those at the end of their careers, the injured, the slow, mediocre breeding mares and poor performing stallions, were turned into meat for human consumption or fed to hunting hounds, whilst others were rendered down to be mixed into everyday products. This massacre of a sport's equine competitors was the result of a lack of foresight and **strategic** planning for the future, the ignorance of potential outcomes, and sheer apathy of a self-regulated industry.

Sherry et al. (2007) discuss how the relationship between sport and business has increased the complexity of ethical issues for sport managers. They note about 'conflict of interest' that:

> The inherent tension within a conflict of interest is the balance between the roles and responsibilities of business; such as: interest, benefit and damage and professional judgment, with the moral values and concepts of ethics; of obligation and duty, voluntary behaviors and **trust**. (2007: 271)

Boatright (2000) also suggested that a conflict of interest arises not merely from conflicting interests, but from a situation where personal interest is in conflict with an obligation to serve the interests of another person or organization.

ACTION LEARNING

- Should the numbers of horses bred for sport by commercial breeders and stallion owners be regulated?
- Do you agree that sport horse welfare would be improved through an independent regulator outside of the sport?
- Access and read the Sherry et al. (2007) article in full. Identify where there have been conflicts of interest in Case Study 12.1.

- What measures should be introduced and by whom to manage these conflicts of interest?
- Are any unique ethical issues presented by the horse-breeding industry, especially taking into account the poor consideration of supply and demand and fundamental economic principles resulting in overproduction?

Review of Anti-Doping Policy for the British Horseracing Industry

The British Horseracing Authority (BHA) announced a review of its 'Anti doping and Medication Control Policy', with changes to be implemented in January 2014.

This follows on from a year of controversy in the sport with one of the biggest global horseracing organizations accused of cheating. In April 2013, in what has been reported as a 'bombshell', trainer Mahmood Al Zarooni accepted responsibility for positive drug tests on 11 horses in his care. Al Zarooni was the trainer for the Godolphin stables, which are owned by Sheik Mohammed, the Prime Minister of the United Arab Emirates and monarch of Dubai.

This is not the first time that this type of controversy has surrounded Sheik Mohammed's stables. In 2012, Al Zarooni was fined £2,000 by the BHA when two of the horses in his care tested positive for propoxyphene, a banned opiate analgesic. The BHA imposed a fine of £1,000 and a disqualification from the respective races on the horses.

In 2006, another trainer, this time of endurance horses, in the employ of Sheik Mohammed, was banned for one year after two horses in his care returned positive tests. In the last few years a total of four endurance horses in the Mohammed stables have tested positive for the banned substance stanozolol, which is also the drug found in the racehorses trained by Al Zarooni. Interestingly Al Zarooni was assistant to Mubarak bin Shafya, who has trained both endurance and racehorses for Sheik Mohammed. Bin Shafya has been in trouble twice for doping offences.

As one of the wealthiest and highest profile men in the world, it would be easy to point the finger at Sheik Mohammed. He is unfortunately not alone, with many other examples, albeit less conspicuous, of doping in equestrian sport. But what is unique to Sheik Mohammed is the reaction of the governing body for horseracing. Sheik Mohammed's horses tested positive in April, and the BHA initiated a review of their policy on drug testing in May 2013.

TOOLS FOR ANALYSIS

As a self-regulated industry, the governance of major equestrian sport is divided between horseracing and all others. The Fédération Equestre Internationale (FEI) is the global governing body for Olympic equestrian sports, with the British Equestrian Federation its UK national representative. Globally, in Britain the British Horseracing Authority is the governing body for horseracing, with each country that participates in horseracing having a national equivalent. These governing bodies have the challenge of collaborating in a sport that operates fluidly across international boundaries. Horses and jockeys can race in different countries and are largely answerable to the local authority.

Riders as well as horses have tested positive for doping and cheating. Frankie Dettori, champion jockey, tested positive for a banned substance and received a six-month ban in 2012. He rode for Sheik Mohammed for 18 years. Kieren Fallon, six-time champion jockey, tested positive in both 2006 and again in 2007. Unique to horseracing is the possibility for a drugged rider to compete on a drugged horse.

Lance Armstrong and Ben Johnson, if they were not already, became household names as the result of the publicity surrounding their downfall. This level of media interest puts sports under pressure to change and may result in immediate responsibility being taken by the athlete and policy changes in governance. There has yet to be a cheating scandal in horseracing on the scale of human athletics but some incidents have been quite high profile and unlike human sport the animal athlete who tests positive cannot be held to blame.

So where does the buck stop in equestrian sport? According to the new rules of the BHA and the Rules of Racing, the trainer is ultimately responsible for the horses in his care! As with coaches for human athletes, this individual does oversee the day-to-day training, although an additional dimension to animal sport is that an athlete can be owned by a third party. Therefore, the trainer is in the employ of the owner and thus, it could be suggested, has a shared level of responsibility.

The case of Mahmood Al Zarooni is an interesting one in respect of the level of responsibility taken by the trainer. He made a public apology to his employer, the emir of Dubai, stating he had made a 'catastrophic error' and accepted total blame for the situation. Both Sheik Mohammad and his racing manager, who stands between the trainer and the owner, quickly stepped away from Al Zarooni. In a statement reported in *Telegraph Sport* (23 April 2013) the Sheik's racing manager claimed his employer was 'absolutely appalled!'.

A feed company has accepted responsibility for another horse owned by royalty which failed a drugs test. BBC Sport broke the news that Estimate, owned by Her Majesty Queen Elizabeth II, the British monarch, tested positive for opiates. The feed manufacturer, who also holds a royal warrant, suggested that one of its product supplied by a third party could contain traces of naturally occurring poppy seeds and be the source for the contamination (*The Independent*, 23 July, 2014). The zero tolerance policy of the BHA will mean a ban and the forfeit of winnings for any horse testing positive, but overall there seems to be a 'these things happen' attitude in this case.

Accidental contamination by rogue poppy seeds was not the case when another of the Queen's horses tested positive for tranexamic acid. In 2009, the Queen's trainer, Nicky Henderson, was banned from racing for three months and heavily fined. He denied using the drug to enhance actual racing performance, but interestingly the BHA investigation found any reference to tranexamic acid had been omitted from the trainer's medication book (*Guardian*, 4 July 2009)

The examples above demonstrate that a range of stakeholders could be accountable when animal athletes test positive for drugs. These examples are from horseracing but the problem is not limited to this sphere of equestrianism. Horses competing in the Olympics have also been caught cheating. The 2008 Games saw four show jumpers banned from competing because of positive drug tests. It is also obvious that there is the potential for a discrepancy between those who should take responsibility and those who are willing to throw themselves on their swords. Corporate manslaughter laws have been implemented in many countries to ensure those culpable were held to account no matter what level they were in the organization. Would the situation be different if everyone involved, from the owner through to the managers, trainers and vets, were all forced to accept some level of responsibility in sports which used animals?

ACTION LEARNING

- Lance Armstrong has put on record that the buck stopped with him. Discuss who must be responsibility (trainer, owner, vets or others) when a non-human athlete tests positive for a banned substance. Does the responsibility extend beyond the athlete in human sport?
- Should human participants in equestrianism (riders and jockeys) be banned or fined for riding a 'drugged' horse?

- Discuss the importance of high profile personalities in sport being caught cheating and whether the media surrounding these events are driving changes in sport policy.
- Could horseracing establish policies and practices similar to those for human sport and the World Anti-Doping Agency?

THINKING POINT 12.2

Oligarchical Control in Horseracing and its Effect on the Thoroughbred Breed

Domination in Europe by three leading breeding and racing operations, Coolmore, Darley/Godolphin and Juddmonte, has led to an oligopoly in the racing and breeding industries. This has had an impact on success at all levels of the sport.

In 2012 the five British Classics (top horse races), the 1,000 Guineas, 2,000 Guineas, the Oaks, the Derby and the St Leger, saw a clean-sweep of wins shared between Coolmore and Darley/Godolphin horses. In the same season, Juddmonte raced the unbeaten Frankel, the best horse of his generation and perhaps of all time, and promptly retired the horse with a stud value of £100 million. In less than 10 years he is likely to sire 1,000 offspring into the racing world. As a group, these giants of the turf have for over 30 years controlled the industry and overshadowed all others in terms of buying power for bloodstock sales, stallion covering figures, successful offspring and racehorse ownership numbers.

TOOLS FOR ANALYSIS

Striving for for supremacy in the world of thoroughbred horseracing has its roots entrenched within the historical record. In contemporary times, the three organizations mentioned above, Coolmore, Darley/Godolphin and Juddmonte, have come to dominate all aspects of racing and breeding to a disproportionate degree. They totally dominate European racing and are expanding their influence into the wider global racing and bloodstock scene. With access to almost unlimited funds they operate linear and integrated businesses in breeding, buying and racing. They have to an extent shaped fashionable bloodlines and now possibly hold the future of the thoroughbred breed in their hands.

The opportunities for breeding racehorses in Ireland improved significantly in 1969 with a tax-free incentive to stallion owners (Popham, 2002). Coolmore's early operations were under the control of the late Robert Sangster. He bought the offspring and blood relations of top North American racehorse and stallion Northern Dancer. From this he established a racing and breeding programme in Ireland. It came to fruition quickly with racing success in Europe. Sangster's triumphs involved a partnership with John Magnier and racehorse trainer Vincent O'Brien. Coolmore's success has proliferated the Northern Dancer line through the thousands of horses they have bred (Morris, 1990).

In the late 1970s Prince Khalid Abdullah of Saudi Arabia was racing horses in his own name and started the Juddmonte Farms breeding empire. By the early 1980s further Middle-Eastern investment by oil-rich Sheikh Mohammed bin Rashid Al Maktoum and his brothers, who rule the emirate of Dubai, immediately established their status as leading players. They formed what is today known as the Darley Stud operation and its racing arm Godolphin.

Both Darley and Juddmonte have focused their operations on a similar fully integrated business model to that of Coolmore. Their dominance, particularly in breeding, has often been at the expense of other talented horses who were mostly rejected as influential stallions, despite their racecourse achievements, because they were either 'unfashionable' or lacking a Northern Dancer bloodline. The origins of this strategy to control the breeding industry date back decades. For example, in 1984 former Derby winner Teenoso was rated 135 by the renowned turf publication *Timeform*. Sadler's Wells, a son of Northern Dancer, whom Teenoso had beaten on the racecourse, was rated 132 (Bull and Griffin, 1985) yet Sadler's Wells went on to become a world-leading sire. For his owners, Coolmore, he was the cornerstone of their empire for nearly a quarter of a century, covering the best mares to become the most prolifically successful stallion Europe had ever seen. Teenoso struggled to attract top mares and was passed down from stud to stud until he disappeared into obscurity.

Coolmore, Darley/Godolphin and Juddmonte have a consistent hold on the most renowned races as well as propagating the most sought-after and expensive stallions. Tables 12.1 and 12.2 show examples of their recent triumphs.

TABLE 12.1 *The leading European stallions (rated by prize-money earned by their offspring)* (Racing Post, 2014)

2013
1   Galileo – Coolmore
2   Dubawi – Darley
3   Oasis Dream – Juddmonte
4   Teofilo – Darley

2012
1   Galileo – Coolmore
2   Montjeu – Coolmore
3   Invincible Spirit – Irish N.S.
4   Exceed and Excel – Darley

2011
1   Galileo – Coolmore
2   Montjeu – Coolmore
3   Oasis Dream – Juddmonte
4   Dansili – Juddmone

TABLE 12.2 *Recent winners of the English Classic Races* (Lowther, 2014)

1,000 Guineas
2013: Sky Lantern – Keswick
2012: Homecoming Queen – Coolmore
2011: Blue Bunting – Darley/Godolphin

2,000 Guineas
2013: Dawn Approach – Darley/Godolphin
2012: Camelot – Coolmore
2011: Frankel – Juddmonte

Oaks
2013: Talent – Dixson
2012: Was – Coolmore
2011: Dancing Rain – Taylor

Derby
2013: Ruler of the World – Coolmore
2012: Camelot – Coolmore
2011: Pour Moi – Coolmore

St Leger
2013: Leading Light – Coolmore
2012: Encke – Darley/Godolphin
2011: Masked Marvel – Nielsen

Regulators of the sport, including the International Federation of Horseracing Authorities, the British Horseracing Authority and the Irish Turf Club, have been silent over the **control** these three have within the sport. They foster the view that they offer vital employment and finance, however they fail to recognize that any competition at the top-end of the sport is being suppressed. In addition, there is little long-term vision by the regulators with regard to the future health of the thoroughbred breed. All racehorses are tied into a closed stud book and this is a restriction on genetic diversity and health that can only have a detrimental effect in the coming years.

ACTION LEARNING

- Should the International Federation of Horse Racing Authorities intervene and regulate to limit and therefore constrain the racing and breeding opportunities of these leading players?
- Research other sports to see if they have a similar dominating group that stifles competition.
- Evaluate the advantages to a sport of having individuals and businesses willing to contribute huge amounts of money towards owning a stake in the industry and the position of compromise this potentially could place on the sport and its governance.
- Has the phenomenal rise of this powerful trio limited opportunities for others in racing? Does their controlling influence on breeding show a disregard for the possible long-term consequences to thoroughbred genetic health?

THINKING POINT 12.3

Support for Retired Athletes

'Brilliant Kingman retired to stud after glittering career on racetrack' reads the headline (Popham, 2002). This horse had been the sole animal among 1000 others to survive injury and natural attrition and have this glamorous end to his career. This was especially rare considering there are less than 300 stallions standing in Britain in total. Although there is a paucity of data provided by the industry on the number and destination of horses leaving racing each year, some of academic literature gives us insight into these numbers. A recent Australian study suggested that the racing industry in this country could be retiring nearly 15,000 horses annually (Thomson et al., 2014).

Considering the accepted industry figure of around 30% of foals success-fully entering racing (4,366 born in 2012 in Britain) and around 4,000 leaving racing every year (ROR, 2014) there are a large number of horses which are termed 'wastage'. These statistics would encourage any aspiring human athlete to think that there is a 30% chance of becoming a professional, but the options for failed and retired human athletes are very different. The fate of horses leaving racing is down to the fickle whims of owners. These fates can extend from the ridiculous ('Retired racehorse learns how to paint': www.cctv-america.com/2014/09/13/retired-racehorse-learns-how-to-paint) to the tragic ('Two 'dead' race horses rescued by RSPCA': www.racingpost.com/news/horse-racing/county-hall-awbeg-beauty-two-dead-racehorses-rescued-by-rspca/610320/#newsArchiveTabs=last7DaysNews).

TOOLS FOR ANALYSIS

It would be wrong to assume that equestrian sports are peripheral and insignificant. These activities contribute £300 billion to the global economy (Wyrick, 2015), with horseracing, as a rural industry, second to agriculture monetarily in the UK providing a quarter of a million jobs (Mayes, 2015). Even the less populous country of Canada has a horse industry worth CAN$19 billion to the national economy. There are estimated to be 1 million horses in the UK and 58 million globally according to the Food and Agriculture Organization of the United Nations. Some of these are animals are bred for work or food but most are intended for some participation in sport.

One of the biggest challenges facing equestrian sport is the management of unwanted animals. The problem is systemic across all aspects of the industry but the scale is most obvious in thoroughbred racing. A third of all thoroughbred horses never see a race and the ones who do generally have a short career. In Australia, for example, only 46% of the horses entering racing saw the second year of their career (Thomson et al., 2014). It should be noted that these would be four-year-old horses that could possibly live well into their 20s.

There is a paucity of specific and precise information provided by the industry on how many horses are retired out of racing every year. A total figure would include young foals that do not enter training or come out of training prior to racing, mares and stallions leaving the breeding industry and horses retiring after a racing career. It is estimated by the author that in Great Britain alone this number exceeds 20,000 animals a year and the global estimate would be many times this figure.

The ultimate fate of retired racehorses is varied. For the some euthanasia is an immediate possibility. There are no real figures on how many horses are killed on retirement every year but it is estimated to be in the thousands. Australia may be 'knackering' about 6% of the horses leaving racing (Thomson et al., 2014) and other countries are killing animals as well. It is known that some of the meat from retired racehorses has entered the human food chain.

Headlines such as 'Burger King reveals its burgers were contaminated in horsemeat scandal' from the *Guardian* newspaper (31 January 2013) might give insights into the fate of some retired equine athletes.

Many horses are rehomed and retrained. The racing industry in Britain places a 10% levy on gambling. The forecast levy for 2015/16 is £66.5m with a small portion of this money being channelled directly to charities who have been established to rehome retired racehorses. The central organization which supports this initiative by the industry is Retraining of Racehorses. This work has been recognized and support by the broader industry and the level of support has been increasing in the past few years. The estate of the late racehorse breeder and philanthropist Paul Mellon recently gave a multi-million pound bequest for retired racehorses. Other significant players in the industry have also contributed, most notably the emir of Dubai, Mohammed bin Rashid Al Maktoum, with a recent gift worth several million dollars.

In spite of the financial support of the industry in helping to rehome and rehabilitate retired equine athletes, official direct responsibility may lie elsewhere. The National Equine Welfare Protocol (2008) was created to allocate responsibility for the wellbeing of horses in the UK equestrian industry. The wording of the documents reads as follows:

> The British Horseracing Authority (BHA) regulates horseracing in the UK and this specifically includes the welfare of horses under the control of those it regulates. Those regulated include owners of horses in training, jockeys and trainers, but do not include thoroughbred horse breeders, or those who keep thoroughbred horses retired from racing, except those in the care of licensed trainers.

According to the Sports Leadership Institute most human professional athletes find the experience of retirement like falling off a cliff. This fall is supported by the governing bodies of the individual sports and other organizations like the IOC Athlete Career programs. *Sports Illustrated* recently published the fact that in spite of the huge salaries paid to professional footballers in the NFL 78% of them are bankrupt two years after retirement. These difficulties faced by human athletes are an interesting theoretical comparison to those of animal athletes.

However, there are those who would suggest an equally or more significant problem for animal athletes. Animal rights campaigners would claim animals should have equal consideration. The term 'speciesism', as coined by philosopher Peter Singer, suggests a moral philosophy which places animal needs as equal to those of humans (Singer, 1975) and the problems faced in retirement could be considered in light of this philosophy.

Equestrianism and other animal sports must be progressive if they are to survive an increasing level of intense scrutiny and criticism. The glamorous image of the Sport of Kings may be changing, with many people associating it with cruelty, death, injury and wastage (Winter and Young, 2014). The American Horse Publications' 2009/10 Equine Industry Survey concluded that the top challenge facing the industry was dealing with unwanted horses. Quite rightly, many historic blood sports have been abolished and outlawed in civilized countries. With a historical prospective, and an awareness of the anthropomorphic tendencies of a large portion of the population, it might be concluded that the illegalization of animal sports is inevitable. This could then set a strong precident for the abolition of human sports, such as boxing, that were deemed detrimental to participants' health and wellbeing.

ACTION LEARNING

- Human professional athletes are generously remunerated for their participation but animal athletes are not. Discuss if unsalaried animal athletes should be guaranteed monetary compensation to support their post-career welfare in consideration of the economic significance of their sport.

- Should we apply an anthropomorphic term like 'retirement' to animal athletes?
- A broken stick in hockey, a crashed F1 car or a broken tennis racket are all quickly disposed of and replaced. Are animal athletes disposable and replaceable?

CONCLUSION

Animals in sport, animals for sport and the complex ethical issues that emerge from commercialization are the subjects of this chapter. We have sought to enlighten readers as to the events which have shaped and continue to influence industries involving animals and sport. Whether directly involved in horseracing or considering a sponsorship relationship, using the greyhound races as a corporate night out, or managing an athlete found guilty of illegal betting on dog fights, there is a need for aspiring sport managers to think about and understand the issues surrounding animals in sport. The use of animals in sport also makes an interesting case study to compare with human athlete management issues.

REFERENCES

BBC Sport (22 July 2014) Queen's horse Estimate tests positive for morphine. Available at: www.bbc.com/sport/0/horse-racing/28430528 (last accessed 9 November 2015).

Berry, F. (2003) Irish economic development over three decades of EU membership. Available at: www.tcd.ie/business/staff/fbarry/papers/papers/Finance%20a%20Uver.pdf (last accessed 20 May 2014).

Boatright, J.R. (2000) *Ethics and the Conduct of Business*, 3rd edn. Englewood Cliffs, NJ: Prentice-Hall.

Bull, P. and Griffin, R. (1985) *Timeform Racehorses of 1984*. Halifax, England: Portway Press. pp. 875–9.

Driver, A. (2013) Irish company 'sold mislabelled horse meat to Czech Republic. Available at: www.farmersguardian.com/home/latest-news/irish-company-sold-mislabelled-horse-meat-to-czech-republic/53637.article (last accessed 20 May 2014).

Guardian (4 July 2009) Nicky Henderson gets ban and fine for doping Queen's horse. Available at: www.theguardian.com/sport/2009/jul/04/nicky-henderson-doping-horse-racing (last accessed 9 November 2015).

Guardian (31 January 2013) Burger King reveals its burgers were contaminated in horsemeat scandal. Available at: www.theguardian.com/business/2013/jan/31/burger-king-horsemeat (last accessed 22 October 2015).

Griffiths, R. (2011) HRI chief responds to horse death numbers. Available at: www.racingpost.com/news/horse-racing/#newsArchiveTabs=newsArchiveTab (last accessed 20 May 2014).

Leadon, D.P., O'Toole, D. and Duggan, V.E. (2012) A demographic survey of unwanted horses in Ireland 2005–2010. Available at: www.irishvetjournal.org/content/65/1/3 (last accessed 20 May 2014).

Lowther, R. (2014) *Horses in Training 2014*. Compton: Raceform Ltd.

Mayes, B. (2015) Changes affecting the equine sector. *The Veterinary Record*, *176*(18): 457–60.

Morris, T. (1990) *Thoroughbred Stallions*. Ramsbury: Crowood. p. 4.

National Equine Welfare Protocol (2008) Available at: www.britishhorseracing.com/wp-content/uploads/2014/03/National_Equine_Welfare_Protocol.pdf (last accessed 22 October 2015).

Popham, M. (2002) Stallion tax exemption in Ireland is threatened. Available at: www.bloodhorse.com/horse-racing/articles/12766/stallion-tax-exemption-in-ireland-is-threatened (last accessed 20 May 2014).

Racing Post Staff (2014) Top Flat Racing Sires. Available at: http://bloodstock.racingpost.com/statistic/leading_lists.sd#leadingListsTabs=top_flat_racing_sires (last accessed 20 May 2014).

ROR (2014) Retraining of Racehorses. Available from: www.ror.org.uk/rehoming-sourcing/ (last accessed 9 November 2015).

Sherry, E., Shilbury, D. and Wood, G. (2007) Wrestling with 'conflict of interest' in sport management. *Corporate Governance: The International Journal of Business in Society, 7*(3): 267–7.

Singer, P. (1975) *Animal Liberation*. New York: HarperCollins.

Sports illustrated (31 March 2009) How (and why) Athletes Go Broke. Available from: www.si.com/vault/2009/03/23/105789480/how-and-why-athletes-go-broke (last accessed 9 November 2015).

The Independent (23 July 2014) Estimate's failed drug test: red faces but no real scandal for racehorse owned by The Queen. Available at: www.independent.co.uk/sport/racing/estimate-s-failed-drug-test-red-faces-but-no-real-scandal-for-racehorse-owned-by-the-queen-9624444.html (last accessed 9 November 2015).

The Telegraph (23 April 2013) Trainer at centre of Godolphin drugs scandal, Mahmood Al Zarooni, admits 'I made a catastrophic mistake'. Available at: www.telegraph.co.uk/sport/horseracing/10012211/Trainer-at-centre-of-Godolphin-drugs-scandal-Mahmood-Al-Zarooni-admits-I-made-a-catastrophic-mistake.html (last accessed 9 November 2015).

Thomson, P.C., Hayek, A.R., Jones, B., Evans, D.L. and McGreevy, P.D. (2014) Number, causes and destinations of horses leaving the Australian Thoroughbred and Standardbred racing industries. *Australian Veterinary Journal*, 92(8): 303–11.

Whelan, K. (2013) Ireland's economic crisis: the good, the bad and the ugly. Available at: www.ucd.ie/t4cms/WP13_06.pdf (last accessed 20 May 2014).

Winter, C. and Young, W. (2014) Fashion, fantasy and fallen horses: alternate images of thoroughbred racing. *Annals of Leisure Research*, 17(4): 359–76.

Wyrick, J. (2015) Today's Equine Industry. ALLTECH Symposium, ALLTECH Industries. Available at: www.alltech.com/blog/posts/todays-equine-industry (last accessed 20 May 2014).

PART TWO
NATIONAL ISSUES

PART MAP

In this part there are a variety of contemporary issues relevant to the sport manager. These are located here to demonstrate how the implications for sport managers of each contemporary issue largely depend on the countries in which that issue is examined or how its extent is dependent upon the national context.

13

SPORT POLICY

JIANDONG YI

Chinese soccer on upswing with new talent and big investment.
(*Washington Post Online*, 10 April 2015)

China: 'Square dancers' face official choreography.
(British Broadcasting Corporation Online, 24 March 2015)

Sports focus: China's Wanda Group acquires In front on way to build sports empire.
(Xinhua News Agency Online, 10 February 2015)

LEARNING OUTCOMES

Upon completion of this chapter, students will be able to:

- Discuss the benefits and limitations of the development of sport policy in China, a developing country.

- Discuss the differences between sport policy in other countries, compared to China.

- Understand and discuss some of the research that has been conducted in relation to sport policy.

INTRODUCTION

Many countries now have national policy objectives focused on sport. Developed nations primarily concentrate on developing elite sport and/or grass roots sport. In developing countries, including China, governments are confronted with difficulties in how to correctly and effectively benefit from sport management. Such difficulties are rooted in two sources. On the one hand, they originate from the industrialized countries who evaluate the emerging Chinese professional sports market with their existing high standards. Meanwhile, the highly professional, **commercialized** sports products, such as the National Basketball Association (NBA) and the Football Association (FA) Premier League, have been introduced in China, and have been significantly influencing the growing Chinese sports market accordingly. On the other hand, those difficulties could be attributed to the limitations of the Chinese sport system. Following the 2008 Beijing Olympic Games, the *Chinese Gold Medal Theory* created in the founding of China in 1949, i.e. the unique Chinese sport system funded by national finance and pursuing gold medals in all competitions, has not adapted to the actual development of the country's economy (Xu, 2009).

Globally, policy has been increasingly adopted by government as a primary tool to promote the development of sport, and this very issue has attracted heavy attention from many researchers, especially in Europe, Australia and Canada. For example, Houlihan attempted to investigate sport policy as a government tool and interpret its relevant characteristics (Houlihan, 1997; Houlihan and White, 2002, 2013). Moreover, other researchers have attempted to investigate the emergence and development of specific sport policy, and further to discover the correlations and underlying meanings of various sport policies. Some researchers have even aimed to find out the significance of the existence of a sport policy. For example, Bloyce and Smith (2010) focused on the UK's development of sport policies for youth sport, community sport, elite sport and **mega-events sport**, while Stewart et al. (2004) reviewed the historical roots of sport policy in Australia and based on that they proposed and interpreted a possible concept of sport policy – *better than design*. In addition, based on their analysis of the practical experience in designing sport policy and developing sport, both Hoye et al. (2010) and Nicholson et al. (2011) investigated the effectiveness of sport policy in Australia.

For less economically developed countries whose governments primarily focus on accelerating development of the economy the situation is different. They put more emphasis on sport policy research on how to stimulate the sport industry, or how to make huge profits via that industry. From this it can be inferred that the aforementioned research themes, especially the issues of regulating and stimulating the sport industry in developing countries, have gained less attention in the prevailing research.

Therefore, in order to present an objective interpretation of the Chinese policy on the sport industry, as well as provide a supplementary aspect to the international research on sport policy, this chapter primarily focuses on China's policy on sports but also demonstrates how policy is a contemporary issue for all nations and particularly for developing nations. From the perspective of public policy, the chapter firstly reviews the history of China's policy for the sport industry. Following four perspectives, i.e. the policy on industrial structure, the policy on industrial organization, the policy on industrial technology and the policy on industrial layout, the chapter identifies contemporary issues within China's sport industry. Finally, it analyses empirically a template policy, *Guidance for Accelerating the Development of the Sport Industry* (CPG, 2010), which is one of the most influential policies in Chinese sports.

CASE STUDY 13.1

Evolution

Chinese policy on the sports industry can be considered in four phases, namely the infant stage (1978–1992), the early stage (1992–1998), the norming stage (1998–2008) and the rising stage (2008–present), and this section in turn will discuss the development and evolution of the policy since the beginning of the Chinese economic reform in 1978.

The infant stage (1978–1992): After the economic reform started in 1978, China was aware of generating funds from social resources to support the development of social undertakings (e.g. sport) and proposed that 'marketization is an effective means to assist the maintenance and development of sports industry' (Yi, 2011). Accordingly, the awareness of industry in China's sport-related area emerged. During this period, the focus was inclined to a self-examination of the sport industry per se. In addition to the pre-existing sport

administrations, commercial organizations entered into the sport industry. Thus the control mechanism of the sport industry was no longer limited to administrative means. Notably, the former sport-related business operations were not yet fully market-oriented, and the primary purpose of the business operations dominated by sport-related administrations was to make up budget deficits through sport, rather than making profits. The Chinese economy was not sufficiently developed to facilitate the formation of the necessary conditions and circumstances that were suitable for growth in the sport industry. Partly estimated, from 1978 to 1992, the gross income for China's sport industry exceeded 1.6 billion Chinese Yuan. In 1992, only 10% of the income gave credit to the business operations. Therefore, during this stage, China did not have a strictly recognized sport industry.

The early stage (1992–1998): China's economic reform, transiting from a planned economy towards a more market-oriented economy, provided a favourable context for the development of the sport industry. The opening of the 14th National Congress of the Communist Party of China in 1992 symbolized the actual formation of the industry when the Chinese government officially declared the implementation of the socialist market economic reform. At that time, the sport industry was regarded not only as a sole means either to provide supplementary funding for the sport-related administrations or to raise bonuses for all staff and workers, but also as a key component of the national economy, which could both increase the gross domestic product (GDP) and create jobs for the whole society.

In June 1995, *the Program for the Development of Sports Industry (1995–2000)* was formulated by the General Administration of Sport, which divided the sport industry into three groups. Firstly, the principal industry, in which the business operations could give full play to both the operating functions and the values inherent in sport, e.g. the operating activities of performance, drilling, fitness, recreation, consulting and training for sport competitions. Secondly, the associated industry, which generally refers to the economic departments that could serve the sporting activities, e.g. the production and marketing of sports equipment and accessories. Thirdly, the peripheral industry, that is the business operations that were undertaken by the sport administrations, aiming at giving financial assistance to the development of the sport industry.

The norming stage (1998–2008): During this period, standardization and intense change became two popular issues in the Chinese sport industry. On the one hand, the high rate of growth reflected the boom in China's sport industry; on the other hand, both the increasing corruption and the growing failure in regulation

highlighted the inadequate preparations for an emerging sport industry. Therefore, the requirement for normalization, standardization and legalization marked the former prevailing characteristics of the policy on Chinese sport.

On 24 March 1998, the plenary meetings of the State Council made a decision to reshuffle the former National Sports Commission, which was accordingly replaced by the General Administration of Sport, a department directly under the State Council. On 6 April an opening ceremony was hosted, which marked the official start-up of the newly established General Administration of Sport. In addition, the reshuffle signified that the sport administrations had appropriately adapted to the changes in both its internal functions and social economic environment, and had proactively made contributions to exploit new marketing opportunities for the industry. Thus the development of the sport industry was greatly enhanced.

In 2002, the National Bureau of Statistics undertook an adjustment to the *Industrial Classification for National Economic Activities*. Compared with the former classification, sport was removed from the auspices of the health, sport and social welfare industry and, together with culture and recreation, became the industry of culture, sport and recreation. In May 2003, the National Bureau of Statistics issued its *Regulations on the Program of the Primary, Secondary and Tertiary Industry*. According to the new classification, the industry of culture, sport and recreation was categorized as the 'tertiary industry'.

The rising stage (2008–present): The norming stage lasted for a decade and the Chinese sport industry had made progress in its commercialization process. After the success of the 2008 Olympic Games in Beijing, the industry had been growing.

Now it entered a new and steady development stage. In March 2010, the State Council issued *Guidance on Accelerating the Development of the Sport Industry (reference No. 22, the State Council, 2010)*, which was regarded as the first official national strategic guidance that formulated both the planning and objectives of the country's sport industry.

In April 2011, the General Administration of Sport issued the *12th Five-Year Program for the Chinese Sports Industry (reference No. 178, the Sport Economy, 2011)*, which laid out the overall planning for the development of the industry. The programme creatively played a distinctive role in accelerating national economic growth, achieving social harmony, boosting cultural prosperity and promoting the holistic development of the sport industry. In October 2013, the State Council issued *Suggestions for Promoting the Development of the Health Services Industry*, which advocated the diversification of the health services industry including consultations on physical examination, national fitness, health, culture and tourism. All the aforementioned policies indicated that the notion of a western sport industry, such as innovation, tourism, health services and ecological industries, had begun to be integrated with the Chinese conceptual framework, and that integration exerted considerable influence on both broadening the horizons of and giving direction to China's sport industry.

TOOLS FOR ANALYSIS

When reviewing the history of China's policy on the sport industry, three distinct features can be identified. First of all, the policy objectives have been changing. For many years, the relevant policies were not oriented toward the healthy development of the industry. Instead, the macroeconomic policy determined the decision making for policy on the sport industry. Secondly, the policy adjustment tool was monolithic with a lack of cooperation between the various governmental departments. Most of the policies aiming at making adjustments were issued by the General Administration of Sport as departmental regulations. There was seldom any cooperation between sport-related administrations and other relevant government sectors such as land, taxation and line ministries. Thirdly, consistency and volatility co-existed within the policy. To a certain degree, the Chinese policy on sports industry simultaneously had maintained both a stable and a transforming status for the previous three decades.

Drawn from the analysis of the aforementioned policies on the industrial structure, organization and layout, several principal limitations both of the Chinese sports industry and its relevant policies were identified by the current research. First of all, the policies on the sport industrial structure were difficult to execute practically and the relevance among the different policies was rather low. The Chinese government primarily focused on formulating programmes for limited industries, such those for sport competition performance, fitness and recreation, and venues. The planning for sport products, sport **media** and sport agency was ambiguous. Legislation (**sport law**) for the sport industry was underdeveloped with low pertinence.

Relevant policies were also lacking in complementary support from other policies such as investment and financing, taxation and land. Moreover, the research examined the implementing effects of some relevant policies, including those on core industries such as sport competition performance and fitness and recreation, and others for peripheral industries such as venues, sport products and the sport lottery. According to the *White Paper for the Development of Chinese Industry of Sport Products*, in 2012 the gross income for the industry was a mere 250 billion Chinese Yuan: 80% of the gross income (more than 190 billion Chinese Yuan) was generated from the production, wholesale and sales of the industry's sport-related products, with business scope for sportswear, shoes and sport equipment. Effectively, these **economic** results were rather low for the relevant industries, such as those for sport competition performance, **sponsorship** and advertising, agency and services.

Secondly, the limitations of the policy on industrial organization led to a serious monopoly in the market for sport competition performance. Low profit margins boosted opportunism in the market and it was extremely difficult for the regulators to carry out their work. All of these limitations then negatively influenced the entire industry's economic results. Viewed from a holistic perspective, this significantly hindered the healthy development of the Chinese sport market. A primary countermeasure could be to have adopted a policy oriented towards increasing competition, including lowering the threshold for market access and fostering competition, and especially encouraging small-and medium-sized enterprises to enter the sport market. Meanwhile, the relevant governmental departments could impose restrictions on the direct involvement of sport-related administrations in the market operation, but instead transformed those involvements into a market regulation-oriented action, such as by strengthening the construction of the infrastructure used for better security protection, and tightening quality control for the sport competition performance, including taking strong measures against fraud, unfair refereeing, violence and hooliganism in sport.

Moreover, the Chinese sport industry lacked a scientific policy on techniques. As an emerging industry, the relevant technical policies on sport exigently needed to be proposed. Although China had previously issued some technical policies on the sport industry, these were macro-oriented. Micro-oriented and niche targeting policies were significantly missing. In addition, most of the relevant policies were inclined towards regulation but not support.

ACTION LEARNING

- What could have been done differently in developing the sport policy for China to make it more successful?

- Critically discuss the implications of sport policy in China for the provision of sport products and services through business and the development of elite athletes.

Implementation of Sport Policy in China

In March 2010, the State Council issued its *Guidance on Accelerating the Development of the Sport Industry*, which was the first official national strategic guidance that formulated both the planning and the objectives of the industry. Accordingly, guided by the national guidance and integrated with local practices, all the local sport administrations respectively formulated their distinctive document entitled *The Implementation of Accelerating the Development of the Sport Industry* (Abbr. *the local implementation*) accordingly.

Reviewing the portfolio of all 17 *local implementations* throughout China, except for three provinces and cities including Fujian, Shanghai and Guangxi, the remaining 14 provinces and cities merely touched lightly on these expressions by the executive body responsible for the policy at either all levels of government, all relevant departments and all relating sectors or sport administrations, with some provinces and cities even neglecting to mention the executive body for the policy. Fujian was the only province that effectively broke down the assignments of the *local implementation*. In order to successfully implement all the tasks in this, the General Office of the Fujian Provincial Government specifically produced an official document entitled *The Notice to Break Down the Assignments Proposed by the Guidance for Accelerating the Development of the Sport Industry*, and allocated every assignment to particular departments and various levels of government.

TOOLS FOR ANALYSIS

Taking a public policy analysis (Weimer and Vining, 2005; Dunn, 2009) approach, we can consider a public policy to have three essential elements, namely the executive body of the policy, the policy objective and the policy measures. From these the current research will investigate the *local implementation* aiming to uncover the overall importance of the specific local policy.

The policy objective is what the policy maker expected to achieve through decision making and it is both a starting point and the end result. Internally, the policy encompasses the measures it may utilize and the planning it may draft. In the local implementation, the objectives for all the districts were expressed either as the overall thinking, a target for development or the key task. In the local implementation also, all the provinces and cities did integrate the policy with its local distinctiveness and all the different targets for development and the key tasks varied.

Firstly, all the local implementations followed the fundamental principles within the national guidance. Secondly, according to its local distinctiveness, different provinces and cities set up different objectives. The four provinces (i.e. Heilongjiang, Shanghai, Guangxi and Shandong) proposed qualitative-oriented objectives such as 'to strikingly raise the ratio of gross income of sport industry to the GDP, to heavily raise the ratio of the industry of sport services to the overall sport industry, to remarkably increase the per capita consumption of sport, and to substantially raise the ratio of employment figures for the sport industry to the whole society'. But all of those objectives were difficult to quantify. Thirdly, all the key tasks represented their local distinctiveness. Henan province focused on *Shaolin Kongfu* (traditional Chinese martial arts) and developed some key projects such as Kongfu training and competitions in *taijiquan* (a kind of traditional Chinese shadow boxing). Since Shanghai had some well-known international competitions such as the F1 Grand Prix, the Shanghai Masters (tennis), the IAAF (International Amateur Athletic Federation) the Diamond League, the Shanghai International Marathon, the International Federation of PGA Tours and the World Snooker Shanghai Masters, the city purposively and vigorously fostered growth in theme tourism and sport competitions related tourism, aiming to develop Shanghai into a nationally famous sport tourist resort.

Policy measures imply the practical methods or proposals necessary to execute *the local implementation*. Four provinces and cities (such as Jiangsu, Sichuan, Qinghai and Shanghai) took creative measures. All of these were suitable for setting up a fund to support the development of the sport industry. In order to constrain proper use of this fund and increase its availability, that fund should be monitored and evaluated. Moreover, they urged integrating training for sport-related personnel with a long-term talent cultivation plan, and by doing so hoped to foster more professional sport-related experts. In general, all the local implementations were in accordance with the measures proposed in the national guidance. From various perspectives (i.e. **financing**, taxation, land, banking, infrastructure, protection of intellectual property in sport-related areas, talents and market regulation), all the local implementations showed their support for developing the Chinese sport industry.

Firstly, the policy objective was slogan-oriented. That objective needed to be distinct, so the policy executors could be guided logically. However, in most of the local implementations the policy makers did not specify a clear statement for the objectives of the sport industry. Instead, abstract expressions such as 'enhancing, strengthening and improving', were used which could not be easily quantified to evaluate the relevant achievements. Therefore, to specify a clear and periodic objective would have been more beneficial to the development of the infant Chinese sport industry. After all, the achievement of a quantified objective would be easier to measure.

Secondly, the executive body for the policy was vague. Except for Fujian, Shanghai and Guangxi, the local implementations for all the remaining 14 provinces and cities lacked a clear statement of the specific assignments allocated to the policy executors. Meanwhile, the indistinct expressions of the executive body such as all levels of government or all relevant departments caused confusion in the executive body of the policy. Without a clear executive body, the effectiveness of the policy implementation would be jeopardized, and also no one would be responsible for examining and auditing whether or not the objectives had been achieved. Moreover, during the development of the local sport industry, the relationship between different policy executors, the consequences to undertake the due obligations and how to determine the levels of obligations were not specified in the local implementation, and so the various departments would inevitably confront or come into conflict with each other.

Thirdly, the policy measures remained ambiguous. Realization of the objectives needed to be supported by the policy measures, which referred to the means by which to guarantee the execution of the local implementation. The policy measures were the practical operating methods by which to apply the particular policy. In the local implementation, the design of the policy measures which aimed to accelerate the development of the sport industry was flawed. Most of the local implementations did mention either the tax preferences, financial support or land concessions, however they still left to one side further specifications such as the standard of the preferential policy, the business scope to enjoy the preferential policies and the share of the supportive financial investment. The generalization of those measures was hard to avoid thus provoking an ineffective outcome. As a result the policy execution was cursory and the effect of government support in developing the sport industry barely noticeable. The policy's ambiguous measures also confused the practical policy executors.

ACTION LEARNING

- From the perspective of public policy analysis, discuss the reasons why professional sport develops slowly in some less economically developed countries, such as China, India and South Africa, and suggest recommendations for each country correspondingly.

- Identify and summarize the sport-related tax policy in the UK (or other country), and discuss how this may be relevant to less economically developed countries.
- Choose a sport policy for another country and compare its aims and objectives with those of China.

CONCLUSION

Within the general context of China's economic transition, social transformation, cultural restructuring and strengthening of the functions of the government's public services, the issue of how to regulate both the Chinese sport industry and its policy is one of great urgency. At present, the policy on the Chinese sport industry has notable limitations, including an unbalanced structure, monolithic measures and a poor running mechanism, and so the Chinese sport industry can barely develop an effective operating environment characterized as 'government dominant, market allocation-oriented, social organizations participating in and public benefiting from'.

In order to achieve legalization, marketization and democratization, and publicize the pluralism in the Chinese sport industry, the country has to respond wisely (Yi, 2011). After all, its sport industry is still in its infant stage and the execution of the policy tools will inevitably experience a process of experimenting and test running. This trial process will certainly provide valuable references and experiences for the development of sports industries in the global developing countries.

REFERENCES

Bloyce, D. & Smith, A. (2010) *Sport Policy and Development: An Introduction*. London: Routledge.

CPG (2010) Guidance for accelerating the development of the sports industry. Available at: www.gov.cn/zwgk/2010-03/24/content_1563447.htm (last accessed 19 September 2015)

Dunn, W.N. (2009) *Public Policy Analysis: An Introduction*. New York: Longman.

Houlihan, B. (1997) *Sport, Policy, and Politics: A Comparative Analysis*. New York: Psychology Press.

Houlihan, B. & White, A. (2002) *The Politics of Sports Development: Development of Sport or Development through Sport?* London: Routledge.

Houlihan, B. & White, A. (2013) *Politics of Sports Development*. London: Routledge.

Hoye, R., Nicholson, M. & Houlihan, B. (2010) *Sport and Policy*. Oxford: Elsevier Butterworth-Heinemann.

Nicholson, M., Hoye, R. & Houlihan, B. (eds) (2011) *Participation in Sport: International Policy Perspectives*. London: Routledge.

Stewart, B., Nicholson, M., Smith, A. & Westerbeek, H. (2004) *Australian Sport: Better by Design? The Evolution of Australian Sport Policy*. London: Routledge.

Weimer, D. & Vining, A. (2005) *Policy Analysis: Concepts and Practice* (4th edn). Upper Saddle River, NJ: Pearson/Prentice-Hall.

Xu, G.Q. (2009) *Olympic Dreams: China and Sports, 1895–2008*. Harvard, CT: Harvard University Press.

Yi, J.D. (2011) Logical bases and value orientation of sport system reform in China. *Journal of Physical Education*, 11(1): 14–25.

USEFUL WEBSITES

General Administration of Sport of the People's Republic of China
www.sport.gov.cn

Hupu Sports Fans Online Club
www.hupu.com

National Bureau of Statistics of the People's Republic of China
www.stats.gov.cn

14

MEGA SPORT EVENTS

KAMILLA SWART

 What did the World Cup do for you, Bafana? In two or 10, or even 20 years' time a visitor to South Africa might turn to a football fan and ask: 'So, what did that 2010 World Cup do for you' Seattlepi?

(www.seattlepi.com/sports/article/What-did-the-World-Cup-do-for-you-Bafana-5199079.php)

One year on, what legacy has the London Olympic Games left us?

That the 2012 Olympics were a success is not in doubt. But will the £8.7bn that was spent on them deliver the legacy that was promised – and in particular, are we any fitter or healthier?

(*Guardian,* www.theguardian.com/uk-news/2013/jul/26/one-year-on-olympic-legacy)

Homophobia: defy Putin with a same-sex kiss at Sochi.

The Olympics in Russia is an opportunity for gay rights to be promoted and pressure should be put on African leaders.

(*Guardian*, www.theguardian.com/commentisfree/2014/feb/01/ homophobia-putin-sex-kiss-sochi-olympics-russia-gay-rights)

LEARNING OUTCOMES

Upon completion of this chapter, students will be able to:

- Appreciate the **politics** of mega sport event bidding.

- Understand the different phases of a mega sport event lifecycle.

- Identify the key issues and impacts of hosting mega sport events on host destinations.

- Understand the challenges associated with assessing mega sport events and maximizing positive legacies.

INTRODUCTION

The bidding for and hosting of mega sport events take place in a highly contested arena, with an increasing number of cities and countries competing against each other for the rights to host events such as the Olympic Games, the FIFA World Cup and the Commonwealth Games. The forces of **globalization** have brought mega sporting events to many different nations. In recent years we have witnessed more developing and emerging destinations being awarded these mega events, such as the Beijing 2008 Olympic Games, the 2010 FIFA World Cup in South Africa, the 2014 World Cup in Brazil, the 2016 Olympic Games in Rio de Janeiro, and the 2018 and 2022 FIFA World Cups in Russia and Qatar, respectively.

Mega sport events have significant popular appeal and are associated with huge attendance figures at the actual event as well as a vast television viewership; hence **sponsorship** is a key source of **funding** for hosts of the Games. These mega events have also grown in attractiveness due to their purported ability to stimulate socio-**economic** development and boost the profile of host destinations. Yet there is much debate about the impacts and legacies of these events, and whether the significant resources required to bid for and host these are justified.

Given the prestige of these mega events, cities and countries will continue to bid for the right to host them, and therefore it is important to consider the complexity of bidding for, planning and staging mega events.

South Africa's Failed Bid for the 2006 FIFA World Cup

South Africa failed in its bid to host the 2006 Football World Cup, losing to Germany by a single vote. President Thabo Mbeki has described the result as a setback in Africa's efforts to gain international sporting recognition. A successful bid by South Africa would have made it the first African nation to host soccer's top international tournament, and it had been widely tipped to succeed. A vote for South Africa was seen as a vote for Africa – which has never hosted a World Cup tournament before, despite exporting some of the world's finest soccer players to Europe and other parts of the world – as well as a vote for developing countries. Many argued that it was time to break the stranglehold that countries in Europe have had on the World Cup. Mr Blatter was elected to the FIFA presidency on a wave of African votes, promising to deliver the World Cup to the continent for the first time.

Source: Why South Africa's bid failed, BBC Sport, 6 July, http://news.bbc.co.uk/sport2/hi/in_depth/2000/2006_world_cup_decision/821888.stm

TOOLS FOR ANALYSIS

Mega sport events are highly political affairs and often influenced by geo-political decision making. They have played a significant socio-political role in post-apartheid South Africa. Such events are regarded as platforms to support governments' nation-building initiatives and at the same time to signal international recognition. Colonial and neo-colonial ties have shaped and continue to affect where these events are hosted. The developed world has dominated the hosting of mega sport events and only recently did Africa host the 2010 FIFA World Cup, and it has yet to host an Olympics Games (after a failed attempt for the 2004 Games). Developing countries use mega events as a way of compensating for their lack of resources, power and influence in the international sphere and so the increased proliferation of developing countries hosting these events is not surprising. A unique feature of the South African bids is its desire to promote South Africa as an African country. The slogan for the 2006 bid was 'It's Africa's turn' and the pan-African notions featured prominently in the 2010 campaign as well as the failed bid for the 2004 Olympic Games.

South Africa lost the awarding of the 2006 FIFA World Cup by one vote due to one member, the President of the Oceania Football Confederation (OCF), controversially abstaining from the last round of voting. He claimed that he was threatened by 'influential European interests' if he voted for South Africa and ignored the OCF decision to vote for South Africa. After South Africa's loss in this manner, FIFA introduced a rotation system whereby only countries on the African continent could bid for the 2010 World Cup and South America for 2014. However, FIFA raised concerns about this system after only one country, Brazil, bid for the 2014 World Cup.

South Africa's 2010 FIFA World Cup was deemed a success from the perspective that the infrastructure required was ready, the concerns regarding safety and security during the event were largely unfounded and perceptions of African pessimism were altered, and this has perhaps inspired other developing countries to also bid for mega sport events. More developed countries assert that it will be more challenging for them to succeed in the future and therefore bidding may be a waste of resources.

As a sport manager it is necessary to be cognizant of the geopolitical context in which mega sport event bidding and hosting take place. It is also important to understand that both the International Sport Federations (ISFs) as well as the governments of host destinations have particular motives for bidding and hosting mega sport events and sometimes (or perhaps often) these are not aligned. Sporting mega events, particularly in the bidding phase, are entwined with a country's **politics**.

ACTION LEARNING

- Would South Africa have been successful in winning the right to host the 2010 FIFA World Cup bid if FIFA had not changed to a continental rotation system? Were there any other factors in South Africa's favour?
- With FIFA's resolve to open up football to new markets, what case can be made for northern European counties to bid

again given England's losing to Russia the hosting of the 2018 FIFA World Cup?
- The Olympic Games have also been rocked by voting scandals in recent years. What steps has the International Olympic Committee (IOC) taken to reduce corruption and bribery with respect to voting to award the Games?

THINKING POINT 14.2

From Bid Committee to Organizing Committee

The Tokyo 2020 Bid Committee was established in September 2011 as a 'specified non-profit corporation' to promote

Tokyo's bid to host the 2020 Olympic and Paralympic Games. The Tokyo 2020 Bid Committee, along with the Tokyo Metropolitan Government (TMG) and the Japanese Olympic Committee (JOC), have assumed the primary roles in Tokyo's bid to host the 2020 Games. The Committee is authorized to represent the city of Tokyo concerning its bid activities.

The Tokyo 2020 Games vision is fully aligned with Tokyo Vision 2020, the new long-term urban strategy for the TMG. Indeed, Tokyo Vision 2020 is a 2020 bid-inspired extension of 'Tokyo's Big Change: the 10-Year Plan', which was developed for the 2016 bid. Tokyo was awarded the right to host the Games in 2013.

In order to ensure smooth cooperation between the various public and private authorities and organizations involved in planning and delivering the Games, committees with direct and strong working links will be established, including a 'Venue Committee', a 'Transport Committee' and a 'Security Committee'. TMG will create the 'Bureau of Olympic and Paralympic Games', as the main contact point for the Tokyo Organizing Committee of the Games (TOCOG), which will be in charge of coordinating all TMG-related work to deliver the Games, including developing TMG-owned sporting venues and coordinating the development of the Olympic village. In addition, the TMG will develop most of the transport infrastructure and related facilities for the Games in accordance with the 'Tokyo Vision 2020' urban strategy.

(Source: Tokyo 2010 Candidature File Volume 1, http://tokyo2020.jp/en/plan/candi dature/dl/tokyo2020_candidate_entire_1_ enfr.pdf)

TOOLS FOR ANALYSIS

The hosting of mega sport events takes years of preparation and planning. The lifecycle of a mega event includes the bidding phase, event implementation and post-event phases (Emery, 2003). The official bidding phase takes place nine years before hosting, however consideration for the feasibility of bidding can take two to three years prior to submitting the bid book. The Olympic Games are generally considered as a benchmark for other mega sport events (Pomfret et al., 2009) and are thus used here as a case study. Given that the bidding for a mega sport event such as the Olympic Games is such a high risk and requires considerable resources, the IOC has reduced the risk by introducing a two-phased bidding system whereby cities respond to an IOC questionnaire as part of the Applicant City during Phase 1 (Swart et al., 2013). Phase 1 is known as the Candidature Acceptance Procedure and centres on undertaking a technical review and the cities' ability to host the Olympics (IOC, 2013a). For the 2020 Games, Baku (Azerbaijan), Doha (Qatar), Istanbul (Turkey), Madrid (Spain), Rome (Italy) and Tokyo (Japan) expressed their interest as Applicant Cities.

The Candidature Procedure is Phase 2 of the bidding process and concentrates on Games' operational matters (IOC, 2013b). Candidate Cities that were short-listed to advance to this Phase for the 2020 Games were Madrid, Turkey and Tokyo. Candidate Cities are requested to submit their Candidature File – which is an in-depth description of their Olympic project and consists of 17 themes ranging from the vision to legal aspects, finance, and the sport and venues, amongst others. Detailed planning takes place in earnest and the Candidature Files essentially represent the Master Plan for organizing the Games (Westerbeek et al., 2006). It underscores the complexity of a mega sport event and requires a strong overall organizational structure that enables close working relationships with the numerous national and local government departments and other stakeholders. Critical path analysis for achieving milestones, detailed planning schedules and clear roles and responsibilities are essential for the timely delivery of a successful Games.

A technical assessment is made by the IOC Evaluation Commission following briefings with the Bid Committee and site visits to the proposed venues (IOC, 2013c). The Commission releases its report one month before the election of the Host City by the IOC members. The success of bidding for a mega sport event is influenced by both the objective (i.e. a technically competent bid) and subjective (i.e. geopolitical support for the bid). Westerbeek et al. (2002) identified the following eight key success factors for bidding: accountability, political support, relationship marketing, ability, infrastructure, bid team composition, **communication** and exposure, and existing facilities. Furthermore, communication throughout the bid process and to internal and external stakeholders is critical to successful bidding (Swart et al., 2013).

Once the right to host a mega sport event has been won, the event implementation phase commences. This phase takes seven years and starts with foundational planning, followed by operational planning whereby the detailed plans for Games' operation evolve about five and a half years prior to the Games and operational readiness planning whereby the host city/ country achieves full preparedness three and a half years prior to hosting the Games (Swart et al., 2013). During this phase the host city/country hosts a series of test events to test operational management systems so as to monitor performance in relation to the plans. The actual hosting of the Games (over two and a half weeks) and transition to the Paralympics are relatively short in comparison to the time required for planning. However, this is the most critical part of the event implementation phase. Anything that goes wrong in this phase can wipe out years of planning and significantly undermine the objectives that the host city/country wanted to achieve by hosting a mega sport event in the first place.

During the post-event phase the organization structure of the organizing committee is dissolved and close-out and evaluation reports are prepared. During this phase lessons learnt are also captured. In recent years, legacy has become more integrated into the bidding, planning and delivering of mega sport events. Legacy is generally viewed as the long-lasting benefits of a host destination after the completion of the event and can be planned or unplanned and has tangible and intangible aspects. The Olympic Games have been at the forefront of legacy planning through their Olympic Games Knowledge Management Platform (OGKM) (IOC, 2013d), but other mega sport events are also taking up the challenge. For example, FIFA has initiated environmental programmes such as Green Goal, and has set up Legacy Trusts in South Africa and Brazil to support social development projects. The Glasgow bid for the 2014 Commonwealth Games was won in 2007 and in 2009 the Scottish Government started putting legacy strategies in place focusing on four national themes (Morrison, 2013). These themes included flourishing (enhance the growth of the Scottish economy), active (become more active citizens), connected (strengthen learning and culture at home and internationally) and sustainable (demonstrate environmental responsibility) (Morrison, 2013). While legacy planning is laudable it is often the case that the positive impacts on host communities and destinations are often not realized (this will be explored further in the rest of the chapter).

ACTION LEARNING

- Review the recent bidding process for the FIFA World Cup. What are the similarities and differences in this process compared to that for the Olympic Games?
- Review the Candidature File of the failed Istanbul bid for the 2020 Olympics and analyse their Master Plan in relation to Tokyo's offering for 2020.
- Legacy can mean very different things to different people. What do you think have been the legacies of the London 2012 Olympic Games?

CASE STUDY 14.1

Costs and Benefits of Hosting Mega Sport Events – An Under-utilized Cape Town Stadium But a Thriving Urban Park, Albeit at a Cost

Sail Stadefrance, the management company appointed to operate Cape Town's R4 billion World Cup stadium, walked out on a 30-year lease to manage the property in October 2010. Sail Stadefrance had projected 'substantial losses' if it took up the project as the maintenance costs were way above expectations. It was estimated that the operational and maintenance costs, including management of the adjacent Green Point Park, were around R46.5 million a year. Other factors which led to this decision included the failure to secure an anchor tenant and 'business constraints' as the land was not commercially zoned.

The City argued that they had no choice but to build its World Cup stadium in Green Point as cheaper sites at Athlone and Newlands were 'not suitable' for FIFA. The City had been in ongoing discussions with Western Province Rugby about whether it would move from Newlands and host its games at the Cape Town Stadium. One of Western Province Rugby's main concerns about the Stadium had been its lack of corporate suites. The City has over-management of the Stadium until it can find a feasible way forward.

The stadium is situated on the 85-ha Green Point Common. Green Point Common is a significant open space in the heart of Cape Town, and before the construction of the stadium, the area had been used for various sporting and community facilities for more than a century.

The construction of the new stadium necessitated the reconfiguration of Green Point Common, which allowed for the creation of a new 12.5 ha public park, the Green Point Park, on the western edge of the Common, which was designed according to ecological principles. A biodiversity garden showcased the indigenous vegetation of the region, while spring water diverted from the slopes of Table Mountain was stored in ponds and wetlands to replace potable water for irrigation. A hydroturbine generated electricity from the spring water supply. Future developments planned for the park include a Smart Living Centre to promote sustainable living in an urban environment, an indigenous nursery, a horticultural training centre and weekend fresh-food markets. Waste separation at source and recycling is promoted. The park was officially opened to the public on 9 February 2011.

(Sources: www.iol.co.za/news/south-africa/western-cape/what-now-for-cape-town-stadium-1.684199#.U2C3dSgVrFl

2010 FIFA World Cup™ Host City Cape Town Green Goal Legacy Report. www.capetown.gov.za/en/GreenGoal/Documents/Green_Goal_Legacy_Report %20final.pdf)

TOOLS FOR ANALYSIS

It is widely accepted that mega sport events are associated with a range of positive and negative impacts, including economic, socio-cultural, environmental and political impacts, amongst others. The economic impacts have received the most attention but a more balanced approach to assessing mega event impact has emerged in recent years. It is also important to note that many of the impacts are inter-related and can often have concurrent impacts. For example, tourism impacts are strongly linked to economic impacts as well as media impacts. On the one hand, a destination would like to enhance visitor numbers to the mega sport event to generate a positive economic impact, and often (due to demand) airline and accommodation prices sky-rocket just prior to the event, causing negative perceptions of the destination, which could have more long-term negative consequences.

Positive economic impacts are generally concerned with infrastructural upgrades, urban regeneration, increases in government tax revenues and tourism inflows, while negative economic impacts include price inflation, the misuse of public funds and tourism displacement. Positive socio-cultural impacts are often linked to 'feel-good' effects such as national pride and social cohesion but these feelings are often short-lived. Other positive social impacts include skills development, volunteerism and enhanced participation in sport. However, mega events are also associated with more negative social impacts, such as disruption to the lives of local residents, increases in crime and terrorism, prostitution and drug-peddling, and other social ills.

Greening mega events have become more important in recent years in order to raise the environmental awareness of both residents and visitors and to act as a catalyst for environmental restoration. However, mega sport events are also associated with negative environmental impacts such as noise and air pollution and environmental degradation.

The enhanced capacity and human capital to bid for and host mega events fall within the ambit of positive political impacts. Other positive political impacts include strengthening regional cooperation and international positioning. However, negative political impacts can include the damaging media coverage a host destination can receive in the lead-up to a mega sport event. Brazil is a case in point whereby social protests were staged and increased during the 2013 Confederations Cup, thus raising safety and security concerns for the main competition in 2014.

Concerns regarding the potential of mega sport events to contribute to sustainable development and mitigate against negative economic, social and environmental impacts are even more heightened for developing countries, given the deep social and economic disparities, significant infrastructural deficits and environmental problems that are not comparable to their more developed counterparts (Konrad Adenauer Stiftung, 2011). In addition various factors influence the cost–benefit ratio of mega sport events and include the following:

- The financing model.
- The quality of the planning and implementation process for investments.
- The economic, social and environmental impacts.
- The potential contributions of the legacy to the development goals of the host destination.
- The successful mitigation of possible negative environmental effects.

Often large amounts of public funds are invested in these mega sport events and the ISFs such as FIFA and IOC will require a financial guarantee to ensure their success: this is usually provided by government. In addition, the projections to host these mega events are generally under-estimated. Opportunity costs associated with the hosting of mega sport events are especially contested in developing nations although it is difficult to assess the counterfactual. Critics of mega sport events argue that public money can be better spent on education, housing and health as opposed to sport infrastructure. Detractors further contend that the benefits are not equally distributed, often creating further inequalities and social exclusion.

The location of the Cape Town Stadium was highly contested, with Newland Rugby Stadium identified as the quarter final venue in the Bid Book. The City of Cape Town preferred Athlone Stadium due to the socio-economic development opportunities it presented in a disadvantaged area. However, when FIFA conducted a site inspection their preference was for Green Point, a wealthy suburb situated next to the Waterfront, which is the most popular tourist attraction in South Africa, as it was an ideal location to profile the city. Construction delays were heightened due to staged protests and initiated court actions to prevent the City from building the stadium in Green Point (CoCT, 2008). The objections centred around traffic congestion and disruption, noise, the attraction of anti-social elements, the impact on property values and increasing rates bills, cost overruns and escalations, as well as the sustainability of the stadium (CoCT, 2008). Although the stadium remains under-utilized it has resulted in the redevelopment of 80 ha of the Green Point Common into a thriving urban park.

The economic and social contestations of mega events have heightened in many countries and in some referenda are being held to ascertain public opinion about these events. For example, Munich residents opposed a future Winter Olympic Games in 2022 by 52% and the plan was rejected in all four areas where the polls were held (Mackay, 2013). It is therefore not surprising that the debates about mega sport event impacts have moved from more short-term impacts to the longer-term impacts or legacies. Gratton and Preuss (2008) argue that one the reasons for this emphasis is to justify the public resources invested in mega events and that 'positive' legacies maintain the interest of cities wanting to bid for mega sport events. However, there are very few studies that have attempted to measure the long-term impacts, with the Manchester 2002 Commonwealth Games and the 1992 Barcelona Olympic Games providing some ad hoc evidence (Gratton and Preuss, 2008). Gratton and Preuss argue that the IOC's OGGI (Olympic Games Global Impact) study project will enhance the evidence base, but one limitation of this study is that it only assesses impacts two years after the event has been held, whereas it takes 15 to 20 years to measure the true legacy of a mega sport event. Attempts to assess impacts beyond the OGGI project were undertaken in relation to the London Olympic Games, whereby the Department of Culture, Media and Sport conducted a meta-evaluation of the Games (Wilkinson, 2013). It remains to be seen, however, whether there will be the political will to assess legacy far beyond the Games.

Similarly, the Scottish Government has committed resources to evaluate the legacy of the 2014 Commonwealth Games. It has embarked on a 10-year, multi-method study, with 2008 as the baseline for this, and examines outcomes and impacts at the national, city and east-end of Glasgow (i.e. the immediate location) levels, with the final report due in 2019 (Morrison, 2013). Key research questions aligned to the four legacy themes are guiding the study in addition to cross-cutting questions, e.g. on partnership/ governance legacy. Interestingly, the GoEast community study is an ecological study tracking health, social and economic data in the area over the period of the legacy study, and importantly will allow the government to assess whether there was a 'Games effect' as comparative data are also being collected and analysed for four other similar regeneration areas (Morrison, 2013).

ACTION LEARNING

- Research what were the most contentious issues for residents in hosting the FIFA World Cup in Germany in 2006 and how that compares with the experiences in Brazil in relation to hosting both the World Cup in 2014 and the Olympic Games in 2016.
- Assess the bid documents for a few mega events and analyse to what extent legacy planning featured in the respective bids over time.
- As the research manager for your bid to host a mega sport event, outline what steps you would take to put together a research plan to assess the legacy of that particular mega event.

CONCLUSION

This chapter underscored the geopolitical nature of bidding and hosting mega events, which adds to the complexity of bidding, planning and hosting these. Consideration needs to be given to the multitude of stakeholders involved and the collaborative efforts that are required for effective partnership. It is important to recognize that the vision for the bid should be guided and embedded in the broader developmental agendas of host cities and nations. Equally important stakeholders need to be cognizant of the challenges in meeting the objectives of the ISFs versus those of the host nation.

Mega sport events take years of preparation and planning, and the lifecycle of a such an event is around 10 years, including the bid, implementation and post-event stages. Communication with internal and external stakeholders at all phases of the mega event is critical to the successful delivery of a mega sport event.

Such events have a range of impacts that can have detrimental consequences for host nations and communities years after. Thus the importance of understanding and assessing their impacts, particularly in relation to legacy, is recognized. While the allure of hosting mega sport events will continue, there is growing public concern about the opportunity costs of these events in both developed and developing contexts. While many host destinations have put plans in place to measure the short-term impacts, legacy impacts need to be examined in the long term and resources need to be committed to these studies, especially to inform future bidding processes and to provide lessons for leveraging benefits and minimizing the costs associated with bidding and hosting future mega sport events.

REFERENCES

City of Cape Town (COCT) (2008) 2010 Fifa World Cup News: 2010 Stadium. Available at: www.capetown.gov.za/en/2010/news/Documents/Archives/2010_stadium.htm (last accessed 19 september 2015).

Emery, P.R. (2003) Sport event management. In L. Trenberth (ed.), *Managing the Business of Sport*. Wellington, New Zealand: Dunmore.

Gratton, P. & Preuss, H. (2008) Maximising Olympic impacts by building up legacies. *International Journal of the History of Sport*, 25(14): 1922–38.

IOC (2013a) Six applicant cities for the 2020 Olympic Games. Available at: www.olympic.org/news/six-applicant-cities-for-the-2020-olympic-games/138220 (last accessed 19 september 2015).

IOC (2013b) 2020 Candidate Cities to present to IOC members. Available at: www.olympic.org/news/2020-candidate-cities-present-to-ioc-members/202184 (last accessed 19 september 2015).

IOC (2013c) Evaluation Commission. Available at: www.olympic.org/evaluation-commission (last accessed 19 september 2015).

IOC (2013d) Factsheet Legacies of the Games. Available at: www.olympic.org/Documents/Reference_documents_Factsheets/Legacy.pdf (last accessed 19 september 2015).

Konrad Adenauer Stiftung (2011) Sustainable mega-events in developing countries. Experiences and insights from host cities in South Africa, India and Brazil. Print communications: Johannesburg.

Mackay, D. (2013) Munich citizens vote against bid for 2022 Winter Olympics and Paralympics. Available at: www.insidethegames.biz/olympics/winter-olympics/2022/1016892-munich-citizens-against-bid-for-2022-winter-olympics-and-paralympics (last accessed 19 september 2015).

Morrison, A. (2013) Commonwealth Games 2014 legacy evaluation. Presented at Carnival Launch. London, 31 January 2014.

Pomfret, R., Wilson, J.K. & Lobmayr, B. (2009) Bidding for sport mega-events. Paper presented to the First European Conference in Sport Economics at the University of Paris held on 6–8 August 2009.

Swart, K., Bob, U. & Turco, D. (2013) Bidding for major international sporting events. In M. Ben Sulayem, S. O' Connor & D. Hassan (eds), *Sport Management in the Middle East*. Abingdon: Routledge.

Westerbeek, H., Smith, A., Turner, P. & Ingerson, L. (2002) Key success factors in bidding for hallmark sport events. *International Marketing Review*, 19(3): 303–32.

Westerbeek, H., Smith, A., Turner, P., Emery, P., Green, C. & van Leeuwen, L. (2006) *Managing Sport Facilities and Major Events.* London: Routledge.

Wilkinson, A. (2013) London 2012 meta-evaluation. Department of Culture, Media and Sport, London. Available at: www.gov.uk/government/collections/london-2012-meta-evaluation (last accessed 19 September 2015).

USEFUL WEBSITES

Federation Internationale de Football Association
www.fifa.com

Glasgow 2014 Commonwealth Games
www.glasgow2014.com

Olympic Studies Centre
www.olympic.org/olympic-studies-centre

The Scottish Government assessing legacy 2
www.scotland.gov.uk/AssessingLegacy2014

UK Department of Culture, Media and Sport
www.gov.uk/government/organizations/department-for-culture-media-sport

15

SPORT PARTICIPATION

JASON BOCARRO
AND MICHAEL EDWARDS

Sport England: Participation down by 200,000, says survey.

(www.bbc.co.uk/sport/0/22806853)

Big Price Tags Attached to Even the Littlest Leagues.

(www.nytimes.com/2012/04/24/sports/big-price-tags-attached-to-even-the-littlest-leagues.html?pagewanted=all&_r=0)

Pros and cons: Even the Europeans say the American model of youth sports is ideal for the development of elite athletes.

(http://blog.pennlive.com/patriotnewssports/2011/04/pros_and_cons_even_the_europea.html)

LEARNING OUTCOMES

Upon completion of this chapter, students will be able to:

- Discuss the history and development of the increased interest in sport participation and the reasons behind the increased interest.

- Understand some basic data and trends regarding sport participation and demographic characteristics.

- Critically discuss the implications of current trends in participation and the implications for sport managers.

INTRODUCTION

People have participated in sport in nearly every civilization since ancient times. In ancient Greece, male members of the ruling class were encouraged to participate in "warrior sports" such as wrestling, boxing, foot racing and archery as part of religious rituals (Guttman, 1978). As victories in ancient Olympic games became associated with glory for city-states, athletes became more specialized and even professional (Coakley, 2014). Medieval Europe saw a distinct separation in sport participation by social class. Peasants participated in folk games that were often violent in nature (e.g. bear baiting) as well as occupational sports (i.e. sports that replicated activities used in work life) and ball games (Dunning, 1999). Peasant sports were encouraged by the nobility to prevent social unrest. The upper classes benefited from access to specialized sporting equipment and facilities that led to the development of early club and racquet sports. Ownership of horses also allowed the nobility to participate in hunting. Tournaments featuring war-like games were popular among the nobility (Coakley, 2014).

During the Protestant Reformation, sport participation among peasants declined considerably. Puritan leaders were highly influential in political and social life and saw sport as an indulgence that distracted from work and prayer (Struna, 1977). During the Enlightenment, sport participation underwent a revival as physical activity and sport came to be seen as a more positive way to use leisure time. Throughout this time, and parallel to contemporary philosophies, results became more important and participation among all classes became more acceptable (Coakley, 2014).

Much of the promotion of modern sport participation developed from the Muscular Christianity movement that emerged in Protestant Britain in the mid-1800s and during the Industrial Revolution. This era also reintroduced the utilitarian purposes of sport participation seen in ancient times. Proponents of Muscular Christianity believed sport, particularly team sports, was an ideal activity for boys to develop Victorian Christian virtues of manliness, loyalty, patriotism and physical strength (Putney, 2001). During this period, industrialization brought many people into cities and required specific spaces and programs to be developed for sport. Sports became more highly organized and rules became codified.

Since the industrial era, sport participation has been influenced by several significant societal trends. First, the globalization of women's rights movements since the 1970s has increased female sport participation exponentially.

Second, parents and organizations interested in child and youth development have increasingly seen sport as a mechanism for providing positive cognitive, physical and social outcomes. Third, international health promotion has led to the encouragement of participation in sport to increase levels of physical activity. Fourth, the global influence of corporations and media has encouraged mass international participation in some sports (e.g. Olympic sports, basketball and football) in developing countries. Finally, social media and the growth of equipment manufacturers and tailored events have provided new opportunities for the consumption of specialized sport equipment and experiences, as well as the adoption of specific sport lifestyles in many affluent western countries (e.g. runners, cyclists or snowboarders).

Therefore, as we have seen, sport participation is heavily influenced by societal constructions of the value of sport. This process is often officially facilitated directly through governmental policy and funding. Governments historically supported and encouraged sport participation for a variety of reasons, including social control of the lower classes, to encourage specific social values and promote national pride. For example, sport participation was heavily encouraged by the Ancient Greek and Roman governments, who provided legal holidays for games and compensation to victorious athletes. Today, many countries have ministries of sport that promote national participation in sport and support organized sport programs. It is important to remember that not all sport participation is equally supported financially or promoted by governments. Elite sports that have higher levels of media attention and international prestige are more likely to be sponsored by national governments. The needs of elite, competitive sports and athletes are generally more highly prioritized than more informal recreational sports. This also means that in developing countries, participation in native or traditional sports may be less encouraged at higher levels of government than organized sports historically associated with wealthier nations in North America and Europe (Coakley, 2014).

Sport managers should be aware that sport participation is associated with a myriad of community and individual benefits. These include psychological and emotional development (Fraser-Thomas et al., 2005), engaged citizenship (Elley and Kirk, 2002), improved self-esteem and decreased stress (National Center for Education Statistics, 2005), friendship and less social isolation (Barber et al., 2001), short- and long-term fitness (Barnett et al., 2008), economic development (Crompton, 2009) and social capital (Nicholson and Hoye, 2008). The inherent benefits behind sport resulted in the United Nations Educational, Scientific and Cultural Organization (UNESCO) recognizing the right of children and young people to participate and enjoy their involvement in sport.

Thus, tracking sport participation has become a key component of a sport manager's job. Despite inherent challenges and controversies in monitoring sport participation, government, non-profit and private entities have all spent increasing time and resources identifying which sports are popular among different segments of the population.

Increasing Sport Participation Among the Broader Population

The Department of Culture, Media, and Sport and Sport England seeks to collaborate with other governmental European sport entities to develop some policies and strategies to increase broad-based sport participation. The overarching goal is to develop a strategic plan to increase broad-based sport participation as well as strategies related to how sport will be funded, what sports will be funded and how to engage more people in sport, particularly under-represented groups. Sport administrators from various levels will engage in conversations about the future of sport at all levels.

Sport participation generally occurs across three dimensions: youth sport, community sport and elite sport. *Youth sport* generally occurs through physical education, school sport, community sport clubs or recreation (leisure) departments. *Community sport* occurs in multiple types of informal and formal settings, including public parks, non-governmental organizations and commercial recreation centers. *Elite sport* is generally situated in sport clubs and sport-specific developmental programs, but is part of the educational system in the United States. Elite sport is generally focused on developing athletes to compete at the highest national and international levels. Sport participation is often seen as an important mechanism to promote population health. Nations often seek ways to improve public health as a way of reducing government-funded health costs (Coakley, 2014). Finally, sport participation often provides social connections among community members (Nicholson and Hoye, 2008).

Participation in different sports fluctuates as new sports emerge (e.g. some action sports) or gain popularity, while others are perceived as unpopular, too expensive or inaccessible. However, for sport managers the consequences for low participation can have significant consequences. For example, in the UK, low participation rates in football (soccer) and tennis may impact the future public funding that both tennis and football governing bodies receive (Hart, 2013). Sport managers working within these governing bodies realize the long-term impact that increasing or declining participation will have on their sports. This includes the development of world class athletes representing their country, funding through membership fees and sales of athletic equipment associated with the sport, as well as public advocacy. Thus, understanding the reasons why certain demographic groups are more or less predisposed to participate in sport is critical for governing bodies as they develop new initiatives and long-term strategic plans.

TOOLS FOR ANALYSIS

Because of the suggested importance of sport participation and the encouragement of sport participation among governmental and non-governmental agencies, we often seek to understand the rate at which people worldwide participate in sport. What are the interests in participating in particular sports? Have efforts by governments to promote sport participation been successful? What resources may be needed in the future to accommodate sport participation? These questions are particularly important due to the substantial investments many countries and organizations make in promoting sport participation.

Results from global participation surveys indicate that sport participation in European nations is highest among the Nordic countries (e.g. Sweden, Finland and Norway) and lowest in Mediterranean countries (e.g. Italy, Spain and Greece). These results seemed to be confirmed by the 2009 Eurobarometer Survey on Sport and Physical Activity (European Commission, 2010). Conversely, recent data indicated that new EU members in Eastern Europe had lower levels of sport participation. The results of the Eurobarometer survey are presented in Figure 15.1.

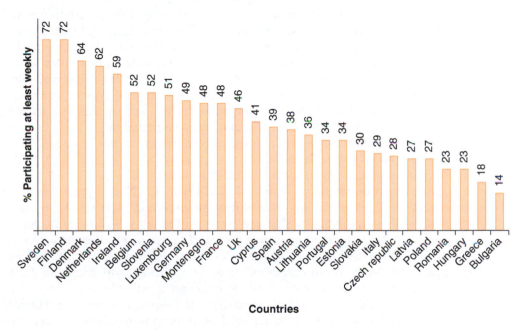

FIGURE 15.1 *Sport participation in EU Member States—2009*

Sport participation rates in the USA, Canada and Australia tend to be similar to those in the UK. In the early 2000s, 60% of Australians and 65% of Americans participated in sport at least once per year (Veal, 2005; Woods, 2011). In Canada, 43.1% of men and 25.8% of women participated "regularly" in sports according to the 2000 National Population Health Survey (Zuzanek, 2005). Less is known about sport participation rates in Asia or in developing countries. One national survey of Japan indicated the rate of sport participation among adults to be 59% (Watanabe et al., 2010). Participation data from India suggest a very different story, that only 1% of the population participate in sport (Mukherjee et al., 2010).

According to survey results, swimming may have the highest participation of any sport. It is the most popular participatory sport in France, the Netherlands and the USA, and the second most popular in many other countries. When included in surveys, walking is often the most popular activity and is the most popular sport in Australia, Canada, Finland and the UK. Other popular sports include aerobics/fitness, cycling and running or jogging. Participation in these informal, casual sports far exceeds participation in team competitive sports. In the USA in 2003, over 96 million people aged six years or older participated in swimming while 35 million played basketball and 18 million played American football (SGMA, 2004). Similarly, participation in walking in the UK was 45% in 1996 compared to 5% for football. Thus, according to the data, team sport participation peaks during childhood and quickly drops off after age 12 (SGMA, 2012). Therefore, while spectatorship of team competitive sports has increased, participation in these sports has either been neutral or declining in recent decades.

Conversely, fitness sports such as yoga, boot camp training, triathlons and adventure racing are growing in popularity. For example, in 2011 there was a 93% increase in US frequent adventure racing participants (defined as participants competing more than 10 times per year) compared to similar figures from 2009 (SGMA, 2012). Analyzing trends related to these data will allow sport managers to more strategically devote resources to growth opportunities or address areas of sport participation decline (see the Action Learning below). However, an important aspect of national participation surveys is the fact that in most countries there is inequity in participation. Three key socio-demographic characteristics, age, gender and social economic status (SES), are related to inequity in sport participation rates.

Age: Sport participation usually declines with age. The physical effects of ageing often prevent many people from maintaining their sport participation, particularly in sports that put stress on the body. Additionally, people are less likely to take up new sports when they are older, preferring to continue participating in familiar activities. Thus, individuals who participate exclusively in sports in childhood or early adulthood which are harder to sustain as they age, are more likely to stop participating later in life.

Gender: Men are more likely to participate in sport than women. Much of sport's gender gap is due to traditional barriers to women's sport participation. Whether related to cultural views related to traditional masculine and feminine gender roles, or nascent medical understanding that led to beliefs that physical activity was harmful to females, women and girls were largely excluded from full participation in sport until the middle of the twentieth century. Women's rights movements and policy changes in many Western countries (e.g. the lifting of the Football Association's ban on women in 1971 and Title IX in the USA in 1972) gave rise to increased opportunities for women to participate in sports. However, their participation in sport still lags behind that of men. One reason may be that the international media attention and prestige afforded to men's sports continue to create disparities in the resources and promotion allocated to sports that are more appealing to women and girls. Another reason may be that in cultures with expectations of more traditional gender roles, women are socialized to view sport as inappropriate or have more requirements for domestic labor during leisure time.

Social Economic Status: Members of higher economic classes are more likely to participate in sports than members of lower economic strata. Economically disadvantaged populations are more likely to live in areas with less access to parks, sports centers, swimming pools and other facilities that support sport and physical activity. Additionally, sport participation often requires financial resources (e.g. for equipment, club membership fees or lessons) and discretionary leisure time that are often less available to disadvantaged populations. Finally, children and adolescents from more disadvantaged backgrounds are often more likely to be encouraged to play sports as a supposed means of economic mobility. Thus, they are more likely to play team sports, often with higher levels of physicality, which seem to offer more opportunities for professionalism. These sports usually require more equipment, organization and time commitment, and therefore are often harder to maintain into adulthood.

ACTION LEARNING

Examine the most recent data relating to a specific country's sport participation (e.g. the Sporting Good Manufacturing Association [USA], or Sport England [UK]).

- Identify three to five key trends that sport agencies and governing bodies need to consider over the next few years.
- Suggest some reasons why participation in specific sports has either increased, decreased or remained the same.

- Based on your trend analysis, if you were making decisions on funding sport in your nation, where would you invest?
- Finally, if you were leading an initiative to increase participation in a specific sport or sports, what recommendations would you make (consider factors such as changing demographics, equity issues and other trends)?

CASE STUDY 15.2

Accept or Reject the Re-structuring of a Community Youth Sports Program

The City of Raleigh's Department of Recreation and Parks soccer program (one aimed at providing summertime recreation for some 1200 youths and adolescents aged 8 to 13) is stirring up a storm. This storm centers around the philosophy and values held by the administrators of the program. The policy states, "the importance of winning should be *de-emphasized*. Instead, the stress should be on playing for the fun of it and each youngster should equally take part in the program." As a result of this philosophy, game scores are not published, there are no uniforms, and there are no awards for specific outcomes (MVP, league championships, etc.). Each team has an adult "mentor," whose job it is to make sure that everyone gets a game and no one gets hurt. The rule states that every member of the team must play at least 15 minutes of a 30-minute game.

The philosophy, however, has met with some strong adult opposition. One protesting parent states, "Since when is this de-emphasis on winning the American way of life?" To tell the youngsters it is not important to play with the intent to win, "is simply knocking out of them the one characteristic that we Americans pride ourselves on having." Another objection is the "everyone must play" philosophy. Would it not give the children the incentive to strive to "make the team on their own ability" rather than just be given a position because it is policy? One irate parent who wrote a letter to the editor of the *Evening Star* newspaper commented, "any boy or girl who enters competitive sports of any type should take the field with one basic principle: to win the game." He further stated, "I personally have no excuse for a good loser. If our youth are trained to just play the game, and forget about winning, what kind of industrialists, doctors, and professional men and women will they become when they reach adulthood?" A local businesswoman who was a former college athlete stated, "let's quit making sissies out of our kids. We should change the philosophy of this program. This is a tough, competitive world that we live in. It isn't too early for 8 to 13 year olds to learn how to win. It's time our kids learned that the way to survive is to learn to win, and there's no better way to learn than through sports."

Opponents of these views had their comments too. One mother stated, "boys and girls in the age 8 to 13 year old age bracket particularly are too young to engage in the mental and physical excitement of competitive sports. There are many more important things than winning a soccer game. The child's health, the instilling of good sportsmanship, the art of getting along with others, and of course the development of the child's physical well-being are important aspects of our recreation program. Let's make our children good citizens first, and competitive athletes second." Another father of a child in the league stated, "competition—that's what these kids will get when they start playing in high school and college. Not everyone will be good enough to make the high school team. This might be the only chance a lot of these kids ever get to play soccer. Why not give them the chance to experience the game, without the pressure of having to be good or having to beat the other team?"

It should also be noted that when asked, the kids who participated in the soccer overwhelmingly responded "it's fun" when asked what they thought of the leagues that they played in. One youth stated, "it's really fun … I like that we all get to play. Sitting on the bench isn't very fun, and besides, how can you get better if you never get the chance? Plus, even though our coaches don't keep score, we all know who really wins, anyway!"

TOOLS FOR ANALYSIS

One philosophy that highlights the value of a positive youth sport experience is the leisure repertoire theory (Iso-Ahola et al., 1994). An individual's leisure repertoire usually consists of activities which they participate in on a regular basis and do well. Therefore this theory suggests that individuals who develop a wider spectrum of activities during childhood are more likely to continue to participate in activities as they get older due to a broader leisure repertoire (and more activities to draw from). However, engaging children in the youth sport experience is not without its challenges. Both Coakley (1992) and Brustad (1996) found that children who perceive parental pressure are likely to experience competitive trait anxiety and sport burnout, resulting in their dropping out of sport at an early age. Furthermore, as national studies (e.g. Hedstrom and Gould, 2004) have found, not having an opportunity to participate and participating not being fun were two of the most prevalent reasons why 8–13 year olds gave up sport.

Applying this theory to youth sport one can see that an important predictor of life-long participation in sport does not appear to be the volume of sport involvement as a child but rather the number of different sports that young people are taught (Roberts and Brodie, 1992) and the positive experiences children have. As adults we become more conservative about our leisure lifestyle and tend to make leisure choices from our own repertoire of skilled activities (Roberts, 1999). Consequently, the greater the repertoire of choices, the more likely individuals will remain committed sports participants when moving from adolescence to adulthood.

ACTION LEARNING

- Should the city continue to restructure youth sports in the manner presented? Why or why not?
- Is there a case to be made for restructuring youth sports in this community? Do the people who are against such restructuring have a point?

- Is there a compromise proposal that might be made here? If you were to propose a compromise, what would your proposal look like?
- How might your decision impact long-term sport participation involvement?

CONCLUSION

There is a growing body of evidence that sport participation can deliver benefits across a wide range of public policy agendas (e.g. health and well-being, economic development, community development). However, for sport managers to capitalize on these wide-ranging benefits, it will be critically important to proactively think about the issues impacting on future sport participation. Below we summarize five key issues and trends.

Access and equity

As sport participation has become more "professionalized," the associated costs have resulted in less accessibility, particularly among already disadvantaged groups (Edwards and Casper, 2012). One area that has seen this occur is in youth sports. John Engh, the CEO of the National Alliance for Youth Sports in the USA, pointed out that in an era of reduced government budgets and the push to include children in organized sports at a younger age, the traditional grassroots sports leagues have virtually disappeared (Tanier, 2012). Furthermore, towns across America have focused resources on new sport venues designed exclusively to accommodate elite-level sport tournaments, making recreation settings designed to provide leisure time physical activity inaccessible to many local residents (Hyman, 2012). In England, the scarcity and increased value of public lands that has resulted in their sale to developers have grassroots sport organizations worried about a permanent loss of opportunity to participate in sport (Gray, 2011).

Sport across the lifespan

In 2011, the number of inactive Americans ages six and older increased to more than 68 million and the inactivity rate rose to almost 24% (SGMA, 2012). Similar trends related to inactivity have been observed throughout the world (Hallal et al., 2012). Within many western countries, participation in youth sport has declined significantly among both adolescent boys and girls (aged around 11–12 years). Two reasons given here are that there are fewer options are available for children of that age who are not advanced athletes (Koplan et al., 2005) and many children no longer enjoy sports, given the competitiveness of organized sports (Seefeldt et al., 1992). Given that time devoted to sport and PE is declining in schools within many western countries, offering avenues to expose children to sport provides sport managers with both an opportunity and a challenge.

Dangers of elite sport

Although inactivity is a global issue, young people are increasingly being encouraged to participate in elite competitive sport at earlier ages. The perception is that advanced entry into elite sport, as well as earlier specialization (i.e. participating exclusively in one sport), will provide children with some type of competitive advantage later in childhood. However, research suggests that early specialization provides little long-term edge for athletes, and instead leads to several negative outcomes (Sagas, 2013). For example, Knobler (2014) tracked the increased prevalence of elbow ligament reconstructive surgeries due to repetitive stress (commonly referred to as Tommy John surgery) and showed a marked increase primarily due to young athletes pitching year-round at the expense of participating in other sports. Additionally, early specialization has been linked with a higher degree of social isolation, increased burnout from sport participation and decreased participation in sport activities in adulthood (Sagas, 2013).

Competition for time

Individuals have limited amounts of free time. It is important for sport managers to recognize that they are competing against many other factors to increase participation in the sport they manage. For example, teenagers' preoccupation with technology has increased; recent statistics show that 71% of teenagers (aged 12–17) own cell phones, 77% own a games console (e.g. an Xbox or PlayStation), 74% own an iPod or MP3 player, 60% own or have access to a desktop or laptop computer and 55% own a portable gaming device (Lenhart, 2009). Thus, understanding the sociological and psychological reasons why different people choose to participate in an activity or the barriers preventing them from participating is critical.

Re-positioning the benefits of sport participation

Sport participation has the potential to positively impact on individuals and communities. As accountability measures become more common, sport managers will need to highlight how participation in the sport they manage provides specific benefits for the community and individuals they serve. For example, in the UK, sports that have seen declining participation (e.g. tennis and football) are at risk of having their lottery funding cut. It is our contention that highlighting the benefits of sport participation around politically important issues will enable sport managers to leverage additional resources and continue to be relevant in the eyes of key stakeholders. Data to provide beneficial evidence will be critical:

- *Health benefits of sport participation* (e.g. physical activity). Although many studies point to sport as reducing inactivity, not all sport is the same. For example, Bocarro et al. (2014) showed that participants in sports such as soccer were significantly more active than in others (e.g. baseball).
- *Academic benefits of participating in sport.* For example, Eccles et al. (2003) showed that participants who were part of a sport team had better educational outcomes than those who were not part of a sport team.
- *Community/social benefits of sport participation.* Cardenas et al. (2009) found that seniors who participated in sport were more likely to be socially and physically active.
- *Economic benefits of sport participation.* Crompton (2009) provides a number of examples of how amateur sport tournaments can show a significant economic return for local communities.

REFERENCES

Barber, B. L., Eccles, J. S. & Stone, M. R. (2001) Whatever happened to the jock, the brain, and the princess? Young adult pathways linked to adolescent activity involvement and social identity. *Journal of Adolescent Research, 16*(1), 429–455.

Barnett, L. M., Van Beurden, E., Morgan, P. J., Brooks, L. O. & Beard, J. R. (2008) Does childhood motor skill proficiency predict adolescent fitness? *Medicine and Science in Sports and Exercise, 40*(12), 2137–2144.

Bocarro, J. N., Kanters, M. A., Edwards, M. B., Casper, J. M. & McKenzie, T. L. (2014) Prioritizing school intramural and interscholastic programs based on observed physical activity. *American Journal of Health Promotion, 28*(sp3), S65–S71.

Brustad, R. (1996) Parental and peer influence on children's psychological development through sport. In F. L. Smoll & R. E. Smith (eds), *Children and Youth in Sport: A Biopsychosocial Perspective* (pp. 187–210). Boston, MA: McGraw-Hill.

Cardenas, D., Henderson, K. A. & Wilson, B. E. (2009) Experiences of participation in senior games among older adults. *Journal of Leisure Research, 41*(1), 41–56.

Coakley (1992) Burnout among adolescent athletes: a personal failure or social problem? *Sociology of Sport Journal, 9*, 271–285.

Coakley, J. (2014) *Sports in Society: Issues and Controversies*. New York: McGraw-Hill.

Crompton, J. L. (2009) *Financing and Acquiring Park and Recreation Resources*. Long Grove, IL: Waveland Press.

Dunning, E. (1999) *Sport Matters: Sociological Studies of Sport, Violence, and Civilisation*. London: Routledge.

Eccles, J. S., Barber, B. L., Stone, M. & Hunt, J. (2003) Extracurricular activities and adolescent development. *Journal of Social Issues, 59*(4), 865–889.

Edwards, M. B. & Casper, J. M. (2012) Sport and health. In G. B. Cunningham & J. D. Singer (eds), *Sociology of Sport and Physical Activity* (2nd edn, pp. 69–98). College Station, TX: Center for Sport Management Research and Education.

Elley, D. & Kirk, D. (2002) Developing citizenship through sport: the impact of a sport-based volunteer program on young sport leaders. *Sport, Education and Society, 7*(2), 151–166.

European Commission (2010) Sport and Physical Activity. Available at: http://ec.europe. eu/public_opinion/archives/ebs/ebs_334_en.pdf (last accessed 9 November 2015).

Fraser-Thomas, J., Cote, J. & Deakin, J. (2005) Youth sport programs: an avenue to foster positive youth development. *Physical Education and Sport Pedagogy, 10*(1), 19–40.

Gray, L. (2011) Hands off our land: football pitches at risk. *Daily Telegraph*. Available at: www.telegraph.co.uk/earth/hands-off-our-land/8769943/Hands-Off-Our-Land-football-pitches-at-risk.html (last accessed 22 September 2015).

Guttman, A. (1978) *From Ritual to Record*. New York: Columbia University.

Hallal, P. C., Andersen, L. B., Bull, F. C., Guthold, R., Haskell, W. & Ekelund, U. (2012) Global physical activity levels: surveillance progress, pitfalls, and prospects. *Lancet, 380*(9838), 247–257.

Hart, S. (2013) Football and tennis face funding cuts as a result of Sport England's "Active People Survey." *Daily Telegraph*. Available at: www.telegraph.co.uk/sport/tennis/10514984/Football-and-tennis-face-funding-cuts-as-a-result-of-Sport-Englands-Active-People-Survey.html (last accessed 22 September 2015).

Hedstrom, R. & Gould, D. (2004) Research in youth sports: critical issues status. Unpublished manuscript, Michigan State University, East Lansing.

Hyman, M. (2012) *The Most Expensive Game in Town: The Rising Cost of Youth Sports and the Toll on Today's Family.* Boston, MA: Beacon Press.

Iso-Ahola, S. E. Jackson, E. & Dunn, E. (1994) Starting, ceasing, and replacing leisure activities over the life-span. *Journal of Leisure Research, 26*(3), 227–249.

Knobler, D. (2014) Baseball's pitching dilemma: "Too hard, too fast, too much, too soon." Available at: http://bleacherreport.com/articles/2080837–baseballs-pitching-dilemma-too-hard-too-fast-too-much-too-soon (last accessed 22 September 2015).

Koplan, J. P., Liverman, C. T. & Kraak, V. I. (2005) *Preventing Childhood Obesity: Health in the Balance*. Washington, DC: The National Academies Press.

Lenhart, A. (2009) Teens and mobile phones over the past five years: Pew Internet looks back. Available at: www.pewinternet.org/Reports/2009/14-Teens-and-Mobile-Phones-Data-Memo.aspx (last accessed 22 September 2015).

Mukherjee, A., Goswami, R., Goyal, T. M., Statija, D. & Gupta, A. (2010) *Sports Retailing in India: Opportunities, Constraints and Way Forward,* Indian Council for Research on International Economic Relations.

National Center for Educational Statistics (2005) *What is the Status of High School Athletes 8 Years After Graduation?* Washington, DC: NCES.

Nicholson, M. & Hoye, R. (2008) *Sport and Social Capital: An Introduction.* Oxford: Butterworth-Heinemann.

Putney, C. (2001) *Muscular Christianity: Manhood and Sports in Protestant America 1880–1920.* Cambridge, MA: Harvard University Press.

Roberts, K. (1999) *Leisure in Contemporary Society.* Wallingford: CABI Publications.

Roberts, K. & Brodie, D. (1992) *Inner-city Sport: Who Plays and What Are the Benefits?* Culemborg: Giordano Bruno.

Sagas, M. (2013) *What Does the Science Say About Athletic Development in Children?* Research Brief. Gainesville, Florida: University of Florida Sport Policy and Research Collaborative for the Aspen Institute Sports & Society Program's Project Play. Available at: www.aspeninstitute.org/sites/default/files/content/docs/events/Athletic%20Development%20in%20Children%20Research%20Brief%20-Aspen%20Inst.pdf (last accessed 22 September 2015).

Seefeldt, V., Ewing, M. & Walk, S. (1992) *Overview of Youth Sports Programs in the United States.* Washington, DC: Carnegie Council on Adolescent Development.

Sporting Goods Manufacturing Association (2004) *2004 Sports, Fitness and Leisure Activities Topline Participation Report.* Jupiter, FL: SGMA Research/Sports Marketing Surveys USA.

Sporting Goods Manufacturing Association (2012) *2012 Sports, Fitness and Leisure Activities Topline Participation Report.* Jupiter, FL: SGMA Research/Sports Marketing Surveys USA.

Struna, N. L. (1977) Puritans and sport: the irretrievable tide of change. *Journal of Sport History, 4,* 1–21.

Tanier, M. (April 12, 2012) Big price tags attached to even the littlest leagues. *New York Times.* Available at: www.nytimes.com/2012/04/24/sports/big-price-tags-attached-to-even-the-littlest-leagues.html?pagewanted=all&_r=2& (last accessed 22 September 2015).

Veal, A. J. (2005) Australia. In G. Cushman, A. J. Veal & J. Zuzanek (eds), *Free Time and Leisure Participation: International Perspectives* (pp. 1–16). Cambridge, MA: CABI Publishing.

Watanabe, K., Fujiwara, N. & Kudo, Y. (2010) *The State of Sports Life Among Japanese Age 20 and Above.* Tokyo: Sasakawa Sports Foundation.

Woods, R. B. (2011) *Social Issues in Sport.* Champaign, IL: Human Kinetics.

Zuzanek, J. (2005) Canada. In G. Cushman, A. J. Veal & J. Zuzanek (eds), *Free Time and Leisure Participation: International Perspectives* (pp. 41–59). Cambridge, MA: CABI Publishing.

USEFUL WEBSITES

The Physical Activity Council's annual study tracking sports, fitness and recreation participation in the USA
www.physicalactivitycouncil.com/pdfs/current.pdf

Sport England website focused on sport participation patterns
www.sportengland.org/research/who-plays-sport

Sport in Canada including participation rates
http://canada.pch.gc.ca/eng/1414151906468/1414151995275

Research report detailing the participation patterns of South Africans,
highlighting trends and figures associated with sport in South Africa
www.srsa.gov.za/pebble.asp?relid=212

National Federation of State High School Associations Sport Participation
Statistics
www.nfhs.org/ParticipationStatics/ParticipationStatics.aspx/

The Aspen Institute's Project Play: Facts about Sports Activity and Children
www.aspenprojectplay.org/the-facts

16

LEADERSHIP

MARK MCDONALD AND KIRSTY SPENCE

Poor leadership dooms sports teams and nations.

(Vallant, 2011)

France's failure is down to poor leadership not a lack of fly-halves: Philippe Saint-André has got it wrong—below par fitness, match edge and decision-making are behind Six Nations woes.

(Kitson, 2013)

Sea Games debacle blamed on inept sports leadership.

(Antipoda, 2013)

LEARNING OUTCOMES

On completion of this chapter, students will be able to:

- Understand how the growing complexity of the sport industry impacts the effectiveness of leadership behavior.

- Understand and be able to apply the All Quadrant All Level (AQAL) model to holistically address sport leadership challenges.

- Define transformational leadership and describe the components of transformational leadership (TL).

- Differentiate between the types of leadership action logics and the interaction of these action logics with TL.

INTRODUCTION

With the increasing complexity of the sport industry and associated organizations, leadership styles and approaches need to adapt to the times. While sport leaders in the past may have been successful utilizing authoritarian "my way or the highway" approaches, complex and fluid sport business environments require leaders who encourage input and collaboration, benefitting from the knowledge, insights and expertise of all company stakeholders. The ability of leaders to successfully adapt is dependent on their worldviews, values and beliefs. For example, if a leader believes or views workers as merely units of production, it is unlikely that that individual will involve employees in discussions and decision making.

In this chapter, a framework is provided for thinking about the interaction of individual motivations, intentions and behavior, organizational culture, and organizational structure and systems, as well as understanding how all of these interactions influence leadership. Furthermore, a model will be presented to aid in understanding the worldviews, values and beliefs of individuals, and the impact on leadership behavior and choices. In the next section, a case study is provided on the relationship between leadership capabilities and the achievement of sustainability outcomes for the Vancouver Organizing Committee (VANOC) of the Vancouver 2010 Winter Olympics. This study is followed by a framework to guide your understanding of the factors impacting on any business situation, which provides useful insights on the various aspects to be considered when building an organization from scratch, and built for a very specific objective.

Case Study 16.2 covers the Basketball Hall of Fame, a sport organization in a state of flux, rocked by internal and external forces. With so many simultaneous challenges needing to be addressed, how does a leader prioritize their time and actions? This is followed by a review of two analysis tools which, when combined, will provide insights on the connection of a leader's personal development to their leadership approach, enhancing readers' ability to analyze the case.

Lastly, the chapter conclusion reviews and ties together this new learning about sport leadership that shows the growing complexity of leading sport organizations, along with theoretical frameworks that provide some analytical tools to apply to leadership challenges.

Leading VANOC's Sustainability Plan

An outcome of the 1992 UN Conference on Environment and Development (UNCED) in Brazil was the development of Agenda 21, a global action plan meant to enact initiatives to preserve the Earth's environment and non-renewable resources, simultaneous to its economic development. In 1999, the IOC developed and endorsed its own Agenda 21 to reflect sustainability as an integrated expression of both the environment and economic development. Since that time, various Olympic Organizing Committees have focused on "Greening the Games" to meet the Olympic ideals on sustainability. In advance of the Vancouver 2010 Winter Games, Vancouver Organizing Committee (VANOC) members envisioned sustainability to mean managing "the social, environmental, and economic impact and opportunities of the Games in ways that would create lasting benefits, locally and globally" (Vancouver Sustainability Report, 2010, p. 5).

Even four years prior to the 2010 Winter Games, Ann Duffy, VANOC's Chief Sustainability Officer (CSO), knew that leaving a legacy on sustainable development was possible, given that sustainability was "dialed into the DNA" of VANOC's corporate Games mission and vision (A. Duffy, personal communication, 30 September 2013). VANOC's vision reflected "a commitment to incorporating sustainability practices into all aspects of Games planning and decision-making" (Vancouver Sustainability Report, 2010, p. 27). VANOC's integrated sustainability plan focused on key areas including: accountability; environmental stewardship and impact reduction; social inclusion and responsibility; aboriginal participation and collaboration; economic benefits; and sport for sustainable living.

Duffy's sustainability team was responsible for overseeing initiatives that were to "conserve natural environments and manage, mitigate, and offset negative impacts" (Vancouver Sustainability Report, 2010, p. 36). Such initiatives included: conscious site selection, venue design and procurement; operating "eco-efficiently" such that energy, water, and material consumption was consciously minimized; and any initiatives to offset unavoidable negative impacts. The Games were a primary vehicle to raise awareness of VANOC's sustainability efforts through a variety of media, such as workshops, signage, information kiosks, media kits and a variety of website pages. Duffy and her team held a main belief that being intelligent about environmental sustainability initiatives could also benefit economic development for VANOC stakeholders. For instance, "more efficient energy consumption translates into reduced operating costs and greater overall energy security" (Vancouver Sustainability Report, 2010, p. 37).

While Vancouver's Expo '86 created substantial regional economic and tourism benefits, vulnerable people living in inner city Vancouver were negatively impacted.

In learning about the various negative impacts from this particular mega event, VANOC was additionally focused on considering "the possible impact of [their] activities on socially or economically disadvantaged communities that, often, do not typically benefit from **mega events** such as Olympic and Paralympic Games" (Vancouver Sustainability Report, 2010, p. 61). As Duffy's team were inspired to develop an integrated sustainability plan, a major challenge was to integrate social inclusion and responsibility elements, given no other Olympic Games Organizing Committee (OGOC) had previously undertaken the task of developing such a plan. As Duffy explains:

> … there's a Human Rights movement, there's a socio-economic development movement, certainly with our inner city, but as an NGO community, they haven't collaborated like the environmental movement has.

To help mitigate the impact of the Games on vulnerable populations, the Vancouver 2010 Bid Corporation collaborated with government partners to develop the joint Inner-City Inclusive (ICI) Commitment Statement (Vancouver Sustainability Report, 2010). In sum, 37 Commitments were outlined, which included initiatives so that the *Games events would be affordable to all* (e.g. 100,000 tickets available for $25 each; 50,000 tickets distributed to disadvantaged individuals through the Celebrate 2010 program; 24,000 tickets distributed to organizations serving Vancouver's inner-city residents); that *recreation and sport would be affordable to all* (e.g. financing the refurbishment of inner-city sport/recreation facilities; 300 single beds, mattresses and linens donated to five summer camp

organizations serving families with financial or physical constraints by the 2010 Winter Games hostel; and executive speaker fees donated to inner-city youth organizations [$20,000 total contribution]); and *provision of employment and training* (e.g. the RONA Vancouver 2010 Fabrication Shop, also known as The Fab Shop: RONA is a Canadian Home Improvement chain and was a National VANOC sponsor), where 64 individuals from priority population groups (i.e. new immigrants, aboriginal adults, women) were trained to learn carpentry skills to make the Games overlay materials (e.g. podiums, ramps, railings).

Often, criticisms are levied against mega-sport events such as the Olympics and Paralympics for exorbitant spending of public monies. When considering such spending, Duffy's team operated with the belief that if managed well the Winter Games could "generate sustainable economic benefits for the communities and regions and countries" (Vancouver Sustainability Report, 2010, p. 87) through job and business development and infrastructure improvements. As such, via sustainable business innovations and transparent and prudent financial practices, VANOC and its partners created economic benefits so these could be integrated with social and environmental goals. For example, VANOC's Buy-Smart program, a formalized set of procedures and activities, was "designed to ensure that sustainability attributes, ethical choices and Aboriginal participation were taken into consideration as part of VANOC's procurement and licensing activities" (Vancouver Sustainability Report, 2010, p. 90), which eventually evolved to include both Licensee (2006) and Supplier (2009) Codes of Conduct, which have been shared with the IOC and future Organizing

Committees as part of knowledge transfer processes.

Even though the 2010 Winter Games are now complete and the numerous legacies from the integrated sustainability plan have been recorded, Anne Duffy recalls vividly:

> Games minus three [years], John Furlong, VANOC's Chief Executive Officer, talked to me about "Anne, these need to be Canada's Games and you need to start thinking about legacies now." … it was just the right kind of tipping point for me to think "Okay, if that's what I need to focus on, how can I do that in a genuine way?"

As CSO, Duffy was faced with a major and primary challenge; her main leadership objective was to match Furlong's challenge to her with the development and implementation of an integrated sustainability plan. If you were in Duffy's position as VANOC's CSO, how would you face this challenge?

TOOLS FOR ANALYSIS

Wilber's All Quadrant, All Level (AQAL) Integral model (Wilber, 1995; 2000), when applied to sport leadership, provides us with an approach that combines and integrates the individual leader's voice as well as the collective group's voice and ways of working. By utilizing such an integral approach to examine our own leadership style or the problems we face, we can better understand the myriad factors that will impact our leadership and how our leadership choices interact with thoughts and feelings, behavior, organizational culture and any interconnected systems. Wilber's Integral approach can assist us in understanding leadership through four perspectives, known as quadrants, which acknowledge the interior and exterior and the individual and collective of any person, situation or problem.

Consider:

1 What are all the organizational issues Duffy must consider to achieve these legacies Furlong speaks about?

2 What resources will Duffy and her team need to address the task in front of them?

3 What challenges might Duffy and her team encounter in developing an integrated sustainability plan focusing on environmental, social, and economic impacts and legacies?

When applying the AQAL model, we can view our reality through upper (individual) and lower (collective) halves. The upper half represents the

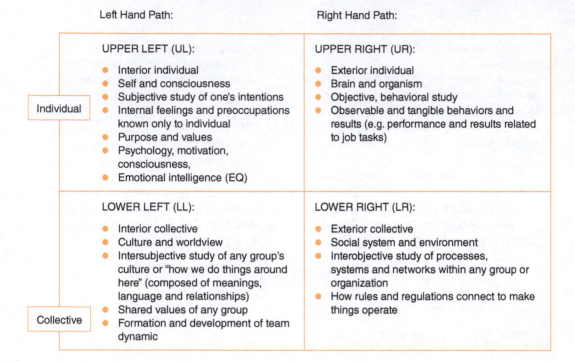

Left Hand Path: Right Hand Path:

UPPER LEFT (UL):	UPPER RIGHT (UR):
Individual • Interior individual • Self and consciousness • Subjective study of one's intentions • Internal feelings and preoccupations known only to individual • Purpose and values • Psychology, motivation, consciousness, • Emotional intelligence (EQ)	• Exterior individual • Brain and organism • Objective, behavioral study • Observable and tangible behaviors and results (e.g. performance and results related to job tasks)
LOWER LEFT (LL):	LOWER RIGHT (LR):
Collective • Interior collective • Culture and worldview • Intersubjective study of any group's culture or "how we do things around here" (composed of meanings, language and relationships) • Shared values of any group • Formation and development of team dynamic	• Exterior collective • Social system and environment • Interobjective study of processes, systems and networks within any group or organization • How rules and regulations connect to make things operate

FIGURE 16.1 *Wilber's AQAL Integral Approach (leadership application)*

Source: Adapted from Wilber (1995, 2000, 2006)

individual internal and external perspectives about any phenomenon, whereas the bottom half represents the collective's internal and external perspectives, again about any phenomenon. Additionally, our reality can be viewed via left- and right-hand quadrants or paths. The right-hand path represents both an individual's and the collective's objective and external understanding of reality and the left-hand path represents both an individual's and the collective's subjective and internal understanding of reality. In Wilber's Integral model, the upper and lower halves and the left- and right-hand paths combine to form four specific yet interrelated quadrants. A description of each quadrant, as applied to sport leaders, is provided below:

Upper Left (UL): The UL quadrant represents the interior and subjective development of an individual leader's consciousness (i.e. any thoughts, feelings, preoccupations and intentions a leader possesses which are available only to the leader him or herself) as well as their level of motivation and experience.

Lower Left (LL): The LL quadrant represents the interior and inter-subjective development of the leader and his/her direct reports or the collective group. This collective can be referred to as the group's culture, which is composed of the combined views, values and language of all group members. The collective culture emerges when the group interacts with the environment in which it is embedded and forms how the group makes meaning, communicates and works.

Upper Right (UR): The UR quadrant represents the exterior and objective or observable aspects of any person, thing or event. For example, a leader may have objective observations of another colleague's behavior (e.g. when the colleague smiles, cries or acts erratically). The leader may also observe the colleague's physiological changes (e.g. when the person displays signs of stress, such as sweating or uneven skin coloring).

Lower Right (LR): The LR quadrant represents the exterior or observable and inter-objective aspects of various different organizational systems or parts and how they work together. For example, such aspects include, but are not limited to, an organization's structure, compensation processes, production methods and technologies, all of which interconnect to form an overall organization system (e.g. when one department connects with another to initiate and implement an organizational project).

Each of these four quadrants is of equal and individual importance to understanding leadership within a sport setting. In addition, each quadrant interacts with the others to provide more comprehensive solutions to the issues leaders face. As Wilber notes, "the quadrants are simply the inside and the outside of the individual and collective, and the point is that all four quadrants need to be included if we want to be as integral as possible" (2006: 23).

ACTION LEARNING

- Anne Duffy, VANOC's Chief Sustainability Officer (CSO), has never been introduced to the AQAL model. After being introduced to the AQAL model and joining Duffy's team, how would you introduce the model to Duffy so you both could use this to initiate your planning and problem solving? What would be your first "moves" using AQAL?

- Wilber notes that people often work from a primary (first favorite) and a secondary (second favorite) quadrant. What are your primary and secondary quadrants? How do you know? Given all of the AQAL quadrants are of equal and powerful worth in solving problems, how would you plan to incorporate all of these, knowing that you otherwise have a primary and secondary preference?

Basketball Hall of Fame

In 2002, the redesigned and relocated non-profit Naismith Memorial Basketball Hall of Fame opened in Springfield, Massachusetts. The total cost of this new facility was over US$45 million, with $25 million coming directly from taxpayers (Turco, 2009). While the predicted annual attendance was between 300,000 and 400,000 visitors, actual attendance has reached approximately 230,000 people annually.

This development project, which includes retail stores, gyms, hotels, restaurants, museums and a river bikeway, was characterized as a poorly planned revitalization strategy by many observers. According to James A. Aloisi of the *Boston Globe* (2005):

> The most egregious example of a botched, albeit well meaning, development decision is the unfortunate siting of the new Basketball Hall of Fame, a potential national tourist attraction, on the edge of the Connecticut River and separated from the downtown by an interstate highway. Simply put: you cannot walk from the downtown to the Hall of Fame without significant effort. Visitors to the Hall of Fame have no feasible way to eat, shop, or do business in the downtown. ... A wasted opportunity for Springfield.

In 2003, excitement about the new facility resulted in revenues of $9.36 million, with profits of $4.3 million (National Centre for Charitable Statistics, 2003). In 2004, the total revenues were only $4.44 million, with unacceptable losses of around $1.1 million (National Centre for Charitable Statistics, 2004). In addition to moving into a new, state-of-the-art building, the organization was in the latter stages of a major transformation involving significant growth in personnel and the implementation of a new organizational ideology. For example, staff in the Hall of Fame historically viewed themselves as caretakers of the game, operating a museum with engaging exhibitions that helped bring this history to life. While admirable, this "caretaker" focus and associated organizational culture were evolving to match the drastically altered operating environment.

At this time, the organization's leader was absent 30% to 35% of the time due to traveling to educate stakeholders (i.e. community members, government agencies, donors and media among others) about the firm's future vision and mission, and also raising money for the organization for future projects. Organizational research conducted during this period indicated that organizational members perceived the leader to be unapproachable due to his busy schedule, and they felt disconnected from him (Spence and McDonald, 2010). Adding additional pressure to this situation, since the new Hall of Fame was partially funded through taxpayer support, the unexpected financial losses resulted in negative publicity.

Under the duress created by these internal and external pressures, the leader and his team began to work on devising new strategies to renew attendance and increase revenues.

Consider:

1 How should the leader prioritize the allocation of his time and effort between

addressing internal versus external organization issues?

2 Given the strong feedback from associates and ongoing organizational transformation, is the leader spending too much time focused on external stakeholders?

3 For the Hall of Fame, what strategies would you recommend for increasing attendance and revenues?

TOOLS FOR ANALYSIS

Transformational leadership

Since the 1980s, the transformational leadership (TL) model has become the foremost framework for the study of leadership effectiveness, and has been widely applied toward leadership development and training within workplace settings (Bass and Avolio, 1997; Stewart, 2006). A transformational leader is defined as one who "looks for the potential motives in followers, seeks to satisfy higher needs, and engages the full person of the follower" (Burns, 1978: 4). Through both transactional leadership behaviors (e.g. an exchange of tasks and rewards that satisfy both leader and follower) and TL behaviors, the transformational leader raises associates' awareness and motivation about issues and problems (Bass, 1985). Motivation cannot be entirely accounted for by an exchange of task accomplishment for payment, but instead incorporates the ability to influence others and "transcend their own self-interest for the good of the group, organization, or country" (Bass, 1985: 15).

Researchers (Avolio et al., 1991; Bass, 1985; Bass and Avolio, 1990; 1994; 1997) have conceived the TL model to include the "four Is" of TL, namely intellectual stimulation (IS), individualized consideration (IC), inspirational motivation (IM) and idealized influence (II). Each of these is described below:

Intellectual Stimulation (IS): The leader enables others to enhance their creative abilities so they may re-examine pressing problems to develop different solutions.

Individualized Consideration (IC): The leader focuses their attention and energies on each associate's needs and motivations and responds appropriately to their issues and challenges.

Inspirational Motivation (IM): The leader turns associates' attention towards a shared vision of organizational excellence, largely through an impassioned articulation of this vision.

Idealized Influence (II): The leader motivates associates towards extraordinary efforts by exhibiting charismatic behaviors (e.g. identifying with associates, gaining their trust and exhibiting confidence).

It is worth noting that Rooke and Torbert (2005) contend that few leaders possess the capacity to effectively transform their associates and organizations to address the challenges of rapidly changing and demanding environmental conditions, such as competition, globalization and technological innovations. Instead of viewing TL as a set of behaviors that can be applied to myriad organizational settings and situations, research indicates that a leader's capacity for TL effectiveness is closely linked with their adult development level. Essentially, leadership development *is* personal development. Insights into levels of development and their connection to TL effectiveness are explored in the next section.

THE LEADERSHIP DEVELOPMENT FRAMEWORK

For many years, organizational trainers, consultants and coaches have focused on developing leaders to obtain certain skills, competencies or "best practices" to solve organizational problems, only to find that developing leaders in this manner as the sole method eliminates their understanding of how leaders can more effectively face the complex problems that inevitably arise (Center for Creative Leadership, 2011). To that end, it is now recognized that there are two ways to develop leaders. First, *lateral development* occurs when individuals acquire knowledge, skills or competencies that translate and deepen their current ways of thinking, seeing or doing things.

Second, *vertical development* occurs when an individual learns how to see the world differently and interprets experience and reality in a completely new way. Oftentimes when we refer to a person as having a new "worldview," this could be indicative of vertical development (Cook-Greuter, 2004). When a leader vertically develops, their worldview becomes more expansive such that they both encompass old assumptions and also transform to take on new and slightly more complex views (Wilber, 2006).

When trainers help to develop leaders, it is ideal for them to incorporate elements of both lateral and vertical development within training programs. That said, the focus in leadership development these past years has been on leaders' lateral development (i.e. skills, competencies) while many consider vertical development to be a more powerful form of integrated leadership development (Spence and McDonald, 2010).

The Leadership Development Framework (LDF) is one effective model to view a leader's vertical development and is composed of seven vertically oriented and different developmental levels called action logics. Rooke and Torbert (1999) explain that a leader's particular developmental level or action logic arises from their assumptions and the relationship between these assumptions and how that person interprets themselves and the world. An individual's developmental level or action logic also affects leadership thinking (i.e. the capacity to which they can make sense of something complex), behavior (i.e. how a leader aligns their purpose and intentions with their behavior or actions) and emotions, as a leader experiences the environment.

As described in Table 16.1, the LDF action logics include the Opportunist, Diplomat, Expert, Achiever, Individualist, Strategist and Alchemist.

According to the LDF, a leader's development may move vertically through these seven action logics, which represent a leader's growth or maturation from the least complex capacities (i.e. displaying less leadership flexibility) to the most complex (i.e. displaying more leadership flexibility) capacities. Metaphorically, vertical development can be seen as a leader climbing a mountain; as a leader climbs to higher vertical altitudes, they acquire both a deeper and a wider view—they essentially see more and are able to attend more because of this deeper and wider view. When a leader has developed this greater (deeper/wider) perspective, and this is combined with targeted lateral development, they can then integrate and influence to a deeper degree than if they are solely engaged in lateral development efforts.

As seen in Table 16.1, the proportion of leaders developmentally located throughout the spectrum of LDF action logics is based on Rooke and Torbert's (2005) work over 25 years. Their research is representative of thousands of leaders and hundreds of diverse American and European private, non-profit and governmental companies.

TABLE 16.1 *Managerial style characteristics of seven LDF action-logics*

Frame name	Managerial style characteristics
Opportunist	Short time horizon; focuses on concrete things; manipulative; deceptive; rejects feedback; externalizes blame; distrustful; fragile self-control; hostile humour; views luck as central; flouts power and sexuality; stereotypes; views rules as loss of freedom; punishes according to "eye for an eye" ethic; treats what they can get away with as legal; forcibly self-interested.
Diplomat	Observes protocol; avoids inner and outer conflict; works to group standards; speaks in clichés and platitudes; conforms; feels shame if violates norms; bad at hurting others; receives disapproval as punishment; seeks membership and status; face-saving essential; loyalty to immediate group, not "distant" organization or principles; needs acceptance.
Expert	Interested in problem solving; seeks causes; critical of self and others based on craft logic; chooses efficiency over effectiveness; continuous improvement and perfection; accepts feedback only from "objective" craft masters; dogmatic; values decisions based on merit; sees contingencies, exceptions, wants to stand out, be unique; sense of obligation to wider, internally consistent moral order.
Achiever	Longer-term goals; future is vivid and important; welcomes behavioral feedback; effectiveness and results oriented; feels like an initiator, not a pawn; appreciates complexity and systems; seeks generalizable reasons for action; seeks some mutuality (as well as hierarchy) in relationships; feels guilt if does not meet own standards, blind to own achieving shadow, to the subjectivity behind objectivity; energized by practical day-to-day improvements based on self-chosen (but not self-created) ethical system.

(Continued)

TABLE 16.1 *(Continued)*

Individualist	Works independently with a high value on individuality; self-curious; freer of obligations and imposed objectives, thus finds new creativity; aware that what one sees depends upon one's worldview and experiments with this; may be a maverick as they experiment with finding their own way; uses power differently; increasingly conscious of the impact they have.
Strategist	Creative at conflict resolution; recognizes importance of principle, contract, theory and judgment—not just rules, customs and exceptions—for making and maintaining good decisions; process oriented as well as goal oriented; aware of paradox and contradiction, unique market niches and particular historical moments; relativistic; enjoys playing a variety of roles; witty, existential humour (as contrasted to prefabricated jokes); aware of dark side, of profundity of evil, and is tempted by its power.
Magician/ alchemist	Disintegration of ego-identity, often because of near-death experience; seeks participation in historical/spiritual transformations; creator of mythical events that reframe situations; anchoring in inclusive present, seeing light and dark, order and mess; blends opposites, creating "positive-sum" games; exercises own attention, researches interplay of intuition, thought, action, and effects on outside world; treats time and events as symbolic, analogical, metaphorical (not merely linear, digital, literal).

Note: Adapted from Fisher, D., Rooke, D., & Tobert, W.R. (2003) *Personal and Organisational Transformations: Through Action Inquiry* (4th edn), p.43.

ACTION LEARNING

- In the Basketball Hall of Fame case study above, the leader in question was objectively measured as operating from a *strategist* action logic. Does knowing the leader's developmental level impact on your conclusions on whether they are spending too much time focused on external stakeholders?

- Do you think a *strategist* mindset is required to address the challenges faced by the HOF and transforming this organization? Or do you think an *achiever* leader would be as, or more, effective?
- How, if at all, does the application of the AQAL model inform your responses to the two questions above?

CONCLUSION

This chapter presented a framework for thinking about the holistic and integrated interaction of individual motivations, intentions and behavior, organizational culture, and organizational structure and systems from the main perspective of how these interactions influence and impact leadership. The AQAL, LDF and transformational leadership models were outlined for you to use as leadership tools to better understand leaders' worldviews, values and beliefs, and their impact on leadership behavior and development. Also in this chapter, we outlined two case studies of sport organizations in which respective leaders face the kind of specific and complex challenges that you too may face in your sport career. It was our hope that the AQAL, LDF and transformational leadership models would serve as analysis tools to help you develop deeper and wider insights on the connection between a leader's personal development and their leadership strategy and behaviors, so as to cull from you a more powerful ability to analyze these leadership problems.

As contemporary sport organizations are embedded within broader environmental and societal contexts that are becoming increasingly more complex, it is imperative that leaders' worldviews and behaviors develop to become more adaptive and agile. Authoritarian styles, which were previously effective for sport leaders, will have severe limitations as leaders face greater fluidity in sport business environments. Leaders will be expected to develop both laterally and vertically in order to exhibit deeper and wider perspectives and behaviors that encourage greater collaboration with key stakeholders. We contend that the integral use of the AQAL, LDF and transformational leadership models will help you expand your perspectives on leadership and encourage you to generate a higher quality of solutions to complex leadership problems. We also hope that you have reached a greater appreciation of the complexity of sport organizations and the world in which these are embedded.

REFERENCES

Aloisi, J.A. (2005) Let's bring Springfield back from the doldrums, *Boston Globe,* 11 July. Available at: www.boston.com (last accessed 10 December 2013).

Antiporda, J. (2013) Sea Games debacle blamed on inept sports leadership, *The Manila Times,* 23 December. Available at: www.manilatimes.net (last accessed 22 April 2014).

Avolio, B.J., Waldman, D.A. & Yammarino, F.J. (1991) Leading in the 1990s: the four I's of transformational leadership, *Journal of European Industrial Training,* 15(4): 9–16.

Bass, B.M. (1985) *Leadership and Performance Beyond Expectations.* New York: The Free Press.

Bass, B.M. & Avolio, B.J. (1990) Developing transformational leadership: 1992 and beyond, *Journal of European Industrial Training,* 14(5): 21–7.

Bass, B.M. & Avolio, B.J. (1994) *Improving Organizational Effectiveness Through Transformational Leadership.* Thousand Oaks, CA: Sage.

Bass, B.M. & Avolio, B.J. (1997) *Full Range Leadership Development: Manual for the Multifactor Leadership Questionnaire.* Redwood City: Mind Garden.

Burns, J.M. (1978) *Leadership.* New York: Harper & Row.

Centre for Creative Leadership (2011) Future trends in leadership development White Paper. Available at Centre for Creative Leadership (last accessed 30 September 2013).

Cook-Greuter, S.R. (2004) Making the case for a developmental perspective, *Industrial and Commercial Training,* 36(7): 275–81.

Kitson, R. (2013) France failure is down to poor leadership not a lack of fly-halves: Philippe Saint-Andre has got it wrong—below par fitness, match edge, and decision-making are behind Six Nations woes, *The Guardian*, 19 March. Available at: www.theguardian.com (last accessed 23 April 2014).

National Centre for Charitable Statistics (2004) *Naismith Memorial Basketball Hall of Fame Form 990*, Internal Revenue Service. Available at: http://dynamodata. fdncenter.org/990_pdf_archive/046/046128892/046128892_200412_990.pdf (last accessed 9 January 2014).

National Centre for Charitable Statistics (2003) *Naismith Memorial Basketball Hall of Fame Form 990*, Internal Revenue Service. Available at: http://dynamodata. fdncenter.org/990_pdf_archive/046/046128892/046128892_200312_990.pdf (last accessed 9 January 2014).

Rooke, D. & Torbert, W.R. (2005) Seven transformations of leaders, *Harvard Business Review*, 83(4): 66–76.

Rooke, D. & Torbert, W.R. (1999) The CEO's role in organizational transformation, *Systems Thinker*, 10(7): 1–5.

Spence, K. & McDonald, M. (2010) Linking developmental action logics to transformational leadership behaviors, *Journal of Integral Theory and Practice*, 5(4): 94–111.

Steward, J. (2006) Transformational leadership: an evolving concept examined through the works of Burns, Bass, Avolio, and Leithwood, *Canadian Journal of Educational Administration and Policy*, 54: 1–29.

Turco, D.M. (2009) *Winning at All Cost? Sport Tourism Financing by the United States State and Local Governments*. Hamburg: Hamburg University Press.

Vallant, L. (2011) Poor leadership dooms sports teams and nations, *Denver Business Journal*, 30 September. Available at: www.bizjournals.com (last accessed 22 April 2014).

Vancouver 2010 Sustainability Report 2009–10. Available at: www.olympic.org Portal (last accessed 30 September 2013).

Wilber, K. (1995) *Sex, Ecology, Spirituality: the Spirit of Evolution*. Boston, MA: Shambala.

Wilber, K. (2000) *Integral Psychology: Consciousness, Spirit, Psychology, Therapy*. Boston, MA: Shambala.

Wilber, K. (2006) *Integral Spirituality: A Startling New Role for Religion in the Modern and Postmodern World*. Boston, MA: Shambala.

17

GENDER

ANNELIES KNOPPERS
AND AGNES ELLING-MACHARTZKI

My time was slower because I started like a woman.

(Male Dutch long distance skater at the World Championship, 2013: Trouw, 19 November 2013)

The women's division at professional football clubs still too often the goat.

(de Volkskrant, 9 March 2015)

We must do more to bring women into sports leadership.

(IOC president Thomas Bach at IWG Conference women and sport, www.olympic.org, 12 June 2014)

LEARNING OUTCOMES

Upon completion of this chapter, students should be able:

- Explain and give examples of what is meant by gender and sport as social constructions.

- Distinguish between the use of gender as a category and as a practice in sport/sport organizations.

- Explain how power shapes gender practices in sport management.

- Give examples of how ideas/ideologies about gender and sport have been reproduced and challenged over time.

- Explain how a disdain for femininity/ womanliness works in sustaining practices that keep women out of sport management.

- Suggest ways in which gender equity can be promoted to ensure more women attain leadership positions in sport.

INTRODUCTION

In this chapter we introduce and discuss several current debates in the issue of gender and sport. We do this by describing a case that focuses on current developments in the professionalization/commercialization of women's football and another that examines the promotion of more gender equity in positions of leadership. We use social constructionism and the concept of unequal power relations as important theoretical perspectives in our analysis. We argue that gender, i.e. men and women, masculinities and femininities, is assigned hierarchical meanings through sports. In addition, sports structures and cultures are still largely gendered, although several transformations towards more gender equity have taken place. Sport therefore continues to be an important field for scholars and practitioners to develop insights as to how gender ideologies and inequalities are reproduced, reconstructed and challenged, and how to promote and create more 'level playing fields' for different groups of women and men.

THINKING POINT 17.1

A Premier League for Women's Football

In 2007 the Royal Dutch Football Federation (KNVB) began a premier league for women's football in the Netherlands, consisting of women's teams affiliated with men's professional football clubs. The purpose of the league was to stimulate the development of women's elite football at a national level and enable women to compete with the international top teams. An earlier initiative in 1996 to start a women's premier league failed, partly because the best women's teams played for amateur clubs. The start of the premier league in 2007 gained much positive media coverage. This attention shifted to a more negative direction when women's football did not meet up to economic expectations during the following years and several clubs withdrew their women's team. However, other famous men's clubs like Ajax began a women's team. In 2012–2013 the Dutch premier league for women's football was integrated into the international women's BENEleague with neighbouring country Belgium.

The beginning of the premier football league for women and its alliance with men's professional clubs have resulted in more development possibilities for young talented players. The quality of performance has improved resulting in the participation of the Dutch national team in the European Championships in 2009 and 2013 and reaching the semi-final in 2009. Such performances have also resulted in more (positive) media coverage. Furthermore the structure and support have increased as has a more positive image of soccer as a suitable sport for girls and women.

Despite these positive developments, women's football in the Netherlands remains in 'second place' for most football clubs and merits only scarce – and sometimes rather ambivalent – media attention when compared to men's football. Moreover, several (male) managers and marketing professionals who promote the women's league still regard women's football as inherently inferior and 'unattractive' – only sold to a male audience by making it 'sexier'.

TOOLS FOR ANALYSIS

We explore the opposition to women's football in particular and the broader issue of gender and sport by using a social construction approach. This means we assume all the meanings we give to phenomena, things, facts, actions, etc. are not fixed but socially constructed. Meanings receive significance through social interactions and in a context of power relations such as gender. Specifically, we look at how people give meanings to gender, to perceived gender differences and to masculinity and to femininity, and how those meanings have become part of sport practice so that it may seem they are common sense. In other words, gender is not only a category but also a verb. We do gender by assigning meanings. Connell (2005) defines masculinity and femininity as practices of gender that are related to each other. This means that what we associate with femininity informs how masculinity is practised or assigned meanings and vice versa. Gender practices work together on a systematic basis to privilege many men and marginalize many women, in interaction with other social power relations such as social class, ethnicity/race and sexuality (Connell, 2005). Our focus in this first case is on how gender is done or assigned meanings at the collective level, in which we use a national sport such as football as an example.

SPORT AS A SOCIETAL INSTITUTION

As an institution, modern sport has historically been framed as a place where competitiveness and physical dominance are most important. In part due to the association commonly made between masculinity and competitiveness and dominance, sport has become a key site for gendered physicality and embodiment (Hargreaves, 1994; Messner and Sabo, 1990). Even though many women participate in a wide variety of sports, sport continues to be an institution that is seen as a place where boys and men can show they are 'real' men, meaning they are not womanly but heterosexual, and superior to women.

Participation and interest in a national sport are often regarded as a rite of passage for young boys that helps them to become seen as and identify with 'real' men (Swain, 2000). A national sport is a place in which many people are involved (as participants and audience) who use it for local and national identification. It also often allows men in particular to associate or identify with a desirable masculinity. In many countries in Europe and worldwide, football for men has developed rapidly during the past century and become the national sport. With the exception of the period around World War One, football for women has long encountered opposition since it was regarded as unfeminine and even dangerous for women, and especially for their 'reproductive function' (see, for example, Magee et al., 2007; Pfister et al., 2002). After separate women's leagues organized outside the umbrella of national federations had become too large to ignore, several European national football federations dropped their ban on women's football in the early 1970s. Women's soccer in the United States is a different story (Knoppers and Anthonissen, 2003), since American football and basketball and baseball are the national sports, not 'soccer'. Consequently American men identify more with other sports than they do soccer/football. Such differences in identification show that the assumption that football (soccer) is a masculine sport is a social construction.

Sports that are constructed as national sports provide men with images and models of masculinity that are assumed to be desirable (Messner, 1990, 2012). By engaging in fanship and by pointing to their history of sport involvement men can identify with a desirable masculinity without having to be outstanding athletes themselves. The assumption that all men are better than women because some men are stronger or faster than most women (and men), gives many men privileges associated with physical superiority including access to resources and **media** attention.

GENDER MARKING

Sport however is no longer confined or limited to male participation and dominance. Women have entered the sporting arena in large numbers, especially as athletes. Currently it is difficult to find a sport in which women do not compete. Yet practices continue that suggest sports in general and especially competitive team and contact sports in particular are still primarily a male domain.

For example, the dominance of men's football and its role in constructions of national and masculine identity mean that men's football has become the norm and is rarely marked by gender. When people talk about the national football team and European and World Championships they tend to automatically refer to men. Women's football, however, needs to be marked to be identified (e.g. the women's national football team). This occurs not only at the elite level but also in schools and at a local club level, where girls and women are still often symbolically excluded from football and 'the first team' most often refers to men (Elling and Knoppers, 2005; Magee et al., 2007; Romijn and Elling, 2009; Scraton et al., 1999). It is as if women's sport and in particular women's football are still insignificant. Nationalism seems to trump gender only when women win Olympic medals or World championships (Wensing and Bruce, 2003). Several studies of gender representation in the mainstream sports media (e.g. Cooky et al., 2013; Koivula, 1999) show that men's sport still largely dominates the sports media and, although several changes have taken place such as less explicit sexualization, the gender stereotyping and trivialization of women's sport continue.

MEN'S FEAR OF 'PLAYING WOMANLY'

The quote by the Dutch skater that prefaced this chapter seems to suggest that women's performance in skating is deficient since they are assumed to start slowly. However, if the skater in the news article wanted to say he began slowly then why did he not use that word instead of referring to women? By doing so he marks women's skating as inferior and denigrates women's sport, which is reproduced in the sports media by quoting his words (see also Knoppers and Elling, 2004). Phrases referring to men such as 'playing like a bunch of girls' or being soft or 'a sissy' work to suggest that acting in ways that are associated with being womanly is not valued. We would argue that it is not women as such who are devalued as much as everything associated with the word 'womanly' (see also Gregory, 2011; Sterk and Knoppers, 2009).

Mariah Burton Nelson (1994) has argued that this fear of what is womanly and the intrusion of women into all of what formerly were seen as male domains are why 'the stronger women get, the more men love football'. This love of football assumes it is a heterosexual practice. This association between males acting womanly and being gay is the antithesis of desirable masculine practices (Connell, 2005; Pronger, 1990). It is not surprising then that boy's and men's football cultures continue to be homophobic (Plummer, 2006). While in many Western countries men are openly gay in different societal domains, including sport, there are no openly gay male football players at the highest competition level. At lower competitive levels, however, changes to more 'inclusive masculine' practices are occurring, even in men's team sports (Anderson, 2011). Gay men are tolerated as long as they also appear and perform in gender normative ways, showing they are 'manly' enough.

Contrary to the absence of openly gay football players at the highest competitive levels, until recently, women footballers in many countries were regarded as 'masculine' and therefore expected to be or accused of being lesbians (Caudwell, 1999; Cox and Thompson, 2000; Elling, 1999). Although 'playing like a man' is implicitly regarded as a compliment for women footballers, they are simultaneously expected to look feminine enough so that they conform to a desirable heterosexual femininity. Obviously then, in both women's and men's football, there is more at stake than just playing high quality football. These sports play a crucial role in society's constructions of femininity and masculinity.

Shifts in dominant gender normative (and heteronormative) ideologies and practices continue to occur, but remain fragile as the developments in women's and men's football illustrate. Further change requires a shift in and transformation of values assigned to dominant constructions of desirable masculinity and of privileged femininity, since these limit the sport participation, talent development and identity development of many man and especially many women. Sport managers can play a crucial role in such transformations since they are continually faced with intersections between sport and gender (and other social inequalities like class, race and ethnicity). They can challenge gender constructions and practices by naming them and trying to deconstruct them. For example, by offering boys and girls similar sporting opportunities in traditional 'masculine' and 'feminine' sports and by fostering a climate that enables greater diversity in doing gender and more inclusiveness to include lesbian, gay, bisexual and transgender people.

ACTION LEARNING

- Have you come across initiatives that include gender diversity in sports? In football? How supportive are you of men who challenge desirable masculine practices? What do you think is needed to further promote gender equality and diversity in football and other sports?
- Thinking Point 17.1: Why is it so difficult for women's football to 'survive' compared to men's football? Which social forces may play a role?
- Do you think women's football (and other women's sports) receive enough media attention and financial resources? Why (not)? What would happen if women's sports received more attention and resources?

CASE STUDY 17.1

A Quota for the Number of Female Board Members?

The first World Conference on Women and Sport was organized by the International Working Group on Women and Sport (IWG) from the IOC, held in Brighton, England, in 1994. The resulting Brighton Declaration provided principles and initiatives that, if implemented, could increase women's involvement in sport at all levels including leadership. It was followed by similar manifests like the Windhoek call for action in 1998 and monitoring instruments like the

Sydney scoreboard in 2000. Targets for increasing the number of females in positions of leadership have been set by national and international organizations. For example, the International Olympic Committee (IOC) wants women to occupy at least 20% of decision-making positions in National Olympic Committees, International and National Sports Federations, and sporting governing bodies belonging to the Olympic Movement. In 2012 about one in three Olympic sports had reached the IOC's target.

The Dutch situation shows how change comes about slowly. In 2001 the Dutch Minister of Sports stated that by 2005 women should comprise 25% of the board members for national sport associations. Subsequent Dutch ministers of sport continued to support projects to stimulate female leadership, but progress was slow. The number of women in Dutch Olympic federation boards had only increased from 10% in 2002 to 13% in 2005, the target year. By 2010 the target number of 25% was within reach (at 21%). In addition, the percentage of federations without any female board members decreased from 53 to 23 (see Figure 17.1).

In most countries men still outnumber women in competitive sports in general. In the Netherlands the overall club sport participation ratio of men to women is 2:1. However, in many sports men and women participate to the same extent and in several sports women outnumber men (e.g. gymnastics, equestrian and volleyball in the Netherlands). Female board membership at the top level continues to lag behind the percentage of female members of sport clubs however. Even in these sports men dominate positions of leadership. In addition, statistics for positions in governance and leadership in sport and outside it suggest that women have moved into middle management positions but have often not advanced further into the top positions (Acosta and Carpenter, 2012; Lapchick, 2010; SHARP Center for Women and Girls, 2013).

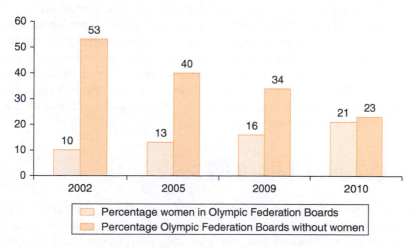

FIGURE 17.1 *Development of gender balance in Dutch national federations of Olympic sports 2002–2010 (Elling et al., 2011)*

TOOLS FOR ANALYSIS

The use of a social constructionist approach requires researchers and sport managers to look at practices in sport organizations that may result in the systematic – though often unnoticed and unwanted – inclusion of men and exclusion of women, especially in top functions of leadership.

As the data in the case and in other international studies (Acosta and Carpenter, 2012) suggest, any change in gender representation in leadership positions in sport comes slowly. Historically, the explanation for this lack of significant change was that women were not selected to positions of governance and administrative positions in sport because they lacked experience in sport (Acosta and Carpenter, 2012). Sport organizations have a poor track record in this aspect, often worse than other non-sport organizations (Knoppers et al., 2013). Gender parity can be developed when sport managers are aware of and create policies and undertake informal measures and actions to change the status quo in which women are under-represented in **sport governance** and management. However, many sport managers still regard gender diversity as a non-issue and are resistant to policy measures (including quotas or targets) that could enhance gender equity.

So how can theory help us understand this phenomenon?

Acker (1990, 2006) has shown how practices of gender in organizations manifest themselves in identity construction, interactions, structure (division of labour and tasks) and culture. She argues that when practices of gender become common sense and systematic, they are difficult to recognize and eradicate. In the following sections we look at each of these dimensions described by Acker and describe how they might work and manifest themselves in sport organizations.

CULTURAL PRACTICES

The study of gender in organizations has shown that sport organizations are places where practices of femininity are often marginalized and those of masculinity valorized (see, for example, Claringbould and Knoppers, 2007, 2008, 2012; Hovden, 2010; Pfister, 2010). Those that are associated with men's physical strength, toughness, perseverance and self-discipline are especially so (Claringbould and Knoppers, 2008; Knoppers, 2011) but not all practices of masculinity are equally valued. Also, when women managers and directors engage in these desirable behaviours the reactions from others tend to be both positive and negative. Women who have shown these qualities have not only been described as good managers, but also as hardnosed, unfeminine and bitchy (Hovden, 2010; Knoppers et al., 2013; Pfister, 2010; Pfister and Radtke, 2009). Moreover, mistakes by women are often ascribed to their gender, whereas this rarely happens to men. They make mistakes but these are usually not attributed to their being men. These cultural practices contribute to the division of labour.

DIVISIONS OF LABOUR AND TASKS

The images that are associated with a position in an organization or a specific task also help determine who fills it. Research shows that those who fit the image of those already holding the majority of these positions have the greatest chance of being selected (e.g. Hovden, 2000, 2010). Positions of paid or volunteer leadership in sport organizations are often associated with heroic masculinity. Those who do the selecting and those who are selected tend to be men. Messner (2009) also found that an informal sorting process based on gender images resulted in men /fathers becoming coaches and women/mothers becoming team parents. This division of labour does not occur automatically. Individuals engage in social interactions to negotiate gender images that contribute to a division of labour.

SOCIAL INTERACTIONS

Daily life in organizations contains interactive practices – including jokes and informal talk – in which people give meaning to gender (Martin, 2003, 2006). Gregory (2011) has described how sports talk used in organizations often disparages indications of femininity, being womanly or gayness in men. Its use suggests a degradation of what is associated with women and means men and women have few alternatives to practising as heroic masculinity (Collinson and Hearn, 1996; Shaw, 2006; Shaw and Hoeber, 2003). Since men tend to dominate these interactions they define what and who are considered normal and different, who is excluded and who is included, and make being anti-feminine/womanly acceptable. These interactions play 'an important role in shaping and normalizing organizational constructions that are part of selection and promotion processes that produce a gendered division of labor and the associated images' (Claringbould and Knoppers, 2013: 179). These interactions also require identity work.

IDENTITY WORK

Identity work is what individuals have to do to fit into an organizational culture. This includes how they give meaning to gender in the way they dress, talk and interact with others. The identity work of women who want to be top managers requires them to enact heroic male and anti-feminine behaviours that are associated with top male managers (Wajcman, 1998). Organizational culture may also require individuals to identify with the organization by working many (extra) hours, and placing the organization ahead of family commitments (Knoppers and Anthonissen, 2008). For women such heroic commitment and identification with the organization are often difficult. Unlike many men who have children, women with families tend not to have someone at home who takes responsibility for the household and children (Dixon, 2008).

As the foregoing shows, gender is a powerful force in sport organizations and involves various layers of an organization and its culture. These layers all impact on each other. This means that change can be complicated. At the same time, it also means that if a change is made somewhere, for example in the forms of identity work or the work structure, this may influence the ways gender is done in the other layers as well. Therefore policy actions to stimulate critical reflection on and to effect change in gendered division of tasks, identity work, cultural practices and/or social interactions may reduce or change the negative impact gender has had on sport organizations. The power of such actions can be increased if these include the empowering and coaching of (potential) women leaders, resistance to and the naming of anti-feminine behaviour and jokes, and the visible support of a broader group of influential (male) managers.

ACTION LEARNING

- With the exception of a few countries like the USA and Canada, most competitive sport participation is organized within and by clubs. Sport clubs and sport associations are usually independent and autonomous. Consequently it is difficult for governments to demand that sport organizations appoint and support more women in positions of leadership. Legislation for change has to come from sport federations or national and international Olympic committees. The IOC has proposed that all decision-making structures should consist of at least 20% women (IOC, 2007).
- Think of a sport organization. Describe its gendered practices using the four dimensions (Acker, 1990) as outlined in this chapter. How could those practices be changed so that more women fill positions of leadership? Which social forces play a role that may support and work against this change?

CONCLUSION

In this chapter we have argued that gender is a powerful force in society and sport organizations, and involves various gender practices that influence the construction and reproduction of gendered sport structures, identities and organizational cultures. Sport has traditionally been strongly related to desirable masculinity, featuring concepts like competitiveness, physical dominance, perseverance and self-discipline, and denigrating forms of femininity.

We have shown that both in terms of participation in sport and in positions of governance and leadership, women have entered the formal male bastions, but gender inequalities continue at all levels. Changes are slow, especially since gender is manifest in different dimensions and at different levels (individuals and groups, organizations, society) and the exclusion of women from (particular) sports or positions of leadership is currently less explicit than in the past. Many people nowadays seem to think that gender is no longer a powerful force, especially when they view events such as the Olympics. They may attribute what they see as gender inequality to biological differences. We hope to have shown that gender troubles in sport need continued scholarly and managerial attention, and require policy measures and concrete actions to further de-gender sports and develop human potential.

REFERENCES

Acker, J. 1990. Hierarchies, jobs, bodies: a theory of gendered organizations. *Gender and Society*, 4(2), 139–158.

Acker, J. 2006. Inequality regimes: gender, class and race in organizations. *Gender and Society*, 20(4), 441–464.

Acosta, R.V. and Carpenter, L.J. 2012. *Women in Intercollegiate Sport: A Longitudinal, National Study 1977–2012.* West Brookfield: Brooklyn College.

Anderson, E. 2011. Updating the outcome: gay athletes, straight teams, and coming out at the end of the decade. *Gender and Society*, 25(2), 250–268.

Burton Nelson, M. 1994. *The Stronger Women Get, the More Men Love Football: Sexism and the American Culture of Sports*. New York: Harcourt Brace.

Caudwell J. 1999. Women's football in the United Kingdom: theorizing gender and unpacking the butch lesbian image. *Journal of Sport and Social Issues*, 23(4), 390–402.

Claringbould, I. & Knoppers, A. 2007. Finding a 'normal' woman: selection processes for board membership. *Sex Roles*, 56(7–8), 495–507.

Claringbould, I. and Knoppers, A. 2008. Doing and undoing gender in sport governance. *Sex Roles*, 58(1–2), 81–92.

Claringbould, I. and Knoppers, A. 2012. Paradoxical practices of gender in sport-related organizations, *Journal of Sport Management*, 26(5), 404–416.

Claringbould, I. & Knoppers, A. 2013. Understanding the lack of gender equity in leadership positions in (sport) organization. In P. Leisink, P. Boselie, D. Hosking and M. van Bottenburg, eds, *Managing Social Issues: A Public Values Approach*, pp. 162–182. Cheltenham: Edward Elgar.

Collinson, D.L. and Hearn, J. eds. 1996. *Men as Managers, Managers As Men: Critical Perspectives on Men, Masculinities and Managements.* London: Sage.

Connell, R. 2005. *Masculinities.* Cambridge: Polity Press.

Cooky, C., Messner, M.A. & Hextrum, R.H. 2013. Women play sport, but not on TV: a longitudinal study of televised news media. *Communication & Sport*, 1(3), 203–230.

Cox, B. & Thompson, S. 2000. Multiple bodies: sportswomen, soccer and sexuality. *International Review for the Sociology of Sport,* 35(1), 5–20.

Dixon, M. 2008. Perspectives on work-family conflict in sport: an integrated approach. *Sport Management Review*, 8(3), 227–254.

Elling, A. 1999. 'Een beetje ruig dat trekt me wel': Over het imago en de beleving van vrouwenvoetbal [A bit of toughness attracts me: the image and experiences in women's soccer]. *Tijdschrift voor Genderstudies*, 2(4), 25–35.

Elling, A., Jong, M. de, Wit, R. de, Notté, R. & Rens, F. van. 2011. *Inventarisatie Diversiteit in Sportbesturen 2010.* Hertogenbosch: W.J.H. Mulier Instituut.

Elling, A. & Knoppers, A. 2005. Sport, gender and ethnicity: practices of symbolic in/exclusion. *Journal of Youth and Adolescence*, 34(3), 257–268.

Gregory, M. 2011. 'The faggot clause': the embodiment of homophobia in the corporate locker room. *Equality, Diversity and Inclusion: An International Journal*, 30, 651–67.

Hargreaves, J. 1994. *Sporting Females: Critical Issues in the History and Sociology of Women's Sports*. London: Routledge.

Hovden, J. 2000. 'Heavyweight' men and younger women? The gendering of selection processes in Norwegian sport organizations. *NORA, Nordic Journal of Women's Studies*, 8(1), 17–32.

Hovden, J. 2010. Female top leaders – prisoners of gender? The gendering of leadership discourses in Norwegian sports organizations. *International Journal of Sport Policy*, 2(2), 189–203.

International Olympic Committee. 2007. *Olympic Charter.* Lausanne, Switzerland: International Olympic Committee.

Knoppers, A. 2011. Giving meaning to sport involvement in managerial work. *Gender, Work and Organization*, 18(1), 1–22.

Knoppers, A. and Anthonissen, A. 2003. Women's soccer in the United States and the Netherlands: differences and similarities in regimes of inequality. *Sociology of Sport Journal,* 20(4), 351–370.

Knoppers, A. and Anthonissen, A. 2008. Gendered managerial discourses in sport organizations: multiplicity and complexity. *Sex Roles*, 58, 93–103.

Knoppers, A., Claringbould, I. & Dortants, M. 2013. Discursive managerial practices of diversity and homogeneity. *Journal of Gender Studies*. DOI:10.1080/0958923 6.2013.833086

Knoppers, A. & Elling, A. 2004. 'We do not engage in promotional journalism': discursive strategies used by sport journalists to describe the selection process. *International Review for the Sociology of Sport*, 39(1), 57–73.

Koivula, N. 1999. Gender stereotyping in televised media sport coverage. *Sex Roles*, 41(7/8), 589–604.

Lapchick, R., Hoff, B. & Kaiser, R. 2010. The 2010 Racial and Gender Report Card: College Sports. University of Central Florida: Institute for Diversity and Ethics in Sport. Available at: www.fsbra.ucf.edu/documents/sport/2010-college-rgrc.pdf (last accessed 27 September 2015).

Magee, J., Caudwell, J., Liston, K. & Scraton, S. eds. 2007. *Women, Football and Europe: Histories, Equity and Experiences.* Oxford: Meyer & Meyer Sport.

Martin, P.Y. 2003. 'Said and done' versus 'saying and doing' – gendering practices, practicing gender at work. *Gender and Society*, 17(3), 342–366.

Martin, P.Y. 2006. Practicing gender at work: further thoughts on reflexivity. *Gender, Work and Organization*, 13(3), 254–276.

Messner, M. 2009. *It's All for the Kids: Gender, Families, and Youth Sports.* Berkeley, CA: University of California Press.

Messner, M. 1990. Masculinities and athletic careers: bonding and status differences. In M. Messner and D. Sabo, eds, *Sport, Men and the Gender Order: Critical Feminist Perspectives,* pp. 97–108. Champaign, IL: Human Kinetics.

Messner, M. 2012. Reflections on communication and sport: on men and masculinities. *Communication and Sport*, 1(1/2), 113–124.

Messner, M. & Sabo, D. 1990. Toward a critical feminist appraisal of sport, men and the gender order. In M. Messner and D. Sabo, eds, *Sport, Men and the Gender Order: Critical Feminist Perspectives,* pp. 1–15. Champaign, IL: Human Kinetics.

Pfister, G. 2010. Are the women or the organizations to blame? Gender hierarchies in Danish sports organizations. *International Journal of Sport Policy and Politics*, 2(1), 1–23.

Pfister, G. and Radtke, S. 2009. Sport, women and leadership: results of a project on executives in German sports organizations. *European Journal of Sport Science*, 9(4), 229–243.

Pfister, G., Fasting, K., Scraton, S. & Vázquez, B. 2002. Women and football – a contradiction? The beginnings of women's football in four European countries. In S. Scraton and A. Flintoff, eds, *Gender and Sport: A Reader,* pp. 66–79. London: Routledge.

Plummer, D. 2006. Sportophobia. Why do some men avoid sport? *Journal of Sport and Social Issues*, 30(2), 122–137.

Pronger, B. 1990. *The Arena of Masculinity.* New York: St. Martin's Press.

Romijn, D. & Elling, A. 2009. *Een prachtige tweede plaats. Een studie naar de stand van zaken van het meisjes-en vrouwenvoetbal in Nederlandse amateurvoetbalverenigingen.* [A beautiful second place: research on the place of girls' and women's football in Dutch amateur football clubs]. Hertogenbosch: WJH Mulier Instituut.

Scraton, S., Fasting, K., Pfister, G. & Brunell, A. 1999. 'It's still a man's game': the experiences of top-level European women footballers. *International Review for the Sociology of Sport*, 34(2), 99–111.

SHARP Center for Women and Girls. 2013. *Women in the Olympic and Paralympic Games: An Analysis of participation and leadership opportunities.* Ann Arbor, MI: SHARP Center for Women and Girls.

Shaw, S. 2006. Scratching the back of 'Mr X': analyzing gendered social processes in sport organizations. *Journal of Sport Management*, 20(4), 510–534.

Shaw, S. and Hoeber, L. 2003. 'A strong man is direct and a direct woman is a bitch': analyzing discourses of masculinity and femininity and their impact on employment roles in sport organizations. *Journal of Sport Management*, 17(4), 347–376.

Sterk, H. & Knoppers, A. 2009. *Gender, Culture and Physicality: Paradoxes and Taboos.* Lanham, MD: Lexington Books.

Swain, J. 2000. 'The money is good, the fame's good, the girls are good': the role of playground football in the construction of masculinities. *British Journal of Sociology of Education*, 21(1), 95–108.

Wajcman, J. 1998. *Managing Like a Man: Women and Men in Corporate Management*. Cambridge: Polity Press.

Wensing, E. & Bruce, T. 2003. Bending the rules: media representations of gender during an international sporting event. *International Review for the Sociology of Sport*, 38(4), 387–396.

18

PERFORMANCE MANAGEMENT

LEIGH ROBINSON
AND MATHIEU WINAND

A company can have a world-class system in place – but it's only as effective as the managers who implement it.

(Oberoi and Rajgarhia, 2014)

Perhaps no talent management process is more important or more reviled than performance management.

(Effron and Ort, 2012)

Rotherham United have been deducted three points and fined £30,000 by a Football Disciplinary Commission for fielding an ineligible player.

(BBC Online, 24 April 2015)

LEARNING OUTCOMES

Upon completion of this chapter, students will be able to:

- Discuss why performance management is important.

- Understand the role of performance evaluation in the management of sport organizations.

- Explain why performance management may not take place in sport organizations.

INTRODUCTION

The management of performance is arguably the most important activity that managers have to carry out in order to ensure the effectiveness of their organizations. Without managing the performance of what they, their staff and the organization deliver on a daily basis, managers run a real risk of their service becoming out of their control. This is because managing the performance of processes, procedures and people is an ongoing, structured activity that allows an organization's strategy to be implemented. Thus, performance management should be an integral part of the operation of all sport organizations. This chapter addresses the need for performance management in the sport sector, with a focus on National Governing Bodies. It considers issues relating to performance management and then discusses performance evaluation and measurement. This discussion is then applied to a case study covering the performance management of the national federations of the Wallonia-Brussels Federation.

CASE STUDY 18.1

A Performance Management Tool for Sport Managers: A Case Study of Belgian Sport Federations

Athletes are accountable for the level of performance they achieve, which can be clearly assessed by indicators such as time, distance, placing and participation at international competitions. Sport organizations also have objectives to achieve; however, their performance is not quite so transparent. Sport managers are accountable for the level of organizational performance achieved by their sport organization. They are liable for securing necessary resources and monitoring their efficient use through organizational processes and activities in order to achieve targeted objectives. This requires a system by which objectives can be set and measured, and actions can be taken, known as a performance management system.

Given the ambiguity of performance, for a performance management system to be effective, it requires consensus on key strategic dimensions and objectives as well as requiring key performance indicators (KPIs) to measure these (explained and set out further in the chapter). The management of sport federation performance has emerged as a priority in Belgium and Figure 18.1 sets out the performance management tool which has been developed for use within Belgian sport federations, which consists of 6+1 strategic dimensions. These dimensions are all core activity domains of sport federations in Belgium and reflect current sport policy priorities. Six dimensions are core operations of sport federations: grassroots sport, elite sport development, societal, organization, communication and finance, while one dimension considers the sport clubs affiliated to sport federations: club quality development – hence 6+1.

The main objective of sport federations is to provide opportunities to take part in

Elite sport development	Grassroots sport	Societal
Obtain international sport results	Enhance the quality of sport services	Attract members
Increase athlete participation at international sport competitions	Enhance the availability of sport services	Increase the number of young participants
Improvement of elite sport services		

Club quality development			
Sport club facilities	Club training pathways	Qualified club representatives	Club members

Organization	Communication	Finance
Improve organizational atmosphere	Promote sport	Acquire financial resources
Improve staff skills	Improve communication with members and clubs	Monitor financial balance
Improve the quality of operating		Manage financial dependence

FIGURE 18.1 *Performance management tool for sport federations: strategic dimensions and objectives*

sport at different levels, primarily amateur and elite. These two dimensions of the performance framework need to be managed and monitored differently. The objective of the grassroots dimension is to enhance the quality and availability of sport services provided to members. The elite sport dimension is concerned with elite athletes and includes international sport results, increasing athlete participation at international sport competitions and improving elite sport services.

The societal dimension has the intention of showing the contribution of the sport federation to society. Sport is considered to be a vehicle for improving health and social wellbeing, and thus the more people taking part in sport, the higher the impact it can have. Public authorities that support sport federations are particularly attentive

to social legitimacy and mass participation in sport. Attracting members and increasing the number of young participants are objectives that show how well a sport federation can promote sport values within the society.

The organization dimension focuses on the functioning of the organization, based on the assumption that highly skilled staff and a good organizational atmosphere are part of the conditions required for sport federations to perform at a high level. The communication dimension covers relations with the external environment of the sport federation and sport federations need to promote their sport and create a positive image in the media. This dimension sets out the need to communicate about their initiatives to society and their members and clubs.

The finance dimension of the model addresses the challenge of acquiring financial resources and monitoring financial balances. Sport federations should seek and get sufficient financial resources to secure their viability and distribute these appropriately. They should also attempt to develop activities in order to decrease their dependence upon public authorities and, thus, increase their capacity for self-investment.

The above dimensions relate to the direct management of sport federations. However, within the assessment of the performance of sport federations, sport clubs and the way they are managed should also be taken into account as they are often responsible for delivering the strategies to meet sport federation objectives. Sport federations should encourage clubs to improve their quality as this could result in the latter's better performance, such as an increase in membership. The club quality development dimension covers the levels of sport club facilities (number and availability of sport club facilities), club training pathways (number of club members trained per year), qualified club representatives (number of trained officials, trainers, coaches of the clubs) and members (number and percentage of young teams of the club).

A sport federation should work to obtain a high percentage of affiliated clubs that meet the minimum level set for each area.

Using the 6+1 dimensions of performance and the associated objectives, sport federations in Belgium are be able to identify how well they should perform based on their previous performance and in line with strategic objectives. The time required for success to be achieved needs to be agreed by those responsible for each objective and targets must be set for the KPIs to indicate achievement. Every year sport federations will measure their performance according to their performance indicators and use this information to identify which objectives have not been met. Following this, plans and actions need to be developed to deal with poor performance. Even if KPIs are met, reflection is also essential in order to identify key success factors and how performance can be sustained.

Note that some of the dimensions or objectives set out above are less relevant than others for some Belgian sport federations. For instance, elite sport results are not relevant to recreational sport federations. In this case the sport federations' managers/volunteer board members can weight dimensions and objectives in order to reflect the organizations' priorities and contexts.

TOOLS FOR ANALYSIS

As set out above, performance management is a comprehensive, albeit relatively straightforward process that relies on the procedures and processes that an organization has, in order to create a performance management cycle. Figure 18.2 shows how a performance management cycle starts with the objectives set out in the strategic plan, which are then used by managers to develop operational plans that help to deliver the objectives set out in the strategic plan. Plans set out the activities that are to be delivered, how these are to be delivered and the resources required, such as money, time and staff. The success of these plans is then evaluated against what they were intended to achieve, using key performance indicators, which have been defined by Taylor et al. (2000: 4) as 'a piece of empirical data representing performance that can be compared over time or with similar organizations'. It is worth noting that it is not enough to carry out an evaluation annually, rather it should be carried out at regular intervals to make sure that the final goal is achieved. For example, in Figure 18.2, which shows a performance management process for qualifying a team for the Olympic Games, the evaluation of plans would need to be done after each competition in order to assess whether qualification for the Olympics is on track.

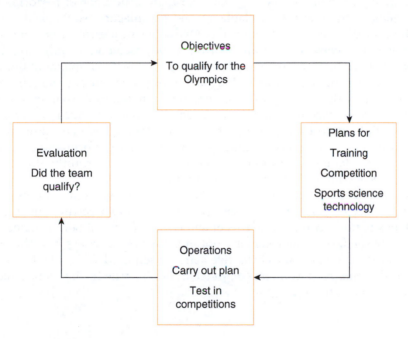

FIGURE 18.2 *Performance management cycle*

(Source: Robinson, 2011)

By following this cycle, managers can use performance management to help them in a number of ways. First, and somewhat obviously, it helps with strategic planning (**strategy**) as it operationalizes the strategies set by organizations. This is because it provides information on how the organization is performing against stated targets and generates information that can be fed into future planning. Indeed, without performance management, planning is a somewhat pointless process. Second, organizations that manage performance are less likely to rely simply on their subjective management judgment as managers have a clear set of objectives to refer to and are being continuously provided with up-to-date information on how well their operation is doing against these. Finally, performance management allows managers to focus on what is important.

It is also necessary to acknowledge the role of performance management in helping to meet stakeholder expectations. Objectives should be set and agreed in consultation with stakeholders, and then the organization can be managed, using plans, to meet those targets. In addition, performance management will also allow managers to demonstrate successes in achieving strategies and implementing policy. Therefore, actively managing performance helps to makes sport organizations more transparent and accountable, which is essential for achieving good governance.

Performance management frameworks have been developed to encourage managers to take a holistic view of the organization's performance, rather than simply focusing on its finances. There are a number of performance management frameworks available to sport managers, such as the one outlined in the case above as well as Quest (www.questnbs.info) and the Balanced Scorecard (Kaplan and Norton, 1996) to mention only two. The choice of which performance management framework to implement doesn't matter in sport organizations as long as the organization has the following features. First, there needs to be an organizational culture that supports a performance management approach. An effective performance management framework is more than just a system of controlling the operations of an organization; it must also encourage staff to consider performance management as a fundamental way of doing business. More importantly, this needs to be embedded in the organization's culture.

Second, in order to be effective, performance management systems must involve effective performance measurement and target setting and this is the focus of the second half of this chapter. If measures of performance are not established, then managers are not in a position to assess how they are doing, or to be able to take corrective action if required. The old adage of *'if you can't measure it, you can't manage it'* is very true in the management of sport organizations.

ACTION LEARNING

- Case Study 18.1: Why is it important to focus on a range of areas of performance?
- What might be the challenges in implementing the 6+1 model?
- What else does this model need in order for the national federations to be able to use it effectively?

- How would you improve the 6+1 performance management model used by Belgium sport federations?
- What do you think is the most important part of the performance management cycle and why?
- What is the most difficult aspect of performance management to introduce into organizations?

Performance Measurement: A Case Study of Belgian Sport Federations

The first case in this chapter set out the performance management framework that is to be followed by the sport federations of the Wallonia-Brussels Federation. The KPIs associated with the strategic dimensions of performance are presented below.

Dimension 1: Elite sport development

- *International sport results per year (e.g. medals or world top eight)*
- *Elite sport expenditure per relevant international sport result*
- *Percentage of athletes participating in international competitions*
- *Athlete participation in international competitions compared to previous year*
- *Percentage of elite sport expenditure compared to total expenditure*
- *Growth of the percentage of elite sport expenditure*

Dimension 2: Grassroots sport

- *Number of qualified sport trainers for 1,000 members*
- *Expenditure on sport services per member*
- *Number of sport activities organized for members per year and their participation rate*

Dimension 3: Societal

- *Growth in membership compared to previous year*

- *Percentage of members under 18 years old*
- *Growth in percentage of members under 18 years old compared to previous year*

Dimension 4: Organization

- *Number of qualified staff within the sport federation*
- *Average years of experience of staff*
- *Staff turnover*
- *Volunteer board member turnover*
- *Percentage of expenditure for non-sport services compared to total expenditure*
- *Percentage of expenditure for non-sport services compared to previous year*

Dimension 5: Communication

- *Percentage of sport promotion expenditure compared to total expenditure*
- *Percentage of members receiving up to date information*
- *Frequency of up-to-date communication to members and clubs through email or website*

Dimension 6: Finance

- *Grants per member*
- *Sponsorship revenue per member*
- *Percentage of management expenditure compared to total expenditure*
- *Financial return to members for sport activities*
- *Grants compared to total expenditure*
- *Grants compared to total revenue*
- *Revenue compared to expenditure*

- Do these KPIs give a comprehensive measurement of performance?
- How 'controllable' are these KPIs?

- Choose one of the dimensions and consider how you would collect the data required to create the KPI.

TOOLS FOR ANALYSIS

Performance evaluation is carried out by comparing what 'is' with what 'ought to be'. Managers in sport organizations set goals and objectives, discuss priorities and set plans for achieving these. Evaluation, using KPIs, measures how well organizations succeed with these plans and evaluates the impact these have on the organization and the sport. Examples of KPIs include number of users, cost of marketing activities and the number of athletes that qualify for championships. In addition, in order to make PIs more useful for management, they are usually associated with a target or level that managers need to obtain. For example, increasing member numbers by 10%, spending £10,000 on marketing and aiming for eight athletes to qualify for the championships.

Research carried out by Holloway (1999) into the value of performance indicators identified the number of roles that they play in terms of evaluation. Performance indicators help to:

- clarify the organization's objectives by setting out how these will be measured;
- evaluate the final outcome of plans and investment and thus enable stakeholders to be informed about performance;
- indicate the contribution of the service towards the organization's objectives;
- act as a trigger for the further investigation of (and possible action to improve) the quality of inputs and outputs;
- assist with managerial decision making when allocating resources;
- provide staff with feedback to enable them to develop and improve operations.

The use of poorly developed or inappropriate performance indicators can have a significant and detrimental impact on an organization and therefore these should be developed and used based on the following criteria:

- The data on which PIs are based must be trustworthy, particularly if those data are being used for external comparison. For example, if financial performance is being measured then financial records must be accurate.

- The data used to form PIs must be collected from the same sources and in the same manner. This will ensure that the performance being evaluated is accurate and allows comparisons. For example, if the success of four events encouraging children to join a sport is being evaluated, a decision has to be made as to whether the numbers attending the event or the numbers joining clubs are the measure of success.

- PIs also need to measure what they are considered to measure, otherwise they may lead to mistakes in decision making. For example, counting the number of members in a National Governing Body is not an accurate reflection of participants in the sport. Membership numbers do not include non-members who play the sport and often include people who are no longer active. This may be an issue with the Societal KPIs set out above.

- PIs should only be used as a guide as they do not provide an explanation for performance. For example, a PI will show that the number of users of a facility is declining, but will not explain why. Managers need to be able to explain both good and bad performance.

- Performance indicators are meaningless unless they are evaluated in comparison with objectives. For example, a manager may be successful in increasing the number of people who use the facility, but may have done this by offering free entry. In this case, the manager has been effective from a membership perspective, but ineffective financially. Actual evaluation of performance has to be done in the context of what is to be achieved.

There is also some debate about whether it is actually possible for organizations to fully manage their performance. Sanderson (1998) presented several concerns regarding the use of performance indicators in public services and these concerns are also applicable to sport organizations. First, he is unconvinced that performance indicators can deal with environmental complexity, which is a characteristic of the operating context within which sport organizations work. For example, not only does a judo club deliver services directly to its members, it may also be working in partnership with other agencies, such as British Judo – the sport's governing body – and schools to increase participation in the sport. To try and identify the contribution the club makes to the partnership, and to measure how effective this is, is considered by Sanderson (1998) to be too complex.

Second, performance management is based on the assumption of *controllability*, which is that all aspects of the organization are under the control of managers. Sanderson (1998) argues that this assumption is also flawed, as managers have no control over a number of features of their environment such as changes in customer tastes, new competition, changed political priorities concerning sport or even athletes' performance. In the case study above there are a number of performance indicators which may be outside of the sport federation's control such as international sport results per year, which may be affected by injury and staff turnover.

Third, and perhaps most importantly, Sanderson (1998) argues that performance management and measurement are based upon a fundamental assumption of *measurability*. The underlying premise of performance management is that all aspects of management can be measured. This assumption is clearly flawed, in that although it is possible to measure many aspects of a sport organization, there are some factors that simply cannot be evaluated. PIs have existed for some time in areas such as customer satisfaction, member numbers and finance. However, they have yet to be fully developed to measure the contribution of sport in combating obesity, or social exclusion or in contributing to 'human capital'. Sanderson (1998) feels that this will lead managers to focus on those aspects of the organization that can be easily measured. For example, measuring the number of children in a swimming class, but not how well they swim, would clearly be to miss the point of the exercise.

It is difficult to present a direct argument against these concerns, however these can be addressed in the way that PIs are interpreted and presented to stakeholders for their review. As long as a balanced set of PIs is collected in a consistent manner and interpreted sensibly, then performance management is a valuable tool for the management of sport organizations.

ACTION LEARNING

- What additional KPIs would you add to those above for sport federations?

- What is the danger with requiring managers to interpret KPIs?
- How can this be overcome?

CONCLUSION

This chapter has considered the role of performance management in the management of sport organizations and has argued that the systematic management of performance results in better planning and strategy delivery, a structured approach to the implementation and monitoring of plans, and an improvement in the subjectivity of management decision making.

Evaluation is fundamental to the performance management process and is reliant on good and appropriately developed performance indicators. This is often difficult to achieve for a variety of reasons, such as the complexity of the operating environment and because managers cannot measure and control all aspects of their organization's performance. The main solution to these concerns is in the interpretation of the performance indicators collected and managers must use such indicators to explain performance, which highlights the need for a holistic programme of performance management and evaluation.

REFERENCES

Effron, M. and Ort, M. (2012) Available at: www.forbes.com/sites/sylviavorhausersmith/2012/12/16/the-new-face-of-performance-management-trading-annual-reviews-for-agile-management (last accessed 27 September 2015).

Holloway, J. (1999) Managing performance. In A. Rose and A. Lawton (eds), *Public Services Management.* Harlow: Pearson Education.

Kaplan, R. and Norton, D. (1996) *The Balanced Scorecard.* Boston, MA: Harvard Business Press.

Oberoi, M. and Rajgarhia, P. (2014) What your performance management system needs most. Available at: www.gallup.com/businessjournal/161546/performance-management-system-needs.aspx (last accessed 9 November 2015).

Robinson, L. (2011) The management and measurement of organizational performance. In L. Trenberth and D. Hassan (eds), *Managing Sport Business.* London: Routledge.

Sanderson, I. (1998) *Achieving Best Value through Performance Review.* Warwick/DETR Best Value series, Paper No. 5. Coventry: Warwick University.

Taylor, P., Robinson, L.A., Bovaird, A., Gratton, C. and Kung, S. (2000) *Performance Measurement for Local Authority Sports Halls and Swimming Pools.* London: Sport England.

19

DOPING

AARON SMITH AND BOB STEWART

> What inspiration does Justin Gatlin give up-and-coming athletes? Take drugs, get caught twice and sign a shoe contract?!
>
> (Kelly Sotherton, Olympic bronze medal-winning heptathlete, 2015)
>
> We need to have independent testing. I was in part the architect of independent, random, wholly out-of-competition testing that is now the template.
>
> (Lord Sebastian Coe, IAAF President, 2015)
>
> I am absolutely determined to use the report to ensure that cycling continues the process of fully regaining the trust of fans, broadcasters and all the riders who compete clean.
>
> (Brian Cookson, UCI President, 2015)

LEARNING OUTCOMES

Upon completion of this chapter, students should be able to:

- Understand the doping issue in sport and its implications for contemporary sport policy.

- Demonstrate a familiarity with the kinds of prominent doping cases in contemporary sport and their consequences.

- Apply key policy theories and concepts to the doping issue in contemporary sport.

INTRODUCTION

Sport's high performance culture delivers innumerable, jaw-dropping and awe-inspiring physical achievements. However, for many sport fans, admiration and inspiration can be undermined by an unsettling suspicion that these remarkable achievements in sport came about because of more than just hard work, mental toughness, flawless skill and thorough preparation. With the omnipresent use of drugs in most societies around the world, and given their capacity to powerfully influence both body and mind, we should not be surprised that drug use in sport has become so endemic that a **global** law enforcement body was established to curtail their use. The formation of the World Anti-Doping Agency (WADA) in 1999, and its inaugural anti-doping policy in 2004, not only reinforced the view that doping in sport constitutes unmitigated cheating, but also assumed that uncontrolled drug use would threaten sport's social and **brand** value. WADA was created with the premise that drug use provides an unfair advantage. Worse, it is blatant cheating, threatens the health and playing longevity of players and athletes, tarnishes the reputation and good standing of sport, and as WADA likes to remind us, devalues the 'spirit of sport'. In short, taking drugs erodes the character-building and social-development properties that accompany sport (WADA, 2011). This chapter highlights the doping issue in contemporary sport, discusses several prominent cases as exemplars, and identifies some theories and concepts that assist in understanding the key policy issues and managerial responses.

CASE STUDY 19.1

Living Strong, Lying and Lance Armstrong

Exposés and scandals involving the illegal use of drugs in sport have been regular affairs. However, none can compare in scale and publicity to the case against Lance Armstrong – probably the world's greatest ever road-racing cyclist – made by the United States Anti-Doping Agency (USADA) in October 2012. For more than a decade Armstrong had indignantly denied ever taking performance-enhancing substances despite consistent claims made by his cycling teammates and competition that he had a long record of use (Coyle, 2006).

Armstrong was born in the US state of Texas in 1971, and by mid-adolescence discovered that he had prodigious ability as an endurance athlete (Armstrong, 2000). In 1988 he became a professional triathlete, and a year later the US Olympic development team invited him to train as a road cyclist. Armstrong showed elite racing potential quickly, and in 1992 represented the United States at the Barcelona Olympic Games. Although he did not win a medal, Armstrong turned professional soon after the Olympics and joined the US-based Motorola cycling team. He made his mark by finishing second in a World Cup race in Switzerland shortly thereafter (Armstrong, 2000). Although Armstrong contested his first Tour de France in 1993, after falling back to 62nd place he withdrew from the event. Nevertheless, he came back with vigour, winning the World Road Race Championship in Norway late in 1993.

By 1996 Armstrong's cycling career had slowed. Despite having earned a lucrative contract with Cofidas, a well-credentialled French team, he was again unable to complete the Tour de France and did not make much impact at the 1996 Atlanta Olympic Games. In late 1996 Armstrong was diagnosed with testicular cancer. To add to this tragic news, shortly after his doctors discovered brain tumours. Armstrong was given a 40% chance of surviving, but after many rounds of chemotherapy emerged cancer-free in early 1997.

Two years later in 1999, Armstrong won the first of seven consecutive Tour de France races as a member of the United States Postal Service team (Armstrong, 2000). After another six successful tours, Armstrong had become recognized as one of the best, and certainly the most famous, road cyclist of all time. Having achieved this extraordinary level of success, he retired in 2005, only to announce three years later that he planned to race once again in the Tour de France in 2009. Remarkably, Armstrong placed third in the race, beaten only by his teammate, Alberto Contador, who had his own drug-use problems to face in the 2010 Tour de France, and Saxo Bank team member Andy Schleck, whose brother Frank was alleged to have taken banned substances at various times during his career. After the race, Armstrong told reporters that he intended to compete again in 2010, with a new team sponsored by Radio Shack.

In a dramatic turnaround in 2012, the USADA brought formal charges against Armstrong and declared their intention of stripping him of his Tour titles. For years Armstrong had vehemently denied doping, meeting the USADA charges with the same off-hand response. He disparaged the new allegations, labelling them 'baseless'. However, in August 2012 Armstrong announced that he was giving up his fight against USADA's charges, advising that he would attempt to reach an arbitrated outcome in order to end the stress and media scrutiny. But the USADA remained unimpressed, announcing that Armstrong would be stripped of his seven Tour titles as well as other honours he had received from 1999 to 2005. With a mass of incontrovertible evidence to show that he had used illegal performance-enhancing substances throughout most of his career, the most successful road cyclist of all time was unceremoniously banned for life and branded as a drug cheat.

Supporting their case, in October 2012 the USADA released a 1,000-page report delivering the damning evidence against Armstrong. It included laboratory test results, emails and monetary payments, which, according to the USADA, showed that the US Postal Service Pro Cycling Team had operated the most sophisticated, professionalised and successful doping programme ever undertaken in professional cycling. In addition, the evidence contained testimony from 26 people, including several former members of Armstrong's cycling team, who claimed that not only had Armstrong used performance-enhancing drugs, but that he had also served as a 'ringleader' for the team's doping efforts (USADA, 2012). Armstrong vehemently disputed the USADA findings at first but later admitted that they were true, including in a much publicized 'tell all' television confession with Oprah Winfrey.

ACTION LEARNING

- Why do you think that the systematic use of drugs in cycling went undetected for so long?
- Do you think that Armstrong's treatment and punishment have been fair and reasonable, including the public response and media coverage as well as formal USADA and WADA sanctions? Explain why.
- What do you think that sport policy makers within cycling and other professional sports must do in order to secure a safe environment for players? Is doping-free professional sport even plausible?

TOOLS FOR ANALYSIS

Formal testing for performance-enhancing drugs was introduced at the Mexico Olympic Games in 1968 in response to the global spread of potent stimulants and anabolic steroids. The International Olympic Committee (IOC) subsequently established a list of prohibited classes of substances and prohibited methods (Dimeo, 2007; Taylor, 1991). However, it took a further 30 years for sport authorities to make the issue of doping an urgent global priority despite the growing number of pharmaceutical products that could improve sport performance, and despite the huge competitive edge that East German athletes secured in the 1970s (Hoberman, 1992; Hunt, 2007). The issue burst into the media spotlight with the Ben Johnson steroids incident at the 1988 Seoul Olympic Games. Doping allegations arising out of the 1996 Atlanta Olympic Games, and the Tour de France Festina team drug scandal of 1998, confirmed that performance-enhancing drug use in sport was widespread (Hanstad et al., 2008; Hoberman, 2001).

For sport officials, the breakthrough occurred in 1999 with the establishment of WADA. WADA became the global voice for the doping problem, identifying itself as the official anti-doping 'watch-dog' (Horvath, 2006: 358–359). The 2003 anti-doping code WADA introduced immediately provided a template for anti-doping policies in international and national governing bodies for sport (WADA, 2003). Three key objectives underpin WADA's mission and policy initiatives: first, to protect athletes' fundamental rights to participate in drug-free sport; second, to promote health, fairness and equality for athletes worldwide; and finally, to ensure harmonized and effective anti-doping programmes at the international and national level incorporating standardized approaches to detection, deterrence and prevention (WADA, 2003). The Code contains a list of banned substances including performance-enhancing drugs like erythropoietin, human growth hormone, anabolic androgenic steroids, the more powerful anti-inflammatory drugs and stimulants, as well as a range of non-performance enhancing, illicit drugs like cannabis, ecstasy and cocaine. Exemptions exist in the Code for athletes who can demonstrate a legitimate therapeutic purpose for a banned substance (WADA, 2003). In these instances, athletes with documented medical conditions like asthma can request a therapeutic use exemption from their national anti-doping agency and national sport governing body.

Under the WADA model, drugs that enhance performance are banned as they allow athletes to cheat. Further, drugs that represent a risk to the athlete's health are also restricted. According to WADA, sport organizations hold a duty of care to the athletes who participate in their competitions, and as a result must be protected through prohibitions on substances incurring health risks. While these first two criteria are clear, the third WADA policy platform is more ambiguous since it outlaws any drug that violates the 'spirit-of-sport'. Under the Code, the spirit-of-sport encapsulates the ideals of Olympism, the celebration of the human spirit, fun and joy, courage, teamwork, excellence in performance, respect for the rules and other participants, dedication and commitment, character and education, community and solidarity, ethics, fair play and honesty (WADA, 2003: 3). These values have been conflated into the initial WADA slogan of 'play-true', and its current mantra of 'drug free sport'. Moreover, if a drug meets two of the above three criteria, it will be listed as a banned substance (WADA, 2003: 15–16).

The WADA Code also distinguishes between drug use in-competition or in-season, and drug use out-of-competition or out-of-season (WADA, 2003). Performance-enhancing drugs are banned both in- and out-of-competition, which means all-year-round. Illicit drugs, on the other hand, are banned only in-competition or in-season (WADA, 2006). As a result, athletes and players can take illicit drugs out-of-competition without a penalty.

The WADA model also prefers punitive values in order to secure compliance through rigid penalties combining shaming with fines, disqualifications and, in extreme cases like that of Lance Armstrong, lifetime exclusion from sport participation. For a first violation involving the use or possession of a prohibited substance, players may be disqualified for up to two years, while for a second violation players can be disqualified for life (WADA, 2003). Some prohibited substances hold 'specified substance' status, and include medicinal products that players may inadvertently use with no intention of securing an improvement in athletic performance. In these cases a first offence may deliver a reprimand or warning, a second offence will incur a two-year suspension, while a third offence will lead to a lifetime ban (WADA, 2003). At worst, the penalties for trafficking can incur a four-year to lifetime suspension even for a first infraction. Illicit drug use delivers less severe penalties. For a first offence players face a 3- to 12-month suspension, for a second offence the penalty can extend to two years, while for a third offence players can be banned from the sport for life.

ACTION LEARNING

- Anti-doping policy relies on the success of drug testing regimes. Do you think these are successful and what other options might policy makers have at their disposal to reduce the incidence of doping in sport?
- Why do you think that WADA is interested in banning illicit, non-performance-

enhancing drugs? Do you think they should test out-of-season as well or not at all?
- Given the systematic and sustained doping undertaken by Lance Armstrong in professional cycling, do you think that the threat of penalties was any form of deterrent?

CASE STUDY 19.2

Baseball to BALCO

One of the highest profile doping cases in sport involved Major League Baseball's (MLB) Mark McGwire, who transformed himself from a lean rookie in 1987 to a heavyweight veteran in 1998, when he claimed the single-season home run record. McGwire admitted that the transformation resulted from a combination not only of hard work, but also the use of an over-the-counter testosterone-producing pill called androstenedione, or 'andro', as it was colloquially known (Bryant, 2005). Although 'andro' had been designated as a banned substance by the IOC, the American National Football League (NFL), the National Hockey League (NBA) and the National Hockey League (NHL), its use was initially permitted in MLB. In fact, a cocktail

of drugs were used by elite baseballers to improve their on-field performances and in 2003 the MLB announced that around 6% of nearly 1,500 anonymous tests on players had come back positive. San Francisco Giants' outfielder Barry Bonds was also linked to the use of a designer steroid, tetrahydrogestrinone, which had the nickname of 'clear' because of its ability to fly under the drug-testing radar (Fainaru-Wada and Williams, 2006). Bonds, who became MLB's home-run record holder, was subsequently indicted for perjury and obstructing justice by telling a federal grand jury he did not knowingly use performance-enhancing drugs, when in fact the evidence demonstrated that he had (Carroll, 2005: 129–132). Bonds had actually been a customer of the Bay Area Laboratory Co-operative (BALCO), a San Francisco Bay company that turned out to be a covert supplier of so-called 'designer' anabolic steroids to professional athletes. BALCO figured prominently in the

►

explosive revelations about the drug use of Marion Jones, one of the greatest female track sprinters of all time. Jones, who won five medals at the 2000 Sydney Olympic Games, pleaded guilty in October 2005 to lying to federal investigators about using anabolic steroids. While Jones had initially pleaded her innocence, her fate was sealed when she became ensnared in the BALCO scandal, which involved the supply of performance-enhancing substances to an array of elite players and athletes. BALCO founder Victor Conte maintained he had seen Jones inject herself with steroids, as had her ex-husband, C.J. Hunter. In addition, Hunter admitted he used steroids, and told a Grand Jury that Jones did too (Assael, 2007; Pampel, 2007).

TOOLS FOR ANALYSIS

From a theoretical viewpoint, two polar models of drug use policy and management can be identified, the first being zero-tolerance, and the second being harm-reduction. The zero-tolerance model, or 'prohibition', is all about eliminating drug use. It aims to reduce the number of people using drugs, curtailing the amount of drugs being used, or both. While zero-tolerance proponents would like to lower the risks of use, they seek to secure a wholesale fall in use as a priority. They understand that this may promote 'collateral harms' by increasing enforcement costs while treading on the rights of athletes, potentially ruining their careers and lifetime earning potential through one doping transgression. However, to zero-tolerance advocates the prohibition calculus represents a reasonable price to pay for maintaining a commitment to drug-free sport and the protection of sport's reputation. The prohibition option finds favour with those who believe in the maxim that sometimes you 'have to be cruel to be kind'. The policy option is underpinned by the assumption that most people are incapable of making rational and informed decisions when it comes to drug use, and that if left to their own devices, will destroy their health, and in some cases their lives or those of others. As a result, the best outcomes will come from having highly restrictive laws over supply and use, criminal sanctions and heavy duty policing. According to the logic of prohibitionists, it may be costly policy, but that is the price to be paid for credible, drug-free sport.

At the other extreme the harm reduction model addresses the negative consequences of use, rather than the act of use itself. The harms associated with drug use include health-related dangers such as the risk of death and serious illness, as well as social stigmatism and loss of personal dignity. While a harm reduction policy may incorporate strategies to promote the reduction of drug use, it aims to do so in a harm sensitive manner so as to avoid unwanted collateral problems. In theory, under the harm reduction model, it could be possible to actually broaden use while still reducing aggregate harms. The concept of tobacco-free cigarettes was once viewed in this light (Taylor, 1984). The free market option meets the aspirations of libertarians, who want the uncontested right to create their own lifestyles in their own ways. Libertarians want no sanctions, no enforcement, and unregulated distribution. They want the freedom to do whatever they wish with their own bodies, and the freedom to ingest whatever substances they desire in light of knowledge about the associated risk and harms. In this policy scenario, knowledge will come through proper packaging and detailed product information as well as widespread educational campaigns. This kind of policy thinking is underpinned by a laissez-faire/neo-liberal economic philosophy, promulgated in an era of diminished anti-monopoly sentiment, lower levels of consumer protection enforcement and a general absence of new regulatory initiatives (Hall, 2011). A laissez-faire/neo-liberal philosophy rests on two beliefs about suppliers, markets and consumers. First, consumers are sovereign in the sense that their purchase intention dictates what and how much should be produced and delivered to market. Second, most market failures could be eliminated or significantly reduced by an increase in intra-market competition. At the same time, this philosophy does not necessarily reduce the occurrence of social market failure, where athletes make decisions to use drugs despite the clear dangers and consequences (Mason and Scammon, 2011).

A middle ground can be found in the regulatory model. Under regulated conditions drugs are neither banned nor freely available. Instead, they are allowed for athletic use under strict conditions. Distribution will be controlled, usually through medical prescription, pharmacy dispensing and specialized outlets. Drug safety will be managed through government bureaucracies. Criminal sanctions may be applied in certain cases, but for the most part sanctions will take the form of fines and penalties. Problems associated with risk, harm and public health will be managed through educational campaigns, counselling and treatment in a proper medical or rehabilitation setting.

At first glance, prohibition appears to be an attractive option given its succinct and decisive interventions. It delivers a punitive edge, which for many people sends an unambiguous signal that doping in sport is wrong and has few redeeming social features. Moreover, in the long haul, drug use costs lives. History reveals that prohibition will never eliminate drug use. It will, however, most probably lower it, delivering a positive contribution to community health. Nevertheless, prohibition comes at a cost since drug quality will be low, exposure to criminal activity will be heightened, the stigma associated with being labelled a user will escalate and people's right to use the drugs of their choice will be curtailed.

A free market model has intuitive appeal since it will take the supply out of the hands of criminals and place it in the hands of the private business sector, which should immediately lead to an improvement in product quality, product knowledge and distribution. On the other hand, there is likely to be an increase in use along with public health risks, as well as an exacerbation of community anxieties. The free market model means that drug use in sport would be accepted as a normal rather than covert part of elite performance.

A regulatory model should, in theory, absorb the better features of the two previous models. At the same time it will be costly since it will demand a bureaucracy to manage the regulations. Still, use will be dampened, and the health problems will probably be lower than under a free market model. Determining the best bundle of tools to use for specific conditions and special circumstances requires a complex set of decisions (Freiberg, 2010). Finding an answer involves reflecting on what the proposed regulations aim to achieve, what types of behaviour and conduct should be punished, what forms of behaviour and conduct should be rewarded, and what social 'goods' or social utility are expected to follow. Few of these variables come into play under the WADA policy perspective where doping is a black and white issue of cheating and moral corruption, about which there should be zero-tolerance.

ACTION LEARNING

- Identify the three policy options for managing doping in sport and explain their underpinning assumptions.
- WADA is committed to the zero-tolerance policy model. Given this philosophical position, what else can WADA do to discourage doping in sport other than get 'even tougher'? Do you think that more severe penalties would decrease doping in sport?
- What kinds of regulatory methods might be employed by clubs, leagues and sport bodies to control doping? Consider options such as education, private drug and health screenings, biological passports, confidential medical support and the strident oversight of supply, for example.

CONCLUSION

The sample of cases we presented in this chapter confirms the seriousness of the drug use problem in sport around the world. While track and field, cycling, cross country skiing, weightlifting and professional team sports are the most vulnerable to drug use, it would be naive to think that other sports are exempt. Some commentators claim that team sports have few drug problems, since skill and strategy rate highly, but the spate of steroid use in MLB tells a different story. In reality, all sports that require strength, endurance, rapid recovery, and the capacity to absorb pain and discomfort present potential sites for performance-enhancing drug use. Moreover, those sports imposing stress and anxiety on their participants will also be conducive to recreational drug use, be it licit or illicit.

This brief snapshot of doping in sport reflects several salient issues driving the problem. First, we should keep in mind that sport has a colourful history of players taking substances to make them perform better, become more engaged, feel less stressed and cope with their social worlds more effectively. Second, doping in sport should come as no surprise, since its use is embedded in our broader society, and is consumed over-the-counter, by prescription or through illicit channels. Third, doping will escalate whenever sport claims additional corporate territory, and its players receive economic incentives to secure a competitive edge. Fourth, no matter what regulations control drug use and attempt to squeeze it out of sport altogether, drugs will always occupy a significant amount of space in sport for the simple reason that they can deliver athletes immense economic, social and personal value.

All of this sport-related drug use takes place in a world driven by two unstoppable forces. The first is technology. The pharmaceutical industry uses billions of dollars of research funds annually to formulate new drugs, medicines and practices that enhance people's quality of life and physical performance (Goldacre, 2012; Weyzig, 2004). As a result, a constant supply of new compounds gives players and athletes a competitive edge. The second is neo-liberalism and its underlying ideology of individualism. Individualism unleashes an insatiable desire for self-improvement where any gain in productivity, cognitive capacity, and physical prowess is never enough (Hall, 2011). This means that every step along the path of enhancement leads to significant economic, social and personal rewards, irrespective of the penalties for being caught. Under such an environment doping is going to be a problem in sport for the foreseeable future.

REFERENCES

Armstrong, L. (2000) *It's Not About the Bike: My Journey Back to Life*. Sydney: Allen and Unwin.

Assael, S. (2007) *Steroid Nation*. New York: ESPN Publishing.

Bryant, H. (2005) *Juicing the Game: Drugs, Power, and the Fight for the Soul of Major League Baseball*. New York: Penguin/Viking.

Carroll, W. (2005) *The Juice: The Real Story of Baseball's Drug Problems*. Chicago, IL: Ivan R. Dee.

Coyle, D. (2006) *Lance Armstrong: Tour de Force*. London: Harper Collins.

Dimeo, P. (2007) *Beyond Good and Evil: A History of Drug Use in Sport*. Abingdon: Routledge.

Fainaru-Wada, M. and Williams, L. (2006) *Game of Shadow: Barry Bonds, BALCO, and the Steroid Scandal that Rocked Professional Sport*. New York: Penguin/Gotham.

Freiberg. A. (2010) *The Tools of Regulation*. Sydney: Federation Press.

Goldacre, B. (2012) *Bad Pharma: How Drug Companies Mislead Doctors and Harm Patients*. London: Fourth Estate.

Hall, S. (2011) The neo-liberal revolution, *Cultural Studies*, 26(6): 706–728.

Hanstad, D., Smith, A. and Waddington, I. (2008) The establishment of the World Anti-Doping Agency: a study of the management of organizational change and unplanned outcomes, *International Review for the Sociology of Sport*, 43(4): 227–249.

Hoberman, J. (1992) *Mortal Engines: The Science of Performance and the Dehumanisation of Sport*. New York: The Free Press.

Hoberman, J. (2001) How Drug Testing Fails: The Politics of Doping Control, in W. Wilson and E. Derse (eds), *Doping in Elite Sport*. Champaign, IL: Human Kinetics, pp. 221–242.

Horvath, P. (2006) Anti-doping and human rights in sport: the case of the AFL and the WADA code, *Monash University Law Review*, 32(2): 358–359.

Hunt, T. (2007) Sports, drugs and the Cold War: the conundrum of Olympic doping policy 1970–1979. *Olympika: the International Journal of Olympic Studies*, 16: 19–41.

Mason, M. and Scammon, D. (2011) Unintended consequences of health supplement information regulations: the importance of recognising consumer motivations, *Journal of Consumer Affairs*, 45(2): 201–223.

Pampel, F. (2007) *Drugs and Sport*. New York: Infobase.

Taylor, P. (1984) *The Smoke Ring: Tobacco, Money and Multinational Politics*. London: Sphere.

Taylor, W. (1991) *Macho Medicine: A History of the Anabolic Steroid Epidemic*. London: McFarland.

United States Anti-Doping Agency (USADA) (2012) *Report on the Proceedings Under the World Anti-Doping Code and the USADA Protocol: United States Anti-Doping Agency (claimant) v. Lance Armstrong (respondent)*. Colorado Springs, CO: USADA.

Weyzig. A. (2004) *Sector Profile of the Pharmaceutical Industry*. Amsterdam: Somo Consulting Group.

World Anti-Doping Agency (WADA) (2003) *World Anti-Doping Code*. Montreal: WADA.

World Anti-Doping Agency (WADA) (2006) *The World Anti-Doping Code: the 2006 Prohibited List International Standard*. Montreal: WADA.

World Anti-Doping Agency (WADA) (2011) *Strategic Plan 2011–2016*. Montreal: WADA.

USEFUL WEBSITES

Doping cases at the Olympics, 1968–2010: http://sportsanddrugs.procon.org/view.resource.php?resourceID=004420

Drugs in sports: Designer Drugs-ESPN.com: http://espn.go.com/special/s/drugsandsports

Global Drug Reference Guide: www.globaldro.com

The World Anti-Doping Code 2012 Prohibited List: www.wada-ama.org/Documents/World_Anti-Doping_Program/WADP-Prohibited-list/2012/

US Anti-Doping Agency: www.usada.org

World Anti-Doping Agency: www.wada-ama.org

20

GAMBLING AND THE SPORTS BETTING INDUSTRY

DAVID FORREST

Betting has a tradition of accompanying football in England in the same way custard goes with English puddings.

(Inside World Football, 12 October 2013)

Football League: Sky Bet named new title sponsors in multi-year deal.

(Skysports.com, 18 July 2013)

Match fixing is cricket's cancer and the corruption refuses to go away.

(*The Mirror*, 1 July 2014)

LEARNING OUTCOMES

Upon completion of this chapter, students will be able to:

- Discuss issues in the sport betting industry that have significant impacts on sport managers in clubs and federations.

- Explain the **legal** status of sport betting in different countries.

- Describe fundamental changes in the sport betting industry and explore how these have implications for sport managers.

- Discuss the influence of **technology** on sport betting.

INTRODUCTION

The worlds of sport and gambling have been intertwined throughout the history of modern sport. Indeed, in at least three of the most popular sports (boxing, cricket and golf) rules were written down for the first time by betting interests who were motivated by the need for it to be very clear who had won a contest so that wagers could be settled without legal dispute. This codification enabled the sports to develop into national and international industries because everyone everywhere started playing by the same rules. Thus betting, in a sense, begat the worlds of sport we know today.

The two sectors, sport and betting, continue to feed off each other. They produce what **economists** term 'complementary goods'. The sports industry provides the events on which gamblers can bet. The gambling industry makes sport more interesting for potential **consumers** (e.g. it is more exciting to view a match if one has a stake in the result as 'neutrals' can make a bet and then care who wins). Hence the audience for the one sector grows whenever there is greater interest in the other.

However, this coincidence of interests is far from guaranteeing harmony between the sports and betting industries. For example, disputes arise because sports seek to gain directly from the growth of interest in betting by lobbying for the payment of royalties for the use of their fixture lists. And a large number of sports have been contaminated by cases of **match fixing** initiated by criminals who can make money on betting markets. Another dark issue in sport, related to betting, is the abnormally high incidence of gambling addiction among professional sportsmen.

This chapter begins to explore the sport betting industry and asks readers to consider three important issues which they may face as the leaders of sport federations. First, can and should the growth of betting on sport be exploited to generate a new revenue stream for sport? Second, how can they safeguard their sports against betting-related match fixing? Third, how should they protect their players against the snare of gambling addiction?

CASE STUDY 20.1

The Legal Status of Betting on Sport

In only a few countries, such as the UK, Ireland and Australia, is sports betting (commonly referring to wagering on events other than horse racing, which is usually treated by the law as a special case) supplied to the market more or less like any other good. In the UK, for example, a network of more than 9,000 bookmaker shops offer betting opportunities on the high street, and residents are permitted to trade with betting websites worldwide without restriction. There is some regulation (such as bookmakers having to comply with rules to prevent under-age play and money laundering) but there is no restriction on the sports offered, the subjects of the bet, and so on, and bookmaker commission rates are left to find their 'free market' level.

In Continental Europe, the model until recently was typically for betting to be legal only with a state-sanctioned monopolist, often the operator of the national lottery. In the Nordic countries particularly, state-owned betting firms, such as Svenska Spel in Sweden, operated large and lucrative betting businesses. In recent years, this model has come under pressure from decisions at the European Court of Justice to the effect that the Single Market provision in the European Economic Area limits the right of member states to protect their markets from entry by betting businesses based in other member states. This has permitted such as British, Irish and Austrian bookmakers to offer betting, either in retail outlets or via the internet, in previously monopolized markets. However, the concessions have often been grudging and limited. For example, France now grants licences for extra-territorial operators to market into France but subject to low maximum limits on the proportion of stakes returned to bettors as winnings. This impedes competition and French bettors who break the law by accessing international websites will still secure much more generous odds.

In the USA, betting on sport is prohibited except in Nevada, where the casinos offer 'sports books'. But the **law** is far from effective in preventing Americans in other states from betting. There has long been a very widespread underground betting industry, estimated by Carpenter (2013) to generate more than 100 times as much turnover as the legal Nevada sports books. Latterly, offshore websites, based in the Caribbean and pitched at the American market, continue to provide another outlet for prospective bettors, despite attempts by the authorities to close them down by making it illegal for American banks to process credit card transactions related to gambling. The long-established prohibitionist legal stance towards sports betting in the USA, vocally supported by sports governing bodies such as the National Football League (NFL) and the National Collegiate Athletic Association (NCAA), was tested in the courts in late 2013 after the State of New Jersey proposed to legalise (and tax) internet sports betting. New Jersey was denied the right to permit sports betting but the case now will be heard by the Supreme Court.

Asia is the region with the highest volume of sports betting in the world even though nearly all jurisdictions there, including China and India, follow prohibition, just like the USA. As in America (and in the UK prior to legalisation in 1961), illegal street bookmakers are ubiquitous. A problem for such small-scale bookmakers is that they may lack sufficient capital reserves to ensure they can pay out if their clients enjoy winning streaks. This has led to the development of a complex pyramid structure to the industry (explained in IRIS, 2012), where bets are passed up to bigger operators, allowing aggregation of bets and spreading of risk. In the modern era, aggregated bets are often placed, at the last stage of a fast electronic journey, with pan-Asian legal operators. The five biggest of these, amongst which SBOBET is the world's largest bookmaker, are licensed in the Cagayan special economic zone in the Philippines. Despite these bookmakers therefore being technically legal, and indeed having a reputation for treating bettors entirely fairly, their activities are often referred to as taking place in 'grey markets' because regulation is very loose and, for example, large bets may be placed anonymously, through agents, which is not permitted in Europe.

TOOLS FOR ANALYSIS

The impact of e-commerce

Over about a dozen years, the internet revolution has transformed the sports betting sector, triggering explosive growth. At the start of this period, potential bettors typically either had to defy legal prohibition or they had to place bets with local operators which faced no competition. Once these bettors were enabled to access suppliers worldwide competition intensified, and predictably they secured much superior value for money. I obtained (from www.football-data.co.uk) closing odds offered by Ladbrokes, the largest British bookmaker, on football matches in the English Premier League between seasons 2000–01 and 2010–11. Over each season there were 380 matches, with home win, draw and away win three possible bets on each match. Placing a one unit stake on each of the 380 × 3 bets would have yielded a loss of 11.13% of stakes in the first season, which is a measure of the bookmaker's commission. By the final season, the bettor's loss had fallen to 6.10%, a near halving of the 'price of betting' (Forrest, 2012). *And* bettors could now reduce average losses even further by using price comparison websites, to get the best odds in the market on each individual bet.

Improved value for money was only one aspect of betting that was making it more attractive. The product had also become more diverse as the market grew, partly due to intense globalised competition and partly because the rapidity of communication online facilitated entirely new modes of betting. Every bookmaker now offers far more subjects for a wager than simply who will win a match. For example, in tennis, all operators routinely offer 30 or more bets on each match (apart from on which player will win) such as: what will be the final score in sets (2–0, 1–2, etc)? how many points will player x win (over or under a specified number)? how many aces will player y serve? Such bets, on subjects other than the final winner, have come to be known as *proposition bets* or *derivatives*. They attract new betting interest from gamblers who like to bet at long odds in sports where players or teams are usually closely matched and the odds on who will win are not far from evens. (The term as used here, and commonly, refers to wagering on events other than horse racing, which is usually treated by the law as a special case.)

Practically, the most important **innovation** has been the availability of 'live' or 'in-play' betting. Rapid communication now makes it feasible for bettors to place bets almost instantly in reaction to events on the field (which they might be watching on television or on a live internet feed). Automated odds-setting systems are programmed to shift the odds immediately in response to key events, such as a try in rugby or a break-point in tennis. The new 'live' product evidently appeals strongly to bettors. Industry sources estimate that 70% of stakes in football, and 90% in tennis, are now placed during a match rather than before play commences.

A final important change associated with the emergence of e-commerce in gambling is that the market has become **globalized**. Professional bettors in Europe can and do place their bets in Asia (where bookmakers' margins are tighter and where high total volumes allow large bets to be accepted).

Betting operators in Asia can and do manage risk by hedging into European markets. The effective integration of the two markets is such that odds movements in Asia are mirrored in Europe in less than a minute. Movements in odds nearly always originate in Asia because it is much the larger segment of the market (typically with twice the volume of Europe for sports events taking place in Europe). So it is the leader and Europe the follower.

The growth in the size of the market

From this betting revolution, then, has emerged a world market the liquidity of which has been increasing very fast. Exactly how fast betting volumes have increased is hard to assess because a high proportion of stakes are placed illegally or in grey markets. But commercial consultancies, with analysts experienced in the betting industry, attempt to produce 'best estimates'. Gross Gambling Yield (GGY) is the amount lost by bettors to bookmakers (i.e. stakes minus winnings) and is therefore interpretable as consumer spending. Estimates by CK Consulting, in SportAccord (2011), point to a more than tripling of the GGY from sports betting between 2000 and 2010, to €19 billion per year.

Such a figure is hard to grasp and comprehend. Perhaps a more vivid illustration of the scale of betting on sport is obtained by asking how much an individual could bet on a match without it attracting suspicion and without it changing the odds unfavourably to the bettor. IRIS asked experienced personnel how much could be placed on the result of a Belgian second division football match through agents in Asia. The consensus was €200,000–300,000. This reflects how much betting volume there is at even a modest level of competition. Football and cricket attract the biggest volumes by sport and liquid markets extend to the lower tiers of competition.

Who bets?

In Great Britain, gambling regulators have carried out three large-scale surveys (The British Gambling Prevalence Survey, BGPS), in 1999, 2007 and 2010, to obtain a rich picture of the country's gambling habits. The data provide an opportunity for finding out, for one jurisdiction at least, which demographic is driving the growth in betting on sport.

The data speak clearly. The market for sports betting is predominantly male, young and relatively affluent. In the BGPS for 1999, 5% of adult men (over-16) and 1% of women self-reported betting with a bookmaker on events other than horses and dogs. By 2010, these figures were 14% and 3%. Over the same period, the prevalence of horse betting was quite stable, reflecting that sport was capturing market share from horse racing. Possibly this reflected improving relative value for money. There was no fall in bookmaker margins on the horses: international websites do not typically offer bets on domestic horse racing programmes and therefore local providers' margins were not driven down as they were in sports betting.

The 2010 data reveal that prevalence of sports betting was 14% for the age-group 16–24 years and 15% for 25–34 year-olds. Participation then fell steadily by age-group to 2% for 65–74. The same heterogeneity by age was not evident in horse betting. So it is participation sports betting rather than betting more generally that is skewed towards the young.

When respondents to the 2010 BGPS were divided into quintiles according to size of personal income, the lowest participation rate in sports betting (8%) was found to be in the bottom quintile and the highest (12%) in the top quintile. There was therefore something of a skew towards the affluent. If 'young, male and affluent' sums up the audience for sports betting, perhaps this makes it similar to that targeted by sport and sports broadcasters. It underlines the intersecting interests of the two industries.

ACTION LEARNING

- What arguments for or against might be put in a national debate in countries like India and the USA on whether prohibition should be lifted and a legal, regulated and taxed legal sports betting sector be permitted?

- Why does organised sport in a country like the USA lobby for a continuation of the prohibition of sports betting?

Can and should sports aim to promote a new revenue stream from betting?

Over the past couple of decades, there have been significant changes in revenue sources for professional sport. At one time, ticket sales at the stadium provided most of a club's income. But in the modern era, broadcasting rights and sponsorship may be of equal or even greater importance. One question which arises is whether sport can tap into the explosive growth of sports betting to turn betting revenue into a fourth pillar of income generation.

The most obvious route would be for sports to charge fees for the use of their fixtures in the commercial operations of the betting industry. Naturally this would not be welcome to betting operators. In Europe, an ongoing battle is being conducted between lobbyists on either side (e.g. the Sports Rights Owners Coalition versus the European Gaming and Betting Association), with each winning occasional victories. But the pan-European legal framework is not generally favourable to the idea of sports organisations having copyright over use of their fixtures. In 2012, the European Court of Justice (Case G604/10) adjudicated in a case between the company that manages data for the English Premier League and betting interests. Consistent with an earlier similar verdict concerning lists of horses in each race fixture (Case C-203-02), it found that the sport had no copyright protection. Copyright law conferred protection only where the product embodied 'originality', and while the technical task of compiling fixtures required 'significant labor and skill', it did not require 'originality'. Not only did the court deny football property rights in this case, it also declared unlawful any legal attempt in any member state of the European Economic Area to assert property rights in sports fixtures, a pre-emptive strike against moves to change national legislation in Europe in favour of sport. Outside Europe, much betting activity of course takes place in illegal or in 'grey' markets, where claiming copyright fees would be liable to be difficult.

However, contemporary sport generates other data than fixture lists and here there is more prospect of securing revenue from the betting industry. Where live betting predominates, betting requires a stream of instantly available data on what is happening in a match and governing bodies are well placed to organise the systematic streaming of such data to betting 'data partners'. The English Premier League has been active in originating and marketing such services. Data on player performance, generated by 'player tracking', may also find a market.

But the main way professional sport is winning revenue from the betting sector is through **sponsorship** and advertising agreements. This is the avenue explored in Case Study 20.2.

CASE STUDY 20.2

Commercial Partnerships between Football Clubs and Betting Firms

Professional football has recognised that it can claim a share of the rapidly growing revenue for betting by entering into commercial relationships with bookmakers. In the English Premier League in season 2013–14, one club, Stoke City, was actually owned by a bookmaker and three others, Aston Villa, Fulham and West Ham United, had betting firms as their principal sponsor. Such sponsorship deals are typically worth £5 million per season to a club (Scott, 2013, quoting sportingintelligence.com). Those four clubs, and indeed all of the other 16 in the league, had additional sponsorship contracts with 'official betting partners'.

Five had contracts nominating SBOBET, the world's largest bookmaker, as their 'official Asian betting partner'. According to the nature of the contractual arrangements in each case, bookmaker names appear on team shirts or perimeter advertising or club websites, and there may be betting concessions within the stadium.

The English Premier League has been notably enthusiastic in embracing betting, but the trend extends to other tiers of competition in England and to other football and sports leagues in Europe and elsewhere. The English Football League is itself sponsored by a bookmaker (and so the next division below the Premier League is the 'Sky Bet Championship'). Examples of new sponsorships elsewhere, announced in late 2013, included: Central Europe's largest betting operator, Fortuna, pledging €1.5 million per season to Polish club Legia Warsaw; SportYes, an Italian betting brand, becoming stadium sponsor at Italian Serie A club FC Livorno; and Swedish bookmaker UNIBET being named as shirt sponsor at Australian Rugby League club Parrametta Eels.

These are just a handful of many examples. Betting has in fact become ubiquitous in football and several other major sports. That the players of celebrated clubs like Real Madrid wear betting brands on their shirts, that television viewers of cricket test matches see betting advertisements on boundary boards whenever a four is scored, that commercial breaks in television coverage of football are dominated by advertisements for gambling websites, all this underlines the close relationship between the sports and betting industries.

Why can sport extract revenue from betting firms? Because the customers for betting are accessible through marketing via the sports events themselves. For example, the trade website Sports Betting Community (23 August 2013) noted that SBOBET's partnerships with five English Premier League clubs secured it perimeter advertising at all home games, amounting effectively to 1,000 minutes of global advertising per season. The League's matches are broadcast in more than 200 countries and viewers will include the young, affluent, interested-in-football audiences that a transnational betting enterprise seeks to reach.

ACTION LEARNING

- If football clubs are owned or funded by betting firms, does this raise any conflict of interest? Might betting firms seek to influence results?
- Gambling is an entertainment to the majority but a harmful and ruinous addiction to some. How does accepting funding in return for promotion of betting products, particularly to young people, fit in with the notion of corporate social responsibility in the sports industry?

THE THREAT FROM MATCH FIXING

While betting interest stimulates an interest in sport, indirectly promoting additional revenue, and as Case Study 20.1 illustrated, providing the prospect of a direct revenue stream as well, it also carries dangers. Where betting markets are liquid enough to absorb large bets, criminals have the potential to win large sums of money by persuading sports insiders to manipulate events on the field in their favour. Of course, successful match fixes may never come to light. Fixes that are discovered are the tip of an iceberg of uncertain size. But certainly revelations have occurred frequently over the last five years, in football, cricket, tennis, handball, darts, snooker, rugby league, sumo wrestling and basketball, amongst other sports. For example, at the end of 2013, criminal trials were in progress charging footballers in

Italy (representing all tiers of competition), Austria (26 players, including from every club in the top division) and Australia, and cricketers from the Indian and Bangladeshi Premier Leagues. Fixing can be on an industrial scale. One gang based in Bochum, Germany, was found guilty of fixing more than 300 football matches in 13 countries. An alleged criminal is charged in Singapore with fixing 600 matches worldwide.

Fixing is of course offensive to the spirit of sport. But does it also pose an existentialist threat to sports leagues and clubs in terms of financial viability? The first risk is that demand from live and television audiences will fall if the product comes to be perceived as contrived and lacking credibility. The second risk is that the value of sponsorship rights will fall because many potential sponsors will not bid if they fear association with a disreputable product. The Chinese Football League collapsed following revelations of widespread fixing: attendances shrunk and the national broadcaster pulled out, as did the League sponsor, Pirelli (IRIS, 2012). In late 2013, Puma withdrew from its partnership with the South African Football Association, explicitly citing its concern over fixing in South African football, while Barclays terminated its sponsorship of the national team (news24.com).

Recent accusations of fixing in football have in fact implicated a majority of FIFA member countries. But Case Study 20.3 focuses on one particular instance reported in 2013, in the Victorian Premier League, which sits in the second tier of the Australian game.

CASE STUDY 20.3

Corruption of Australian Soccer

Australia could be argued to be something of a soccer backwater. And the Southern Stars Club does not even play in its national league. The club's players, a few overseas, many part-time and playing for 'pocket money', compete in a lower level competition in the State of Victoria. They play against clubs like Hulme Green, Green Gully, Pascoe Vale and Oakleigh.

That is a fixture list which might seem unlikely to attract the interest of international criminals. Yet in September 2013, the coach and four of Southern Stars' players were charged by police with fixing its matches against those four clubs.

It was alleged that a new owner had recruited new players who were known to be willing to fix matches (similar cases have been proven in Belgium and Finland). The conspiracy was claimed to be led by a Malaysian national who had been successful in his plan to reap large profits on betting markets (*Herald Sun*, 18 September 2013).

The League in Victoria could not be argued to offer other than a low level of competition. Yet its matches can attract heavy betting volumes in Asia, where the Australian game is a particularly attractive subject for soccer bettors because of the time zones where it takes place. On Friday night, at the start of the weekend, the next football product on offer to an Asian gambler is Australian.

TOOLS FOR ANALYSIS

Economists draw on theory from the economics of crime to organise their thoughts on the issue of fixing. Ehrlich (1996) looked to understand crime in terms of the supply and demand of offences. Forrest (2011, 2014) operationalises the idea with 'the fix' as the offence. The supply of fixes comes from sports insiders, usually players but perhaps referees or coaches. The demand for fixes comes from criminals, often in international organised crime, who buy fixes so they can make money in the betting market.

Supply of offences: The willingness of sports insiders to sell a fix for a given price depends on factors such as how likely they are to be detected, the penalty on detection (e.g. lost earnings from a life ban), the value to them of loss of glory and reputation from playing badly and the cost of a bad conscience (if they have moral scruples). A higher proportion of players will be willing to fix if there is little chance of being caught, if earnings are low in any case, if there is little at stake in the game and if they feel themselves to be badly treated (and they therefore have no moral scruples about cheating their employer).

Demand: The willingness of criminals to pay for fixes depends on how much profit they could make in the betting market from manipulating a match. This in turn depends simply on betting volume. If the market is very liquid, a large bet can be placed and large profits secured, making it worthwhile to offer a high bribe in the market for fixes.

Putting supply and demand together, a particularly dangerous situation is where player wages/prizes are low but betting volumes are high. Examples of such situations are professional darts competitions, second-tier football leagues, American college sports (where player wages are zero!), and matches in major tennis tournaments involving players outside the small number with a genuine chance of reaching the final stages. It is in just such environments where the majority of proven cases of corruption have occurred (Forrest, 2014). Of course, that is not to say that top-tier sport will be entirely immune, as instances in elite Indian cricket and Italian football demonstrate.

The supply–demand framework also aids understanding of which aspects of a match criminals will attempt to fix. For example, players may be very willing to get themselves a yellow card in return for a bribe. But they are unlikely to find a buyer for this offence because, while bookmakers will take wagers on the number of yellow cards, the betting volumes are small and it is not possible to place a large bet or win a large sum of money. In general, criminals will attempt to influence the result of a football match or the total number of goals in the match since these are the high volume betting markets where large bets are possible. Similarly, in cricket, the large markets are on the result and on the number of runs in a session. In basketball, liquidity is high only in markets on the match result and on the total points in the game. Criminal trials show that these are indeed invariably subject to fixes. Probably the most common transaction in the market for fixes is for defenders in football to be paid to concede goals. Defenders can make small, hard-to-detect mistakes that have a high chance of leading to a goal, and substantial profits are to be made in the betting market on total goals in a match.

ACTION LEARNING

- Find out what sorts of policies are pursued by sports in terms of attempting to mitigate risks of fixing. Useful sources include SportAccord (2011) and a collection of readings edited by Haberfeld and Sheehan (2014).

A controversial blog (www.declanhill.com) on match fixing by Canadian journalist Declan Hill, author of *The Fix*, often charges sports federations and clubs with turning a blind eye to fixing – why might they do this?

ACTION LEARNING

- How could management of a sports league assess how vulnerable its competition is to the threat of betting-related fixing?

- What measures might be considered to protect a given sport in a given country from match fixing?

PROBLEM GAMBLING IN THE SPORTS COMMUNITY

The final case deals with a very different issue, that of problem gambling among sports players. Nevertheless, it is tangentially linked to Case Study 20.3 because problem gamblers usually get into debt and are then become particularly vulnerable to approaches from match fixers.

CASE STUDY 20.4

High Incidence of Gambling Disorder Among Athletes

'Problem-' or 'pathological-gambling' is a recognised mental health problem. It is termed 'gambling disorder' in the 5th edition of the *Diagnostic and Statistical Manual* of the American Psychiatric Association. Those suffering from it are documented to experience serious harm that is evident in severely elevated rates of unemployment, divorce, bankruptcy and suicide. Fortunately, its prevalence is estimated as below 1% in most jurisdictions where population surveys monitor gambling behaviour. In the Health Survey for England (2013), the prevalence rate among adults was estimated as 0.4%, using a screen, the Problem Gambling Severity Index, which asks questions designed to reveal dependence on and harm from gambling. Unfortunately, prevalence rates among athletes appear from many indicators to be far above this level.

Certainly it is not hard to find examples of famous and well-paid sportsmen who have got into trouble from excessive gambling. Online, *Business Insider* lists 'ten pro athletes who couldn't stop gambling'. The *Betfair* website also presents cautionary tales of 'seven sportsmen who blew a fortune'. All the names in these lists enjoyed celebrity status and superstar earnings but nevertheless got into very severe problems from betting or casino gaming.

However, the problems extend beyond the elite to the lower levels of professional sport. The British addiction charity Sporting Chance reported treating more sportsmen with gambling than was the case with drink and drug problems (news story, casinos-online, 2013). A propensity to excessive gambling is evident also among serious athletes below professional level. Rhind (2011) notes concern over problem gambling prevalence among college players in America and reports the results of a large survey of British university sports players. Using the same screen as the Health Survey for England, Rhind classified 9.2% of male athletes and 1.1% of female athletes as problem gamblers, suggesting a serious cause for concern.

Why might problem gambling be so extensive among sportsmen compared with the rest of the population? First, the two most firmly established risk factors for problem gambling are 'male' and 'young' (Johanson et al., 2009). The world of sport (and its culture) is of course disproportionately male and young. Personality traits such as a taste for risk and high sensation-seeking are also relevant. There is every reason to suppose that sport attracts risk takers. Sulloway and Zweigenhaft (2010) found that players who engaged more often in risky strategies ended with better career records and longer tenure in Major League Baseball. A taste for risk appears, then, to favour success in sport, and therefore it seems implied that those who are good enough to play professional or college sport will include a high proportion of risk lovers, likely to be drawn to gambling where risk is actually the defining characteristic of the product consumed. Add to this the periods of inactivity that training schedules include, and the willingness of sportsmen to believe that they have above-average knowledge of sport such that they might be expected to win money at betting, and it is easy to appreciate why gambling and gambling disorders are serious issues in the world of sport.

TOOLS FOR ANALYSIS

The sources of gambling disorder and the effectiveness of interventions are the subjects of large literatures, particularly in psychology. Many relevant articles appear in the specialist scientific journals *International Gambling Studies* and *Journal of Gambling Studies*. Johanson (2009) offers a synthesis of empirical studies seeking to identify risk factors.

- In light of problems associated both with match fixing and addictive behaviour, should sports prohibit players from betting with bookmakers?
- To what extent do managers of a sports club or a college athletic programme owe a duty of care to their players? Who in an organisation should intervene if a player appears to be losing control of their gambling? What form might this intervention take?

CONCLUSION

Gambling is pervasive in society and it is therefore unsurprising that it impinges heavily on the world of sport, in many dimensions. This chapter has focused on three issues.

If betting on sport is extensive, many would argue that it is entitled to squeeze as much revenue as it can from the betting sector. For managers in professional sport, the first case examined how lucrative partnerships with betting could be and encouraged readers also to think about and discuss the propriety of conferring legitimacy on betting by presenting it explicitly as part of the sports product.

No matter how high or low profile a sports competition is, it may be the subject of betting whether approved by the sport or not. Commentary around the second case explored the danger that manipulation of a parallel betting market would threaten the integrity of competition.

The final case study focused on the love of gambling evident among many who play sport at a serious level. It sought to raise awareness among managers of professional and student sport programmes of the extent to which gambling may be causing problems in the lives of their athletes.

REFERENCES

Carpenter, K. (2013). The United States and sports betting: the great sports hypocrisy. *Law In Sport* (www.lawinsport.com), 25 June.

Ehrlich, I. (1996). Crime, punishment and the market for offences. *Journal of Economic Perspectives*, 10: 43–67.

Forrest, D. (2011). The threat to football from betting-related corruption. *International Journal of Sport Finance*, 7: 99–116.

Forrest, D. (2012). Online gambling: an economics perspective. In R. Williams, R. Wood & J. Parke (eds), *Routledge Handbook of Internet Gambling*. London: Routledge, pp. 29–45.

Forrest, D. (2014). Match fixing: an economics perspective. In M.R. Haberfeld & D.L. Sheehan (eds), *Match Fixing in International Sports: Existing Processes, Law Enforcement and Prevention Strategies*. Berlin: Springer.

Haberfeld, M.R. & Sheehan, D.L. (eds) (2014) *Match Fixing in International Sports: Existing Processes, Law Enforcement and Prevention Strategies*. Berlin: Springer.

IRIS (2012). *Paris sportifs et corruption: Comment préserver l'intégrité du sport,* IRIS éditions, Institut de Rélations Internationales et Stratégiques, Paris. (English language edition available in electronic format only.)

Johanson, A., Grant, J.E., Kim, S.W., Odlaug, B.L. & Göterstam, K.G. (2009). Risk factors for problematic gambling: a critical literature review. *Journal of Gambling Studies*, 25: 67–92.

Rhind, D.J.A. (2011). Do you want to bet? The prevalence of problem gambling amongst athletes in the UK, London Workshop of Problem Gambling (www.brunel.ac.uk).

Scott, M. (2013). Time to overhaul football's betting relationship. *Inside World Football* (www.insideworldfootball.com), 13 December.

Sport Accord (2011). Integrity in sport: understanding and predicting match fixing, Sport Accord, Moudon, Switzerland.

Sulloway, F. and Zweigenhaft, R. (2010). Birth order and risk-taking in athletics: a meta-analysis and study of Major League Baseball. *Personality and Social Psychology Review*, 14: 402–416.

21

FUNDING FOR SPORT

ELWYN COX

Rio 2016: Weightlifting only winner in UK Sport funding appeals
(BBC Online, 19 March 2014)

FA disappointed by Sport England decision to cut funding
(The FA Online, 27 March 2014)

Football and cricket facing funding cuts by Sport England
(Sky Sports Online, 27 March 2014)

LEARNING OUTCOMES

Upon completion of this chapter, students will be able to:

- Discuss the difference between the funding and financing of grassroots and elite sport in the UK.

- Discuss how funding is allocated to sports in the UK and the importance of sport funding as a national issue.

- Discuss how the public, private and voluntary sectors are involved in funding sport in the UK and some differences in other countries.

- Discuss the implications of national funding policies for longer-term planning for managers of sport organizations where funding is the primary support.

INTRODUCTION

Modern sport uses resources up to the level that was needed to stage the 2012 Olympic Games, the largest sporting **mega event** currently sought after by governments to showcase their countries and achieve their sporting objectives for the nation. It is the job of the sport manager to find such resources needed and to use these as effectively as possible to achieve the required objectives. In developed countries much of sport is professional and entirely **commercialized**, but amateur sport has also needed to embrace sound management principles.

The money to pay for resources can take two forms, i.e. funding or financing. Whilst the concepts are often used interchangeably there is a difference, namely whether or not the sources of monetary support for the sports organization originate from the public or private sector. The focus of this chapter will be on funding, but will also include examples of financing to illustrate the distinction between them. This division has been noted by previous authors (Byers et al., 2012), whilst others focus instead on the challenges of financing facing commercial private sector organizations in sport (Stewart, 2007). In fact Stewart's (2007) consideration is heavily weighted towards effective accounting and organizational aspects of commercial sports enterprises rather than the funding of the public and third sectors that have different agendas including health and wellbeing through participation.

Definitions of funding suggest that such a resource is provided by government or other organizations to be used for a specific purpose. The reason for providing funding will not be to provide a financial profit. This is different from the financing of sport, although the boundaries are sometimes difficult to define. Within athletics there is funding potentially available from grassroots through to elite level participation, but individual iconic events within the sport, such as the London Marathon, will be run on a commercial basis.

The follow examples from the sport of football will illustrate this difference.

Manchester United is internationally known as a highly successful English Premier League football club whose central purpose is to gain financial income from a number of sources with the overall aim of making a profit – they need *financing* for their activities.

In contrast an amateur football team that exists to provide those who are excluded or underprivileged with sporting opportunities that could strengthen their community might apply for *funding*. An example of a potential funding provider in this instance would be Sport Relief's Community Foundation Programme.

Later the more complex situation experienced by contemporary sports organizations will be reviewed.

Case Study 21.1 tracks what has been seen as a very effective use of funding which has brought benefits when allied with good management practice.

CASE STUDY 21.1

British Cycling

Support from UK Sport and Sport England has always been at the heart of British Cycling's Vision and Strategy over the past decade and our performances internationally and growth at grass roots level are as a direct result of that investment. (British Cycling, 2009)

This acknowledgement is taken from British Cycling's *The Whole Sport Plan 2009–2013*. The decade prior to its date of publication would have encompassed the three Olympic Games of Sydney 2000, Athens 2004 and Beijing 2008. Figure 21.1 includes the level of medal success during those three events. Additionally it includes the results of the London 2012 cycling events.

Although there was a fall in the total medal count during London 2012 it represented the achievement of the sport's higher target and has resulted in a further increase in funding for the Rio 2016 Games in Brazil. During the period of Lottery funding for cycling from 1995 to the present day, the tally of Olympic medals stands at 19 gold, 7 silver and 9 bronze from five Olympic Games (see Figure 21.1). In the five Games prior to 1995 the medal count was a single gold for Chris Boardman at the 1992 Barcelona Games.

Overall the total for Olympic medals since National Lottery funding began stands at 35 medals compared to a sole medal in the equivalent number of pre-Lottery Games (www.olympics.org).

The impact of funding on cycling medal success is acknowledged by Sir Chris Hoy, a major figurehead during the period of success:

The bottom line is without UK Sport, the support I received through Lottery funding and the World Class Performance Program I wouldn't be where I am today. I would still be in the sport I'm sure, but there's no chance I'd have achieved these goals. It's simply not possible at this level and in this day and age. (Sir Chris Hoy, quoted on the UK Sport website)

Based on both the medal count and direct acknowledgement from senior representatives within the sport of cycling,

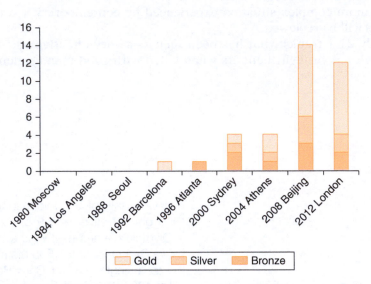

FIGURE 21.1 *British Olympic cycling success 1980–2012*

there would seem to be a clear correlation between effective utilization of the funding provided and the ability to create repeated competitive achievements.

There may also be less obvious consequences. Olympic and World Championship success produced a further catalyst as commercial sponsors became willing to add their support. In particular the media organization Sky created interventions at both the elite and grassroots level.

At the higher echelons the improved training, support structure and experience afforded to these athletes were reflected in success in road cycling that had never been seen before, including the unprecedented British winners of the Tour de France in 2012 and 2013.

Sky also aligned itself with the broader objective of encouraging participation in cycling through its Skyride initiative – again with the cooperation of British Cycling. This more direct involvement is characteristic of a new breed of hybrid sponsors who provide more than money and a brand as they take an active part in developing the sport they fund. Initiatives such as Skyride can boost grassroots cycling participation and help the sport achieve the targets on which future public funding relies.

In this case the target increase in participation as evidenced by the Active People Survey is from 1,962,000 in 2013 to 2,087,000 by 2017, and is a condition of funding set by Sport England (Sport England, 2013).

TOOLS FOR ANALYSIS

To obtain sport funding, the network of influences that act upon funding policy need to be understood. The case study of the sport of cycling in Britain suggests a clear correlation between levels of funding and international success in competition, plus evidence of an increase in non-competitive cycling. However, not all funded sports have achieved such success. Houlihan (2005) expressed concern at the lack of critical academic evaluation of sport policy. Green (2006) noted a shift from broad access to a sport provision to a sharper twofold focus on the 'active citizen' and a 'No Compromise' approach to winning medals. Neither author questions the principle of funding sport, but instead considers the basis for deciding fund allocation.

However, Grix and Carmichael (2012) go further and question whether the central assumptions about the intrinsic value of government support for sport are valid. They conclude that the idea of elite sporting success leading to mass participation is suspect at best. Trimble et al. (2010) further review changing government policy and consider how the public, private and third sector all contribute to the provision of sport.

In some cases private sector funding can replace or reinforce that of the public sector as with the growth of sponsorship. More recently, the changing nature of the sponsor's contribution might involve direct engagement within coaching and development as well as more traditional kit or stadia naming rights. This was illustrated at several levels within the case study above.

THE TRANSIENT NATURE OF FUNDING

The availability of funding is a function of two factors: the willingness to provide that funding combined with the actual ability to do so. Changes in government can bring changes in policy priorities that will present problems for long-term planning for sport overall. Governments themselves may need to temper their ambitions in response to global pressure, such as the recent global recession. Rising national debt will compromise the ability to spend on encouraging active lifestyles even if the willingness to do so is still present.

Green (2006) and Houlihan and Green (2008) noted a shift from a Sport for All approach to a much tighter twin focus on targeting children and young people to become active citizens and go on to international medal success. This 'No Compromise' approach to elite competition demands a clear return on investment. The drive to a more professional, business-like approach to the use of funds channelled through UK Sport and Sport England has resulted in their organizational objectives becoming narrower. If the aims of funding change then the criteria for qualification might also change as a consequence.

The shifting framework of funding is not limited to the public sector. Opportunities are often equally short term in the private sector.

SOURCES OF FINANCE

If a broader definition of funding were to include financing then there are many commercial options available to sports (or other) organizations to raise capital, pay for operational costs and help secure a profit for stakeholders.

Figure 21.2 shows those elements which can contribute a substantial percentage of the total revenue or income.

Not all options apply in all circumstances. One of the challenges that will face the sport manager is to research, identify and then access the most relevant potential sources of income.

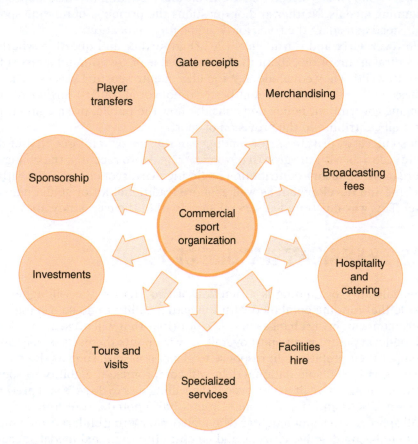

FIGURE 21.2 *Potential sources of financial revenue for professional sports organizations*

Gate receipts from supporters make an important contribution to revenue, although they are often aggregated with catering and other elements into an overall match day category in published accounts. For Manchester United these were 30% of all their revenue in the season 2012–13.

Media rights at elite sports level are also an increasing part of total revenue. Often these are part of a collective agreement. In England, the English Premier League (EPL) signed a television broadcasting deal with Sky and British Telecom (BT) in 2012 that was estimated to be worth over $5 billion for the first time once overseas deals had been finalized (*Guardian*, 2012).

Hospitality provides a premium experience, but at a premium price. The provision can be permanent corporate boxes which are part of the stadium structure or event specific such as the tented village that accompanies major rugby union international games at Twickenham, London, or at the hosting golf club of a major. In the USA the growth of the luxury box has been noted since the 1990s and can provide between 5–20% of total team revenue (USAToday.com, 2012).

Sponsorship within sport is again a projected growth area following recovery from the impact of global recession upon sponsors (PriceWaterhouseCoopers, 2011). The total value of shirt sponsorship deals for season 2013–14 within the EPL increased 12.5% to £165 million (*Independent*, 2013). Stadia-naming rights have also proved a fruitful source of income. Manchester City Football Club made £10 million a year when they sold their naming rights to the airline Etihad (*Telegraph*, 2011).

Sale of players to other clubs is only a source of revenue to the selling club. Expenditure in the EPL was a record £630 million, although £400 million of this went to clubs outside the league (bbc.co.uk).

There are also *bank loans or shareholder investment*, as well as the return on other investments such as that of Arsenal who built much more than just the stadium when they moved from Highbury to the Emirates stadium. The revenue from the sales of residential properties was reported as £156.9 million in figures covering the year to May 2010 (BBC, 2010).

The opportunity to *hire sports facilities* for social, conference or corporate events exists such as organized visits to the stadium and club museum or trophy room. Specialized services and equipment such as sports physiotherapy are available through Perform within Hampshire Cricket Club's Ageas Bowl as is the chance to see open-air concerts (ageasbowl.com).

SOURCES OF FUNDING

It was estimated in 2013 that there were an estimated 151,000 sports clubs within the UK (Sport and Recreation Alliance, 2013). Only a small percentage can look to commercial solutions to fully supply their income. The same survey shows a depressing picture, with a 15% drop in average annual income between 2008 and 2010. Average adult membership fell 11% from 2008–11, while average junior membership fell 8% in the same period. Of course this period coincided with the global economic recession that started in 2008 and it is perhaps to be expected that sport, leisure and recreation would be impacted on as much as any other area.

No two sports clubs are exactly the same and the sources of revenue shown in Figure 21.3 are illustrative only. At first glance it can be seen that many options for securing income available to the commercial sports organization are also available to the voluntary club. *Sponsorship* can be global or a small, local business whose target audience is the immediate local community. *Memberships and subscriptions* are the equivalent of season tickets or gate entry fees. A small golf club is likely to offer food and drink for players to buy throughout the day.

Local authority support in the UK manifests itself in the provision of playing fields or other facilities, although there may also be enticements to attract professional teams such as the leasing of the local authority-owned KC stadium to Hull City FC and Hull RLFC.

FIGURE 21.3   *Potential sources of financial revenue for voluntary sports clubs*

What is not as easily available to commercial sports concerns, but can be accessed by not-for-profit sports groups, is the opportunity to apply for *funding grants* such as those that originate from the National Lottery. Sport managers in either the private or public sector have to be realistic as to what sources are likely to be available and justify why their organization merits being a worthwhile candidate to receive them. With the growth of professionalism expected of the beneficiaries of funding their many aims and objectives need to be shown as SMART (**S**pecific, **M**easurable, **A**chievable, **R**elevant/**R**ealistic and **T**ime-bound), which should help establish clarity and focus.

WHAT IS FUNDING FOR?

Funding is there to support that which is considered beneficial, but for which private finance is not available. The term 'good causes' is often used in conjunction with funding, suggesting that the money granted will be used in a worthwhile manner. As is shown in Figure 21.4 the National Lottery has provided substantial funding to sport organizations and events since 1995. Large, if variable contributions have also been made by the Exchequer and other charitable organizations.

In each case the provider of such funding may have different aims or objectives to be met and this should be taken into account by applicants. With each funding source those aims may change and may include shorter-term initiatives, including the staging of the London 2012 Olympics. Sport England's Annual Report for 2011–12 included their 'new Youth and Community Strategy', i.e. the creation of 'a new community sport activation fund', and in terms of strategic outcomes, it talks of 'our new strategy' which is to run from 2012–17. This was reviewed in the 2013–14 report (SportEngland). Without commenting on the justification for these changes the fact that they are new means there has been a change which could compromise longer-term planning.

As a further example Sport England administered an initiative called the Innovation Fund which was funded by the Exchequer and was intended to support breakthrough ideas to transform the look and feel of community sport, but only ran during 2009/10.

A difficulty for the public sector is that there are conflicting calls for funding. Governments are faced with requests to provide more facilities, to support elite athletes in their quest for success, to enable talented individuals to progress through the stages towards elite level, and also to get the majority of the populace participating in sport or exercise.

Sources of funding are finite and decisions must be made. Is international success in sporting competitions of real importance? Should people need a government to encourage them to eat less and walk more? At present the answers would be yes, but governments and attitudes can change.

For the past two decades the National Lottery has been instrumental in supporting direct government funding from the Exchequer in achieving these aims and a more detailed consideration of its work and value is required.

THE IMPACT OF NATIONAL LOTTERY FUNDING ON UK SPORT

The total value of grants awarded since Lottery funding began in 1995 was £28,316,957,174 (as of 19 November 2013). Of this total sport has received £5,150,016,926 (see Table 21.1).

TABLE 21.1 *Lottery funding for sport 1995–2012*

Date	Funding	Date	Funding
1995	113,465,210	2004	221,851,242
1996	143,680,296	2005	235,025,685
1997	220,791,199	2006	261,093,232
1998	357,852,339	2007	149,029,576
1999	316,127,361	2008	137,313,642
2000	380,140,336	2009	469,672,416
2001	516,379,186	2010	131,057,794
2002	447,672.457	2011	186,933,275
2003	209,123,725	2012	170,146,246

(Source: lottery.culture.gov.uk)

To understand why such funding may be allocated, revised or withdrawn it is useful to first understand the aims and targets associated with any provision. Additionally the structure and agencies involved with distribution need to be known.

Lottery funds are administered by 12 separate organizations which are notionally independent of the government, but overall national concerns with health and lifestyle are nonetheless influencing factors in funding sport.

The National Lottery funding for Good Causes comprises 28% of Lottery income split between different sectors (including sport) based upon the following percentages as guidelines:

- 40% health, educational, environmental and charitable trusts
- 20% sport
- 20% arts
- 20% heritage

There are five distributors of the sports funding, namely UK Sport and the four national bodies of Sport England, Sport Northern Ireland, Sport Wales and sportscotland. There was a temporary additional distributing organization, which played a major role in the funding of the 2012 Olympic and Paralympic Games, i.e. the Olympic Lottery Distributor.

DOES FUNDING BRING BENEFITS?

Money from the National Lottery Fund is distributed funding to voluntary sports clubs to help achieve the aims and targets established by the Department for Culture, Media and Sport. However, Garrett (2004) questioned whether an undoubted enthusiasm for the funding was matched by the ability or willingness of such clubs to realize those aims. An uneven pattern of success and development since would support that question in relation to some sports, but not all.

What is considered an acceptable level of success?

Within this there are criticisms that performance-based targeting can bring about a number of unwanted consequences. Sam (2012) looks at this from a New Zealand perspective, but draws parallels with the UK. If a body fails to meet targets and is considered ineffective funding can be cut and often is. The problem is that this may make the gaps between the 'haves' and 'have-nots' even wider as they now have to show improvement with fewer resources to work with. Table 21.2 looks at a sample of summer Olympic sports and measures their cumulative success over the four Games between 2000 and 2012.

TABLE 21.2 *Average cost per medal for a sample of summer Olympic sports*

	Sydney	Athens	Beijing	London	Total	Funding	Cost per medal
Athletics	6	4	4	5	24	73,661,000	3,069,208
Canoeing	2	3	3	4	12	38,998,700	3,249,892
Diving	0	1	0	1	2	14,708,700	7,354,350
Gymnastics	0	0	1	4	5	29,806,600	5,961,320
Judo	1	0	0	2	3	22,445,000	7,481,667
Rowing	3	4	6	9	24	73,529,600	3,063,733
Swimming	0	2	6	3	13	59,103,600	4,546,431

(Sources: Olympic.org and UKsport.gov.uk)

This is a simplified model that does not give any weighting to the category of medal. Against that medal return the total funding over that period is measured and the cost per medal calculated. As can be seen from the analysis athletics, canoeing and rowing represent a much better return on investment than diving or judo, with gymnastics and swimming falling between those two groups. If a 'No Compromise' approach was taken to a more extreme degree could there be a case for cutting funding and redirecting the balance to the sports with cheaper medals?

Sport England is responsible for encouraging greater numbers to take up sport and exercise more. This is at a grassroots level, but with scope for progression along the development continuum for those with the appropriate talent and skill potential.

UK Sport funds the elite level programmes of sport. National Governing Bodies (NGBs) coordinate all levels within their own sport. Each body that receives funding will have to periodically produce a Whole Sports Plan to justify that that their funding is merited.

Funding can make a difference, but that difference is not guaranteed. Archery for example gained two medals in the span of the five Games since National Lottery funding began, but achieved three medals in the five Games prior.

Elite level tennis does not receive Lottery funding as it is considered to be sufficiently self-resourced. There is little yet to show that the existing and historic investment in tennis is succeeding, with the senior British player, Andy Murray, having developed his game outside the Lawn Tennis Association's coaching schemes.

It is also worth considering whether excessive funding brings with it excessive pressure to perform which, in part, contributes to the problems of **corruption** such as **doping** and **match fixing** in sport. Highly **commercialized** sport with high funding levels from government, sponsors or other sources means greater consideration of the ethical and moral issues related to how a sport or athlete is funded.

INTERNATIONAL DIMENSION

Within most developed economies government support for sport will include funding, but there is no single global approach to funding.

Australia has a model that is very similar to that of Great Britain and the central issue of allocation is the same, as can be encapsulated by the newspaper headline 'Lack of Government Funding Blamed for Poor Olympics for Australia' (*Independent*, 2012).

The involvement of federal (central) government followed an uneven path from the 1970s when a series of short-term initiatives started and finished. The Australian Sports Commission (ASC) was formed in 1985 as an independent authority empowered by statute. In 1989 the Next Step initiative passed most of an A$239 million package to promote both grassroots and elite sport, roles which have been split within the UK. The tension between funding elite sport for international success and national pride or mass participation for health and social benefits was shown as critics and supporters of the changing initiatives frequently communicated.

In 2010–11 the government responded to the Crawford Report, an in-depth review of sport that had been published in 2009. Their priorities mirrored many from within the UK system, such as:

- 'A Sport and Education Strategy to improve the number of children participating in sport.
- Changes to National Sporting Organizations' (NSO) agreements with the ASC to require a greater focus on participation outcomes as part of funding agreements.

- New funding and measures to address issues affecting women's participation, advancement and leadership in sport.

- Increased funding for the talent identification program to ensure future champions are discovered and assisted to reach their full potential.

- Assistance for high performance athletes to attend and compete strongly in international competition' (Adapted *from Australian Sport Funding: A Balancing Act*, 2013)

However, following a perceived failure for Australia at the London 2012 Olympics the focus of how funding was to be gained and maintained became tighter and more target-driven.

One significant difference between Australia and countries such as New Zealand or the UK is in its lack of support to use a lottery system for funding. A tax benefit system to encourage donations is in place to supplement government funds.

The current initiative is called the 'Winning Edge' and is a 10-year strategy that will stay in place until 2022. To receive funding sports organizations face a detailed scrutiny of their plans and abilities to meet specific targets set over this period. Again there are similarities here with the UK's sometimes controversial 'No Compromise' approach.

A brief consideration is given to three further examples. In the USA there is greater pressure for public sector provision of stadia, but Kelley (2012) talks of the need for schools, universities and youth sport organizations to cast their nets far wider than the public sector for financial support.

Chappell (2007) notes that Cuba still invests 2% of its gross domestic product in sport, although the original socialist manifesto may be weakened as former Eastern European allies have moved more to a free market economy. Kenya is explained as a country without a clear overall framework for public investment in sport, although their runners of both sexes are expected to continue to dominate middle- and longer-distance running in the immediate future.

CONCLUSION

Funding and financing can be defined as separate activities, but the boundary between the two can be unclear in specific circumstances. Distribution of funding in the UK is via UK Sport and the national body (such as Sport England). UK Sport looks at the elite level while national bodies focus on the lower levels including grassroots. A drive for professionalism, encouraged by governments, has resulted in a performance-based system. Funded sports must produce a plan and targets against which their success or failure can be measured. Some success is more costly than others. There are critics who warn that this can bring significant problems. Funding does not in itself guarantee success, but some sports have used it very effectively. Funding streams do not always stay consistent and longer-term planning can be difficult.

The National Lottery is not the only source of funding, which may also come from the Exchequer or charitable associations. Globally there is a broad spectrum of approaches to funding and its organization.

REFERENCES

BBC (2010) Arsenal property deals send profits to record high, 24 September, accessed 2 August 2014, www.bbc.co.uk/news/business-11403202.

British Cycling (2014) Annual Report 2009, accessed 5 August, www.britishcycling.org.uk/zuvvi/media/bc_files/press/British_Cycling_Annual_Report_2009.pdf.

Byers, T., Slack, T. and Parent, M. (2012) *Key Concepts in Sport Management*. London: Sage.

Chappell, R. (2007) *Sport in Developing Countries.* London: International Sports Publications, Football Association.

Garrett, R. (2004) The response of voluntary sports clubs to Sport England's Lottery funding: cases of compliance, change and resistance. *Managing Leisure,* 9(1): 13–29.

Green, M. (2006) From 'Sport For All' to not about 'sport' at all? Interrogating sport policy interventions in the United Kingdom. *European Sport Management Quarterly,* 6(3): 217–238.

Grix, J. and Carmichael, F. (2012) Why do governments invest in elite sport? A polemic. *International Journal of Sport Policy and Politics,* 4(1): 73–90.

Guardian (2012) Premier League TV rights set to top £5bn for first time, 12 November.

Houlihan, B. (2005) Public sector policy developing a framework for analysis. *International Review for the Sociology of Sport,* 40(2): 163–185.

Houlihan, B. and Green, M. (2008) *Comparative Elite Sport Development: Systems Structures and Public Policy.* London: Elsevier.

Independent (2012) Lack of government funding blamed for poor Olympics for Australia, 3 August.

Independent (2013) Premier League shirt sponsors pour record £166m into top-flight bank accounts – with Arsenal seeing the biggest rise, 26 August, accessed 3 August 2014, http://blogs.independent.co.uk/2013/08/26/premier-league-shirt-sponsors-pour-record-166m-into-top-flight-bank-accounts-with-arsenal-seeing-the-biggest-rise.

Kelley, D.J. (2012) *Sports Fundraising*. Abingdon: Routledge.

PriceWaterhouseCoopers (2011) Changing the game: outlook for the global sports market to 2015, accessed 4 August 2014, www.pwc.com/sportsoutlook.

Sam, M. (2012) Targeted investments in elite sport funding: wiser, more innovative and strategic? *Managing Leisure,* 17(2–3): 207–220.

Sport and Recreation Alliance (2013) *Sports Club Survey 2013*, accessed 6 March 2014, www.sportandrecreation.org.uk/policy/SSC.

Sport England (2013) Sports measurable by APS in 2013–17, accessed 5 August 2014, www.sportengland.org/media/116626/Agreed-NGB-WSP-targets-1-.pdf.

Sport England (2014) Sport England annual report and financial statements 2013–14, www.sportengland.org/media/339673/annual-report-2013-14.pdf.

Stewart, B. (2007) *Sport Funding and Finance*. Oxford: Butterworth-Heinemann.

Telegraph (2011) Manchester City's £10m deal with Etihad for stadium naming rights, 7 July.

Trimble, L., Buriamo, B., Godfrey, C., Grecic, D. and Minten, S. (2010) *Sport in the UK*. Exeter: Learning Matters.

USAToday.com (2012) Luxury suites rule in professional sports revenue, 4 February, accessed 3 August 2014, http://usatoday30.usatoday.com/money/economy/story/2012–02–04/cnbc-super-bowl-suites/52948968/1.

22

MATCH FIXING IN INTERNATIONAL SPORT

ANDREW HARVEY AND HAIM LEVI

> They are both trying to lose, and that is unforgivable! This is the Olympic Games, they owe a duty, this is what all athletes swear to: to comply with the Olympic Code of Conduct. … What I have seen tonight was not sport. It was a disgrace.

(BBC Sport, 1 August 2012)

> I met my agent at a restaurant called Big Chefs three days before the game upon his request. He told me that Fenerbahçe SK offered me $100,000 for not scoring a goal against them.

(Ibrahim Akın, Istanbul BB player, Public Prosecutor Office, 15 July 2011)

> Substantial illegal bets placed by footballers last year on their own team to lose a league match are 'just the tip of the iceberg' of a far-reaching, organised scam.

(Nick Harris, *The Independent*, 24 April 2009)

LEARNING OUTCOMES

Upon completion of this chapter, students will be able to:

* Appreciate the global nature of the problem of match fixing in sport.

- Identify the different forms that match fixing can take and define why it is problematic to sport and those who manage sport.

- Discuss the advantages and disadvantages of different mechanisms to monitor and control match fixing in sport.

INTRODUCTION

All traditions are invented and it seems from the literature on match fixing that it has become 'traditional' to commence any report or study with an acknowledgement that it has been around for as long as sport and most certainly as long as sport and gambling have been closely associated. It is usual to note that corruption in sport was known to the Ancient Greeks and it is *de rigeur* to mention the notorious 'Black Sox' scandal in the Major League Baseball Championship of 1919, perhaps still the most prominent example of corruption at the apex of professional sport.[1] The tradition extends to an observation that, while match fixing may be nothing new, both gambling and non-gambling related match fixing are now said to be far more widespread than at any time in the past, to the extent that Forrest and his colleagues were able to warn that, 'the apparent increase in cases of fraud in sport, in particular those connected with betting activities, is threatening the very essence of sport'.[2] This chapter introduces the reader to the major forms of match fixing, including matches manipulated for the purposes of betting

THINKING POINT 22.1

Badminton – the London Olympics 2012

Before the London Games, the Badminton World Federation (BWF) introduced a round-robin stage to a normally straightforward knockout competition. In the round-robin format, the top two ranked in each group qualify for a second-stage single-elimination tournament. The second-seeded team in the competition, Tian Qing and Zhao Yunlei of China, suffered an unexpected loss to a Danish team in the first stage. As a result, they were placed as one of the lowest-seeded teams in the second-stage tournament. At that point it became advantageous for the remaining teams that had already secured a second-stage berth to lose their final first-stage match in order

[1]For more details on these and other historical cases, see, for example, Maennig (2008).

[2]IRIS (2012), p.4.

to avoid being paired against Qing and Yunlei in the first round of the second stage.

The final match in group A between the first-seeded Chinese and a South Korean pair began with both pairs having already secured their qualification to the quarter-finals. In order to maximize their chances of progressing to the final, both teams wanted to avoid playing against the other Chinese duo. The match came under scrutiny after being played exceptionally poorly by the two pairs and a sense of anger started spreading around the Wembley Arena, culminating in loud boos from the 6,000 spectators who had paid good money to watch a world-class competition. The subsequent match, held just one hour later, saw a second South Korean duo and an Indonesian pair who had also already qualified for the knockout stages, playing in the same way, with both teams overtly keen to lose in order to avoid the Chinese pair in the next round.

A disciplinary hearing followed where it was decided that the four women's doubles teams, two from South Korea, the Chinese and the Indonesian, would all be disqualified from the tournament and effectively expelled from the Games. According to the BWF the four teams had infringed its code of conduct by 'not using one's best efforts to win a match' and 'conducting oneself in a manner that is clearly abusive or detrimental to the sport'.[3]

as well as for 'sporting' reasons and for other non-gambling related reasons. Case studies and Thinking Points are presented for each of the main forms of match fixing followed by a discussion. The first Thinking Point is the women's badminton competition in the London 2012 Olympics, which is an example of attempted match fixing that was motivated by purely 'sporting' reasons.

TOOLS FOR ANALYSIS

In this case, the attempted 'fix' was not for **gambling** purposes nor was it **corrupt** given the level of transparency in perpetrating the 'fix'. It is open to argument whether adopting a particular tactic in order to maximize the chances of progression to a later stage of a competition is match fixing at all. The goal of competing in the Olympics is to win a gold medal, and, arguably, it is legitimate to pursue tactics that maximize the potential to do so. Despite these arguments, there is a clear sense that it is un**ethical** and contrary to the spirit of sport not to try to win every game irrespective of the wider circumstances. From the perspective of spectators, television audiences, sponsors and the Games organizers, the effect was largely the same as if the 'fix' had been for non-sporting reasons: a contest had not taken place. Overcoming this type of scenario is relatively straightforward since it merely requires the rules of the competition to be designed in such a way that it is not beneficial for a competitor to lose a game in order to maximize

---

[3]Badminton World Federation, 1 August 2012.

the prospects of progressing in the competition. However, relying on competition design alone to overcome the problem of match fixing for sporting reasons is insufficient because it will not always be possible to design competitions, especially league competitions played over a number of weeks or months, in such a way as to ensure that there no possibility of asymmetrical benefits for each competitor or team – i.e. that victory is more important to one side than the other. Measures to counter match fixing, for whatever motives, must include an ethical injunction that trying to win every game is important since it is only in that way that the sport, participants, fans and viewing public, broadcasters, sponsors and others are respected.

The inability of competition rules to provide a complete answer to all non-gambling related match fixing is highlighted by cases in which there is an asymmetrical benefit in winning, but where financial considerations are in play rather than purely 'sporting' reasons. The notorious 'calciopoli' scandal in Italy in 2006[4] is such an example, and investigative reporter Declan Hill alleges that he has uncovered similar practices involving deals between senior club officials in the Russian football leagues.[5] More recently, similar practices have come to light in Turkey, which forms our case study below.

CASE STUDY 22.1

Turkey Match Fixing Scandal, 2011

In one of the most widespread match fixing cases in the history of football, 93 people were arrested early in July 2011 by the Turkish police, with various charges including fraud, match fixing and establishing a criminal organization. Among them were senior executives of several football clubs, board members, current and former managers, coaches and players.

The scandal was brought to light during an undercover investigation where some 1,028 wiretaps had been used as evidence, with 103 of these tied to Fenerbahçe SK President, Aziz Yildirim. Eight Turkish clubs, including Fenerbahçe, Trabzonspor and Beşiktaş J.K., were investigated by the Turkish Football Federation's Professional Football Disciplinary Board (PFDK). Yildirim was charged with trying to have favourable referees assigned to his team's games, paying opposition players to underperform against his team and other chairman-to-chairman match fixing offences,[6] such as

---

[4]See 'Calciopoli Scandal 2006' blog for details of the Italian match fixing scandal.

[5]See Hill (2009).

[6]'Chairman-to-chairman' fixing is a common practice in the Balkans, Eastern Europe and Russia, especially when a win is very important to one club and less so for a rival (IRIS, 2012).

'incentive premiums' to opponents from Trabzonspor and Bursaspor, their closest rivals for the championship.[7] Placed in third place and therefore not in a position to qualify for the Champions League, a remarkable run of 16 wins in the season's last 17 games saw Fenerbahçe win the title, thus securing participation in Europe's blue-ribbon competition. One of the matches investigated was Fenerbahçe's win of 4–3 against Sivasspor in the very last match of the 2010–2011 season.

In early 2011 the government introduced Law 6222 on the Prevention of Violence and Disorder in sports events, which lays down a penalty of between 5 and 12 years' imprisonment for, *inter alia*, match fixing offences. Shortly after the scandal erupted, allegedly due to the powerful nature of some of those implicated, the Turkish Parliament voted almost unanimously (284 votes in favour, six against and one abstention) for the penalty to be reduced to between one and three years' imprisonment.

The European Commission then responded, reflecting the mood within the wider environment with respect to the way the authorities in Turkey were addressing the scandal, stating that, 'this relaxation can only give rise to strong reservations and increase suspicions that this law protects the illicit financial interests of a powerful lobby'.[8]

The Turkish Football Federation (TFF) decided in the wake of the new law to discuss changing the article in its disciplinary code that mandates relegation to a lower division for any club found guilty of match fixing. An initial suggestion to allow clubs involved in match fixing to avoid relegation was first rejected by the General Convention of the TFF only to be reverted, and in April 2012 the TFF amended Article 58 in its Disciplinary Code to allow clubs to remain in competitions while charged with match fixing attempts. This process saw the resignation of the TFF President.

In May 2012 the TFF cleared all 16 clubs involved in the match fixing scandal. The first report by the TFF's PFDK found no evidence that any wrongdoing had materialized into a fix. Nevertheless, the federation did not spare the individuals who were implicated, as 10 suspects were banned from the game, among them officials from Fenerbahçe, İstanbul BB and Eskişehir SK and two players, while an appeal tribunal saw some of the bans dropped or altered.

In July 2012 a Turkish court sentenced Yildirim to more than six years in prison only to see him serving one year, pending an appeal, which he lost in 2014. In November 2013 he was re-elected as the club's president, but was forced to step down as a result of the failed appeal. In 2013 the European football governing body, UEFA, launched an investigation through its Control and Disciplinary Board (CDB), culminating in a decision to ban Fenerbahçe from participating in its European club competitions starting from 2013/2014 for two years plus one year suspended for five years. UEFA banned Beşiktaş for one year, a decision which was later upheld by the Court of Arbitration for Sport (CAS). Fenerbahçe's appeal in 2014 to the Swiss Federal Supreme Court was also rejected, while later in 2014 two other Turkish clubs were found guilty of influencing matches during the 2010/2011 season, and were excluded from participating in European competitions in the 2014/2015 season.[9]

[7]*NY Daily News*, 13 February 2013.

[8]Brasseur (2012), p. 8.

[9]UEFA, 7 July 2014.

TOOLS FOR ANALYSIS

This case shows how a culture of corruption appears to have spread throughout the Turkish game, involving senior club officials and the governing body as well as referees and players. One of the major challenges with corrupt non-betting related match fixing is the difficulty in detection, without recourse to the sophisticated and expensive wire-tapping procedures adopted in the Turkey case. As Gorse and Chadwick rightly state, 'there is no clear form of detection system akin to WADA or the sophisticated technological integrity systems employed by European licensed betting operators to identify non-betting related match-fixing'.[10] In the same report the authors caution that such difficulties of detection may mean that non-betting related match fixing is more prevalent than its betting-related cousin. However, the same problems mean that such determinations remain largely within the realm of speculation.

In interviews with representatives of the Professional Footballers' Association in England, respondents were confident that non-gambling related match fixing was unlikely to be a problem in the English professional leagues due to the structure of the leagues, which maintain a competitive edge to the games throughout the season, with a number of these vying for promotion or play-off places or trying to avoid relegation often up until the last day of the season.[11] However, as we noted above, no design, however sophisticated, can make all matches wholly meaningful at all times. Where matches lose their competitive edge, the conditions become more fruitful for match fixing, either for non-gambling financial reasons or for gambling-related reasons. However, as the case above shows, non-gambling related match fixing may even occur where there is a competitive league, for example where one team (or their owner/president) values Champions League football above all else. In the Turkey case it appears that the President's motives were a mixture of financial gain and the kudos to be had from participating in the UEFA Champions League.

There has been a link between sport, money and corruption for almost as long as sport has been a business. In *The Black Diamond* (1921), a novel set in the years leading up to the First World War, Francis Brett Young comments that 'although league football had not sunk in those days to its present depths of unabashed commercialisation … the result of a match was sometimes decided in accordance with the bookmaker's instructions'.[12] Money is certainly implicated in the majority of match fixing incidents. Walsh and Giulianotti (2007) recount the case of Hanse Cronje, where the disgraced former South African cricket captain went on record to say that his match fixing exploits were motivated by money. The impact of his corruption on the value of the game on spectators and others is demonstrated by his now notorious decision to offer England a victory target in the Test Match in February 2000.

---

[10]Chadwick and Gorse (2011).

[11]Harvey and Levi (2014).

[12]Young (2004), p. 36.

His declaration was lauded at the time as a piece of remarkable sportsmanship that earned the coveted 'champagne moment' from the BBC Test Match Special radio commentary team. When the corrupt reason for his apparent beneficence became clear 'most commentators bemoaned the fact that their enjoyment of the game had been based on a deception; they had been duped … the philosophical point then is that commodification is pathological if incorporation into the commercial world of the market leads athletes and sports administrators to regard the pursuit of wealth as their primary aim, thereby evacuating or subverting the internal goals [of sport].'[13]

CASE STUDY 22.2

Accrington Stanley v Bury, Division Two, England, July 2008

Accrington Stanley FC played the last game of the 2007/2008 season against Bury FC, with both clubs playing in English fourth tier league – Division 2. The game had no significant implications for the clubs' near future in the competition as none of them had a chance of being promoted to Division 1, nor were they under the threat of relegation. Winning or losing, to put it simply, meant little to either side.

Before the game, several betting operators stopped taking bets on the game after noticing unusual betting activity; almost £300,000 worth of bets were being placed before kick-off, a remarkably large amount for a Division 2 game. One bookmaker, Betfair, took £281,000 on Accrington Stanley to lose, which was believed to be 14 times more than they would normally expect. Most matches at a similar level on the same weekend saw a total of around £20,000 being staked. William Hill

suspended betting when large stakes were still being wagered even when the odds had been cut to 10/11 on a Bury win.

The bookmakers then reported the suspicious activity to the Football Association (FA), who immediately launched an investigation. In a last-minute attempt to prevent external influence on the outcome of the match, the FA changed the referee and assistants, making sure, as far as possible, that the game was not affected by one of its own officials. Bury went on to win the match 2–0 while the post-match reaction from Accrington Stanley's manager John Coleman suggested nothing wrong: 'We gave our very best for 90 minutes', he said.

However, the FA investigation revealed a different story: examination of security camera tapes from betting shops in the north-west area, together with extracted personal information from accounts of online bookmakers, and interviews and interrogations, concluded with five players being charged with breaching the Football Association's rules on betting. Ultimately, the players were found guilty with all of them betting on Bury to win the match. They were each given fines and suspensions:

---

[13]Walsh and Giulianotti (2007), p. 42.

CONTEMPORARY ISSUES IN SPORT MANAGEMENT

James Harris, an Accrington player, received the longest suspension (one year) and was also fined £5,000. David Mannix, also an Accrington player, was fined £4,000 and given a 10-month suspension, while Robert Williams was fined £3,500 and suspended for eight months. Andrew Mangan, a Bury player, was fined £2,000 and suspended for five months. Peter Cavanagh, Accrington Stanley's captain, was suspended for eight months and fined £3,500.

Bury player Andrew Mangan returned to the case a couple of years later, suggesting that the problem was still rife in the lower leagues. He claimed that the ban persuaded him to tackle his own serious gambling problems. Strikingly, he pointed out, young players are particularly vulnerable to falling into this trap[14]: 'The younger players look at the wealthy ones who are on a lot more and think: "I would like a lot more money"'.

The pursuit of wealth with disregard for the internal goals of the sport is seen in clear relief in our second case study, which concerns players betting on a game in which they were involved with a view to fixing the result in advance in order to make a gain in the betting market.

TOOLS FOR ANALYSIS

This case illustrates a simple form of match fixing in which players bet on a match in which they are involved. The football authorities in England and Scotland have taken steps to prevent betting on football by players, officials and others working in the game in order to protect the integrity of the sport. In England, the FA introduced a worldwide ban on betting on football from August 2014. Article E8 of the 'Rules of the Association'[15] prohibits betting, either directly or indirectly by participants, on the result, progress or conduct of any match or competition played in any part of the world. The worldwide ban on betting is extended to betting on other related information other than the match outcome 'for example and without limitation, the transfer of players, employment of managers, team selection or disciplinary matters'. Inciting to bet or providing bettors with inside information (which is not publicly available) is also prohibited by this section of the rules.[16] The FA has produced a video explaining the new rules, which have applied since the beginning of the 2014/2015 season, including possible sanctions that apply to transgressors.[17]

The Scottish FA has similar rules on betting. Disciplinary rule 22 (rule 33 in updated Judicial Panel Protocol for season 2013/2014) states that:

---

[14]*Daily Mail Online*, 25 February 2011.

[15]*The FA Betting Rules 2014–15*.

[16] Ibid., pp. 115–116.

[17]The FA, Betting. www.thefa.com/football-rules-governance/rulebookanalysis/betting.

'No club, official, Team Official or other member of Team Staff, player, match official or other person under the jurisdiction of the Scottish FA shall bet in any way on a football match (except authorized and registered football pools)'.[18] The effect of the rule, as in England, is that betting is prohibited on any football match, played at any time in any part of the world.

A more ambiguous form of corruption is where players, or others with inside knowledge of a club or team, share information with friends and acquaintances, who are then able to place bets with the benefit of price-sensitive knowledge that is not available to the wider betting public. The individual concerned may have no financial incentive nor even be aware that the information will be used by others for attempted financial gain. They may not even be aware that the information they share is price sensitive. However, in a betting market where legal bookmakers now have low profit margins due to the intense competition from global competitors, inside information may be crucial in tipping the balance of the odds in favour of the gambler, although of course it comes with no guarantees of any kind: a weakened team may obviously still win a game of football. Gorse and Chadwick found that sharing inside information can lead to substantial gains on the betting markets for perpetrators even where no actual 'fix' had taken place.[19] If the case of the Olympic badminton players above was a case of a 'fix' without corruption, then sharing inside information might be seen as the opposite – corruption without a 'fix'.

Our second Thinking Point considers what has perhaps become the major threat to sport – externally organized 'fixes' instigated by highly proficient criminals.

THINKING POINT 22.2

Wilson Raj Perumal, Finland 2011

Finland is not a destination where the average football fan expects to hear of an ongoing match fixing problem. However in recent years several scandals have prompted several investigations. One of the biggest scandals was masterminded by Wilson Raj Perumal, already a convicted match fixer by the time he arrived Finland, who had perfected his *modus operandi* in the late 1990s in countries like Ghana and Zimbabwe. Fixing matches with Finnish football club Rovaniemen Palloseura (RoPS) for some years prompted Perumal's syndicate to buy the club in 2008, in a mission to strengthen the control over the fixes.[20] The club was extremely attractive due to its links with Zambia, which had seen

---

[18]PFA Scotland, Gambling awareness. http://pfascotland.co.uk/advice/pfa-scotland-on-gambling.

[19]See *Supra* note 9, p. 21.

[20]Forrest, 28 May 2012.

the club featuring many players from the African country. Following a tip-off by one of his own lieutenants with whom he had fallen out, Finnish police followed Perumal to one of the RoPS matches. They witnessed a heated exchange with three RoPS players. This provoked their curiosity and prompted them to contact football officials, who in turn asked for FIFA's input. The response was unequivocal: Perumal is the most prolific criminal match fixer in international football. The investigation rolled out quickly and nine players, seven Zambian and two Georgian, were arrested. In February 2011 Perumal was arrested by Finland's National Bureau of Investigation, trying to leave the country on a fake passport.

The investigation uncovered bribes ranging from €1,000 to €40,000 per player. In two instances Perumal paid €80,000 to eight RoPS players to lose to VPS and Tampere United by a specified margin. Perumal did not limit himself to RoPS games; in Oulu two players admitted accepting €50,000 from Perumal as a bribe to fix a first division match. The players were also sentenced to conditional imprisonment ranging from 5 to 20 months. The Lapland District Court concluded that 24 of the club's matches had been fixed, and that Perumal's direct involvement was proven in seven of these. According to the prosecution, three other match fixers were involved in the case but they had not been able to establish their identities. He was subsequently sentenced to two years in prison. In a later interview with CNN[21] Perumal commented on the extent of his life's work: 'I never really counted, but I think it should be between 80–100 football matches.'

TOOLS FOR ANALYSIS

Several determinants make Finland a fertile ground for fixes, particularly those rooted in the betting market.[22] Firstly, low-waged players are most vulnerable since bribes may be worth more than an annual salary. In Finland, footballers are paid about half of a full-time employed male's average earnings. Secondly, low interest in the league in terms of match attendance and TV viewing ratings and newspaper coverage means poor performances are rarely scrutinized. Thirdly, the criminal law in Finland punishes offences of bribery and corruption with fines and imprisonment of up to four years. This was considered low by a European Commission study in 2012, and in reality, sentences are even lower. Lastly, and perhaps of most importance to the case at hand, Finnish football is played throughout the summer months, when most European leagues are in their off-season. This vacuum is prey for the global betting market, and consequently, Finnish football attracts a disproportionate amount of betting activity which a fixer will be interested in as it allows them to manipulate matches for profit.

---

[21]CNN, 26 August 2014.

[22]Koivula, 2 October 2013.

As a consequence, research for FIFPro showed that players in Finland have been susceptible to match fixing, with 20% of those surveyed reporting that they had played in a match that they believed to have been fixed.[23] To combat the threat of match fixing in Finland, the Finnish professional footballers' association (JPY) has introduced a mobile app that allows players to report anonymously any illegal approaches or other suspicious behaviour.[24]

Gambling-related match fixing perpetrated by criminals, acting either alone or in concert with others, has become a major challenge to the football and law enforcement authorities. By way of a benchmark, the Europol VETO investigation that ran from July 2011 to January 2013 alleged that a 'total of 425 match officials, club officials, players, and serious criminals, from more than 15 countries, are suspected of being involved in attempts to fix more than 380 professional football matches'.[25] We use the word 'alleged' because the Europol report provided little by way of evidence to support its claims, citing on-going investigations as the reason. However, there is little doubt that match fixing has become a highly profitable and relatively risk-free criminal activity even if its precise extent cannot be discerned.

Since 2014, numerous steps have been taken to combat the threat of match fixing to sport in Europe. To help regulate the expanding online betting industry, in July 2014 the European Commission adopted the Recommendation on Principles for the Protection of Consumers and Players of Online Gambling Services and the Prevention of Minors from Gambling: 'The Recommendation encourages Member States to pursue a high level of protection for consumers, players and minors through the adoption of principles for online gambling services and for responsible advertising and sponsorship of those services.'[26] In order to base future policy making on a firmer evidential footing, in September 2014 the European Commission published two research studies it had commissioned. The first study, by TMC Asser Instituut, reported on Member States' regulation and self-regulation of sports-related gambling, offering a comparative study for the identification of good practice. The second report, carried out by Oxford Research and VU Amsterdam, 'focuses on the regulation of information collection, storage, and sharing of information on suspicious sports betting activity, examining both formal regulations imposed through the legal and official regulatory system in each of the EU 28 Member States, along with industry-led self-regulatory approaches'.[27]

---

[23]Harvey and Levi (2014), p. 29.

[24]FIFPro, Finnish match-fixing app shows its value. www.fifpro.org/en/news/finnish-match-fixing-app-shows-its-value.

[25]Europol, 6 February 2013.

[26]European Commission. http://ec.europa.eu/growth/single-market/services/gambling/initiatives/index_en.htm.

[27]European Commission, Studies on betting-related match-fixing now available. http://ec.europa.eu/sport/news/2014/betting-related-match-fixing_en.htm.

To strengthen the regulatory environment to tackle match fixing, the Council of Europe adopted the Convention on the Manipulation of Sports Competitions in September 2014. Article 1 states that the objectives of the Convention are:

a) to prevent, detect and sanction national or transnational manipulation of national and international sports competitions;
b) to promote national and international co-operation against manipulation of sports competitions between the public authorities concerned, as well as with organisations involved in sports and in sports betting.'[28]

Taken together, these measures may provide an impetus for greater coordination between agencies across Europe in the fight against match fixing (for an updated overview of match fixing policy developments see Carpenter, 2015).

Another type of gambling-related match fixing is the 'spot fix', where a particular incident in a game is the subject of bets. In 2012 Essex cricketer Mervyn Westfield was convicted of accepting a £6,000 bribe to give away a certain number of runs in a particular over.[29] His case followed soon after the conviction of three Pakistani cricketers for 'spot fixing' in the Test match series against England in 2010. However, due to the reluctance of bookmakers to take bets on single events such as a no-ball or a wide in cricket, the 'spot fix' is not as common as is sometimes believed.[30]

These cases show that gambling-related match fixing can take many different forms and involve many different instigators. These include external agents, acting alone or in concert with criminal gangs and internal club officials. The perpetrators of a fix will usually include players, but referees or other match officials may also be involved. Occasionally a fix may involve non-playing actors, such as the corruption of stadium staff to turn off the floodlights in games involving West Ham and Charlton in the late 1990s.[31] The lesson to be drawn here is that there are numerous motivations for match fixing and an array of techniques and methods available to the match fixer. Match fixing also involves a large number of different actors in sport – club owners, managers, players, referees and coaches – while supporters can act as violent enforcers. It is the sheer diversity of operations that makes the problem an acute one for the authorities and one that is difficult to tackle.

---

[28]Council of Europe, *Convention on the Manipulation of Sports Competitions*. http://conventions.coe.int/Treaty/en/Treaties/Html/215.htm.

[29]*Guardian*, 12 January 2012.

[30]Kumar (2013).

[31]For a summary of types of cases of match fixing see 'The unfortunates of match-fixing', available at www.onlinebetting.com/match-fixing.

TOOLS FOR ANALYSIS

Match fixing and activities related to it, such as sharing inside information, fall under a number of distinct categories. From the discussion above, these are:

- Non-corrupt, non-gambling related match fixing, or match fixing undertaken for 'sporting' reasons, such as to advance in a competition. To be non-corrupt the 'fix' will need to be transparent.

- Corrupt, non-gambling related match fixing where the object of the 'fix' is to obtain a financial advantage through sporting success, such as winning a league, gaining promotion or avoiding relegation, for example.

- Corrupt, gambling-related match fixing that involves influencing the result of a game, or an incident within the game, for the purposes of gaining an advantage in the betting markets.

- Other gambling-related activities, such as sharing inside information or betting on a sport in breach of the rules, but which does not involve a 'fix'.

How might these diverse manifestations of 'match fixing' (including those that do not involve an actual 'fix') be thought about? **Economic** approaches, such as that proposed by Caruso, favour an incentive-based analysis of and solution to match fixing.[32] Caruso confines his discussion to non-gambling related incidents of alleged match fixing, including the 1982 World Cup game between West Germany and Austria, where apparent collusion between the teams meant that both progressed to the later stages of the completion at the expense of Algeria.[33] He argues that a system of incentives and rewards that favour performance over participation would eliminate the economic gains to be made by match fixing. In his study he implies that such a system would also be applicable to gambling-related match fixing where there are explicit economic incentives. Arguing along similar lines, Preston and Szymanski maintain that 'match fixing occurs 'either because one side "needs" to win to the extent that it is willing to make side payments to persuade the other side not to make an effort or to persuade the referees to make biased decisions, or because players or officials stand to gain financially from gambling on the outcome of a match'.[34] Preston and Szymanski offer a model that assumes that match fixing arises out of an evaluation of the risks of doing so against the potential financial gains. Thus, they maintain that the relatively small amounts of money (approximately $20,000) acquired by Hanse Cronje would not be sufficient to tempt players in more financially rewarding sports, such as football or basketball, to engage in match fixing. Certainly,

---

[32]Caruso (2009).

[33]Doyle (2010).

[34]Preston and Szymanski (2003: 617).

low wages, wages not paid on time and other economic detriments that many professional footballers face outside of the top leagues, are a major problem that helps to create the conditions under which corruption might take place.[35] A Good Practice Guide to help tackle match fixing in football, published as a result of research conducted for FIFPro in 2014, showed that decent wages and wages that are paid on time are vital external conditions that can help prevent match fixing.[36]

The existence of poor working terms and conditions features prominently in Forrest's identification of a number of factors that tend to lead to match fixing. He and his colleagues concluded that this is most likely to occur where:

1 betting volume is high;
2 the athletes are poorly paid;
3 the fixing involves the actions of individuals rather than a complex interactive sequence of events;
4 the scrutiny on the competition is less intense, for example the match is played out at a lower league level;
5 the outcome of the match does not affect the final placing in for example a tournament;
6 the match fixing does not involve losing;
7 the salary level is regarded as unjust;
8 there is a high level of corruption generally in the society.[37]

Forrest's identification of the conditions under which match fixing for financial gain is likely to take place usefully moves the analysis beyond a simple cost/benefit assessment and takes other factors such as cultural conditions into account. As has been seen in the brief survey and case studies above, match fixing is a complex and disparate phenomenon and needs to be understood in multi-disciplinary terms, including criminology, law, education and sociology. Placing the fight against match fixing on firm ethical grounds is also vital in order to provide a platform of shared values from which to develop policy and practices.[38] Similarly, solutions to match fixing will need to be equally sophisticated and nuanced towards the specific conditions and ways in which it manifests itself in different countries and cultures. The challenge for academics and researchers will be to provide a more comprehensive understanding of the complexities of match fixing in order to inform policy responses.

---

[35]FIFPro (2012).

[36]Harvey (2014), p. 16; Harvey and Levi (2014).

[37]Serby (2012), p. 8.

[38]For a more detailed discussion on the ethics of match-fixing, see Harvey (2015).

ACTION LEARNING

- In what ways does match fixing undermine the integrity of sport?
- What measures should sporting authorities take to counter match fixing?

- What might be the impact of match fixing on the future of sport?

CONCLUSION

Match fixing and manipulation have become prominent threats to sport across the globe. While there is little solid empirical evidence to show that corruption in sport is at higher levels now than in the past, there is a view that the rapid growth and globalization of gambling markets and the vulnerability of sport to manipulation for the purposes of betting are serious problems that have the potential to undermine the value of sport if not tackled effectively. In response to these threats there has been a greater interest taken in the phenomenon of match fixing from academics, policy makers and journalists.

As has been seen in the brief survey and cases mentioned above, match fixing is a complex and disparate phenomenon and needs to be understood in multi-disciplinary terms, including criminology, law, education and sociology. Placing the fight against it on firm ethical grounds is also vital in order to provide a platform of shared values from which to develop policy and practices.[39] Similarly, solutions to match fixing will need to be equally sophisticated and nuanced towards the specific conditions and ways in which it manifests itself in various countries and cultures. The challenge for academics and researchers will be to provide a more comprehensive understanding of its complexities in order to inform policy responses.

REFERENCES

Badminton World Federation (1 August 2012). 'Four badminton pairs have been disqualified'. *Badminton World Federation.* Retrieved from: www.bwfbadminton. org/news_item.aspx?id=65297 [Accessed 15 November 2013].

BBC Sport (1 August 2012). 'Olympics badminton: Fans jeer players for not trying'. *BBC Sport.* Retrieved from: www.bbc.co.uk/sport/0/olympics/19073935 [Accessed 22 November 2013].

Brasseur A. (2012). 'The need to combat match-fixing'. *Council of Europe, Committee on Education Culture, Science and Media.* Retrieved from: www. assembly.coe.int/Communication/070312_BrasseurReportE.pdf [Accessed 22 November 2013].

'Calciopoli Scandal 2006'. Available at http://calcioitaliascandal.blogspot.co.uk [blog].

---

[39]For a more detailed discussion on the ethics of match-fixing, see Harvey (2015).

Carpenter, K. (13 May 2015). 'An overview of the latest match-fixing policy developments in 2015'. *Lawinsport.com*. Retrieved from: www.lawinsport.com/blog/kevin-carpenter/item/an-overview-of-the-latest-match-fixing-policy-developments-in-2015 [Accessed 28 September 2015].

Caruso, R. (2009). 'The basic economics of match-fixing in sport tournaments'. *Economic Analysis and Policy*, 39(3): 255–377.

Chadwick, S. and Gorse, S. (2011). 'The prevalence of corruption in international sport – a statistical analysis', Coventry University Centre for the International Business of Sport.

CNN.com (26 August 2014). 'Wilson Raj Perumal: The man who fixed football'. CNN.com. Retrieved from: http://edition.cnn.com/2014/08/26/sport/football/match-fixing-wilson-raj-perumal-corruption/index.html [Accessed 22 March 2015].

Council of Europe (18 September 2014). *Convention on the Manipulation of Sports Competitions*. Retrieved from: http://conventions.coe.int/Treaty/en/Treaties/Html/215.htm [Accessed 18 March 2015].

Daily Mail Online (25 February 2011). 'Players are still gambling on matches! Wrexham striker Mangan insists FA threats aren't taken seriously'. Daily Mail Online. Retrieved from: www.dailymail.co.uk/sport/football/article-1360478/Wrexham-striker-Andy-Mangan-insists-players-gambling-matches.html [Accessed 18 November 2013].

Doyle, P. (13 June 2010). 'The day in 1982 when the world wept for Algeria'. *Guardian*. Retrieved from: www.theguardian.com/football/2010/jun/13/1982-world-cup-algeria [Accessed 11 November 2013].

European Commission (2014). 'Initiatives'. European Commission. Retrieved from: http://ec.europa.eu/growth/single-market/services/gambling/initiatives/index_en.htm [Accessed 18 March 2015].

European Commission (17 September 2014). 'Studies on betting-related match-fixing now available'. European Commission. Retrieved from: http://ec.europa.eu/sport/news/2014/betting-related-match-fixing_en.htm [Accessed 18 March 2015].

Europol (6 February 2013). 'Results from largest football match-fixing investigation in Europe'. Europol. Retrieved from: www.europol.europa.eu/content/results-largest-football-match-fixing-investigation-europe [Accessed 18 November 2013].

FIFPro (2012). *FIFPro Black Book Eastern Europe*. Hoofddorp: FIFPro.

FIFPro (25 April 2014). 'Finnish match-fixing App shows its value'. FIFPro. Retrieved from: www.fifpro.org/en/news/finnish-match-fixing-app-shows-its-value [Accessed 18 March 2015].

Forrest, B. (28 May 2012). 'All the world is staged'. *ESPN The Magazine*. Retrieved from: http://brettforrest.com/wp-content/uploads/Match-Fixing.pdf [Accessed 21 November 2013].

Guardian (12 January 2012). 'Cricketer Mervyn Westfield pleads guilty to spot fixing in county match'. *Guardian*. Retrieved from: www.theguardian.com/sport/2012/jan/12/cricketer-mervyn-westfield-spot-fixing [Accessed 22 November 2013].

Guardian (22 September 2013). 'The fix is in (the genes?): why a love of risk may lead some athletes astray'. *Guardian*. Retrieved from: www.theguardian.com/society/blog/2013/sep/22/gambling-sport-risk-taking [Accessed 17 November 2013].

Harvey, A. (2014). *Protect our Game: A Good Practice Guide for Professional Football Players' Associations to Tackle Match-fixing in Football*. Hoofddorp: FIFPro.

Harvey, A. and Levi, H. (2014). *Don't Fix It: Players Questionnaire Results and Analysis*. Hoofddorp: FIFPro.

Harvey, A. (2015). 'Match-fixing: towards an ethical framework', *Journal of the Philosophy of Sport*, 42(3): 393–407.

Hill, D. (2009). 'To fix or not to fix? How corruptors decide to fix football matches', *Global Crime*, 10(3): 157–177.

Institut de Relations Internationales et Strategique (IRIS) (2012). 'White Paper on ports betting and corruption: how to preserve the integrity of sport'.

Koivula, A. (2 October 2013). 'Realities of football match-fixing – case Finland'. LawInSport.com. Retrieved from: www.lawinsport.com/articles/anti-corruption/item/realities-of-football-match-fixing-case-finland [Accessed 15 November 2013].

Maennig, W. (2008). 'Corruption in international sports and how it may be combated'. In P. Rodriguez, S. Kesenne and J. García (eds), *Threats to Sports and Sports Participation*. Oviedo: Servicio de Publicaciones de la Universidad de Oviedo. pp. 83–111.

NY Daily News (13 February 2013). In Turkey, trial of Fenerbahce owner Aziz Yildirim shows that soccer's match-fixing scandal goes all the way to the top. *NY Daily News*. Retrieved from: www.nydailynews.com/sports/more-sports/fenerbach-scandal-shows-match-fixing-straight-top-article-1.1263144 [Accessed 22 November 2013].

PFA Scotland (n.d.). 'Gambling awareness', PFAScotland.co.uk. Retrieved from: http://pfascotland.co.uk/advice/pfa-scotland-on-gambling [Accessed 18 March 2015].

Preston, I. and Szymanski, S. (2003). 'Cheating in contests'. *Oxford Review of Economic Policy*, 19(4): 612–624.

Serby, T. (2012). 'Gambling related match-fixing: a terminal threat to the integrity of sport?' *The International Sports Law Journal*, 1(2): 7–12.

The FA Betting Rules (2014). The FA Rules of the Association 2014–2015 (2014). TheFA.com. Retrieved from: www.thefa.com/~/media/files/thefaportal/governance-docs/rules-of-the-association/2014–15/fa-handbook-2014-complete.ashx [Accessed 22 March 2015].

UEFA (7 July 2014). 'Eskişehirspor and Sivasspor decisions welcomed'. UEFA.org. Retrieved from: www.uefa.org/disciplinary/news/newsid=2122197.html [Accessed 22 March 2015].

Walsh, A. and Giulianotti, R. (2007). *Ethics, Money and Sport: This Sporting Mammon*. Abingdon: Routledge.

Young, F.B. (2004, First published 1921). *The Black Diamond*. Thirsk: House of Stratus.

RECOMMENDED BIBLIOGRAPHY

Books

Hawkins, E. (2012). *Bookie Gambler Fixer Spy*. London: Bloomsbury.

Haberfeld, M.R. and Sheehan, D. (eds) (2013). *Match-Fixing in International Sports: Existing Processes, Law Enforcement, and Prevention Strategies*. Berlin: Springer.

Hill, D. (2008). *The Fix: Organized Crime and Soccer*. Toronto: McClelland & Stewart.

Hill, D. (2013). *The Insider's Guide to Match-Fixing in Football*. Toronto: Anne McDermid & Associates.

Rowbottom, M. (2013). *Foul Play: the Dark Arts of Cheating in Sport*. London: Bloomsbury.

Articles

Aquilina, D. and Chetcuti, A. (2014). 'Match-fixing: the case of Malta'. *International Journal of Sport Policy and Politics*, 6(1): 107–128.

Carpenter, K. (2012). 'Match-fixing: the biggest threat to sport in the 21st century?'. LawInSport.com. Retrieved from: www.lawinsport.com/articles/anti-corruption/item/match-fixing-the-biggest-threat-to-sport-in-the-21st-century-part-1?

Harvey, A. (2015). 'Match-fixing: towards an ethical framework'. *Journal of the Philosophy of Sport*, 42(3): 393–407.

Rodenberg, R.M. (2012). '(Non)gambling corruption in sports'. *Wake Forest Review Online*, 2: 45–53.

Shepotylo, O. (2006). Three-point-for-win in soccer rule: are there incentives for match-fixing? In O. Shepotylo, 'Three Essays on Institutions and Economic Development'. Dissertation. College Park, MD: University of Maryland, Department of Economics.

Reports

Bozkurt, E. (2012). 'Match-fixing and fraud in sport: putting the pieces together'. Emine Bozkurt, Member of the Special Committee on organised crime, corruption and money laundering. Retrieved from: www.europarl.europa.eu/document/activities/cont/201209/20120925ATT52303/20120925ATT52303EN.pdf.

De Speville, B. (2012). 'A review of the anticorruption arrangements of the International Cricket Council'. ICC. Retrieved from: http://icc-live.s3.amazonaws.com/cms/media/about_docs/518b7096b002c-Bertrand%20de%20Speville%20Report%20-%20A%20Review%20of%20the%20Anti-Corruption%20Arrangements%20of%20the%20ICC.pdf.

KEA European Affairs (2012). 'A mapping of criminal law provisions in EU27'. European Commission. Retrieved from: http://ec.europa.eu/sport/library/studies/study-sports-fraud-final-version_en.pdf.

Report of the Sports Betting Integrity Panel (2010). DCMS. Retrieved from: www.sportsbettinggroup.org/docs%5Creports_sports_betting_integrity_panel.pdf.

Transparency International (2009) 'Working paper: corruption and sport: building integrity and preventing abuses'. Retrieved from: www.transparency.org/whatwedo/pub/working_paper_no.03_2009_corruption_and_sport_building_integrity_and_preven.

Interventions

Australian Sports Ministers (2011). 'National policy on match-fixing in sport'. Retrieved from: www.health.gov.au/internet/main/publishing.nsf/Content/F6DB8637F05C9643CA257C310021CCE9/$File/National%20Policy%20on%20Match-Fixing%20in%20Sport%20(FINAL).pdf.

Harvey A. (2014). *Protect Our Game: A Good Practice Guide for Professional Football Players' Associations to Tackle Match-fixing in Football*. FIFPro, Birkbeck, University of London, UEFA, European Commission. Retrieved from: www.sportbusinesscentre.com/wp-content/uploads/2013/12/Dont-Fix-It-Protect-Our-Game-A-Good-Practice-Guide-for-Professional-Football-Players-Associations-to-tackle-match-fixing-in-football.pdf.

The Nordic Game authorities (2013). 'Match-fixing in the Nordic countries'. Retrieved from: www.lotteriinspektionen.se/Global/nyhetsdokument/MATCH%20FIXING%20IN%20THE%20NORDIC%20COUNTRIES.PDF.

USEFUL WEBSITES

www.transparency.org/whatwedo/activity/staying_on_side_education_and_
prevention_of_match_fixing
www.playthegame.org/theme-pages/match-fixing/
www.interpol.int/Crime-areas/Integrity-in-Sport/Integrity-in-sport

23

DISABILITY SPORT

IAN BRITTAIN

No Ramps, Dirty Toilets: Paralympic Meet Nightmare for Differently-Abled Athletes.

(NDTV website, 22 March 2015)

Paralympic medal winner Olivia Breen: 'Sport has been my lifeline.'

(*Daily Express*, 28 December 2014)

Pistorius: I wouldn't want to run if I was cheating. I believe in the purity of sport.

(*Daily Mail Online*, 14 February 2013)

LEARNING OUTCOMES

On completion of this chapter, students will be able to:

- Appreciate some of the problems faced by people with disabilities around the world in becoming involved in and benefitting from sport.

- Identify some of the complex issues around taking part in sport for people with disabilities at all levels.

- Begin to understand the role that they might be able to play as a potential future worker/manager in the sports industry in increasing the inclusion of people with disabilities within the sporting structure.

INTRODUCTION

The concept of disability sport is a contemporary and growing issue for sports management. Increasing media coverage and growing acceptance of the validity of disability sport and the abilities of athletes with disabilities have meant that sports managers are having to play catch-up in order to understand this increasingly important area of sport. Within disability sport there are a number of issues that not only make this inclusion process difficult at times, but also make it a very interesting and fertile area for research. In order to really understand the importance of sport and its impacts upon the lives of people with disabilities it is necessary to first understand the role(s) it may play in their lives. Sir Ludwig Guttmann (1976: 12–13), internationally recognized founder of the modern-day Paralympic movement, highlighted three main areas in which **participation** in sport could benefit people with disabilities.

Sport as a curative factor

According to Guttmann, sport represents the most natural form of remedial exercise and can be used to successfully complement other forms of remedial exercise. Sport can be invaluable in restoring the overall fitness, including strength, speed, coordination and endurance of someone who has received a disabling injury. Tasiemski et al. (1998) point out how sport can be of particular benefit to individuals with certain disabilities. Following a pilot study on individuals recovering from a spinal cord lesion, they state:

> Systematically practised physical activity and sports allows the disabled person to keep the high level of physical fitness that was obtained during rehabilitation. It also helps to maintain compensatory processes and prevent complications caused by inactivity. Physical activity and sports are amongst the most important factors that determine the effectiveness and final outcomes of physical rehabilitation. (Tasiemski et al., 1998; unpublished)

They also found that the frequency of hospital readmissions per year following discharge was three times less in athletes than it was in non-athletes, adding weight to their claim that those involved in activities away from the home, especially physical ones such as sport, are physically fitter, more independent and have fewer avoidable complications.

The recreational and psychological value of sport

Guttmann claims that the big advantage of sport for the disabled over other remedial exercises lies within its recreational value in that it restores 'that passion for playful activity and the desire to experience joy and pleasure in life, so deeply inherent in any human being' (1976: 12). Guttmann also points out that much of the restorative power of sport is lost if the person with the disability does not enjoy their participation in it. As long as enjoyment is derived from the activity, then sport can help develop an active mind, self-confidence, self-dignity, self-discipline, competitive spirit and camaraderie, all of which are essential in helping someone overcome the all-consuming depression that can occur with sudden traumatic disability.

Sport as a means of social re-integration

There are certain sports where people with disabilities are capable of competing alongside their non-disabled peers, e.g. archery, bowls, table tennis, as Neroli Fairhall of New Zealand proved when she competed from a wheelchair in archery at the 1976 Olympic Games in Montreal. This helps create a better understanding between people with disabilities and their non-disabled peers and aids their social re-integration through the medium of sport.

More recent research in the field appears to continue to add credence to Guttmann's claims. Berger (2008: 650) claims that the benefits gained from participation in sport include improved physical conditioning and a sense of bodily mastery, along with a heightened sense of self-esteem and personal empowerment that spills over into other social pursuits. These comments appear to concur with the findings of Sporner et al. (2009), who investigated the psychosocial impact of participation in the 2006 National Veterans Wheelchair Games and Winter Sports Clinic for 132 veterans with disabilities. Key findings included that 84% felt that participation in these events led them to a greater acceptance of their own disabilities and 77.1% felt it led to their greater participation in society.

These processes do not just apply to people with disabilities in developed nations with strong sporting structures. There are examples of this process at work for children with disabilities in places such as former African conflict zones, although such examples are few and far between. PlayAble, an organization based in the Netherlands, works on sporting projects with children with disabilities in Kenya, Mozambique and Uganda. They not only work with the children, they also train coaches and try to involve the local community as much as possible. As an example of the potential impact of sport for children with disabilities on the re-integration process, they cite the following case:

> Ismail is one of the coaches who manage to use the platform of sport as a powerful tool to spread positive messages about the rights and abilities of people with disabilities. In one of the slum areas in Nairobi (Kenya), outreach activities for children with all abilities were organized every other week. Some of these children had to be picked up from their homes where parents locked them up in fear of discrimination and sexual abuse. Since the activities

were new and novel, community members came to watch and the coaches also invited teachers from a local school and the local governor. After a couple of activities they sat together to talk about the right of education. Once they had seen and realized the great abilities of the children, they together decided to open a special unit in the local school to allow 20 children with disabilities to enroll in the school. (PlayAble website, 2011)

,

THINKING POINT 23.1

Participation in Disability Sport – the Sport England Active People Survey 2012–13

The number of countries participating in the summer Paralympic Games has risen dramatically over the past 25 years from 60 in Seoul 1988 to 164 in London 2012. This can likely be attributed partly to the fact that in Seoul, and ever since, the Paralympic Games have been hosted in the same host city and venues as the Olympic Games. However, according to the Sport England Active People Survey 2012–13 only 18.2% of people with disabilities in the UK are playing sport at least once a week compared to 35.2% for the overall population. In order to be counted an individual must take part in at least 30 minutes of sport at moderate intensity at least once a week.

Therefore, despite the apparent rapid growth of elite sport for people with disabilities, participation at the grassroots level still lags a long way behind their non-disabled counterparts. However a recent survey by the English Federation of Disability Sport (EFDS) published in September 2013 found that 70% of those interviewed said they would like to do more sport and physical activity. The EFDS survey also found that the most popular sport for people in the survey to take part in was swimming at 46%, significantly ahead of going to the gym (29%) in second place, and cycling and walking (22%) in joint third.

TOOLS FOR ANALYSIS

If the benefits of taking up sporting activities for the persons with a disability are potentially so high and a large proportion of people with disabilities, in the UK at least, would like to do more sport and physical activity (EFDS, 2013), then why aren't more of them involved in sport? There are myriad reasons why this is the case, many of which are the same or very similar to the reasons a lot of non-disabled individuals do not take up sport (see Taylor, 2011: 41). Sharkey (1996) puts forward five key barriers to participation that prevent, or make it very difficult for, persons with a disability to take part in sporting activities.

Transportation difficulties

Being able to get to where a particular activity is taking place is something that non-disabled individuals mostly take for granted. Although the public transport system may not be exactly convenient, if they do not have their own transport, being able to access that public transport can, generally, be achieved with relatively minor inconvenience. However for those in wheelchairs, the visually impaired, those who cannot walk very far and many others with various disabilities getting to a particular venue can be a very major hurdle in itself.

Restricted physical access

As with transportation, problems with physical access are compounded for those with restricted physical mobility. This can be overcome, to a certain degree, with the use of specially adapted equipment, but as DePauw and Gavron (2005) point out, this can often be prohibitively expensive.

Cost of activity against level of disposable income

According to the Office for Disability Statistics (2013), in the UK in 2012, 46.3% of working-age people with disabilities were in employment compared to 76.4% of working-age non-disabled people. Sharkey (1996) claims that for those people with disabilities in employment their jobs tend to be low status, poorly paid and in uninteresting sheltered positions. Facility pricing policies will, therefore, have a significant effect upon the participation rates of persons with disabilities, particularly those on a low income.

Poor communication causing a lack of awareness of a facility or programme of activities

Making persons with a disability aware of the fact that a particular programme or sporting activity is available is not simply a matter of advertising it in the same way as one might for a non-disabled programme. The form of communication used to get that message across can make all the difference. It is pointless advertising an activity for the blind using a small advert in a newspaper or an activity for the deaf on the radio and hoping that someone will tell them about it. Poor communication stems from a lack of overall understanding about the actual impacts of various forms of disability (Holmes, 1997; Sharkey, 1996).

Management and staff attitudes towards disability

Low self-esteem and fear of failure are often cited as reasons why persons with a disability are reluctant to take up sporting activities (Brittain, 2004;

DePauw and Gavron, 2005). This problem is often compounded by the negative attitudes of others towards persons with a disability and can often be more of an obstacle to participation than the problems of access (Thierfeld and Gibbons, 1986). According to Torkildsen (1986) a positive, proactive and friendly attitude from management and staff towards persons with a disability can often overcome many of the problems posed by access to a particular programme or facility.

In addition to the above, gender also appears to play a key role in participation rates amongst persons with disabilities. According to the Sport England Adults with a Disability and Sport National Survey (2000–2001) excluding walking, disabled men (44%) were more likely to have participated in at least one sport than disabled women (33%). Even when walking was included, disabled men (56%) were still more likely to have participated in at least one sport than disabled women (47%). This can be partially accounted for by the fact that the 1980 national census in America revealed that more men are permanently injured through accidents while more women have chronic disabling conditions that are not accident related (Grimes and French, 1987). Thierfeld and Gibbons (1986) showed that in competitive sports considerably fewer women are involved than men. They cite the case of the membership lists of the National Wheelchair Athletic Association's (NWAA) membership list for 1985 in America, where of 1,600 members only 35% were women. They suggest that this is due to the fact that men do more dangerous things. They are more daring, have more accidents and become disabled. However, according to many authors, the problem goes much deeper than that. Henderson and Bedini (1997) and Guthrie (1999) all discuss the problems persons with disabilities, and women with disabilities in particular, face in any attempts to become involved in any kind of sporting activity. These include the following:

- Generally men grow up playing sport and are encouraged to do so by everyone around them. Women, however, generally do not and are not encouraged to do so. This is equally true of non-disabled girls and women, and so if they are not encouraged young women with disabilities are even less likely to play sports, as they face the double discrimination of being both disabled and a woman.
- It is rare for women who were not active in sports prior to becoming disabled to turn to them afterwards for fitness, especially as those who influence them are unlikely to encourage them in that direction.
- Disabled women and girls often face enormous emotional problems. Issues of low self-esteem, inexperience with sports, fear of success and failure, which are already documented for non-disabled women, are even greater problems for disabled females.
- A lack of female role models with disabilities to counteract rolelessness plays a major part as they provide tangible proof of what is attainable.

Type of disability also has a role to play in participation rates in sport and physical activity. The English Federation of Disability Sport Disabled People's Lifestyle Survey (2013: 17) found that 'people with visual impairment and those with a learning disability or social or behavioral issues are more likely to be limited by the fact that they need support to take part in sport and physical'. According to Brittain (2010) the impact of a combination of the above mentioned factors not only affects recruitment into grassroots disability sport, but also at the very highest levels. Brittain (2004) claims that from 1992 to 2000 only one new visually impaired athlete joined the Great Britain Paralympic track and field squad. In addition, of the nine visually impaired track and field athletes representing Great Britain in Sydney only one was under 30 years of age.

ACTION LEARNING

- If you were to work in the sports industry in your country in the future what could you do to make access to sports and physical activity for people with disabilities easier?

- What strategies might you employ to attract people with disabilities to take part in your programmes or events?

THINKING POINT 23.2

Disability Sport for Development and Peace – the Case of Sierra Leone.

Between 1991 and 2001, about 50,000 people were killed in Sierra Leone's civil war. Hundreds of thousands of people were forced from their homes, and many became refugees in Guinea and Liberia. In 2001, UN forces moved into rebel-held areas and began to disarm rebel soldiers. By January 2002, the war was declared over. By 2004, the DDR (disarmament, demobilization and reintegration) process was complete. However, throughout the 10 years of civil war, many thousands of people, both combatants and non-combatants, suffered disabling injuries as a result of the conflict.

This included many youths (children at the time) who, in most cases, were forced to become child soldiers and either became injured in combat or had limbs hacked off for disobeying orders or even just as a warning to others. Add to this those people born with birth defects due to the severe poverty and those disabled by accidents, and the number of disabled young people in Sierra Leone becomes disproportionately high compared to other countries that have not undergone a recent conflict. Trani et al. (2009: 13) claim research by Unicef in 2005 estimated that the prevalence of disability in Sierra Leone could be as high as 24% for children.

According to Gottschalk (2007) the common greeting in Sierra Leone is 'How de Body?', which she claims reflects a culture that places its social and communal identity in the physical realm. According to Heeren (2003) amputees have reported that they feel rejected by society in post-conflict Sierra Leone because the public do not want to be reminded of what they have done to them. The introduction of amputee football has had a major impact on these perceptions by changing attitudes towards individuals who are amputees and thus giving them back a sense of self-respect. In addition, the use of mixed-tribal teams has helped break down, or at least blur, some of the lines of conflict along which the original war was fought. However, this only deals with amputees, and only single amputees at that (i.e. one limb), as these form part of the criteria for competing in amputee football. Other impairments such as paralysis or visual impairments are still to a large degree overlooked and so there are still many opportunities for sport to be used as a re-integration tool for people with disabilities all over Africa.

TOOLS FOR ANALYSIS

One of the main impacts of armed conflict is that there is a high level of disabilities caused by small arms and light weapons (SALW), including anti-personnel landmines. Young people, both as civilians and combatants, appear to be one of the most affected groups who become disabled, and it is often the case that there are no adequate socio-economic services and opportunities in post-conflict environments to help deal with the many issues raised by these conflict-induced disabilities. However, research relating to the impact of conflict-induced disability, particularly with regard to children, is scarce, although this may be partly due to the difficulties of carrying out such research in the often challenging situation of a post-conflict society. Indeed, it is equally important not to overlook the issues for those who received their disabilities as a result of accidents or birth defects, otherwise there would be a risk of further marginalizing an already marginalized group. People, and particularly children, with disabilities do not have equal opportunities and equal access regarding most parts of life. Handicap International claim this lack of access includes basic services (especially education and health) because of their physical inaccessibility to the buildings, a lack of information in adapted formats (e.g. Braille) and discriminatory behaviour within society.

In addition, individuals with disabilities tend to suffer disproportionately during and after conflict situations have occurred. They are often the most exposed to protection risks, including physical and sexual violence, exploitation, harassment and discrimination (Reilly, 2010). This is particularly true for females. Research by the United Nations indicates that violence against children with disabilities occurs at annual rates at least 1.7 times greater than for their non-disabled peers. Finally, they also lack options for making a living and therefore the opportunity to transcend out of poverty, which often means they either remain a burden on their families or are forced to beg to make a living. Disability and poverty are also closely linked to insecure living conditions, a lack of access to basic services, malnutrition and other dimensions of poverty, not only leading directly to disabilities, but also making life much harder for those who are born with or acquire disabilities through accidents or as a result of conflict. Add to these facts the issue of the perceived stigma attached not only to the person with a disability, but also their families, which can cause parents to try and conceal their disabled children, and it is clear that life for a person with a disability in former conflict zones in Africa is very difficult indeed. The rehabilitation of children with conflict-induced disabilities also needs to bear in mind a set of additional issues, such as the context of poverty, social stigma, cultural values and traditions prevalent within the society under investigation. Moreover, as there are always many priorities for reconstruction in post-conflict affected environments, and people with disabilities and particularly children are far less likely to have access to decision-making processes, means of production and financial capital, they tend to be further marginalized within society.

One further issue for people with disabilities in conflict zones is that they often become displaced from their villages and local communities, either forcibly or out of fear for their own safety, and often end up in internal displacement camps where conditions are often far from ideal to meet their needs. However, once the resettlement process is under way, the devastation caused by the conflict in terms of the destruction of villages and infrastructure often means that people with disabilities are one of the hardest groups to re-settle. They also often meet other people with disabilities in the camps that enable them to achieve some sort of camaraderie, which is often preferable to the isolation they can feel back in their own villages where they can be shunned or stigmatized by their acquired disability (Duerden, 2010).

Estimating accurate numbers for the disabled population in a given country in a post-conflict situation is often almost impossible. A lack of consistency in terminology and the methodologies for data collection, cultural differences in definitions and concepts of disability, and a lack of training or disability awareness amongst data collection staff will all affect the accuracy of the data. This is also compounded by some of the issues highlighted above regarding stigma and the hiding away of the people with disabilities, the difficulties of researching in isolated (and sometimes dangerous) rural areas, and the general administrative and bureaucratic chaos that follows a prolonged conflict situation. In short, life for children and young people with disabilities in a post-conflict environment often means marginalization, exclusion, disparity, poverty and ostracization. It is, therefore, very important for them to have opportunities to address these challenges. Sport can be a low-cost and effective means to foster positive health and well-being, social inclusion and community building, for people with a disability.

ACTION LEARNING

- What are the similarities and differences between the lives of people with disabilities in post-conflict zones such as in Africa and developed nations such as the UK, Canada or the USA, particularly in terms of the role that sport might play in their lives?
- What problems might you encounter in trying to set up a sports programme in a post-conflict zone?

THINKING POINT 23.3

Technology and Disability Sport – Oscar Pistorius and the Beijing Olympic Games

With the massive improvements in performance standards currently occurring in disability sport some athletes have reached a standard that might allow them to qualify for the Olympic Games. However, the technology they use in terms of adapted equipment in order to enable them to compete has raised questions regarding the advantages such equipment might give them over their non-disabled counterparts. This has led to the coining of such terms as 'technological doping' or 'cyborg athlete'. The most notable example of this is, of course, Oscar Pistorius, the South African double-below the knee amputee who uses carbon fibre blade prosthetic limbs to allow him to compete.

The Pistorius case has been covered heavily by both the media and academics worldwide (see Howe, 2008). Pistorius, a Paralympic gold medallist and world record holder, decided he wished to compete against non-disabled athletes in open competition and if possible qualify to compete in the 400 metres at the Olympic Games in Beijing. He had come within half a second of the qualifying standard when in March 2007 the International Association of Athletics Federation (IAAF) introduced a rule regarding 'technical aids' that brought into question the use of such prosthetic limbs within the Olympic Games, as it was felt these gave users an unfair advantage when compared to the capabilities of the human leg. Following an appeal to the Court of Arbitration for Sport (CAS) , which challenged the veracity of the tests carried out by the International Olympics Committee (IOC) and the IAAF, it was decided by CAS that Pistorius should be allowed to compete (but only using the technology which he had used in the original tests). In the end Pistorius failed to reach the qualifying time for the individual event, but still hoped to make his country's relay team, at which point the IAAF Secretary General Pierre Weiss is cited as saying 'we'd prefer that they don't select him for reasons of safety. ... Pistorius will risk the physical safety of himself and other athletes if he runs in the main pack of the relay event' (CBC Sports, 2008). In the end Pistorius was not selected for the South African team as four other athletes posted faster times. However, he did qualify and compete in the 400 metre and 400 metre relay events at the London 2012 Olympic Games – without incident.

TOOLS FOR ANALYSIS

The fear then, in the case of Pistorius, for the IOC and the IAAF, was not the usual prejudice most people with disabilities have encountered at some point in their lives of being considered 'less than human', but in fact the complete opposite – the fear of being 'more than human'. The very devices society has devised to allow individuals to walk in the upright position like everyone else, and to compete in running events in a similar style and manner as their non-disabled counterparts, are now considered to give an unfair competitive advantage. Pistorius went from a fine Paralympic athlete whose achievements were to be applauded, albeit perhaps in a slightly patronizing manner, to a kind of 'Robocop' of the track who might not only have an unfair advantage over athletes not wearing his prosthetic limbs, but also might heap danger and injury upon both himself and his fellow relay competitors.

Swartz and Watermeyer (2008) ascribe this reaction to the fact that Pistorius is effectively challenging a key underlying ethos of sport – that of bodily perfection. He is challenging culturally ascribed definitions of bodily perfection based around non-disabled conceptions. To have someone whose body is less than perfect (i.e. missing limbs) potentially beating athletes whose bodies far more readily meet the requirements laid down by society for bodily perfection is a challenge to the virtues of those who hold power, especially when that body has been 'technologically accessorized' with prosthetic limbs. It is somewhat ironic that the term 'prosthetic' is derived from the Greek meaning 'an addition designed to remove physical stigma' (Howe, 2008: 127), when in Pistorius's case it appears to have resulted in removing the stigma of being disabled and adding another stigma of being 'more than human' in athletic ability, but 'less than human' in physical appearance, i.e. some kind of cyborg. This then begins to raise numerous questions around the difference between being human and being a machine.

In contrast to Pistorius it should be pointed out that another South African, swimmer Natalie Du Toit, a single leg amputee, did qualify to represent South Africa in the 10 kilometre Open Water swimming event at the Beijing Olympic Games, and there was no such reticence regarding her participation from either the IOC or FINA, as she does not use any kind of prosthetic when she swims, although she does so for daily living.

ACTION LEARNING

- Is there a difference between the prosthetic **technology** worn by athletes such as Oscar Pistorius and the equipment used in sports such as cycling by the wealthiest and most developed sporting nations?

- Should athletes with disabilities be allowed to compete at both the Olympic and Paralympic Games in the same year?

Cheating in Disability Sport – the Sydney 2000 Eligibility Scandal

On 21 October 2000 the Spanish intellectually disabled basketball team won the gold medal at the Sydney Paralympic Games beating Russia 87–63 in the final. This victory capped Spain's best ever performance at a Summer Paralympic Games winning 107 medals and finishing third in the medal table. However, triumph was to turn into disaster in late November when Carlos Ribagorda, a member of the gold medal-winning basketball team and, as it turned out, also a journalist with a Madrid-based business magazine, *Capital*, wrote an article chronicling long-term and widespread fraud and cheating within intellectually disabled sport in Spain. The pinnacle of his revelations was that 10 of the 12 gold medal-winning Spanish basketball players actually had no intellectual disability at all, and had been deliberately recruited to increase the strength of the team in order to win medals and thus guarantee future funding. It also turned out that this was not a new occurrence, but had been going on for a number of years. It later transpired that four members of the Spanish intellectually disabled basketball team that had won the gold medal at the World Championships in Brazil also had no disability. The potential cheating was apparently not restricted to the sport of basketball either. One member of Spain's intellectually disabled track and field team, two swimmers and one table tennis player were suspected of not having a disability and went on to win medals.

As a result of a Spanish Paralympic Committee investigation the International Paralympic Committee set up an investigation commission in December 2000 to examine the allegations. The commission concluded that the eligibility verification of athlete registration forms at both a national and international level had been seriously mismanaged and administered. Based upon these findings, on 29 January, 2001 the IPC Management Committee suspended all athletes with an intellectual disability and their international governing body (INAS-FID) from all IPC activities, including until such times as they could come up with a process of assessment, verification and certification of intellectually disabled athletes that was workable and could be trusted. Athletes with disabilities did not compete again at the Paralympics Games until London 2012, such were the problems in achieving the new certification process.

TOOLS FOR ANALYSIS

Many people find it hard to believe that cheating occurs in sport for the disabled. This possibly reflects a perception of sport for the disabled that is grounded more in 'pity for these poor unfortunate individuals' than one that views them as athletes who simply happen to have an impairment. The growing media coverage and increasing rewards now available to individuals who are successful at the highest levels of disability sport, as well as the increasing importance placed on being successful at the Paralympic Games by national governments, mean that the pressure to succeed leads to a win-at-all-costs mentality amongst some individuals. Although the above case highlights an issue of non-disabled individuals cheating within disability sport, many of the forms of cheating that have long been known about in international non-disabled sport are now also prevalent in elite sport for the disabled. Although cheating is to be deplored in any sport, disabled or non-disabled, what it does highlight is that athletes with disabilities are as human as everyone else, with the same wants, desires and potential character flaws that may lead them to cheat. There are four main areas within disability and Paralympic sport where cheating has occurred.

Doping

Much has been written about the illegal use of drugs for performance enhancement (doping) purposes within non-disabled sport. Drugs cheats also occur in disability sport. However, the problem is made far more difficult in disability sport by the fact that some athletes actually need to take drugs on a regular basis for health reasons. Given the nature of some impairments certain individuals may be required to take substances or use treatment methods, under doctors' orders, that are prohibited by the World Anti-Doping Agency (WADA) code. Under such circumstances, if the individual wishes to continue competing in their chosen sport, they must apply to either the IPC Therapeutic Use Exemption Committee or their own national anti-doping agency for a therapeutic use exemption certificate at the latest on the final day of entry for the competition they wish to compete in. However, in extraordinary circumstances, such as an injury during training or illness just prior to competition, an emergency therapeutic use exemption (TUE) may be granted. The TUE Committee to which the application has been made, and consisting of at least three members, then evaluates the request in accordance with the WADA International Standards for Therapeutic Use Exemptions and renders a decision. This decision is then communicated to both the athlete and WADA. At this point WADA may, at the request of the athlete concerned or of their own volition, review the decision, and in exceptional circumstances may even overturn it. The outcome of this is that an athlete who is granted a Therapeutic Use ExemptionTUE may then compete in a sporting competition and if drug tested the testers will know to expect to find the allowed banned substance in the sample and the expected levels of that substance.

Dope testing at the Summer Paralympic Games appears to have begun at the Stoke Mandeville Games in 1984 when eight urine samples all tested negative. Since then the number of tests taken at each Games has increased dramatically, with over 1,000 tests being carried out at Beijing 2008. The five Summer Paralympic Games from 1992 to 2008 returned a total of 27 positive tests. In the same period there were 48 positive tests at the Olympic Summer Games. Perhaps a little surprisingly this means that the Summer Paralympic Games have returned one positive test for every 121 tests carried out, whereas the rate for the Summer Olympic Games is one positive test for every 285 tests carried out. However it should be pointed out that the vast majority of these positive tests (70%) have all occurred in one sport – powerlifting (Brittain, 2010).

Boosting

'Boosting' is the colloquial terminology for self-induced autonomic dysreflexia,[1] which is considered to be a performance-enhancing technique (Harris, 1994). Boosting refers to a technique potentially employed by athletes with a spinal cord injury at the T6 level or above. The resultant effect is similar to that produced by ergogenic aids.[2] Boosting has, therefore, been banned in sport for the disabled. Reported methods for boosting by some athletes include temporarily blocking their own urinary catheter, drinking large amounts of fluids prior to their event to distend the bladder, tightening clothing and sitting for long periods of time. According to Grey-Thompson (2008) it can boost performance by up to 25%. Potential complications of prolonged boosting are the same as for non-self-induced autonomic dysreflexia, such as stroke, seizure, irregular heart rhythm, heart attack and potentially death (Malanga, 2008). Boosting is therefore banned, not just on ethical grounds but also health grounds.

Classification

The most obvious and clear-cut case of cheating the classification system is the one outlined in Thinking Point 23.3 above. However, given that in Beijing there were 99 functional reclassifications, 63 visual impairment reclassifications and 13 athletes reclassified again after their first appearance in front of the classifiers, it clearly shows that classification is not an exact science. Two athletes were actually reclassified to such an extent that they were deemed to be not sufficiently disabled enough to compete in Paralympic sport, one of them after having won a silver medal. The inexactness of the classification system clearly opens up opportunities for individuals to try and get themselves classified into a group that would give them a competitive advantage or to be simply wrongly classified and the mistake not get spotted.

Tampering with technology

Grey-Thompson (2008) claims that there have been instances where wheelchair track athletes have felt that their racing chairs, and in particular their compensators, which they calibrate themselves to help them go around the

---

[1]Autonomic dysreflexia is unique to individuals with lesions above T6 and can lead to an uncontrolled rise in systolic and diastolic blood pressure, which in a sporting situation can lead to improved blood flow to working muscles and thus better performance. However, there is potential for a stroke or intracranial haemorrhage, which, in extreme cases, may lead to death.

[2]Ergogenic aids are any external influences that can be determined to enhance performance in high-intensity exercises including, but not limited to steroids, that may lead to a competitive advantage.

two bends on the track, have been tampered with. A slight change in the calibration might mean that the chair would either not turn in correctly, forcing the chair out wide, or might turn in too sharply, causing the chair to hit the curb on the inside of the track. For this reason Grey-Thompson claims she also guarded her racing chair very closely whenever she was racing.

ACTION LEARNING

- For a country of your choice carry out some desk-based research to find out what programmes are in place to educate about and deter people from cheating in sport?

- List some of the reasons why people might cheat in sport and discuss some of the ways you might try to prevent cheating in sport amongst your peer group?

CONCLUSION

This chapter has highlighted a selection of issues that people with disabilities face in becoming involved in sport, as well as some of the benefits they can accrue from their participation. The chapter also highlighted that for someone interested in carrying out research in sport the area of sport for people with disabilities offers very fertile and in many cases untouched ground. Any issue that has been researched in non-disabled sport can be re-researched and re-analysed in the context of disability sport, with an extra list of interesting issues to add to the mix, making the results both new and useful given the rising prominence of sport for people with disabilities within society.

By training the sports managers of the future and providing them with the knowledge necessary to facilitate sporting opportunities for people with disabilities it should be possible to greatly increase the participation of people with disabilities within sport. This in turn may help break down some of the societal barriers people with disabilities face on a daily basis and assist with their greater inclusion in the their local communities and beyond.

REFERENCES

Berger, R.J. (2008) Disability and the Dedicated Wheelchair Athlete: Beyond the "'Supercrip'" Critique, *Journal of Contemporary Ethnography*, 37(6): 647–678.

Brittain, I. (2004) Perceptions of Disability and Their Impact Upon Involvement in Sport for People with Disabilities at All Levels, *Journal of Sport and Social Issues*, 28(4): 429–452.

Brittain, I. (2010) *The Paralympic Games Explained*. Abingdon: Routledge.

CBC Sports (2008) Pistorius falls short in last-chance run. Available at: www.cbc.ca/news/story/2008/07/16/pistorius-lucerne.html (last accessed 9 December 2008).

DePauw, K.P. & Gavron, S.J. (2005) *Disability and Sport* (2nd edn). Champaign, IL: Human Kinetics.

Duerden, S. (2010) Displacement limbo in Sierra Leone. Available at: www.
  fmreview.org/disability/Duerden.doc (last accessed 15 September 2010).
EFDS website (2013) Disabled People's Lifestyle Survey. Available at: www.efds.
  co.uk/assets/0000/7297/Disabled_People_s_Lifestyle_Survey_Report_Sept_2013.
  pdf (last accessed 18 September 2013).
Grey-Thompson, T. (2008) Cheating does happen in the Paralympics. Available
  at: www.telegraph.co.uk/sport/othersports/paralympicsport/2798515/
  Cheating-does-happens-in-the-Paralympics-Paralympics.html (last accessed
  10 February 2009).
Grimes, P.S. & French, L. (1987) Barriers to Disabled Women's Participation in
  Sports, *JOPERD*, 58(3): 24–27.
Gottschalk, P. (2007) 'How are we in this world now?' Examining the experiences
  of persons disabled by war in the peace processes of Sierra Leone. Unpublished
  Master's thesis, University of Victoria, Canada.
Guthrie, S.R. (1999) Managing Imperfection in a Perfectionist Culture: Physical
  Activity and Disability Management Among Women with Disabilities, *Quest*,
  51: 369–381.
Guttmann, L. (1976) *Textbook of Sport for the Disabled.* Oxford: Alden.
Harris, P. (1994) Self-induced Autonomic Dysreflexia ('Boosting') practised by
  Some Tetraplegic Athletes to Enhance their Athletic Performance, *Paraplegia*,
  32(5): 289–291.
Heeren, N. (2003) Sierra Leone and civil war: Neglected trauma and forgotten
  children, *Revue Humanitaire,* Vol. 9. Paris: Medicins du Monde.
Henderson, K.A. & Bedini. L.A. (1997) Women, Leisure, and 'Double Whammies':
  Empowerment and Constraint, *Journal of Leisurability*, 24(1): 36–46.
Holmes, S. (1997) Aspire to Success, *Recreation*, September: 30–31.
Howe, P.D. (2008) *The Cultural Politics of the Paralympic Movement: Through an
  Anthropological Lens.* London: Routledge.
Malanga, G.A. (2008) Athletes with disabilities. Available at: www.emedicine.com/
  sports/TOPIC144.HTM (last accessed 20 November 2008).
Office for Disability Issues (2013) Disability facts and figures. Available at: http://
  odi.dwp.gov.uk/disability-statistics-and-research/disability-facts-and-figures.
  php#imp (last accessed 18 September 2013).
Reilly, R. (2010) Disabilities among refugees and conflict-affected populations.
  Available at: www.fmreview.org/disability/FMR35/08-10.pdf, (last accessed 15
  September 2010).
Sharkey, P. (1996) Equal Rights, *Recreation,* 55(8): 31–33.
Sporner, M.L., Fitzgerald, S.G., Dicianno, B.E., Collins, D., Teodorski, E., Pasquina, P.F.
  & Cooper, R.A. (2009) Psychosocial Impact of Participation in the National Veterans
  Games and Winter Sports Clinic, *Disability and Rehabilitation*, 31(5): 410–418.
Sport England website (2013) Active People Survey 7. Available at: http://archive.
  sportengland.org/research/active_people_survey/active_people_survey_7.aspx
  (last accessed 18 September 2013).
Sport England (2001) Adults with a Disability and Sport National Survey
  (2000–2001) (Headline Findings). Available at: http://archive.sportengland.org/
  research/tracking_trends.aspx (last accessed 15 September 2010).
Swartz, L. & Watermeyer, L. (2008) Cyborg Anxiety: Oscar Pistorius and the
  Boundaries of What it Means to Be Human. *Disability and Society*, 23(2): 187–190.
Tasiemski, T., Bergstrom, E., Savic, G. & Gardner, B.P. (1998) 'Sports, Recreation
  and Employment Following Spinal Cord Injury – a Pilot Study' (unpublished).
Taylor, P. (ed.) (2011) *Torkildsen's Sport and Leisure Management* (6th edn).
  Abingdon: Routledge.

Thierfeld, J. & Gibbons, G. (1986) From Access to Equity: Opening Doors for Women Athletes in Sports, *Spokes*, May/June: 21–23.

Torkildsen, G. (1986) *Leisure and Recreation Management* (2nd edn). London: Spon.

Trani, J.-F., Bah, O., Bailey, N., Browne, J., Grace, N. & Kett, M. (2009) *Disability: In and Around Urban Areas of Sierra Leone*. London: Leonard Cheshire and University College London.

PART THREE
ORGANIZATIONAL ISSUES

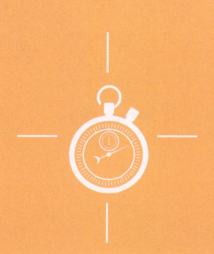

24

OWNERSHIP

JOHN BEECH

Dozens of Blackpool fans stepped up their campaign against chairman Karl Oyston by holding a protest outside his home.

(*The [Blackpool] Gazette* online, 12 April 2015)

Bernie Ecclestone likens F1 to an 'old house' that needs repairing.

(Sky Sports, 30 March 2015)

Chinese company launches crowdfunding to buy AC Milan.

(*Business Standard*, 9 April 2015)

LEARNING OUTCOMES

Upon completion of this chapter, students will be able to:

- Appreciate the differing motivations of owners at the time of purchase of a club and during their subsequent period of ownership.

- Evaluate the strengths and weaknesses of different models of the regulation of ownership.

- Consider the implications of ownership regulation in an external environment.

INTRODUCTION

When organized club sport first emerged in the nineteenth century, a club was simply a loose organization based on members who, to a large extent, shared the same values and organizational goals. Any concept of 'ownership' was really restricted to an implicit 'psychological' ownership. As sports and the clubs within each sport became professionalized, the cash flow within the club increased markedly, and the issue of legal liability for debts prompted the vast majority to turn themselves into limited liability private companies. In this post-professionalized era ownership now meant 'legal ownership' (Beech, 2013).

While there tended to be relatively little trading of the shares in the limited liability company, over time many clubs found themselves owned either by a small group of local businessmen or perhaps a single owner. Profits were not a motivation for these owners – any profits were ploughed back into the club, either in terms of improved infrastructure, such as a new stand, or in the purchase of new players to bolster the club's performance. In the case of English professional football, dividends were severely restricted so that there was no financial incentive to buy shares as an investment.

The most significant change in sport as business has been the onset of **commercialization**. This has seen the involvement of external stakeholders in sport, with the injection of large sums of money, both directly to clubs in the form of **sponsorship** and stadium-naming rights, and indirectly to clubs via their league through broadcasting rights. With the relaxation of dividend caps there is now a significant attractiveness to an external investor to acquire ownership of a club, particularly if that club plays in one of the wealthier leagues such as football's English Premier League. Sports which have reached a post-commercialized phase include football, the North American major sports leagues, Formula 1 motor racing and cycling. It might be intuitively reasoned that increases in capital and a variety of new owners would create positive market forces and a healthy ownership environment. We shall see that there is clear evidence of quite the opposite.

Another consequence of the injection of money from these external stakeholders, and in many cases the injection of capital, either as equity or as 'soft loans',[1] has been a 'vertical financial stretching' in the various pyramids of leagues. In other words, rich clubs have become significantly richer than previously and significantly richer than clubs lower down the pyramid. Competitive balance at a given level in a pyramid becomes dependent on similar cash injections into each club from its owners, a situation which has been largely unregulated, and which has accelerated reduced uncertainty of outcome. It has also made it progressively more difficult for clubs to climb up a pyramid, and has often led to relegated clubs facing

---

[1]Debt for which there is little pressure for repayment, and for which little or no interest is paid. This is in contrast to 'hard debt', in the form of a loan from a bank, for example, where commercial rates of interest are charged and repayments must be made against a pre-agreed schedule.

insolvency if they failed to adjust their costs downwards to allow for the reduced scale of revenues in their new lower league. The Premier League has deemed it necessary to introduce 'parachute payments' for relegated clubs, thus potentially exacerbating the disruption of competitive balance in the division below.

In the following sections we will consider the motivations of owners and how these impact differently on clubs and leagues. Through this discussion, readers will also note how ownership has implications for the **funding and financing** of sport clubs. Next we explore the different ownership models that have emerged, looking at how governance within a league has shaped the types of owners that have become involved, and then we conclude with an overview of the developing contemporary scene.

Owners' motivations

The underlying principle assumed in the study of management is that the owner of a business will seek to maximize their profit. The case of sport as business, and in particular the ownership of clubs, precludes such an assumption. This is perhaps not surprising in light of the 'specificity of sport' concept. This term features in the Treaty of Lisbon and was coined to highlight the fact that sport is different from other areas of economic activity (Commission of the European Communities, 2007).

It might be expected that owners of clubs might adopt one of three attitudes towards profit as a motivation:

- To maximize profit in order to reinvest in the club by buying the best available players and by developing optimal infrastructure.
- To be prepared to sink further money into the club in order to maximize utility (i.e. to achieve the best possible performance on the field) and hence to be relatively unconcerned about profit.
- To maximize profit in order to take such profits out of the club.

It might also be expected that an owner might try to seek profit maximization *and* utility maximization at the same time, but as George Zipf has pointed out (Zipf, 1965), it is not possible to compare meaningfully the achievement of two superlative objectives simultaneously. In elaborating his 'Fallacy of the Dual Superlatives', he cites as an example the case of U-boat commanders instructed to sink the maximum tonnage of enemy shipping in the shortest possible time. With the exception of a case where a single commander achieved both superlatives, it is impossible to determine who has been most successful – the double superlative 'renders the problem completely meaningless and indeterminate' (1965: 3).

In further policy elaborations (EU Council, 2011; European Commission, 2011) ownership is recognized implicitly as an issue, in that the emphasis in European sports policy has been placed on club licensing and on combatting **corruption** in sport. In the case of money laundering, a deeply corrupt activity, a report by the Financial Action Task Force (FATF, 2009) laid out a clear argument as to why sport, and football in particular, was vulnerable to this. Sport is thus vulnerable to those who wish to become owners of a club in order to engage in corrupt practices.

Although at the European Union level there is recognition of the societal dimension of sport, there is no recognition of a further possible type of motivation in those owning sports clubs – the lure of the publicity associated with ownership of a sports club. This may be the desire to be recognized in the community as a benefactor, or at a more base level to be recognized as a celebrity in the local community.

Individual motivation is difficult to determine in any definitive sense, but an indicative determination of the motivation of an individual owner can be established via the study of a range of secondary sources. Research by the author into the ownership of over 300 English football clubs, which are covered in great depth by national and local newspapers, has revealed a typology of ownership, based on two dimensions of classification, shown in Tables 24.1 and 24.2. Table 24.1 shows a simple classification based on the background from which the owner has emerged and the intent which they project. It should be noted however that applying this classification to a specific pairing of club and owner is only possible as a point-in-time exercise – motivations can change over time, and the financial resources to continue in perpetuity propping up a club which runs at an operational loss would require infinitely deep pockets and unswerving commitment. Table 24.2 shows classifications based on the emergent behaviour of the owner over time.

TABLE 24.1 *A typology of 'benefactor' owners at the point of taking ownership of a club*

TYPE I BENEFACTOR	Owner is a local businessman with a loyalty to both the club and the locality
TYPE II BENEFACTOR	Owner is an entrepreneur with no immediately obvious attachment to the locality or the club

TABLE 24.2 *A typology of 'benefactor' owners over time*

TYPE A BENEFACTOR	Benefactor has both the funds and the personal commitment to engage in long-term support in spite of continuing lack of financial sustainability of the club without continuing injections of funding
TYPE B BENEFACTOR	Benefactor runs out of (1) funds, and/or (2) commitment, and seeks to exit; or (3) through age seeks to disengage
TYPE C BENEFACTOR	Benefactor emerges as having no intention of 'doing good' and begins, for example, to asset strip
TYPE D BENEFACTOR	Benefactor emerges as never having had (1) the funds, (2) the commitment, or (3) the business acumen to bring stability and success to the club

If all benefactor owners were Type I and Type A, all would be well for a club in terms of economic sustainability. Leagues therefore have a responsibility to vet potential owners in order to ensure that, for example, a Type C or Type D 'benefactor' does not gain control of a club. In the case of the English Football Association (FA), regulations have been framed to require potential owners to submit to an Owners' and Directors' Test (formerly known as, and still sometimes referred to colloquially as, the 'Fit and Proper Persons' Test).

THE REGULATION OF CLUB OWNERS BY LEAGUES

FA regulations for the approval of owners and directors set out the following rationale for their existence:

> Why does football have an Owners' and Directors' Test?
>
> Those holding positions of responsibility at clubs are required to meet obligations placed on them under the law. Football believes that such persons should meet standards over and above the law so as to better protect clubs and the reputation and image of the game.

The Regulations then define who is required to pass the Test:

> The Test applies to any person that is defined as an Officer of a club and includes any person operating the powers that are usually associated with those of:
>
> - a director of a company incorporated under the Companies Act; or
> - direct or indirect control over a Club including a shareholding of 30% or more; or
> - an officer of an Industrial & Provident Society; or
> - a Chairman, Secretary or Treasurer of a Club that is an unincorporated association.

Arguably two potential loopholes for prospective owners arise. Firstly there is, on the face of it, an imprecision as to what does and does not constitute indirect control. Secondly, it would seem that a potential director who would fail the test might sidestep having to pass it by instead passing some of his shareholding, at least nominally, to close family members or business colleagues who might be expected to vote at board meetings in a consistent and supportive way, while simultaneously denying that that individual has indirect control.

In the case of English football, where the FA is, at least in theory, the ultimate governing body, there are similar Owners' and Directors' Tests within the Premier League and the Football League. The Football League, controller of Tiers 2, 3 and 4 (the Championship, League 1 and League 2 respectively), has a slightly different listing for who must submit to the Test:

1 Directors of the Club
2 Directors of any associated, parent or group companies
3 Shadow directors
4 Persons in accordance with whose directions or instructions the Club's management are 'accustomed to act'
5 Persons exercising 'control' over the Club.

This constitutes a broader sweep than the Football Association requires. It explicitly adds 'Directors of any associated, parent or group companies', and explicitly includes 'Shadow directors', a term which has a status in law. The issue of 'Indirect control' is recognized by the use of inverted commas with 'control' in the final bullet point, and attempts to resolve it by defining this as:

- A 30% or more shareholding in the Club
- The regulations also allow us to consider shareholders holding less than 30% if they are acting 'in concert' with others and together they go over 30%

  For example, if there is a 25% shareholder and they are someone in accordance with whose instructions the Board of the Club are 'accustomed to act' they still qualify as a Club Director and have to submit to the Test.

The Regulations then explain how the Football League decides who is required to submit to the Test:

- Information collated from Clubs at the start of the season
- Companies House filings
- Copies of information supplied to the Football Association
- Club's returns

  Note: The onus is on the Club to ensure it has submitted the appropriate forms for ALL persons who are subject to the test.

Two measures of the effectiveness of league regulation of ownership of clubs are:

1 How frequently prospective owners fail the Owners' and Directors' Test or its equivalent.
2 Whether prospective owners who fail can successfully appeal the league's decision.

English football has a poor track record with the former measure. Very few prospective owners have failed the test (see Case Study 24.1). One intriguing example is that of Ali Al Faraj, purchaser of Portsmouth FC in 2009.

His persistent failure to even visit the club prompted speculation as to whether he actually existed – see for example, Davies (12 January 2010), Anon. (2010) or Lipton (2010). His predecessor as owner, Sulaiman Al Fahim, had already provoked considerable criticism of the ineffectiveness of the Test – see, for example, White (2009) (see Case Study 24.2). Whatever the truth may be regarding Al Faraj's existence, the Premier League now requires prospective owners to present themselves in person.

CASE STUDY 24.1

The Banning of a Rotherham United Owner

Rotherham United is a long-established football club in northern England.

By 1987 the club had fallen into financial difficulty and was placed into administration, i.e. the process of seeking protection through the courts from creditors. It was rescued by a wealthy local businessman, Ken Booth, who proved to be a Type IA benefactor. By 2003 the club had been shored up with 'soft debts' in the form of loans from Mr Booth to the extent of approximately £3 million. As a result it was not financially self-sustainable, and annual losses had reached £730,000.

Ken Booth was by then in his 80s and looking to sell the club as his two sons had interests away from football. To extract his loans, his sons sought to acquire ownership of the stadium and its training ground, the club's main assets.

Ownership of the club proved difficult to pass on. Attempted buy-outs by first a former director, Neil Freeman, and then the club's sponsor, a local company, Earth Mortgages, fell through. Eventually it was acquired by a consortium of local businessmen. They made a modest investment into the club, and arranged a sale-and-lease-back arrangement with Ken Booth's sons.

Attempts to break even proved unsuccessful, and the club was bought by a second consortium of local businessmen, headed by Dennis Coleman. In order to achieve the take-over, the parlous state of affairs led very quickly to the club having to negotiate a court-backed Company Voluntary Agreement (CVA) with creditors, which included the tax authority, Her Majesty's Customs and Excise (HMRC).

Further investment was not forthcoming, and in March 2008 the club was again forced to seek court protection from its creditors by going into administration.

As a result, notwithstanding his continued commitment to trying to keep the club alive, Dennis Coleman became the first person to fail what is now the Owners' and Directors' Test because the club had fallen into a second proscribed insolvency event under his ownership.

Worse was to follow for the club. The Booth Brothers pressured the club financially to the extent that the next owner, Tony Stewart, also a local businessman, felt he had no alternative but to take the club into exile at Sheffield's Don Valley stadium. The club received a 17-point deduction because of the latest insolvency event.

In spite of these troubles the club returned to Rotherham, to a new stadium funded by a mix of private investment and public funding.

TOOLS FOR ANALYSIS

Use the typology of benefactors in Table 24.2 and the regulations stated above to analyse the case.

ACTION LEARNING

- Did the banning of Dennis Coleman serve the following stakeholders well? Give your reasons.

  (a) Rotherham United?
  (b) The other clubs in the Football League?
  (c) Dennis Coleman?

- Do you consider the current ownership of Rotherham United to be significantly more sustainable financially than under the previous ownerships?

- Using examples of owners of clubs with which you are familiar, assess whether they are/were Type I or II benefactors, and whether they are/were Type A, B, C or D. Consider whether they have changed their classification over time.

CASE STUDY 24.2

The Trials and Tribulations of Portsmouth FC and its Various Owners

Portsmouth was, like Rotherham United, rescued from administration, but by a non-local benefactor. Ownership of the club had been acquired by a local businessman, John Deacon, who in turn sold the club to a London-based businessman, Jim Gregory, in 1988. As was the case with so many football clubs, Portsmouth struggled to be sustainable financially, and in 1997 it was sold to Terry Venables, who had been initially brought in as a consultant by Gregory, for £1. Venables failed to turn the club around financially, and in December 1998 it was placed into administration.

Milan Mandarić, a Serbian-American businessman and previously the owner of football clubs in the USA, Belgium and France, bought the club from the administrator for a reported £5 million, and set about turning it around. He brought in the well-known manager Harry Redknapp. During his ownership of Portsmouth Mandarić invested roughly a further £20 million, and with Redknapp investing in experienced players the club returned to the Premier League, where they had last played in the 1950s.

In 2006 Mandarić sold 50% of his shares in Portsmouth to French-Israeli businessman Alexandre Gaydamak, and subsequently resigned as chairman, selling the other 50% to Gaydamak. Mandarić is reported to have made approximately £25 million for the sale of his shares, and thus he broadly neither made a profit out of owning the club, nor did he lose money by doing so.

Under Gaydamak's ownership expensive signings continued to be made and these resulted in some successes. For example, they brought about the club's foray into European football. However, the revenues never met the high costs of players. In May 2009 Gaydamak tired of subsidizing the club and sold it to Suleiman Al Fahim, a businessman from the United Arab Emirates, for a reported price of around £60 million.

Funding was not, it is reported, free flowing, and shortly after came reports of players not being paid. Top (and expensive) players such as Peter Crouch, Sylvain Distin, Glen Johnson and Niko Kranjčar were sold in a desperate attempt to bring some financial stability to the club. In September 2009 Al Fahim declared that he would bring serious new funding to the club, and the following month 90% of the club's shareholding was acquired by the enigmatic Ali Al Faraj and a company based in the British Virgin Islands, Falcondrone.

At the end of October, the club received a loan of £17 million from a company, Portpin, owned by Balram Chainrai, a Hong Kong-based Nepalese-born British passport-holding businessman, even though Chainrai had at that time never met Al Faraj. This loan did little to alleviate the serious cashflow problems, and by the turn of the year HMRC had issued a winding-up petition over non-payment of VAT, Gaydamak had announced that he was still owed £28 million by the club, and there were once again delays in paying the players.

Early in the new year Chainrai became a reluctant owner, buying Al Faraj's 90% shareholding, and Al Fahim left the club. Having failed to find a new owner, in February 2010 Chainrai placed the club once again into administration. This resulted in a nine-point deduction, but had no bearing on the club's relegation from the Premier League at the end of the season.

In June 2011 the club once again had a new owner – CSI Sports, a company owned by a London-based Russian businessman, Vladimir Antonov. However, in November Antonov was arrested for alleged forgery, which resulted in CSI being placed into administration.

In January 2012 HMRC again issued a winding-up petition, and for the second time in two years the club was placed into administration, incurring an automatic 10-point deduction from the Football League. In April the Administrator reported the club as having debts of £58 million, including £3.5 million owed to the playing staff and £2.3 million to HMRC.

In May Balram Chainrai, still owed £17 million by the club, offered to buy it through his company Portpin with a settlement of 2p in the pound to creditors, prompting a counterbid by the newly formed Supporters' Trust. Matters came to a head in October when the Administrator, Trevor Birch, announced that Pompey Supporters' Trust was his preferred bidder. It might have been expected that Chainrai would have failed the Directors' and Owners' Test for having placed the club into administration twice, but the situation was complicated by a grey area over his involvement, via Portpin, in the case of the second administration.

Chainrai held a debenture over the ownership of the club's stadium, Fratton Park, which he valued at £17 million, a figure at great variance with the independent valuation obtained by the Pompey Supporters' Trust of between £3 million and £3.5 million. The High Court ruled against the Chainrai valuation, and in April 2013 ownership of the club passed to the Pompey Supporters' Trust. By this time, the club had suffered three consecutive relegations, having fallen from the Premier League to English football's fourth tier, League 2.

TOOLS FOR ANALYSIS

Use the typology of benefactors in Table 24.2 and the regulations stated above to analyse the case.

ACTION LEARNING

- Did the Premier League and the Football League apply rigorous enough measures in assessing the suitability of the various owners?
- Should the test of ownership apply to both the club and its stadium?
- What challenges present themselves when a club is under foreign ownership?

THE EFFECTIVENESS OF REGULATING OWNERSHIP IN ALTERNATIVE GOVERNANCE REGIMES

The two cases above raise issues over the effectiveness of the regulation of ownership by governing bodies. As both cases refer to examples in English football, it is necessary to look more widely to see whether more effective regulation is possible.

Ultimately effectiveness will depend on the relative powers of the governing body and the would-be owner. The three mini-cases which follow provide contrasting examples:

1 *Governance in the Big 4 North American sports – the National Basketball Association (NBA) and Clippers*

In April 2014 an audio tape was circulated which, it was alleged, had Donald Sterling telling his girlfriend not to 'bring black people to my games' (Associated Press, 2014). Sterling, who had owned the Clippers since 1981 and was at the time the longest-serving owner in the NBA, had in November 2009 agreed to pay $2.73 million (£1.62 million) to settle allegations by the government that he refused to rent apartments to Hispanics and black people and to families with children.

As the comment on the audio tape referred specifically to NBA games, the NBA, which operates a rigorous licensing system, acted swiftly and banned Sterling for life (isportconnect, 2014) and put the franchise up for sale. Financial backers had already begun to withdraw their support for Sterling (BBC, 2014).

At the time of writing, in early May 2014, it was unclear whether Sterling would take legal action against the NBA in an attempt to overturn the ban.

2 *The Austrian Bundesliga*

The governing body of Austrian football and operator of the top two league levels, the Austrian Bundesliga, operates a strict licensing system for member football clubs. In the past it has been known to force two clubs to merge – LASK was forced to merge with a financially ailing long-term local rival VOEST (latterly known as FC Linz) to form Linz LASK in 1997.

More recently, the Bundesliga denied renewals for licence applications for no fewer than six out of a total of 24 of the clubs (Sport Business Global, 2013).

3 *The Football League, Leeds United and Massimo Cellino*

In early 2014 Massimo Cellino sought to buy financially troubled Leeds United. He had a long track record as an owner of the Italian football club Cagliari. On the downside, however, he had two prior criminal convictions, for cheating the Italian Ministry of Agriculture out of £7.5 million in 1996 and for false accounting at Cagliari in 2001 (Fahy, 2014). Additionally he was about to be found guilty of tax evasion and fined €600,000 (£500,000) for failing to pay €388,500 in tax on a yacht seized by Italian police and customs officials in June 2012.

Under existing regulations the earlier offences were considered spent, but the Football League initially banned him from taking over Leeds United. However Cellino appealed and the Football League appointed an independent QC to consider the appeal. The result was that the appeal was upheld and Cellino took over the club (Warshaw, 2014).

These three contrasting examples when considered together suggest some guiding principles for the regulation of ownership of clubs:

- Transparency of ownership is a precursor of accountability, but does not in itself guarantee appropriate accountability.
- Annual licensing systems offer much more rigorous control than tick-box initial tests.
- The structure of the relevant governing body determines whether it acts more in the collective interests of the member clubs or more in the interests of the individual club being considered.
- Regulation of ownership has to take place in the external legal environment of the relevant country. Each country may have stricter or laxer company law, and provide greater or lesser grounds for appealing decisions in court.

An alternative form of ownership: fan ownership

The emphasis in this chapter has been on 'benefactor ownership', whether this is a committed local businessman on the one hand, or an external financial investment body on the other. In either case the owner is solely responsible for the conduct of the club and unanswerable to fans of the club. In many cases the wishes of the owner, who has legal ownership, may be at odds with the fans' wishes, who have what has been termed 'psychological ownership' (see, for example, Sumida et al., 2012). The difference between these and those of the owner may be extreme enough to provoke a protest or even a boycott. Examples of the latter include the formation of FC United of Manchester by disgruntled fans of Manchester United, owned by the USA-based Glazer family, and on a much smaller scale, the formation of FC Blau-Weiss Linz, a resurrection club formed by disenchanted ex-fans of FC Linz.

In both of these cases the new clubs have been founded on the principle of fan-ownership.

In the UK two forms of mutual, or cooperative, have been used as the legal basis for the ownership and operation of a club. In England the generally preferred form is that of a Supporters' Trust (ST), while in Scotland the preferred form is a Community Interest Company (CIC). Both forms emphasize fan ownership, normally with a restriction on the number of shares an individual fan is allowed to own, and the notion of social enterprise. The main difference in practical terms lies in the voting rights of shareholders – with an ST each shareholder is entitled to one vote, whereas with a CIC each share carries a vote.

The advantages of this form of ownership are many. They include building strong relations with the community, and (re)establishing the bond and **loyalty** with fans embedded in their sense of identity defined by place, greater transparency and democratic accountability.

Ownership of large clubs is obviously a challenge for such 'crowd-funded' enterprises, and for such clubs a hybrid model has been adopted. In the case of the new owners of Portsmouth, for example, as well as some 2,000 fans having bought £1,000 shares in the club, a small number of High Net Worth Individuals (HNWIs) had been allowed to invest larger amounts. The HNWIs have a voice on the board of the company in addition to that of the regular fan shareholders, but a golden share precludes the HNWIs having the power to determine, for example, whether to sell the stadium.

In Germany, a significantly greater emphasis has been placed on the advantages of fan ownership. The German Bundesliga has what is colloquially known as 'the 50 + 1 rule', which requires share holding to be on the basis of at least 50% in the hands of members (fans) plus one further share to ensure those members always have a majority holding in any vote.

Fan ownership in German clubs is generally credited as resulting in:

- lower ticket prices;
- higher attendance figures;
- few foreign star players;
- stronger youth academies;
- a stronger national team.

(See, for example, Dietl and Franck, 2007; Conn, 2012.)

The model is not perfect however. As the 50 +1 rule is applied to the two top tiers of the German pyramid only, it is still possible for benefactors to fund the climbing of a club until it nears the summit of the pyramid, a classic claim being that of Hoffenheim and its backing by Dietmar Hopp, the former Chief Executive Officer of SAP, the well-known producer of finance software.

Another form of fan ownership is that employed in what is known as the Spanish model. Again the basis of ownership is through the formation of members' clubs. Democratic though this may seem, fans elect a president every four years who has considerable power, and can, if he chooses to do so, run the club autocratically throughout his period of office. The concomitant lack of transparency and immediate accountability are at least in part the cause of many Spanish clubs building up massive tax debts, which may well prove unsustainable in the future.

CONCLUSION

The particular form of ownership model used by a particular league has far-reaching consequences. If the regulation of ownership is too light-handed, unsuitable owners may gain control of clubs. In extremis, a 'benefactor' like John Batchelor may buy a club like York City with the covert plan to simply asset strip by selling the stadium to property developers (Carroll, 2008).

The key to operating a successful system of regulating club ownership is striking the right balance between a system that is too lax to exclude unsuitable owners and one which is so strict that it deters suitable persons from attempting to buy a club.

Of the various forms of ownership, the fan-owned model provides serious benefits for the sustainability of both the individual club and the league. It is, however, no 'magic wand', and is likely to need to be hybridized if large clubs are the target for purchase.

REFERENCES

Anon (2010). Never mind fit and proper, does Ali al Faraj even exist? *The News [Portsmouth]*. Portsmouth: Johnston Press PLC.

Associated Press (2014). LA Clippers owner allegedly says: 'Don't bring black people to my games'. *Guardian,* 26 April.

BBC (2014, 29 April). Backers withdraw LA Clippers support in racism row. Retrieved 1 May 2014 from www.bbc.co.uk/sport/0/basketball/27201275.

Beech, J. (2009). Finance in the Football Industry. In S. Hamill and S. Chadwick (eds), *Managing Football: an International Perspective*. Oxford: Elsevier.

Beech, J. (2013). Introduction: The commercialisation of sport. In J. Beech and S. Chadwick (eds), *The Business of Sport Management*. Harlow: Pearson Education.

Carroll, S. (2008). Former City owner's amazing admission. *The Press [York]*.

Commission of the European Communities (2007, 11 July). White Paper on Sport. Retrieved 1 February 2014 from http://new.eur-lex.europa.eu/legal-content/EN/TXT/?qid=1389190214279&uri=CELEX:52007DC0391.

Conn, D. (2012). German model bangs the drum for club, country and the people's game. *Guardian,* 2 December.

Davies, A. (12 January 2010). So does Ali Al-Faraj actually exist? Retrieved 30 April 2014 from www.bbc.co.uk/dna/606/A61740218.

Dietl, H.M. and Franck, E. (2007). Governance Failure and Financial Crisis in German Football. *Journal of Sports Economics,* 8(6): 662–669.

EU Council (2011). *The Communication on Developing the European Dimension in Sport.* Brussels: EU Commission.

European Commission (2011). *Developing the European Dimension of Sport.* Brussels: EU Commission.

Fahy, D. (2014). Who is Massimo Cellino? The controversial Italian vying to take over Leeds United. *The Independent,* 4 February.

FATF (2009). *Money Laundering Through the Football Sector,* report, July.

Football Italia Staff (28 January 2014). Qataris negotiate Cagliari takeover. Retrieved 1 February 2014 from www.football-italia.net/44431/qataris-negotiate-cagliari-takeover.

isportconnect (2014, 30 April). LA Clippers owner Donald Sterling banned for life, NBA pushes sale. Retrieved 1 May 2014 from www.isportconnect.com/index. php?option=com_content&view=article&id=26523:la-clippers-owner-donald-sterling-banned-for-life-nba-pushes-sale&catid=58:top-news&Itemid=167.

Sport Business Global (2013). Austrian football Bundesliga denies license to six clubs. Retrieved 14 April 2014 from www.sportsbusinessdaily.com. GlobalIssues/2013/05/02/Leagues-and-Governing-Bodies/Bundesliga-licenses.aspx.

Sumida, K., Wooliscroft, B. and Sam, M. (2012). Sports fans' psychological ownership: the team as a cultural institution, 20th EASM Conference, Aalborg, 18–21 September.

Warshaw, A. (2014). Cellino wins appeal and declared 'fit and proper' to takeover at Leeds. Retrieved 14 April 2014 from www.insideworldfootball.com/world-football/europe/14429-cellino-wins-appeal-and-declared-fit-and-proper-to-takeover-at-leeds.

White, J. (2009). Portsmouth circus shows 'fit and proper person' test is just a joke, *Daily Telegraph,* 9 October.

Zipf, G.K. (1965). *Human Behavior and the Principle of Least Human Effort.* New York: Hafner.

25

SOCIAL MEDIA CHALLENGES
SEBASTIAN KOPERA

Social media today are the key to gaining access to young people.

(Bach, 2013: 11)

It's hard to get away from knowing that—with Twitter and Facebook and the media and everything you obviously know what's at stake.

(Luke Donald, www.espn.co.uk/espn/sport/quote/index.html?search=s;quoteSrcBox=social+media, 23 April 2011)

In an age of ever-tightening athletic budgets and increasing diffusion of traditional media audiences, social media provides a comparatively inexpensive personal connection with fans, through services already offered by third parties, such as ... Facebook, Twitter, and others.

(Clavio, 2011: 310)

LEARNING OUTCOMES

Upon completion of this chapter, students will be able to:

- Understand the complexity of the social media concept from a sport management research perspective.

● Discuss the challenges and risks of managing social media in sport.

● Recognize and evaluate opportunities for the use of and research in social media in sport management.

INTRODUCTION

Social media can be defined as "a group of Internet-based applications that build on the ideological and technological foundations of Web 2.0, and that allow the creation and exchange of User Generated Content" (Kaplan and Haenlein, 2010). This "group" expands daily, and covers a wide span of different tools that often pervade each other, such as social networking sites, media-sharing sites, blogging and microblogging sites, wikis, social review sites, social bookmarking sites, forums and discussion groups, web auctions, interactive applications, webinars, virtual work spaces and instant messaging systems (Kopera, 2009; Woodcock et al., 2011; Baird and Parasnis, 2011a). Very important and distinctive features of social media (in relation to most other information and communication technologies (ICT)) are web communities, i.e. internet-based groups of individuals or organizations that cluster together to interact in different interest or problem areas (Plant, 2004). Social media enable and facilitate the emergence and functioning of web communities through their various tools for communication, collaboration, resource sharing, etc.

In a situation where 72% of adult internet users are active on social networking sites (Brenner and Smith, 2013), it is quite natural that sport organizations and athletes open up to the Web 2.0 ideology and solutions. Although social media belong to one group of solutions they are diversified as far as their characteristics, functionality and popularity are concerned. Those differences result in different business goals and functions that can be supported by each solution.

According to the intersectoral survey conducted by IBM Institute for Business Value in 2011, the most popular applications of social media in business refer to customer engagement through communication, responding to customer questions, promoting events, generating sales leads, selling products and services, etc. (Baird and Parasnis, 2011a). Companies also use social media in their innovation processes: 48% use it to solicit customer reviews, 46% capture customer data and brand monitoring, 43% do customer research and 40% solicit customer ideas (Baird and Parasnis, 2011a). Although the "engagement orientation" prevails in this second group applications are growing dynamically. There are also some other applications (e.g. recruitment or employee interactions) but these are less popular than those previously mentioned.

The IBM survey had displayed some of the general trends in business applications for social media, and these were quite typical for most of the sectors. It refers also to the sport sector in which social media are used for promotion (Pedersen, 2012; Newman et al., 2013), building relationships with external stakeholders (O'Shea and Alonso, 2011; Eagleman, 2013), brand building (Ioakimidis, 2010), interacting with fans (Kassing and

Sanderson, 2012), etc. But certainly, when it comes to details the sectoral specificity of social media applications can be discovered.

Social media utilization in sport business is a dynamically emerging field within research and practice. There are many challenges involved here and some of the most important will be addressed in this chapter. The first section is devoted to the issue of social media competencies of athletes and sport professionals, which are key to success in the current social media environment. They are also a necessary stepping stone for future developments in this field, including social media intelligence.

There is a growing number of sport organizations undertaking different social media activities, but these cannot be considered to be separate from the wider social media ecosystem: channels are used by their sport teams, sponsored athletes, sport journalists and fans. The second section discusses the opportunities involved in this "extended perspective" for different marketing initiatives, particularly those related to branding and image building.

Contemporary fans spend a significant part of their lives being "online" in some way. New media are becoming an inherent part of their lives, and being "connected" is a fundamental requirement. Responding to this societal and technological changes rising number of sport organizations, including top sport clubs and arenas and even the International Olympics Committee (IOC), are working on a "digitally-enriched fan experience". This is discussed in the third section below, together with related technological and organizational challenges.

The final section will cover other issues of growing importance for the sport sector, including social media intelligence and innovation processes, and new business models based on the Web 2.0 environment. All of these have still to be addressed in a more in-depth manner by sport organizations and athletes who wish to profit from their social media presence, as well as by scientists who conduct research within this dynamic field.

THINKING POINT 25.1

Social Media Competencies

A friendly match between the national teams of Poland and the Slovak Republic was observed by Mateusz Klich, the Polish midfielder. His team were performing poorly. He was disappointed, but not so much with the play of his team mates as with the behavior of the fans, who—in his opinion—were giving no support to the losing team. After the match he strongly criticized these Polish fans on his Twitter account. This resulted in a (mostly) negative response from the sport community: fans, sports journalists and media, as well as other athletes. Worth noticing is the fact that his light-hearted comments brought criticism not only to him alone, but also to other footballers from the national squad as well as their new coach. On this occasion—once again—the famous words of Herm Edwards directed to NFL rookies, "Don't press send," confirmed their validity.

(Source: Jachimiak, 2013)

ACTION LEARNING

- What kind of competencies did this Polish footballer lack?
- What would you do as the coach or team manager in a similar situation?

- Discuss some preventive measures that could be applied to overcome such situations in the future.

TOOLS FOR ANALYSIS

A very important and characteristic feature of social media is that in most cases these can be utilized with only scant investment. This makes them available and affordable to almost every sport organization or athlete and is particularly important for low-budget sport organizations (including national governing bodies, voluntary sports organizations, etc.) which can benefit from their utilization of social media (Eagleman, 2013). But this availability involves a drawback: the low costs of IT solutions provoke an unprofessional implementation and utilization of social media, and don't enforce high standards in their management, as has been observed on various occasions (Stoldt, 2012; Eagleman, 2013). As presented in the first case its results can be positive or negative.

Although the dynamics of social media cannot be fully steered or **controlled** by the athletes who engage in interactions with fans and other stakeholders their digital literacy can make a significant difference here (Kassing and Sanderson, 2012). The virtual competency of individuals—strengthened by their experience—is crucial for the effectiveness of **communication** performed in digital settings (Wang and Haggerty, 2009). Knowledge of how to use particular social channels and be effective in virtual communication with fans and other stakeholders is an important stepping stone for engaging in social media space. But it is not enough for building strategic advantages in the complex environment of sport business, such as long-lasting relationships with fans, **loyalty** or a positive brand image. For this reason sport organizations should provide this training "focused on how they can strategically use new media resources" (Kassing and Sanderson, 2012: 13). The training should involve all athletes and other sport professionals utilizing social media for maintaining any relationship with the external world.

It is worth noticing that the "new media resources" are not limited to functionalities facilitating conversation but also cover the acquisition of information and knowledge encompassed in user generated content. At present, the acquisition of valuable information and ready-to-use knowledge from SM is still seen as a time, energy and resource consuming activity (Akehurst, 2009). For this reason the issue of "social media intelligence" appears only in a small number of sport organizations, and with a limited scope. Nevertheless it is the emerging idea that will play a significant role in the future, because in the age of innovation social media Big Data are (and will continue to be) a rich source of knowledge and information that can be utilized by sport organizations to fuel their innovation processes.

In the context of social competencies fan perspective should also be considered by sport managers, as this environment is all about participation and interaction mostly with this particular group. However, before a sport organization begins to generate content and gets into interactions with fans it should first consider the level of social media adoption in the target group. Sometimes this requires some previous training in the utilization of particular tools (Clavio, 2011). Otherwise all the effort to set up and maintain a conversation will fail.

ACTION LEARNING

- What are the limits to athletes' "privacy" in the social media space?

- How can sport organizations educate fans on new forms of social media interactions and behaviors?

THINKING POINT 25.2

The Social Media Ecosystem

Montrail is a Richmond, California-based manufacturer of running and recovery footwear. It is a wholly owned subsidiary of the Columbia Sportswear Company known to amateur and professional runners worldwide. As a company functioning in a niche sport market (it is particularly well known among trail runners) it cannot count on an extensive mainstream media presence. As with other niche sport organizations social media appear to be a very important platform for its marketing activities with a worldwide reach.

Montrail builds a fan community and promotes its activities through various social media channels, including a company blog, a Facebook fanpage and Twitter. Additionally fans are kept up to date through a Rich

Site Summary (RSS) channel. All of these solutions are integrated on the company webpage. What is more, Montrail sponsors a group of runners who feature as the "Montrail team." Most of the athletes presented on the company web-site have their social media presence on Facebook and a blogging platform. Some of them also use Twitter and Vimeo. Links to those channels can be also accessed from the Montrail site. All of those channels are elements of a social media ecosystem for a brand that can be used in praise of that company's brand and image. However, to activate this ecosystem it is necessary to engage the sponsored athletes in the creation of brand-supporting content in line with the company's marketing strategy. And this requires a significant effort by the Montrail marketing department to provide adequate assistance to the sponsored individuals.

(Source: www.montrail.com)

- How can the company support cooperating athletes to help them contribute to its marketing efforts?

- What is the risk of the fact that cooperating athletes are active in their own social media infospace?

Kietzmann et al. (2012) have identified seven basic functionalities of social media: identity, presence, relationships, reputation, groups, conversation and sharing. Although the authors concentrated on the individual user perspective, presented functionalities can be also used for structuring an understanding of the Web 2.0 phenomenon in an organizational context. Sport organizations and athletes use social media to mark and confirm their presence in the minds of their fans and other stakeholders (*presence*); to build their image and brand name awareness (*identity*); to strengthen and sometimes defend a reputation that is threatened in the offline world (*reputation*); to build or join virtual communities of fans, supporters and partners (*groups*) with which they can engage in dialogue (*conversation*) and exchange content (*sharing*); and what this results in is a strengthening of the bonds with—the mostly external—environment (*relationships*).

Although the ways by which different types of social media contribute to a brand image and reputation may vary, their role in this process is nowadays evident and unquestioned (Greenberg, 2010). They are the most influential tools for companies, which in an age of convergence are being included in transmedia storytelling (Jenkins, 2006) and eagerly employed also by sponsors in their marketing campaigns. However, the specificity of social media that are dominated by user generated content results in decreasing **control** over marketing communication in comparison to other new media belonging to the first internet wave (e.g. traditional websites). Most of the popular clubs or athletes, next to their official social media profiles, websites, blogs, forum, etc. have those created by their fans. In most cases the result of this "presumption" is positive, i.e. enlarged brand awareness and engagement among fans. But this can easily prove problematic when any kind of conflict or disagreement appears between fans and the sport organization or professional. An example of this "dysfunctional" fan activity can be the hashtag #LeBroning, created to make fun of a top basketball player who is famous for his foul simulation. Amusing content usually has very big viral potential, as can be observed in the case of the social media buzz around LeBron James. It is worth noticing also that extreme satisfaction and dissatisfaction are part of the significant factors influencing the voluntary sharing of digital content (De Bruyn and Lilien, 2008).

Thinking Point 25.2 presented the basic elements of a social media ecosystem for a sport sector company, that included next to the organizational channels ones run by the sponsored athletes. Organizations should strive toward their synchronization according to company's marketing strategy. But this "synchronicity" is something valuable from the sponsored athletes' point of view as well. From their perspective the sponsor's social media significantly enlarge the reach of their own brands. When we consider that a single athlete or team may have many more sponsors, the related social media ecosystem appears to be in full swing. Or almost full swing, because there is still one very significant element missing here: sport journalists.

Sport journalists "have always been important cultural intermediaries between sports and society" (Boyle, 2012: 92). Boyle called them "the myth makers" to underline their role in the creation of an athlete's image. Although they have always played this role, it has been changing with the popularization of social media. Sheffer and Schultz, investigating the utilization of Twitter among journalists, found that they use it mostly for presenting their own opinions and commentaries (Sheffer and Schultz, 2010). This is hardly a surprise—social media create additional content that is accessible, free and uncontrolled by mainstream media channels for communication. They are not restricted by the time limitations inherent in traditional broadcasting. They are also more personal as the sender—whoever that person is—can present their own sometimes contraversial opinions. Thus social media narration run by sport journalists is growing in importance, challenging traditional media. While in the case of the most popular sports the latter still dominate, in the case of niche or non-professional sports the social media domain has already outpaced mainstream coverage. For this reason it is necessary to include social media journalism as the ecosystem element that is vital for the realization of a marketing strategy.

Independence in the social media domain that is greater than that found in traditional media with greater control over the broadcasted content, constitutes a great opportunity not only for journalists but also for sport professionals. It is particularly evident in crisis situations, when clubs or athletes have to withstand a stream of negative publicity from traditional media space. Brand protection online together with the utilization of social media currently are among the most important challenges facing the PR industry (Boyle, 2012: 94). Sport professionals, more and more often supported by PR specialists, can maintain a parallel storytelling, thus strengthening the mainstream media coverage or withstanding it in times of crisis. The latter application of social media has been highlighted by Hambrick et al. (2013), who analyzed the image repair strategies applied by Lance Armstrong in the most contentious period of his **doping** scandal across traditional and social media (another interesting example of a top athlete coping with his image threats via Twitter is provided in Sanderson, 2010).

The analysis of the case of Lance Armstrong's use of Twitter provides some insights into the potential threats from social media utilization by athletes to sponsors (Hambrick et al., 2013). Cooperation with low performing or controversial athletes may result in challenging their image and reputation (Hambrick et al. 2013). The threats to sponsors are related also to unpredictability in the online behavior of athletes, who may feel the social media domain to be "private" and might result in their feeling released from their obligations toward sponsors. They also may not feel obliged to follow the official PR policy of their organizations, which can lead to significant problems in relations with their organizations as well as with their environment (Hambrick et al., 2010). Some organizations will try to go as far as banning athletes from using social media in order to protect their image and sponsors' rights, and so violating such regulation may result in high fines (Anon., 2010). However, it seems that educating athletes on their strategic use of social media, which was discussed in the first section, is a more rational alternative.

ACTION LEARNING

- Provide some ideas on how to set up and maintain relationships with sport journalists active in the social media domain.
- Discuss specific issues involved in the creation of a social media ecosystem for a sport event. How do these differ in the case of company or team brand ecosystems?

- Many athletes have started employing PR professionals to run their conversations in social media. What are the pros and cons of this practice?
- Discuss strategies or activities which could be undertaken by sponsors to minimize the risk related to social media activity by sponsored athletes.

THINKING POINT 25.3

Enriched Sport Experience

In 2013 Manchester City joined the growing group of stadiums which are "connected." This emerging idea has meant the provision of all the necessary digital infrastructure to enable fans to experience unbounded inter-actions in the social media domain during any stadium event together with support for many facility operations.

Central to the solution implemented in cooperation with Cisco and O2 is high speed internet access via a high density Wi-Fi network. This is also a platform for other solutions, like StadiumVision Mobile,

which provides fans with instant delivery of live video and information content, as well as access to many channels with replays and alternate views, and a dynamic data channel with stats, real-time contests and MPGs straight to their mobile devices. The new infrastructure also solves the problem of a mobile network overload on match days.

The cooperation of the Etihad Stadium with its technology partners resulted in many innovations providing an enriched and immensely "connected" experience for fans, extended marketing and PR opportunities for the club, and improved match-day management for the stadium.

(Source: Cisco 2013)

TOOLS FOR ANALYSIS

Social media issues in sports encompass not only the activities performed by clubs and athletes on the web, they more and more involve the integration of offline and online realities to interact with fans in real time, particularly during big events. The trend of "socializing" sporting events has already become traditional and so have its infrastructural problems. During the Olympic Games in London 2012 organizers had encouraged fans to engage in social media conversations during different contests. This activity together with organizers' efforts to provide Web 2.0 platforms for the participants—The Olympic Athletes' Hub (http://hub.olympic.org)—earned it the name "socialympics." Fans responded enthusiastically by going to their social profiles, posting messages and uploading live shots from the event. However, in some cases (i.e cycling events) this resulted in the obstruction of the telecommunication infrastructure to a level at which even licensed broadcasting media had problems with providing seamless coverage, which in turn brought many protests to the organizers' door (Jones, 2012).

More and more clubs and organizers of sport events are striving to engage fans in social media interactions. The leaders of this process can be found among the most popular team sports clubs and stadiums. This trend leads to developments in the "social media stadium" (Walsh, 2013), which aim to engaging fans in social media interactions on match days. The idea of a "social media stadium" should be considered in relation to the concept of a "connected stadium" with regard to the development of the network infrastructure necessary to connect the internet in order to use social media and other online services. As in the previously mentioned case of the London 2012 cycling events, lacking this or having an inefficient infrastructure can result in the failure of any great idea. It is worth noting that this infrastructure is also a key platform enabling the application of new services supporting facility and security management.

Technical infrastructure is necessary to create a "social stadium" but it is not enough to make social networks "crowded" on a match day. It implies the need for innovative ideas on how to engage fans and provide sufficient multimedia content to feed social media channels. Fan engagement is becoming more difficult to induce due to the rise in fan expectations against the benefits they can access for online interactions with brands (Ioakimidis, 2010). However, this is the necessary element of any business application of social media and it should be addressed by the social media strategy of the organization or sport professional.

There are already some good examples of how match-day social media activity can be fueled and maintained. One of these is the "Indian Social Suite" (ISS)—an idea developed by the Cleveland Indians baseball team (Olenski, 2012). The club has created a special Wi-Fi enabled suite in its stadium, which is a place where social media-loving fans can engage in and moderate online conversations with other fans. To be invited to the ISS it is necessary to undergo an application process. All chosen fans receive free tickets to a match. Social media conversations and interactions with fans are more authentic and—what also matters—less expensive than those facilitated by professional PR specialists. Another good example comes from the New Jersey Devils, who in 2011 introduced their "Mission Control" initiative— a **control** center for managing, monitoring and measuring fan engagement (Burns Ortiz, 2011). The Mission Control team's activity covers all the social media channels utilized by the team and its stadium—the Prudential Center.

Although social media are quite inexpensive (at least in a basic form), their application always involves some kind of investment: in employee training, additional staff dedicated to run social media conversations, related organizational change or even an athlete's time. This is even more evident in the case of the aforementioned network infrastructure for sport arenas. This initial and/or continuous social media investment—as with any other business investment—should bring visible business results that are consistent with the general business **strategy**.

There are many new business opportunities involved in the development of social media. For example, investments in the "connected stadium" open up new opportunities in the form of sponsorship and advertising via social channels, and customized and targeted promotions with a precise timing, as well as paid exclusive fan services (Cisco, 2011). The results can and should be measured and translated into business benefits. The monetization of social media investments evokes the attention of sport experts, and it is expected that since 2014 a greater focus will be attributed not only to monitoring social media traffic, but also to identifying the social media return on investments (Walsh, 2014).

ACTION LEARNING

- Enabling participants to be connected during big sport or entertainment events creates the potential to increase their engagement—this is key to business success in and through the social media environment. But giving the opportunity itself will not result in growth of engagement. Provide innovative ideas on how to engage fans both inside and outside the stadium on a match day in social media interactions.
- Discuss the pros and cons of encouraging fans to go online during sport events, adapting the perspectives of the sport club, its sponsors and fans.
- Name some most important business results to be achieved through the application of social media. How would you measure those results?

CONCLUSION

Social media give enormous power to fans, and those who cannot or do not want to be responded to that way. Using social channels it is possible to keep controversial issues alive for a long time, unlike in the passing age of traditional media, when "breaking news" pushed out older hot topics. There are many examples of the persistent actions of virtual communities that gave sport professionals sleepless nights. One notable example here is the case of the NFL team, the Washington Redskins, who were consequently pushed by the online community to change the team's name because many of their opponents regarded it as offensive and racist (Gianatasio, 2013). Another example is virtual fan communities' outcry against the new design of the Cy-Hawk trophy that swept over social media in 2011 and led to the abandonment of the initial idea (ESPN, 2011). All sport organizations and professionals will have to make themselves ready for social media lobbying and develop suitable strategies.

However, the power of fan communities may also play a significant supportive role by contributing to the development of new business models and supporting sport entrepreneurship. A good example of this is social media crowdfunding. Crowdfunding itself can be perceived as a kind of crowd-sourcing, with the broader idea based on the assumption that a community has something valuable for an organization that is worth their while to acquire. To those who can benefit from it—next to the start-ups and small enterprises – belong all kind of voluntary organizations and events. Although the idea of raising funds from a community is not new, social media have given it additional leverage, and if applied properly, can amplify crowdsourcing initiatives by sport organizations and professionals.

Crowdsourcing can also cover ideas, information and knowledge. But even without organized and—to some extent—formalized sourcing initiatives, social media represent a vast collection of valuable information and knowledge and information on and from customers, partners, competitors, etc. The "marketization" of social media activities however can cloud their potential as a learning and education space—for the sport business as well as for fans. The first group may develop social media intelligence supporting innovation and competitiveness building processes. The second one can benefit from acquiring valuable knowledge from the followed channels. In this context benefits can be also attributed to institutional creators of content, including national sport governing bodies. They can utilize those tools in accomplishing their missions, promoting sports and healthy lifestyles among youngsters, and educating society with regard to common sport pathologies, like doping.

Finally, it is necessary to keep in mind here that social media are still only a tool for the creation of business value. This "tool" induces sometimes significant costs with regard to infrastructure, staff and services. As with any other ICT-based solutions it should earn for itself by producing valuable results for business. To achieve satisfactory return on investment two aspects should be addressed. The first is rationalization of the social media sphere in business to avoid unnecessary costs. The second refers to the creation of measurable business results that will translate into increased income streams. At the end of the day it will not matter how many followers an organization has or how entertaining it is for its fans, but how much it can earn thanks to its social media engagement in the form of higher sponsors' contracts, increased events attendance, or direct sales. Finding an innovative way to reforge social media success into measurable business results, including the various aspects of organizations' functioning, is going to be a top priority challenge for sport managers and athletes in the years to come.

REFERENCES

Akehurst, G. 2009. User generated content: the use of blogs for tourism organizations and tourism consumers. *Service Business*, 3(1): 1–12.

Anon., 2010. Chad Ochocinco fined $25K. ESPN.com. Available at: http://sports. espn.go.com/nfl/trainingcamp10/news/story?id=5493157 (last accessed 10 November 2013).

Bach, T. 2013. Unity in diversity, 43(3). Available at: www.olympic.org/Documents/ IOC_President/Manifesto_Thomas_Bach-eng.pdf (last accessed 28 September 2015).

Baird, C.H. & Parasnis, G. 2011a. *From Social Media to Social CRM: Reinventing the Customer Relationship, Part 2*, IBM Institute for Business Value.

Baird, C.H. & Parasnis, G. 2011b. *From Social Media to Social CRM: What Customers Want, Part 1*, IBM Institute for Business Value.

Boyle, R. 2012. Reflections on communication and sport: on journalism and digital culture. *Communication and Sport*, 1(1–2): 88–99.

Brenner, J. & Smith, A. 2013. 72% of Online adults are social networking site users: groups continue to increase their engagement. Available at: http://pewinternet.org/ Reports/2013/social-networking-sites.aspx (last accessed 28 September 2015).

Burns Ortiz, M. 2011. Devils fans power "Mission Control", 2 May. Available at: http://sports.espn.go.com/espn/page2/story?page=burnsortiz/110502_nhl_ social_media (last accessed 28 September 2015).

Cisco, 2011. The new fan experience is here. Available at: www.cisco.com/web/strategy/ docs/sports/fan_experience_brochure.pdf (last accessed 28 September 2015).

Cisco. 2013. Manchester City to become first Premier League team to offer high density stadium WiFi and the latest fan mobile video solution. Press Release. Available at: http://newsroom.cisco.com/release/1181486/Manchester-City-to-Become-First-Premier-League-Team-to-Offer-High-Density-Stadium-WiFi-and-the-Latest-Fan-Mobile-Video-Solution (last accessed 28 September 2015).

Clavio, G. 2011. Social media and the college football audience. *Journal of Issues in Intercollegiate Athletics*, 4: 309–325.

De Bruyn, A. & Lilien, G.L. 2008. A multi-stage model of word-of-mouth influence through viral marketing. *International Journal of Research in Marketing*, 25(3): 151–163. Available at: http://linkinghub.elsevier.com/retrieve/pii/ S0167811608000414 (last accessed 10 January 2014).

Eagleman, A.N. 2013. Acceptance, motivations, and usage of social media as a marketing communications tool amongst employees of sport national governing bodies, *Sport Management Review,* 16: 1893–2083.

ESPN. 2011. Controversial Cy-Hawk trophy dumped, 24 August. Available at: http:// espn.go.com/college-football/story/_/id/6889208/controversial-cy-hawk-trophy-replaced (last accessed 28 September 2015).

Gianatasio, D. 2013. Will social media force the NFL's third-most valuable franchise to change its name? An issue that won't die, Adweek, September. Available at: www.adweek.com/news/advertising-branding/will-social-media-force-nfl-s-third-most-valuable-franchise-change-its-name-152765 (last accessed 28 September 2015).

Greenberg, P. 2010. *CRM at the Speed of Light: For Engaging Your Customers* (4th edn). New York: McGraw-Hill.

Hambrick, M.E., Frederick, E.L. & Sanderson, J. 2013. From yellow to blue: exploring Lance Armstrong's image repair strategies across traditional and social media. *Communication and Sport*. Available at: http://com.sagepub.com/lookup/doi/10.1177/2167479513506982 (last accessed 9 December 2013).

Hambrick, M.E., Simmons, J.M., Greenhalgh, G.P. and Greenwell, T.C. 2010. Understanding professional athletes' use of Twitter: a content analysis of athlete tweets. *International Journal of Sport Communication*, 3: 454–471.

Ioakimidis, M. 2010. Online marketing of professional sports clubs: engaging fans on a new playing field. *International Journal of Sports Marketing and Sponsorship*, 11(4): 271–283.

Jachimiak, Ł. 2013. Reprezentacja. Klich: Na trybunach masakra. Kosecki: Żenada, Klich ma rację. *Sport.pl*, 1 November. Available at: www.sport.pl/pilka/1,65037, 14963337,Reprezentacja__Klich__Na_trybunach_masakra__Kosecki_.html (last accessed 28 September 2015).

Jenkins, H. 2006. *Convergence Culture Where Old and New Media Collide.* New York and London: New York University Press.

Jones, C. 2012. Olympics 2012: Twitter users blamed for disrupting BBC's cycling coverage. *Guardian*, 29 July. Available at: www.theguardian.com/media/2012/jul/29/olympics-2012–twitter-bbc-cycling (last accessed 28 September 2015).

Kaplan, A.M. & Haenlein, M. 2010. Users of the world, unite! The challenges and opportunities of social media. *Business Horizons*, 53(1): 59–68.

Kassing, J.W. & Sanderson, J. 2012. Playing in the new media game or riding the virtual bench: confirming and disconfirming membership in the community of sport. *Journal of Sport and Social Issues*: 1–16. Available at: http://jss.sagepub.com/cgi/doi/10.1177/0193723512458931 (last accessed 9 December 2013).

Kietzmann, J.H., Silvestre, B.S., McCarthy, I.P. and Pitt, L.F. 2012. Unpacking the social media phenomenon: towards a research agenda. *Journal of Public Affairs*, 12(2): 109–119.

Kopera, S. 2009. Social software in information environment of tourist enterprise. In B.F. Kubiak & A. Korowicki, eds, *Information Management*. Gdańsk: Gdańsk University Press.

Newman, T. et al. 2013. *Social Media in Sport Marketing*. Scottsdale, AZ: Holcomb Hathaway.

Olenski, S. 2012. Cleveland Indians offer social media suite. Available at: http://espn.go.com/blog/playbook/trending/post/_/id/403/cleveland-indians-offer-social-media-suite (last accessed 28 September 2015).

O'Shea, M. & Alonso, A.D. 2011. Opportunity or obstacle? A preliminary study of professional sport organisations in the age of social media. *International Journal of Sport Management and Marketing*, 10(3/4): 196–212.

Pedersen, P.M. 2012. Reflections on communication and sport: on strategic communication and management. *Communication and Sport*, 1(1–2): 55–67. Available at: http://com.sagepub.com/lookup/doi/10.1177/2167479512466655 (last accessed 9 December 2013).

Plant, R. 2004. Online communities. *Technology in Society*, 26: 51–65.

Sanderson, J. 2010. Framing Tiger's troubles: comparing traditional and social media Tiger Woods' s precipitous fall from grace. *International Journal of Sport Communication*, 3: 438–453.

Sheffer, M. & Schultz, B. 2010. *Paradigm Shift or Passing Fad? Twitter and Sports Journalism* (2008), pp. 472–484.

Stoldt, G.C. 2012. The impact of social media on college athletics communications. College Sports Information Directors of America website. Available at: http://cosida.com/media/documents/2012/7/Social_media_impact_2012_Stoldt_study.pdf (last accessed 14 January 2014).

Walsh, S. 2013. Manchester City take a step closer to the "Social Media Stadium". Available at: http://digital-football.com/featured/manchester-city-take-a-step-closer-to-the-social-media-stadium/#comment-457641 (last accessed 28 September 2015).

Walsh, S. 2014. Sports social media has to focus on monetization in 2014. Available at: http://digital-football.com/featured/sports-social-media-has-to-focus-on-monetization-in-2014/ (last accessed 14 January 2014).

Wang, Y. & Haggerty, N. 2009. Knowledge transfer in virtual settings: the role of individual virtual competency. *Information Systems Journal*, 19(6): 571–593.

Wilson, B. 2012. Barcelona uses new media to sell its brand to fans. *BBC News*, 21 May. Available at: www.bbc.co.uk/news/business-18065300 (last accessed 28 September 2015).

Woodcock, N., Green, A. & Starkey, M. 2011. Social CRM as a business strategy. *Journal of Database Marketing and Customer Strategy Management*, 18(1): 50–64. Available at: www.palgrave-journals.com/doifinder/10.1057/dbm.2011.7 (last accessed 31 January 2013).

USEFUL WEBSITES

http://digital-football.com
http://socialmediatoday.com
www.socialbakers.com
www.adweek.com
http://hub.olympic.org
www.sociagility.com
www.sportsnetworker.com
www.sporttechie.com

26

MANAGING SOCIAL MEDIA IN SPORT

OLAN SCOTT, KATHERINE BRUFFY AND MICHAEL NAYLOR

'By definition, a "twitter" is a series of short, high-pitched calls or sounds. In the past five years, those brief bursts of noise have steadily increased in volume to significantly alter what was already a loud sporting landscape.

(Kirs Shannon, *NZ Herald*, 21 May 2013)

The IOC actively encourages and supports athletes and other accredited persons at the Olympic Games to take part in social media and to post, blog and tweet their experiences.

(Sochi 2014, *IOC Social Media Guidelines*)

Disseminating information digitally and promoting itself via social media are a centre piece of a five-year plan NASCAR has implemented in hopes of attracting a younger demographic to the sport.

(Nate Ryan, *USA Today*, 17 November 2012)'

Upon completion of this chapter, students should be able to:

- Recognize and explain the importance of social media in sport organizations.

- Demonstrate an understanding of the various approaches used for developing and implementing social media marketing strategies.

- Appreciate the importance of branding, marketing and building relationships through social media.

INTRODUCTION

In 2013, sport comprised just 1% of television content, yet nearly half of all Tweets produced during that period were sport related (Nielsen Holdings, 2014). Other social media are used extensively in conjunction with sport consumption as well. It is more important than ever for sport organizations and athletes to prioritize these platforms in an overall marketing strategy. SNSs have profoundly impacted how fans access information and interact with their favorite teams. Social media have enabled organizations across the sport industry to have an unfiltered voice in the marketplace. The majority of content is no longer vetted by journalists, editors or producers. Sport organizations have responded to this change by incorporating social networking sites (SNS) into their communications, promotion and sponsorship strategy. As this relatively new communication platform evolves, it is necessary for those involved in the management and marketing of sport to understand some of the key issues that have arisen from the utilization of social media. In this chapter readers will be introduced to the various ways in which sport organizations use social media to build a brand, develop relationships with stakeholders, and market products and services.

The advent and proliferation of social media have altered the media landscape like never before. SNSs allow individuals to "(a) construct a public or semi-public profile within a bounded system, (b) articulate a list of other users with whom they share a connection, and (c) view and traverse their list of connections and those made by others within the system" (Boyd and Ellison, 2007: 211). Social media users are simultaneously consumers and producers of media content (Mahan and McDaniel, 2006; Booth, 2010). Until the creation of SNSs, communication between sport organizations and fans was typically one-way—organization to fan. The gate-keeping role of the media made it very difficult for sport consumers to gain an immediate connection with the producers of sport (Arsenault and Castells, 2008; Scott et al., 2012). SNSs enable sport organizations, athletes and consumers to bypass the gate-keeping role of the media and "disseminate an unfiltered message" (Scott et al., 2012). The potential for sport organizations and athletes to connect with their fans through SNSs is a point of difference from traditional marketing methods because sport fans not only read content, they also share it with their online network, and/or generate further messages (Bradley, 2010, cited in Williams and Chinn, 2010).

Research has shown that sport fans are particularly avid users of technology (Kelly, 2013). In fact, fans now express themselves and access information across multiple technology devices at the same time. For example, they may follow their team on television while using their computer, tablet, or smartphone to view real-time statistics of the game or communicate with other fans watching the same contest. This is termed "second-screen consumption" and can often also include the use of SNSs such as Twitter, Facebook and Instagram. The popularity of second-screen viewing, and simultaneous engagement through social media, justifies the incorporation of SNSs into a broader marketing strategy. Many sport fans no longer wait for the media to interpret what has happened after a game. Social media allow sport fans to create their own narrative during the game, and then share it with others.

Adapting SNSs into the overall marketing strategy of an organization or athlete is no easy task. Allocating sufficient resources to support a social media strategy is one challenge, whilst equipping employees with the skills to be confident and comfortable implementing that strategy is another. When organizations get past these and other barriers, social media can enhance brand equity by creating additional opportunities to connect with the sport consumer. In order to illustrate the contemporary importance of social media in sport organizations, a real-world example is needed.

The New Zealand Breakers are based in Auckland and are one of eight teams in the (Australasian) National Basketball League (NBL). The NBL was founded in 1979 and is the preeminent basketball league in Australia and New Zealand. The Breakers entered the league in 2003 and later won the league championship three seasons in a row (2011–2013). The authors have consulted with the Breakers on social media strategy in an on-going and multi-stage framework of inquiry and action. Discussions in the remainder of the chapter are accompanied by practical examples that are reflective of the Breakers' social media strategy. The chapter is organized into three sections: (1) creating an online brand profile; (2) relationship building; and (3) leveraging engagement for benefit.

THINKING POINT 26.1

Creating an Online Brand Profile

Social media enable **brands** to post messages without influence from a third party, such as journalists, editors and producers of media content. As a result, sport organizations can now produce their own content and publish online. The following post shows how the New Zealand Breakers are using Facebook to brand the organization, create a unique online profile and exploit the benefits of social media platforms to brand the organization. In the example below the Breakers posted a video message featuring two of its players discussing their taller (known as the "bigs") teammates. This message enabled the organization to display players' personalities via a video posted to the team's Facebook page.

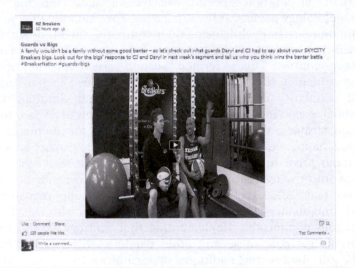

◀

ACTION LEARNING

- Using the example above, how does your favorite (sport) organization use its social media posts to give it a brand personality?

TOOLS FOR ANALYSIS

The New Zealand Breakers have created and cultivated a brand image on social media. The team is able to show off its players' personalities, promote its marketing efforts and engage fans on social media platforms. Aaker (2004: 91) suggested that organizations should "participat[e] in the emerging market niches that represent future growth." With the rise of social media, sport organizations have had an opportunity to create an online brand profile. Keller (2003) suggested that companies need to investigate consumer preferences, satisfaction and purchase behavior. As a result, sport teams should identify which product and service features are meaningful to its fans (or clients). Effective presentation of salient components of sport brands such as colors and logos can lead to competitive advantage and should be highlighted in any social media strategy (Keller, 2003).

Evans (2010) suggested that for effective online brand management, an organization needs to utilize social media effectively. Through various social media platforms, such as Facebook, Twitter, blogs, Instagram and many others, sport organizations can communicate in new and innovative ways with consumers and enable companies to "gain maximum leverage in strengthening and building long-term relationships" (Williams and Chinn, 2010: 435). Prior to the popularization of social media, it was very difficult for individuals to communicate with their favorite sport team or athlete. Through the use of social media, fans are able to interact with their favorite brand, which was not possible in the past.

In order to build long-term relationships with consumers through social media, Shih (2011) suggests that organizations need to move away from a mass market approach toward one in which an organization listens to its customers and engages them in a more personal manner. Further, Shih highlighted the importance of brand authentication on social media platforms. For example, sport organizations are able to have a more human voice (Zimmerman, 2012). As illustrated in Figure 26.1 below, the Los Angeles Kings National Hockey League account tweeted on 12 April 2012, "To everyone in Canada outside of BC [British Columbia], you're welcome," when the Kings defeated the Vancouver Canucks in a playoff series. The Vancouver Canucks are disliked by many NHL fans, especially in Canada (Fong, 2012; Stockley, 2012). Thus, the LA Kings' tweet was quite timely in terms of connecting with other hockey fans who may have been cheering for the LA Kings to defeat the Canucks. The Kings' brand benefitted from this heightened fan engagement through social media, as coverage of the tweet spilled into more mainstream media (Zimmerman, 2012).

In this new age of social media, customers expect their favorite brands to engage them. As a result, organizations need to have an active voice to facilitate customer engagement online (Shih, 2011). Further, organizations can create additional marketing opportunities and expose followers to its products and services. At the beginning of the 2013–2014 NBL season, the NZ Breakers wanted to create a hashtag that both it and its Twitter followers could use when discussing the team online. In our discussions with the marketing team, it was suggested that the Breakers post a tweet asking fans for their input on the season's hashtag (shown in Figure 26.2) rather than the marketing team creating the hashtag. As a result, the Breakers' tweet was replied to many times and frequently retweeted. The purpose

FIGURE 26.1 *Los Angeles Kings you're welcome tweet*

We're thinking of using a hash tag
throughout the season, something that
represents us as a team - any suggestions?

↩ Reply   ⇄ Retweeted   ★ Favorite   ••• More

FIGURE 26.2   *New Zealand Breakers hashtag suggestion tweet*

of the suggestion tweet was to drive communication with the team and if possible increase engagement amongst fans of the Breakers. Followers of the Breakers responded with many different hashtags and the team chose #breakernation as the official hashtag for the season. As a result, fans can now follow the various discussions about the NZ Breakers online by searching for the #breakernation hashtag.

Monitoring fans' comments is fast and easy using social media. Therefore a sport organization like the Breakers can respond to fans quickly, which has been identified as a key element in building successful brands via online technologies (Shih, 2010). In this digital age, consumers expect a real-time response from a query that was made on social media. With the proliferation of mobile devices and Wi-Fi availability, customers are able to be online throughout the day. As a result, Evans (2010) suggests that social media branding efforts should be looked at from a "return on conversation" perspective rather than the older "return on investment" adage. Sport organizations need to invest in online customers by engaging in conversations and harnessing the power that its followers have to obtain success on social media (Evans, 2010). One of many drawbacks to social media is that responding to fans' posts or moderating content on various social media platforms can be time-consuming for under-resourced organizations. Further, social media postings on a sports team's game day must be in real time to have any engagement for fans. For example, the social media team for the Breakers have, in some instances, stayed up all night posting scores and highlights of games, and in particular when the Breakers play in Perth which is five hours behind New Zealand time. Another issue for sport organizations to consider is how much (and how quickly) they respond to fans' social media comments and feedback. Being responsive is important from a branding perspective, but it can consume significant organizational resources – particularly when things are not going well, because fans will take to social media to voice their displeasure online (Dragon, 2013). As a result, social media marketers need to have a plan in place for either ignoring or deflecting negative fan messages.

This section has reviewed some of the new opportunities that organizations have to brand themselves through social media. Sport organizations are now able to humanize themselves in the online environment, respond to customer inquiries in real time, and know what people are saying about the brand. Social media pose many new and unique business prospects.

- Is bringing a brand to life through social media only possible in professional sport? What about non-profit/club sport? Athletes?

- What are the challenges that grassroots sport organizations face when using social media to build a brand?
- How can social media be different from other media in presenting brand associations?

THINKING POINT 26.2

Relationship Building

A photo of primary school students attending a November 2013 match was posted on the New Zealand Breakers' Facebook page. This is one example of the Breakers using social media to build relationships with fans. The students had been promised tickets to the third game of the NBL Championship series during the previous season, but the game was not required because the Breakers won the first two games of this three game series. The strategy here is that by bringing attention to this group of fans, the team hope to foster relationships with both those who benefitted from this experience and others who were simply made aware of it through social media. Social media are uniquely suited to communicate messages of this type.

NZ Breakers shared a link.
November 20 ⚲

Remember Papatoetoe South School? Huge supporters of the SKYCITY Breakers who had never been to a game, we gave them tickets to the 3rd Grand Final last season which they didn't get to come to after the Championship was won in Perth. They finally got their chance last Friday – check out their experience Thanks to Campbell Live below.

Papatoetoe South School were part of over 1500 school kids and their families who got to experience SKYCITY Breakers game night at Vector Arena on Friday through our Hoop Dreams programme – giving kids and their families tickets, travel to the game on public transport and donating basketballs and coaching to the schools involved. If you would like to nominate a school to be involved in Hoop Dreams, or your company would like to sponsor a school, email hayden@nzbreakers.co.nz for more information.

Primary kids' first ever basketball game
www.3news.co.nz

ACTION LEARNING

- What are some of the examples of the key stakeholder relationships a sport

organization can create and maintain using social media?

TOOLS FOR ANALYSIS

Thus far the use of social media to build brands has been explored. Sport managers can also use social media to build relationships with a variety of stakeholders. These stakeholders may include fans, athletes, other sport organizations or organizations outside sport. Building relationships with fans through social media is common practice amongst sport organizations. Building relationships with other stakeholders is part of the broader sport marketing framework and also of strategic importance. In addition there is an opportunity for sport organizations to use social media to implement a corporate social responsibility (CSR) strategy as well as foster sponsor relations. In this section, the focus is on the use of social media to build relationships.

Although social media embedded within marketing strategies are still a recent phenomenon in the sport industry, the use of relationship marketing strategies is not new. The concept of relationship marketing was first put forward in the service marketing field (Berry, 1983) but has also been discussed in the sport industry (e.g. Bee and Kahle, 2006). Abeza et al. defined relationship marketing in the context of sport as "retaining customers through the achievement of long-term mutual satisfaction by businesses and their customers" (2013: 120). Kim (2008) focused on quality in his exploration of relationship marketing. His findings supported the link between seven relationship-quality constructs (trust, commitment, satisfaction, love/liking, intimacy, self-connection and reciprocity) and sport consumption behaviors (media consumption, the purchase of licensed merchandise and attendance). Kim's findings justify sport managers' attempts to strengthen relationships. Although not explicitly identified by Kim, there is the potential for social media to facilitate enhanced trust and reciprocity—key to building relationships. Stavros et al. (2008) have advanced our understanding of relationship marketing in sport settings within the context of an increasingly sophisticated practice environment. One component of the Breakers' changing and increasingly sophisticated environment is social media.

A sport organization may attempt to build relationships by posting content related to another geographically proximal or related sport organization. This is common practice in the off-season when timely content may be scarce. For example, the Breakers have "liked" the New Zealand Warriors on Facebook. The New Zealand Warriors are a professional rugby league team also based in Auckland. The strategy here is based on creating an overlap of fans. The Breakers also follow other New Zealand-based sport organizations on Twitter. In the 2013 off-season, the Breakers marketed ticket sales to a Tall Blacks/Tall Ferns double header taking place in Auckland, which is shown in Figure 26.3. This was done for the purpose of building/maintaining a relationship with New Zealand Basketball—the national sporting organization for the sport and an important stakeholder in the Breakers.

An organization may also build relationships with organizations outside sport. This may be done through a CSR framework. CSR refers to initiatives related to an organization's responsibility beyond generating a financial surplus. One common example across the professional sports sector is teams visiting children's hospitals in an effort to raise awareness

FIGURE 26.3   *New Zealand Breakers promoting national teams' ticket drive*

FIGURE 26.4   *New Zealand Breakers promotion with charitable organization*

and lift spirits. Babiak (2010) is among many sport management scholars who have emphasized the opportunity for sport organizations to simultaneously work towards organizational and CSR objectives. Likewise, sponsors are important stakeholders for sport organizations and with whom relationship quality is paramount. Social media can facilitate the creation and maintenance of relationships between sport organizations and external stakeholders—including charitable organizations and sponsors. Figure 26.4 illustrates a Facebook post that is reflective of the New Zealand Breakers' efforts to build relationships with both a charitable organization (the Salvation Army) and a sponsor (Crown Relocations). Fans, geographically proximal sport organizations, sponsors and charitable partners are just some of the stakeholders with whom a sport organization like the Breakers may use social media to build relationships.

ACTION LEARNING

- Think about an example of a sport organization using social media in a CSR initiative. Was it effective? Why or why not?

- How have you seen social media used to enhance trust and reciprocity amongst key stakeholders?

THINKING POINT 26.3

Leveraging Social Media Engagement

Contractual agreements with sponsors often include guaranteed social media activation, where the sponsors would like to leverage their relationship through the Breakers' social media platforms to engage Breakers' fans. Our research has shown that posting marketing messages from a sponsor generates limited engagement, whereas creating a link, such as a unique promotion between the sponsor and the Breakers, can produce significant engagement in fans as measured by likes, comments and sharing behavior. The following example illustrates the marketing link between the New Zealand Breakers and its sponsor, Gatorade.

NZ Breakers
Liked · December 3 ·

Courtesy of Gatorade New Zealand we've got the ultimate Christmas gift for a Breakers fan who has everything, one of only a handful of singlet's made to commemorate the world's fastest man's visit to our training facility last year, signed by Usain Bolt himself. All you need to do is tell us who your favourite SKYCITY Breakers player is and your favourite Gatorade Flavour to be in win this great prize. Get in fast, entries close at 9.58 tomorrow morning!

Like · Comment · Share

ACTION LEARNING

- Is social media a suitable platform for sport organizations to promote their product or endorse a sponsor? Why or why not?
- Are fans interested in social media messages related to sponsors, ticket announcements, price discounts or competitions? Or do fans simply ignore these types of social media communication?
- How is consumer engagement generated through social media?

TOOLS FOR ANALYSIS

Professional sport organizations, sporting leagues and athletes use social media as marketing and communication tools. Social media has been used as a platform to sell tickets, offer discounts, activate sponsorship, provide live game updates, share "insider" pictures and videos, and converse with fans. The relatively low cost of social media is advantageous, especially for organizations with small budgets (Eagleman, 2013), which is perhaps one of the reasons social media have become mainstream. This section suggests online networks and meaningful online engagement with stakeholders are key for sport organizations and athletes in using social media effectively.

Relationships built and maintained online with stakeholders are vital in order to generate an online community. An online network determines the reach of online communications. The more extensive a network, the more potential eyes there are to see an online message. The networks formed provide access not only to established relationships (i.e. fans, sponsors, and stakeholders) but also to friends of the established network ("friend extensions"). The social network allows fans to promote an organization's product as they use social media to communicate with their friends about their experiences at the game. This word-of-mouth selling has been shown to be effective in building a brand and selling products (Coyle, 2010; Emmons, 2012). Facilitating engagement with stakeholders through social media, and subsequently benefitting from that engagement, are important for maximizing the reach of online messages.

Research has shown meaningful fan engagement on social media can improve brand equity, increase ticket and merchandise sales, and heighten fan loyalty (Coyle, 2010; Ioakimidis, 2010). The challenge for marketers using social media is to produce content that generates this consumer engagement. Based on our preliminary research with the Breakers, direct marketing messages receive very limited engagement. However, when a marketing message is combined with a message about the team or an athlete, fan engagement increases greatly. For example, a message including the final score of a game with a mention to buy tickets to the next home game has a greater consumer response and reach than simply making a direct marketing post to purchase tickets. The combination of the two types of messages is a strategy to create more leverage within social media postings.

A key stakeholder in sport organizations are the athletes who play for the team. These athletes are part of the organization's brand, yet they also represent their own image and brand. Sport organizations leverage benefit from athletes by linking up with the athletes' online presence. The benefits from associating with athletes are to further build an online presence, foster online relationships and generate a larger social network. Athletes use social media, particularly Twitter, to promote themselves (Hambrick et al., 2010). Although the benefits of using social media for athletes are similar to those of sporting organizations, athletes generate engagement with their fans differently. Athletes regularly promote themselves by providing information about their personal lives (Frederick et al., 2012). They will often describe their daily activities, such as what they ate for dinner, or announce

Thomas Abercrombie @tomabo10 · Jan 12
New fave game on the ps4 #dontstarve. So frustrating though!! #PS4share
pic.twitter.com/Qopg9ZfCqJ

FIGURE 26.5   *Screenshot of videogame Tweet by Thomas Abercrombie*

their vacation destination. Personal posts are regularly combined with information about the athlete's sport life (Frederick et al., 2012). For example, Thomas Abercrombie's tweets about playing PlayStation 4 (see Figure 26.5) and recovering from training at the beach (Figure 26.6) are examples of the effective content that athletes post on social media. These posts are more personal and individual than those of sport organizations, enabling the athlete to connect with their fans.

Activating sponsorship through social media is a domain that is becoming more prevalent for athletes and sport organizations. Linking sponsorship and social media is financially advantageous. Pegoraro (2010) suggests there is room for athletes to use social media as a platform for individual revenue generation through endorsement and sponsorship. The value of online social networks was previously discussed, so it should be no surprise that

Thomas Abercrombie @tomabo10 · Feb 20
Nice little recovery down at the beach in Wollongong after a travel day. Getting ready for tomorrow #breakernation pic.twitter.com/3sP8FFb62J

FIGURE 26.6   *Picture of recovery session at the beach by Thomas Abercrombie*

Daryl Corletto @DarylCorletto · Sep 24
Mmmm barny banana protein! Thanks guys @SciMXNZ @kiwibodybilder
pic.twitter.com/RNQYiyli7p

FIGURE 26.7 *Sci-MX Tweet by Daryl Corletto*

sponsors desire access to the social media networks of those they sponsor. Key to successful activation is aligning social media messages with the wants of the social media consumer. For example, Daryl Corletto tweeted images of sponsor products, Sci-MX protein powder (Figure 26.7) and Barkers clothing (Figure 26.8). Corletto's tweets are activating sponsorship deals, but the messages are still relevant to his followers because the products relate to sport and everyday activity. The benefit of such posts may include fans becoming aware of the products and/or encouraging product usage.

The project the authors are conducting with the New Zealand Breakers has revealed a need to develop marketing strategies and practices to manage sponsors' social media desires and requirements. In the Breakers' experience they have found sponsors often approach sponsorship activation with a quid pro quo mentality, where the sponsor pays for a specific number of

Daryl Corletto @DarylCorletto · Sep 9
Thanks to @barkers for the gifts at training last week. Nice to meet you guys at the quiz night! pic.twitter.com/PkYGRyNOFI

FIGURE 26.8 *Tweet of Barkers Clothing by Daryl Corletto*

social media posts. This type of arrangement can be detrimental to the sport organization and hinders effectiveness because of the importance of providing consumers with information that they would actually want to read. Simply posting a sponsor message to sport fans could clutter the consumer's social media feeds with unwanted messages while also interfering with the sport organization's brand. Marketers need to be creative when activating sponsorship messages to fans, because of the importance of creating a message that generates fan interaction. Social media packages, which include elements such as naming rights for final score posts, product placements in photos and sponsor messages, are being created to streamline expectations between the sponsor and the sport organization or figure, while also respecting the fan's social media space (Fisher, 2013). Social media sponsorship deals are another opportunity for sport teams and individuals to generate revenue, however the fit between sponsor and message must be relevant.

ACTION LEARNING

- If you were a professional athlete, would you use social media to directly promote attendance at one of your competitions?
- How could an athlete use social media to successfully market a sporting event?
- Describe a social media posting you have recently seen that contains either a promotion or a sales message. Did fans engage with the message?
- Did the marketing post encourage sport consumption? Explain why the message was or was not successful.

CONCLUSION

This chapter outlined three ways in which sport organizations use social media for branding purposes, to communicate with and to consumers, and to leverage engagement on these social networking platforms. It is important for sport organizations and sport managers to continue to be proactive in how social media are used to achieve a return on conversation through engagement with fans. Social media platforms are increasingly being utilized by sport organizations for online brand management by communicating directly with consumers. Sport organizations are able to directly engage their consumers through the use of social media by having an active voice, which can help to facilitate consumer engagement. Further, social media can also be used to create relationships with key stakeholders, implement CSR activities and foster sponsor relations. This chapter outlined how sport organizations can use social media posts for both profit-oriented goals and to show charitable works. The third section of the chapter outlined several ways in which social media are used to meet communication and marketing goals. Successful social media branding and fan engagement can be highly profitable for the sport organization through increased sales of tickets and merchandise. Further, the branding of a team's athletes can be an key tool in leveraging the engagement with fans. Athletes represent the team and often on social media they will show insider content, such as pictures of what they are doing or eating that can enable fans to become more engaged with the athlete and/or team.

The challenge for sport organizations moving forward is to use social media tools and unlock their potential to strengthen relationships with fans and other stakeholders (Williams and Chinn, 2010). Whilst professional teams such as the Breakers have done well in this area, there is room for improvement and growth. This chapter has been built on an example from professional sport—the New Zealand Breakers. It is necessary to remember that social media are *and should be* used by other non-elite entities within the broader sport industry, including non-profit and grassroots organizations.

REFERENCES

Aaker, D. (2004) *Brand Portfolio Strategy.* New York: The Free Press.

Abeza, G., O'Reilly, N. and Reid, I. (2013) Relationship marketing and social media in sport. *International Journal of Sport Communication*, 6(2): 120–142.

Arsenault, A. and Castells, M. (2008) Switching power: Rupert Murdoch and the global business of media politics: a sociological analysis. *International Sociology,* 23: 488–513.

Babiak, K. (2010) The role and relevance of corporate social responsibility in sport: a view from the top. *Journal of Management and Organization*, 16: 528–549.

Bee, C.C. and Kahle, L.R. (2006) Relationship marketing in sports: a functional approach. *Sport Marketing Quarterly*, 15(2): 102–110.

Berry, L.L. (1983) Relationship marketing. In L.L. Berry, G.L. Shostack and G. Upah (eds), *Emerging Perspectives on Services Marketing*. Chicago, IL: American Marketing Association. pp. 25–28.

Booth, P. (2010) *Digital Fandom: New Media Studies.* New York: Peter Lang Publishing.

Boyd, D. and Ellison, N.B. (2007) Social network sites: definition, history, and scholarship. *Journal of Computer-Mediated Communication,* 13: 210–230.

Coyle, P. (2010, 4 January) Teams active in social media build strategic advantage. *Sports Business Journal*. Retrieved from www.sportsbusinessdaily.com/Journal.

Dragon, R. (2013) *Big brand theory: Boston Celtics*. Available at: http://socialmediatoday.com/Big_Brand_Theory/boston-celtics.

Eagleman, A. (2013) Acceptance, motivations, and usage of social media as a marketing communications tool amongst employees of sport national governing bodies. *Sport Management Review*, 16(4): 488–497.

Emmons, B. (2012) Interview with Kathleen Hessert, Founder and President of Buzz Mgr and SportsMediaChallenge. *International Journal of Sport Communication*, 5: 454–456

Evans, L. (2010) *Social Media Marketing: Strategies for Engaging in Facebook, Twitter and Other Social Media.* Que Pub.

Fisher, E. (2013) Social media sponsorship deals. *Sports Business Journal*. 3–9 June 2013. Retrieved from www.sportsbusinessdaily.com/Journal/Issues/2013/06/03/In-Depth/Social-media-sponsorships.aspx.

Fong, P. (2012) Vancouver Canucks could be NHL's most despised team. Retrieved from www.thestar.com/sports/hockey/2012/04/08/vancouver_canucks_could_be_nhls_most_despised_team.html.

Frederick, E., Lim, C.H., Clavio, G., Pedersen, P.M. and Burch, L. (2012) Choosing between the one-way or two-way street: an exploration of relationship promotion by professional athletes on Twitter. *Communication and Sport,* published online 12 December.

Hambrick, M., Simmons, J., Greenhalgh, G. and Greenwell, T. (2010) Understanding professional athletes' use of Twitter: a content analysis of athlete tweets. *International Journal of Sport Communication*, 3: 454–471.

Ioakimidis, M. (2010) Online marketing of professional sports clubs: engaging fans on a new playing field. *International Journal of Sports Marketing and Sponsorship*, July: 271–283.

Keller, K. (2003) Brand synthesis: the multidimension of brand knowledge. *Journal of Consumer Research,* 29: 595–600.

Kelly, S.M. (2013) Avid sports fans 52% more likely to own a tablet. Retrieved from http://mashable.com/2013/01/22/sports-digital-technology.

Mahan, J.E. III. and McDaniel, S.R. (2006) The new online arena: sport, marketing, and media converge in cyberspace. In A.A. Raney and J. Bryant (eds), *Handbook of Sports and Media.* Mahwah, NJ: Erlbaum. pp. 409–434.

Nielsen Holdings (2014) *Year in Sports Media Report 2013.*

Pegoraro, A. (2010) Look who's talking—athletes on Twitter: a case study. *International Journal of Sport Communication*, 3: 501–514.

Scott, O.K.M., Hill, B. and Zakus, D.H. (2012) Framing the 2007 National Basketball Association finals: an analysis of commentator discourse. *International Review for the Sociology of Sport,* forthcoming.

Shih, C. (2010) *The Facebook Era: Tapping Online Social Networks to Market, Sell, and Innovate.* New York: Pearson Education.

Stavros, C., Pope, N.K. and Winzar, H. (2008) Relationship marketing in Australian professional sport: an extension of the Shani framework. *Sport Marketing Quarterly*, 17(3): 135–145.

Stockley, R. (2012) 5 Reasons why fans hate the Vancouver Canucks. Retrieved from http://bleacherreport.com/articles/1059414–five-reasons-to-hate-the-vancouver-canucks.

Walsh, S. (2012) Why is digital social media so important? 8 March. Retrieved from http://digital football.com/opinion/why-is-social-media-so-important-for-sports.

Williams, J. and Chinn, S.J. (2010) Meeting relationship-marketing goals through social media: a conceptual model for sport marketers. *International Journal of Sport Communication*, 3: 422–437.

Zimmerman, M.H. (2012) Interview with Pat Donahue, Coordinator of Digital Media, Los Angeles Kings. *International Journal of Sport Communication*, 5: 457–460.

USEFUL WEBSITES

List of NBL Teams social media accounts
www.nbl.com.au/social-media

Nike outscores Adidas at the social Olympics (London 2012)
www.l2thinktank.com/nike-outscores-adidas-in-social-olympics/2012

3 ways sport organizations use social media to increase fan loyalty
http://socialbusiness.hootsuite.com/rs/hootsuitemediainc/images/3-ways-sports-organizations-use-social-media-to-increase-fan-loyalty.pdf

The NBA and social media
www.slideshare.net/AdamVincenzini/the-nba-and-social-media-a-case-study

Year in sports media report: 2013
www.nielsen.com/us/en/reports/2014/year-in-the-sports-media-report-2013.html

New Zealand Breakers' Twitter account
https://twitter.com/nzbreakers

New Zealand Breakers' players' Twitter accounts:

- C.J. Bruton https://Twitter.com/cbj4real
- Casey Frank https://Twitter.com/kseefrank
- Kerron Johnson https://twitter.com/kjbbruin03
- Daryl Corletto https://twitter.com/DarylCorletto
- Thomas Abercrombie https://twitter.com/tomabo10
- Mika Vukona https://twitter.com/M1kaV

27

BRAND MANAGEMENT IN SPORT

JONATHON EDWARDS

> There's no second chances in this scenario, no second first-impressions on prospective fans, sponsors, players, agents and the like. Once the brand is revealed, a sports team's reputation begins to take shape.
>
> (Matisz, 2015)

> "Consumers have known us for other things throughout the years," said Reebok President Matt O'Toole. "We are slowly and surely reintroducing them to Reebok. A lot of it is traced to when we decided to return Reebok to its fitness roots about five years ago. Reebok started in the early 80's in its modern form as a fitness brand that was giving women, in particular, the incentive to sweat and workout. Our view is this version of fitness that we are part of today is similar in a lot of ways. Fitness is much more experimental."
>
> (Heitner, 2015)

> More children in England and Scotland recognize the beer brand Foster's than certain makes of biscuit, crisps or ice-cream, a survey has found, while 50% linked beer brands to football teams and sports events.
>
> (*RTE News*, 2015)

On completion of this chapter, students will be able to:

- Gain an understanding of brand equity and the brand equity model in a practical application.

- Develop some comprehensive branding building strategies.

- Be able to critique and evaluate branding strategies.

- Gain an understanding of brand extensions and how these can be used effectively.

- In the context of brand building, understand how a manager establishes brand loyalty.

INTRODUCTION

Branding has been and is considered to be an integral facet of the sporting industry for marketers, sponsors and management. The term became popular during the mid-1990's and is typically focused on the spectator sport industry (Mullin et al., 2013). O'Reilly and Séguin (2013) stated that "A brand is the most intangible asset" (p. 153); and Aaker (1992) and Keller (2003) were discussed in O'Reilly and Séguin (2013) as regards a brand being a company's greatest asset. A sport brand can ignite customer emotion, loyalty, passion for a team, organization, league and/or manufacturer, which is not typically found within other industries. Essentially, "For customers, brands can simplify choice, promise a particular quality level, reduce risk, and/or engender trust" (Keller and Lehmann, 2006: 740). Within team sport organizations, whether that is professional or non-profit, the strategic focus of management is on winning, which is a short-term outcome as opposed to the long-term marketing and sponsorship strategies around building a brand (Ross, 2006). As a result marketers and management often underestimate the power of a brand and its impact on customer consumption, where the focus is often on the product.

A brand is understood to be a name, logo, slogan, sound and/or a unique symbol that distinguishes a product, service or organization from that of competing organizations operating within the same or similar environment (Mullin et al., 2013; O'Reilly and Séguin, 2013). In the context of sport, then, the brand "means that a product or a service, such as a type of sport (e.g. basketball) or an event (world championships) or a person (athlete), and institution (club, federation) can be perceived as a brand" (Pedersen, 2004: 47). By establishing a strong brand identity and/or image, consumers and producers are essentially protected from competitors with similar products and/or services (Aaker, 1991). Some examples of the most valuable brands in sport can be seen in Table 27.1.

Brands and brand strategy can be further categorized in three ways: *corporate branding*, *mixed branding* and *house of brands*. *Corporate branding*

TABLE 27.1 *The top 10 most valuable sports brands in the world (Forbes, 2014)*

Ranking	Brand name	Brand value
1	Nike	$15,000,000,000.00
2	ESPN	$11,500,000,000.00
3	Adidas	$5,000,000,000.00
4	Sky Sports	$3,000,000,000.00
5	Gatorade	$2,500,000,000.00
6	Reebok	$1,500,000,000.00
7	Under Armour	$1,000,000,000.00
8	EA Sports	$625,000,000.00
9	YES Network	$600,000,000.00
10	MSG (Madison Square Gardens)	$500,000,000.00

covers those brands where the "corporate name is dominant in endorsing all or part of the firm's product and service brands" (Rao et al., 2004: 127). An example here would be Nike. Conversely, *mixed branding* is when "firms typically employ a set of house or family brands, such as subsidiary names, in their brand portfolio, in addition to using the corporate name for certain products" (p. 127). For example, Maple Leaf Sport and Entertainment is the main brand, but also owns the Toronto Maple Leafs (National Hockey League, NHL), the Toronto Raptors (National Basketball Association, NBA), Toronto FC (Major League Soccer, MLS) and the Toronto Marlies (American Hockey League, AHL). The final type of strategy is *house brands* where the brand will keep their corporate name "in the background and use individual brands for their product lines" (p. 127). For example FGL Sports, who have corporate banners, includes Sport Chek, Atmosphere, National Sports, Hockey Experts, S3 and Nevada Bob's Golf.

Building on the definition of a brand, O'Reilly and Séguin (2013: 156) described the concept of branding as the creation of "a brand with an image that perfectly matches the image that the target market (s) seeks association with." While it is important that the brand image matches the image the target market seeks, the brand itself has to set itself apart from its competition within the environment that sport organizations operate. For example, in baseball the New York Yankees of Major League Baseball (MLB) has one of the strongest team and global brands in professional sport, where fans purchase merchandise (e.g. baseball jerseys, bobble heads, mini baseball bats) with the Yankees logo throughout the world. The strength of the Yankee logo transcends national US borders and is in fact a global brand. Other brands within MLB and even other professional sports do not have the brand image and power of the Yankees' brand. Essentially branding and a brand invoke trust among customers, sponsors and stakeholders within a sport organization. This chapter builds on definitions of a brand and branding, and discusses concepts such as brand equity, brand extensions, brand loyalty and branding strategies.

Knowing When to Rebrand Your Organization—Reebok Looks to Increase their Brand Equity among Consumers

Reebok International Ltd has been in direct competition with Nike since the 1980s. Reebok was initially founded in 1890 by a shoemaker, J.W. Foster, in Lancashire, England. In 2005 it was acquired by the German foot apparel company Adidas as a means of competing with Nike (see Figure 27.1). While the initial merger produced some initial positive results (i.e. financial profit) Reebok, however, continued to lose revenue in 2006 and beyond. In 2012 the 10-year contracts that Reebok had with the National Football League came to an end. Currently, losses for Adidas were estimated at €293 million in the last quarter.

The continual financial losses forced Reebok to rethink their brand strategy and market position and contemplate rebranding. As a result, Reebok management has recently decided to rebrand their image. This was done by releasing a new logo, which is not referred to as a logo but a symbol (see Figure 27.2). The Reebok symbol depicts a delta which is reflective of the change that fitness can bring to an individual's life (see Figure 27.2):

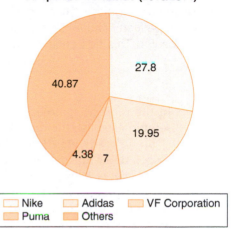

Market share sports goods and sportwear companies worldwide (2013/2014)

27.8
40.87
19.95
4.38   7

Nike   Adidas   VF Corporation
Puma   Others

FIGURE 27.1 *A graph depicting the market share with sporting good company's worldwide (MBAskool. com, 2015)*

FIGURE 27.2 *The change in the symbol for Reebok (MBASkool.com, 2015)*

"The newfound purpose of the brand, now, is to serve the pursuit of fitness. The three arms of the delta in the symbol are meant to represent the three changes—physical, mental and social fitness would inspire in an individual" (MBASkool.com, 2015). This rebranding campaign is being delivered as the "Be More Human" campaign where

Reebok is urging consumers to "live up to their full potential" (Heitner, 2015: 1).

Reebok, after many years of financial losses, has taken the initiative to rebrand the logo to what is now they call a symbol. Their focus has also shifted to the "Be More Human" campaign, which has allowed for strategic partnerships to be forged with various endurance events (e.g. Spartan Race), combat sport athletes (e.g. Jon Jones, Johny Hendricks), the Ultimate Fighter Championship (UFC) competition, and a commitment to the CrossFit. This has contributed to significant growth over the past year. The management attitude at the company has focused on a tough fitness mentality. This "tough fitness mentality" was recognized by Reebok marketing executives when they identified that there was a high percentage (approximately 35 million) of customers using combat sports to stay fit (MBASkool.com, 2015). It is apparent that Reebok has reached the maturity or decline stage in the product life cycle (e.g. introduction, growth, maturity and decline), which has forced executives into a position of rebranding.

In the rebranding process, it becomes important that management needs to set and establish the direction for **marketing** activities. This process is known as brand positioning. In the Reebok case, the rebranding position involves the association with companies such as the UFC, CrossFit and various endurance-based events. This provides Reebok with unique brand position in comparison to other products offered by their competitors (e.g. Nike and Under Armour). Keller and Lehmann (2006) paraphrased Keller et al. (2002) and offered this explanation: "Brand positioning involves establishing key brand associations in the minds of customers and other important constituents to differentiate the brand and establish (to the extent possible) competitive superiority" (2006: 740). In the case of Reebok, management's **strategy** has been to enter into an environment with little competition and ability to differentiate themselves from their competition. There are two areas that are relevant to brand positioning, which are brand intangibles and the corporate image and reputation.

Brand intangibles are those assets of an organization that transcend the physical/tangible aspects of a product. Examples of brand intangibles include the user imagery, purchase and consumption imagery, organizational history, heritage and experiences (Keller and Lehmann, 2006). When positioning the brand in comparison to the competition, existing organizational history, heritage and consumption patterns can provide a starting point when an organization such as Reebok is looking to rebrand. In this case, Reebok is seeking to maintain some of those intangible assets, but are really looking to differentiated themselves and establish themselves in an environment.

Establishing a corporate brand reputation is understood to be based on a firm's past performance, which will dictate future **performance** (Deephouse and Suchman, 2008). Keller and Lehmann (2006) further explained the brand reputation in the context of brand credibility, where Keller and Aaker (1992, 1998) were paraphrased as corporate credibility is the "extent to which consumers believe that a company is willing and able to deliver products and services that satisfy customer needs and wants" (Keller and Lehmann, 2006: 742).

One of the ways to create credibility and build the reputation of the brand is for management to utilize brand extensions, which can lead to enhancing brand perceptions in a positive manner to the customers. In the case of Reebok, their brand extension is linked to whom Reebok is associating with (i.e. UFC, CrossFit and various endurance events).

One of the visual tools that can be used to analyse the brand position is a brand map. A brand map is based on two variables and is used to evaluate the competitive market, where the current brand is positioned, and where the brand can be positioned to optimize revenues. The first step in creating a brand map is to determine the variables that will comprise the X and Y axis. Some examples of different variables that can be established include price (high and low), accessibility (high and low) and/or visibility (high and low). After determining the variables, the X and Y axis are labelled using variables; for example, your X axis may be labelled as price (high and low) in correlation with your Y axis, which is labelled as accessibility (high and low). This creates four quadrants that will be used to depict your brand in conjunction with the competition. In the second step, the current brand position is labeled within one of the quadrants. The next step is to label the brand's current direct and indirect competition within the applicable quadrant. The final step is to label where the brand would like to be positioned. This is an important consideration, as marketers do not want to position the brand in a quadrant where there is too much competition or the environment is saturated.

ACTION LEARNING

- Do you believe that Reebok's rebranding strategy will succeed? Why or why not?
- How would you develop a brand map and which variables would you use to illustrate Reebok's rebranding strategy?

- How and which brand extensions should Reebok be utilizing?
- Is Reebok's rebranding strategy a short- or long-term solution?

THINKING POINT 27.2

Building a Brand in a Non-Hockey Market

Rumours throughout the professional hockey industry are that the NHL board of governors and the commissioner, Gary Bettman, are contemplating team expansion to Las Vegas. Currently there are 30 NHL teams, which comprise 23 US-based teams and seven Canadian teams. The interest in Las Vegas by the NHL dates back to 1991, when the NHL hosted the first outdoor hockey game of the modern era between the Los Angeles Kings and the New York Rangers at Caesar's Palace. For a short period of time there was a professional minor league hockey team between 1993 and 1999; when the lease agreement with the Thomas & Mack Center concluded the team management decided not to continue operating in the city.

Currently, there is no professional sport team in Las Vegas: as Allen (2015) explained, "Las Vegas is an attractive venue for a variety of reasons, not the least of which is that it is a high-profile city without any franchises in the three other major sports. The arena, which will seat about 18,000 for hockey, will be completed in April 2016." Currently there are about two million people who reside in the Las Vegas area. The city is considered to be a resort where the focus is on entertainment, gambling, shopping and fine dining.

In August of 2014, rumours began to surface about a possible expansion to Las Vegas, due to the construction of a new arena that is a joint venture between Anschutz Entertainment Group and MGM Resorts International. This was further augmented "when billionaire businessman Bill Foley and former Sacramento Kings owners Joe and Gavin Maloof launched a season-ticket drive for their proposed NHL team" (Allen, 2015). As Allen (2015) reported, "If we sell 10,000 season tickets, I believe we will go a long ways to getting the franchise," Foley told USA TODAY Sports. "Ten thousand is our number."

TOOLS FOR ANALYSIS

Building a brand is an important aspect for any team entering into a new environment. Sport organizations need to take into consideration their direct and indirect competition in order to understand the viability of entering into such an environment. In analyzing a brand-building strategy for establishing an NHL hockey team in Las Vegas, we can apply the brand equity model established by Aaker (1991). Brand equity is "a set of assets and liabilities linked to a brand, its name and symbol that adds to or subtracts from the value provided by its product or service to a firm and/or to that firm's customers" (Aaker, 1991: 12). Ross (2006) paraphrased Aaker (1991) by stipulating that "brand equity provides increases the probability of brand choice, customer (retailer) retention, profit margins, willingness to pay premium prices, customer search, marketing communication effectiveness, positive word-of-mouth brand licensing opportunities, and brand extensions" (1991: 23). Thus the elements of the brand equity model consist of brand loyalty, brand awareness, perceived quality, brand association and other proprietary brand assets:

1 Taking on the strategy of attempting to pre-sell 10,000 season tickets is an example of attempting to establish brand loyalty. As O'Reilly and Séguin (2013: 160) stated, if "they [customers] continue to purchase the brand, even in the face of competitors with superior features, price, and

convenience, substantial value exists in the brand." There are a number of ways that **brand loyalty** can be established, which consist of meeting the customers' expectations, introducing innovative products, designing brand loyalty programs, and making sure that marketing departments and management support the brand loyalty initiatives.

2   Brand awareness is arguably the first component in building brand equity. It is important to establish the brand with the consumers so they are aware of the brand and the product(s). Pre-selling tickets can be an effective marketing strategy in creating brand awareness. This becomes key for brand equity in that awareness can increase the possibility that the brand is considered for consumption by consumers, can be influential in brand associations and can "affect decisions about brands in the product category or consideration set" (O'Reilly and Séguin, 2013: 158). Because of the emergence of the internet in the early 1990s, information about product(s) and brands is more readily accessible to customers, meaning that it becomes vital for organizations entering into a new environment that there is brand awareness to establish brand loyalty.

3   Another element of brand equity is the perceived quality of the product(s). Perceived quality is understood to be the overall perception by the consumers with regard to a specific product in comparison to similar products within same industry (Aaker, 1991; O'Reilly and Séguin, 2013). This is a challenging aspect for the potential Las Vegas team above as there are no other professional sport franchises to compare, and essentially they are comparing a team that "might" be in Las Vegas with an established entertainment industry with superstar performers, such as Celine Dion, for example. Furthermore, the question becomes "Will individuals go to Las Vegas to watch NHL hockey, which they can do in 30 other cities, or are they going to come for the gambling and entertainment?"

4   Brand association is the intangible set of associations that are created with the brand. Thus brand association can be understood by the consumer's experience with the product and the symbolic benefits of that product (i.e. does the product satisfy the underlying need for social approval? See O'Reilly & Séguin, 2013). Brand association is also linked with brand image, which is the perception of the brand by consumers. Drawing on the case study, brand association can occur in two ways: (1) the team focus is on the Las Vegas experience, as opposed to just coming to a NHL hockey game; and/or, (2) the team can associate themselves with previous professionals and build on their successes.

5   The final brand equity element is other proprietary brand assets, and in the case of the Las Vegas example, this is the competitive advantage that the potential NHL Las Vegas team has over other professional franchises. There are currently no other professional franchises in sport to compete with a hockey team. This is not the case in most large markets. For example, most large cities have at least an MLB team, NBA team, National Football League (NFL) team and/or MLS team. These teams are therefore all competing for customers to consume their products.

When applying the brand equity model to team sport brand equity, three areas affect the elements discussed above. The first is team related, which refers to the success of the team, the head coach or a star player. The second is organization related, covering areas such as organizational reputation, scheduling, product delivery (i.e. the overall customer experience in attending the event) and the overall entertainment package. The final area is market related, which is media coverage, geographic location, competitive forces and support (Gladden, 2014; O'Reilly and Séguin, 2013). The result of the three areas in correlation with the elements can be an increase in local and national media exposure, merchandise sales, corporate support, atmosphere and ticket sales, which then leads to shaping customer' perceptions (O'Reilly and Séguin, 2013). This illustrates the importance of marketers understanding the concept of brand equity in building a brand.

ACTION LEARNING

- Which brand marketing strategy would you use to build your brand and why?
- In applying the brand equity model to team sports, what potential consequences are a result of applying the team sport brand equity to initiating a team in Las Vegas?
- If Las Vegas were to be awarded a team, which branding strategy would you initiate to create brand equity?

- Do you believe that the branding strategy that is already in place is an effective approach?
- Comparatively, is there another environment that would be more effective in hosting an NHL franchise? Apply the brand equity model to support your answer.

CONCLUSION

This chapter set out to outline the concepts of brand positioning, equity, loyalty and strategies by examining two case studies: the rebranding of Reebok, and building a brand in a non-hockey market. As discussed in the introduction to this chapter, branding is an integral facet of the sport industry. Due to the ever-changing environment, whether it is social, political, economic, technological and/or legal, the sport brand is the "staple" of the organization that provides organizational stability.

To obtain organizational stability through a sports brand, marketers and management have to be concerned with the position of the brand within the context of the environment and competition. This is vital for both new brands entering a new market, and those established brands in the process of evaluating. In the case of Reebok, their strategy involves a new rebranding initiative with a focus and message that have not been capitalized on by their competitors (i.e. Nike). It is for this reason that understanding brand positioning becomes essential for management in developing strategic responses that will differentiate the organization from their competitors.

Building on the brand position, brand equity plays a role in measuring the value of the brand. The key elements of building brand equity are brand loyalty, brand awareness, perceived quality, brand awareness and other proprietary brand assets. When determining brand equity for a team, Gladden (2014) indicated that the areas of a team that have an impact on the elements of brand equity are the success of the team, organization related and market related. The outcomes or consequences of these areas and elements include national media exposure, merchandise sales, corporate support, atmosphere and ticket sales (Gladden, 2014; O'Reilly and Séguin, 2013). Overall the power of a brand in the sport industry can provide organizational stability and competitive advantage, and ultimately generate millions of dollars in revenue.

REFERENCES

Aaker, D.A. (1991). *Managing Brand Equity: Capitalizing on the Value of a Brand Name*. New York: The Free Press.

Aaker, D.A. (1992). The value of brand equity. *Journal of Business Strategy, 13*(4): 27–32.

Allen, K. (2015). Ticket drive to test if NHL could work in Las Vegas. Retrieved from www.usatoday.com/story/sports/nhl/2015/01/19/las-vegas-market-expansion-bill-foley/22026309.

Arshad, S. (2013). Tom Brady net worth 2014 salary endorsement deals income. Retrieved from www.tsmplug.com/richlist/tom-brady-net-worth.

Deephouse, D.L. & Suchman, M. (2008). Legitimacy in organizational institutionalism. In R. Greenwood, C. Oliver, K. Saline & R. Sunday (eds), *The Sage Handbook of Organizational Institutionalism* (pp. 49–77). London: Sage.

Forbes (2014). The Forbes Fab 40: The world's most valuable sports brands. Retrieved from www.forbes.com/pictures/mlm45jemm/the-most-valuable-company-brands.

Gladden, J. (2014). Managing sport brands. In B.J. Mullin, S. Hardy & W.A. Sutton (eds), *Sport Marketing* (4th edn) (pp. 161–178). Champaign, IL: Human Kinetics.

Heitner, D. (2015). Reebok reveals massive "Be more human" brand campaign. Retrieved from www.forbes.com/sites/darrenheitner/2015/01/28/reebok-reveals-massive-be-more-human-brand-campaign.

Keller, K.L. (2003). *Strategic Brand Management* (2nd edn). Upper Saddle River, NJ: Prentice Hall.

Keller, K.L. & Aaker, D.A. (1992). The effects of sequential introduction of brand extensions. *Journal of Marketing Research, 29*(1): 35–50.

Keller, K.L. & Aaker, D.A. (1998). The impact of corporate marketing on a company's brand extension. *Corporate Reputation Review, 1*(4): 356–378.

Keller, K.L. & Lehmann, D.R. (2006). Brands and branding: research findings and future priorities. *Marketing Science, 25*(6): 740–759.

Keller, K. Sternthal, B. & Tybout, A. (2002). Three questions you need to ask about your brand. *Harvard Business Review, 80*: 80–89.

Matisz, J. (2015). Flint OHL team should avoid temptation, ignore "Tropics". Retrieved from www.ottawasun.com/2015/02/12/flint-ohl-team-should-avoid-temptation-ignore-tropics-nickname.

MBASkool.com. (2015). Reebok's rebranding: a comprehensive analysis. Retrieved from www.mbaskool.com/business-articles/marketing/9995–reeboks-rebranding-a-comprehensive-analysis.html.

Mullin, B.J., Hardy, S. & Sutton, W.A. (2007). *Sport Marketing*. Windsor, Ontario: Human Kinetics.

O'Reilly, N. & Seguin, B. (2013). *Sport Marketing: a Canadian Perspective* (2nd edn). Toronto, Ontario: Nelson Education.

Pedersen, L.H. (2004). Why is branding so important? Retrieved from www.fiba.com/asp_includes/download.asp?file_id=406.

Rao, V.R., Agarwal, M.K. & Dalhoff, D. (2004). How is manifested brand strategy related to the intangible value of a corporation? *American Marketing Association, 68*(4): 126–141.

Ross, S.T. (2006). A conceptual framework for understanding spectator-based brand equity. *Journal of Sport Management, 20*: 22–38.

RTE News (2015). Study: 50% of children link beer brands to sports. Retrieved from www.rte.ie/news/2015/0205/677948–alcohol.

28

CRISIS MANAGEMENT

STACEY HALL

Mourning, resolve and quest for answers after deadly Boston Marathon bombs.

(Greg Botelho, CNN, 17 April 2013)

1989: Football fans crushed at Hillsborough.

(BBC News, 15 April 2005)

Sports programs experience slow renewal after Katrina.

(Steve Wieberg, *USA Today*, 26 August 2010)

LEARNING OUTCOMES

Upon completion of this chapter, students will be able to:

- Define crisis management and develop a crisis communication message.

- Discuss the importance of planning, training, and exercising safety and security procedures.

- Identify potential threats and common vulnerabilities for sporting events and venues.

- Identify protective measures to enhance security and explain the various types of exercises available to a sport manager.

INTRODUCTION

This chapter provides an overview of crisis management principles, with an emphasis on risk management, planning, training and exercises, and crisis **communications**. It addresses the collaborative work of safety and security teams, and the importance of developing a communication plan. Communication strategies and implementation methods are discussed and sample communication messages are highlighted as a learning tool for emergency preparedness representatives.

CASE STUDY 28.1

Boston Marathon Bombing, 2013

During the 117th Boston Marathon on 15 April 2013, two pressure cooker bombs exploded near the finish line killing three people and injuring an estimated 264 others. The bombs exploded about 13 seconds and 210 yards (190 m) apart, with more than 5,700 runners yet to finish the race. At least 14 people required amputations, with some suffering traumatic amputations as a direct result of the blasts. As the attack occurred at the finishing line, Emergency Medical Technicians (EMTs) and triage stations were available to respond quickly to the immediate aftermath of the explosions. Casualties were treated in 27 different local hospitals.

Officials had swept the area for bombs twice before the explosions, with the second sweep occurring one hour before the bombs detonated. The blasts blew out windows on nearby buildings but did not cause any structural damage. The marathon was halted abruptly. Police, following emergency plans, diverted the remaining runners away from the finish line and evacuated nearby buildings. Many people dropped backpacks and other bags as they fled, requiring each to be treated as a potential bomb. Police closed down a 15-block area around the blast site. As a precaution, the Federal Aviation Administration restricted airspace over Boston and issued a temporary ground stop for Boston's Logan International Airport.

The Massachusetts Emergency Management Agency suggested people trying to contact those in the vicinity use text messaging instead of voice calls because of crowded cellphone lines. The American Red Cross helped concerned family and friends receive information about runners and casualties. The Boston Police Department also set up a helpline for people concerned about relatives or acquaintances to contact, and a line for people to provide information. Google Person Finder activated their disaster service under *Boston Marathon Explosions* to log known information about missing persons as a publicly viewable file.

The Federal Bureau of Investigation led the investigation, assisted by the Bureau of Alcohol, Tobacco, Firearms and Explosives, the Central Intelligence Agency, the National Counterterrorism Center and the Drug Enforcement Administration. US government officials stated that there had been no intelligence reports that indicated such a bombing would take place.

(Sources: Boston Marathon Bombings (2013) Retrieved from http://en.wikipedia.org/wiki/Boston_Marathon_bombings.

Todt, K.E. (2013) Lessons in response and resilience from the Boston Marathon bombing. *International Center for Sport Security Journal*, 1(2).

ACTION LEARNING

- What suggestions would you recommend for securing open-access events?
- What additional training would you suggest for crowd management personnel?
- Do you think surveillance efforts should be increased at all open-access events? Why?

TOOLS FOR ANALYSIS

Crisis management

A crisis is an event that occurs unexpectedly, may not be in the control of management, and may cause harm to an organization's' reputation and viability (Crisis and Emergency Risk Communication, 2002). The three underlying characteristics of a crisis are the element of surprise, the creation of threatening circumstances (i.e. the sustainability of the sport organization) and the short response time. Intentional incidents at sporting events may include an active shooter, improvised explosive device (IED) or fan/player violence. The 2013 Boston Marathon bombing reinforced the notion that major sporting events are attractive targets for terrorists. Unintentional incidents include inclement weather, logistical failure or emergency medical assistance. Hurricane Katrina, one of the worst natural disasters in US history, impacted on several college and professional sports teams in the Gulf Coast and New Orleans region. Effective crisis communications is vital in these circumstances to inform staff and athletes of response plans and the continuity of operation procedures.

Providing a safe environment is a priority for all stakeholders involved in delivering a sporting event (Schwarz et al., 2010). It is also a **legal** requirement to provide a "duty of care" for those consuming your products/services. The high profile of major sport events increases the risk of exposure for spectators, participants, and other entities such as sponsoring agencies (Stevens, 2007). Sport stadia operators world-wide implement safety and security preparedness measures to mitigate the consequences of all-hazard incidents (natural and/or man-made). Over US$2 billion is spent each year globally on security efforts, although during years when mega-events occur (i.e. the Olympics) the figure rises to $6 billion (Culf, 2006). Security efforts include conducting risk assessments, training personnel, exercising plans and implementing crisis/emergency communication systems. Crisis communications in particular has become a critical component of the overall event safety and security system that requires the collaboration of sport marketing and media departments (Sport Event Risk Management, 2010).

Critical Role of First Responders When dealing with an open access event, locations where spectators and athletes are the most vulnerable, and where officials are most prepared for dealing with a crisis, must be identified. Enhancing the security of an event may include an increased EMT presence and actively recruiting volunteers who have backgrounds in emergency response. Qualified EMTs and associated resources in close proximity to an incident ensure injuries are treated quickly and effectively.

Evolving Role of Surveillance Officials are able to observe assets, athletes and the crowd during an event, and are also able to return to the time of a security breach to collect evidence. Video **technology** can be a key asset in emergency response, recovery and crisis management throughout a post-event investigation. Following the Boston Marathon bombings, there may be a greater need and demand for tightening formal **controls** such as additional surveillance at open-access sporting events.

Crowd Management Personnel Training Open-access sporting event officials may decide to distribute their focus and attention equally between the athletes, the event and the crowd/spectators.

Community Education Programs Empowering communities and providing them with the tools, education and awareness knowledge to identify suspicious behaviors and anomalies is critical in a constantly evolving threat environment. Cooperation between the community and law enforcement is fundamental in identifying and preventing potential terrorist threats.

ACTION LEARNING

- Do you believe communities have the necessary tools, education and awareness to know what their role is in community safety and security? If not, what needs to be done?
- What kinds of community-based education programs are available in your local community (or at the regional/national level) to assist the public in identifying and/or reporting suspicious behavior?
- How can sport managers and event planners learn from the Boston Marathon bombing to develop their crisis management skills?

RISK MANAGEMENT

Managing organizational and facility risks is arguably one of the most important aspects of the sport management profession. A risk assessment will provide insight on the current security profile of the sport event/venue, specifically highlighting the strengths and weaknesses in safety and security processes. The outcome of this assessment helps to develop a justification of cost-effective countermeasures and increase security awareness among staff members (Broder, 2006). The risk assessment process involves several steps, including asset identification (physical, financial and human), a threat assessment, vulnerability assessment, consequence evaluation and countermeasure improvement recommendations.

Protecting sport events requires the collaboration and coordination of many individuals and agencies. The sport event/venue command group (CG) serves as the core functional group for all security efforts, including incident management, risk management, staff training, developing and implementing plans and protective measures, conducting exercises, and coordinating response, recovery and continuity efforts. The CG includes representatives from facility management, law enforcement, emergency management, fire and hazardous materials (hazmat), EMS, public health and safety, and sport media/public relations (Hall et al., 2012). It is important to establish this multi-disciplinary team prior to the sport season (or event day), and this group should continue to meet on a regular basis. Input from the CG during the risk assessment process is imperative. The CG defines: (1) the essential functions of the facility; (2) undesired incidents that would interrupt facility operations; (3) the consequences of such incidents; and (4) the potential liabilities incurred. Decisions for the CG are presented in Figure 28.1.

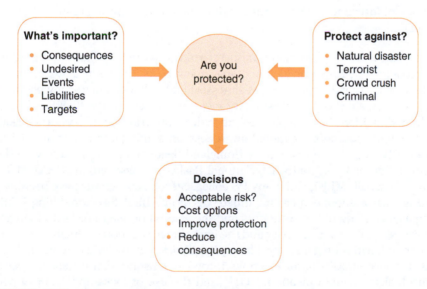

FIGURE 28.1 *Risk management decisions*

Potential threats and facility vulnerabilities compromise the security system (Biringer et al., 2007). Threat information can be obtained from various local, state and federal sources, brainstorming sessions with key personnel, table top exercises, modeling and simulation, and facility walk-throughs pre-event and during the event (Stevens, 2007). Threats may include terrorism, natural catastrophes, crowd control, vandalism, theft, fire, fraud, personal assault, traffic incidents, facility intrusion and technological problems. Terrorism has been cited as one of the most common threats to sport venues (Stevens, 2007). International, domestic and lone-wolf terrorists have considered stadia as targets since such facilities present open access and the opportunity to achieve their objectives of mass casualties, economic damage and social/psychological impact (Office of Intelligence and Analysis, 2009). Hall et al. (2007) identified the following common vulnerabilities at major sport venues that could possibly place an organization at risk:

- Lack of emergency response and evacuation plans specific to their facility.
- Inadequate searching of the facility prior to an event.
- Inadequate lock-down procedures.
- Inadequate searches of fans and their belongings.
- Unsecure concession areas.
- Inadequate signage concerning searches and restricted items.
- Lack of Closed Circuit Television (CCTV) coverage of the sport facility or surrounding areas.
- Storage of dangerous chemicals inside the sport facility.
- Lack of accountability for vendors and their vehicles.
- Lack of security notification system for fans, players, staff, etc.
- Inadequate training of staff members.
- Lack of interoperable communication capabilities among responding agencies.

Countermeasure improvements (also referred to as risk reduction strategies) are recommendations provided to management based on venue assessments to address security vulnerabilities (weaknesses) and enhance emergency planning and recovery efforts. Possible security measures to reduce the likelihood of an undesired incident include physical upgrades, staff training, preventative facility maintenance and educational awareness programs (Ammon et al., 2010). Since 2010, the US Department of Homeland Security in conjunction with the National Football League (NFL), National Basketball Association (NBA), Major League Baseball (MLB), and many US college athletics programs have been promoting an awareness campaign entitled "See Something, Say Something." This campaign is marketed to spectators and the general public in order to increase awareness of suspicious activity and the importance of reporting incidents to the proper authorities on game day. Physical upgrades may include detection, delay and response strategies: for example, intrusion sensors, identity check access control, alarm communication, CCTV, and the use of locks and security personnel stationed at restricted access areas of the venue (Biringer et al., 2007).

Technology improvements may be cost-prohibited, however simple procedural changes such as additional staff training and increasing the number of facility walk-throughs to detect hazards are alternative options for managers.

PLANS, POLICIES AND PROTECTIVE MEASURES

An all-hazard emergency response plan (ERP), inclusive of an evacuation plan (partial, shelter-in-place and full) as well as a business continuity plan, is essential in the planning process. Venue policies should also include (but not be limited to) alcohol, communications, credentialing, emergency medical services, fan conduct, missing child/person, parking, prohibited items, search policy, tailgate (pre-event activities), ticket taking and special accommodations.

Many sport entities have developed security best practice guidelines for their members. In the USA, after the tragic events of September 11, 2001, the NFL, NBA and National Hockey League (NHL) developed a best practices guideline of protective security measures to assist league members (Schwarz et al., 2010). Security management was also enhanced at the intercollegiate level. The National Collegiate Athletic Association (NCAA) issued a Security-Planning Options guideline for university athletic events (Schwarz et al., 2010). In Europe, many sport entities must adhere to a set of standards; for example, in the UK, venue operators must be in compliance with the safety criteria set forth by the *Guide to Safety at Sports Grounds* (also known as the Green Guide) in order to be open to the general public. Previous research also presented protective security measures for sport entities to consider implementing in the following key areas (Hall et al., 2012: 90).

Physical security

- Security zones and perimeters established including countermeasures for vehicle borne improvised explosives devices (VBIEDs).
- Uniformed law enforcement presence prior, during, and after the event.
- Secure buildings surrounding the stadium.
- Secure all heating ventilating and air conditioning, mechanical, gas, fuel and drainage systems.

Technical security

- Utility areas to be alarmed and contain secure access points.
- Adequate closed circuit television and monitoring room at the stadium.
- Adequate facility lighting.
- Interoperable communications with back-up systems in place and tested.
- Cyber security to prevent computer intrusion.
- Utilize telephone trap and trace.

Access control

- Public access through designated checkpoints, including searches for prohibited items.
- Media, VIPs, concessions, game day personnel and teams are searched.
- Tickets electronically scanned.
- Law enforcement present at each entry point.
- Scheduled secure delivery times for vendors.
- Lock down stadium prior to event.
- Background checks required for all game day staff.
- Issue photo credentials to all game day staff.

Emergency management

- Develop an Emergency Action Plan with annexes for emergency response, evacuation and business continuity.
- Establish primary and secondary command posts.
- Establish mutual aid agreements with local, state and federal emergency response agencies.
- Conduct briefing and debriefing game management meetings.
- Conduct a risk assessment that includes the identification of critical assets, threats, vulnerabilities and consequence reduction proposals.
- Include relative intelligence in periodic threat assessments.

Training and exercises

- Security and game day staff are provided by licensed and certified providers.
- Conduct routine emergency response evacuation exercises.
- Train all game day staff relative to their specific job responsibilities.
- Train all game day staff in security awareness and evacuation procedures.

Training techniques and exercises

Once safety and security plans, policies and procedures have been developed, key staff and facility personnel responsible for implementation should be trained and tested. The three primary levels of staff training include the CG (multiagency team), supervisors and event staff (i.e. ticket takers, ushers, checkers, parking attendants). Training techniques may include seminars/workshops, practice drills, pre-post event briefings and providing hand-held cards for event staff containing information pertinent to emergencies and specific roles and responsibilities (Hall et al., 2012). It is also necessary to include external public agencies (i.e. police, fire, public health, media relations and local hospitals) in training sessions as they will play a significant role in emergency response operations.

The CG should conduct exercises to test plans and promote awareness of roles, responsibilities and position assignment during an incident scenario: "An exercise is a focused practice activity that places the participants in a simulated situation requiring them to function in the capacity that would be expected of them in a real event" (FEMA, 2008: 2). Exercises improve readiness by evaluating operational capabilities: specifically, these help venue managers to (1) clarify roles and responsibilities; (2) improve interagency coordination and communication; (3) reveal resource gaps; (4) develop individual performance; and (5) identify opportunities for improvement (FEMA, 2009).

The US Department of Homeland Security Exercise and Evaluation Program (HSEEP) promotes seven different types of exercises, categorized as either discussion-based or operations-based. *Discussion-based* exercises familiarize participants with current plans and policies, and may be used to develop new plans, policies and procedures. Discussion-based exercises include seminars, workshops, table-top exercises or game simulations. *Operations-based* exercises are more complex than discussion-based exercises. Operation-based exercises validate plans and policies, clarify roles and responsibilities, and identify resource gaps in security operations and capabilities. Operations-based exercises normally involve the deployment of resources and personnel: these include drills, functional exercises and full-scale exercises (HSEEP, 2007).

Crisis communications

Sport organizations must be able to manage communications both during an incident and post-incident. The organization's response with factual communication to its stakeholders and public is critical, as their initial response and subsequent communications will be scrutinized (Crisis and Emergency Risk Communication, 2002). Crisis communication planning is important for the following reasons: (1) adherence to industry best practices promotes a safe environment; (2) planning, training and implementation of a crisis communication plan can reduce potential damage and loss; (3) documentation of a crisis communication plan minimizes liability to the facility, owners and operators; and (4) good planning practices minimize negative media exposure and enhance the image of the venue (Center for Venue Management Studies, 2002).

A sport event crisis, either intentional or unintentional, requires an effective communication plan. There is no one best way to reach everyone in a venue during a crisis. However, sport marketers should work closely with the CG to communicate a consistent and clear message to spectators, players and staff (Sport Event Risk Management, 2010). This ultimately minimizes any panic or chaos that may result in further injury or harm. Emergency communications will include pre-event messaging circulated throughout the season before every game, and emergency messaging delivered during an incident via the public announcement systems. Pre-event messaging can be delivered on the back of tickets, inside game day programs and media guides, through public service announcements, and on message boards and Jumbotrons. The latter can be used to deliver public address announcements with the help of coaches or athletes featured in a video safety message before game time and during halftime promotions. No matter what the modality, instructions need to be clear, concise, accurate and actionable (Sport Event Evacuation Training and Exercise, 2011: 95):

> *Clear:* Messages need to be clear of distortion and ambiguity and clearly communicated, visually and aurally. This will limit spectator confusion and maintain trust during the incident. If spectators do not trust the message, they will not act on the direction.
>
> *Concise:* Messages need to be concise so they can be quickly delivered and easily understood. A format of 3–9–27, three main ideas, nine words each, 27 words total, is a useful guideline. Messages need to be repeated until new information requires the delivery of updated messages.
>
> *Accurate:* Messages need to be accurate in order to build and maintain spectator trust. Spectators need to know what is happening so they can trust the directions they are provided with.
>
> *Actionable:* Messages need to inform spectators what to do. There needs to be an action piece that provides them direction.

Emergency information is vitally important and can mean the difference between life and death, or the calm reassurance that response and recovery efforts are underway. Unfortunately, people find it difficult to hear messages during an emergency due to stress or the change of routine (Communicating in an Emergency, 2005). An example of an incident and venue announcement following the above guidelines is presented below (Hall et al., 2012).

A bomb threat is received at a sport venue, and local law enforcement deem the threat credible. A search ensues within the venue to locate a suspicious package. Within 10 minutes a backpack containing explosive devices is located. Management decides to conduct a full evacuation of the venue. The marketing team releases the following public address announcement in coordination with law enforcement and emergency management:

> Ladies and gentlemen, may I have your attention: Officials have chosen to suspend play on the field and are implementing a full evacuation of the stadium. Please remain calm and exit the venue as directed by officers and venue staff.

The announcement is clear, concise and does not panic the fans by offering explicit directions to exit the venue. Identifying a problem to the public through an announcement could potentially cause mass chaos or hysteria, which may lead to further injury or harm. The wrong instructions can cost lives; for example, overcrowding and a lack of communication between police authorities and gate attendants resulted in 97 deaths during the 1989 Hillsborough Football Disaster. This incident was a pivotal moment in the UK's governance of sports. The resulting action mandated safety legislation requiring all major sport venues to adhere to a set of safety criteria in order to be operationally accepted and open to the public (Schwarz et al., 2010).

The CG must develop a notification sequence that ensures event staff involved with managing the movement of patrons are in position before the announcement is made to spectators. Special consideration should be given to the notification of game day officials so they can stop play, and athletes and staff can be escorted from the playing area. This can be accomplished via public address announcements and on-field verbal commands from event staff. Typically, spectators will not leave a venue while athletes are still in view. Athletes and team officials leaving the playing area provide a visual cue that supports the message being sent to spectators (Sport Event Evacuation Training and Exercise, 2011).

The communication plan needs to provide multiple methods for delivering emergency messages by taking advantage of the venue's public address system, display boards and stadium TV screens. The purpose for doing so is to cut down reaction time and reduce confusion during an incident and to mitigate legal liability (Sport Event Evacuation Training and Exercise, 2011). Today's technology affords new vehicles for communicating via cell phones, text messaging and social media outlets. Social media such as Twitter, YouTube and Facebook are essential tools for crisis communication and can be used to monitor what is being said about a program/event, anticipate potential crises and communicate to stakeholders during a crisis (Ulmer et al., 2011).

The NFL has implemented a text messaging system that allows fans to report drunk or disorderly fans without confronting them. Fans send a text message to the stadium's command center for security to respond. The system enables teams to compile databases of complaints, how those complaints were resolved and identify areas in a stadium where complaints are frequent (Hall et al., 2012). Furthermore, with upgraded Wi-Fi and cellular networks in venues, management will be able to serve fan bases with new, targeted experiences. Venue-specific apps can be downloaded by fans to their personal devices. This will enable facility operators to stream video and data directly to each fan's device. Communication opportunities that become possible using a closed-venue app include video streaming on program content; direct access to interact with the team and sponsor marketing objectives; facility navigation for way-finding and egress; and direct emergency communication messaging to fans by operations staff (Abelson, 2011).

Ideally, messages should be delivered in synchronized video, text and audio form. Most facilities these days employ some form of video coverage that should be a valuable source for situational awareness. The methods identified for delivering messages need to be regularly tested before an incident occurs. A critical concern during testing is determining if selected methods have alternative power sources. The communication plan should identify means for delivering messages without use of the technology available in the venue. Efficient communication plans take into account system failures and provide for human intervention, such as verbal commands (Sport Event Evacuation Training and Exercise, 2011).

Most venues built today include a command center with communication capabilities for the CG to monitor activities inside and outside the venue perimeter. Command center capabilities include coordinating internal responses to minor incidents; referring support requests to external agencies for major incidents; managing all event communications; recording venue incidents; and directing/managing venue evacuations (Hall et al., 2012). Sport organizations should have an interoperable communication system in place with access to the venue's command center. An interoperable communication system requires certain equipment such as hand-held portable multi-channeled radios, cell phones and/or pagers (Protective Measures Guide for U.S. Sports Leagues, 2008). All responding agencies must be able to communicate with each other on the same network to coordinate response efforts.

CONCLUSION

Sport organizations and their CEOs may face legal or moral/ethical culpability for a crisis event and inevitably the public will judge an organization's response to a crisis. It is imperative for the sport entity to protect their brand reputation and minimize negative public perception as presented through the media. Therefore sport organizations must identify a CG, conduct a venue risk assessment, develop plans and policies, and train and exercise staff on roles and responsibilities. Furthermore, a well-developed crisis communication system with consideration for the message delivery method and the intended audience must be established.

REFERENCES

Abelson, D. (2011). Can teams, venues meet fans' technology expectations? *Street & Smith's Sports Business Journal,* 5 September.

Ammon, R., Southall, R. & Nagel, M. (2010). *Sport Facility Management: Organizing Events and Mitigating Risks*. Morgantown, WV: Fitness Information Technology

Biringer, B.E., Matalucci, R.V. & O'Connor, S.L. (2007). *Security Risk Assessment and Management*. Hoboken, NJ: Wiley.

Broder, J.F. (2006). *Risk Analysis and the Security Survey* (3rd edn). Oxford: Butterworth-Heinemann.

Center for Venue Management Studies (2002). *Best Practices Planning Guide Emergency Preparedness*. International Association of Assembly Managers (IAAM) Safety and Security Task Force.

Communicating in an Emergency (2005). In *Basic Communication Skills: Independent Study*. Emergency Management Institute, Federal Emergency Management Agency (FEMA).

Crisis and Emergency Risk Communication (2002, October). Centers for Disease Control and Prevention.

Culf, A. (2006, 19 January). The six-billion dollar sports security industry. *Guardian*. Retrieved from www.guardian.co.uk/sport/2006/jan/19/football. newsstory.

Federal Emergency Management Agency (FEMA) (2008). Introduction to Exercise Design. In *Exercise Design: IS-139*. Washington, DC: Emergency Management Institute, FEMA.

Federal Emergency Management Agency (FEMA) (2009). Exercise Basics. In *An Introduction to Exercises: IS-120.A*. Washington, DC: Emergency Management Institute, FEMA.

Hall, S., Marciani, Cooper, W.E. & Rolen, R. (2007). Introducing a risk assessment model for sport venues. *The Sport Journal*, *10*(2), 1–6.

Hall, S., Cooper, W.E., Marciani, L. & McGee, J.A. (2012). *Security Management for Sports and Special Events—An Interagency Approach*. Champaign, IL: Human Kinetics.

HSEEP (2007) *Homeland Security Exercise and Evaluation Program*. The US Department of Homeland Security, Washington, DC.

Office of Intelligence and Analysis (2009, 26 January). *Threats to College Sports and Entertainment Venues and Surrounding Areas*. US Department of Homeland Security, Washington, DC.

Protective Measures Guide for US Sports Leagues (2008). Department of Homeland Security, Washington, DC.

Schwarz, E.C., Hall, S. & Shibli, S. (2010). *Sport Facility Operations Management: A Global Perspective*. Oxford: Butterworth-Heinemann.

Sport Event Evacuation Training and Exercise (2011, March). The US Department of Homeland Security, Washington, DC.

Sport Event Risk Management (2010, April). The US Department of Homeland Security, Washington, DC.

Stevens, A. (2007). *Sports Security and Safety: Evolving Strategies for a Changing World*. London: Sport Business Group.

Ulmer, R.R., Sellnow, T.L & Seeger, M.W. (2001). *Effective Crisis Communications: Moving from Crisis to Opportunity*. Thousand Oaks, CA: Sage.

USEFUL WEBSITES

www.ncs4.com
www.icss.org
www.iavm.org
www.dhs.gov

29

SEXUALITY: HOMOHYSTERIA AND COMING OUT IN SPORT

RYAN SCOATS AND ERIC ANDERSON

> Gay Kentucky basketball player comes out at a game, gets chased by opposing team.
>
> (*Outsports*, 1 April 2015)
>
> Brittney Griner: Growing up, I always got 'She's a man'.
>
> (NPR, 8 April 2014)
>
> Justin Collins: I was focused on: It's time. I was ready, and I was tired of waiting for some other guy who was still active in sports to do it.
>
> (*New York Times*, 27 June 2014)

LEARNING OUTCOMES

Upon completion of this chapter, students will be able to:

- Understand the origins of homophobia in men and women's sport.

- Apply homohysteric theory to explain cultural attitudes towards homosexuality.

- Understand the different cultural climate for high level male and female athletes coming out in sport.

- Discuss how managers of sport are affected by and can influence homohysteria in sport.

INTRODUCTION

Sport has been heralded as an important institution for men in western societies because it mirrored an esteemed form of masculinity brought on by twentieth-century industrialisation. Its principal purpose has been to socialise men into conservative sexual values: sexism, physical violence, compulsory heterosexuality, the normalisation of aggression, homophobia and femphobia (Anderson, 2009).

The desire for men to distance themselves from femininity is based upon the patriarchal notion that masculinity is superior to femininity (Crosset, 1990), and the belief that any association with femininity will decrease one's masculinity (Bird, 1996). If men desire to be seen as masculine in other men's eyes, they must therefore distance themselves from feminin-ity. This also led to a situation where, for decades, women were excluded from sport in the twentieth century. Their presence was thought to unsettle the legitimacy of the myth regarding men's natural athleticism and women's supposed frailty (Burton-Nelson, 1994).

As well as adhering to the culturally generated norms of masculinity, men must also establish their own heterosexuality (Adams et al., 2010) if they are to be esteemed in the eyes of other men. Because homosexuality is mostly invisible, men have done this by policing the behaviours of other men, in a king-of-the-hill style competition, where suspected homosexual males were relegated down-hill (Anderson, 2005). While this jockeying often included physical domination, homophobic discourse has been the primary weapon to regulate the behaviours of teammates, question their heterosexuality and steer them away from perceived feminine behaviours (Anderson, 2009; Plummer, 2006). This homophobia helps defend one-self against homosexual suspicion whilst ensuring others adhere to the endorsed form of masculinity within the institution of sport. In women's sport it is the opposite. Distancing oneself from masculinity guards against homosexual accusations (Anderson and Bullingham, 2013; Griffin, 1998; Shire et al., 2000).

This chapter first outlines the cultural landscape that allowed for con-temporary norms of masculinity to take hold, before outlining Anderson's (2009) theory of homohysteria. This theory is then used to explain atti-tudes towards homosexuality, from the 1980s until the present day, and how this relates to **media** reaction to basketball player Jason Collin's coming out. Homohysteria is then applied to women in sport, and the relative quietness surrounding basketball player Brittney Griner's coming out.

NBA, Jason Collins

In 2013, professional National Basketball Association (NBA) player Jason Collins became the first athlete within the four most popular American major professional sports leagues (National Football League, NFL; NBA, Major League Baseball, MLB; and National Hockey League, NHL) to come out as gay and still desire to continue his sporting career. Since that time, he has received support and praise from (but not limited to) President Barack Obama, former President Bill Clinton, fellow NBA player and Olympic gold medalist Kobe Bryant, and multinational sports corporation Nike.

TOOLS FOR ANALYSIS

Masculinity in the nineteenth and twentieth century

A rapid shifting away from an agrarian economy to an industrial one in the latter half of the nineteenth and early part of the twentieth century led to a situation where a large proportion of the population was now living in cities. This industrial revolution had profound implications for society, including the awareness of homosexuality. Freud observed that the urbanisation of western cultures led to an increase in same-sex behaviours, ascribing this to the separation of children from their male role models. With men away working in the factories, the role of children's socialisation fell upon women (Hartmann, 1976). Thus, Freud (1905: 146) wrote, '… the presence of both parents plays an important part. The absence of a strong father in childhood not infrequently favors the occurrence of inversion.'

In other words, Freud positioned sexuality as being acquired rather than innate. He placed particular importance on a dominant mother and the absence of a father figure in engendering homosexuality (what he called 'inversion') amongst boys. Freud's theories, along with an increased public awareness of homosexuality, led to a moral panic regarding masculine socialisation: one that demanded a solution. It was this fear of feminisation amongst boys within society that helped legitimate sport as a domain by and for men. This epoch should thus be considered a time in history of increasing homohysteria (Anderson, 2009).

Homohysteria

Homohysteria is a theoretical tool for examining the societal zeitgeist towards homosexuality within an historical frame. It is understood as the cultural fear of being homosexualised (McCormack, 2011), i.e. labelled homosexual by both society, and/or those in close proximity to you for the wrongdoing of gender. In the formation of a homohysteric society three factors need to align with each other: (1) a broad cultural understanding that homosexuality exists throughout society as a static sexual orientation; (2) a cultural zeitgeist of homophobia; (3) the condemnation of those who transcend what are considered 'traditional gender roles', i.e. men who adopt femininity, or women who adopt masculinity, as these practices are associated with homosexuality. Anderson's (2009) theory also describes three stages of homohysteria that a society or culture may potentially move through, with these being homosexual erasure, homohysteria and inclusivity.

In a culture of homosexual erasure, homophobia is so high that citizens do not accept that homosexuality is pervasive within their society. Demonstrating this, Anderson argues that much of the Islamic world, as well as parts of Africa, view homosexuality as 'only' a western problem (Frank et al., 2010). Dlamini (2006: 135) suggests that it was colonialists that introduced the denial and intolerance of homosexuality into Africa, and 'Only when native people began to forget that same-sex patterns were ever part of their culture did homosexuality become truly stigmatized.' Using another example, in 2007 Iranian president Mahmoud Ahmadinejad stated '… in Iran we don't have homosexuals like in your country' (cited in Anderson, 2009: 86).

Anderson suggests that extremely high levels of homophobia in Iran mean that people are more likely to stay in the closet, helping to give the perception that homosexuals don't exist within their society and alleviate suspicions that someone they know could be homosexual (because it's statistically unlikely). This culture-wide denial that homosexuals exist in significant numbers leads to a situation where men have less need to distance themselves from homosexual suspicion, and therefore can engage in physical, same-sex behaviours such as hand-holding or kissing on the cheek. However, when this extreme homophobia combines with the realisation that anyone could be homosexual, this paves the way for a shift towards a homohysteric culture.

Homohysteria in the 1980s

During the 1980s, both Britain and the USA reached their peak of homohysteria. During this epoch, the increased visibility and growing normality of homosexuality combined with extreme homophobia. This led to cultures heavily steeped in homohysteria. Within the USA, increasingly loud Christian fundamentalists aimed to demonise homosexuality (Anderson, 2011a), a demonising which managed to gain cultural impact through the increased visibility of HIV/AIDS and the large percentage of even gender-typical men who acquired it through same-sex sex. AIDS brought with it an elevated visability of homosexuality, and also bringing the cultural realisation that it permeated American culture (Anderson, 2009).

It is within this epoch of high homohysteria that men needed to re-establish themselves as heterosexual by distancing themselves from homosexuality, and by extension, femininity. Similar to the time of the industrial revolution, and the utilisation of sport to instill masculinity, Anderson argues that sport (particularly in the years 1983–1993) served as a vessel by which men could demonstrate their *heteromasculinity* (Pronger, 1990). Anderson (2009) suggests that this explicit display of masculinity is needed because sexual orientation, unlike race or gender, is not immediately visable. Furthermore, because one's 'performance' of masculinity (West and Zimmerman, 1987) can never be a permanently achieved, but instead needs constant re-establishment (Anderson, 2009), continual participation in sport could be used as a means to continually prove one's masculinity. Within this context, men needed to align their gendered behaviours with acceptable perceptions of masculinity, and masculinity essentially 'became homophobia' (Kimmel, 1994).

Overt homophobia helped men to defend accusations of homosexuality. Kimmel wrote, 'The fear – sometimes conscious, sometimes not – that others might perceive us as homosexual propels men to enact all manner of exaggerated masculine behaviors and attitudes to make sure that no one could possibly get the wrong idea about us' (Kimmel, 1994: 133).

Inclusivity

Homohysteria, however, cannot exist within a society that is no longer homophobic. In 1987, the British Social Attitudes Survey (BSA) found that 66% of respondents viewed sexual relations between two same-sex adults to be always wrong. The equivalent survey in the USA, the General Social Survey (GSS), found the response to the same question in the same year to be 75%. Comparing with data from 2010, these numbers have now fallen to 20% and 43.5%, respectively. These large-scale data, combined with a growing body of research, suggest that both Britain and the USA (and western culture in general), has/is moving towards an era of post-homohysteria in many areas of society. Nowhere is this more true than among those born after 1990.

With this shift in attitudes within western society, we have seen men now adopting more 'inclusive' behaviours (Anderson, 2009), because they no longer feel the need to distance themselves from homosexuality/femininity. If they do not fear being culturally homosexualised, this allows for their gendered behaviours to be drastically different (McCormack, 2012). Evidencing this, McCormack (2012) found boys in three different further education settings able to demonstrate pro-gay attitudes and homosocial tactility without fear of retribution. Anderson et al.'s (2011) work also looked at sport team initiation rituals within the UK where behaviours were monitored over a seven-year period. During the beginning of this period, low level, same-sex sexual behaviours were used as punishments for new recruits. But as time passed, these behaviours lost their stigmatising factor and capacity to punish, and eventually lost utility as a hazing tool. Towards the end of the study, men were voluntarily kissing as a form of homosocial bonding, rather than a penalty. Elsewhere, Adams (2011) found university soccer players able to espouse gay friendly attitudes, as well as partake in once homosexualised activities (like being concerned about their grooming) without a homosexualising judgement.

Jason Collins

Whilst homohysteria does not necessarily diminish uniformly across all areas of society – meaning that it will still exist within homophobic groups – this cultural shift into post-homohysteria has been far enough to facilitate Jason Collins's confidence in coming out as gay. He stated, 'I'm glad I'm coming out in 2013 rather than 2003. The climate has shifted; public opinion has shifted. And yet we still have so much farther to go' (Collins and Lidz, 2013: 3). This reflection of how culture has shifted can be illustrated with the case of Justin Fashanu, who in 1990 became the first gay professional footballer to come out (Cashmore and Cleland, 2011). The resulting fallout was disastrous, with abuse coming from his manager, fans, fellow players and even members of his own family. Fashanu spent the remainder of his career playing in minor leagues outside of England (Cashmore and Cleland, 2011) and, following his suicide in 1998, the coroner argued that he had been overcome by the extent of the discrimination he suffered.

However, since Fashanu's coming out in the 1990s there have been other athletes who have done so and continued to play successfully. In Britain these have also been from sports of comparable popularity to America's 'big four' such as cricket (Stephen Davies) and rugby (Gareth Thomas). But whilst America has seen athletes come out and continue to play such as Robbie Rogers (soccer), Patrick Jeffery (diving) or Rudy Galindo (figure skating), none has been from the most revered of sports, the 'big four'.

Collins was considered different from many previous male athletes who had come out of the closet in America, in that he comes from one of the big four American sports and had the desire to continue playing, rather than coming out after retirement, and therefore potentially leaving himself open to harassment both on and off the court (Anderson, 2002), as well as threats to his career. The big four exemplify and embody what many consider to be some of the key tenants of masculinity such as physicality (Luciano, 2007), violence (Burstyn, 2000) and domination over others (Sabo and Runfola, 1980), suggesting that those within these sports were least likely to be considered as potentially homosexual. But the illusion that sport 'guards' against homosexuality by instilling masculinity effectively diminishes when it is seen that some of those at the highest levels, in the most revered sports, are in fact gay.

ACTION LEARNING

- In what ways as a sports manager/coach can you help foster an environment allowing for players/co-workers to come out of the closet?
- How might a sports manager/coach with very 'traditional' views on masculinity impact on all areas of sports team or organization?
- What role does sport **governance** play in managing these issues?

Brittney Griner

Nearly two weeks before Jason Collins came out, Brittney Griner, the number one draft pick for the Women's National Basketball Association (WNBA), also came out in an interview with the *Sports Illustrated* online website, SI.com. Prior to entering the WNBA, Griner played college basketball for Baylor University in Waco, Texas; for the US national team in Europe; and amassed an all-time National Collegiate Athletics Association (NCAA) record of 748 blocks across her career; as well as a host of other awards and records (see Wikipedia for the full list). It was at her time at Baylor that, according to an interview with *ESPN* the magazine and espnW, that Griner was encouraged not to be open about her sexuality. She stated that, 'The coaches thought that if it seemed like they condoned it, people wouldn't let their kids come play for Baylor', and 'It was more of a unwritten law [to not discuss your sexuality] … it was just kind of, like, one of those things, you know, just don't do it' (ESPNgo.com).

TOOLS FOR ANALYSIS

Homohysteria in women's sport

As team sports, particularly those involving heavy contact, can be thought of as 'the last bastion of male domination' (Burton-Nelson, 1995: 6), this has generated problems for a competitive sport with physical contact, women manage to disrupt traditional gender boundaries. Concerning female involvement in rugby, Wright and Clarke (1999: 299) proposed that it could 'be expected to challenge fundamentally what it means to be a male and female'. If women are able to participate in predominantly male team sports, then this upsets the cultural notions of masculinity associated with sport; or conversely, encourages society to question women's involvement, and their femininity.

Hargreaves (1994: 171) argued that women participating in male-dominated sports were vulnerable to 'the greatest criticism and exposure to ridicule'. Exemplifying the position many women in sport find themselves in, Lenskyj (1986: 95) stated that, 'femininity and heterosexuality [were] seen as incompatible with sporting excellence: either sport made women masculine or sportswomen were masculine from the outset'. Evidencing this perceived inconsistency between women in sport and their femininity/heterosexuality, Cox and Thompson (2001) found that female footballers were presumed lesbian because of their decision to participate in a traditionally male sport.

In order to distance themselves from lesbian suspicion and reduce the 'controversy' over their participation, Griffin (1998) argues that women have been shown to promote heterosexual identities, as well as using overt homophobic discourse to demonstrate their own heterosexuality. Demonstrating this discourse, Shire et al. (2000: 49) described the behaviours of heterosexual members within a female hockey team, writing, 'They joked about the lesbian women in order to reinforce their heterosexuality to others.' Anderson and Bullingham (2013) also find more hostile examples of homophobia ranging from verbal abuse to destruction of property and assault.

The promotion of particularly feminine identities has allowed women playing traditionally male sports to do so with reduced lesbian suspicion; similar to how men in sport were able to accrue masculine capital in one domain that allowed them to transgress gender expectations in another (Anderson, 2005; DeVisser and Smith, 2007). Griffin (1998: 68) writes that 'femininity has become a code word for heterosexuality', comparable to Kimmel (1994) describing masculinity as heterosexuality for males. Accordingly, women were forced to adopt hyper-feminine identities in order to gain societal support for their participation in sport (Lenskyj, 2003). This attempted denial and silencing of lesbians in sport permits discrimination and stereotypes of lesbianism to go unchecked (Krane and Barber, 2003).

This erasure of lesbianism via the promotion of hetero-femininity has been termed the 'apologetic', and it occurs because women are participating in a male domain. Felshin (1974: 36) contends that 'because women cannot be excluded from sport and have chosen not to reject sport, apologetics develop to account for their sport involvement in the face of its social unacceptability'. The apologetic can take forms such the formation and adherence to a traditional feminine identity, trying to cultivate a heterosexual image, or even literal apologies for aggressive behaviours on the pitch (Davis-Delano et al., 2009; Ezzell, 2009). Looking at how the apologetic still manifests itself in contemporary female sport suggests that while homohysteria has reduced within male sport, the same may not necessarily be true for women (Anderson and Bullingham, 2013).

Brittney Griner

With homohysteria still present in female sports, this raises questions as to why a woman coming out in sport is 'less newsworthy' than a man who does the same? When Jason Collins, who has frequently been described as an average basketball player (see Buzinski, 2013; Magary, 2013; Megdal, 2013; Towel, 2013), came out it was reported as a 'ground-breaking story sending shockwaves through the sports world' (ABC News, 2013), but when Brittney Griner, the top pick for the WNBA draft, came out, there was considerably less fanfare. As Sam Borden of the *New York Times* stated, 'Female star comes out as gay, and the sports world shrugs' (Borden, 2013). This is likely because the idea of a lesbian in sport may be considered predictable as it aligns with gendered assumptions about women in sport.

When Griner came out as a lesbian in an interview, this was done so in the past tense, suggesting that it was knowledge previously known to all:

> I wouldn't say I was hiding or anything like that. I've always been open about who I am and my sexuality. So, it wasn't hard at all. If I can show that I'm out and I'm fine and everything's OK, then hopefully the younger generation will definitely feel the same way. (ESPN.go.com, 2013)

This example demonstrates an internalised understanding by Griner that women in sport are linked with masculinity (Lenskyj, 1986) and that she is 'obviously' lesbian (Cox and Thompson, 2001). Additionally, because Griner has often being described as a 'masculine' player (curvemag.com, 2010), and has a propensity not to perform the apologetic, this has likely led to assumptions from others that she is a lesbian; for example, when Notre Dame coach Muffet McGraw stated 'I think she's one of a kind. I think she's like a guy playing with women', Griner responded 'I take it as a compliment' (Larimore, 2012).

Furthermore, unlike Collins, she is not the first athlete actively playing in her sport to come out: Michele Van Gorp (2004), Sheryl Swoopes (2005), and Seimone Augustus (2012) all preceded her. With other basketball players already out of the closet, coupled with the expectation of unfeminine women in sports to be lesbian (Griffin, 1998), and sport media's 'dominant ideology which claims that male sport is more important and more interesting than female sport' (Müller, 1999: 126), these factors may have rendered this story seemingly inconsequential compared to Jason Collins, at least in the eyes of sport journalists. Whilst Collin's actions defied traditional assumptions about men in sport, Griner's simply upheld the female stereotype.

ACTION LEARNING

- How might the apologetic be detrimental to a sports team or organisation?

- How can a sports manager/coach be supportive of lesbian players/co-workers within a team or organisation?

CONCLUSION

Anderson (2009) has contended that during the 1980s men's sport reached its apex of homohysteria. During this time men used sport and homophobia to reinforce their masculine capital and guard against accusations of homosexuality. Drawing on both qualitative and quantitative research, he argues that homohysteria is reducing, and we are moving into a post-homohysteric period within men's sport (Anderson, 2009). Here, men are not afraid to associate with femininity as it no longer homosexualises them.

However, the same conclusions cannot be drawn from women's sport. Until we see further widespread reduction in female homohysteria, it is likely that women who refuse to perform the feminine apologetic will continue to be assumed lesbian. This enduring situation may suggest cultural differences between men and women's sports. Finally, Anderson (2005) argues that whilst the presence of a gay athlete on a male team does not bring into question the sexuality of his teammates, a lesbian doing the same does.

REFERENCES

ABC News (2013). Gay in the NBA: Jason Collins comes out. [Video Online] Available at: http://abcnews.go.com/US/video/jason-collins-comes-out-as-gay-in-the-nba-19066550 [Accessed 16 October 2013].

Adams, A. (2011). 'Josh wears pink cleats': Inclusive masculinity on the soccer field. *Journal of Homosexuality*, 58(5), pp. 579–596.

Adams, A., Anderson, E. & McCormack, M. (2010). Establishing and challenging masculinity: the influence of gendered discourses in organized sport. *Journal of Language and Social Psychology*, 29, pp. 278–300.

Anderson, E. (2002). Openly gay athletes: contesting hegemonic masculinity in a homophobic environment. *Gender and Society*, 16, pp. 860–877.

Anderson, E. (2005). *In the Game: Gay Athletes and the Cult of Masculinity*. Albany, NY: State University of New York Press.

Anderson, E. (2009). *Inclusive Masculinity: the Changing Nature of Masculinities*. London: Routledge.

Anderson, E. (2011a). The rise and fall of Western homohysteria. *Journal of Feminist Scholarship*, 1(1), pp. 80–94.

Anderson, E. (2011b). Updating the outcome: gay athletes, straight teams, and coming out in educationally based sport teams. *Gender and Society*, 25, pp. 250–268.

Anderson, E. & Bullingham, R. (2013). Openly lesbian team sport athletes in an era of decreasing homohysteria. *International Review for the Sociology of Sport*, 50(6), pp. 647–660.

Anderson, E., McCormack, M. & Lee, H. (2011). Male team sport hazing initiations in a culture of decreasing homohysteria. *Journal of Adolescent Research*, 20, pp. 1–22.

BBC Sport (2014). Casey Stoney: England captain reveals her sexuality for first time. [Online] Available at: www.bbc.co.uk/sport/0/football/26084748 [Accessed 13 April 2015].

Bird, S.R. (1996). Welcome to the men's club: homosociality and the maintenance of hegemonic masculinity. *Gender and Society*, 10, pp. 120–132.

Borden, S. (2013). Female star comes out as gay, and sports world shrugs. [Online] Available at: www.nytimes.com/2013/04/19/sports/ncaabasketball/brittney-griner-comes-out-and-sports-world-shrugs.html?_r=0&adxnnl=1&adxnnlx=1381928348-zHaslZH2+GrAqg8uOHb1Zg [Accessed 16 October 2013].

Burstyn, V. (2000). *The Rites of Men: Manhood, Politics, and the Culture of Sport*. Toronto: University of Toronto Press.

Burton-Nelson, M. (1995). *The Stronger Women Get the More Men Love Football: Sexism and the American Culture of Sports*. New York: Avon Books.

Buzinski, J. (2013). Jason Collins on the sidelines as NBA camps open and the reasons why are varied. [Online] Available at: www.outsports.com/2013/10/2/4796698/jason-collins-gay-nba-training-camps [Accessed 16 October 2013].

Cashmore, E. & Cleland, J. (2011). Glasswing butterflies: gay professional footballers and their culture. *Journal of Sport and Social Issues*, 20(10), pp. 1–17.

Collins, J. & Lidz, F. (2013). Why NBA center Jason Collins is coming out now. [Online] Available at: http://sportsillustrated.cnn.com/magazine/news/20130429/jason-collins-gay-nba-player/#ixzz2fEnwpGIe [Accessed 16 October 2013].

Cox, B. & Thompson, S. (2001). Facing the bogey: women, football and sexuality. *Football Studies*, 4, pp. 7–24.

Crosset, T. (1990). Masculinity, sexuality, and the development of early modern sport. In M. Messner & D. Sabo (eds), *Sport, Men, and the Gender Order: Critical Feminist Perspectives*. Leeds: Human Kinetics, pp. 45–54.

Curvemag.com. (2010). Brittney Griner may push gender boundaries, but not on purpose – playing for our team-web articles 2010. [Online] Available at: www.curvemag.com/Blogs/Playing-for-Our-Team/Web-Articles-2010/Brittney-Griner-May-Push-Gender-Boundaries-But-Not-on-Purpose/ [Accessed 16 October 2013].

Davis-Delano, L., Pollock, A. & Ellsworth Vose, J. (2009). Apologetic behavior among female athletes. *International Review for the Sociology of Sport*, 2–3, pp. 131–150.

De Visser, R.O. & Smith, J.A. (2007). Alcohol consumption and masculine identity among young men. *Psychology and Health*, 22(5), pp. 595–614.

Dlamini, B. (2006). Homosexuality in the African context. *Agenda: Empowering Women for Gender Equity*, 20(67), pp. 128–136.

ESPN.go.com (2013). Griner: No talking sexuality at Baylor. [Online] Available at: http://espn.go.com/wnba/story/_/id/9289080/brittney-griner-says-baylor-coach-kim-mulkey-told-players-keep-quiet-sexuality [Accessed 16 October 2013].

Ezzell, M.B. (2009). 'Barbie dolls' on the pitch: identity work, defensive othering, and inequality in women's rugby. *Social Problems*, 56, pp. 111–131.

Felshin, J. (1974). The triple option … for women in sport. *Quest*, 21, pp. 36–40.

Frank, D.J., Camp, B.J. & Boutcher, S.A. (2010). Worldwide trends in the criminal regulation of sex, 1945 to 2005. *American Sociological Review*, 75, pp. 867–893.

Freud, S. (1905). Three essays on the theory of sexuality. *Complete Psychological Works* (vol. 7). London: Hogarth.

Griffin, P. (1998). *Strong Women, Deep Closets.* Leeds: Human Kinetics.

Hargreaves, J.A. (1994). *Sporting Females.* London: Routledge.

Hartmann, H. (1976). Capitalism, patriarchy and job segregation. *Signs: Journal of Women in Culture and Society*, 1(3), pp. 137–169.

Kimmel, M. (1994). Masculinity as homophobia: fear, shame and silence in the construction of gender identity. In H. Brod & M. Kaufman (eds), *Theorizing Masculinities: Research on Men and Masculinities Series*. Thousand Oaks, CA: Sage , pp. 119–141.

Krane, V. & Barber, H. (2003). Lesbian experiences in sport: a social identity perspective. *Quest*, 55, pp. 328–346.

Larimore, R. (2012). Brittney Griner plays like a man. That doesn't make it OK to call her a man. [Online] Available at: www.slate.com/blogs/xx_factor/2012/04/04/brittney_griner_plays_like_a_man_that_doesn_t_make_it_ok_to_call_her_a_man_.html [Accessed 16 October 2013].

Lenskyj, H.J. (1986). *Out of Bounds: Women, Sport and Sexuality.* Ontario: The Women's Press.

Lenskyj, H.J. (2003). *Out on the Field: Women, Sport and Sexualities.* Toronto: Women's Press.

Luciano, L. (2007). Muscularity and masculinity in the United States: a historical overview. In J.K. Thompson & G. Cafri (eds), *The Muscular Ideal: Psychological, Social and Medical Perspectives*. Washington, DC: American Psychological Association, pp. 41–65.

Magary, D. (2013). Why does it matter if Jason Collins is a 'bad' pro basketball player? [Online] Available at: http://deadspin.com/why-does-it-matter-if-jason-collins-is-a-bad-pro-bask-484587396 [Accessed 16 October 2013].

McCormack, M. (2011). The Declining significance of homohysteria for male students in three sixth forms in the south of England. *British Educational Research Journal*, 37(2), pp. 337–353.

McCormack, M. (2012). *The Declining Significance of Homophobia: How Teenage boys are Redefining Masculinity and Heterosexuality*. New York: Oxford University Press.

Megdal, H. (2013). Jason Collins: average N.B.A. player, extraordinary potential acquisition. [Online] Available at: www.capitalnewyork.com/article/sports/2013/04/8529527/jason-collins-average-nba-player-extraordinary-potential-acquisition [Accessed 16 October 2013].

Müller, A. (1999). Women in sport and society. In. J. Riordan & A. Krüger (eds), *The International Politics of Sport in the 20th Century*. London: E & FN Spon, pp. 121–149.

Plummer, D. (2006). Sportophobia why do some men avoid sport? *Journal of Sport and Social Issues*, 30(2), pp. 122–137.

Pronger, B. (1990). *The Arena of Masculinity: Sports, Homosexuality, and the Meaning of Sex*. New York: St. Martin's Press.

Sabo, D.F. & Runfola, R. (1980). *Jocks: Sports and Male Identity*. Upper Saddle River, NJ: Prentice Hall.

Shire, J., Brackenridge, C. & Fuller, M. (2000). Changing positions: the sexual politics of a women's field hockey team 1986–1996. *Women in Sport and Physical Activity Journal*, 9, pp. 35–64.

Towle, A. (2013). Who will sign gay NBA player Jason Collins? [Online] Available at: www.towleroad.com/2013/07/who-will-sign-gay-nba-player-jason-collins.html [Accessed 16 October 2013].

Vaughan, B. (2013). The RG3 outtakes [Online]. Available at: www.gq.com/blogs/ the-feed/2013/08/rg3-gq-cover-story-interview-outtakes.html [Accessed 16 October 2013].

West, C. & Zimmerman, D. (1987). Doing gender. *Gender and Society*, 1, pp.125–151.

Wright, J. & Clarke, G. (1999). Sport, the media and construction of compulsory heterosexuality. *International Review for the Sociology of Sport*, 34, pp. 227–248.

USEFUL WEBSITES

www.ericandersonphd.com
www.glisa.org
www.gaygames.org
www.gaysport.info
www.outsports.com

30

FAN LOYALTY IN SPORT

JOERG KOENIGSTORFER

Loyal Knicks Fans May Deserve a Medal. But a Refund?
(*New York Times*, 21 January 2015)

When teams lose fans tackle fatty food.
(*New York Times*, 16 September 2013)

Which team has the most loyal fans? Science says it's the Dallas Cowboys.

(Yahoo, 16 August 2013)

LEARNING OUTCOMES

Upon completion of this chapter, students will be able to:

- Learn to define and conceptualise fan loyalty, name antecedents and consequences of fan loyalty.

- Relate fan loyalty to the concept of customer lifetime value from the perspective of different stakeholders.

- Appreciate the importance of the concept of loyalty to the management and marketing of sport.

INTRODUCTION

This chapter explains how fan loyalty develops in sports, what fan loyalty means, and what the consequences of loyalty are from the perspective of teams (or athletes), club or (athlete) management, sponsors and other consumers. It highlights key peculiarities in the customer relationship management of sporting organisations, showcasing two German football clubs (FC Bayern München and FC St. Pauli). The implications help sporting organisations generate a strong fan base that is loyal to the club despite the ups and downs in service delivery that are inherent with sports games. As the above media headlines indicate, understanding loyalty is an important and contemporary issue from the perspective of sports clubs. Managers of sports clubs may have to deal with one of the following questions: Why are sports fans loyal to certain teams (or athletes)? Why and when do sports fans stick to their favourite teams (or athletes) despite low sporting success, given that wins make fans happy and losses make them sad? And how do teams (or athletes) and other stakeholders profit from a loyal fan base? This chapter aims to provide answers to these questions by showcasing the loyalty of sports fans to two German football teams: FC Bayern München and FC St. Pauli.

Loyalty does not just mean that fans regularly follow the games of a particular team. Loyalty also means that fans form attitudes towards anything that matters to 'their' team. This includes the game experience (e.g. whether the team wins), the identity of the team (e.g. the values the team stands for), and the perception of rivals of the team (e.g. rival fans) – among many other factors. These formation processes are referred to as attitudinal loyalty.

The concept of attitudinal loyalty implies that fans build a relationship between themselves and the team. In this relationship fans are not always being entertained, but they do take an active role in supporting their team, similar to the role they have in a family or a partnership: 'it [fandom] is about duty, obligation, blood, sweat and tears' (Richardson and Turley, 2006: 178; Wann et al., 2001). In what follows next, I will describe how strong bonds between fans and teams develop and what the facets of fan loyalty are. Two Thinking Points will be presented to illustrate the practical relevance of fan loyalty.

THINKING POINT 30.1

FC Bayern München

FC Bayern München is the most successful football team in the history of the German Bundesliga. Attendance figures for their games (and thus the revenue from ticket sales) have been consistently high since the 1972/73 season, when the Olympic Stadium (with an original capacity of 80,000 spectators) became the venue for the team's home games. In 2006, the newly built Allianz Arena (with a capacity of 71,000 spectators) became their new home. It has been sold

FC Bayern München

Date founded:	27 February 1900		Achievements of the club:
Club members:	217,241		First division Bundesliga since 1965/66
Revenues:	€332.2 Million. (FC Bayern AG) €373.4 Million. (entire group)		22 Bundesliga championship titles since then (thereof 6 in the last 10 years)
Sponsorship profit:	€82.3 Million.		16 DFB National Cup titles
Player's value:	€483.7 Million. (in 2013)		Five Champions League titles (including pre-Champions League European Cup)
			Most successful club in Germany

Reference: 2012/13 season except players' value (as of beginning 2013/14 season)

FIGURE 30.1 *FC Bayern München: statistics*

out since its opening, and a large percentage of fans own season tickets.

Although the team has been playing in the most modern of arenas and has had a history of past successes, its fans have been criticised for remaining silent during home games and not contributing to the atmosphere in the stadium. In other words, the fans' behavioural loyalty does not translate into singing, chanting and making noise, for example, according to media reports and FC Bayern München representatives. To address this, the club may answer the following questions as a starting point:

1 How is loyalty defined and what facets does attitudinal fan loyalty have?

2 Why does behavioural loyalty not always go along with attitudinal loyalty?

3 What can the club do to increase the attitudinal loyalty of their fans? Please refer to each of the facets of attitudinal loyalty.

TOOLS FOR ANALYSIS

The loyalty continuum

Consumer loyalty is the psychological process that makes consumers feel attached to an entity (Fournier, 1998). In the sports context, loyalty is defined as 'an allegiance or devotion to a particular team that is based on the spectator's interest in the team that has developed over time' (Wakefield and Sloan, 1995: 159). Fan loyalty may result from early experiences in childhood, social affiliation with other fans of the team, sporting success or the regional history of the team (Funk and James, 2001; Tapp, 2004). However, there is no binary classification for individuals being either loyal or not loyal to the team (or athlete). Fan loyalty is a continuous measure and fluctuates over time. For example, a fan's loyalty may be higher when the team is successful or when the fan has more free time, whereas it may be lower when moving away from the region where the team is located. At the same time, another fan may become even more loyal when the team loses games (e.g. after relegation), because she thinks that the team needs her support, or when she misses the team more than ever after having moved abroad. These examples highlight that loyalty can change over time, and that both actual behaviour and fan perception and attitudes affect consumer loyalty. I therefore would make the following distinction between behavioural and attitudinal loyalty in order to describe the loyalty of fans:

> (1) *Behavioural loyalty*, i.e. the behaviour of consumers in terms of re-purchasing goods and services (here: following games repeatedly in the stadium or via media), purchasing other goods and services from the entity (e.g. following games of one club's other sports teams, buying merchandise or becoming a member of the club), and engaging in positive word-of-mouth behaviour (e.g. talking about the team in social media or with family members).
>
> (2) *Attitudinal loyalty*, i.e. consumers' favourable evaluation of the entity based on both emotional and cognitive factors, as well as conscious and unconscious attitude formation processes that make consumers feel attached to the team.

Although attitudinal loyalty is considered a predictor of behavioural loyalty, there are some situational constraints that prevent consumers from re-buying or re-patronising (De Wulf et al., 2001). For example, attitudinal loyalty does not translate to behavioural loyalty if a Bayern München fan has moved to the USA and cannot attend the games any more, or if the fan cannot access the game's broadcast due to a missing internet connection/no TV access. Behaviours may also influence attitudes. Again, behavioural loyalty does not necessarily increase attitudinal loyalty (e.g. a Bayern München fan attends the stadium because her friends attend the game and she likes to socialise with them, without feeling close to the team); it is likely that the fan changes her behaviour in a situation where the behavioural incentive is not present any more (e.g. when she makes new friends that have other interests than sports). Marketers will therefore try to capture, and increase, consumers' attitudinal loyalty (beside their actual behaviours).

The facets of attitudinal loyalty

Sports fans are individuals with an abiding interest in sport and/or the teams (or players) associated with these (Wann et al., 2001). Although sports fans are often described as being highly enthusiastic about their fandom (Sloan, 1989; Zillmann and Paulus, 1993) and considering their favourite team as a partner for life (Madrigal and Dalakas, 2008; Richardson and O'Dwyer, 2003), there are some fans whose bond to the team is superficial and lacks the characteristics of a genuine relationship. One may ask the question of how many fans would still support FC Bayern München if the team did not win a single championship within the next decade, for example. To answer questions like these, I consider four facets of attitudinal loyalty:

1 *Satisfaction*, i.e. the fan's evaluation of the perceived quality of an entity (here: the team, the games) after consumption as opposed to prior to consumption.

2 *Self-connection*, i.e. the activation of a person's identity system reflecting the degree to which a team delivers on important identity concerns, tasks or themes, expressing a significant aspect of a person's identity.

3 *Intimate commitment*, i.e. the enduring desire to continue a deep and personal relationship with the team.

4 *Emotional achievement*, i.e. the feeling of personal achievement by fans when their team is successful, and the positive emotion of pride associated with this.

Each of these facets is part of the attitudinal loyalty of sports fans (Koenigstorfer et al., 2010). I will first refer to consumer satisfaction. Satisfaction is defined as 'a postconsumption evaluation of perceived quality relative to prepurchase performance expectations about quality' (Homburg et al., 2005: 85). It is considered to be an antecedent of behavioural loyalty (Bodet and Bernache-Assollant, 2011). Several authors have built upon this assumption and developed satisfaction-loyalty models that are grounded in the confirmation/disconfirmation paradigm (Laverie and Arnett, 2000; Madrigal, 1995; Martínez and Martínez, 2007; Trail et al., 2005; Van Leeuwen et al., 2002; Wakefield and Blodgett, 1994). The confirmation/disconfirmation paradigm postulates that consumer expectations, coupled with perceived performance, lead to post-purchase (dis)satisfaction. Satisfaction results from positive disconfirmation (performance $\geq$ expectations), while dissatisfaction results from negative disconfirmation (performance < expectations; Oliver, 1980). However, fans do not necessarily experience dissatisfaction when experiencing the (objective) failures of their favourite team, such as relegation to a lower league. Fans feel like going through the battle against relegation together with their club and are even more satisfied with the performance, despite relegation, if the team improves its style of play, gave its best and eventually encounters more regional rivalries in the lower league than before (Koenigstorfer et al., 2010). Thus, satisfaction may be a less important predictor of behavioural loyalty for highly (versus lowly) attached fans (Bodet and Bernache-Assollant, 2011).

Self-connection is high when fans claim that they are fans of a specific team ('I am an FC Bayern München fan') and that their club expresses the attributes and values that are important to them, such as success, leadership, sportsman-like behaviour, never giving up and risk taking. Wann et al. (2001: 4) state that, 'highly identified fans often view it [the role as team follower] as a reflection of themselves'. Self-connection is important to fans because the team allows them to maintain their self-concept (Dimanche and Samdahl, 1994; Laverie and Arnett, 2000). Fans even maintain their self-connection when their favourite team is relegated to a lower league (Koenigstorfer et al., 2010). Being a fan of a sport club is something that can give meaning to a fan's life (Tapp, 2004). Their fandom is about expressing their identity and attitude to life. Teams achieve their highest self-connection with fans when they share the same values and identity.

A genuine relationship between fans and their clubs is not only associated with high levels of commitment, but also with intimacy, mutuality, interaction and **trust** (Harris and Ogbonna, 2008). Intimate commitment captures the depth of intimacy of the relationship between fans and sport teams, and the degree to which fans build up reciprocal, close relational ties with their teams. Fandom is about knowing everything about the club, sharing intimate details with it and experiencing intense emotions that other spectators do not experience in the same way. Richardson and Turley (2006: 178) argue that highly committed fans want to assert that their fandom is more authentic compared with other supporters, because it is real, as well as 'about duty, obligation, blood, sweat and tears'. Intimate commitment has been shown to increase in response to a relegation, whereas it decreased in fans of teams that were not relegated, most likely due to the fact that those fans did not perceive the urgency for their devotion to the same extent as the fans whose clubs were relegated and in the midst of a crisis (Koenigstorfer et al., 2010). Thus intimate commitment represents the glue that sticks fans and teams together.

Emotional achievement represents fans' feeling of personal triumph after their team's performance. Fans feel proud and relate their team's wins to a greater extent to internal and stable causes than to external and unstable causes (Madrigal, 2008; Wann and Dolan, 1994; Wann and Schrader, 2000). This facet of attitudinal loyalty is affected most by the outcome of the game or the outcome of the season. For example, emotional achievement was negatively affected by relegation (Koenigstorfer et al., 2010). Whereas emotional achievement captures fans' internal states, basking in reflected glory occurs when consumers express their emotions after wins to others. I will refer to 'basking in reflected glory' below.

Transgressions and attitudinal loyalty

Transgressions are violations of the implicit or explicit rules that guide the performance and evaluation of a relationship (Aaker et al., 2004). From the fan perspective, a transgression may include the use of **doping**, **corruption**, unethical on- or off-field behaviour, game fixing and even a poor sporting **performance** (e.g. relegation). These transgressions can arise both from incidents that occur in the contextual environment (not directly related to the service delivery) and those that occur in the delivery process, such as during the game (Königstorfer and Uhrich, 2009). Transgressions can affect both the attitudinal and behavioural loyalty of sport fans.

Single game outcomes have also been related to the behaviour of loyal fans. After a win, fans tend to 'share in the glory of a successful other with whom they are in some way associated' (Cialdini et al., 1976: 366). This is referred to as 'basking in reflected glory'. The process of doing so describes the rise in fans' self-esteem by decreasing the psychological distance between themselves and successful teams. Conversely, fans protect their self-image when clubs lose games by increasing the psychological distance between themselves and the unsuccessful teams. They tend to cut off reflected failure in order to prevent harm to their self-esteem or public image (Snyder et al., 1986). They also tend to eat more fatty food to cope with defeats (Cornil and Chandon, 2013). However, there is also evidence that there are sport fans who are not basking in reflected glory after wins, because they want to protect themselves from being disappointed in the future when the team will be less successful (Wann et al., 1995). Also, fans – as an act of symbolism – will stand against other groups of spectators (e.g. fair-weather fans) and justify their fandom (Richardson and Turley, 2006). They feel that they have to stand by the team and what the team stands for, especially in bad times, similar to a partnership, and even increase their tendency to bask in reflected glory when sporting performance is low (Koenigstorfer et al., 2010).

To conclude, I can state that fans vary with respect to both behavioural and attitudinal loyalty, and that both loyalty dimensions develop, and change, over time. Attitudinal loyalty can be captured via four facets that describe the attachment to the team (or athlete). Situational factors can affect these facets positively or negatively.

ACTION LEARNING

- If you were asked to measure attitudinal loyalty repeatedly every season (in order to derive managerial implications), how would you do this?
- Which facets of attitudinal fan loyalty in your opinion, are most relevant to fans' contribution to the stadium atmosphere via singing, chanting and making noise? Why?
- Given that your aim is to increase attitudinal loyalty in your fan base to increase sales, how could you find out whether high attitudinal loyalty actually transfers to high behavioural loyalty?

THINKING POINT 30.2

FC St. Pauli

The German football team of FC St. Pauli is based in the St. Pauli area in Hamburg. The club is recognised for its unique fan culture. Many FC St. Pauli fans are involved in left-wing politics and regard themselves as anti-racist, anti-fascist, anti-homophobic and anti-sexist (as outlined in their club's official principles). Fans have adopted the skull and crossbones as their own unofficial emblem.

Ultra fans of FC St. Pauli have a friendship with FC Bayern München's Schickeria fan club. A win against FC Bayern München, the 2001 World Club Champions, made the fans produce shirts stating '*Weltpokalsiegerbesieger*'. However, FC St. Pauli has gone through tough times since then. The club faced bankruptcy in 2003, which was only prevented due to extensive fund-raising activities. FC Bayern München also helped rescue the club by playing a friendly game.

It is expected that FC St. Pauli will only be promoted to the highest division of the Bundesliga again if they can attract more sponsors and generate constant revenues from ticket sales; that is, when the reconstructed stadium (capacity of 30,000) is filled with behaviourally loyal fans no matter what the short-term game outcome is. To reach this goal, the club may answer the following question: what is the customer lifetime value of a fan?

FC St. Pauli

Date founded:	15 May 1910		Achievements of the club:
Club members:	18,500		Eight first division Bundesliga season appearances since 1963/64
Revenues:	€24.25 Million. (soccer team) €30.25 Million. (entire group)		No championship titles and eight relegations since then (to both second and third divisions)
Sponsorship profit:	€6.82 Million.		
Player's value:	€15.2 Million. (in 2013)		2001/02 Weltpokalsiegerbesieger ('World Club Champion beaters') after a 2–1 win against FC Bayern München

Reference: 2012/13 season except players' value (as of beginning 2013/14 season)

FIGURE 30.2   *FC St. Pauli: statistics*

TOOLS FOR ANALYSIS

Customer lifetime value

Managers have realised that (loyal) customers are the greatest assets to their company. Without customers, there is little potential for future profits. This is also true in sports: (loyal) fans are the reason for most of the revenues generated by the teams, including revenues from ticket sales, merchandising, sponsorship and broadcasting in the media. However, fans are not of equal worth to sport organisations, and this is why they segment fans, target them and position themselves as brands to offer the 'right'products and services to the 'right' consumers. Imagine a fan sitting in a heated grandstand lounge (including catering) while watching a sport game versus a fans standing in the fan curve among thousands of others. It is likely that the first type of fan allows teams to generate more monetary value than the second type. The concept of customer lifetime value (CLV) puts this into numbers.

(CLV) is 'the present value of expected benefits (e.g. gross margin) less the burdens (e.g. direct costs of servicing and communicating) from customers' (Dwyer, 1997: 7). Customer lifetime value is a tool to segment and prioritise customers according to profitability and then calculate the return on the marketing investment (Rust et al., 2004).

The basic equation for calculating the lifetime value of a customer is as follows (Venkatesan and Kumar, 2004):

$$CLV_i = \sum_{t=1}^{n} \frac{(Future\ contribution\ margin_{it} - Future\ cost_{it})}{(1+r)^t}$$

where
i = customer index,
t = time index,
n = forecast horizon and
r = discount rate.

The components of customer lifetime value include future purchase frequency, future contribution margin and future marketing costs. Some of the antecedents of purchase frequency and contribution margin (e.g. marketing communications, sponsorship) are under the control of organisations' management and in turn affect the variable costs for managing customers. These antecedents are therefore used to maximise customer lifetime value (Venkatesan and Kumar, 2004). The present and future lifetime values of each customer sum up to customer equity, which is a measure of the performance of the operational business of an organisation (Gupta et al., 2004).

Behavioural loyalty means that consumers have a high purchase frequency. Imagine a fan that owns a season ticket, travels to away games and follows all the international games in which her team may compete, for example. The fan spends more money the higher the frequency of attending games. The contribution margin and the costs involved, however, will depend on several factors, such as the sports under consideration (e.g. the contribution margin will be higher for football than for baseball because of the differences in demand in Europe) and the level of standardisation in the communication to fans. Also, fans may spend money on products and services other than tickets, such as merchandising articles and club memberships, or they may donate to the team in fundraising activities. This can increase the contribution margin further.

Although fans are important revenue sources for sport teams, as they generate a large part of the clubs' income by attending games, buying merchandise, paying to watch games on television or the internet and attracting sponsors, they also contribute to factors that are less easily quantifiable in monetary terms, such as the atmosphere in sport stadia, the identity of the teams and what makes them attractive to other fans. These factors often result from fans' high attitudinal loyalty (such as self-connection and intimate commitment) and lead to a high attachment that often goes beyond the attachment found in typical buyer–seller relationships. Without the extremely high attitudinal loyalty levels of their fans, FC St. Pauli would not have had success in their 'Retteraktion' (i.e. the fund-raising activities to prevent the club's bankruptcy).

Imagine an arena that is just filled with fans sitting in heated grandstand lounges. At first glance, the stadium might appeal to marketers, because the spectators might be most profitable due to their high willingness to pay for tickets. However, such a stadium would not appeal to most of the spectators – even those in the grandstand lounges – and stakeholders (Uhrich and Benkenstein,

2010; Uhrich and Koenigstorfer, 2009). It is often the fans with little to medium customer lifetime value (e.g. those buying the cheapest tickets) that make other fans become loyal to the club by performing certain behaviours such as singing the team's anthem before the game or by contributing to the identity of the club (Charleston, 2009; Uhrich and Benkenstein, 2012). Thus, they co-create value for other spectators. Other spectators may like the atmosphere produced by fans with high attitudinal loyalty and may feel as if they were part of their rituals. Therefore, sport managers should be cautious about prioritising customers based on hard monetary figures only.

In what follows next, I will focus on the relationship between fan loyalty and the success of sponsorship of brands that support the fans' favourite team. In sponsorship, an entity different from the team hopes to profit from the experience of spectators who follow the team and that team's games. Merchandising, broadcasting, and ticketing revenues are closely related to the core product and service and the team involved. Therefore, it is not surprising that high attitudinal or behavioural loyalty go along with higher merchandising, broadcasting and ticketing revenues. The relationship is well established in the literature: see Fisher and Wakefield, 1998; Wann and Branscombe, 1993. I will therefore focus on the effects of fan loyalty on sport sponsorship in the next paragraph.

The role of fan loyalty for sponsorship effects

One important question that is raised by sponsors of sports teams is whether high (attitudinal and/or behavioural) fan loyalty also produces positive effects for the sponsor. The identification of sport spectators with their team predicts a number of behaviours including game attendance (Fisher and Wakefield, 1998) and the amount of money spent on team-licensed merchandise (Fisher and Wakefield, 1998; Wann and Branscombe, 1993), but does increasing fan loyalty also produce greater sponsorship success?

The basic assumption of many sponsors is that those fans who are most attached to the team may also be most loyal to the sponsors of the team (Crimmins and Horn, 1996). This may be for several reasons. First, fans may form positive attitudes to a sponsor because they acknowledge that the sponsor supports their favourite team financially. Second, by supporting the sponsor the fans act in a way that is consistent with the goals and values of the team (i.e. an important characteristic of self-connection). Madrigal (2000, 2001), Cornwell and Coote (2005), and Gwinner and Swanson (2003) use social identity theory to explain how consumers connect to teams and, in turn, sponsors via the formation of in-group identities. Their findings support the claim made above: as team identification (often measured as a single dimension on a five- or seven-item scale) increases, so do the intentions to purchase products from corporate sponsors. The process through which this happens is as follows. Team identification influences the group norms, i.e. highly identified fans are more likely to form behavioural intentions that are congruent with the goals and objectives of the group than they are with personal factors such as attitudes towards the behaviour. This strengthens their identity as a team member (Madrigal, 2000, 2001). The findings indicate the role of normative pressure that is produced by referent information: higher purchase intentions will be more likely if intentions are perceived as important to other members of the group.

Gwinner and Swanson (2003) show that highly identified sport fans are more likely to recognise the sponsor have a positive attitude towards the sponsor, be satisfied with the sponsor and have higher purchase intentions for the sponsor's products. There is recent evidence that team performance also matters in this context. Fans with low team identification levels respond more negatively in terms of decreasing purchase intentions for the sponsor's products to a losing team than highly identified fans, because they tend to lower the basking in reflected glory and increase their cutting off reflected failure. Ngan et al. (2011) reason that lowly identified fans are attracted to the sport and the team for pleasure and stress relief, or for opportunities for social interactions within the community; their attachment relates to the entertainment value of the sport rather than to the team itself.

The sponsorship of rival teams also affects the relationship between fan loyalty and sponsorship effects. Davies et al. (2006) show that involvement with the team and attitudes towards (or preferences for the sponsor) do not correlate when a brand sponsors both the favourite team and the rival team (such as for the Glasgow football teams). The highly involved supporters were either Celtic or Rangers fans. They were more likely to reject the joint sponsorship. The rejection of the joint sponsorship is also positively though less strongly associated with changes in attitudes and brand preferences. The authors conclude that, 'there seemed to be a fine balance of positive and negative feelings towards NTL [the sponsor] among those supporters with greater emotional involvement, while for those who were able to consider the situation more rationally, accepting the need for a joint sponsor, the response was more positively weighted. This is a clear contrast to the single sponsorship situation' (Davies et al., 2006: 46).

To conclude, I can state that sponsors likely profit from a loyal fan base. Although there is no evidence for a direct effect of sponsorship on sales (given that isolating the effect of sponsorship from other activities within the promotion mix or from variables in the market is nearly impossible), highly (vs. lowly) loyal consumers seem to be more aware of the sponsorship, form more positive attitudes towards the sponsor, and have higher purchase intentions for the sponsor's products and services. It remains to be seen which attitudinal loyalty measures are most relevant in this context, and how CLV differences from the perspective of teams affect the sponsor's customer relationship management.

ACTION LEARNING

- How can you make sure that loyalty to the team translates into loyalty to the sponsor? Does the distinction between attitudinal and behavioural loyalty matter? Why?
- Do you assume that fans with the highest customer lifetime value for the club are also those with the highest customer lifetime value for the sponsor? To what degree do the goals and values that the team (versus the sponsor) stands up for matter in this relationship? Why?

CONCLUSION

This chapter elaborated on attitudinal and behavioural fan loyalty development in sports. It explained how fan loyalty can be described (in terms of dimensions and facets), how different factors contribute to fan loyalty and how stakeholders profit from a loyal fan base. While the case studies were drawn from football (i.e. the most popular sport in Germany), the loyalty dimensions and facets may be replicated in fans of different sports (e.g. team sports and individual sports).

REFERENCES

Aaker, J., Fournier, S. & Brasel, S.A. 2004. When good brands do bad. *Journal of Consumer Research,* 31, 1–16.

Bodet, G. & Bernache-Assollant, I. 2011. Consumer loyalty in sport spectatorship services: the relationships with consumer satisfaction and team identification. *Psychology and Marketing,* 28, 781–802.

Charleston, S. 2009. The English football ground as a representation of home. *Journal of Environmental Psychology,* 29, 144–150.

Cialdini, R.B., Borden, R.J., Thorne, A., Walker, M.R., Freeman, S. & Sloan, L.R. 1976. Basking in reflected glory: three (football) field studies. *Journal of Personality and Social Psychology,* 34, 366–375.

Cornil, Y. & Chandon, P. 2013. From fan to fat? Vicarious losing increases unhealthy eating but self-affirmation is an effective remedy. *Psychological Science,* 24, 1936–1946.

Cornwell, T.B. & Coote, L.V. 2005. Corporate sponsorship of a cause: the role of identification in purchase intent. *Journal of Business Research,* 58, 268–276.

Crimmins, J. & Horn, M. 1996. Sponsorship: from management ego trip to marketing success. *Journal of Advertising Research,* 36, 11–21.

Davies, F., Veloutsou, C. & Costa, A. 2006. Investigating the influence of a joint sponsorship of rival teams on supporter attitudes and brand preferences. *Journal of Marketing Communications,* 12, 31–48.

De Wulf, K., Odekerken-Schröder, G. & Iacobucci, D. 2001. Investments in consumer relationships: a cross-country and cross-industry exploration. *Journal of Marketing,* 65, 33–50.

Dimanche, F. & Samdahl, D. 1994. Leisure as symbolic consumption: a conceptualization and prospectus for future research. *Leisure Sciences,* 16, 119–129.

Dwyer, R.F. 1997. Customer lifetime valuation to support marketing decision making. *Journal of Interactive Marketing,* 11, 6–13.

Fisher, R.J. & Wakefield, K. 1998. Factors leading to group identification: a field study of winners and losers. *Psychology and Marketing,* 15, 23–40.

Fournier, S. 1998. Consumers and their brands: developing relationship theory in consumer research. *Journal of Consumer Research,* 24, 343–353.

Funk, D.C. & James, J. 2001. The psychological continuum model: a conceptual framework for understanding an individual's psychological connection to sport. *Sport Management Review,* 4, 119–150.

Gupta, S., Lehmann, D. & Ames Stuart, J. 2004. Valuing customers. *Journal of Marketing Research,* 41, 7–18.

Gwinner, K. & Swanson, S.R. 2003. A model of fan identification: antecedents and sponsorship outcomes. *Journal of Services Marketing,* 17, 275–294.

Harris, L.C. & Ogbonna, E. 2008. The dynamics underlying service firm: customer relationships insights from a study of English Premier League soccer fans. *Journal of Service Research,* 10, 382–399.

Homburg, C., Koschate, N. & Hoyer, W.D. 2005. Do satisfied customers really pay more? A study of the relationship between customer satisfaction and willingness to pay. *Journal of Marketing,* 69, 84–96.

Koenigstorfer, J., Groeppel-Klein, A. & Schmitt, M. 2010. 'You'll never walk alone': How loyal are soccer fans to their clubs when they are struggling against relegation? *Journal of Sport Management,* 24, 649–675.

Königstorfer, J. & Uhrich, S. 2009. Riding a rollercoaster: the dynamics of sports fans' loyalty after promotion and relegation. *Marketing – Journal of Research and Management,* 31, 71–83.

Laverie, D.A. & Arnett, D.B. 2000. Factors affecting fan attendance: The influence of identity salience and satisfaction. *Journal of Leisure Research,* 32, 225–246.

MadrigaL, R. 1995. Cognitive and affective determinants of fan satisfaction with sporting event attendance. *Journal of Leisure Research,* 27, 205–227.

Madrigal, R. 2000. The influence of social alliances with sports teams on intentions to purchase corporate sponsors' products. *Journal of Advertising,* 29, 13–24.

Madrigal, R. 2001. Social identity effects in a belief–attitude–intentions hierarchy: implications for corporate sponsorship. *Psychology and Marketing,* 18, 145–165.

Madrigal, R. 2008. Hot vs. cold cognitions and consumers' reactions to sporting event outcomes. *Journal of Consumer Psychology,* 18, 304–319.

MadrigaL, R. & Dalakas, V. 2008. Consumer psychology of sport: more than just a game. In Haugtvedt, C.P., Herr, P.M. & Kardes, F.R. (eds), *Handbook of Consumer Psychology.* New York: Taylor and Francis Group/Lawrence Erlbaum Associates.

Martínez, C.L. & Martínez, G.J.A. 2007. Cognitive–affective model of consumer satisfaction. An exploratory study within the framework of a sporting event. *Journal of Business Research,* 60, 108–114.

Ngan, H.M., Prendergast, G.P. & Tsang, A.S. 2011. Linking sports sponsorship with purchase intentions: team performance, stars, and the moderating role of team identification. *European Journal of Marketing,* 45, 551–566.

Oliver, R.L. 1980. A cognitive model of the antecedents and consequences of satisfaction decisions. *Journal of Marketing Research,* 17, 460–469.

Richardson, B. & O'Dwyer, E. 2003. Football supporters and football team brands: a study in consumer brand loyalty. *Irish Marketing Review,* 16, 43–52.

Richardson, B. & Turley, D. 2006. Support your local team: resistance, subculture, and the desire for distinction. *Advances in Consumer Research,* 33, 175–180.

Rust, R.T., Lemon, K.N. & Zeithaml, V.A. 2004. Return on marketing: using customer equity to focus marketing strategy. *Journal of Marketing,* 68, 109–127.

Sloan, L.R. 1989. The motives of sports fans. In Goldstein, J.H. (ed.), *Sports, Games, and Play: Social and Psychological Viewpoints,* 2nd edn. Mahwah, NJ: Lawrence Erlbaum Associates.

Snyder, C.R., Lassegard, M. & Ford, C.E. 1986. Distancing after group success and failure: basking in reflected glory and cutting off reflected failure. *Journal of Personality and Social Psychology,* 51, 382–388.

Tapp, A. 2004. The loyalty of football fans. We'll support you evermore? *Journal of Database Marketing and Customer Strategy Management,* 11, 203–215.

Trail, G.T., Anderson, D.F. & Fink, J.S. 2005. Consumer satisfaction and identity theory: a model of sport spectator conative loyalty. *Sport Marketing Quarterly,* 14, 98–111.

Uhrich, S. & Benkenstein, M. 2010. Sport stadium atmosphere: formative and reflective indicators for operationalizing the construct. *Journal of Sport Management,* 24, 211–237.

Uhrich, S. & Benkenstein, M. 2012. Physical and social atmospheric effects in hedonic service consumption: customers' roles at sporting events. *The Service Industries Journal,* 32, 1741–1757.

Uhrich, S. & Koenigstorfer, J. 2009. Effects of atmosphere at major sports events: a perspective from environmental psychology. *International Journal of Sports Marketing and Sponsorship,* 10, 325–344.

Van Leeuwen, L., Quick, S. & Daniel, K. 2002. The sport spectator satisfaction model: a conceptual framework for understanding the satisfaction of spectators. *Sport Management Review,* 5, 99–128.

Venkatesan, R. & Kumar, V. 2004. A customer lifetime value framework for customer selection and resource allocation strategy. *Journal of Marketing,* 68, 106–125.

Wakefield, K.L. & Blodgett, J.G. 1994. The importance of servicescapes in leisure service settings. *Journal of Services Marketing,* 8, 66–76.

Wakefield, K.L. & Sloan, H.J. 1995. The effects of team loyalty and selected stadium factors on spectator attendance. *Journal of Sport Management,* 9, 153–172.

Wann, D.L. & Branscombe, N.R. 1993. Sports fans: Measuring degree of identification with their team. *International Journal of Sport Psychology,* 24, 1–17.

Wann, D.L. & Dolan, T.J. 1994. Attributions of highly identified sports spectators. *Journal of Social Psychology,* 134, 783–792.

Wann, D.L. & Schrader, M.P. 2000. Controllability and stability in the self-serving attributions of sport spectators. *Journal of Social Psychology,* 140, 160–168.

Wann, D.L., Hamlet, M.A., Wilson, T.M. & Hodges, J.A. 1995. Basking in reflected glory, cutting off reflected failure, and cutting off future failure: the importance of group identification. *Social Behavior and Personality: an International Journal,* 23, 377–388.

Wann, D.L., Melnick, M.J., Russell, G.W. & Pease, D.G. 2001. *Sport Fans: The Psychology and Social Impact of Spectators.* New York: Routledge.

Zillmann, D. & Paulus, P.B. 1993. Spectators: reactions to sports events and effects on athletic performance. In Singer, R.N., Murphey, M. & Tennant, K.L. (eds), *Handbook of Research on Sport Psychology.* New York: Macmillan.

USEFUL WEBSITES

www.theguardian.com/football/2005/sep/02/sport.blueprintforabetterfootball

www.nytimes.com/2000/08/11/sports/sports-psychology-it-isn-t-just-a-game-clues-to-avid-rooting.html?pagewanted=all&src=pm

www.thefootballsupernova.com/2012/02/story-behind-youll-never-walk-alone.html

http://well.blogs.nytimes.com/2013/09/16/when-teams-lose-fans-tackle-fatty-food/?r=2

http://sports.yahoo.com/blogs/nfl-shutdown-corner/team-most-loyal-fans-science-says-dallas-cowboys-171057776.html

31

TRUST AND CONTROL IN SPORT ORGANIZATIONS

TERRI BYERS AND ALEX THURSTON

ECB says lack of trust ended Kevin Pietersen's England career.
(www.telegraph.co.uk/sport/cricket/kevinpietersen/10627449/ECB-says-lack-of-trust-ended-Kevin-Pietersens-England-career.html)

Redknapp says lack of trust at QPR made him quit.
(http://uk.reuters.com/article/2015/04/10/uk-soccer-england-redknapp-idUKKBN0N10U220150410)

Bayern Munich team doctor quits over lack of trust.
(www.sportsmole.co.uk/football/bayern-munich/news/bayern-doctor-quits-over-lack-of-trust_217565.html)

LEARNING OUTCOMES

Upon completion of this chapter, students will be able to:

- Define the concepts of control and trust to understand the importance of trust in the management of sport.

- Identify how trust can fail in sport and the implications of this for sport organization control.

- Discuss the complex relationship between trust and control in sport and articulate the implications of this to managers, athletes and fans.

INTRODUCTION

Trust and control and the relationship between the two terms are key concepts for sport managers to consider. The world of sport is inherently emotional, with passionate yet divergent motivations and goals of multiple stakeholders for involvement in sport organizations. It is important we can trust in leagues and teams and individual athletes to perform honestly and to the best of their ability. The **governance** of sport is about its control and regulation and there is an assumption/trust that governing bodies will provide **strategic** leadership to develop sports appropriately. In essence we trust in the sport system and the people who work/volunteer within it to behave in responsible and **ethical** ways. We also construct control mechanisms to ensure ethical, transparent and responsible behaviour. Voluntary sport organizations comprise a large proportion of the sport sector in many countries and these informal groups often rely on trust and social interaction to organize rather than formal mechanisms of coordination (Byers, 2013). However, we know that trust in sport and sport organizations is delicate and vulnerable to violations where a breach in trust is experienced, such as **athlete transgressions**, abuse or the overproduction of **animals** (who lack a voice to protest) in sport and other unethical practices. When trust is breached, there are serious consequences for commercial organizations (and perceptions of their consumers), athletes (and their **sponsorship** relationships), governing bodies and voluntary sport organizations, not to mention the confidence of many of stakeholders concerning sport organization's control and **governance** of a sport. This lack of trust most often leads to some change in structures, systems or personnel, and sport managers are left to wonder how to control for these new developments and rebuild trust in their organization, sport or athletes.

Trust can be breached through **athlete transgressions**, un**ethical** decision making in **governance** and other forms of **corruption** such as **match fixing**. With increasing and/or rapid commercialization in sport, control in sport organizations has changed from largely informal, social control systems to bureaucratic professional/formally controlled, and some may suggest this formality demonstrates a lack of trust for volunteers to perform in a 'professional' manner. Control within and of sport organizations is integral to the management of sport. But the concept of control is often misunderstood to refer to 'a management function' (Byers and Thurston, forthcoming 2016). Sport organizations are controlled by their internal and external environments (Slack and Parent, 2007), by a variety of stakeholders including governance structures/organizations, management, staff, volunteers, customers, suppliers, competitors and many others. They are not controlled solely by managers. Within sport organizations, control mechanisms and processes are both formal and informal, cultural and derived from personal self-motivational factors.

This chapter briefly introduces the concept of control as a complex issue for managers but focuses on the concept of trust, its importance to sport and the implications for the control of sport organizations when trust fails. Trust and control in sport is indeed a very contemporary issue, and we draw primarily on literature outside of sport to begin to understand the issue and its impact on the management of sport.

Voluntary Sport Clubs in the UK

There are approximately 151,000 sport clubs in the UK. The size and structure of these organizations vary across England, Scotland, Wales and Northern Ireland, from very small informal clubs with memberships of less than 50 people, to larger more professionally operated clubs with hundreds of members. Regardless of the size or structure, voluntary sport clubs are considered the life blood of sport, with important social and economic impacts for people of all ages. Clubs are also often founded on social/common interests and many have been in existence for more than 40 years. However, clubs are increasingly under pressure to professionalize their operations and adopt more formal procedures to demonstrate good governance and quality management of sport. Sport England (SE) operates 'Clubmark' quality accreditation. According to the SE website (see http://www.clubmark.org.uk, last accessed 7 May 2015):

It shows that a 'Clubmarked' club provides the right environment which ensures the welfare of members and encourages everyone to enjoy sport and stay involved throughout their lives.

An accredited club is recognized as a safe, rewarding and fulfilling place for participants of all ages, as well as helping parents and carers know that they're choosing the right club for their young people.

Over 14,000 clubs have achieved this, with another 4,000 clubs in the process of Clubmark accreditation. Based on four key areas of club development it centres around:

- Activity/playing programmes: this includes, for example, coaching qualifications required, insurance and coach-to-participant ratios.
- Duty of care and welfare: appropriate risk assessments, health and safety policies, training, compliance and child protection policies.
- Knowing your club and its community: this ensures that your club is committed to fairness and equity in respect of the way in seeks to attract and retain members from your local community.
- Club management: which covers issues to do with club and committee structures and the general running of the organization.

Sport clubs are voluntary organizations, with limited resources, and achieving increased professionalization comes with challenges. Volunteers in sport clubs in England have expressed concern over the increasing amount of paperwork and 'red tape' involved in volunteering. Growing use of the 'volunteer agreement', compliance with national policy on child protection, data protection and other policies is difficult in small voluntary organizations that rely on a few people to give up their time and expertise for a few hours per week. Voluntary sport clubs in the UK are managed by committee structures of approximately 10–12 people, whereby the majority of work in a club is done by the officers (secretary, chairperson(s), treasurer) of the club. Some clubs may be structured for other responsibilities including membership, fundraising, teams or Youth. However, it is necessary to remember that many of these volunteers will have full-time jobs and be constrained in the number of hours they can devote to the operation of the club. Often, committee members will also have friends and family members (including their children) who are part of the club as well. There can be conflicts of interest when family members are responsible for making decisions on competition structures, team selection, etc., when their child is also subject to those decisions.

Most sport clubs are composed of people with a common passion for sport, but not necessarily a passion for organizing or managing an organization. Sport clubs are very social and part of the way the work of the club gets done is through interpersonal discussions/negotiation rather than rigid policies and procedures as would be found in a commercial business. While there is a need for some rules and regulations to help clarify roles and guide appropriate behaviour, excessive use of these in voluntary sport clubs can decrease volunteers' enjoyment and satisfaction. Striking a balance can be difficult.

ACTION LEARNING

- Do you volunteer for a sport club and have you noticed any changes in how they operate in recent years? If so discuss how these have changed and why.

- Discuss whether you think the changes in your club have been beneficial or have caused problems for the club.

TOOLS FOR ANALYSIS

Control mechanisms

There is a difference between 'controls' and control. Controls refer to the specific mechanisms in an organization that may have a role in directing individual and group behaviour. How those mechanisms are developed and implemented constitutes the process of control and this can be a complex issue to address (Byers and Thurston, forthcoming 2016). Hopwood (1974) identified three categories of control (administrative, social and self) which operate in all organizations. Byers (2013) recognized that these mechanisms are referring to different levels of analysis in organizations when applying the concepts to understanding control in voluntary sport organizations, specifically voluntary equestrian clubs. Administrative mechanisms are the formal, tangible controls that are often designed by managers such as agendas, policies, procedures, disciplinary codes and performance appraisals. Social controls are the intangible norms and values which develop through human interaction. This is similar to the notion of culture in an organization. Self-controls are the individual personal motivations and feelings which guide human behaviour such as emotion and identification. Control mechanisms change over time, they emerge from social negotiation, and may also be subject to approval structures, historical contexts and institutional pressures. In sport organizations that have voluntary and paid staff, whose motivations for being in the sport organization are different (although they may share some passion for the sport itself), the development of control mechanisms may be more reliant on social norms than on the formal mechanisms of decision making.

The process of control

The various levels of control signify to sport managers that what and indeed who control sport organizations are a combination of tangible and intangible mechanisms that exert influence over a period time. Whether a control mechanism is effective or not is dependent upon many factors, including who is exerting the control, when, on whom, and in what social context (Byers, 2013; Byers et al., 2015). What is certain is that excessive administrative controls can quickly become ineffective as they are not developed through social processes or internalized by individuals as valuable or relevant. Hopwood (1974) suggested that to be truly effective, any administrative mechanism must become a social control mechanism (supported and encouraged through informal channels) and then a self-control mechanism whereby the mechanism is internalized/valued by an individual and they act according to the formal control because they want to (as it is consistent with their own values), not because they have to, to avoid punishment or sanctions.

Traditional views of 'control' were focused on management, creating rules and monitoring their use, and rewards and sanctions used according to an individual's behaviour and to maintain control in line with organizational goals. In some settings, this may largely be the case. However, it ignores the political nature of organizations and the emotional nature of human behaviour. The process of control is therefore more accurately depicted as a 'holistic and dynamic phenomenon' involving complex structures and agents who challenge, produce and reproduce the mechanisms which control individuals and groups within organizations.

Control mechanisms, process and change

Because control mechanisms can change over time, as individuals interact and challenge existing ways of organizing, there is often resistance to change and a significant factor in that resistance is a lack of trust or understanding of the change (Slack and Parent, 2007). Ways of managing this include using participation and consultation when implementing any new policy or administrative mechanism in an organization. This gives managers the chance to understand sources of resistance and resolve misunderstandings or address trust issues if these are identified as problematic.

- What control mechanisms operate in small voluntary sport clubs in the UK?
- What control mechanisms are encouraged by SE?
- How can Hopwood's (1974) classification be useful to policy makers who wish to influence (in the UK, over 150,000) sport clubs?

- What do SE need to do to increase the number of clubs who adopt 'Clubmark'?
- What are the implications of an organization like SE trying to change the nature of control within clubs from informal, social mechanisms to administrative, formal mechanisms? Who benefits from this change?

CASE STUDY 31.2

International Scandal Threatens the Integrity of Sport: The Control of Doping in Sport and Trust Repair

Organization control often focuses on what managers 'do' to coordinate direct and ultimately 'control' the direction and purpose of their organization. The primary purpose of sport National Governing Bodies has been to provide leadership, coordination and, some would argue, to 'control' their respective sports. International Sport Federations take this mandate to a higher level to ensure consistency and 'good governance' across National Governing Bodies and the delivery/production of sporting competitions across the globe. Fuelled by an alarming trend in sport, doping, a new set of sport organizations has emerged to attempt to control the situation. the World Anti-Doping Agency (WADA) has led the charge, producing international standards, rules, protocols, prohibitive substance lists, sanctions and education to eradicate/control the use of performance-enhancing sub-

stances in sport. WADA also coordinates anti-doping activities globally through its central clearing house Anti-Doping and Administration Management System (ADAMS). With its programme Regional Anti-Doping Organizations, (RADO) WADA has the following objectives:

- To help countries and organizations develop anti-doping programmes that are compliant with the World Anti-Doping Code in regions of the world where no quality anti-doping activities have been established.
- To bring together several countries and stakeholders within a geographic area to mobilize and pool resources for anti-doping under the umbrella of an independent RADO.
- To increase worldwide testing and promote the long-term sustainability of testing and anti-doping education.
- To ensure that all athletes in all countries and in all sports are subject to the same anti-doping protocols and processes.
- To have all countries in the world engaged in anti-doping activities.

There are hundreds of National Anti-Doping Organizations (NADOs), education programmes, policies and formal systems in place to discourage doping in sport, catch those who are doping and, through sanctions/penalties, eradicate doping. However, doping prevalence (or perhaps detection) has increased steadily in recent years. There is hardly a sport not touched by a doping scandal. The systematic and prevalent use of performance enhancing drugs (PED) in USA cycling was the subject of extensive media coverage which played a role in highlighting the damage of doping to sponsorship deals, public confidence and trust in athletes and the organizations who represented sport, once a 'clean' respectable endeavour encouraged for its character building, wholesome values of hard work and performance, fair play and social good. More recently, the media have been focusing on Russia, suggesting children are doping at school (*Guardian*, 2015) and increasing concern and scrutiny by, for example, the International Association of Athletics Federation (IAAF) (BBC Sport, 2015) regarding the banning of five athletes for drug violations.

While most athletes would agree doping is wrong and damaging to individuals, teams and compromises the integrity/values of sport itself, the research indicates that athletes' attitudes to the management of doping in sport are that the current formal systems and processes are inadequate, invasive and take the joy out of being an elite athlete. For example, Overbye and Wagner (2014) conducted a study to measure athletes' attitudes to the whereabouts reporting system and showed that attitudes were largely ambivalent. The majority accepted the system as necessary, a duty or consequence of their performance level, but also felt it strongly and negatively impacted on their daily life: 75% thought the system was too time-consuming and fear of a warning was the largest concern as a result of it. They perceived the system as 'surveillance' and did not trust that it operated consistently across other countries. Quite remarkably, this distrust seemed to increase after athletes had personal experience of whereabouts reporting.

The Lance Armstrong scandal was the largest, most powerful shock the sporting world had experienced in relation to the problem of doping in sport. For years, doping in cycling has been documented throughout the world but the realization that this doping was organized, systematic and integral to the governance and management of a sport signified that trust in the athletes and the whole sport system was in question. The media played an integral role by making the case a social, public issue and focusing on a single person as the scapegoat. However, cases of doping and positive tests for banned substances are increasingly prevalent in sport and a parallel development is the decreasing participation in organized sport, the decreasing engagement and retention of volunteers in sport, and the increasing commercialization and changing values from amateurism to professionalism. Is this a coincidence or could the commercialization be a causal factor in doping leading to a widespread distrust of sport by parents and society generally, meaning that sport is no longer viewed as a powerful force for personal development but merely a means to an end for personal wealth, fame and exploitative opportunity?

Athletes who dope do not do so in isolation, they do not act alone. Cultures, both national and sport specific, influence an athlete to dope. Personal attitudes and goals may influence whether an athlete purposely takes a performance-enhancing substance. Social pressure from friends, fans or teammates may play a role. The support team around a high performance athlete would be knowledgable about doping.

ACTION LEARNING

- Which control mechanisms are operating in this case?
- Who exerted these controls and to what effect?

- What do you think the implications of doping scandals in sport are as regards participation and volunteering in sport?

TOOLS FOR ANALYSIS

Trust

'Trust is a psychological state comprising the intention to accept vulnerability based upon positive expectations of the intentions or behaviors of another' (Rousseau et al., 1998: 395). Two key features of this definition are that individuals have a willingness to be vulnerable and the expectation of some beneficial treatment by another party (Colquitt et al., 2007; Ferrin et al., 2008). Trust is an important concept to understand as it is associated with the long-term success of organizations and is a central component of effective work relationships (Sousa-Lima et al., 2013). Two forms of trust can be distinguished: *interpersonal trust*, i.e. trust between people, and *institutional trust*, i.e. trust in the functioning of organizational, institutional and social systems (Bijlsma-Frankema and Costa, 2005). Trust is itself vulnerable, it can increase or decrease depending on interactions and contexts. If those who are trusted live up to those expectations trust increases, and if those expectations are violated trust decreases (March and Olsen, 1975; Buskens, 1999; Gautschi, 2002). Trust is thought to smooth relations among actors (Dirks and Ferrin, 2002), and encourage belief in information and acceptance of influence (Smith and Barclay, 1997), leading to high levels of cooperation and performance (Costa, 2003).

'Trust, in some sense of the word, is implicated in most of our sporting relationships' (Jones, 2001: 96). Whether this is interpersonal trust of athletes as role models, heroes or representatives of a brand, or institutional trust in governing bodies, sport event organizers and sponsors, there is an abundance of opportunity/risk for trust to be broken in sport. However, it can also prove a 'poisoned chalice' (Skinner et al., 2013), in that when trust is high there can be negative consequences for organizations and individuals, such as what Gargiulo and Ertug (2006) called the 'dark side' where trust becomes poor judgement. In other words, actions and behaviours of others goes unchecked, unquestioned as appropriate and this may then be revealed incorrect and detrimental to a wide variety of stakeholders. Trust can refer to three objects of trust:

- *individual* (based on face-to-face contacts, long-term acquaintance and mutual interests.
- *institutions* (a focus on formal rules and their continuity).
- *institutional arrangements* (trust in organizations, their structures or contracts).

(Source: Edelenbos and Klijn, 2007)

Trust can be acquired via different sources:

- *Competence-based trust* (of an individual or an organization's experience and/or knowledge).
- *Goodwill trust* (in someone to make things work).
- *Cognition-based trust* (based on knowledge of others' attitudes/behaviour, developed over time).
- *Affect-based trust* (based on affection stemming from loyalty and empathy).

Researchers interested in the management of sport have yet to explore the issue of trust as fully as other industries and no research exists on the relationship between trust and control in sport to date, either to document if sport managers are aware of the implications of trust or the consequences of trust failure and how these are managed in different contexts. Sport offers an interesting context in which to explore issues and misuses of trust, given its centrality for the sporting world.

Trust and control

There is a growing body of research around the relationship between trust and control. The notion that trust and control are related has emerged after several decades of academic inquiry focused on formal control's role in governing behaviour in organizations.

Vlaar et al. (2007) discussed the evolution of trust, distrust and formal coordination/control (in interorganizational relationships). They indicate that several different relationships between trust and control have been evidenced in the literature, including:

- Trust and (formal) control mechanisms are substitutes, i.e. if we have trust, we do not need formal controls.
- Trust and formal controls may complement one another, i.e. to formalize an aspect of organizing is to make this explicit, demonstrating trust in a relationship.
- Trust and formal control have a variety of effects on performance, i.e. trust can be beneficial and it can also be detrimental to organizations.
- Trust and control may develop by self-reinforcing cycles, i.e. trust can shape human interactions, which in turn can control the mechanisms adopted, which then influences trust, and a cycle of trust and control relationships ensues.

(For more detailed information on the above see Macaulay, 1963; Zand, 1972; Zucker, 1986; Gulati, 1995; Sitkin, 1995; Zaheer and Venkatraman, 1995; Ghoshal and Moran, 1996; Deakin and Wilkinson, 1998; Dyer and Singh, 1998; Kern, 1998; Das and Teng, 2001; Luo, 2002; Poppo and Zenger, 2002; Sydow and Windeler, 2003; Inkpen and Currall, 2004; Mayer and Argyres, 2004).

Edelenbos and Eshuis (2011) studied the relationship between trust and control in governance processes, a context particularly relevant to sport management students aspiring to work in sport governing bodies. They reveal that the relationship between trust and control is complex and explain this complexity through the concept of coevolution. The results of their study suggest that formal and informal controls can contribute to trust, depending on the initial situation in which the relationship between trust and control develops. When trust is established, with an understanding of how control is enacted, that trust can be decreased if those control mechanisms are not adhered to (see Byers and Edwards, 2015 on control of doping). For example, a sport club trusts in their governing bodies to provide information and advice to help them develop the club, increase membership and manage their business. They do this however with the understanding that clubs are fairly autonomous in how they operate. If governing bodies begin to implement increased amounts of formal control mechanisms such as recruitment targets or structural changes, clubs may begin to distrust governing bodies and their intension to support clubs individually as opposed to meeting their own objectives for efficiency.

Repairing trust violations

Trust violations are due to an individual, team or organization acting in a way that diverges from the formal or informal expectations of other stakeholders. In sport, this may be when a board member ignores conflict of interest policy and lobbies for decisions that put personal gain over the wellbeing of the organization or sport. When an athlete is found guilty of match fixing or doping, this undermines the amateur values and ethical principles on which sport is arguably founded. When a sport celebrity such as Tiger Woods makes a personal indiscretion of infidelity (which is totally unrelated to his sport performance), this has implications for the image of the athlete as a brand in whom sponsors place immense monetary and corporate image value. These situations represent a breach of trust, either due to **athlete transgression** or management **corruption**. Steps are usually taken to 'manage' these situations, to mitigate against the negative consequences of the trust violation for those who were in violation and for those who trusted. But to repair trust after it has been violated is a complex and often difficult, if not impossible, task. Research has identified at least two reasons why the process of repairing trust may be more difficult and require different strategies than building trust initially (see Kim et al., 2004).

Kim et al. (2006) discuss the implications of different types of trust violations. They suggest that there can be *competency trust* violations, i.e. the breach of trust was due to a person's lack of skill or knowledge, or *integrity trust* violations, i.e. the breach of trust was due to a person's lack of moral obligation and unethical decision making. Strategies to repair trust will often include apologies and Kim et al. (2006: 49) suggest that trust can be repaired:

> ... more successfully mistrusted parties apologized with an internal, rather than external, attribution when the trust violation concerned matters of competence, but apologized with an external, rather than internal, attribution when the trust violation concerned matters of integrity.

Research suggests that an apology may not always be beneficial to rebuild trust because it is an admittance of guilt (Riordan et al., 1983; Sigal, 1988).

ACTION LEARNING

- What intended affect would restructuring a sport following a doping scandal have on trust by the public, sponsors or international sporting federations?
- How can trust be 'a poisoned chalice' for sport governing bodies?
- How can trust be positive and beneficial for sport organizations?
- What control mechanisms are being developed/implemented to control doping in sport? Are these successful? Why or why not?

- What recommendations would you suggest based on understanding control in sport organizations and the implications of trust in sport for different strategies to control doping in sport?
- Can doping be controlled or is sport doomed to maintain a tarnished image of cheating, corruption and scandal? Outline what and where you see the key problems and some potential solutions. Use Vlaar et al.'s (2007) suggested relationships between trust and control to discuss their relationship in the context of sport governance.

CONCLUSION

This chapter introduced the notion of trust as important in the management of sport. We also suggested that trust and control within organizations were key concepts for sport managers to consider. A brief insight into some of the research on trust and control has been included but readers are encouraged to explore the very large bodies of literature on trust and control, and the smaller amount of knowledge on trust and control in the mainstream management literature, and consider how this may or may not apply in a sporting context.

This chapter also looked at the importance of trust and control in voluntary sport clubs and national governing bodies, but the issue of trust is certainly significant within a variety of other sport management issues such as fan loyalty (Wu et al., 2012) and brand loyalty in sport and fitness (Filo et al., 2008). There are many contexts in sport where trust can and has been violated, including child sexual abuse cases, athlete transgressions and human trafficking around mega-sporting events. This is an area that is virtually untouched by research on trust and more needs to be done to understand how trust and the trust–control nexus operate in sport.

REFERENCES

BBC Sport (2015). IAAF concerned over Russian doping cases. Available at www. bbc.com/sport/0/athletics/30921021 (last accessed on 11 February 2015).

Bijlsma-Frankema, K. and Costa, A.C. (2005). Understanding the trust-control nexus. *International Sociology*, 20(3): 259–282.

Buskens, V. (1999). The social structure of trust. *Social Networks*, 20: 2655–2689.

Byers, T. (2013). Using critical realism: a new perspective on control of volunteers in sport clubs. *European Sport Management Quarterly*, 13(1): 5–31.

Byers, T. and Edwards, J. (2015). Why DON'T you Dope?: A preliminary analysis of the factors which influence athletes decisions NOT to dope in sport. *Choregia*, 11(2): 1–19.

Byers, T. and Thurston, A.J. (forthcoming 2016) Organization control in sport organizations, in T. Slack (ed.), *Understanding Sport Organizations*. Champaign, IL, Human Kinetics.

Byers, T., Anagnostopoulos, C. and Brooke-Holmes, G. (2015). Understanding control in nonprofit organisations: moving governance research forward?. *Corporate Governance*, 15(1): 134–145.

Byers, T., Slack, T. and Parent, M.M. (2012). *Key Concepts in Sport Management*. London: Sage.

Colquitt, J.A., Scott, B.A. and LePine, J.A. (2007). Trust, trustworthiness, and trust propensity: a meta-analytic test of their unique relationship with risk taking and job performance, *Journal of Applied Psychology*, 92(4): 909–927.

Costa, A.C. (2003). Work team trust and effectiveness. *Personnel Review*, 32(5): 605–622.

Das, T.K., and Teng, B.-S. (2001). Trust, control, and risk in strategic alliances: an integrated framework. *Organization Studies*, 22: 251–283.

Deakin, S. and Wilkinson, F. (1998). Contract law and the economics of interorganizational trust, in C. Lane and R. Bachmann (eds), *Trust Within and Between Organisations* (pp. 146–172). Oxford: Oxford University Press.

Dirks, K.T. and Ferrin, D.L. (2002). Trust in leadership: meta-analytic findings and implications for research and practice. *Journal of applied psychology*, 87(4): 611.

Dyer, J.H. and Singh, H. (1998). The relational view: cooperative strategies and sources of interorganizational competitive advantages. *Academy of Management Review*, 23: 660–679.

Edelenbos, J. and Eshuis, J. (2011). The interplay between trust and control in governance processes: a conceptual and empirical investigation, *Administration and Society*, 44(6): 647–674.

Edelenbos, J. and Klijn E.H. (2007). Trust in complex decision-making networks, a theoretical and empirical exploration. *Administration and Society*, 39: 25–50.

Ferrin, D.L., Bligh, M.C., and Kohles, J.C. (2008). It takes two to tango: an interdependence analysis of the spiraling of perceived trustworthiness and cooperation in interpersonal and intergroup relationships. *Organizational Behavior and Human Decision Processes*, 107(2): 161–178.

Filo, K., Funk, D.C. and Alexandris, K. (2008). Exploring the role of brand trust in the relationship between brand associations and brand loyalty in sport and fitness. *International Journal of Sport Management and Marketing*, 3(1), 39–57.

Gargiulo, M., and Ertug, G. (2006). The dark side of trust, in R. Bachmann and A. Zaheer (eds), *Handbook of Trust Research* (pp. 165–186). Cheltenham: Edward Elgar Publishing.

Gautschi, T. (2002). *Trust and Exchange: Effects of Temporal Embeddedness and Network Embeddedness on Providing and Dividing a Surplus*. Thela Thesis, Amsterdam.

Ghoshal, S. and Moran, P. (1996). Bad for practice: a critique of the transaction cost theory, *Academy of Management Review*, 21: 13–47.

Guardian (2015). Russian child athletes are doping at school. Available at: www.theguardian.com/sport/2015/feb/03/russian-child-athletes-doping-school-sports-minister (accessed 7 July 2015).

Gulati, R. (1995). Does familiarity breed trust? The implications of repeated ties for contractual choice in alliances, *Academy of Management Journal*, 38: 85–112.

Hopwood, A.G. (1974). *Accounting and Human Behaviour*. London: Prentice Hall.

Inkpen, A.C. and Currall, S. (2004). The coevolution of trust, control, and learning in joint ventures. *Organization Science*, 15: 586–599.

Jones, K. (2001). Trust in sport. *Journal of the Philosophy of Sport*, 28(1): 96–102.

Kern, H. (1998). Lack of trust, surfeit of trust: some causes of the innovation crisis in German industry, in C. Lane and R. Bachmann (eds), *Trust Within and Between Organisations* (pp. 203–213). Oxford: Oxford University Press.

Kim, P.H., Ferrin, D.L., Cooper, C.D. and Dirks, K.T. (2004). Removing the shadow of suspicion: the effects of apology versus denial for repairing competence-versus integrity-based trust violations. *Journal of Applied Psychology*, 89(1): 104.

Kim, P.H., Dirks, K.T., Cooper, C.D., and Ferrin, D.L. (2006). When more blame is better than less: The implications of internal vs. external attributions for the repair of trust after a competence- vs. integrity-based trust violation. *Organizational Behavior and Human Decision Processes*, 99(1): 49–65.

Luo, Y. (2002) Contract, cooperation and performance in international joint ventures. *Strategic Management Journal*, 23: 903–909.

March, J.G., and Olsen, J.P. (1975). The uncertainty of the past: organizational learning under ambiguity. *European Journal of Political Research*, 3(2): 147–171.

Macaulay, S. (1963). Non-contractual relations in business: a preliminary study. *American Sociological Review*, 28: 55–67.

Mayer, K.J. and Argyres, N. (2004). Learning to contract: evidence from the personal computer industry, *Organization Science*, 15: 394–410.

Overbye, M. and Wagner, U. (2014). Experiences, attitudes and trust: an inquiry into elite athletes' perception of the whereabouts reporting system. *International Journal of Sport Policy and Politics*, 6(3): 407–428.

Poppo, L. and Zenger, T. (2002). Do formal contracts and relational governance function as substitutes or complements? *Strategic Management Journal*, 23: 707–725.

Riordan, C.A., Marlin, N.A. and Kellogg, R.T. (1983). The effectiveness of accounts following transgression, *Social Psychology Quarterly*, 46: 213–219.

Rousseau, D.M., Burt, R.S., Sitkin, S.B. and Camerer, C. (1998). Not so different after all: a cross-discipline view of trust. *Academy of Management Review*, 23: 393–404.

Sigal, J., Hsu, L., Foodim, S. and Betman, J. (1988). Factors affecting perceptions of political candidates accused of sexual and financial misconduct. *Political Psychology*, 9(2): 273–280.

Sitkin, S. (1995). On the positive effect of legalization on trust, in R.J. Bies, R.J. Lewicki and B.H. Sheppard (eds), *Research on Negotiation in Organizations* (Vol. 5, pp. 185–217). Greenwich, CT: JAI press.

Skinner, D., Dietz, G. and Weibel, A. (2013). The dark side of trust: when trust becomes a 'poisoned chalice'. *Organization*, DOI: 1350508412473866.

Smith, J.B. and Barclay, D.W. (1997). The effects of organizational differences and trust on the effectiveness of selling partner relationships. *The Journal of Marketing*, 3–21.

Slack, T. and Parent, M.M. (2007). *Understanding Sport Organizations*. Champaign, IL, Human Kinetics.

Sousa-Lima, M., Michel, J.W. and Caetano, A. (2013). Clarifying the importance of trust in organizations as a component of effective work relationships. *Journal of Applied Social Psychology*, 43(2): 418–427.

Sydow, J. and Windeler, A. (2003). Knowledge, trust, and control. *International Studies of Management and Organization*, 33: 69–99.

Vlaar, P.W.L., Van den Bosch, F.A.J and Volberda, H.W. (2007). On the evolution of trust, distrust, and formal coordination and control in interorganizational relationships: towards an integrative framework. *Group and Organization Management*, 32(4): 407–428.

Wu, S.H., Tsai, C.Y.D., and Hung, C.C. (2012). Toward team or player? How trust, vicarious achievement motive, and identification affect fan loyalty. *Journal of Sport Management*, 26(2): 177–191.

Zaheer, A. and Venkatraman, N. (1995). Relational governance as an interorganizational strategy: an empirical test of the role of trust in economic exchange, *Strategic Management Journal*, 16: 373–392.

Zand, D.E. (1972). Trust and managerial problem solving. *Administrative Science Quarterly*, 17: 229–239.

Zucker, L.G. (1986). Production of trust: institutional sources of economic structure, in B.M. Staw and L.L. Cummings (eds), *Research in Organizational Behavior* (Vol. 8, pp. 53–111). Greenwich, CT: JAI.

32

SPONSORSHIP IN SPORT

NICOLAS CHANAVAT
AND GUILLAUME BODET

What [Qatar], did, in sponsoring Paris Saint-Germain (PSG), was choose the only football franchise in the most iconic city in the world.

(Frédéric Longuépée, Deputy Managing Director, Paris Saint-Germain (see Desbordes and Chanavat, 2014))

The world is changing. We must open up our hearts and minds. We must invite people to our country so we can learn from them and they can learn from us. Tourism is the gateway to the world. Focusing on tourism will also enable us to improve our infrastructure and visitor facilities and services.

(Issa Bin Mohammed Al-Mohannadi, Qatar Tourism Authority chair, 2014)

We set out with a huge promise to the world: to deliver the most sustainable Olympic Games of Modern Times. Seven years, 9 million visitors and 2,484 medals later, that's exactly what we achieved. London 2012 wouldn't have reached the level of sustainability that it did without the support and commitment of our Partners.

(David Stubbs, Head of Sustainability, London Organising Committee of the Olympic and Paralympic Games, LOCOG)

Upon completion of this chapter, students will be able to:

- To introduce the concept of sponsorship and its role in the management of sport.

- To understand the reasons for a large sponsorship deal between a foreign state and a French football club.

- To analyze the inclusion of CSR objectives in sporting event sponsorship.

INTRODUCTION

As advertising and marketing strategy have evolved over the past 30 years, possibly no one approach that organizations use to reach consumers has undergone more transformation than sponsorship. Indeed, sponsorship arrangements have been one of the fastest growing forms of promotional activities. The International Events Group (IEG) estimates that global sponsorship expenditures reached US$53.3 billion in 2012 (IEG, 2013). This represents an increasingly popular field in marketing practice and research and now accounts for a significant part of the marketing mix. It is seen as a strategic decision to achieve "a position of sustainable competitive advantage" (Amis et al., 1997: 81), and differs from other ways of doing marketing even if they are not mutually exclusive.

According to Gardner and Shuman (1988: 44) "sponsorship may be defined as investments in causes or events to support corporate objectives (by enhancing corporate image) or marketing objectives (such as increasing brand awareness)." Therefore, "sponsorship has the capacity to achieve a range of goals, such as corporate image, **corporate social responsibility**, brand exposure, marketing sales, and effects (e.g., image building, goodwill generation, attitude change). Moreover, a company's sponsorship activities are able to impact simultaneously on internal and external publics, such as general public, internal staff, politicians/regulators, **media**, target market, self/peers" (Meenaghan, 2005: 246). However, while organizations enter into sponsorship arrangements for a variety of reasons, one of the most important ones is to "establish, strengthen, or change **brand** image" (Gwinner and Eaton, 1999: 47).

Gauging the value of sponsorship's return on investment is certainly achievable but challenging. As with other communication tools, sponsorship should be measured against clearly expressed objectives that can be agreed prior to the commencement of activities. It is against these goals that the success or failure of a sponsorship program should be assessed. Obviously, objectives need to be set in such a way that performance can be fairly gauged. The underlying aim is for organizations to obtain a tangible return through the link that is established between the sponsorship property and the company or brand. Overall, sponsorship aims to modify or enhance cognitive, affective or conative reactions of the consumer regarding brands (Chanavat et al., 2009).

A look at the latest trends in sponsorship, focusing on what has recently emerged and what the implications are for 2014, identifies the following issues: digital marketing, social media, in stadia naming, ambush marketing, multiple sponsorship, corporate social responsibility (CSR), etc. In addition, there is development in the nature of the entities involved in sponsorship activities: states and regions, non-profit organizations, etc. Therefore, this chapter highlights two different kinds of sponsorships in sport (i.e. foreign state sponsorships and CSR sponsorship) and seeks to understand the potential impact of this marketing approach in these contexts.

CASE STUDY 32.1

Sponsorship, Marketing and Place Administration

Qatar has turned its attention towards sport and particularly football. In 2011 the Qatar Investment Authority took over the French professional football club of Paris Saint-Germain (PSG). In 2013, the club officially announced their sponsorship deal with the Qatar Tourism Authority (QTA), which would net the French Ligue 1 champions up to €200 million a year. The agreement was publicly confirmed making PSG the first official club to be sponsored by a state. Thanks to this, the French club made it into the top five of the Deloitte's Money League (2014), recording the highest ever commercial revenue for a football club. In fact, PSG's €254.7 million' commercial revenue represents the highest ever total from a single revenue stream in the history of the Money League because of the sponsorship activities. For Qatar, most investments are long-term strategic investments. They all contribute to the Qatar National Vision 2030, which seeks to shift the country from a carbon economy to a knowledge economy.

Sponsorship alone is limited, as the process requires the synergy of communication that can make it interesting (Cornwell et al., 2006). This case study allows a deeper understanding of how a state can use sponsorship in sport as a strategic tool in its marketing program. States, countries, regions or cities all over the world are faced with the consequences that economic and cultural globalization and other major trends pose for the environment that these places operate in, and are challenged by changes in their economic, cultural and social mosaic. One of these consequences is increased competition among places, which is apparent in various levels and fields of activity. Nowadays, fierce competition for resources, for business relocation, for foreign investment, for visitors and even residents seems to be evident (Kotler et al., 1999). In order to respond to the demands of competition and attract the desired target groups, place administrators have recognized in marketing theory and practice a valuable ally. They are following ideas and utilizing practices developed by marketing peculiar environment and translating concepts according to their needs and characteristics (Barke, 1999). Therefore, Ashworth and Voogd (1990) highlight that theoretical emergence of place marketing is attributed to the development of marketing in non-profit organizations, of social marketing and of image marketing, all of which contribute to the emancipation of traditional marketing thought from goals and practices attached to this initial field of application. Overall, there is an evident shift towards branding, which has been recognized widely in the literature (Hauben et al., 2002; Trueman et al., 2004). It seems to be and is apparent in the practice of place marketing (Kavaratzis, 2004).

In light of the literature, it also seems that place branding represents a complex subject that encompasses five trends. Place of origin branding (Kotler and Gertner, 2002; Gerke et al., 2013) concerns the usage of the place of origin in branding a product. Nations branding (e.g. van Ham, 2001) act as advisors to national governments that have realized the potential advantages of branding their territory but do not have the knowledge and skills necessary to design and implement branding campaigns and strategies. Destination branding (Morgan et al., 2002) represents the most developed in theory and the most used in practice trend within place branding has been investigation of the role of branding in the marketing of tourism destinations. Entertainment branding (Hannigan, 2004) is the examination of the impact of cultural, sport and entertainment branding on the physical, economic and social environment of cities. Place/city branding discusses the possibilities of exploiting branding as an approach to integrate, guide and focus place management (Hankinson, 2004; Kavaratzis, 2004).

TOOLS FOR ANALYSIS

Qatar, sport and sponsorship

'One of the things we always forget is that Qatar has chosen sports as a vehicle to promote the country. Football is probably one of the greatest [sports], it's the most watched sport in the world and Qatar has decided to invest a lot of energy, time and money into promoting the country through football. (Frédéric Longuépée, see Desbordes and Chanavat, 2014)'

The Al Thani family has ruled Qatar as an absolute and hereditary emirate since the mid-nineteenth century. It was a British protectorate until it gained independence in 1971. Since then, it has become one of the region's wealthiest states due to its massive oil and natural gas revenues. In 1995 Sheikh Hamad bin Khalifa Al Thani became Emir when he deposed his father in a peaceful coup d'état. As ruler of Qatar for 18 years, he has since transferred the "reins of power" to his son in June 2013. The outgoing emir made the announcement to hand over power to Sheikh Tamim bin Hamad Al Thani, 33. Qatar tops Forbes' list of the world's richest countries (Forbes, 2013). With a small citizen population of fewer than 300,000 people, foreign workers by far outnumber native Qataris.

In this context, in 2005, the Qatar Investment Authority (QIA), which controls more than US$100 billion of assets, was founded by the state of Qatar to reinforce the emirate's economy by varying this within new asset classes. Constructing on the heritage of Qatar investments dating back more than three decades, its developing portfolio of long-term strategic investments helps complement the state's huge wealth in natural resources. Qatar's objective has been to become a major international center for finance and investment management, a vision shared by its government, people and institutions. Indeed, Qatar wants to exercise soft power influence in a troubled region via attraction. Headquartered in Doha, the QIA is structured to operate at the very highest levels of global investment. As a world-class investor, the QIA adheres to the strictest financial and commercial disciplines. It has a strong track record of investing in different asset classes, including listed securities, property, alternative assets and private equity in all the main capital markets, as well as the newer emerging markets. So what does Qatar look for when choosing where to invest its vast wealth? Most investments are long-term strategic investments, but they all contribute to the Qatar National Vision 2030, which seeks to shift the state from a carbon economy to a knowledge economy. Indeed, the Qatar National Vision 2030 builds a bridge from the present to the future. It wants to transform the country into an advanced state, sustaining its development and providing a high standard of living for all of its people for generations to come. Hence, it is looking to increase the number of tourists. There were approximately 2.5 million visitors in 2011 and Qatar is trying to increase this figure to 7.4 million by 2030 (*Doha News*, 2014): "Tourism is a means to enhance the image and identity of a country worldwide," said QTA chair Issa Bin Mohammed Al-Mohannadi (*Doha news*, 2014). The QTA plans to focus its promotional and funding efforts on tourism products and services that fall into several categories: (1) culture, authentic Qatari and Arab experiences; (2) urban, shopping, entertainment, dining and relaxation; (3) meetings, conferences and exhibitions; (4) sun and beach; (5) health and wellness; (6) nature: wildlife, desert dunes and bodies of water; (7) sports; and (8) education (*Doha News*, 2014).

Overall, Chanavat and Desbordes (2014) stress that the sovereign wealth fund, Qatar Investment Authority, through its organ dedicated to the sport industry, Qatar Sports Investments, has developed a strategy of influence throughout sports based on the following main activities: the acquisition of professional sport clubs (Paris Saint-Germain and Paris Handball); the organization of recurring events (Open Tennis Doha, the Tour of Qatar, Qatar Masters golf, etc.) and one-off events (the 2006 Asian Games, the 2010 World Indoor Athletics Championships, the 2022 FIFA World Cup, etc.); the acquisition of television and broadcasting rights (Ligue 1 Orange, UEFA Champions League, etc.), the creation of a sporting goods manufacturer (Burrda Sport); contractual partnerships (FC Barcelona, Qatar Prix de l'Arc de Triomphe, the Tour de France, etc.). In any event, multiplication of the association, partnership and activation with different sport brands with named multiple sport sponsorship (Chanavat et al., 2009, 2010) could have complex cognitive, affective and conative impacts. Qatar's strategy moves beyond the scope of the emirate itself to influence the entire international perception of the Middle East. The development of a Qatar brand can make a tiny state a diplomatic and economic reference in a region with powerful states like Saudi Arabia and the United Arab Emirates. However, it still seems difficult to measure the effectiveness of this new strategy based on sponsorships.

In 2011, the Qatar Investment Authority took over the French professional football club of Paris Saint-Germain. This investment is part of the overall development strategy of Qatar, which has made sport a cornerstone of this strategy to develop its brand image and its affect on consumers and policy makers around the world: "So both the 2030 plan and the plan to increase the number of visitors by 2020 are long-term and I trust QSI will invest on a long-term basis with Paris Saint-Germain as well if you look at the way Qatar is investing through QSI (which is a corporate strategy) and the way the Qatar Tourism Authority is a partner of Paris Saint-Germain, I don't think it's too much considering the return on investment, which is pretty efficient" (Frédéric Longuépée, see Desbordes and Chanavat, 2014). The tourism strategy places an emphasis on setting up more tourism-related attractions outside Doha. As part of its efforts to woo more tourists from Europe, the Qatar Tourism Authority has announced a new partnership deal with Paris Saint-Germain. This formal announcement comes nearly a year after media reports first surfaced about the tie-in. The deal will help PSG, which is owned by QSI, an entity of the state's sovereign wealth fund, to comply with the new financial fair play rules for European clubs that require them not to spend more than they earn. In a statement, the PSG CEO Jean-Claude Blanc declared: "Our association with QTA allows us to have the means necessary to develop the club in the direction that we envision. The club's image clearly benefits from it and so do our results. We are able to give our supporters all around the world a high level of performance matching their expectations and our ambitions" (*Doha News*, 2013).

Association with Paris Saint-Germain

The sponsorship literature has shown that it is essential for the sponsor to be associated with a sponsee that shares its values and where the degree of congruence is acceptable and thus closer to its target (Becker-Olsen and Simmons, 2002). The association component and especially the emotional association are particularly necessary for sponsorship, as the sponsee may be linked in memory with the sponsoring brand (Keller, 1993). Chanavat et al. (2010) highlight that football is perceived as a "democratic" sport because it is popular across all socio-economic levels and has a truly global reach. It combines "passion" with "fun" and represents a positive way to emotionally connect commercial brands with people. For example, many people in many countries around the world stop all their activities for 90 minutes in order to watch some matches in the context of the FIFA World Cup. Beyond the generations, families, women and children celebrate the magic of this social event happening together. In this context, the French football Ligue 1 is recognized as one of the five major European leagues, along with the English Premier League, German Bundesliga 1, Italian Serie A and Spanish Liga 1. It represents a championship organized by the French professional football league

(Ligue de Football Professionnel, LFP). Two characteristics condition sporting stakes and thus team situations in the standing: the existence of continental competitions and relegations (Scelles et al., 2013).

"First of all, one objective of Paris Saint-Germain—and we do not communicate this widely—is to become one of the biggest sports properties in the world in the next five to eight years" (Frédéric Longuépée, see Desbordes and Chanavat, 2014). In this sense, in January 2013, the arrival of David Beckham at PSG has created a craze hitherto never seen in France for an athlete. It is a further step in the globalization of French football, the globalization of the PSG brand, and consequently the globalization of Qatar. In other words, beyond the sporting aspect, the arrival of superstar players contributes to the overall strategy of business and marketing club owners. Then 38 years old, he continues to be the most famous football player, particularly in Asia and North America. At the time of the announcement of his signing, PSG instantly gained 5,700 followers on Twitter and 23,591 fans on Facebook. And more than 150 journalists attended the press conference. One consequence is that the club sold 400,000 jerseys in 2012–2013, an increase of 60% in one year, and became one of the richest clubs in the world. His contract with PSG seems to fit within this logic of making Qatar more attractive, and encouraging sport tourism. It seems that Beckham and his brand will help make Doha more international, more showbiz, more glamorous. In this sense, Frédéric Longuépée (see Desbordes and Chanavat, 2014) highlighted that:

> David Beckham is probably one of the most iconic people in the world when it comes to sport and fashion. He's on the front cover of sports newspapers and he's in fashion magazines. So he helps the club to get out of the sporting industry and enter into the fashion industry, which is all about people. This obviously helps the club to be seen by people other than just the pure football fans. From an international point of view it helps to be seen by people all over the world because when Beckham signed for Paris Saint-Germain, there was a huge buzz across the world.

More than just talent or experience, the player added some brand star power to PSG and Qatari investors. Beckham's new contract perfectly illustrates Qatar's long-term strategy outlined in the Qatar National Vision 2030. The fact that the Qatar Tourism Authority (QTA) has once again become sponsors of PSG seems to bolster this hypothesis.

The Deloitte Money League (2014) had a number of interesting changes. Nevertheless, the main development was the emergence of PSG, who reached fifth place with €398.8 million, climbing above Chelsea FC (seventh) and Arsenal FC (eighth). Indeed PSG, owned by Qatar Sports Investments (QSI), signed a huge sponsorship deal with the Qatar Tourism Authority. This represented an innovative association in the context of sponsorship. Income from the deal, which will reportedly be retroactively active from 2012, is said to increase incrementally year-on-year up to a reported maximum of €200 million come 2016.

In this perspective, PSG recorded the highest ever commercial revenue for a football club. In fact, PSG's €254.7 million commercial revenue is the highest ever from a single revenue stream in the history of the Money League. PSG have been able to increase their revenue almost five-fold since the season of 2009–2010, while Bayern Munich's commercial income reached €237 million and Real Madrid's €211.6 million (Deloitte, 2014). In substance, the Fair Value rule is UEFA's way to ensure that owners do not artificially inject cash into the club as a way of getting round the financial fair play rules. It represents a pivotal clause in the financial fair play rules because without it it could be easy for owners to bypass those rules by getting their companies to pour millions into their teams. For two years now, QTA has put up to €200 million a year into Paris Saint-Germain under an advertising contract designed only to help the French club meet UEFA's financial fair play rules. Even if the QTA sponsorship deal with PSG does not include shirt sponsorship or stadium-naming rights, this innovative association seems to have had a potential massive impact for the emirate. In this way, Frédéric Longuépée (see Desbordes and Chanavat, 2014) argues, I have met with people from the Qatar Tourism Authority. They are really willing to develop the country as a tourist destination and the analysis we've done recently shows that when you survey football fans, they are much more aware of Qatar than non-fans and much more willing to go to Qatar. This shows that the partnership and the activation we implemented through QTA are efficient."

ACTION LEARNING

- In what ways can sport marketers develop a sport sponsorship from a place administration?
- How and why did other territory use this marketing strategy recently?

- How can a sport marketer measure the efficiency of this innovative sponsorship deal?
- Why has Qatar chosen Paris in order to promote the state and why does this deal make sense for PSG?

THINKING POINT 32.1

Coca-Cola and Corporate Social Responsibility

As a worldwide TOP (The Olympic Partner) partner for the Olympic movement and the 2012 London Olympics in the non-alcoholic beverages category, Coca-Cola aimed to encourage consumers to lead more active, healthy and sustainable lifestyles. This corporate social responsibility objective associated with sponsorship of the Games was made possible with the partnership of a charity organization StreetGames, which provided sporting opportunities for young people from disadvantaged communities across the UK.

TOOLS FOR ANALYSIS

Sponsors' motives and objectives

The reasons why organizations and companies engage in sport sponsorship activities are broad and strongly vary between contexts. If commercial motives might appear as the most obvious reasons as mentioned in the introduction, these are certainly not the only ones, and many other motives can be identified. Among them, personal motives and interest (Polonsky et al., 1996), which can be associated with liking a specific sport or team (Burton et al., 1998) or with the advance of personal interests and agendas (Cornwell et al., 2001), have also been identified. Philanthropic, altruistic and social (Shaw and Amis, 2001), or patriotic motives, particularly in relation to the hosting of major sporting events such as the Olympic Games (Papadimitriou et al., 2008) have also been recognized in the literature. Finally, commercial motives have been widely identified and are associated with the advantages sponsorship can provide in comparison with traditional media (Ferrand et al., 2007; Meenaghan, 1991).

Motives and objectives are often used interchangeably in the literature (Charalambous-Papamiltiades, 2013) and although many of these do correspond (e.g. commercial motives are likely to lead to commercial objectives), this is not always the case. For instance, even with commercial and branding motives, not all sponsors set clear and measurable objectives (Chadwick and Thwaites, 2005). Also, the first reason to enter into a sport sponsorship agreement could be a personal motive with or without setting specific commercial objectives. Furthermore, certain motives (e.g. advancing personal agendas or political orientation) cannot necessarily be translated into explicit sponsorship objectives. Although objectives, when they exist, can clearly be expressed, this is not always the case for motives. As for branding and commercial sponsorship objectives, these can be categorized into four main types, which are increasing brand awareness, brand image, sales and internal communication (Desbordes and Tribou, 2007).

As for the brand awareness objective, Coca-Cola already benefits from very high worldwide brand awareness and it is unlikely that this objective was set as a priority by the brand. However, as a corporation owing a portfolio of more or less known brands (e.g. Schweppes Abbey Well, Innocent, Powerade, etc.), awareness may have been a secondary objective when supplying non-alcoholic beverages within the Olympic Park. Brand image objectives rely upon the potential transfer of positive image and associations (Gwinner and Eaton, 1999) from the sport event to the sponsor, and therefore from the Olympics to Coca-Cola in this particular case. This objective is probably the primary one for Coca-Cola considering the negative image soft drinks can have due to the amount of calories they contain and their consequent possible impact on people's health and alleged contribution to obesity among young people. It is in light of this that the partnership with StreetGames aiming to increase sport opportunities and participation for young people should be examined. Considering the sales objectives, this may depend on the nature of the sponsors' products and services and this can be related to enhancing repeat purchasing and the concept of brand loyalty. As the official supplier of non-alcoholic beverages for Coca-Cola in the Olympic Park sales were certainly an objective as well as enhancing brand loyalty.

Finally, internal communication objectives aim to gather sponsors' employees and sometimes collaborators around a project and values to better perform, enhance a team spirit and make employees proud to work for their organization (Desbordes and Tribou, 2007). As for Coca-Cola, it is difficult to know if it has used its sponsorship of the London Olympics to achieve this objective, but we could note that the Olympics certainly represent a great platform from which to achieve these objectives considering its worldwide appeal and the positive values generally associated with Games and Olympism (e.g. excellence, inclusivity, diversity, efforts, achievements, etc.) (Ferrand et al., 2012).

Sponsorship and corporate social responsibility (CSR)

As for sponsors' motives, not all objectives are commercial, and more and more sponsorships are associated with philanthropic and social objectives, which probably fall into line with the increasing importance that corporate social responsibility (CSR) is having for firms and brands. CSR has proven difficult to define and for Crane et al. (2008: 6) "the subject of the social obligations and impacts of corporations in society" lies at the core of debates about its definition. This idea of social obligation is also at the heart of the debate between motives and objectives, and if one sponsor feels obliged to set social objectives, no one can really know whether it corresponds to social and philanthropic motives, to commercial motives of brand protection, or a mix of both. This is confirmed by Bradish and Cronin (2009: 692) when they state that "CSR is not pure philanthropy, but rather, a holistic business mindset, much like a corporate culture, where the 'socially responsible' obligations of the firm could and indeed, should incorporate both social and economic interests."

In the case of Coca-Cola's sponsorship of the Olympics, the social and altruistic objective was to "inspire change, participation and a lasting legacy" (Coca-Cola, 2012). This objective can be considered as social as it does not directly and/or explicitly respond to commercial objectives and aim to improve sport participation, which is often seen to have positive impacts on health, social interaction and integration (Smith and Westerbeek, 2007), especially for deprived areas and communities in the UK. This philanthropic aspect was evident when Coca-Cola claimed that it aimed to help people lead active and healthy lives and provide sporting opportunities for those from disadvantaged areas. However, despite this social dimension, it is not possible to exclude any commercial interest from it, as improving sport participation could be seen for Coca-Cola as a way to justify the consumption of their products and counter criticisms regarding their high-calorie nature. These CSR programs would then improve the image of the corporation and its products, which corresponds to Bradish and Cronin's (2009) comment about the dual (i.e. philanthropic and business) nature of CSR.

Although many Olympic event sponsors engage with CSR programs (Bretherton, 2014), the particularity of this case is the strong involvement of StreetGames, a charity organization, which was responsible for the operational aspects of the program and the organization of the sport sessions in those deprived areas. StreetGames brought their expertise and network to the partnership but also brought legitimacy to Coca-Cola reinforcing its corporate and brand image. In this case, these CSR activities can also be considered as activation and leveraging activities which are perceived as crucial to maximize the benefits a sponsor can accrue from these partnerships (Ferrand et al., 2007). This also corresponds to the latest trends in terms of sponsorship activation, which have seen increasing partnerships and brand alliances between various sport events' stakeholders to maximize the benefits for all involved (Ferrand et al., 2012).

ACTION LEARNING

- What are the differences between sponsors' motives and objectives?
- Which other sponsors were involved in CSR activities during the 2012 London Olympics and in recent major sporting events? Which objectives and strategies did they have?
- What kind of non-CSR-related activation and leveraging activities have sport events' sponsors recently been engaged in?

CONCLUSION

Once considered a simple financial contribution, sponsorship is now an integral part of the marketing strategies of organizations. It meets the same evaluation criteria as a campaign advertising or promotion. It seems that sponsorship represents the most emotional of all communication mediums. No other medium could compare with the strength of emotional attachment that consumers have with the sports entities (events, players, clubs, etc.) and properties they so dearly love. It would seem that to simply rely on an equivalent media value for evaluating sponsorship would miss the uniqueness of this relationship, which has become increasingly collaborative between sponsors and sponsee and is increasingly involving other stakeholders.

REFERENCES

Amis, J., Pant, N. & Slack, T. (1997). Achieving a sustainable competitive advantage: a resource-baced view of sport sponsorship. *Journal of Sport Management,* 11(1): 80–96.

Ashworth, G.J. & Voogd, H. (1990). *Selling the City: Marketing Approaches in Public Sector Urban Planning.* Belhaven Press: London.

Barke, M. (1999). City Marketing as a Planning Tool, in M. Pacione (ed.), *Applied Geography: Principles and Practice*. London: Routledge.

Becker-Olsen K. & Simmons C.J. (2002). When do social sponsorships enhance or dilute equity? Fit, message source, and the persistence of effects, *Advances in Consumer Research*, 29: 287–289.

Bradish, C. & Cronin, J.J. (2009). Corporate social responsibility in sport, *Journal of Sport Management*, 23: 691–697.

Bretherton, P. (2014). Corporate social responsibility at London 2012: the dynamics of sport and activity promotion at the Olympic Games. Unpublished doctoral thesis, Loughborough University.

Burton, R., Quester, P.G. & Farrelly, F.J. (1998). Organizational power games, *Marketing Management*, 7(1): 26–36.

Chadwick, S. & Thwaites, D. (2005). Managing sport sponsorship programs: lessons from a critical assessment of English soccer, *Journal of Advertising Research*, September: 328–338.

Chanavat, N. & Desbordes, M. (2014). Le parrainage sportif multiple événementiel: atouts, défis et conditions de succès, *Revue Gestion (HEC Montréal)*, 38(4): 27–36.

Chanavat, N., Martinent, G. & Ferrand, A. (2009). Sponsor and sponsees interactions: effects on consumers' perceptions of brand image, brand attachment and purchasing intention, *Journal of Sport Management*, 23(5): 644–670.

Chanavat, N., Martinent, G. & Ferrand, A. (2010). Brand images causal relationships in a multiple sport event sponsorship context: developing brand value through association with sport sponsees, *European Sport Management Quarterly*, 10(1): 49–74.

Charalambous-Papamiltiades, M. (2013). Sport marketing in Cyprus: the dynamics of the sport sponsorship context: Emergence, development and management practices in the football industry. Unpublished doctoral thesis, Loughborough University.

Coca-Cola (2012). *London 2012: Our Sustainability Legacy*. London: Coca-Cola.

Cornwell, T.B., Humphreys, M.S., Maguire A.M., Weeks C.S. & Tellegen, C.L. (2006). Sponsorship-linked marketing: the role of articulation in memory, *Journal of Consumer Research*, 33(December): 312–321.

Cornwell, T.B., Pruitt, S.W. & Van Ness, R. (2001). The value of winning in motorsports: sponsorship-linked marketing, *Journal of Advertising Research*, 41(1): 17–31.

Crane, A., McWilliams, A., Matten, D., Moon, J. & Siegel, D. (2008). The Corporate Social Responsibility Agenda. In A. Crane, A. McWilliams, D. Matten, J. Moon & D. Siegel (eds), *The Oxford Handbook of Corporate Social Responsibility* (pp. 3–18). Oxford: Oxford University Press.

Deloitte (2014). *Football Money League 2014 Report*. London: Deloitte.

Desbordes, M. & Chanavat, N. (2014). Interview with Frederic Longuépée, Deputy Managing Director, Paris-Saint-Germain, *International Journal of Sport Marketing and Sponsorship*, 15(2): 79–88.

Desbordes, M. & Tribou, G. (2007). Sponsorship, Endorsements and Naming Rights. In J. Beech and S. Chadwick (eds), *The Marketing of Sport*, pp. 267–291. Harlow: Pearson Education.

Doha News (2013). QTA announces deal with Paris Saint Germain to promote country's brand. Available at: http://dohanews.co/qta-announces-deal-with-paris-saint-germain-to-promote-countrys-brand.

Doha News (2014). Qatar aims to attract 7.4 million annual visitors by 2030. Available at: http://dohanews.co/qatar-aims-to-attract-7-4–million-annual-visitors-by-2030.

Ferrand, A., Chappelet, J.L. & Séguin, B. (2012). *Olympic Marketing*. Abingdon: Routledge.

Ferrand, A., Torrigiani, L. & Camps Povil, A. (2007). *Routledge Handbook of Sports Sponsorship: Successful Strategies*. Abingdon: Routledge.

Forbes (2013). The World's Top-Saving Countries, 2013. Available at: www.forbes.com/sites/danalexander/2013/11/08/worlds-top-saving-countries-2013.

Gardner, M. & Shuman, P. (1988). Sponsorships and small business, *Journal of Small Business Management*, 26(4): 44–52.

Gerke, A., Chanavat, N. & Benson-Rea, M. (2014). How can country-of-origin image be leveraged to create global sporting goods brands, *Sport Management Review*, 17: 174–189.

Gwinner, K.P. & Eaton, J. (1999). Building brand image transfer through event sponsorship: the role of image transfer, *Journal of Advertising*, 28(4): 47–57.

Hankinson G. (2004). Relational network brands: towards a conceptual model of place brands, *Journal of Vacation Marketing*, 10(2): 109–121.

Hannigan J. (2004). Boom towns and cool cities: the perils and prospects of developing a distinctive urban brand in a global economy. Paper presented at the Leverhulme International Symposium: The Resurgent City, London School of Economics: April.

Hauben, T., Vermeulen, M. and Patteeuw, V. (eds) (2002). *City Branding: Image Building and Building Images*. NAI Uitgevers: Rotterdam.

International Events Group (2013). *IEG Sponsorship Report.* IEG.

Kavaratzis, M. (2004). From city marketing to city branding: towards a theoretical framework for developing city brands, *Place Branding*, 1(1): 58–73.

Keller K.L. (1993). Conceptualizing, measuring, and managing customer-based brand equity, *Journal of Marketing*, 57: 1–22.

Kotler, P. & Gertner, D. (2002). Country as brand, product, and beyond: a place marketing and brand management perspective, *Brand Management*, 9(4–5): 249–261.

Kotler, P., Asplund, C., Rein, I. & Heider, D. (1999). *Marketing Places Europe: Attracting Investments, Industries, Residents and Visitors to European Cities, Communities, Regions and Nations*. London: Pearson.

Meenaghan, T. (1991). The role of sponsorship in the marketing communications mix, *International Journal of Advertising,* 10(1): 35–47.

Meenaghan, T. (2005). Sport Sponsorship in a Global Age. In J. Amis and T.B. Cornwell (eds), *Global Sport Sponsorship*, pp. 243–246. Oxford: Berg.

Morgan, N., Pritchard, A. and Pride, R. (eds) (2002). *Destination Branding: Creating the Unique Destination Proposition*. Oxford: Butterworth-Heinemann.

Papadimitriou, D., Apostolopoulou, A. & Dounis, T. (2008). Event sponsorship as a value creating strategy for brands, *Journal of Product and Brand Management*, 17(4): 212–222.

Polonsky, M., Sandler, D., Casey, M., Murphy, S., Portelli, K. & Van Velzen, Y. (1996). Small business and sport sponsorship: the Australian experience, *Journal of Promotion Management*, 3(1, 2): 121–139.

Scelles, N., Durand, C., Bonnal, L., Goyeau, D. & Andreff, W. (2013). Competitive balance versus competitive intensity before a match: Is one of these two concepts more relevant in explaining attendance? The case of the French football Ligue 1 over the period 2008–2011, *Applied Economics*, 45(29): 4184–4192.

Shaw, S. & Amis, J. (2001). Image and investment: sponsorship and women's sport. *Journal of Sport Management* 15(3): 219–246.

Smith, A. & Westerbeek, H. (2007). Sport as a vehicle for deploying corporate social responsibility, *Journal of Corporate Citizenship*, Spring: 1–12.

Trueman, M., Klemm, M. & Giroud, A. (2004). Can a city communicate? Bradford as a corporate brand, *Corporate Communications: An International Journal*, 9(4): 317–330.

van Ham, P. (2001). The rise of the brand state: the post-modern politics of image and reputation, *Foreign Affairs*, 80(5): 2–6.

USEFUL WEBSITES

www.deloitte.com
www.forbes.com
www.sponsorship.com
www.uefa.com

33

ATHLETE TRANSGRESSIONS: IMPLICATIONS FOR SPORT MANAGERS

KATE WESTBERG, CONSTANTINO STAVROS, BRADLEY WILSON AND AARON SMITH

Adidas's criticism of Liverpool's Luis Suárez may hit where it hurts.

(*Guardian*, 23 April 2013, www.theguardian.com/sport/blog/2013/apr/22/adidas-criticism-liverpool-luis-suarez)

Patriots were "taken aback" by murder charge.

(*The Boston Globe*, 29 June 2013, www.bostonglobe.com/sports/2013/06/28/patriots-had-inside-knowledge-murder-charge-before-cutting-aaron-hernandez/efZRO6DxYpy6AZd7SMH3OL/story.html)

PGA Tour begins to pay a price for Tiger Woods's transgressions.

(*The Wall Street Journal*, 25 January 2010, www.wsj.com/articles/SB10001424052748703699204575017550261245506)

LEARNING OUTCOMES

Upon completion of this chapter, students should be able to:

- Identify the potential impact on relationships between a sport organization and their sponsors as a result of athlete transgressions.

- Understand the factors that influence the impact on sponsorship relationships.

- Appreciate the fan and community response to athlete transgressions and the implications.

- Understand the strategies that managers within sport organizations can use to manage athlete transgressions.

INTRODUCTION

The steady growth of professional sport has been fueled by the explosion of media channels facilitating greater consumption and commercialization opportunities. Consumers now are experiencing unprecedented levels of exposure to sport, for example, by spectating using a variety of media, through sport images in marketing as well as through sport-related merchandise (Cashmore, 2010). The increased exposure of sport has also triggered the rise in profile of sport teams and their athletes. Given the interest in professional sports people, the media have responded with extensive coverage of athletes' sporting performance as well as their activities outside of sport. As such, sport entities and athletes have become desirable properties on many levels and this status is reflected in the media attention and the significant sponsorships and endorsements both athletes and their teams can attract. Sponsorship has been recognized as a powerful platform for building brands (Cliffe and Motion, 2005), and sponsors are keen to associate their brands with the passion and profile garnered by sport, which can entail a significant investment. However, with this elevated status of sport, and in particular individual athletes, comes increasing pressure to maintain that position, not only as it relates to their performance on the field but in all aspects of their lives.

Unfortunately, in recent years, many major sport organizations around the world have been challenged by incidents of inappropriate and illegal behavior perpetrated by athletes as well as the subsequent media scrutiny those incidents attract. These incidents, or transgressions, can include sexual assault, drug use, driving while intoxicated, speeding, unauthorized gambling, assault and on-field violence. Transgressions can be described as a violation of the implicit or explicit rules guiding relationship behavior. The breaking of rules or overstepping the standards of normative behavior can have a significant impact on sport organizations and their stakeholders (Westberg et al., 2011).

This chapter explores the implications of athlete transgressions for sport management in terms of the potential impact on relationships with sponsors, fans and the community in general.

CASE STUDY 33.1

Insuring Sponsorship Success

The Transport Accident Commission (better known as the TAC) is a government-operated insurer based in the state of Victoria, Australia. The TAC assists people and families affected by traffic accidents by providing financial compensation and support. In the 2011/12 financial year, the TAC paid out almost AUS $1 billion in benefits and compensation to over 44,000 people.[1]

The TAC is somewhat unique in that it is best known in the community for its long-standing and award-winning marketing activities aimed at creating awareness of road safety issues and modifying the behavior of motorists. Numerous powerful advertising campaigns have highlighted dangerous transport practices, including those related to alcohol, speed and fatigue. This approach has had the effect of significantly reducing the number of injuries and deaths on Victorian roads.

One platform that the TAC considers useful for its safe driving messages is sport sponsorship. Whilst this is appropriate for targeting many audiences, the TAC is particularly interested in reaching young male drivers, who are statistically more likely to be involved in dangerous driving practices than other demographic groups. Sport sponsorship is an ideal channel to target this group.

The TAC has sponsored a number of teams and sports. One of the most notable is Australian football through the TAC Cup, which is an elite Under 18's competition that the TAC has supported since the Cup commenced in 1992. Many of the players in this league will go on to play in the Australian Football League (AFL), which is arguably the most successful professional sporting code in Australia and features 10 teams from the State of Victoria.

The TAC has also sponsored several AFL teams over the years—including Richmond and Collingwood, two of the most popular teams in the league. However these sponsorships have created controversy at times as the safe driving messages promoted by the TAC conflict with player transgressions relating to speeding and drink driving. Ultimately the relationship with these teams and the TAC ended after a string of player driving offences led many in the community to question the appropriateness of a sponsorship that provided an organization with several hundreds of thousands of dollars each year to promote a message that some of its own employees could not follow. Whilst the TAC initially warned and then fined the teams, increasing pressure to sever ties grew as the transgressions continued, despite the best efforts of the teams involved to curb the negative player behavior.

---

[1]www.tac.vic.gov.au/about-the-tac/our-organization/what-we-do.

- For a sport organization that is being sponsored by a company, such as the TAC, who espouses responsible driving, what actions could they undertake to promote appropriate and positive behavior amongst their athletes?

- It is arguable that some poor driving behavior is almost inevitable amongst a large group of athletes. What could an organization such as the TAC do to deal with such outcomes, other than warnings and fines? Should it avoid sponsoring sport altogether given the risks?

TOOLS FOR ANALYSIS

Sport sponsorship has been described as a strategic business relationship between a sponsor and a sport organization, entity or athlete which is mutually beneficial (Farrelly and Quester, 2005). Sponsorships generally are entered into by sponsors seeking brand-related benefits through association with a sport or athlete. The brand image of the sport organization or event is used to define or enhance the perceptions of the sponsor's brand in the minds of their customers and other important stakeholders (Farrelly et al., 2006). For a sport organization, this means that a strong brand can attract potentially sizable sponsorship fees as well as increased exposure in the media and consequently greater exposure to potential sponsors. Therefore, active management of the sport entity brand is essential to develop successful relationships with sponsors (Cornwell et al., 2005). As depicted in the preceding case, transgressions involving athletes representing the sport entity may threaten the brands of both sport and sponsor and weaken or even ultimately dissolve the partnership. One of the key concerns for sponsors in relation to these transgressions is the potential for negative image transfer, i.e. that the actions of the sponsored entity will have an unfavorable "spill-over" effect on the sponsor's brand (Votolato and Unnava, 2006). Effective management of these incidents is critical to protecting the sport entity's brand equity, as well as that of the sponsor's, and ultimately the relationship (Kahuni et al., 2009).

It has been suggested that business-to-business relationships, like sponsorship arrangements, can be altered as a result of different types of interactions or experiences which can either be positive, negative or neutral (Schurr, 2007). A negative experience has been described as a degenerative episode which threatens the relationship by potentially reducing trust, cooperation and mutual understanding (Schurr et al., 2008). This change in the relationship can either be incremental, whereby the nature of the relationship is changed, or radical, which can result in termination of the relationship. The terms "critical event" or "critical incident" have also been used to describe an event that causes a radical change in a business environment (Halinen et al., 1999). Negative critical incidents have the ability to cause stakeholders to review long-term relationships and can also cause destabilization.

Research suggests that player transgressions can act as a degenerative episode in the relationship between the sport organization and their sponsor(s), resulting in potential change and even damage to the relation-ship (Westberg et al., 2011). For example, as a result of a transgression, or series of transgressions, sponsors have requested that behavioral clauses be added to the sponsorship agreement or contract. Violation of these clauses may then lead to fines or termination of the sponsorship arrangement. Other outcomes include non-renewal of the sponsorship agreement or ter-mination. However, it should be noted that an abrupt termination prior to the end of the contract may or may not be preceded by a number of warn-ings or discussions related to player behavior, as in the case of the TAC.

The type of change in relationship as a result of a player transgression depends upon a number of factors relating to the circumstances surround-ing the incident as well as the existing quality of the relationship (Westberg et al., 2011). Regarding the incident itself, for example, the potential for damage to a **sponsorship** partnership is influenced by the sponsor's perception of the severity of the incident; for example, drunken public behavior where no one is harmed versus driving while intoxicated or committing a sexual assault. The sponsor's perception of this severity may be influenced by the anticipated views and responses of their target audience, the company's values and/or the nature of their business. It is important for sport organizations to recognize that their sponsors may have different "zones of tolerance" related to the same transgres-sion. Further, the sponsor's reaction can relate to their attribution of blame.

Attribution theory explains how people interpret behavior and it is sug-gested that negative or unexpected events are subject to greater attributional analysis (Folkes, 1988; Kelly and Micheala, 1980). In the context of player transgressions, sponsors will seek to assess blame, in particular whether the sport organization is accountable for preventing or better managing the trans-gression in question. Sponsors are more likely to lay blame on the sport entity if these types of incidents occur frequently, as that may be seen to reflect poor management or a fundamental problem with the organization's culture. Finally, player transgressions which attract greater or more prolonged media coverage are of more concern to sponsors. Media scrutiny of a sport scandal can result in a sponsor's brand receiving significant negative exposure.

In addition to the circumstances surrounding the transgression, the impact on the sport-sponsor relationship also can be influenced by the quality of the relationship prior to the incident (Westberg et al., 2011). The key tenets for most relationships, whether business or personal, include communication, **trust** and commitment. A strong relationship between a sport organization and its sponsors can mitigate the damage to a relationship as a result of any negative episodes. Strong relationships are characterized by clear communication of expectations by the sponsor and a shared understanding of the sport organization's strategies to manage and prevent transgressions. Commitment to a sponsorship rela-tionship can be reflected by length of sponsorship and size of the sponsorship investment, as well as the degree to which the sponsorship relationship has been leveraged. The latter refers to specific relationship investments which are unique to the partnership and therefore non-transferable, and have been linked to suc-cessful alliances. However, the level of commitment, particularly in terms of sponsorship investment, may be outweighed by the severity of the transgression or the extent of media scrutiny. Further, the organization's inability to prevent repeated transgressions is likely to erode sponsor **trust**.

Finally, the impact on the sport–sponsor relationship is also determined by how the incident is managed by the sport organization. Characteristics of successful episode management include transparency and timeliness of **communication**, proactivity and good media management (Westberg et al., 2011). Management of athlete transgressions will be discussed further in the final section of this chapter.

ACTION LEARNING

- Considering the factors that influence the impact of a player transgression on the relationship between a sport organization and its sponsors, how might sponsorship from a bank differ from that of an athletic apparel brand, in terms of the likely response of the sponsor and the impact on the relationship?

- Research athlete transgressions that have been reported in the media to identify the different ways in which sponsors respond to these incidents. In examples where sponsorships have been terminated, what do you think motivated the sponsor to respond in this way?

CASE STUDY 33.2

Back from the Doghouse

In one of the more extraordinary cases of athlete transgressions to ever reach the public spotlight, Michael Vick was sent to prison for 23 months in 2007 for his role in a dog-fighting ring. Vick, a highly regarded quarterback, was signed by the Atlanta Falcons as the number one pick of the 2001 National Football League (NFL) Draft. In six seasons with the franchise, he was selected to the Pro-Bowl three times and led the Falcons to the play-offs twice.

Wishing to return to the NFL after his incarceration, Vick's prospects were thought to be bleak, with ESPN columnist John Clayton speculating in 2007 that it would be a "public relations nightmare" to sign Vick and that there might be a backlash from season ticket holders and corporate box holders (Clayton, 2007).

The situation was further complicated by the Falcons, who having signed Vick to a long-term contract in 2004 sought to have some of the signing bonus they paid him returned, whilst indicating they would not take Vick back as a player. Eventually the Philadelphia Eagles signed Vick in 2009 after the Falcons released him as an unrestricted free agent.

Not surprisingly, Vick's endorsements dried up after news of the nature of his transgression surfaced. Nike, one of his major sponsors, severed his contract in 2007. In a remarkable reversal, they then re-signed Vick in 2011 noting that whilst they did not condone his actions, they supported the positive changes he had made since the incident. Vick was awarded the title of "NFL Comeback Player of the Year" in 2010 by the Associated Press and the Professional Football Writers of America and was selected for his fourth Pro Bowl.

The decision by Nike caused widespread discussion, with some consumers seeking to boycott the brand, whilst others supported the tale of redemption. Nike's action was perhaps reflective of its penchant for supporting athletes through adversity. In another example in 2009, whilst other companies re-evaluated their relationship, Nike stood by Tiger Woods after he became embroiled in an infidelity scandal that saw him announce a break from golf that lasted almost four months.

ACTION LEARNING

- Nike's decision to re-sign Vick would have come after careful deliberation of the pros and cons of such an action. Outline what you think these pros and cons would have been for Nike specifically.
- In signing Vick, the Philadelphia Eagles needed to deal with the "public relations nightmare" that this decision would attract from a large range of stakeholders. What strategies would the Eagles have needed to undertake in order to manage this situation? In thinking of responses, first list and then consider the diverse range of groups who may have voiced their concern about Vick's signing.

TOOLS FOR ANALYSIS

Athlete transgressions have the potential to impact not only on the relationship between the sport organization and their sponsors, but also on the brands of both parties as well as the individual athlete. As seen in the preceding case study, Nike's actions generated a negative response from some consumers, who may have perceived the company's support of the athlete as either approval, or at the very least a lack of disapproval, regarding Vick's behavior.

With the increasing **commercialization** of the sport industry, organizations need to strategically manage a range of stakeholders in addition to their sponsors. Key constituents include the sport consumer, especially fans with high levels of **loyalty** or team identification, as well as the larger community in which the organization operates. With regard to highly identified fans, research suggests that off-field offenses committed by athletes can negatively impact on team identification (Fink et al., 2009). Social identity theory provides some insight into this response as it suggests that people join social groups which enhance self-esteem and therefore their own personal identity. Negative behavior by athletes may prompt highly identified fans to distance themselves from the team as this behavior is inconsistent with their expectations and their own identity. However, it has also been suggested that a strong response from team management clearly communicating the unacceptable nature of these incidents can help mitigate the potential for a negative response (Fink et al., 2009). As a result, sport managers need to be aware that, similar to sponsors, fans respond both to the transgression and the sport organization's management of the incident.

The perceived role of the athlete in society has also been shown to influence both fans and the general community in their response to athlete transgressions (Westberg et al. 2013). It has been noted that people are increasingly turning to the world of sport for their heroes and role models (Parry, 2009). Research suggests that the expectations of those who view athletes as role models extend beyond their on-field performance to include how they conduct themselves off-field (Westberg et al. 2013). These people may even hold athletes to a higher standard of behavior if they perceive them to be in a privileged position that carries significant financial rewards.

However, similar to sponsors, the fan and community response toward athlete transgressions is shaped by a number of factors, including the perceived severity of the transgression, the age and personal circumstances of the athlete concerned, and the perceived role of external influences (Westberg et al. 2013). Again, attribution theory is useful in explaining how consumers make sense of transgressions, i.e. if events do not conform to expectations then people will undergo a more elaborate examination of potential causes which in turn influences their ultimate reaction. Regarding the severity of an incident, research indicates that consumers, not surprisingly, are likely to be less tolerant of transgressions that are clearly in violation of the law, such as sexual assault and driving while intoxicated. However, more compassion may be extended in instances where the behavior is deemed to violate social norms, depending on the attributions made in relation to the behavior. The severity of the incident may also be judged according to the impact on others, either in relation to the sport or outside the sport. For example, in the case of assault, if an innocent bystander is injured in a brawl, a harsher judgment is a likely outcome. Similarly, if the incident has on-field implications, for example if the incident affected the athlete's playing ability, thereby impacting on the team and fans, this could result in a more critical evaluation of the transgression.

Greater compassion may be garnered for athletes who are young and therefore susceptible to the mistakes of youth. Similarly, an athlete's circumstances, such as an underprivileged upbringing or a struggle with addiction, may engender more understanding and tolerance. In general, sport consumers may be more moderate in their response if they can attribute blame to factors outside an athlete's control. However, this attribution of blame may transfer to the sport organization if they are perceived to have either facilitated the event; for example, team functions involving excessive alcohol consumption, or if they have not taken steps to prevent potential transgressions, for example by educating players or assisting them with rehabilitation. The attributions of sport consumers, and in particular highly identified fans, may result in damage to **fan loyalty** or team identification (Fink et al., 2009). The impact is not always visible in the form of complaint behavior or customer exit, but can impact on commitment to the relationship. In sport, damaged relationships can lead to apathy resulting in reduced attendance and spectatorship (Kim and Trail, 2011).

A key external factor, which can shape the attitudes of sport consumers to these transgressions, is the role of the **media** in creating awareness of these incidents (Westberg et al., 2013). The increased scrutiny, both from traditional media as well as the "smartphone" wielding public, is increasingly invasive. Further, it has also been observed that there is a disproportionate coverage of negative behavior as opposed to highlighting the positive contributions of sports people to the community. While the media have been credited with much of the commercial success enjoyed by professional sport, it is also recognized that the intense media focus increases the pressure on both athletes and sport organizations. As a result, the media have a significant influence on the perception of the brand of the sport organization and require careful management, as will be discussed in the next section.

ACTION LEARNING

- Given the factors which can influence the sport consumer response to athlete transgressions, as outlined in the preceding section, which factors are sport organizations most likely to be able to control or influence?

- Using the preceding discussion as a starting point, consider more broadly the advantages and disadvantages of the media's interest in sport. In particular, what are some of the potential avenues for managing transgressions, considering both traditional media channels as well as social media?

CASE STUDY 33.3

When is Enough, Enough?

We are no longer convinced that the international professional world of cycling can make this a clean and fair sport. We are not confident that this will change for the better in the foreseeable future.

Those words by Bert Bruggink, a board member of Rabobank, a Dutch multinational financial services company, were reported in the media on 19 October 2012.[2] This statement was made to help explain why the company was severing

▶

---

[2]www.reuters.com/article/2012/10/19/us-cycling-rabobank-idUSBRE89I0DC   2012 1019 and www.bbc.com/sport/0/cycling/20001685.

the long-standing ties to its professional cycling team.

The Rabobank decision came at a particularly tumultuous time for professional cycling. Just over a week earlier the United States Anti-Doping Agency had released an explosive report that had cast the already embattled sport in a poor light. The detailed investigation stated that the US Postal Service Pro Cycling Team, which included Lance Armstrong, ran "… the most sophisticated, professionalized and successful doping program that sport has ever seen."[3]

Given the popularity of cycling in the Netherlands, Rabobank's involvement with the sport had been a golden opportunity to integrate their brand into the community in a positive and dynamic manner. Major sponsors in professional cycling typically have their brand name become the team name, making it easy to establish awareness and identification. Considering their overall involvement, it was estimated that Rabobank invested €15 million a year into professional cycling as part of a strategy that had lasted almost two decades.

While Rabobank planned to continue its involvement in amateur and youth cycling, its decision to curtail its involvement in professional cycling was not altogether unexpected. There had been ongoing speculation as to how sponsoring brands could continue to manage the negative publicity that had surrounded elite cycling for some time. Despite this, the decision was criticized on social media by David Millar, a professional rider from Britain who was suspended for two years in 2004 for doping. Millar tweeted, "Dear Rabobank, you were part of the problem. How dare you walk away from your young clean guys who are part of the solution. Sickening."

ACTION LEARNING

- Millar's tweet outlines the "go or stay" paradox facing major sponsors in sports where transgressions have occurred. Detail this dilemma for an organization such as Rabobank that has made a considerable investment in professional cycling, and consider what factors need to be considered in making a decision to "go or stay".
- Some commentators have called for sports, such as cycling , to allow certain levels of doping in a medically controlled environment. How would the instigation of such an approach affect sponsors?

TOOLS FOR ANALYSIS

As has been discussed, athlete transgressions present significant challenges for sport organizations and their sponsors. As a result, sport managers need to proactively develop strategies and contingency plans both to prevent and manage these events (Wilson et al., 2010). These plans could

---

[3]http://cyclinginvestigation.usada.org.

be considered a form of risk/crisis management. As has been depicted in the case studies, these incidents can arouse the ire of fans and the community, threaten the brand image of all parties concerned and have the potential to cause relational damage.

Sponsors are prepared to terminate a sponsorship arrangement in the event of what they perceive to be a severe transgression, especially where the relationship with and trust of the sport organization/athlete has been weakened by factors such as repeated offences or poor communication (Westberg et al., 2011). Other less radical changes to the relationship, if the transgression is perceived as less severe and has occurred within a strong partnership, include relational adaptation such as amending the sponsorship agreement to include exit clauses, fines or other specifications regarding player or sport entity behavior. Sport entities need to be aware that these requests can signal a change in the relationship that may in fact represent the initiation of an exit strategy. They should also be aware of other signs, such as reduced communication and investment, which may precede relationship dissolution (Alajoutsijarvi et al., 2000).

Sponsors and sport entity managers need to protect their brands by being prepared for the occurrence of athlete transgressions. It is unrealistic to expect that player behavior will be beyond reproach all of the time. A proactive approach can reduce the impact and duration of the controversy or the media scrutiny surrounding the incident, as well as preserving the relationship between the two parties (Wilson et al., 2008). The presence of a prevention program also can help to manage the expectations of the sponsor and thus reduce the threat to the partnership, as well as the damage to corporate reputations and brand equity. Such a program can also serve to decrease the degree of responsibility attributed to the sport organization for an individual athlete's transgression as well as increase the likelihood of the organization being perceived positively after the incident. For example, some organizations have introduced codes of conduct to explicitly promote appropriate behavior, while others have implemented formal education sessions to discuss how players can avoid potentially compromising situations. These sessions can extend to briefing players on the nature of sponsors' businesses and strategic priorities. Whatever form the prevention program takes, the sport organization needs to create a culture amongst the team that encourages responsible behavior both on and off the field (Westberg et al., 2008).

Sponsors can also introduce their own programs aimed at assisting sport organizations to formalize preventative measures. This can include fully briefing the sport organization of their expectations, and clearly stating their sensitivities (zone of tolerance) and the measures that will be taken if they are breached. This understanding will assist sport entities to adopt a more strategic brand and relationship management approach.

Finally, the media have been shown to play a critical role in how the negative behavior is presented, the degree of scrutiny and coverage an incident receives, and thus the ultimate impact upon the associated brands. Sport organizations need to manage the media effectively at such times, and be proactive in cultivating ongoing positive relationships with specific media vehicles and reporters (Wilson et al., 2008). Media management can be complicated in sport organizations as representatives such as coaches, presidents, players (both past and present), agents, various team administrators and employees all may be sought for comment and all may feel empowered to speak on an issue. Without careful coordination, conflicting messages about the sport entity brand and its values may occur, fueling media attention and potentially putting pressure on sponsors to respond publicly. Further, athlete transgressions are often reported in the media before the sport organization can gather all the facts and formulate a response. Managers should consider alternate media channels, such as their website and social media forums, to clarify the facts of the incident and their response to it (Taylor and Perry, 2007). In particular, these are powerful vehicles for communicating and interacting with fans and other sport consumers.

ACTION LEARNING

- Research the websites of major sport teams or organizations to find examples of player codes of conduct. Identify any specific aspects of those codes that explicitly or implicitly extend to conduct off the field.

- What additional measures, other than those noted in this chapter, could sport organizations put in place to prevent or manage athlete transgressions?

CONCLUSION

This chapter has explored the implications of athlete transgressions for sport managers. In particular it has focused on the response to these incidents by two key stakeholder groups: sponsors and sport consumers. It has been identified that inappropriate athlete behavior can generate a range of negative outcomes for the sport organization in terms of their relational bonds with these stakeholders. However, these outcomes are influenced by a range of factors related to the transgression itself as well as the organization's management of those transgressions. Sport managers need to consider a range of strategies to proactively prevent and manage these, and in doing so reduce the potential for both brand and relational damage.

REFERENCES

Alajoutsijarvi, K., Moller, K. & Tahtinen, J. (2000) Beautiful exit: How to leave your business partner, *European Journal of Marketing*, 34(11/12): 1270–1290.
Cashmore, E. (2010) *Making Sense of Sports*, 5th edn. Hoboken, NJ: Taylor & Francis.

Clayton, J. (2007) Vick's NFL future could be bleak. ESPN. Available at: http://sports.espn.go.com/nfl/columns/story?columnist=clayton_john&id=2977162 (last accessed 9 November 2015).

Cliffe, S. & Motion, J. (2005) Building contemporary brands: a sponsorship based strategy, *Journal of Business Research*, 58(8): 1068–1077.

Cornwell, T.B., Weeks, C. & Roy, D.P. (2005) Sponsorship-linked marketing: opening the black box, *Journal of Advertising*, 31(2): 21–42.

Farrelly, F. & Quester, P. (2005) Investigating large-scale sponsorship relationships as co-marketing alliances, *Business Horizons*, 48(1): 55–62.

Farrelly, F., Quester, P. & Burton, R. (2006) Changes in sponsorship value: competencies and capabilities of successful sponsorship relationships, *Industrial Marketing Management*, 35(8): 1016–1026.

Fink, J.S., Parker, H.M., Martin, B. & Higgins, J. (2009) Off-field behavior of athletes and team identification: using social identity theory and balance theory to explain fan reactions, *Journal of Sport Management*, 23: 142–155.

Folkes, V. (1988) Recent attribution research in consumer behavior: a review and new directions, *Journal of Consumer Research*, 14(March): 548–565.

Halinen, A., Salmi, A. & Havila, V. (1999) From dyadic change to changing networks: an analytical framework, *Journal of Management Studies*, 36(6): 779–794.

Kahuni, A.T., Rowley, J. & Binsardi, A. (2009) Guilty by association: image "spill-over" in corporate co-branding, *Corporate Reputation Review*, 12(1): 52–63.

Kelley, H.H. & Michela, J.L. (1980) Attribution theory and research, *Annual Review of Psychology*, 31: 457–501.

Kim, Y.K. & Trail, G. (2011) A conceptual framework for understanding relationships between sport consumers and sport organizations: a relationship quality approach, *Journal of Sport Management*, 25(1): 57–69.

Parry, K.D. (2009) Search for the hero: an investigation into the sports heroes of British sports fans, *Sport in Society: Cultures, Commerce, Media, Politics*, 12(2): 212–226.

Schurr, P.H. (2007) Buyer-seller relationship development episodes: theories and methods, *Journal of Business and Industrial Marketing*, 22(3): 161–170.

Schurr, P.H., Hedaa, L. & Geersbro, J. (2008) Interaction episodes as engines of relationship change, *Journal of Business Research*, 61(8): 877–884.

Taylor, M. & Perry, D.C. (2007) Diffusion of traditional and new media tactics in crisis communication, *Public Relations Review*, 31: 209–217.

Votolato, N.L. & Unnava, H.R. (2006) Spillover of negative information on brand alliances, *Journal of Consumer Psychology*, 16(2): 196–202.

Westberg, K., Stavros, C. & Wilson, B. (2008) An examination of the impact of player transgressions on sponsorship B2B relationships, *International Journal of Sports Marketing and Sponsorship*, 9(2): 125–134.

Westberg, K., Stavros, C. & Wilson, B. (2011) The impact of degenerative episodes on the sponsorship B2B relationship: implications for brand management, *Industrial Marketing Management*, 40(4): 603–611.

Westberg, K., Stavros, C., Wilson, B. & Smith, A. (2013) Consumer attributional and emotional responses to transgressions: who's to blame?, European Association for Consumer Research Conference. IESE Business School and the

Barcelona School of Management of the Universitat Pompeu Fabra Barcelona, Spain, 4–7 July.

Wilson, B., Stavros, C. & Westberg, K. (2008) Player transgressions and the management of the sport sponsor relationship, *Public Relations Review*, 34(2): 99–107.

Wilson, B., Stavros, C. & Westberg, K. (2010) A sport crisis typology: establishing a pathway for future research, *International Journal of Sport Management and Marketing*, 7(1/2): 21–32.

34

CORPORATE SOCIAL RESPONSIBILITY *OF* AND *THROUGH* SPORT

CHRISTOS ANAGNOSTOPOULOS AND DIMITRIOS KOLYPERAS

Sports has this enormous capacity … to really make an important contribution. And we should be severely criticized if we don't take advantage of it. … We should be talking about it as an obligation.

(NBA Commissioner David Stern in *Beyond Sport Summit and Awards*, 2013).

Football Works is a great initiative using sport as a tool for personal development, education and employability. There is a high level of unemployment today, particularly among young people, and programs like this will hopefully provide a positive destination for those involved.

(Sir Alex Ferguson backing up the Football Works initiative, 2012)

It would be better for everyone—for fans, for clubs, for the communities they serve and for the broadcasters pouring billions into their pockets—if the huge allure that currently attracts ever larger commercial deals could also power so-called community projects on a more ambitious scale. Clubs are more than just businesses and fans more than mere consumers but even the corporate world recognises the value of significant CSR investment.

(*Guardian*, "Five ways for the Premier League to use its new £5bn deal for good," 11 February 2015)

Upon completion of this chapter, students should be able to:

- Define the different meanings of CSR on the part of sport organizations.

- Appreciate the relevance and significance of CSR-related activities in the sport sector.

- Describe the distinction between CSR *of* sport and CSR *through* sport.

- Consider the advantages that sport organizations have/ hold (compared to other sectors perhaps) in relation to CSR.

- Identify and discuss key managerial issues for the implementation of CSR *of* and *through* sport.

INTRODUCTION

One aspect of managing sport organizations that has attracted considerable interest in recent years by both scholars and practitioners has been the concept of "corporate social responsibility" (CSR). Although dating back to the early twentieth century when businesses first begun donating funds to improve social conditions, the concept of CSR has today become of significant for modern sport organizations, often generally referring to a duty of these organizations to maximize the long-term positive impact on society, while simultaneously minimizing the negative impact. The aim of this chapter is to introduce readers to the concept of CSR and how it is managed/utilized within the sport industry. For a better understanding of the concept itself, however, we address its two major thrusts: (1) CSR *of* sport, and (2) CSR *through* sport.

Sport provides an ideal context and means for implementing as well as demonstrating CSR initiatives. Whether *of* or *through* sports, Smith and Westerbeek (2007) see several reasons why sport organizations should deploy CSR:

- The popularity and global reach of sport can ensure that these practices have mass media distribution and communication power.
- Sport has youth appeal, thus children's engagement in programs designed to tackle or contribute toward the above-mentioned issues becomes easier if such programs are associated with a sports organization or a well-known athlete.
- By its very nature, sport offers the perfect platform to encourage activity, including health awareness and anti-obesity campaigns as well as disease prevention.
- Linked with the previous reason, social interaction can be thus facilitated by group participation in sports activities.

- Environmental and sustainability awareness and consciousness can be further reinforced, especially with the hosting of **mega-sporting events** (e.g. Olympic Games, the Football (Soccer) World Cup).

- Sport may also lead to enhanced cultural understanding and integration.

- Both active and passive participation in sport offer immediate gratification benefits with unclear social advantages, albeit scarcely unimportant.

Considering the above elements, this chapter begins by focusing on the first aspect of CSR in the sport industry. It does so by introducing a case study that illustrates how a newly established basketball franchise in the UK uses CSR-related programs to address a number of local social issues. The chapter then discusses key issues relating to CSR *of* sport and the different structural shapes and forms CSR *of* sport can take. The second aspect of the CSR concept (i.e. CSR *through* sport) is discussed by focusing on one of Western Union's CSR initiatives. The chapter then offers relevant literature with the goal of assisting readers to place the exemplar case study in a critical conversation addressing the key managerial issues that CSR *through* sport may entail.

CASE STUDY 34.1

Birmingham Knights and the Birmingham Sports and Education Foundation (BSEF)

The recent launch of the 2013/2014 British Basketball League (BBL) season marked the welcome return of a team for the city of Birmingham (UK), the Birmingham Knights. The Knights bring with them a new era of basketball for the nation's second largest city, one that has been deprived of top-level basketball since the Birmingham Bullets back in 2006. Whilst some observers may suggest performances on the court have not yet reached the levels fans would aspire to, it is off court where the Knights have made their biggest impact. Since the franchise was relaunched in 2011, the Birmingham Knights have placed a heavy emphasis on establishing a presence in the wider Birmingham community. Acknowledging that the club would not have the financial backing to compete with some of the larger clubs across the country, the owners have used their vast experience in sport and the charitable sector to fully embed the team into the lives of people across the city. The team's charity partner, the Birmingham Sports and Education Foundation (BSEF), set up in 2012, has played a major role in this community presence. Utilizing basketball as a delivery tool, BSEF was created to aid disadvantaged people from across Birmingham in overcoming the barriers they face to leading successful, prosperous lives. It is fair to say BSEF has been considerably successful in working toward this target. Utilizing the power of basketball and other sports to achieve change, BSEF has delivered an extensive number of projects which target issues such as religious, racial and cultural tensions, anti-social behavior and crime, social exclusion and exceedingly high levels of deprivation—all of which are highly prevalent in Birmingham. Alongside this, at the time of writing the charity has delivered over 1,200 sport sessions in schools across the city, bringing free, high quality physical activity to the next generation of basketball fans, which has helped to develop and increase their interest and participation in basketball and other sports across Birmingham. Summarizing this inspiring story, Jo Aldridge, Director of the Birmingham Knights, states:

> Our community program is now well established and proving a great success, continuing to grow at an impressive rate. As this was an integral part of our overall objectives when we first took over the franchise, we are delighted with the impact we're having within the local community and will endeavour to continue to grow this side of the club as a fundamental component of the team's activities.

Whilst the impact of the Knights' community programs has exceeded expectations, there have of course been a few problems and barriers which have proven difficult to overcome. The (at times) poor quality community work delivered by former Birmingham BBL franchises in the past has led to a degree of reluctance and cautiousness on the part of schools and local organizations to working with the Knights and BSEF. Fortunately, the current delivery and continued commitment to providing a high quality service have begun to turn this around. Birmingham has been one of the hardest hit cities in the UK by the economic recession, and whilst this has further exemplified the need for the Knights and SEF to support the community, it has also presented a fierce financial challenge. To counter this, BSEF has managed to successfully obtain a number of grants which have enabled the continued provision of positive outcomes to the many beneficiaries across the city. The Funding and Development Coordinator at BSEF, Rahul Bissoonauth, explains:

> Over the last 12 months, we have spent a considerable amount of time developing positive relationships with funders and building a strong network of partners such as StreetGames and Sporting Equals across Birmingham who substantially strengthen the quality of our work and our community impact. These relationships have helped us to successfully secure over £100k in grant funding that has enabled us to continue and enhance the great work being done by our delivery team in helping disadvantaged people overcome the barriers in their lives.

In overcoming these barriers, BSEF and the Birmingham Knights have shown their commitment to a long-term impact across the city. Whilst the Knights have now begun their first professional season, the community focus has not relented. In fact, many of the professional players play an active role in the community coaching being delivered through BSEF, providing positive, aspirational role models to disadvantaged young people across Birmingham. With this in mind, the next 12 months are certain to be an exciting period of growth for BSEF and the Birmingham Knights—basketball in the nation's second largest city is truly back.

ACTION LEARNING

- What has been the role of the BSEF in the building up of this new basketball franchise?
- Visit Birmingham Knights' website and identify three community programs that

are being currently implemented by the BSEF. Suggest ways that each of these programs can have a greater social (i.e, for the BSEF itself) and business (i.e. for the team/franchise) impact.

TOOLS FOR ANALYSIS

CSR *of* sport

Several factors that make the sport sector a distinctive type of business have been documented (Hassan, 2012; Smith and Stewart, 2010; Stewart & Smith, 1999) and discussed in the introduction. It is this distinctiveness that allows sport to manifest a number of unique features with regard to CSR (Smith and Westerbeek, 2007). But what responsibilities should be considered as CSR? In other words, what are sport organizations responsible for? Following Carroll's seminal proposition (1979), four facets of CSR *of* sport are discussed: economic, legal, ethical and social responsibilities.

Firstly, with regard to **economic** responsibility, sport organizations are facing mounting criticism for a number of actions and practices. Excessive spending on transfers and athlete salaries, along with insolvency issues, changes in **ownership** and a tendency to live beyond their means, to name but a few, have led sport organizations to consider thoroughly their economic responsibilities. Issues of governance in terms of transparency and recruitment processes, or mechanisms to ensure financial sustainability and eschew money laundering, have risen up the corporate agenda (see Financial Fair Play (FFP), the newly introduced policy by the Union of European Football Associations, UEFA), whereas policies for physical, social and personal development have also appeared, given that qualified and accredited personnel are required in the production of professional sport.

Secondly, in today's globalized sports arena, **gambling**, hooliganism and **match fixing** have harmed the sector enormously. Due to these scandals, financial problems, racial vilifications, bribing, illegal gambling and unsocial labor conditions, organizations in the sport industry are expected to act and behave in a socially responsible way, perhaps more than any other businesses in a variety of industries. For these and other reasons, they have adopted several legal and semi-legal regulatory frameworks (for instance, in terms of the physical safety of all participants and spectators, with a particular emphasis on the protection of the young participants against potential physical, sexual and verbal abuse), some of which have set the scene outside the sporting sphere (see the Bosman judgment; charters of **ethical** behavior and dress code for professional athletes; severe penalties for anti-racism anti-equality behaviors). These legal responsibilities all require socially responsible decisions to be made.

In addition to the development and implementation of effective mechanisms to ensure uncertainty of outcome and competitive balance, sport teams and athletes have long been the focus of much adulation and hero-worship, demonstrating a *trust* and *loyalty* in sport organizations and athletes that are envied by other commercial firms outside of the sport sector. Emerging from within societal groups, these have become "hubs" for social and cultural exchange, and a place where notions such as fair play, diversity, access or equality have found room to flourish. Given that sports are embedded in community environments, this very nature has led them take action toward ethical and social responsibilities. Regardless of programs designed to better understand those communities and their social needs (for instance educational programs with star players reading books in school and deprived areas), several sports organizations have accepted responsibility for the impact they have on air, land and water. Solar panels on roofs, water and waste management systems, along with the idea of "cleaner" stadia and "greener" events, have been just a few of the issues recently addressed within the debate on CSR *of* sport.

A useful way to better understand CSR *of* sport is to further break it down into CSR *of*: associations and leagues (e.g. UEFA; the National Football League (NFL), the English Premier League, etc.); professional team sport organizations (e.g. Barcelona FC); and athletes (e.g. the Didier Drogba Foundation). By way of an example, UEFA has developed a CSR partnership portfolio to address specific issues, including racism, reconciliation and peace, violence, health and humanitarian issues, and it is doing so by allocating 0.7% of its annual revenue (Walters and Anagnostopoulos, 2012). In the USA all major leagues have begun to address environmental concerns, with endeavors focusing on offsetting carbon emissions and recycling during games and major events (Trendafilova et al., 2013). Furthermore, in English football, clubs are now delivering social inclusion- and educational-based initiatives showing that professional teams can play a positive role within their communities. In Spain and Greece, in conjunction with Barcelona's and Olympiakos' charitable foundations respectively, Unicef's logo appears on team shirts, highlighting the quest by both parties to address the problems of children in vulnerable situations. It has also been argued that the perception of a professional sport team's CSR extends beyond its own corporate activities to include those of its professional athletes (Babiak et al., 2013). This line of thinking can be seen as reasonable if one considers that athletes are public figures, product endorsers, ambassadors for worthy causes, and thus role models with positive as well as negative connotations, both for themselves and the corporations (clubs, sponsors) they represent.

Given that interest in CSR *of* sport is accelerating (Trendafilova et al., 2013), so have more integrative and strategic approaches to CSR management. This might be able explain the current proliferation of sport-related charities and the ever-increasing application of CSR *of* sport via charitable foundations. This trend has grown over the past decade, with more and more professional teams across a range of sports and national contexts modifying their organizational structure by establishing foundations to deliver their CSR (Anagnostopoulos and Shilbury, 2013; Babiak and Wolfe, 2009; Bingham and Walters, 2013; Kolyperas and Sparks, 2011).

In the context of professional team sport organizations in particular, it has been argued that partnership-building as a tool to implement CSR can occur in a more strategic fashion by the establishment of such charitable foundations (Walters, 2009). In addition, the charitable foundation model has been identified as the ideal format through which commercial organizations outside sport (see further: CSR *through* sport) can deliver CSR objectives (Walters and Chadwick, 2009). This latter work posits that establishing a charitable foundation offers strategic advantages for professional teams, such as the removal of commercial and community tensions, reputation management, brand building, local authority partnerships, commercial partnerships and player identification. As attested by key managers in the Birmingham Knights' case discussed earlier, it was through the BSEF that the new franchise managed to build a new and strong network of partners.

However, such charitable institutions, although encompassing the general characteristics of foundations (e.g. non-membership-based, private, self-governing, non-profit-distributing and public-benefit-purposed: see Anheier, 2001; European Foundation Centre, 2005), they also (1) depend on the "parent" company for funding, (2) have close ties with the "parent" company (e.g. a name, logo) and (3) nearly always have executives of the "parent" company as members of their board of trustees (Pedrini and Minciullo, 2011). Bingham and Walters (2013), while referring to English football charitable foundations, highlight the same problem, emphasizing the need for these organizations to reduce their reliance on (mainly public) grant funding and instead seek sponsorship opportunities with commercial organizations. The main points of all these three works by Walters and colleagues have been that such a practice could bring additional funding and resources, financial stability and the expansion of operations, as well as creating a community and business network hub. It seems, therefore, that for these charitable organizations resource constraints and securing funding are proving to be the greatest obstacles for taking CSR-related content further (Pallotta, 2008).

This consideration is echoed by Breitbarth et al. (2015) as well as Paramio-Salcines et al. (2013), all of whom point out the importance of a well-defined structure as to achieving the most significant impact. Husted (2003), for instance, identified three different forms of organizational structure that impact how organizations strategically implement CSR. The first form involves organizations outsourcing CSR through charitable contributions. In the second form, organizations seek to internalize CSR through in-house projects. The third way that CSR can be implemented is through a collaborative or partnership model. Therefore, a relevant question could deal less with *why* sport context offers great potential for CSR (Godfrey, 2009; Smith and Westerbeek, 2007) and more with *how* sport organizations can indeed become the vehicle for deploying CSR agendas for companies that come from outside sport. This last point takes our discussion from CSR *of* sport to CSR *through* sport. To this thrust of CSR, therefore, is where this chapter now turns its attention.

- What are the CSRs of sport organizations? Do these vary by country, size, level or culture?
- Amongst the three forms/models of how organizations can strategically implement CSR (Husted, 2003), which one would be the most suitable for professional team sport organizations? Would that choice be appropriate for both European and US professional teams, or would the sporting structural differences between the two continents also require a different form/model for CSR implementation?

- Some studies have suggested that the establishment of charitable foundations in the context of professional teams contributes toward the removal of intra-organizational tensions between the commercial and community departments (Walters and Chadwick, 2009); other studies have demonstrated that such separation actually brings along more challenges which potentially increase these organizational tensions (Anagnostopoulos et al., 2014; Anagnostopoulos and Shilbury, 2013). Critically discuss.

TOOLS FOR ANALYSIS

CSR *through* sport

An increasing number of businesses that exist and operate outside or in parallel to the sport industry have now started manifesting their social responsibility through sport (Bason and Anagnostopoulos, 2015). Without necessarily restricting their initiatives in the local communities where they mainly reside, more and more businesses see meaning in employing CSR through a sport, sport organizations or athletes, in order to achieve their own commercial or social ends.

A characteristic case that exemplifies the role of CSR within the contemporary sports scene is that of Nike. Over the past decade or so, there has been a considerable degree of negative profile in the media relating to use of child labor. Nike's response was to intensify its support for various international development initiatives, such as the "Together for Girls" initiative which runs in refugee camps in East Africa and promotes empowerment of women through leadership training.

From a more proactive point of view, Barclays' program "Spaces for Sport" made them the biggest corporate investor in grassroots sport in the UK (£30 million for the period 2004–2007). Barclays, which is one of the largest financial services companies in the world, won the 2009 Peace and Sport award for the CSR Initiative of the Year when it expanded the program in disadvantaged communities in South Africa, Spain, the USA and Zambia.

Western Union and the "PASS" initiative

Established in 1851, Western Union is now a global industry leader, offering an assortment of financial services including money transfer, prepaid and business services. With over 8,000 employees and locations in more than 200 countries and territories, it is clear that Western Union demonstrates a truly global presence. In 2001 it established the Western Union Foundation as a vehicle for driving its CSR worldwide. Since its formation, the foundation has dedicated in excess of US$85.2 million in grants to over 2,591 non-governmental organizations (NGOs) across the world (Western Union Holdings Inc., 2013). Western Union's main charitable focus is on the need for education as a passageway to economic opportunities. Through the foundation, the company provides grants to NGOs worldwide in order to link economic opportunity with families. Over the past five years, the Western Union Foundation has handed 545 grants to NGOs in a bid to support education, an impressive US$17,904,589 worth. The education grants span a total of 80 countries, supporting over 2.15 million students (WU PASS, 2012). Western Union Vice President Marc Audrit has recently identified two platforms (music and football) as potential drivers for the company to demonstrate its social responsibility while at the same time strengthening its brand image. Western Union has therefore chosen one of the leading football tournaments, the Europa League, as an obvious fit for the implementation of its new initiative. Formerly known as the UEFA Cup, this league is framed in such a way that it is much more inclusive than the Champions League, hosting 48 clubs representing 25 countries in the group stages alone. In one of the last editions of the UEFA Europa League over 1,400 players were involved, demonstrating its global reach. The league is incorporating one of the most enterprising football partnerships ever undertaken, with Western Union having signed a three-year agreement to become the Presenting Sponsor between 2012 and 2015. As well as the Europa League finals, it also includes the UEFA Futsal Cup finals within the same time period. As a fundamental theme to this partnership, Western Union launched their "PASS" initiative, aiming to provide over one million days of education over the next three competitions. From the start of the UEFA Europa League group stages, in autumn 2012, up until the final in May 2013, every pass completed by every player taking part would equate to a charity donation of one day's worth of education. The initiative is aimed at providing education for underprivileged children in 11 countries worldwide. "PASS" aims to span the globe in addressing barriers to education, initially focusing on Brazil, China, Columbia, Jamaica, Mexico, Morocco, Nigeria, Senegal, Romania, Russia and Turkey. In addition, the Western Union Foundation will donate a minimum of $1.8 million (or €1.5million) over three years to

Unicef's education programs. Western Union and the Western Union Foundation will work with non-profit, NGOs that specialize in areas such as increasing enrolment, and addressing teacher shortages. Using the latest technology, Opta (one of the leading sports data companies in the world) was responsible for monitoring every pass in the Europa League competition, before analyzing and distributing the information back to Western Union. Each pass was assigned a specific financial value depending on the stage of the tournament, and went into a fund allocated to the 11 countries via these NGO partnerships. These NGOs then decided how the money was spent to deliver the number of days' education that Western Union funds on a quarterly basis. As of 4 November 2013 the teams in the UEFA Europa League had made a total of 240,349 passes, equating to an equal sum of 174,495 days' education. With an overall objective of one million days of education over three competitions, it will be a challenge for Western Union to match this expectation. The "PASS" initiative of course does not use sport as a delivery method as such, but utilizes the global appeal and profile of European football and the Europa League competition to enhance the credibility of its cause and highlight Western Union's commitment to addressing inequality.

ACTION LEARNING

- What long-term benefits can Western Union expect to see from this CSR strategy in terms of their brand image?

- Using the "PASS" initiative as a model, could this be successfully implemented with other sporting competitions and what implications could develop from this?

TOOLS FOR ANALYSIS

MacDonald et al. (2009), studying the indexed multinational companies with the highest CSR performance rankings, found that CSR through sport activities entails an aspect of sponsorship firstly, followed by a focus on philanthropic funding, volunteers, health, disability, grassroots initiatives, underprivileged groups and the environment. Levermore (2010) addresses the same subject from a more critical perspective, identifying some of the limitations involved in employing CSR *through* sport. For Levermore, although the sporting context provides a platform for building partnerships between institutions that would not normally work together, this development is most often driven by the needs of the donor (and thus may be too brand-centric) rather than those of the community the program is supposed to serve. Most of these initiatives fall into the category of discretionary or philanthropic activities, while some border on improving the ethical situation for the stakeholders with whom they come into contact.

Although a company's reputation can be enhanced through philanthropy—in light of increased public skepticism following a number of corporate scandals—it is those companies that "demonstrate a significant impact on a social problem that will gain more credibility" (and thus, ultimately, a competitive advantage), rather than those who "are merely big givers" (Porter and Kramer, 2002: 67). Bruch and Walter (2005) phrase Porter and Kramer's latter point as *peripheral philanthropy*, i.e. an engagement which is unrelated to the core business activities, but they also offer three more types of corporate philanthropy: *constricted philanthropy*, in which companies form synergies between their core business and their charitable activities, but largely neglect their external stakeholders; *dispersed philanthropy*, a piecemeal approach consisting of small projects run on an ad hoc basis and with no guiding theme; and *strategic philanthropy*, which integrates internal (i.e. core business) and external (i.e. stakeholders) perspectives and applies the same professional management principles to these as to any other field of business operations.

Porter and Kramer's (2006) work is, somehow, in line with Bruch and Walter's (2005) typology. For them, once organizations have ranked social issues, then a corporate social agenda can be created. Such an agenda, however, should not restrict itself to a *responsive CSR*, which occurs when a company becomes involved in a generic social issue that is not related to operations, or when it structures its value chain to avoid any negative social impacts (Werther and Chandler, 2011), but rather to a *proactive/strategic CSR* in which a company's operations have a direct effect on society and vice versa. This means that businesses should identify which social issues and stakeholders they have the ability to influence, as well as identify a fit between the cause, the stakeholders involved and the sporting vehicle (what sport, what level) used to deploy CSR.

The above mentioned observations by influential scholars in the field of strategic management may call into question the nature and scope of CSR *through* sport. This is, by no means, to say that sport does not provide a very useful platform upon which CSR-related programs can be implemented. What CSR *through* sport may, however, require is ever more strategic thinking (in the comparison to CSR *of* sport) so as it moves away from a *peripheral philanthropy* or *responsive CSR* exercise towards a *strategic philanthropy* (Bruch and Walter, 2005) or '*strategic CSR*' (Porter and Kramer, 2006) engagement.

ACTION LEARNING

- Drawing on Bruch and Walter's (2005) typology of CSR, how would you characterize Western Union's PASS initiative? Why?
- Read the article by Bason and Anagnostopoulos (2015: see References).

Identify companies that deploy CSR *through* sport. Classify their programs according to the terms "peripheral philanthropy," "constricted philanthropy," "dispersed philanthropy" and "strategic philanthropy." Critically discuss.

CONCLUSION

This chapter introduced readers to the concept of CSR in sports along with its two major thrusts. This consideration of the changes and challenges of CSR in sporting settings allows us to summarize the key issues of CSR *of* sports and CSR *through* sports. CSR *of* sports has been an ongoing matter for sport managers and researchers, revolving around the economic, legal, social and ethical issues sport organizations should constantly address and strategically incorporate in their business reality. Notwithstanding the importance of economic viability and legitimacy seeking from various legal and ethical stakeholders in the wake of scandals, the very social nature of sport organizations ordains social initiatives and outreach programs. More and more sport organizations realize such nature and ability and, despite a variety of types and forms currently dominating the industry, a shift toward formulating charitable foundations is apparent.

However, the realization that sport holds a strong socially responsible and community embedded nature has grown in importance not only within but also outside the sporting sphere. This may be able to explain the ever-increasing number of corporations who now see sport organizations, events or athletes as appropriate vehicles to achieve their own social and commercial ends. On that basis, social sponsorships and partnerships have been developed and new products are launched through an aspect of donation. Whether fad or best practice, such activity depicts a shift toward a more proactive and strategic use of the CSR concept *through* sports, with various corporations rethinking the way they collaborate with sport entities and charitable set-ups so as to achieve competitive advantage.

REFERENCES

Anagnostopoulos, C. & Shilbury, D. (2013). Implementing corporate social responsibility in English football: towards multi-theoretical integration. *Sport, Business and Management: an International Journal*, 3(4): 268–284.

Anagnostopoulos, C., Byers, T. & Shilbury, D. (2014). Corporate social responsibility in team sport organisations: toward a theory of decision-making. *European Sport Management Quarterly*, 14(3): 259–281.

Anheier, K. (2001). Foundations in Europe: a comparative perspective. In A. Schlüter, V. Then & P. Walkenhorst (eds), *Foundations in Europe*. London: Directory of Social Change.

Babiak, K., Heinze, K., Lee, S. & Juravich, M. (2013). A foundation for winning: athletes, charity, and social responsibility. In J.L. Paramio-Salcines, K. Babiak & G. Walters (eds), *The Handbook of Sport and Corporate Social Responsibility* (pp. 221–235). New York: Routledge.

Babiak, K. & Wolfe, R. (2009). Determinants of corporate social responsibility in professional sport: internal and external factors. *Journal of Sport Management*, 23(6): 717–742.

Bason, T. & Anagnostopoulos, C. (2015). Corporate social responsibility through sport: a longitudinal study of the FTSE-100 companies. *Sport, Business and Management: an International Journal*, 5(3): 218–241.

Bingham, T. & Walters, G. (2013). Financial sustainability within UK charities: community sport trusts and corporate social responsibility partnerships. *VOLUNTAS: International Journal of Voluntary and Nonprofit Organizations*, *24*(3): 606–629.

Breitbarth, T., Walzel, S., Anagnostopoulos, C. & van Eekeren, F. (2015). Corporate social responsibility and governance in sport: "Oh, the things you can find, if you don't stay behind!" *Corporate Governance: the International Journal of Business in Society*, *15*(1): 254–273.

Bruch, H. & Walter, F. (2005). The keys to rethinking corporate philanthropy. *MIT Sloan Management Review*, *47*(1): 49–55.

Carroll, A.B. (1979). A three-dimensional conceptual model of corporate performance. *Academy of Management Review*, *4*(4): 497–505.

European Foundation Centre (2005). *Foundation Facts and Figures across the EU—Associating Private Wealth for Public Benefit*. Brussels, Belgium.

Godfrey, P. (2009). Corporate social responsibility in sport: an overview and key issues. *Journal of Sport Management*, *23*(6): 698–716.

Hassan, D. (2012). The social and cultural management of sport: contemporary arguments concerning the case for specificity. In L. Trenberth & D. Hassan (eds), *Managing Sport Business: An Introduction* (pp. 32–46). London: Routledge.

Husted, B. (2003). Governance choices for corporate social responsibility: to contribute, collaborate or internalize. *Long Range Planning*, *36*(5): 481–498.

Kolyperas, D. & Sparks, L. (2011). Corporate social responsibility communications in the G-25 football clubs. *International Journal of Sport Management and Marketing*, *10*(1/2): 83–103.

Levermore, R. (2010). CSR for development through sport: examining its potential and limitations. *Third World Quarterly*, *31*(2): 223–241.

MacDonald, S., Smith, A. & Westerbeek, H. (2009). Using sport and physical activity (PA) in corporate social responsibility programs: an analysis of indexed multinationals. In P. Rodríguez, S. Késenne, & H. Dietl (eds), *Social Responsibility and Sustainability in Sports* (pp. 111–134). Oviedo: Universidad de Oviedo.

Pallotta, D. (2008). *Uncharitable: How Restraints on Nonprofits Undermine Their Potential*. Medford, MA: Tufts University Press.

Paramio-Salcines, J.L., Babiak, K. & Walters, G. (2013). *Routledge Handbook of Sport and Corporate Social Responsibility*. London: Routledge.

Pedrini, M., & Minciullo, M. (2011). Italian corporate foundations and the challenge of multiple stakeholder interests. *Nonprofit Management and Leadership*, *22*(2): 173–197.

Porter, M. & Kramer, M. (2006) Strategy and society: the link between competitive advantage and corporate social responsibility, *Harvard Business Review*, 84: 78–92.

Smith, A. & Stewart, B. (2010). The special features of sport: a critical revisit. *Sport Management Review*, *13*(1): 1–13.

Smith, A. & Westerbeek, H. (2007). Sport as a vehicle for deploying corporate social responsibility. *Journal of Corporate Citizenship*, *25*: 43–54.

Stewart, B. & Smith, A. (1999). The special features of sport. *Annals of Leisure Research*, 2: 87–99.

Trendafilova, S., Babiak, K., & Heinze, K. (2013). Corporate social responsibility and environmental sustainability: why professional sport is greening the playing field. *Sport Management Review*, *16*(3): 298–313.

Walters, G. (2009). Corporate social responsibility through sport: the community sports trust model as a CSR delivery agency. *Journal of Corporate Citizenship*, *35*: 81–94.

Walters, G. & Anagnostopoulos, C. (2012). Implementing corporate social responsibility through social partnerships. *Business Ethics: a European Review*, *21*(4): 417–433.

Walters, G. & Chadwick, S. (2009). Corporate citizenship in football: delivering strategic benefits through stakeholder engagement. *Management Decision*, *47*(1): 51–66.

Werther, J. & Chandler, D. (2011). *Strategic Corporate Social Responsibility: Stakeholders in a Global Environment* (2nd edn). Thousand Oaks, CA: Sage.

WU PASS (2012) Western Union unveils new education initiative around UEFA europa League to deliver one million school days. [Online]. Available at: http://ir.westernunion.com/news/PressReleases [last accessed 28 April 2013].

Western Union Holdings Inc. (2013) Corporate social responsibility. [Online]. Available at: http://foundation.westernunion.com/corporate_social_responsibility.htm [last accessed 26 April 2013].

USEFUL WEBSITES

www.bsef.co.uk
Birmingham Sport and Education Foundation/Birmingham Knights Basketball team
www.csr-insport.com
http://community.responsiball.org

PART FOUR
EMPLOYABILITY

35

CONCLUSIONS: THE EMPLOYABILITY 'RACE' IN SPORT MANAGEMENT

TERRI BYERS

LEARNING OUTCOMES

Upon completion of this chapter, students will be able to:

- Understand what is meant by 'employability' generally and discuss the issue of employability in the context of opportunities in the sport industry.

- Identify how knowledge of contemporary issues in sport management contributes to employability in sport.

- Discuss the public, private and voluntary sector's values and role in the sport industry.

- Critically evaluate the nature of the sport industry and the contribution you can make to the values of sport business and organizations.

INTRODUCTION

The purpose of this chapter is to draw on all the chapters that make up this book to discuss the concept of employability and demonstrate to students embarking on their education and future careers in sport management that the employment market for sport jobs is truly *global or glocal* (see Chapter 1)*, competitive and dynamic*. This is both a positive and negative for job seekers! This chapter on employability also highlights that 'working' in sport is not just about the highly commercialized (Chapter 2) context of professional sport and mega events (Chapter 14). There are rewarding opportunities in the public and voluntary sectors and there is a need for students to think critically about the ethical (Chapter 6), sustainable and responsible management of sport (and recreation). There is also a need for managers and academics to focus on what is happening in the public and voluntary sectors, to critically reflect on whether we as a profession are comfortable with the direction of their development, and what if anything should be done to influence those developments.

The sport industry is dynamic and always changing, and this means there are plenty of opportunities for innovation and entrepreneurship, although savvy entrepreneurs will recognize the superiority of focusing on sustainability and responsible contributions aimed at social and cultural development as well as commercial gain. The capitalist exploitation of sport is opportunistic, unsustainable and detrimental to the growth of sport as a trusted and valued institution. The Edleman (2015) Trust Barometer indicates the importance of trust for consumers, businesses, government and others who either serve the public or wish to profit from society. Trust in some sectors is declining and it would serve the sport management community to recognize the salience of considering how our actions may positively or negatively impact on trust in sport. Without trust, sport organizations, coaches, athletes, governing bodies and entrepreneurs cannot achieve their objectives. Without trust in sport and the management of sport, there is a serious risk of continuing the trend of decreasing participation and volunteering in sport.

The global economy for sport (Chapter 5) has expanded considerably in recent years, providing opportunities for employment and various careers in different aspects of the sport industry. Numerous chapters in this book have highlighted the negative consequences for sport due to commercialization such as corruption (Chapter 4), doping (Chapter 19), match fixing (Chapter 22), gambling (Chapter 20) and player transgression (Chapter 33). Broader than this, the chapter on ethics (Chapter 6) illustrates how commercialization can change and increase the ethical demands and challenges for sport managers. Sport *can* have a positive and powerful impact on communities and personal and professional development, as well as national pride, economic development and cultural inclusiveness, hence this is why the politics of sport and its governance (Chapter 7) have become a global issue. Chapter 13 illustrates the use of sport policy in a specific national context, i.e. China.

However, the role and impact of sport in our societies depend upon how we manage it! This book introduces students to sport management by focusing on the key contemporary issues facing the field. There are some opportunities for employment, personal/professional development and entrepreneurial endeavours. There are also some real and worrying threats to sport in the form of corruption, poor governance, rapid commercialization and a lack of trust, and sport managers should not underestimate the complexity of the industry, the growing list of stakeholders to whom sport is important, and the various pressures from within and outside their organizations to behave and 'manage' in certain ways. Of all of these I would say this: think critically about the implications of your actions, look at the long term and not just the immediate benefits … and take responsibility when making a contribution to the management of sport. Sport managers need to think more about 'what I put in' rather than just 'what I get out' if the industry is to continue to grow economically but still make positive social and cultural impacts throughout the world.

Sport is unique in that there are many opportunities for voluntary work which enable students to experience the field, different sporting contexts or sectors, and grow their skill set and understanding of the industry, as well as contribute to their communities. This last point is particularly significant. With the increasing commercialization, professionalization and globalization of sport, it can be argued that the traditional values of sport, volunteering, amateurism and participation (Chapter 15) are becoming diluted or even side-lined. This in itself is a contemporary issue, and it is the responsibility of current students, future leaders and their colleagues to ensure this does not happen and that sport has large positive effects on individuals, society, and economies through critical, sustainable management practices. Chapter 31 looks at the implications of not addressing these challenges, such as the lack of trust and control in sport.

Sport is facing a number of serious and potentially fatal challenges, as identified in this book, such as corruption, doping and match fixing, but also declining sport participation (Chapter 15), and the challenges of managing disability sport (Chapter 23), including creating sport systems/programmes that are inclusive and accessible. Gender issues (Chapter 17) and sexuality in sport (Chapter 29) continue to be challenges that sport managers have yet to fully define and articulate as our perceptions of what is appropriate also evolve. There is increasing recognition of the need for corporate social responsibilities (Chapter 34) and consideration for ethical decision making (see Chapter 6), and as the sport landscape becomes more complex with delivery systems in public, private and voluntary sectors as well as cross-sector partnership delivery, increases in legal considerations (Chapter 8), managing brands (Chapter 27) and consumer loyalty (Chapter 30) become a challenge requiring detailed systematic knowledge of the latest research evidence and market research techniques. In addition, the subject of technology and innovation (Chapter 3) in sport is growing, and learning when and how to be innovative is a particular challenge that more and more sport management students will face directly. Related to this is the increasing role of media and communications (Chapter 9) and the ability of sport organizations to think and act strategically (Chapter 11), and understand the economic pressures (Chapter 5) and political objectives (Chapter 7). As you may have realized, there is no particular order in which to read this book – chapters are numbered but the issues are interdependent and your appreciation of sport management will benefit from reading and re-reading around the issues, thinking about the relationships between concepts. There is some benefit in reading the global section first, followed by the national section and then the organizational, but moving back and forth between different chapters will also only further enhance your understanding and skill set.

This chapter draws on the concepts presented in the book and begins a discussion of how contemporary issues provide a unique, innovative and engaging introduction to the management of sport. We hope this book inspires critical thinking, and specifically, this chapter aims to facilitate that process through discussing the relationship between contemporary issues and employability in sport management.

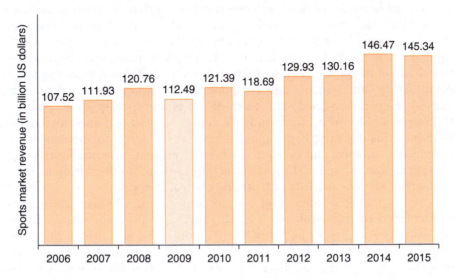

FIGURE 35.1 *Global sports market – total revenue from 2006 to 2015 (in billion US dollars)*

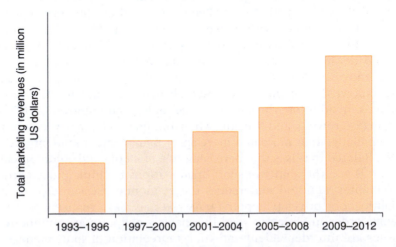

FIGURE 35.2 *Total Olympic Games marketing revenues from 1993 to 2012 (in million US dollars)*

UNDERSTANDING EMPLOYABILITY

Hillage and Pollard (1998: 2) define employability as 'the capability to move self-sufficiently within the labor market to realize potential through sustainable employment'. In other words, employability is not just about getting a job but also includes the ability to maintain one's employment, consistently, over time. Achieving this requires both skills and knowledge of the industry/sector in which you wish to work. There is much research on what employability skills are, how to develop them and why they are important (Brewer, 2013; Chavan and Surve, 2014). Individual job adverts also reveal the set of skills each employer is seeking to attract and these will vary according to the specific job requirements and position level. More senior management roles require evidence of leadership, managing teams, motivating staff and strategic vision, whereas entry-level positions usually concentrate on fundamental interpersonal skills such as communication, working in a team or individually, presentation skills and basic computer knowledge. Employability has become a very political term, with governments developing programmes and training to increase the employability of individuals as a solution to high unemployment rates. However, unemployment is not solely a factor of an unskilled workforce but a more complicated consequence of economic and political development. Employability in sport has not received extensive attention, but there is some concern over educating sport managers and the role of employability skills as well as how to ensure graduates possess the correct skills. The next section discusses some of this research in the context of this book.

ACTION LEARNING

- Considering your education, experience and volunteering, conduct a SWOT (strengths, weaknesses, opportunity [for development] and threats [limitations]) analysis of your skills/experience and discuss what makes you 'employable' generally, regardless of the industry or sector within which you wish to work. Discuss how your skills and abilities allow you to contribute to society and how those skill sets may be lacking.

CONTEMPORARY ISSUES IN SPORT MANAGEMENT AND EMPLOYABILITY

An examination of the structure and content of this book illustrates three main characteristics of the sport industry that we suggest are important to consider in relation to employability: *global or glocal*, *competitive* and *dynamic*. Those readers interested in gaining employment in sport management need to consider the concept of employability as previously discussed, but they also need to consider the nature of the industry in which they seek employment. Students of sport management can also look to a small body of literature on employability in sport (see Byers et al., 2012: 56–59, for a brief discussion) for an understanding of what is being done through education programmes to increase graduate' employability. Mathner and Martin (2012) discuss the career expectations of graduates and practitioners, providing some useful suggestions for students to help prepare them for better career decisions.

The term 'employability' becomes more complex when applied to the sport industry because of the diversity and complexity of the industry, as well as its rapid growth and competitive job market (Byers, 2009). You may also consider the role of sport participation/engagement (active participant, volunteering, coaching, leadership, etc.) in enhancing your employability. Allen et al. (2013) studied the impact of engagement in sport on the employability of graduates from the perspectives of graduates themselves, senior higher education management and employers. The results demonstrated the overall positive effects of sport engagement on employability, salary (personal and household income) and continuous employment throughout one's career (avoiding periods of unemployment).

This book introduces the management of sport using three levels of analysis: by looking at global, national and organizational contemporary issues in sport, we highlight how the sport industry is incredibly diverse, with some issues for managers being at an organizational level such as managing a brand (Chapter 27) or crisis (Chapter 28), but understanding the forces that influence your management decisions on those issues comes from understanding the economic (Chapter 4), social/ethical (Chapters 1 and 6), legal (Chapter 8) and political (Chapter 5) context in which you are working or volunteering. Employability in sport management is about not only having global knowledge and understanding the big issues and forces driving our industry, it is also about being able to appreciate how those forces are manifest at a more local, regional or national level. It is worthwhile exploring in some more detail here the notions of global/glocal, competitive and dynamic in relation to working (or volunteering) in sport.

Global or glocal?

On one hand, there are opportunities in every corner of the globe to work in sport (see Chapter 1), which means travel, new cultures and the chance to experience a way of life that is different from what you may be accustomed to. From the chapters in this book you will have read case studies from the UK, Canada, China, India, South Africa and more. Whether it is a developed nation like Canada, or a developing country like South Africa, sport is growing in importance as a key contributor to the economic and social fabric of societies. This diversity may be seen as a challenge for some as different skills are required for work in international contexts. Languages, changes to behaviour, working conditions and rates of pay may vary greatly from one job to the next.

The various sectors (public, private and voluntary) that comprise the sport industry can also be found globally and so obtaining employment can require that you identify the sector you are most interested in as these have different values in relation to their relationship with sport. While this is a global trend, there are differences in the way sport is organized in the public private and voluntary sectors in different countries. For example, in Canada and the UK, the voluntary sector includes many small voluntary sport clubs which deliver sport opportunities to the population. In the USA this is not the case however and more sport services are provided through private sector clubs and publically funded facilities. In China, there is virtually none of the 'community' sport that we see in much of Europe (particularly Scandinavian countries) and Canada. Although no specific chapter has been included related to volunteering, this contemporary issue has been highlighted in several chapters throughout the book.

There are also increasing numbers of alliances and partnerships between sectors due to the highly competitive and complex nature of delivering sport products and services. This means that, although you may work in one sector, it is likely you will interact with people working in the other sectors, and so an understanding of the values and constraints of each is useful as an introduction to working in sport management. We will touch on this more shortly in discussing the structure of the sport industry by its public, private and voluntary sectors.

Competitive

The job market in sport management is also competitive, due to the growth of commercial opportunities in sport, realized through the involvement of television and other media. Related to this, there is increasing innovation and use of technology (Chapter 3) in sport such as the use of social media (Chapters 25 and 26), which means the delivery of sport products and services is reliant upon knowledge of how to employ technology successfully as well as the challenges in doing so. This is steadily and continuously contributing to the complex and therefore competitive (in order to survive) environment in which most sport organizations operate. The positive side of this is increased opportunities for individuals and businesses (commercial or social) to grow and contribute to the sport industry.

There are an increasing number of opportunities in sport including professional sport (see Chapter 24 on ownership), mega-sporting events (Chapter 14), and corporate responsibility through sport (see Chapter 34), as well as jobs as a result of transgression (Chapter 33) and corruption (Chapter 4) in sport which require expertise in governance (Chapter 7) and control (Chapter 31). Some people even leave existing careers in which they are unhappy to work in sport where they have passion and intrinsic interest in the subject. However, this passion is not always what employers are seeking. Employers are looking for graduates and employees with skills that can apply to sport, and a passion for work but not a passion that will interfere with their job (i.e. a 'fan' of a professional athlete is not likely to be employed as their agent). Sport management jobs are increasingly 'professional', and employers are looking for people who can conduct themselves in a professional manner with excellent communication skills (see Chapter 9 on the importance of communication in sport management).

Professionalization often means decreasing emotive behaviour and increasing rational, systematic, evidence-based decision making. This contemporary and critical book highlights the importance of understanding the field of sport, and one of the best ways to do this is to keep oneself up to date on the research developing in sport management. There is a growing literature around employability generally and on sport management specifically. This chapter draws on knowledge of contemporary issues in the field, and research being conducted on concepts relevant to sport managers, to offer readers an introduction to the academic side of sport management as well as a basic practical industry structure perspective that can be understood by looking at each sector and how they utilize sport. Sport is unique in that it is 'delivered' and produced by the public, private and voluntary sectors as well as through partnerships and alliances between those sectors. Organizations (e.g. 'leagues') cooperate in order to compete, while other organizations use sport for different purposes, such as a commercial business delivering sporting goods or a government-funded sport governing body delivering services to members to participate in sport, and so 'sport' is the most diverse and complex 'product' imaginable.

Dynamic

The sport industry is changing, evolving, daily, weekly, monthly, and as such it is subject to sharp, sizable changes in economics (Chapter 5), such as a recession, politics (Chapter 7), such as a change in government (and government funding for sport: see Chapter 21), or more incremental and slow-paced changes like social trends that can only be analysed over a longer period of time, and so often the implications of these changes can only be managed reactively. Participation is one example, whereby data concerning trends in participation (Chapter 15) indicate there are problems here. The solutions have traditionally come through a focus on policy and national strategic initiatives, but if we consider how dynamic and interconnected the sport industry is, and think more innovatively and critically about the problem, then perhaps the changing demographics (an ageing population) and individual motivational factors or socio-economic status are not the only factors at play here. This book identifies a number of serious issues in sport that are challenging the image and reputation of sport, such as corruption, doping, match fixing, increasing commercialization and professionalization. Have leaders in our industry thought how these could be impacting on parents and grandparents who desire to place children in this 'new sport environment', characterized by transgression, unethical behaviours and intense media criticism?

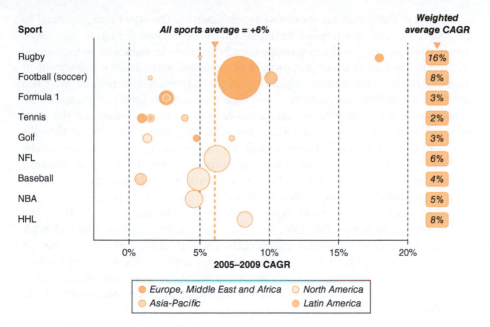

FIGURE 35.3 *Major sports growth*

Source: Collignon et al. (2011)

Notes: CAGR is compound annual growth rate; NFL stands for National Football League; NBA stands for National Basketball Association; NHL stands for National Hockey League.

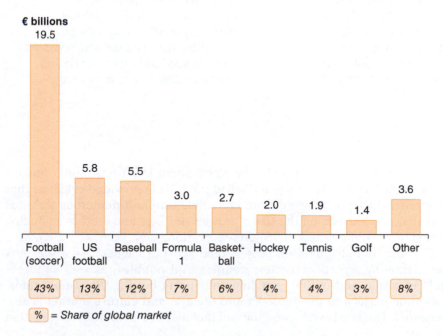

FIGURE 35.4 *Worldwide sport event market in 2009*

Source: Collignon et al. (2011)
       A.T. Kearney analysis

Some critical questions about the development of the sport industry need to be discussed, such as what are the impacts of the professional, high performance levels of sport on grassroots participation? Are the decreases in volunteering related to the increased expectation of commercial gains from involvement in sport? Are the pressures on athletes from the commercialization of sport the driving force behind corruption, or are there more multi-level complications to understanding how unethical behaviours in sport seem to overtaken the view of sport as positive and beneficial to social development? It is often thought that the grassroots level of sports feeds into the elite and professional levels, but what if the current practices in elite/professional sport are in fact having a detrimental effect on parents' and children's perception of sport and are part of the problem of decreasing participation and volunteering in sport …

These questions and more have yet to be addressed in research on the management of sport. To date, we have primarily been concerned with increasing effectiveness and efficiencies (see Byers et al., 2012, for an overview of research in sport management), despite calls for more critical perspectives. To further explore the dynamism (and resultant diversity) of the sport industry, we now examine its size and structure and some of the key changes/trends that have occurred.

ACTION LEARNING

- Make a list of the 'jobs' you would like to pursue in the sport industry. Discuss how you may evaluate what skills and experience you will need to acquire such employment. Have you considered different 'paths' of employment you may take through different sectors (public, private, voluntary) or within one sector?
- Aside from which career you would like from the sport industry, what do you intend to contribute to the industry?

Size

The sport industry is estimated to be worth about US$1.5 trillion (Plunkett Research Ltd, 2014). Milano and Chelladurai (2011) provided evidence that the sport industry is growing at an incredible rate and numerous websites exist that provide data on the size of various markets and sectors, including www.statista.com/markets/409/sports-recreation.

This site includes data on professional sports (leagues), sports events and marketing, sports activities, wellness and hobbies, as well as topics such as casino and online gambling and sports betting. Statistical information on parks and the outdoors and the arts and culture market is also presented. The site is very engaging and includes useful market information such as:

- Total market revenue from 2006–2015 for the global sports market.
- Total Olympic Games' marketing revenue from 1993–2012.

Industry overviews like this can be indicative of the size and growth in the sport sector but should not be the sole influence on sport managers' actions and decisions. National governments may also provide data on aspects of the sport industry, such as:

Statistics Canada
www.ic.gc.ca/eic/site/026.nsf/eng/h_00078.html
The European Commission
http://ec.europa.eu/sport/policy/economic_dimension/sport_statistics_ en.htm

The statistics above are just an indication of the diversity and potential in the sport industry (and often included here is 'recreation'). Understanding the size of a market for a particular sport and where in the world that market exists is also important for sports entrepreneurs and business people. Yet statistics often do not differentiate between the different sectors which provide sport products and services within the industry (or they are more focused on the commercial industry and do not compare this value to the public or voluntary sectors).

Structure

The public, private and voluntary sectors are each vital to the operation of the sport industry. Each has its own purpose and values with regard to sport yet they are increasingly working together to achieve their objectives (Frisby et al., 2004). The *private sector* has a core mission to profit from sport products and services. The *public sector* aims to achieve broader social and economic goals through sport services and participation such as reduced health care costs, decreased crime, increased national identity and social inclusion. The *voluntary sector* often has the same values as amateur sport, such as encouraging access to sport opportunities, equipment and training for all, sportsmanlike behaviour and ethical, sustainable sport business practices. Although the objectives/values of profit (commercial sector), sport for wider social/economic benefits (public sector) and amateurism (voluntary sector) may seem at odds, sport organizations from these different sectors often collaborate to achieve their aims. Public sector facilities in the UK have partnered with voluntary trusts/foundations to deliver services through more efficient means (great financial savings through different tax rates for voluntary organizations), and governments and voluntary sport clubs/governing bodies work together in Canada to deliver provincial-wide sport opportunities.

TRENDS: CHANGES IN SIZE STRUCTURE AND CONTEMPORARY ISSUES

Key trends that impact on employability include the changes in the size of the sport industry, changes in structure (the increasing role of the state, innovative new business models, etc.) and what new contemporary issues are emerging.

Changes in size

A.T. Kearney (The Sports Market, 2011) suggested that the (commercial) sport market is one of the fastest growing sectors, developing more rapidly than the GDP (gross domestic product, a common measure for a countries value) for most countries. They suggest that the worldwide sport event market is particularly strong and growing in size/value. This trend is embraced by governments and business people for any growth in economic value lies at the heart of their existence and strategies. However, trends in the public sport sector include government-funding cuts, restructuring/downsizing and changes in programmes and services which add inconsistency and uncertainty to sport provision. In the voluntary sport sector, there is evidence that the 'life blood' of the sector (numbers of volunteers) is decreasing in many countries around the world including Germany, Norway, the UK and Australia (Cuskelly, 2004; Cuskelly and O'Brien, 2013; Seippel, 2002; Wicker and Breuer, 2011). The pressures on voluntary sport clubs are well documented (Byers, 2013; Nichols et al., 2005; Vos et al., 2011) and in part have been thought to have played a role in driving away volunteers in sport. Pressures on voluntary sport clubs include increases in bureaucracy, formalization and compliance with legislation such as child protection; a reliance on decreasing numbers of volunteers to manage club operations; and complex and changing funding sources which are not linked to clubs' needs but to government priorities. Voluntary sport clubs are also experiencing decreasing participation (and volunteering), primarily because of the rising costs of participating in sport, such as those for equipment, facility usage and coaching, but as noted by Cuskelly and O'Brien (2013), decreasing numbers of participants may also mean less demand for volunteers to run events, programmes or activities.

Due to the size and complexity of the sport industry, trends will vary according to the specific sector. But one thing is certain: the environment for sport, sport business and sport products and services is dynamic, and always changing as new businesses emerge, innovative materials, ways of working and delivering sport are developed. This indicates that the sport industry is developing commercially/economically and so is a positive trend for job seekers and those who wish to build a career in sport. However, with this growth come increasing pressures to consider the responsibilities that arise from increased commercialization, and increased numbers of stake-holders who have different interests in sport from the use of sport for social development to the exploitation of athletes as commodities for the production of a sport team or league.

Zeigler (2007) was one to suggest that the rampant growth in the commercial sector of sport has not necessarily been of benefit to sport participants or facilitated growth in socially desirable consequences of sport, such as increases in social capital, more volunteering and community cohesion. Some hope can be seen in the increasing practice of **corporate social responsibility** (Chapter 34) in the programmes of professional sports and commercial organizations. Yet a critical view of these programmes is that they are still for commercial gain, with social impacts of secondary importance.

Milano and Chelladurai (2011) recognized that sport has become a dominant aspect of society, yet sport management researchers have taken a greater interest in the economic value and commercial impacts of sport. This is understandable given the growth of the commercial sector; however, sport management scholars can also shape and raise awareness of other sectors of the sport industry rather than just be reactive to external industry forces. Yes, the commercial sport sector has seen the largest growth but this is an indication that sport managers and scholars need to question what the implications of this growth may be to the voluntary and public sectors. Phillips and Newland (2014) offer an insightful glance into what could be the unfortunate future of sport – controlled and operated by corporate/commercial interests and devoid of voluntary, 'traditional' governance. They present an 'emergent model of sport development and delivery' (2014: 107) and discuss a case study of triathlon in Australia and the USA whereby governing bodies have emerged as irrelevant in favour of third party organizations (TPO) in the form of profit-driven event management companies. The TPO provide sport for high performance athletes, generate a profit from doing so, and then use that money to develop their own business (as opposed to grassroots sport and encouraging participation). The business model incorporates novice and elite athletes in the same event for efficiencies. The implications of this are that triathlon is open for innovation and capitalist investment and sport managers need to be aware that new models of sport development are emerging (Phillips and Newland, 2014). These models are, in part, contributing to the changes in the structure of the sport industry that we are seeing and will continue to experience over the coming decades. We now turn to discussing some of these structural changes and their implications for sport managers.

Changes in structure

The structure of the sport industry is changing and sport organizations are changing their structures in order to adapt to an increasingly complex and dynamic external environment. Beech and Chadwick (2014) offer a model that illustrates the development of sport as a business, as depicted in Figure 35.5.

Sport organizations start at the foundation stage where there is little formalization of their operations (*foundation*). As participation in the sport grows, there is an increasing need for consistency in how the game is played, regulated and controlled (*codification*). As participation spreads geographically (through forces of *globalization*), structures, leagues and tournaments also expand (*stratification*). Next, a sport gains such popular appeal that spectators are willing to pay to watch live or televised versions and this demand has led broadcasting and media companies to invest, purchasing the rights to games, leagues and sporting competitions. This influx of money is then used to pay players, sport managers, administrators, agents and such professional positions to manage the complexities brought by increasing participation, spectatorship and finance (Chapter 21).

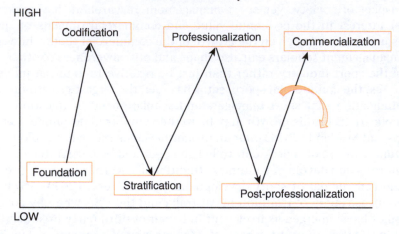

FIGURE 35.5 *The development of sport as a business*

Source: adapted from Beech and Chadwick (2014)

Post-professionalization occurs when there is a relatively stable senior and junior level to the sport. It is then that commercialization starts to take hold – the rising interest in stakeholders leads business (sponsors, governments, etc.) to take an interest in sport to further their own interests and objectives. This is often seen as desirable among sports as it means influxes of more money, resources and interest, which on one hand provide greater stability, but on the other serious challenges that need to be managed if sport is to retain (or in some cases rebuild) the trust and admiration of diverse groups in society.

Statistics reporting sport voluntary activity are conflicting. While some report sources show a decline in sport volunteering (Environmental Scan, 2010) and indicate a number of challenges for the management of voluntary sport organizations, other sources indicate a slight increase in sport volunteering hours (as opposed to number of people) (Stats Canada, 2013). Individual countries will produce their own statistics on volunteering and sport-related volunteering. In my experience, in the UK and Canada, sport organizations tell me they are struggling to attract and retain volunteers; they struggle to manage this resource in a sustainable manner. The commercialization and professionalization of sport are partly responsible for this – increasing levels of bureaucracy for sport clubs make volunteering more formal, less enjoyable.

Public sectors (government), through increased media exposure of corruption and unethical use of funds combined with a general downturn in the economy since 2007, continually look to reduce budgets and refine internal structures to be lean and efficient. This often means budget cuts for sport provision, facilities and programmes, or an increasing tendency to look to the private sector to fund infrastructure and provide services. Without public sector services, the provision of sport and recreation for disadvantaged groups or those who cannot 'pay' will decline because they are not economically viable.

There are many and constant changes in the structures of sport organizations as they adapt to changing external environments. Participation in organized sport is declining in many areas of the world yet increasing in recreational, less competitive sporting activities. Sport organizations, through guidance from national governing bodies and international federations and central governments, have been encouraged to focus on the pathway from grassroots to elite, but what if this is not what people want? Why should grassroots sport organizations not place more emphasis on 'play', recreational sport and physical activity through sport, and not place the pressure to progress on young children? How many sport clubs do you know that have programmes for adults? Or programmes for families? Our sport clubs have been influenced in a top-down fashion for too long by external forces and there needs to be greater innovation to allow them to respond to community needs. There is also a strong need for more research on sport clubs and associations to understand what they do and why, informing policy rather than constrained by it. Decreases in birth rates and the number of children in some areas mean that sport organizations may need to consider their viability, or if they can merge/cooperate with other clubs to remain sustainable and responsive to their communities.

Changes in contemporary issues

We have highlighted throughout this book a number of contemporary issues in the management of sport. These issues represent a wide variety of skills and knowledge that will serve sport management graduates well in seeking and retaining employment. Yet recent research by Minten and Forsyth (2014) indicated that sport graduate careers are dynamic and evolutionary, meaning that students will need to understand how to manage their careers and the changes that will inevitably occur as they progress in employment. As you change jobs, and perhaps even industry sectors, the issues of relevance to succeeding in that sector may be different. Moving from a career in sport law (private sector) to academia (public sector) is possible but requires a shift in values from commercialism to education and reflective practice. If you are in a position to be managing human resources (Chapter 10) or the performance (Chapter 18) of your organization, you should also be aware of the tendency for turnover and change in your organization as well as what is 'normal' for the industry and excessive/detrimental due to poor management practices.

Whichever career or sector of the sport industry you choose, it is likely you will need to understand developments in the private, public and voluntary sectors, as in sport these all interact and changes in one can lead to significant changes in another. If political parties change, sport funding (Chapter 21) policy may also shift from elite to community/grassroots: a downturn in the economy can lead to increased competition and decreased resources in the private sport sector, and sport services once provided by the public/voluntary sector (sport governing bodies) may cease in favour of a private sector, commercially driven model. It is therefore important to remember that everything you do matters because it has implications at various levels, be that immediate, medium- or long-term impacts on individuals, groups, organizations and values within sectors generally. Your choices, values and decisions will shape our industry, so please choose wisely.

CONCLUSION: THE REST IS UP TO YOU

We sincerely hope you have enjoyed reading this book – a collection of contemporary issues, some of which have been around for a long time (i.e. commercialization) but are still 'contemporary', and some of which are not talked about enough (i.e. animals in sport; see Chapter 12)! We have tried to stress the importance of understanding sport management on different levels (global, national, organizational) but also to appreciate that to be an effective manager you need to think of the sport industry from a multi-level, interconnected perspective.

Chapter 31 on trust and control in sport goes some way to drawing together the issues on how sport management is developing and is controlled, and how the implications of trust need to be given consideration for commercial as well as ethical reasons. And yet this book is *just an introduction* – a fascinating array of issues, giving rise to other issues and problems that have been presented in its case studies, theoretical models, and the research used to analyse and discuss what sport managers should do and how to shape the sport industry in a sustainable, responsible manner.

We can't control everything that happens in sport but we hope this book goes some way to influencing you, your attitude to and leadership in (Chapter 16) sport management. Its chapter authors have provided you with incredible diversity, clarity and thought-provoking material. What you do with all of this is up to you! Finally, we wish you well in your endeavours and hope this book will remain part of your 'reading list', whether you are a student, a new manager or an experienced sport manager looking for some new and innovative ideas.

REFERENCES

Allen, K., Bullough, S., Cole, D., Shibli, S. and Wilson, J. (2013). *The Impact of Engagement in Sport on Graduate Employability*. London: British Universities and Colleges Sport (BUCS).

Beech, J. and Chadwick, S. (2013). Introduction: the commercialization of sport, in *The Business of Sport Management* (2nd edn). Essex: Pearson Education.

Brewer, L. (2013). *Enhancing Youth Employability: What? Why? And How? Guide to core work skills.* Geneva: International Labour Office. Available at http://embargo.ilo.org/wcmsp5/groups/public/-ed_emp/-ifp_skills/documents/publication/wcms_213452.pdf (last accessed 23 April 2015).

Byers, T. (2009). *Enhancing Employability in Postgraduate Sport Management Students*. Available at www.heacademy.ac.uk/sites/default/files/141_byer_enhancing_employability_in_postgraduate_students.pdf.

Byers, T. (2013) Using critical realism: A new perspective on control of volunteers in sport clubs. *European Sport Management Quarterly,* 13(1): 5–31.

Byers, T., Slack, T. and Parent, M.M. (2012). *Key Concepts in Sport Management*. London: Sage.

Chavan, R.R. and Surve, A.Y. (2014). Assessing parameters of employability skills: an employer's perspective. *Asian Journal of Management Research*, 5(2): 254–260.

Collingon, H., Sultan, N. and Santander, C. (2011). *The Sports Market: Major trends and challenges in an industry full of passion*. Available at www.atkearney.com/documents/10192/6f46b880-f8d1-4909-9960-cc605bb1ff34 (last accessed 23 February 2015).

Cuskelly, G. (2004). Volunteer retention in community sport organisations. *European Sport Management Quarterly*, 4(2): 59–76.

Cuskelly, G. and O'Brien, W. (2013). Changing roles: applying continuity theory to understanding the transition from playing to volunteering in community sport. *European Sport Management Quarterly*, 13(1): 54–75.

Edleman (2015). *Edleman Trust Barometer 2015*. Available at www.scribd.com/doc/252750985/2015-Edelman-Trust-Barometer-Executive-Summary# (last accessed 10 June 2015).

Environmental Scan (2010). *Trends and Issues in Canada and in Sport*. Policy Research Group, Department of Canadian Heritage. Available at http://sirc.ca/sites/default/files/content/docs/pdf/general_-_escan_sportincanada_final_en.pdf (last accessed 10 June 2015).

Frisby, W., Thibault, L. and Kikulus, L. (2004). The organizational dynamics of under-managed partnerships in leisure service departments. *Leisure Studies*, 23(2): 109–126.

Hillage, J. and Pollard, E. (1998). *Employability: developing a Framework for Policy Analysis*. London: DfEE.

Mathner, R.P. and Martin, C.L.L. (2012). Sport management graduate and undergraduate students' perceptions of career expectations in sport management. *Sport Management Education Journal*, 6: 21–31.

Milano, M. and Chelladurai, P. (2011). Gross domestic sport product: the size of the sport industry in the United States. *Journal of Sport Management*, 25(1): 24–35.

Minten, S. and Forsyth, J. (2014). The careers of sports graduates: implications for employability strategies in higher education courses. *Journal of Hospitality, leisure, Sport and Tourism*, 15: 94–102.

Nichols, G., Taylor, P., James, M., Holmes, K., King, L. and Garrett, R. (2005). Pressures on the UK voluntary sport sector. *Voluntas: International Journal of Voluntary and Nonprofit Organizations*, 16(1): 33–50.

Phillips, P. and Newland, B. (2014). Emergent models of sport development and delivery: the case of triathlon in Australia and the US. *Sport Management Review*, 17(2), 107–120.

Plunkett Research Ltd (2014). *Sports Industry Overview*. Available at www.plunkettresearch.com/sports-recreation-leisure-market-research/industry-statistics (last accessed 21 July 2014).

Seippel, Ø. (2002). Volunteers and professionals in Norwegian sport organizations. *Voluntas: International Journal of Voluntary and Nonprofit Organizations*, 13(3): 253–270.

Stats Canada (2013). *Canada Survey of Giving, Volunteering and Participating*. Available at www.statcan.gc.ca/pub/11-008-x/2012001/c-g/11638/c-g03-eng.htm (last accessed 5 May 2015).

Wicker, P. and Breuer, C. (2011). Scarcity of resources in German non-profit sport clubs. *Sport Management Review*, 14(2): 188–201.

Vos, S., Breesch, D., Késenne, S., Van, J., Hoecke, B. V. and Scheerder, J. (2011). Governmental subsidies and coercive pressures: evidence from sport clubs and their resource dependencies. *European Journal for Sport and Society*, 8(4): 257–280.

Zeigler, E.F. (2007). Sport management must show social concern as it develops tenable theory. *Journal of Sport Management*, 21(3): 297.

USEFUL WEBSITES

Sport as a means to develop employability skills

www.sportanddev.org/en/learnmore/sport_and_economic_development/
sport_as_a_means_to_build_skills_for_employability

Fit for the Workplace: collaborative approaches to enhancing graduate employability in sport

http://blogs.heacademy.ac.uk/social-sciences/2014/06/10/fit-for-
the-workplace-collaborative-approaches-to-enhancing-graduate-
employability-in-sport

Employability: Transferable skills that matter

www.eaie.org/blog/employability-transferable-skills-that-matter

INDEX

Bold indicates an entry in a table. Italic indicates an entry in a figure.

CONTEMPORARY ISSUES IN SPORT MANAGEMENT

CONTEMPORARY ISSUES IN SPORT MANAGEMENT